Frommer's®

D0978278

POSTCARDS

FROM

MAUI

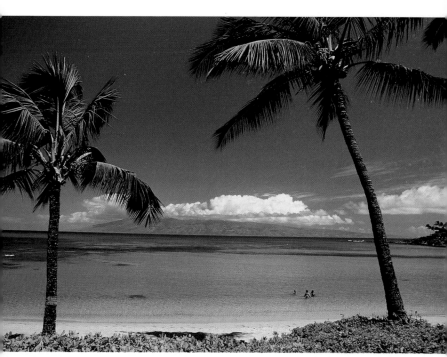

For coverage of the best beaches on Maui, see chapter 6. © David Olsen/Tony Stone Images.

You may spot a spinner dolphin while whale watching or ocean rafting, or even from shore. See chapter 6. © Stuart Westmorland/Tony Stone Images.

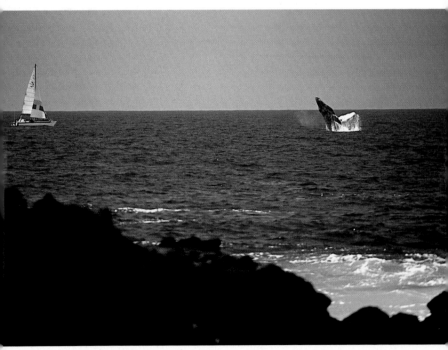

If you're lucky, you'll see a humpback whale breaching. See chapter 6. © Charla Thompson/ Photo Resource Hawaii.

Some of the many species visible to snorkelers and divers include the threadfin butterfly fish (© Jeff Hunter/Image Bank) and the green sea turtle (© Mike Severns/Tony Stone Images). See chapter 6.

Maluaka Beach (Makena Beach), a palm-fringed crescent of golden, grainy sand set between two black-lava points. See chapter 6. © Douglas Peebles Photography.

The Emerald Course at Wailea, designed by Robert Trent Jones, Jr. See chapter 6. © George Fuller/Photo Resource Hawaii.

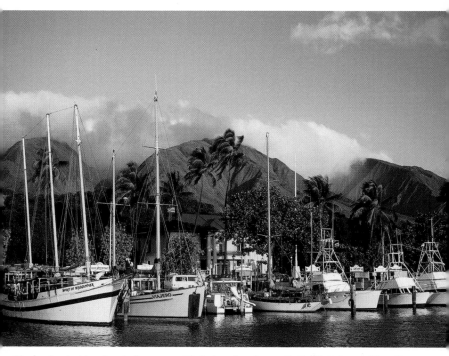

Harbor in the historic whaling town of Lahaina. See chapter 7. © Chris Bryant/Tony Stone Images.

Sunrise at Haleakala National Park. See chapters 6 and 7. © Jim Cazel/Photo Resource Hawaii.

Cinder cones in the crater of Haleakala, the world's largest dormant volcano. See chapters 6 and 7. © Jon K. Ogata/Photo Resource Hawaii.

The snaky Haleakala Crater Road climbs from sea level to 10,000 feet, passing through puffy cumulus clouds like these. See chapters 6 and 7. © Robert Holmes Photography.

There are more than 25 miles of hiking trails in the crater, where the terrain ranges from burnt-red cinder cones to ebony-black lava flows. See chapters 6 and 7. © John Elk Photography.

Four-mile-long Kaanapali Beach, one of the best beaches on the island. See chapter 6. © Greg Vaughn/Tony Stone Images.

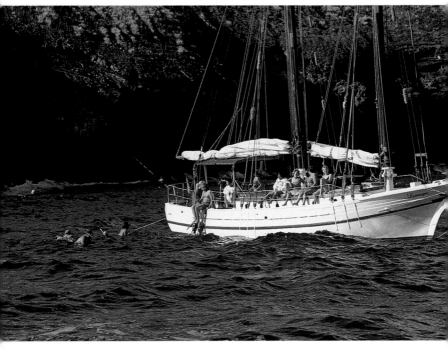

A snorkel cruise to Molokini, a natural sanctuary for tropical fish and one of the most popular snorkel spots. See chapter 6. © Mark E. Gibson Photography.

Hawaiian traditions live on in Maui. Luaus often feature hula performances. See chapter 9.
© Cliff Hollenbeck Photography.

Making traditional leis. See "The Welcoming Lei," in chapter 2.
© Hollenbeck Photography.

Driving through a verdant rain forest on the Road to Hana. See chapter 7. © Cliff Hollenbeck Photography.

On your way to Hana, you'll see sweet-smelling ginger everywhere. See chapter 7. © John Elk Photography.

Maui's rain forest is dotted with waterfalls. See chapter 7 for waterfall pools on the way to Hana. © Jerry Alexander/Tony Stone Images.

Taro and banana patches along the Hana coast. See chapter 7. © Greg Vaughn/Tony Stone Images.

Hamoa Beach, one of Hana's best beaches, is popular with sunbathers, surfers, and snorkelers alike. See chapters 6 and 7. © David Olsen/Tony Stone Images.

Oheo Gulch (often called Seven Sacred Pools) at Kipahulu, just beyond Hana. More than 20 waterfall pools and cataracts cascade into the sea. See chapter 7. © Cliff Hollenbeck Photography.

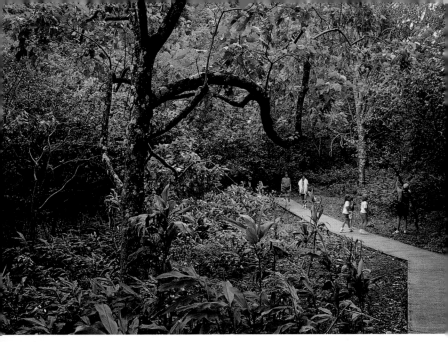

Iao Valley, a state park in the West Maui Mountains, offers easy trails perfect for family hikes. See chapter 7. © Mark E. Gibson Photography.

The highest sea cliffs in the world, along Molokai's north shore. See chapter 10. © Franco Salmoiraghi/Photo Resource Hawaii.

There's no better way to see Molokai's Kalaupapa National Historic Park than from the back of a mule. See chapter 10. © Douglas Peebles Photography.

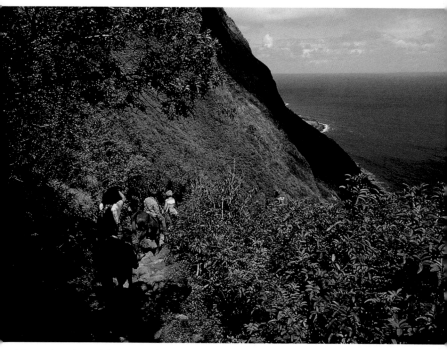

The mule ride to Kalaupapa takes you down 26 switchbacks on a narrow, 3-mile trail. See chapter 10. © Franco Salmoiraghi/Photo Resource Hawaii.

*Waterfall in the lush West Maui Mountains. See chapters 6 and 7. © Randy Wells/
Stone Images.*

Frommer's® 2000

Maui
with Molokai
and Lanai

by Jeanette Foster & Jocelyn Fujii

with Online Directory by Michael Shapiro

MACMILLAN • USA

ABOUT THE AUTHOR

A resident of the Big Island, **Jeanette Foster** has skied the slopes of Mauna Kea—during a Fourth of July ski meet, no less—and scuba dived with manta rays off the Kona Coast. A prolific writer widely published in travel, sports, and adventure magazines, she's also a contributing editor to *Hawaii* magazine.

Kauai-born **Jocelyn Fujii,** a resident of Honolulu, is one of Hawaii's leading journalists. She has authored *Under the Hula Moon: Living in Hawaii* and *The Best of Hawaii,* as well as articles for *The New York Times, National Geographic Traveler, Islands, Condé Nast Traveller, Travel Holiday,* and other national and international publications.

In addition to this guide, Jeanette and Jocelyn also co-author *Frommer's Hawaii, Frommer's Hawaii from $60 a Day,* and *Frommer's Honolulu, Waikiki & Oahu.*

MACMILLAN TRAVEL

Macmillan General Reference USA, Inc.
1633 Broadway
New York, NY 10019
Find us online at **www.frommers.com**

Copyright © 1999 by Ahsuog, Inc.
Maps copyright © by Ahsuog, Inc.

ISBN 0-02-862986-8
ISSN 1076-2817

Editor: Leslie Shen
Production Editor: Michael Thomas
Photo Editor: Richard Fox
Design by Michele Laseau
Staff Cartographers: John Decamillis and Roberta Stockwell
Additional Cartography: Robin D'Amato
Page Creation by Ellen Considine and Pete Lippincott
Front Cover Photo: Kaanapali beaches and coastline

SPECIAL SALES

Bulk purchases (10+ copies) of Frommer's and selected Macmillan travel guides are available to corporations, organizations, mail-order catalogs, institutions, and charities at special discounts, and can be customized to suit individual needs. For more information write to Special Sales, Macmillan General Reference, 1633 Broadway, New York, NY 10019.

Manufactured in the United States of America

5   4   3   2   1

Contents

List of Maps

An Invitation to the Reader

In researching this book, we discovered many wonderful places—hotels, restaurants, shops, and more. We're sure you'll find others. Please tell us about them, so we can share the information with your fellow travelers in upcoming editions. If you were disappointed with a recommendation, we'd love to know that, too. Please write to:

Frommer's Maui 2000
Macmillan Travel
1633 Broadway
New York, NY 10019

An Additional Note

Please be advised that travel information is subject to change at any time—and this is especially true of prices. We therefore suggest that you write or call ahead for confirmation when making your travel plans. The authors, editors, and publisher cannot be held responsible for the experiences of readers while traveling. Your safety is important to us, however, so we encourage you to stay alert and be aware of your surroundings. Keep a close eye on cameras, purses, and wallets, all favorite targets of thieves and pickpockets.

What the Symbols Mean

✪ Frommer's Favorites

Our favorite places and experiences—outstanding for quality, value, or both.

The following abbreviations are used for credit cards:

AE	American Express	EURO	Eurocard
CB	Carte Blanche	JCB	Japan Credit Bank
DC	Diners Club	MC	MasterCard
DISC	Discover	V	Visa
ER	EnRoute		

Find Frommer's Online

Arthur Frommer's Outspoken Encyclopedia of Travel (**www.frommers.com**) offers more than 6,000 pages of up-to-the-minute travel information—including the latest bargains and candid, personal articles updated daily by Arthur Frommer himself. No other Web site offers such comprehensive and timely coverage of the world of travel.

The Best of Maui   1

by Jeanette Foster & Jocelyn Fujii

Maui, also called the Valley Isle, is but a small dot in the vast Pacific Ocean, but it has the potential to offer visitors dreamlike, even surreal, experiences: floating weightless in a rainbowed sea of tropical fish, standing atop a 10,000-foot volcano watching the sunrise color the sky, listening to the raindrops in a bamboo forest.

From around the globe, travelers are drawn to Maui, each in search of a unique encounter. Next to Waikiki, Maui is Hawaii's best-known destination, welcoming some 2½ million people each year to its sunny shores. As soon as you arrive at Kahului Airport, a huge banner greets you with the news that the readers of *Condé Nast Traveller* voted Maui the best island *in the world*—and they've done so 4 years running. As a result, sometimes Maui feels a little *too* well known—especially when you're stuck in bumper-to-bumper traffic around the airport. However, the congestion here pales in comparison to big-city Honolulu; Maui is really just a casual collection of small towns. Once you move beyond the resort areas, you'll find a slower, more peaceful way of life, where car horns are used only to greet friends, posted store hours mean nothing if the surf's up, and taking time to watch the sunset is part of the daily routine.

Whether you want to experience the "real" Hawaii, take part in heart-pounding adventure, or simply relax on the beach, this book is designed to help you find the paradise of your dreams. It can be bewildering to plan your trip with so many options vying for your attention; to make your task easier, this chapter highlights what we consider the very best that Maui has to offer.

1 The Best Beaches

- **D. T. Fleming Beach Park:** This quiet, out-of-the-way beach cove, located north of the Ritz-Carlton Hotel, starts at the 16th hole of the Kapalua golf course (Makaluapuna Point) and rolls around to the sea cliffs on the other side. Ironwood trees provide shade on the land side. Offshore, a shallow sandbar extends out to the edge of the surf. Generally, the waters are good for swimming and snorkeling, but sometimes, off near the sea cliffs, the waves build enough for bodyboarders and surfers to get a few good rides in. See chapter 6.
- **Kapalua Beach:** On an island of many great beaches, this one takes the prize. A golden crescent with swaying palms protected

The Hawaiian Islands

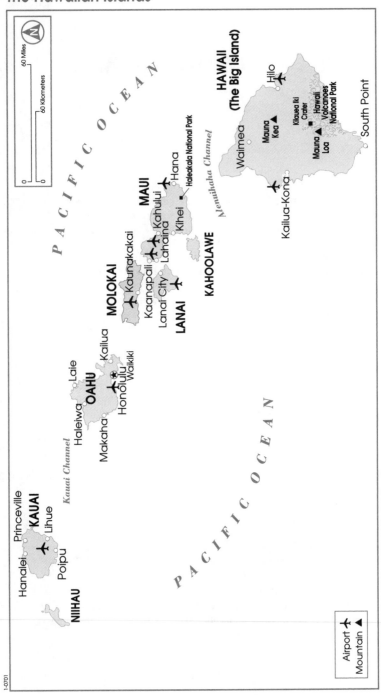

from strong winds and currents by two outstretched lava-rock promontories, Kapalua has calm waters that are perfect for snorkeling, swimming, and kayaking. Even though it borders the Kapalua Bay Hotel, the beach is long enough for everyone to enjoy. Facilities include showers, rest rooms, and lifeguards. See chapter 6.

- **Kaanapali Beach:** Four-mile-long Kaanapali stands out as one of Maui's best beaches, with grainy gold sand as far as the eye can see. Most of the beach parallels the sea channel, and a paved beach walk links hotels and condos, open-air restaurants, and the Whalers Village shopping center. Summertime swimming is excellent. The best snorkeling is around Black Rock, in front of the Sheraton; the water is clear, calm, and populated with multitudes of tropical fish. See chapter 6.

- **Wailea Beach:** This is the best gold-sand, crescent-shaped beach on Maui's sunbaked southwestern coast. One of five beaches within Wailea Resort, Wailea is big, wide, and protected on both sides by black-lava points. It serves as the front yard for the Four Seasons Wailea and the Grand Wailea Resort Hotel & Spa, respectively Maui's most elegant and outrageous hotels. From the beach, the view out to sea is magnificent, framed by neighboring Kahoolawe and Lanai and the tiny crescent of Molokini. The clear waters tumble to shore in waves just the right size for gentle riding, with or without a board. From shore, you can see Pacific humpback whales in season (December through April), as well as unreal sunsets nightly. See chapter 6.

- **Maluaka Beach (Makena Beach):** On the southern end of Maui's resort coast, development falls off dramatically, leaving a wild, dry countryside punctuated by green kiawe trees. The wide, palm-fringed crescent of golden sand is set between two black-lava points and bounded by big sand dunes topped by a grassy knoll. Makena can be perfect for swimming when it's flat and placid, but it can also offer excellent bodysurfing when the waves come rolling in. Or, if you prefer, it can be a place of serenity, with vistas of Molokini Crater and Kahoolawe off in the distance. See chapter 6.

- **Waianapanapa State Park:** The 120 acres of this state park offer 12 cabins, a caretaker's residence, a picnic area, a shoreline hiking trail, and, best of all, a black-sand beach (actually small black pebbles). Swimming is generally unsafe, though, due to strong waves breaking offshore, which roll into the beach unchecked, and strong rip currents. But it's a great spot for picnicking, hiking along the shore, and simply sitting and relaxing. See chapter 6.

- **Hamoa Beach:** This half moon–shaped, gray-sand beach (a mix of coral and lava) in a truly tropical setting is a favorite among sunbathers, snorkelers, and bodysurfers in Hana. The 100-foot-wide beach is three football fields long and sits below 30-foot black-lava sea cliffs. An unprotected beach open to the ocean, Hamoa is often swept by powerful rip currents. Surf breaks offshore and rolls ashore, making it a popular surfing and bodysurfing area. The calm left side is best for snorkeling in the summer. See chapter 6.

2 The Best Maui Experiences

- **Take the Plunge:** Don mask, fins, and snorkel, and explore the magical world beneath the surface, where kaleidoscopic clouds of tropical fish flutter by exotic corals; a sea turtle might even come over to check you out. Molokini is everyone's favorite snorkeling destination, but the shores of Maui are lined with magical spots as well. Can't swim? No problem: Hop on the **Atlantis Submarine**

(☎ **800/548-6262**) for a plunge beneath the waves without getting wet. See chapters 6 and 7.

- **Hunt for Whales on Land:** No need to shell out megabucks to go to out to sea in search of humpback whales—you can watch these majestic mammals breach and spy hop from shore. We recommend scenic McGregor Point, at mile marker 9 along Honoapiilani Highway, just outside Maalaea in South Maui. The humpbacks arrive as early as November, but the majority travel through Maui's waters from mid-December to mid-April. See chapter 6.

- **Watch the Windsurfers:** Sit on a grassy bluff or stretch out on the sandy beach at Hookipa, and watch the world's top-ranked windsurfers twirling and dancing on the wind and waves like colorful butterflies. World-championship contests are held at Hookipa, which is known around the world as one of the greatest windsurfing spots on the planet. See chapters 6 and 7.

- **Experience Maui's History:** Wander the historic streets of the old whaling town of Lahaina, where the 1800s are alive and well thanks to the efforts of the Lahaina Restoration Society. Drive the scenic Kahekili Highway, where the preserved village of Kahakuloa looks much as it did a century ago. Stand in awe at Piilanihale, Hawaii's largest *heiau* (temple), located just outside Hana. See chapter 7.

- **Greet the Rising Sun from Haleakala's Summit:** Bundle up in warm clothing, fill a thermos full of hot java, and drive up to the summit to watch the sky turn from inky black to muted charcoal as a small sliver of orange forms on the horizon. Something about standing at 10,000 feet, breathing in the rarefied air, and watching the first rays of light streak across the sky makes this a mystical experience of the first magnitude. See chapter 7.

- **Explore a Different Hawaii—Upcountry Maui:** On the slopes of Haleakala, cowboys, farmers, ranchers, and other country people make their homes in serene, neighborly communities like Makawao, Kula, and Ulupalakua—worlds away from the bustling beach resorts. Acres of onions, lettuce, tomatoes, carrots, cabbage, and flowers cover the hillsides. Maui's only winery is located here, offering the perfect place for a picnic and a chance to sample the tropical varieties of paradise. See chapter 7.

- **Drive through a Tropical Rain Forest:** The Hana Highway is not just a "drive" but an adventure. Stop along the way to plunge into icy mountain ponds filled by cascading waterfalls; gaze upon vistas of waves pummeling soaring ocean cliffs; inhale the sweet aroma of blooming ginger; and take a walk back in time, catching a glimpse of what Hawaii looked like before concrete condos and fast-food joints washed ashore. See chapter 7.

- **Take a Day Trip to Lanai:** From Lahaina, join **Trilogy Excursions**' snorkel cruise to Lanai (☎ 800/874-2666), or take the **Expeditions Lahaina/Lanai Passenger Ferry** and rent a four-wheel-drive Jeep on Lanai from **Red Rover** (☎ 808/565-7722). It's a two-for-one island experience: Board in Lahaina Harbor and admire Maui from offshore, then get off at Lanai and go snorkeling in the clear waters, tour the tiny former plantation island, and catch the last ferry home. See chapters 6 and 11.

3 The Best of Natural Maui

- **Volcanoes:** Maui was conceived by two volcanoes: Puu Kukui, in the West Maui Mountains, and Haleakala, in the east, which flowed together to create the island. Don't miss seeing **Haleakala National Park.** A bird's-eye view into this long-dormant volcanic crater—big enough to contain Manhattan!—is more than just staring at a big hole in the ground. You'll see otherworldly swirls of burnt-red, orange, brown, and black cinders; lava tubes; and Haleakala's own minimountain range. See chapters 6 and 7.

- **Waterfalls:** Rushing waterfalls thundering downward into sparkling freshwater pools—they're some of Maui's most beautiful natural wonders. The Hana Highway offers numerous viewing opportunities and chances to stop for swims at the deep pools. At the end of the road you'll find **Oheo Gulch** (also known as the Seven Sacred Pools), some of the most dramatic and accessible waterfalls in the islands. See chapter 7.

- **Gardens:** The islands radiate the sweet smell of flowers. For a glimpse of Hawaii's spectacular range of tropical flora, we suggest spending an afternoon at one of Maui's lush gardens. At **Kula Botanical Garden,** you can take a leisurely self-guided stroll through more than 700 native and exotic plants, including orchids, proteas, and bromeliads. In Hana, numerous gardens display everything from tropical natives to exotics from around the globe. See chapter 7.

- **Marine Life Conservation Areas:** These preservation areas, submerged in a Neptunian underworld, possess a sensual serenity that's unmatched in the world above the waves. Four underwater parks are spread across Maui County: Honolua-Mokuleia Marine Life Conservation District and Ahihi-Kinau Natural Area Reserve, both off the shores of Maui (see chapters 6 and 7); Molokini Marine Life Conservation District, off Maui's southwest coast (see chapter 6); and Manele-Hulopoe Marine Life Conservation District, on Lanai (see chapter 11). Be sure to take your snorkel to at least one of these wonderful places.

- **Garden of the Gods:** Out on Lanai's north shore lies the ultimate rock garden: a rugged, barren, beautiful place full of rocks strewn by volcanic forces and shaped by the elements into an infinite variety of shapes and colors—brilliant reds, oranges, coheres, yellows. Scientists explain how these boulders got here with phrases like "ongoing posterosional event"; the ancient Hawaiians, however, considered this desolate, windswept place an entirely supernatural phenomenon. Natural badlands or mystical garden? Take a four-wheel-drive trip out here and see for yourself. See chapter 11.

4 The Best Maui Adventures

Branch out while you're in Maui; do something you wouldn't normally do—after all, you're on vacation. Below are a list of adventures we highly recommend. They may be a bit pricey, but these splurges are worth every penny.

- **Try Scuba Diving:** You're in love with snorkeling and the chance to view the underwater world, but it's just not enough—you want to get closer and see even more. Take an introductory scuba dive; after a brief lesson on how to use the diving equipment, you'll be down swimming with the tropical fish and eyeball to eyeball with other marine critters. See chapter 6.

- **Skim Over the Ocean in a Kayak:** Glide silently over the water, hearing only the sound of your paddle dipping beneath the surface. This is the way the early Hawaiians traveled along the coastline. You'll be eye level and up close and personal with the ocean and the coastline, exploring areas you can't get to any other way. Venture out on your own, or go with an experienced guide—either way, you won't be sorry. See chapter 6.

- **Explore a Lava Tube:** Most people come to Maui to get outdoors and soak up some Hawaiian sunshine, but don't miss the opportunity to see firsthand how volcanic islands were formed. With **Maui Cave Adventures** (☎ 808/248-7308), you can hike into the subterranean passages of a huge, extinct lava tube with 40-foot ceilings—an offbeat adventure and a geology lesson you will not soon forget. See chapter 6.

- **See the Stars from Inside a Volcanic Crater:** Driving up to see the sunrise is a trip you'll never forget, but to *really* experience Haleakala, plan to hike in and spend the night. To get a feel for why the ancient Hawaiians considered this one of the most sacred places on the island, you simply have to wander into the heart of the dormant volcano, where you'll find some 27 miles of hiking trails, two camping sites, and three cabins. See chapters 6 and 7.
- **Hike to a Waterfall:** There are waterfalls and there are waterfalls, but the hike to the magnificent 400-foot Waimoku Falls, in Oheo Gulch outside of Hana, is worth the long drive and the uphill hike. The falls are surrounded by lush green ferns and endemic orchids, and you can even make a pit stop at the pool at the top of Makahiku Falls on the way. See chapter 6.
- **Fly Over the Remote West Maui Mountains:** Your helicopter streaks low over razor-thin cliffs, then flutters past sparkling waterfalls and down into the canyons and valleys of the inaccessible West Maui Mountains—it's like flying in your dreams, except there's so much beauty to absorb that it all goes by in a rush. You'll never want to stop flying over this spectacular, surreal landscape—and it's the only way to see the dazzling beauty of the prehistoric area of Maui. See chapter 7.
- **Take a Drive on the Wild Side:** Mother Nature's wild side, that is—on the Kahekili Highway on Maui's northeast coast. This back-to-nature experience will take you past ancient Hawaiian heiau (temples); along steep ravines; and by rolling pastures, tumbling waterfalls, exploding blowholes, crashing surf, and jagged lava coastlines. You'll wander through the tiny Hawaiian village of Kahakuloa and around the "head" of Maui to the Marine Life Conservation Area of Honolua-Mokuleia and on to the resort of Kapalua. You'll remember this adventure for years. See chapter 7.
- **Ride a Mule to Kalaupapa:** Even if you have only one day to spend on Molokai, spend it on a mule. The **Molokai Mule Ride** (☎ 800/567-7550) trek from "topside" Molokai to the Kalaupapa National Historic Park, Father Damien's world-famous leper colony, is a once-in-a-lifetime adventure. The cliffs are taller than 300-story skyscrapers—but Buzzy Sproat's mules go up and down the narrow 3-mile trail daily, rain or shine, without ever losing a rider or mount on 26 switchbacks. See chapter 10.

5 The Best of Underwater Maui

An entirely different Maui greets anyone with a face mask, snorkel, and fins. Under the sea, you'll find schools of brilliant tropical fish, lumbering green sea turtles, quick-moving game fish, slack-jawed moray eels, and prehistoric-looking coral. It's a kaleidoscope of color and wonder.

- **Black Rock:** This spot, located on the Kaanapali Beach just off the Sheraton Maui Resort, is excellent for beginner snorkelers during the day and for scuba divers at night. Schools of fish congregate at the base of the rock and are used to snorkelers that they go about their business as if no one were around. If you take the time to look closely at the crannies of the rock, you'll find lion fish in fairly shallow water. At night, lobsters, Spanish dancers, and eels come out. See chapter 6.

- **Molokini:** Shaped like a crescent moon that fell from the sky, this islet's shallow concave side serves as a sheltering backstop against sea currents for tiny tropical fish; on its opposite side is a deep-water cliff inhabited by spiny lobsters, moray eels, and white-tipped sharks. Neophyte snorkelers report to the concave side; experienced scuba divers, the other. Either way, the clear water and abundant marine life make this islet off the Makena coast one of Hawaii's most popular dive spots. See chapter 6.
- **Ahihi-Kinau Natural Preserve:** Fishing is strictly *kapu* (forbidden) in Ahihi Bay, and the fish know it; they're everywhere in this series of rocky coves and black-lava tide pools. The black, barren, lunar-like land stands in stark contrast to the green-blue water, which is home to a sparkling mosaic of tropical fish. Scuba divers might want to check out **La Pérouse Pinnacle** in the middle of La Pérouse Bay; clouds of damsel and trigger fish will greet you on the surface. See chapter 6.
- **Hawaiian Reef:** Scuba divers love this area off the Kihei-Wailea coast because it hosts a good cross-section of topography and marine life typical of Hawaiian waters. Diving to depths of 85 feet, you'll see everything from lava formations and coral reef to sand and rubble, plus a diverse range of both shallow and deep-water creatures. See chapter 6.
- **Third Tank:** Scuba divers looking for a photo opportunity will find it at this artificial reef, located off Makena Beach at 80 feet. This World War II tank acts like a fish magnet: Because it's the only large solid object in the area, any fish or invertebrate looking for a safe home comes here. Surrounding the tank is a cloak of schooling snapper and goat fish just waiting for a photographer with a wide-angle lens. For its small size, the Third Tank is loaded with more marine life per square inch than any site off Maui. See chapter 6.
- **Olowalu:** When the wind is blowing and the waves are crashing everywhere else, Olowalu, the small area 5 miles south of Lahaina, can be a scene of total calm—perfect for snorkeling and diving. You'll find a good snorkeling area around mile marker 14. You might have to swim about 50 to 75 feet; when you get to the large field of finger coral in 10 to 15 feet of water, you're there. You'll see a turtle-cleaning station here, where turtles line up to have small cleaner wrasses pick small parasites off. This is also a good spot to see crown-of-thorns starfish, puffer fish, and lots of juvenile fish. See chapter 7.

6 The Best Golf Courses

- **Kaanapali Courses** (☎ **808/661-3691**): All golfers, from high handicappers to near-pros, will love these two challenging courses. The North Course is a true Robert Trent Jones Jr. design: an abundance of wide bunkers; several long, stretched-out tees; and the largest, most contoured greens on Maui. The South Course is an Arthur Jack Snyder design; although shorter than the North Course, it does require more accuracy on the narrow, hilly fairways. Just like its sister course, it has a water hazard on its final hole, so don't tally up your score card until the final putt is sunk. See chapter 6.
- **Kapalua Resort Courses** (☎ **808/669-8044**): Kapalua is probably the best nationally known golf resort in Hawaii, due to the PGA Kapalua Mercedes played here each January. The Bay Course and the Village Course are vintage Arnold Palmer designs, whereas the new Plantation Course is a strong Ben Crenshaw/Bill Coore design. All are sited on Maui's windswept northwestern shore, at the rolling foothills of Puu Kukui, the summit of the West Maui Mountains. See chapter 6.

- **Makena Courses** (☎ 808/879-3344): Here you'll find 36 holes by "Mr. Hawaii Golf"—Robert Trent Jones Jr.—at his best. Add to that spectacular views: Molokini islet looms in the background, humpback whales gambol offshore in winter, and the tropical sunsets are spectacular. The South Course has magnificent views (bring your camera) and is kinder to golfers who haven't played for a while. The North Course is more difficult but also more spectacular. The 13th hole, located part way up the mountain, has a view that makes most golfers stop and stare. The next hole is even more memorable: a 200-foot drop between tee and green. See chapter 6.
- **Wailea Courses** (☎ 808/879-2966): On the sunbaked south shore of Maui stands Wailea Resort, *the* hot spot for golf in the islands. You'll find great golf at these three resort courses: the Blue course is an Arthur Jack Snyder design, and the Emerald and Gold courses are both by Robert Trent Jones, Jr. All boast outstanding views of the Pacific and the mid-Hawaiian Islands. See chapter 6.
- **The Lanai Courses** (☎ 808/565-GOLF): For quality and seclusion, nothing in Hawaii can touch Lanai's two golf-resort offerings. **The Experience at Koele,** designed by Ted Robinson and Greg Norman, and **The Challenge at Manele,** a wonderful Jack Nicklaus effort with ocean views from every hole, both rate among Hawaii's best courses. Both are tremendous fun to play, with the Experience featuring the par-four 8th hole, which drops some 150 yards from tee to fairway, and the Challenge boasting the par-three 12th, which plays from one cliff side to another over a Pacific inlet—one of the most stunning holes in Hawaii. See chapter 11.

7 The Best Luxury Hotels & Resorts

- **Sheraton Maui** (☎ 800/STAY-ITT): Offering the best location on Kaanapali Beach, the most recent renovations, and a great "hassle free" experience, the Sheraton is our pick of Kaanapali hotels. This is the place for travelers who just want to arrive, have everything ready for them, and get on with their vacation (Sheraton has a "no hassle" check-in: The valet takes you and your luggage straight to your room, which means no time wasted standing in line at registration). See chapter 4.
- **Ritz-Carlton Kapalua** (☎ 800/262-8440): With its great location, style, and loads of hospitality, this is the best Ritz anywhere. Situated on the coast below the picturesque West Maui Mountains, this grand, breezy hotel overlooks the Pacific and Molokai across the channel. The natural setting, on an old coastal pineapple plantation, is the picture of tranquillity. The service is legendary; the golf courses are daunting; and the nearby beaches are perfect for snorkeling, diving, and just relaxing. See chapter 4.
- **Four Seasons Resort Wailea** (☎ 800/334-MAUI): This is the ultimate beach hotel for latter-day royals, offering excellent cuisine, spacious rooms, gracious service, and Wailea Beach—one of Maui's best gold-sand beaches, right outside the front door. Every room has at least a partial ocean view from a private lanai. The luxury suites are as big as some Honolulu condos, and full of marble and deluxe appointments. See chapter 4.
- **Grand Wailea Resort Hotel & Spa** (☎ 800/888-6100): Grand is right—in fact, this place borders on the grandiose—but after all, you're on vacation, and you might as well treat yourself to some fantasy. This megaresort boasts 10,000 tropical plants in the lobby; an intricate pool system with not only pools, slides, waterfalls, and rapids, but also a water-powered elevator to take you to the top;

a floating New England–style wedding chapel; and nothing but ocean-view rooms. And it's all crowned with $30 million worth of original art, much of it created expressly for the hotel by Hawaii artists and sculptors. There's also a fantastic beach in the front yard. See chapter 4.

- **Renaissance Wailea Beach Resort** (☎ **800/9-WAILEA**): This is the kind of place for visitors craving the luxury of a Wailea hotel in a smaller, more intimate setting. Located on 15 acres of rolling lawn and tropical gardens, the resort has the feel of a small boutique hotel. Maybe it's the U-shaped design, or the spacious rooms, or the series of small coves and beaches on the property; whatever the reason, it just doesn't feel crowded here. See chapter 4.

- **Manele Bay Hotel** (☎ **800/321-4666**): This is Lanai's only hotel at the beach—not just any beach, but overlooking Hulopoe Beach, one of Hawaii's best stretches of golden sand. The U-shaped, Mediterranean-style hotel steps down the hillside to the pool and that great beach, then fans out in oceanfront wings separated by gardens with lush flora, artificial waterfalls, lotus ponds, and streams. Bordered on the other side by golf greens on a hillside of dry land scrub, the hotel is a real oasis against the dry Arizona-like heat of Lanai's arid south coast. See chapter 11.

8 The Best Moderately Priced Accommodations

- **Aston Maui Islander** (☎ **800/367-5226**): This wooden complex isn't on the beach, but it is on a quiet side street (a rarity in Lahaina) and within walking distance to restaurants, shops, attractions, and, yes, the beach (just 3 blocks away). The good-sized, comfortable, and quiet units are one of Lahaina's great buys—especially those with kitchenettes. The entire complex is spread across 10 landscaped acres and includes tennis courts (with night lights until 10pm), pool, sundeck, barbecue, and picnic area. See chapter 4.

- **Lahaina Inn** (☎ **800/669-3444**): If the romance of historic Lahaina catches your fancy, a stay here will really complete the experience. Built in 1938 as a general store, it has been restored as a charming, Victorian antique–filled inn right in the heart of town. Downstairs you'll find one of Hawaii's most popular storefront bistros, David Paul's Lahaina Grill. See chapter 4.

- **Plantation Inn** (☎ **800/433-6815**): Attention, romantic couples: You need look no further. This charming inn looks like it's been here 100 years or more, but looks can be deceiving. The Victorian-style hotel is actually of 1990s vintage—an artful deception. The rooms are romantic to the max, tastefully done with period furniture, hardwood floors, stained glass, ceiling fans, and four-poster canopy beds. The rooms wrap around the large pool and deck; also on site are a spa and an elegant pavilion lounge, where breakfast is served. See chapter 4.

- **Napili Bay** (☎ **888/661-7200**): One of Maui's best-kept secrets (until now, that is), this intimate, two-story condo complex is located right on half-mile-long white-sand Napili Beach. The beach here is so beautiful that people staying at the much more expensive resort down the street frequently haul all their beach paraphernalia here to set up for the day. The compact studio apartments, which have everything you need, start at just $65—unbelievable! See chapter 4.

- **Aston Maui Lu Resort** (☎ **800/92-ASTON**): At the quieter, northern end of Kihei, the Polynesian-style Maui Lu offers a nostalgic old Hawaii atmosphere on its 28 green acres by the sea. The rooms are big and airy, with beach units right on the sand; they definitely don't make them like this anymore. The rest of the resort is across the road and up on a rise, situated around a swimming pool in the shape of the island of Maui. See chapter 4.

- **Punahoa Beach Apartments** (☎ **800/564-4380**): This small ocean-side Kihei condo is hidden on a quiet side street; the grassy lawn out front rolls about 50 feet down to the beach. You'll find great snorkeling just offshore and a popular surfing spot next door, with shopping and restaurants all within walking distance. Every well-decorated unit features a lanai with fabulous ocean views. See chapter 4.

9 The Best Bed-and-Breakfasts

- **Old Wailuku Inn at Ulupono** (☎ **800/305-4899**): Located in historic Wailuku, this restored 1924 former plantation manager's home is the place to stay if you're looking for a night in the old Hawaii of the 1920s. The guest rooms are wide and spacious, with exotic ohia-wood floors and traditional Hawaiian quilts. The morning meal is a full gourmet breakfast served on the enclosed back lanai, or on a tray delivered to your room if you prefer. See chapter 4.
- **Guest House** (☎ **800/621-8942**): This is one of the great bed-and-breakfast deals in Lahaina: a charming inn offering more amenities than the expensive Kaanapali hotels just down the road. The spacious home features floor-to-ceiling windows, parquet floors, and a large swimming pool. Guest rooms have quiet lanais and romantic hot tubs. Breakfasts are a gourmet affair. See chapter 4.
- **What a Wonderful World B&B** (☎ **808/879-9103**): One of Kihei's best B&Bs offers a great central location in town—just a half mile to Kamaole II Beach Park, 5 minutes from Wailea golf courses, and convenient to shopping and restaurants. All rooms boast cooking facilities and private entrances, private bathrooms, and phones. A family style breakfast (eggs Benedict, Alaskan waffles, skillet eggs with mushroom sauce, fruit blintzes) is served on the lanai, which has views of white-sand beaches, the West Maui Mountains, and Haleakala. See chapter 4.
- **Makena Landing** (☎ **808/879-6286**): This gem, one of the island's best B&Bs, offers a fabulous location (right on the ocean at Makena Landing); incredible views (sunsets to die for); and some of the best swimming, snorkeling, diving, and shoreline fishing just outside your bedroom. To complete the picture, add private entrances, full kitchens, and the nicest hosts you'll ever meet. See chapter 4.
- **Olinda Country Cottages & Inn** (☎ **800/932-3435**): Breathe the crisp, clean air of Olinda at this charming B&B, located on an 8½-acre protea farm on the slopes of Haleakala and surrounded by 35,000 acres of ranch lands (with miles of great hiking). The 5,000-square-foot Tudor mansion, refurbished and outfitted with priceless antiques, has large windows with incredible panoramic views of all of Maui. In addition to the guest rooms in the country house, two cozy cottages and a romantic country suite are also available. See chapter 4.
- **Silver Cloud Ranch** (☎ **800/532-1111**): Old Hawaii lives on at Silver Cloud Ranch, founded in 1902 by a sailor who jumped ship when he got to Maui. Located in Kula at 2,800 feet, the former working cattle spread offers a commanding view of four islands and features antique-filled guest rooms, quaint studios, and even a romantic honeymooners' cottage. See chapter 4.
- **Maui Tradewinds** (☎ **800/262-9912**): No expense was spared in the construction of this 1,000-square-foot studio apartment in the rolling hills of Haiku. Floor-to-ceiling windows capture the ocean view, while features such as blonde wood floors, recessed lighting, bamboo furniture, laundry facilities, top-of-the-line

kitchen equipment, outdoor Jacuzzi, and full bath with dry/steam sauna make this accommodation a cut above. See chapter 4.

- **Huelo Point Flower Farm** (☎ **808/572-1850**): Here's a little Eden by the sea in remote Huelo, on a spectacular 300-foot sea cliff near a waterfall stream. The 2-acre estate, which overlooks Waipio Bay, contains two guest cottages, a guest house, and a main house, all available for rent. Facilities include a pool and an oceanfront hot tub. Homemade scones, tree-ripened papayas, and fresh-roasted coffee are available to start your day, and you're welcome to pick fruit, vegetables, and flowers from the extensive garden. See chapter 4.
- **Ekena** (☎ **808/248-7047**): Situated on 8½ acres in the hills above Hana, this Hawaiian-style wooden pole house, with 360° views of the coastline, the ocean, and Hana's verdant rain forest, is perfect for those in search of a quiet, peaceful vacation. Inside, the elegantly furnished home features floor-to-ceiling sliding-glass doors and a fully equipped kitchen; outside, hiking trails into the rain forest start right on the property. Beaches, waterfalls, and pools are mere minutes away. See chapter 4.
- **Hamoa Bay Bungalow** (☎ **808/248-7884**): This enchanting retreat sits on 4 verdant acres within walking distance of Hamoa Beach, just outside Hana. The romantic, 600-square-foot, Balinese-style cottage has a full kitchen and hot tub. This very private place is perfect for honeymooners—even the tropical breakfast of fruit, yogurt, and muffins is left out daily to eat at your leisure. See chapter 4.

10 The Best Restaurants

- **A Pacific Cafe Maui** (☎ **808/879-0069**): Jean-Marie Josselin's pan-seared mahimahi with garlic and sesame, pan-seared scallops, tiger-eye sushi tempura, and a roster of daily specialties are only part of the reason diners flock to this Kihei magnet. You never know what to expect from this energetic chef—only that it will be good. The offerings are always an adventure into the freshest resources of the region. Word has it that Josselin's new A Pacific Cafe Honokowai is equal to the challenge. See chapter 5.
- **A Saigon Cafe** (☎ **808/243-9560**): Jennifer Nguyen's unmarked dining room in an odd corner of town is always packed, a tribute to her clean, crisp Vietnamese cuisine—and the Maui grapevine. Grab a round of rice paper and wrap your own Vietnamese "burrito" of tofu, noodles, and vegetables. Lemongrass shrimp, curries, and the Nhung Dam, the Vietnamese version of fondue, are among the solid hits. See chapter 5.
- **Café 'O Lei** (☎ **808/573-9065**): What Casanova is to nightlife, Café 'O Lei is to lunch: reliable, exciting, and tirelessly creative. Makawao merchants come daily for the rainbow of salads (Asian, greens, quinoa) and the breathtaking sandwiches that utilize fresh Maui vegetables marinated and grilled, served on focaccia with goat cheese. Served on hand-painted ceramic dinnerware, on a narrow terrace cooled by mountain breezes, the meal is an uplifting experience. See chapter 7.
- **Casanova Italian Restaurant** (☎ **808/572-0220**): Yes, we still love Casanova in Makawao, and for more than one reason: garlic spinach topped with Parmesan and pine nuts, polenta with radicchio, tiramisu, the spaghetti fra diavolo. This is pasta heaven and the center of nightlife on this half of the island. See chapter 5.
- **David Paul's Lahaina Grill** (☎ **808/667-5117**): It's a tough call on this island, but most people choose David Paul's as their favorite Maui eatery. No one seems

to tire of his kalua duck, Kona coffee–roasted rack of lamb, or tequila shrimp. We love the Kula salad, eggplant napoleon, and lobster risotto, along with his marvelous presentations of fresh Maui produce. The menu changes often, but thank goodness the room doesn't; its pressed-tin ceilings and 1890s decor continue to satisfy. See chapter 5.

- **Haliimaile General Store** (☎ 808/572-2666): It's an oasis in the middle of the pineapple fields, an erstwhile plantation-style house that for a decade has been one of Maui's most popular haunts. Bev's Boboli topped with crab dip, paniolo ribs, ahi tartare, and the house salad—with Mandarin oranges, toasted walnuts, and blue-cheese crumble—are part of the Haliimaile legend. See chapter 5.

- **Hula Grill** (☎ 808/667-6636): You can wander straight off the beach into this Whalers Village restaurant, where you'll be met by the welcoming embrace of Peter Merriman's firecracker mahimahi, crab and corn cakes, and, at lunch, down-home sandwiches and salads. During the day, watch sailboats bob on the horizon; at night, flickering torchlight warms the koa walls and Hawaiian canoes. Hula Grill is not intimate—in fact, it's big and bustling—but it's an upbeat place to enjoy top-notch island cookery with a storybook view. See chapter 5.

- **Maui Bake Shop** (☎ 808/242-0064): Guiltless gourmets flock to Wailuku for these European pastries, homemade soups, sandwiches on fresh-baked bread, buttery brioches, and other simple pleasures. The brick oven is one of Maui's oldest, installed in 1935. There are a couple of tables as well as a counter, where regulars pick up their birthday cakes and then try, unsuccessfully, to leave without the white-chocolate macadamia-nut cheesecake, the ultimate dessert. See chapter 5.

- **Pauwela Cafe** (☎ 808/575-9242): Out in the boonies of east Maui, in the industrial sailboard-manufacturing center of the Islands, Becky and Chris Speere serve sandwiches, salads, and inexpensive island cuisine with culinary finesse. The kalua turkey sandwich is the best, but the black-bean chili comes close. It's a long drive out for breakfast, but the eggs chilaquile (layers of tortilla, beans, chiles, and cheese, topped with egg custard) are a handsome reward. See chapter 5.

- **Roy's Kahana Bar & Grill/Roy's Nicolina Restaurant** (☎ 808/669-6999): It's odd that they're right next to each other, have the same menu, and are both so successful. Roy Yamaguchi has perfected his Euro-Asian cookery and snap-to service so that people get what they expect. The staples: fresh fish (eight or nine choices), rack of lamb, roast chicken, and dozens of specials on the daily changing menu. See chapter 5.

- **Sansei Seafood Restaurant** (☎ 808/669-6286): Furiously fusion and relentlessly popular, Sansei serves sushi, and then some: hand rolls warm and cold, udon and ramen, and the signature Asian rock-shrimp cake with the oh-so-complex lime chile butter and cilantro pesto. This Kapalua choice is flavor central—simplicity is not the strong suit, so be prepared for some busy tasting. See chapter 5.

11 The Best Shops & Galleries

The best news in this department is the imminent arrival of a cultural and retail icon, **Sig Zane Designs** of Hilo. When Zane moved from a more obscure location in Hilo to the Hilo Bayfront, suddenly the whole area came alive. Watch for his new shop of aloha wear and Hawaiian lifestyle treasures, on Market Street in historic Wailuku.

- **Bailey House Gift Shop** (☎ 808/244-3920): You can travel Hawaii and peruse its past with the assemblage of made-in-Hawaii items at this museum gift shop.

A Night to Remember: Maui's Top Luau

The **Old Lahaina Luau** (☎ **808/667-1998**) promised more, not less, of those qualities we'd come to love in its former location, where authenticity, intimacy, hospitality, cultural integrity, and sheer romantic beauty made this Maui's top luau and one of our two favorites in the state. The good news is that Old Lahaina Luau is an even bigger hit—often sold out a week or two in advance—at its new 1-acre site just ocean side of the Lahaina Cannery. We thought it couldn't get any better, but it did.

Local craftspeople display their wares only a few feet from the ocean. Seating is provided on lauhala mats for those wishing to dine as the traditional Hawaiians did, but there are tables for everyone else. Staging has been thoughtfully planned, so that the audience faces the ocean as well as the show; hidden underground dressing rooms allow the dancers dramatic entrances and exits. Thatched buildings, amphitheater seating, and the backdrop of a Lahaina sunset are among the event's unforgettable features.

The luau begins at sunset and features Tahitian and Hawaiian entertainment, including ancient hula, hula from the missionary era, modern hula, and an intelligent narrative on the dance's rocky course of survival into modern times. The sophisticated entertainment is both educational *and* riveting, even for jaded locals, and the top-quality food is as much Pacific Rim as authentically Hawaiian, served from an open-air thatched structure. Dishes include imu-roasted kalua pig, baked mahimahi in Maui onion–cream sauce, guava chicken, teriyaki sirloin steak, lomi salmon, poi, dried fish, poke, Hawaiian sweet potato, sautéed vegetables, seafood salad, and the ultimate taste treat, taro leaves with coconut milk. (No watered-down mai tais, either; these are the real thing.) You won't soon forget the genuine hospitality and enthusiasm of the staff. The cost is $65 for adults, $30 for children, plus tax.

Tropical preserves, Hawaiian music, pareus, prints by esteemed Hawaii artists, cookbooks, hatbands, and magnificent wood bowls reflect a discerning standard of selection. Unequaled for Hawaiian treasures on Maui. See chapter 8.

- **Brown-Kobayashi** (☎ **808/242-0804**): At this quiet, tasteful, and elegant Asian shop, the selection of antiques and collectibles changes constantly but reflects an unwavering sense of gracious living. There are old and new European and Hawaiian objects, from koa furniture (which disappears fast) to lacquerware, Bakelite jewelry, Peking glass beads, and a few priceless pieces of antique ivory. Every square inch is a treasure trove. See chapter 8.

- **Hui No'eau Visual Arts Center** (☎ **808/572-6560**): Half the experience is the center itself, one of Maui's historic treasures: a strikingly designed 1917 kamaaina (old-timers) estate on 9 acres in Makawao; two of Maui's largest hybrid Cook and Norfolk pines; and an art center with classes, exhibitions, and demonstrations. The gift shop is as memorable as the rest of it. You'll find one-of-a-kind works by local artists, from prints to jewelry and pottery. See chapter 8.

- **Ki'i Gallery** (☎ **808/871-4557** in Kahului; ☎ **808/871-4557** in Wailea): The Kahului shop focuses on South Pacific pearls, handmade jewelry and hand-turned wooden bowls, and marvelous gift items and works of art, including studio glass, a Ki'i specialty. The Wailea gallery is a gleaming corner space of museum-quality glass and wood vessels—just a few pieces, but big in size, spirit, and visual impact. See chapter 8.

- **Ola's Makawao** (☎ **808/573-1334**): Imaginative, bright, and impeccably tasteful, the selection represents the work of more than 100 artists from Hawaii and the mainland. Ola's celebrates craftsmanship at its finest, from studio glass to wood turning, painting, porcelain, fabrics, and jewelry. See chapter 8.

- **Old Daze** (☎ **808/875-7566**): What fun to browse this eclectic collection of Hawaiian collectibles and 19th-century Americana. Chockablock with collections of Depression glass, old washboards, county-fair souvenir plates, and assorted memorabilia, it's a riotous celebration of the old days. See chapter 8.

- **Summerhouse** (☎ **808/871-1320**): Bright and sassy tropical wear, and the jewelry and accessories to go with them, are a cut above at Summerhouse. T-shirts are tailored and in day-to-evening colors, while dresses are good for both the office and a night out. See chapter 8.

- **Viewpoints Gallery** (☎ **808/572-5979**): We love this airy, well-designed gallery and its helpful staff, which complement the fine Maui art: paintings, sculpture, jewelry, prints, woods, and glass. This is Maui's only fine-arts cooperative, showcasing the work of dozens of local artists. See chapter 8.

- **Village Galleries** (☎ **808/669-1800** in Kapalua; **808/661-4402** in Lahaina): Maui's oldest galleries have maintained high standards and the respect of a public that is increasingly impatient with clichéd island art. On exhibit are the finest contemporary Maui artists in all media, with a discerning selection of hand-crafted jewelry. In Lahaina, the new contemporary gallery has a larger selection of jewelry, ceramics, glass, and gift items, as well as paintings and prints. See chapter 8.

Planning a Trip to Maui   2

by Jeanette Foster

Maui has so many places to explore, things to do, sights to see—where to start? That's where we come in. In the pages that follow, we've compiled everything you need to know to plan your ideal trip to Maui: information on airlines, seasons, a calendar of events, how to make camping reservations, and much more (even how to get married in the islands).

1 The Island in Brief

CENTRAL MAUI

This flat, often windy corridor between Maui's two volcanoes is where you'll most likely arrive—it's where the main airport is. It's also home to the majority of the island's population, the heart of the business community, and the local government (courts, cops, and county/state government agencies). You'll find good shopping and dining bargains here, but very little in the way of accommodations.

KAHULUI   This is "Dream City," home to thousands of former sugarcane workers who dreamed of owning their own homes away from the plantations. A couple of small hotels located just 2 miles from the airport are convenient for 1-night stays if you have a late arrival or early departure, but this is not a place to spend your vacation.

WAILUKU   With its faded wooden storefronts, old plantation homes, and shops straight out of the 1940s, Wailuku is like a time capsule. Although most people race through on their way to see the natural beauty of **Iao Valley,** this quaint little town is worth a brief visit, if only to see a real place where real people actually appear to be working at something other than a suntan. This is the county seat, so you'll see men and women in suits on important missions in the tropical heat. Beaches surrounding Wailuku are not great for swimming, but the old town has a spectacular view of Haleakala, a couple of hostels and an excellent historic B&B, great budget restaurants, a tofu factory, some interesting bungalow architecture, a Frank Lloyd Wright building on the outskirts of town, and the always-endearing Bailey House Museum.

WEST MAUI

This is the fabled Maui you see on postcards. Jagged peaks, green valleys, a wilderness full of native species—the majestic West Maui Mountains are the epitome of earthly paradise. The beaches here are

Maui

Pacific Ocean

Central Maui

Kahului Airport
To Hana

Amala Rd.
Keolani Pl.
Hana Hwy. 36

36
370
Hansen Rd.

Kahului Bay

340
32
Puunene Ave.
Kaahumanu Ave.
Lono Ave.
350
Dairy Rd.
Maui Marketplace
Alexander & Baldwin Sugar Museum
Puuene

Kuihelani Hwy.
Mokulele Hwy.

Kahului

Wailuku

Honoapiilani Hwy.
Waiale Rd.
380
311

30
Waikapu

Maui Tropical Plantation

Kealia Pond National Wildlife Preserve
To South Maui

Kealia Pond

To West Maui
31
Maalaea Beach

Maalaea   Maalaea Harbor

Waipio Bay

36
365
360
Haiku
Huelo
Kailua

Makawao Hwy.
Hana Hwy.
Keanae

Makawao
UPCOUNTRY MAUI
Koolau
Nahiku
Hana Airport
360
Hana Hwy.

Pukalani
377
Makawao Forest Reserve
Olinda
PINE FORESTS

Forest

Reserve

EAST MAUI

Waianapanapa State Park

Hana

Kula Hwy.
Haleakala Hwy.
37
378
377
Haleakala Crater Rd.

Kula

Puu Ulaula
Science City
Haleakala National Park

Hana Forest Reserve

Hamoa

Hamoa Beach

Kula Forest Reserve

Kahikinui Forest Reserve

Kipahulu Forest Reserve

31

Polipoli Springs State Rec. Area

Oheo Gulch
Kipahulu

Piilani Hwy.
31
Kaupo

Alenuihaha

Kailio Point

Channel

Channel

some of the islands' best. And it's no secret: This stretch of coastline along Maui's "forehead," from Kapalua to the historic port of Lahaina, is the island's most bustling resort area (with South Maui close behind).

If you want to book into a resort or condo on this coast, first consider which community you'd like to base yourself in. Starting at the southern end of West Maui and moving northward, the coastal communities are as listed below.

LAHAINA   This old whaling seaport teems with restaurants, T-shirt shops, and a gallery on nearly every block, but there's still lots of real history to be found amid the gimcrack. This vintage village is a tame version of its former self, when whalers swaggered ashore in search of women and grog. The town serves as a great base for visitors: A few old hotels (like the newly restored 1901 Pioneer Inn on the harbor), quaint B&Bs, and a handful of oceanfront condos offer a variety of choices. This is the place to stay if you want to be in the "center" of things: oodles of restaurants, shops, and nightlife.

KAANAPALI   Farther north along the West Maui coast is Hawaii's first master-planned family resort. Pricey midrise hotels, which line nearly 3 miles of gold-sand beach, are linked by a landscaped parkway and separated by a jungle of plants. Golf greens wrap around the slope between beachfront and hillside properties. **Whalers Village**—a seaside mall with such fancy names as Tiffany and Louis Vuitton, plus the best little whale museum in Hawaii—and other restaurants are easy to reach on foot along the waterfront walkway or via resort shuttle, which also serves the small West Maui airport just to the north. Shuttles also go to Lahaina, 3 miles to the south, for shopping, dining, entertainment, and boat tours. Kaanapali is popular with meeting groups and families—especially those with teenagers, who will like all the action.

FROM HONOKOWAI TO NAPILI   In the building binge of the 1970s, condominiums sprouted along this gorgeous coastline like mushrooms after a rain. Today, these older ocean-side units offer excellent bargains for astute travelers. The great location—along sandy beaches, within minutes of both the Kapalua and the Kaanapali resort areas, and close enough to the goings-on in Lahaina town—makes this area an accommodations heaven for the budget-minded.

In **Honokowai** and **Mahinahina,** you'll find mostly older units that tend to be cheaper; there's not much shopping here aside from convenience stores, but you'll have easy access to the shops and restaurants of Kaanapali.

Kahana is a little more upscale than Honokowai and Mahinahina. Most of the condos here are big high-rise types, built more recently than those immediately to the south. You'll find a nice selection of shops and restaurants in the area, and Kapalua West Maui Airport is nearby.

Napili is a much-sought-after area for condo seekers: It's quiet; has great beaches, restaurants, and shops; and is close to Kapalua. Units are generally more expensive here (although we've found a few hidden gems at affordable prices; see the Napili Bay entry in chapter 4).

KAPALUA   North beyond Kaanapali and the shopping centers of Napili and Kahana, the road starts to climb and the vista opens up to fields of silver-green pineapple and manicured golf fairways. Turn down the country lane of Pacific pines toward the sea, and you could only be in Kapalua. It's the very exclusive domain of two gracious and expensive hotels, set on one of Hawaii's best gold-sand beaches, next to two bays that are marine-life preserves (with fabulous surfing in winter).

Even if you don't stay here, you're welcome to come and enjoy Kapalua. Both of the fancy hotels provide public parking and beach access. The resort champions innovative environmental programs; it also has an art school, three golf courses, historic features, a collection of swanky condos and homes (many available for vacation rental at astronomical prices), and wide-open spaces that include a rain-forest preserve—all open to the general public. Kapalua is a great place to stay put. However, if you plan to "tour" Maui, you will spend a lot of your vacation driving from this location and might want to consider a more central place to stay, because even Lahaina is a 15-minute drive away.

SOUTH MAUI

This is the hottest, sunniest, driest, most popular coastline on Maui for sun worshippers—Arizona by the sea. Rain rarely falls, and temperatures stick around 85°F year-round. On former scrub land from Maalaea to Makena, where cacti once grew wild and cows grazed, are now four distinct areas—Maalaea, Kihei, Wailea, and Makena—each appealing to a different crowd.

MAALAEA   If the western part of Maui is a head, Maalaea is just under the chin. This windy, oceanfront village centers around the small boat harbor (with a general store and a couple of restaurants) and the newly opened **Maui Ocean Center,** an aquarium/ocean complex. This quaint region offers several condominium units to choose from, but visitors staying here should be aware that it is often—as in 350 days a year—very windy (all the wind from the Pacific is funneled between the West Maui Mountains and Haleakala, coming out in Maalaea).

KIHEI   Kihei is less a proper town than a nearly continuous series of condos and minimalls lining South Kihei Road. This is Maui's best vacation bargain: Budget travelers swarm like sun-seeking geckos over the eight sandy beaches along this scalloped, condo-packed, 7-mile stretch of coast. Kihei is neither charming nor quaint; what it lacks in aesthetics, though, it more than makes up for in sunshine, affordability, and convenience. If you want latte in the morning, beach in the afternoon, and Hawaii Regional Cuisine in the evening—all at budget prices—head to Kihei.

WAILEA   Only 25 years ago, this was wall-to-wall scrub kiawe trees, but now Wailea is a manicured oasis of multimillion-dollar resort hotels situated along 2 miles of palm-fringed gold coast. It's like Beverly Hills by the sea, except California never had it so good: warm, clear water full of tropical fish; year-round sunshine and clear blue skies; and hedonistic pleasure palaces on 1,500 acres of black-lava shore. Amazing what a billion dollars can do.

This is the playground of the stretch-limo set. The planned resort development—practically a well-heeled town—has a shopping village, three prized golf courses of its own and three more in close range, and a tennis complex. A growing number of large homes sprawl over the upper hillside, some offering excellent bed-and-breakfast units at reasonable prices. The resorts along this fantasy coast are spectacular, to say the least. Next door to the Four Seasons, which is the most elegant, is the Grand Wailea Resort Hotel & Spa, a public display of ego by Tokyo mogul Takeshi Sekiguchi, who dropped $600 million in 1991 to create his own minicity. There's nothing like it in Hawaii, maybe even on the planet. Stop in and take a look—it's so gauche you've gotta see it.

Appealing natural features include the coastal trail, a 3-mile round-trip path along the oceanfront with pleasing views everywhere you look—out to sea and to the neighboring islands, or inland to the broad lawns and gardens of the hotels. The trail's south end borders an extensive garden of native coastal plants, as well as ancient lava-rock house ruins juxtaposed with elegant oceanfront condos. But the chief attractions, of course, are those five outstanding beaches (the best is Wailea).

MAKENA   Suddenly, the road enters raw wilderness. After Wailea's overdone density, the thorny landscape is a welcome relief. Although beautiful, this is an end-of-the-road kind of place: It's a long drive from Makena to anywhere on Maui. If you're looking for an activity-filled vacation, you might want to book somewhere else, or spend a lot of time in your car. But if you crave a quiet, relaxing respite, where the biggest trip of the day is from your bed to the beach, Makena is your place.

Beyond Makena you'll discover Haleakala's last lava flow, which ran to the sea in 1790; the bay named for French explorer La Pérouse; and a chunky lava trail known as the King's Highway, which leads around Maui's empty south shore past ruins and fish camps. Puu Olai stands like Maui's Diamond Head on the shore, where a sunken crater shelters tropical fish, and empty golden-sand beaches stand at the end of dirt roads.

UPCOUNTRY MAUI

After a few days at the beach, you'll probably take notice of the 10,000-foot mountain in the middle of Maui. The slopes of Haleakala ("House of the Sun") are home to cowboys, growers, and other country people who wave back as you drive by; they're all up here enjoying the crisp air, emerald pastures, eucalyptus, and flower farms of this tropical Olympus—there's even a misty California redwood grove. You can see 1,000 tropical sunsets reflected in the windows of houses old and new, strung along a road that runs like a loose hound from Makawao, an old-paniolo-turned–New Age village, to Kula, where the road leads up to the crater and **Haleakala National Park.** The rumpled, two-lane blacktop of Highway 37 narrows on the other side of Tedeschi Winery, where wine grapes and wild elk flourish on the Ulupalakua Ranch, the biggest on Maui. A stay upcountry is usually affordable and a nice contrast to the sizzling beaches and busy resorts below.

MAKAWAO   Until recently, this small, two-street upcountry town consisted of little more than a post office, gas station, feed store, bakery, and restaurant/bar serving the cowboys and farmers living in the surrounding community; the hitching posts outside storefronts were really used to tie up horses. As the population of Maui started expanding in the 1970s, a health-food store sprang up, followed by boutiques, a chiropractic clinic, and a host of health-conscious restaurants. The result is an eclectic amalgam of old paniolo Hawaii and the baby-boomer trends of transplanted mainlanders. **Hui No'eau Visual Arts Center,** Hawaii's premier arts collective, is definitely worth a peek. The only accommodations here are reasonably priced bed-and-breakfasts, perfect for those who enjoy great views and don't mind slightly chilly nights.

KULA   A feeling of pastoral remoteness prevails in this upcountry community of old flower farms, humble cottages, and new suburban ranch houses with million-dollar views that take in the ocean, isthmus, West Maui Mountains, Lanai and Kahoolawe off in the distance, and, at night, the string of pearls that lights the gold coast from Maalaea to Puu Olai. Everything flourishes at a cool 3,000 feet (bring a jacket), just below the cloud line, along a winding road on the way up to Haleakala National Park, and everyone here grows something—Maui onions, carnations, orchids, and proteas, that strange-looking blossom that looks like a *Star Trek* prop. The local B&Bs cater to guests seeking cool tropic nights, panoramic views, and a rural upland escape. Here you'll find the true peace and quiet that only rural farming country can offer—yet you're still just 30 to 40 minutes away from the beach and an hour's drive from Lahaina.

EAST MAUI

ON THE ROAD TO HANA   When old sugar towns die, they usually fade away in rust and red dirt. Not **Paia.** The tangle of electrical, phone, and cable wires hanging overhead symbolizes the town's ability to adapt to the times—it may look messy, but it works. Here, trendy restaurants, eclectic boutiques, and high-tech windsurf shops stand next door to the ma-and-pa grocery, fish market, and storefronts that have been serving customers since the plantation days. Hippies took over in the 1970s; although their macrobiotic restaurants and old-style artists' co-op have made way for Hawaii Regional Cuisine and galleries featuring the works of renowned international artists, Paia still manages to maintain a pleasant vibe of hippiedom. The town's main attraction, though, is **Hookipa Beach Park,** where the wind that roars through the isthmus of Maui brings windsurfers from around the world, who come to fly over the waves on gossamer wings linked to surfboards. A few B&Bs are located just outside Paia in the tiny community of **Kuau.**

Ten minutes down the road from Paia and up the hill from the Hana Highway— the connector road to the entire east side of Maui—sits **Haiku.** Once a pineapple-plantation village, complete with cannery (today a shopping complex), Haiku offers vacation rentals and B&Bs a quiet, pastoral setting: the perfect base for those who want to get off the beaten path and experience a quieter side of Maui, but don't want to feel too removed (the beach is only 10 minutes away).

About 15 to 20 minutes past Haiku is the largely unknown community of **Huelo.** Every day, thousands of cars whiz by on the road to Hana, but most passengers barely glance at the double row of mailboxes overseen by a fading HAWAII VISITORS BUREAU sign. But down the road lies a hidden Hawaii: a Hawaii of an earlier time, where Mother Nature is still sensual and wild, where ocean waves pummel soaring lava cliffs, and where an indescribable sense of serenity prevails. Huelo is not for everyone—but those who hunger for the magic of a place still largely untouched by "progress" should check into a B&B or vacation rental here.

HANA Set between an emerald rain forest and the forever-blue Pacific is a village probably best defined by what it lacks: golf courses, shopping malls, McDonald's. Except for two gas stations and a bank with an ATM, you'll find little of what passes for progress here. Instead, you'll discover the simple joys of fragrant tropical flowers, the sweet taste of backyard bananas and papayas, and the easy calm and unabashed small-town aloha spirit of old Hawaii. What saved "Heavenly" Hana from the inevitable march of progress? The 52-mile **Hana Highway,** which winds around 600 curves and crosses more than 50 one-lane bridges on its way from Kahului. You can go to Hana for the day—it's a 3-hour drive (and a half century away)—but 3 days are better. The tiny town has a first-class resort, a handful of great B&Bs, and some spectacular vacation rentals (where else can you stay in a tropical cabin in a rain forest?).

2 Visitor Information & Money

VISITOR INFORMATION

For advance information on traveling in Maui, contact the **Maui Visitors Bureau,** 1727 Wili Pa Loop, Wailuku, Maui, HI 96793 (☎ **800/525-MAUI** or 808/ 244-3530; fax 808/244-1337; www.visitmaui.com). Once you're on the island, to get here from the airport, go right on Highway 36 (the Hana Highway) to Kaahumanu Avenue (Highway 32); follow it past Maui Community College and Wailuku War Memorial Park onto East Main Street in Wailuku; at North Market Street, turn right, and then right again on Mill Street; go left on Imi Kala Street and left again onto Wili Pa Loop.

The **Kaanapali Beach Resort Association** is at 2530 Kekaa Dr., Suite 1-B, Lahaina, HI 96761 (☎ **800/245-9229** or 808/661-3271; fax 808/661-9431; www.maui.net/~kbra).

The state agency responsible for tourism is the **Hawaii Visitors and Convention Bureau** (HVCB), Suite 801, Waikiki Business Plaza, 2270 Kalakaua Ave., Honolulu, HI 96815 (☎ **800/GO-HAWAII** or 808/923-1811; www.gohawaii.com). The HVCB also has a U.S. mainland office at 180 Montgomery St., Suite 2360, San Francisco, CA 94104 (☎ **800/353-5846**). All other HVCB offices on the mainland have been closed due to budget constraints.

If you want information about working and living in Hawaii, contact **The Chamber of Commerce of Hawaii,** 1132 Bishop St., Suite 200, Honolulu, HI 96815 (☎ **808/545-4300**).

INFORMATION ON MAUI'S PARKS

NATIONAL PARKS   Both Maui and Molokai have one national park each: Haleakala National Park, P.O. Box 369, Makawao, HI 96768 (☎ **808/572-9306;** www.nps.gov/hale); and **Kalaupapa National Historical Park,** P.O. Box 2222, Kalaupapa, HI 96742 (☎ **808/567-6802;** www.nps.gov/kala). For more information, see "Hiking & Camping" in chapters 6 and 10.

STATE PARKS   To find out more about state parks on Maui and Molokai, contact the **Hawaii State Department of Land and Natural Resources,** 54 S. High St., Wailuku, HI 96793 (☎ **808/984-8109;** www.hawaii.gov), which provides information on hiking and camping, and will send you free topographic trail maps on request.

COUNTY PARKS   For information on Maui County Parks, contact **Maui County Parks and Recreation,** 1580-C Kaahumanu Ave., Wailuku, HI 96793 (☎ **808/243-7380;** www.mauimapp.com).

MAUI ON THE WEB

More than 200 Web sites now originate from Hawaii, making it one of the most "wired" places in the country. You can book a hotel room, get the weather report, order Maui-grown coffee or exotic tropical flowers, check on surf conditions, see Maui's beaches, and much more. Many Maui B&Bs are now on the Internet as well; we've included their Web sites in the accommodations listings in chapter 4.

Here are some useful links to Hawaii:

- **Hawaii Visitors and Convention Bureau:** www.gohawaii.com
- **Hawaii State Vacation Planner:** www.hshawaii.com
- **Hawaii State Tourism Office:** www.hawaii.gov/tourism
- **Travel and Visitor Information:** www.planet-hawaii.com/travel
- **Maui Information:** www.maui.net
- **Maui Visitors Bureau:** www.visitmaui.com
- **Kaanapali Beach Resort Association:** www.maui.net/~kbra
- **Molokai Information:** www.molokai-hawaii.com
- **Hawaii Yellow Pages:** www.surfhi.com
- **Weather Information:** www.weather.com/weather/us/states/Hawaii.html or www.cnn.com/WEATHER/cities/us.hawaii.html or http://lumahai.soest.hawaii.edu/index.html

MONEY

Hawaii pioneered the use of automated teller machines (ATMs) more than 2 decades ago, and now they're everywhere. You'll find them at most banks, in supermarkets, at Long's Drugs, and in some resorts and shopping centers like Whalers Village in Kaanapali. It's actually cheaper and faster to get cash from an ATM than to fuss with traveler's checks, and credit cards are accepted just about everywhere. To find the ATM location nearest you, call ☎ **800/424-7787** for the **Cirrus** network or ☎ **800/843-7587** for the **Plus** system. You can also locate Cirrus ATMs on the Web at www.mastercard.com/atm and Plus ATMs at www.visa.com/atms.

3 When to Go

The majority of visitors don't come to Maui when the weather's best in the islands; rather, they come when it's at its worst everywhere else. Thus, the **high season**—when prices are up and resorts are booked to capacity—generally runs from mid-December through March or mid-April. The last 2 weeks of December in particular are the prime time for travel to Maui; if you're planning a holiday trip, make your reservations as early as possible, count on holiday crowds, and expect to pay top dollar for accommodations, car rentals, and airfare.

The **off-seasons,** when the best bargain rates are available, are spring (from mid-April to mid-June) and fall (from September to mid-December)—a paradox, since these are the best seasons in terms of reliably great weather. If you're looking to save money, or if you just want to avoid the crowds, this is the time to visit. Hotel rates tend to be significantly lower during these off-seasons. Airfares also tend to be lower—again, sometimes substantially—and good packages and special deals are often available.

Note: If you plan to come to Maui between the last week in April and mid-May, be sure to book your accommodations, interisland air reservations, and car rental in advance. In Japan, the last week of April is called Golden Week, because three Japanese holidays take place one after the other; the islands are especially busy with Japanese tourists during this time.

Due to the large number of families traveling in **summer** (June through August), you won't get the fantastic bargains of spring and fall. However, you'll still do much better on packages, airfare, and accommodations than you will in the winter months.

CLIMATE Since Maui lies at the edge of the tropical zone, it technically has only two seasons, both of them warm. The dry season corresponds to summer, and the rainy season generally runs during the winter from November to March. It rains every day somewhere in the islands at any time of the year, but the rainy season can cause "gray" weather and spoil your tanning opportunities. Fortunately, it seldom rains for more than 3 days straight.

The **year-round temperature** usually varies no more than 15°F, but it depends on where you are. Maui is like a ship in that it has leeward and windward sides. The **leeward** sides (the west and south) are usually hot and dry, whereas the **windward** sides (east and north) are generally cooler and moist. If you want arid, sunbaked, desertlike weather, go leeward. If you want lush, often wet, junglelike weather, go windward. Your best bet for total year-round sun are the Kihei-Wailea and Lahaina-Kapalua coasts.

Maui is also full of **microclimates,** thanks to its interior valleys, coastal plains, and mountain peaks. If you travel into the mountains, it can change from summer to winter in a matter of hours, since it's cooler the higher up you go. In other words, if the weather doesn't suit you, go to the other side of the island—or head into the hills.

HOLIDAYS When Hawaii observes holidays, especially those over a long weekend, travel between the islands increases, interisland airline seats are fully booked, rental cars are at a premium, and hotels and restaurants are busier than usual.

Federal, state, and county government offices are closed on all federal holidays: January 1 (New Year's Day); third Monday in January (Martin Luther King Jr. Day);

third Monday in February (Presidents' Day, Washington's Birthday); last Monday in May (Memorial Day); July 4 (Independence Day); first Monday in September (Labor Day); second Monday in October (Columbus Day); November 11 (Veterans' Day); fourth Thursday in November (Thanksgiving Day); and December 25 (Christmas).

State and county offices also are closed on local holidays, including Prince Kuhio Day (March 26), honoring the birthday of Hawaii's first delegate to the U.S. Congress; King Kamehameha Day (June 11), a statewide holiday commemorating Kamehameha the Great, who united the islands and ruled from 1795 to 1819; and Admission Day (third Friday in August), which honors Hawaii's admission as the 50th state in the United States on August 21, 1959.

Other special days celebrated by many people in Hawaii but that do not involve the closing of federal, state, or county offices are Chinese New Year (in January or February), Girls' Day (March 3), Buddha's Birthday (April 8), Father Damien's Day (April 15), Boys' Day (May 5), Samoan Flag Day (in August), Aloha Festivals (in September or October), and Pearl Harbor Day (December 7).

Maui Calendar of Events

Please note that, as with any schedule of upcoming events, the following information is subject to change; always confirm the details before you plan your schedule around an event. For a complete and up-to-date list of events throughout the islands, point your Internet browser to **www.hawaiian.net/~mahalo/calendar/current.html**.

January

- **PGA Kapalua Mercedes Championship,** Kapalua Resort, Maui. Top PGA golfers compete for $1 million. Call ☎ **808/669-0244.** First weekend after New Year's Day.

- **Hula Bowl Football All-Star Classic,** War Memorial Stadium, Maui. An annual all-star football classic featuring America's top college players. Call ☎ **888/716-HULA** or 808/947-4141. Sunday before the Super Bowl.

- **Maui Pro Surf Meet,** Hookipa Beach and Honolua Bay, Maui. The top professional surfers from around the globe compete for some $40,000 in prize money. Call ☎ **808/575-9264.** Mid-January.

- **Celebration of Whales,** Four Seasons Resort, Wailea, Maui. Cetacean experts host discussions, whale-watching excursions, social functions, art exhibits, and entertainment. Call ☎ **808/847-8000.** Last weekend in January.

- ✪ **Ka Molokai Makahiki,** Kaunakakai Town Baseball Park, Mitchell Pauole Center, Kaunakakai, Molokai. Makahiki, a traditional time of peace in ancient Hawaii, is re-created with performances by Hawaiian music groups and hula halau (dance troupes), ancient Hawaiian games and sporting competitions, and Hawaiian crafts and food. A wonderful chance to experience the Hawaii of yesteryear. Call ☎ **800/800-6367** or 808/553-3876. Late January.

February

- ✪ **Chinese New Year,** Wo Hing Temple, Front Street, Lahaina, Maui. The Chinese New Year is ushered in with a lion dance, food booths, Chinese calligraphy, firecrackers, and other activities. Call ☎ **808/667-9175** or e-mail: action @maui.net.

March

- **Whalefest Week,** West Maui. A weeklong celebration with seminars, art exhibits, sailing, snorkeling and diving tours, and numerous events for children to celebrate Maui's best-known winter visitors, the humpback whales. Call ☎ **808/667-9175** or e-mail: action@maui.net. Usually early March.

- **Maui Marathon,** Kahului to Kaanapali, Maui. For nearly 3 decades, runners have lined up at the Maui Mall before daybreak and headed off for Kaanapali, some 26.2 miles across the island. Call ☎ **808/871-6441.**

- **St. Patrick's Day Parade,** Kaanapali Parkway, Kaanapali Resort, Maui. Everyone becomes Irish for a day when this hometown parade makes its way through the Kaanapali Resort area. Call ☎ **808/661-3271.** March 17.

- **East Maui Taro Festival,** Hana, Maui. Here's your chance to taste taro in its many different preparations, from poi to chips. Also on hand are Hawaiian exhibits, demonstrations, and food booths. Call ☎ **808/248-8972.** Usually the last weekend in March.

- **Queen Kaahumanu Festival,** Kaahuman Center, Kahului, Maui. A day of celebration for Kamehameha's first wife, with Hawaiian exhibits, entertainment, games, and storytelling. Call ☎ **808/877-3369.**

- **Prince Kuhio Celebration.** Various festivals throughout the state commemorate the birth of Jonah Kuhio Kalanianaole, born March 26, 1871. He might have been one of Hawaii's kings, if not for the U.S. overthrow of the monarchy and Hawaii's annexation to the United States. Prince Kuhio was elected to Congress in 1902. Molokai has a daylong event; call ☎ **808/553-5215.** End of March.

- ✪ **Annual Ritz-Carlton Kapalua Celebration of the Arts,** Ritz-Carlton Kapalua, Maui. Contemporary and traditional artists give hands-on lessons. Call ☎ **808/669-6200.** End of March or early April.

- **Molokai Hawaiian Paniolo Heritage Rodeo,** Molokai Rodeo Arena, Maunaloa, Molokai. A celebration of Hawaii's *paniolo* (cowboy) heritage. Call ☎ **808/552-2791.**

April

- **Buddha Day,** Lahaina Jodo Mission, Lahaina, Maui. This historic mission holds a flower-festival pageant honoring the birth of Buddha. Call ☎ **808/661-4303.** April 6.

- **Polo Season,** Olinda Polo Field, Makawao, Maui. Polo matches featuring Hawaii's top players, often joined by famous international players. Call ☎ **808/572-7326.** Most weekends throughout the summer.

- **Molokai Earth Day,** Mitchell Pauole Center, Kaunakakai, Molokai. A daylong event honoring the natural resources and beauty of the island of Molokai. Call ☎ **808/553-5236.** Mid-April.

- **Da Kine Hawaiian Pro Am Windsurfing,** Hookipa Beach Park, Maui. The top competitors from around the globe flock to the world-famous windsurfing beach for this annual competition. Call ☎ **808/575-9264.**

- ✪ **Maui County Agricultural Trade Show and Sampling,** Ulupalakua Ranch and Tedeschi Winery, Ulupalakua, Maui. The name might be long and cumbersome, but this event is hot, hot, hot. Local product exhibits and sampling, food booths, and live entertainment. Call ☎ **808/875-0457** for this year's schedule.

May

- ✪ **Annual Lei Day Celebration.** May Day is Lei Day in Hawaii, celebrated with lei-making contests, pageantry, arts and crafts, and concerts throughout the islands. Call ☎ **808/879-1922** for Maui events. May 1.

- **Molokai Kayak Challenge,** Molokai to Oahu. Kayakers race 38 grueling miles from Kaluakoi Resort on Molokai to Hawaii Kai's Koko Marina. Call ☎ **808/537-8660.** Mid-May.

✪ **Molokai Ka Hula Piko,** Papohaku Beach Park, Kaluakoi, Molokai. A daylong celebration of the creation of hula on the island where it was born, featuring performances by hula halau, musicians, and singers from across the state. See demonstrations of Hawaiian crafts, including quilting, woodworking, feather work, and deer-horn scrimshaw. Hawaiian foods, including Molokai specialties, are also available. Call ☎ 800/800-6367 or 808/553-3876.

• **Outrigger Canoe Season,** all islands. From May to September, nearly every weekend, canoe paddlers across the state participate in outrigger canoe races. Call ☎ **808/961-5797.**

• **In Celebration of Canoes,** A Street Festival, Front Street, Lahaina, Maui. Daylong events with food booths, music, parades, cultural demonstrations, and more, all in celebration of the Hawaiian canoe. Call ☎ **808/667-9175.**

• **Maui Music Festival,** Kapalua Resort, Maui. Weekend of events featuring the top musicians in the state. Call ☎ **808/661-3271.**

June

✪ **King Kamehameha Celebration,** statewide. It's a state holiday with a massive floral parade, *hoolaulea* (party), and much more. Call ☎ **808/667-9175** for Maui events or ☎ **808/552-2791** for Molokai events. First weekend in June.

• **Cowhorse Classic,** Molokai Rodeo Arena, Maunaloa, Molokai. The island's cowboys celebrate Hawaii's paniolo heritage. Call ☎ **808/552-2791.**

July

• **Makawao Parade and Rodeo,** Makawao, Maui. The annual parade and rodeo event has been taking place in this upcountry cowboy town for generations. Call ☎ **808/572-9565** or 808/572-2076 for this year's date.

✪ **Hoolaulea O Ke Kai—A Molokai Sea Fest,** Kaunakakai, Molokai. Canoe races, windsurfing competition, and Hawaiian music and food at this daylong celebration of the sea. Call ☎ **800/800-6367** or 808/553-3876 for this year's date and schedule.

✪ **Kapalua Wine Symposium,** Kapalua, Maui. Famous wine and food experts and oenophiles gather at the Ritz-Carlton and Kapalua Bay hotels for formal tastings, panel discussions, and samplings of new releases. Call ☎ **800/669-0244** for this year's dates and schedule.

August

• **Pineapple Festival,** Lanai City, Lanai. Some of Hawaii's best musicians participate in Lanai's liveliest event, celebrating the golden fruit with everything from fishing tournaments to pineapple-cooking contests, food and craft booths, water activities, and demonstrations by well-known chefs. Call ☎ **808/565-7600.**

• **Maui Onion Festival,** Whalers Village, Kaanapali, Maui. Everything you ever wanted to know about the sweetest onions in the world. Food, entertainment, tasting, and Maui Onion Cook-Off. Call ☎ **808/661-4567.** First week in August.

• **Admissions Day,** all islands. Hawaii became the 50th state on August 21, 1959, so the state takes a holiday; all state-related facilities will be closed. Third Friday in August.

• **Molokai Museum and Cultural Center Annual Music Festival,** Meyer Sugar Mill and Museum Grounds, Kalae, Molokai. An outdoor music festival featuring top Hawaiian musicians. Call ☎ **808/567-6436.** Saturday following Admissions Day.

September

○ **Aloha Festivals,** various locations statewide. Parades and other events celebrate Hawaiian culture. Call ☎ **800/852-7690,** or 808/545-1771 for a schedule of events.

○ **Great Molokai Mule Drag and Hoolaulea,** Kaunakakai, Molokai. As part of the Aloha Festivals celebration on Molokai, the local residents honor the importance of the mule to the island's heritage with a mule race (which is sometimes a mule-dragging contest) down the main street of Kaunakakai. Call ☎ **800/ 800-6367** or 808/553-3876.

• **Maui Writer's Conference,** Grand Wailea Resort, Wailea, Maui. Workshops, lectures, and panel discussions with writers, agents, and publishers. Call ☎ **808/879-0061.** Labor Day Weekend.

○ **Earth Maui,** Kapalua Resort, Kapalua, Maui. A weeklong series of events to encourage appreciation of Maui's natural environment, plus hiking and snorkeling trips. Call ☎ **800/527-2582** or 808/669-0244 for this year's schedule of events.

• **A Taste of Lahaina,** Lahaina Civic Center, Maui. Some 20,000 people show up to sample 35 signature entrees of Maui's premier chefs during the weekend-long festival, which includes cooking demonstrations, wine tastings, and live entertainment. The weekend kicks off with "Maui Chefs Presents" on Friday, an elegant dinner by Maui's top chefs. Call ☎ **808/667-9175** or e-mail: action@maui.net. Usually mid-September.

• **Hana Relays**, Hana Highway. Hundreds of runners, in relay teams, will crowd the Hana Highway from Kahalui to Hana (you might want to avoid the road this day). Call ☎ **808/871-6441.** Usually the third Saturday in September.

• **Na Wahine O Ke Kai,** Molokai to Waikiki. A women's 40.8-mile outrigger canoe race from Molokai to Oahu. Departs from Hale O Lono, Molokai, and finishes at Duke Kahanamoku Beach, Hilton Hawaiian Village, Waikiki. Call ☎ **808/262-7567.** End of September.

• **Tour of Champions Mountain Bike Race,** Molokai Ranch, Molokai. Invited elite mountain-bike racers flock to Molokai to compete for some $100,000 in prize money in this prestigious race. Call ☎ **808/552-2791.**

October

• **Run to the Sun,** Paia to Haleakala, Maui. The world's top ultramarathoners make the journey from sea level to the top of 10,000-foot Haleakala, some 37 miles. Call ☎ **808/871-6441.**

• **Maui County Fair,** War Memorial Complex, Wailuku, Maui. The oldest county fair in Hawaii features a parade, amusement rides, live entertainment, and exhibits. Call ☎ **808/242-2721.** Early October.

○ **Aloha Classic World Wavesailing Championship,** Hookipa Beach, Maui. The top windsurfers in the world gather for this final event in the Pro Boardsailing World Tour. If you're on Maui, don't miss it—it's spectacular to watch. Call ☎ **808/575-9151.**

• **Molokai Hoe,** Molokai to Oahu. The season's biggest canoe race, this men's 40.8-mile outrigger contest crosses the channel from Molokai to finish at Fort DeRussy Beach in Waikiki. Call ☎ **808/261-6615.** Mid-October.

○ **Halloween in Lahaina,** Maui. There's Carnival in Rio, Mardi Gras in New Orleans, and Halloween in Lahaina. Come to this giant costume party (some 20,000 people show up) on the streets of Lahaina; Front Street is closed off for the party. It'll be the greatest memory of your trip. Call ☎ **808/667-9175.**

November

- **Hawaii International Film Festival,** various locations on Maui. A cinema festival with a cross-cultural spin, featuring filmmakers from Asia, the Pacific Islands, and the United States. Call ☎ **808/528-FILM** or www.hiff.org. Mid-November.
- **Molokai Ranch Rodeo and Great Molokai Stew Cookoff,** Molokai Rodeo Arena, Maunaloa, Molokai. The island's cowboys celebrate Hawaii's paniolo heritage. Call ☎ **800/800-6367** or 808/552-2791.
- **Festival of Art & Flowers,** Lahaina, Maui. The weekend before Thanksgiving is celebrated in Lahaina with flowers: cut flower displays, floral arrangements, demonstrations, lei-making contests, art exhibits, and entertainment. Call ☎ **808/667-9175** or e-mail: action@maui.net.
- **Maui Invitational Basketball Tournament**, Lahaina Civic Center, Maui. Top college teams vie in this annual preseason tournament. Call ☎ **312/755-3577.**
- **Kapalua Betsy Nagelsen Pro Am Tennis Invitational**, Kapalua Tennis Garden, Maui. Top women pro tennis players compete in this prestigious event. Call ☎ **808/669-5677.**

December

- **Old-Fashioned Holiday Celebration,** Lahaina, Maui. The second Saturday in December, in the Banyan Tree Park on Front Street, is a day of Christmas carolers, Santa Claus, live music and entertainment, a crafts fair, baked goods, and activities for children. Call ☎ **808/667-9175** or e-mail: action@maui.net.
- **Festival of Lights,** island-wide. Festivities include parades and tree-lighting ceremonies. Call ☎ **808/667-9175** on Maui, or 808/567-6361 on Molokai. Early December.
- ✪ **First Night,** Maui Arts and Cultural Center, Maui. Hawaii's largest festival of arts and entertainment takes place on three different islands. For 12 hours, musicians, dancers, actors, jugglers, magicians, and mimes perform, food is available, and fireworks bring in the New Year. Alcohol-free. Call ☎ **808/242-7469.** December 31.

4 What to Pack

Maui is very informal: You'll get by with shorts, T-shirts, and sneakers at most attractions and restaurants; a casual dress or a polo shirt and khakis is fine even in the most expensive places. Dinner jackets are required only at a very few resorts, such as the Lodge at Koele on Lanai, and they'll cordially provide a jacket if you don't bring your own. Don't forget a long-sleeved cover-up (to throw on at the beach when you've had enough sun for the day), rubber water shoes or flip-flops, and hiking shoes and several pairs of good socks if you plan to do any hiking.

The tropical sun poses the greatest threat to anyone who ventures into the great outdoors, so be sure to bring **sun protection:** sunglasses, strong sunscreen, a light hat (like a baseball cap or a sun visor), binoculars (if you have them), and a canteen or water bottle if you'll be hiking—you'll easily dehydrate on the trail in the tropic heat, so figure on carrying 2 liters of water per day on any hike. Campers should bring water purification tablets or devices. Also see "Staying Healthy," below.

Don't bother overstuffing your suitcase with 2 whole weeks' worth of shorts and T-shirts: Maui has **laundry facilities** everywhere. If your accommodation doesn't have a washer and dryer or laundry service, there will most likely be a laundry nearby. The only exception to this is Hana; the tiny town has no Laundromat, so either check with the place you're staying beforehand, or do a load of laundry before you arrive.

One last thing: **It really can get cold on Maui.** If you plan to see the sunrise from the top of Haleakala, bring a warm jacket—40°F upcountry temperatures, even in summer when it's 80°F at the beach, are not uncommon. It's always a good idea to bring long pants and a windbreaker, sweater, or light jacket. And be sure to bring along rain gear if you'll be in Maui from November to March.

5 The Active Vacation Planner

If you want nothing more on your vacation than a fabulous beach and a perfectly mixed mai tai, you're in luck—Maui has some of the most spectacular beaches (not to mention the best mai tais) in the world. But Maui's wealth of natural wonders is hard to resist; the year-round tropical climate and spectacular scenery tend to inspire even the most committed desk jockeys and couch potatoes to get outside and explore.

If you have your own snorkel gear or other water-sports equipment, bring it if you can. However, if you don't have it, don't fret; everything you'll need is available for rent. We discuss all kinds of places to rent or buy gear in chapter 6.

SETTING OUT ON YOUR OWN VERSUS USING AN OUTFITTER

There are two ways to go: Plan all the details before you go and schlepp your gear 2,500 miles across the Pacific, or go with an outfitter or a guide and let them worry about the details.

Experienced outdoors enthusiasts can follow their nose to coastal campgrounds or even trek into the rain forest on their own, but it's often preferable to go with a local guide who is familiar with the conditions at both sea level and the summit, knows the land and its flora and fauna in detail, and has all the gear you'll need. It's also good to go with a guide if time is an issue. If you really want to see native birds, for instance, an experienced guide will take you directly to the best areas for sightings. And many forests and valleys in the interior of the islands are either on private property or in wilderness preserves that are accessible only on guided tours. If you go with a guide, plan on spending at least $100 a day per person; we recommend the best local outfitters and tour-guide operators in chapter 6.

But if you have the time, already own the gear, and love doing the research and planning, try exploring on your own. Chapter 6 discusses the best spots to set out on your own, from the best offshore snorkel and dive spots to great daylong hikes, as well as the federal, state, and county agencies that can help you with hikes on public property; we also list references for spotting birds, plants, and sea life. We recommend that you always use the resources available and inquire about weather, trail or surf conditions, water availability, and other conditions before you take off on your adventure.

For hikers, a great alternative to hiring a private guide is taking one of the guided hikes offered by the **Nature Conservancy of Hawaii,** 1116 Smith St., Honolulu, HI 96817 (☎ **808/537-4508** on Oahu; 808/573-4147 on Maui; 808/553-5236 or 808/524-0779 on Molokai), and the **Hawaii Chapter of the Sierra Club,** P.O. Box 2577, Honolulu, HI 96803 (☎ **808/573-4147** on Maui; www.hi.sierraclub.org). Both organizations offer guided hikes on preserves and special places during the year, as well as 1- to 7-day work trips to restore habitats and trails and root out invasive plants like banana poka, New Zealand flax, nonnative gorse, and wild ginger. It might not sound like a dream vacation to everyone, but it's a chance to see the "real" Maui—including wilderness areas that are usually off-limits.

All Nature Conservancy hikes are free. However, you must reserve a spot, and a deposit is required for guided hikes to ensure that you'll show up; your deposit is refunded once you do. The hikes are generally offered once a month on Maui,

Safety Tip

Be sure to see "Staying Healthy," below, before setting out on any adventure; it includes useful information on hiking, camping, and ocean safety. Even if you just plan to lie on the beach, check out the box "Don't Get Burned: Smart Tanning Tips," on page 34, to learn how to protect yourself against the sun's harmful rays— a must for *everyone* in Maui.

Molokai, and Lanai (call the Oahu office for reservations). There's also no charge for the trips to restore habitats. Write for a schedule of guided hikes and other programs.

The Sierra Club offers weekly hikes on Maui. Hikes are led by certified Sierra Club volunteers and are classified as easy, moderate, or strenuous. These half-day or all-day affairs cost $1 for Sierra Club members, $3 for nonmembers (bring exact change). For a copy of the newsletter, which lists all outings and trail repair work, send $2 to the address above.

USING ACTIVITIES DESKS TO BOOK YOUR ISLAND FUN

If you want to go with an outfitter or a guide—especially if you're interested in an activity that requires an outfitter or a guide, such as horseback riding, whale watching, or sportfishing—and you'd like to save some money, you might want to consider booking your activity through a discount activities center or activities desk. These agents—whose sole business it is to act as a clearinghouse for activities, much like a consolidator functions as a discount clearinghouse for airline tickets—can often get you a better price than you'd get by booking an activity directly with the outfitter.

Discount activities centers will, in effect, split their commission with you, giving themselves a smaller commission to get your business—and passing, on average, a 10% discount on to you. In addition to saving you money, good activities centers should be able to help you find, say, the snorkel cruise that's right for you, or the luau that's most suitable for both you *and* the kids. But it's in the activities agent's best interest to sign you up with outfitters from which they earn the most commission; some agents have no qualms about booking you into any activity if it means an extra buck for them. If an agent tries to push a particular outfitter or activity too hard, be skeptical. Conversely, they'll try to steer you away from outfitters that don't offer big commissions. For example, Trilogy, the company that offers Maui's most popular snorkel cruises to Lanai (and the only one with rights to land at Lanai's Hulupoe Beach), offers only minimal commissions to agents and does not allow agents to offer any discounts at all; as a result, most activities desks you speak to on Maui will automatically try to steer you away from Trilogy even if you say you want to book with it.

Another important word of warning: Be careful to avoid those activities centers offering discounts as fronts for time-share sales presentations. Using a free snorkel cruise or luau tickets as bait, they'll suck you into a 90-minute presentation—and try to get you to buy into a Maui time-share in the process. Not only will they try to sell you a big white elephant you never wanted in the first place, but—since their business is time-shares, not activities—they also won't be as interested, or as knowledgeable, about which activities might be right for you. These shady deals seem to be particularly rampant on Maui. Just do yourself a favor and avoid them altogether.

On Maui, we recommend **Tom Barefoot's Cashback Tours** (e-mail: barefoot@maui.net), at Dolphin Shopping Center, 2395 S. Kihei Rd., Kihei (☎ **808/879-4100**), and at 834 Front St., Lahaina (☎ **808/661-8889**). Tom offers a 10% discount on all tours, activities, and adventures when you pay in cash or with traveler's checks. If you pay with a credit card or personal check, he'll give you a 7%

discount. The two showrooms are loaded with pictures and maps of all the activities the company books. We found Tom's to be very reliable and honest.

OUTDOOR ETIQUETTE

Act locally, think globally, and carry out what you carry in. Find a trash container for all your litter (including cigarette butts; it's *very* bad form to throw them out of your car window). Observe *kapu* (taboo) and NO TRESPASSING signs. Don't climb on ancient Hawaiian *heiau* (temple) walls or carry home rocks, all of which belong to the Hawaiian volcano goddess, Pele. Some say it's just a silly superstition or coincidence, but each year the National and State Park Services get boxes of lava rocks in the mail, sent back to Hawaii by visitors who have experienced unusually bad luck.

6 Staying Healthy

Maui is one of the most healthful places in the world to visit. People who live here have a longer life expectancy than anywhere else in the United States (74 years for men and 78 years for women). However, there are some natural hazards you should be aware of so that, if necessary, you can take the proper steps to prevent them from blooming into full-scale problems.

ON LAND

As in any tropical climate, there are lots of bugs in Maui. Most of them won't harm you; however, three insects—mosquitoes, centipedes, and scorpions—do sting, and they can cause anything from mild annoyance to severe swelling and pain.

MOSQUITOES   These pesky insects aren't native to Hawaii, but arrived as larvae stowed away in the water barrels on the ship *Wellington* in 1826. There's not a whole lot you can do about them, except to apply commercial repellent to keep them off you, burn mosquito punk or citronella candles to keep them out of your area, or apply sting-stopping ointments (available at any drugstore) after they've stung you to ease the itching and swelling. Most bites disappear in anywhere from a few hours to a few days.

CENTIPEDES   These segmented insects with a jillion legs come in two varieties: 6- to 8-inch-long brown ones and the smaller 2- to 3-inch-long blue guys; both can really pack a wallop with their sting. Centipedes are generally found in damp, wet places, like under wood piles or compost heaps; wearing closed-toe shoes can help prevent stings if you accidentally unearth a centipede. If you're stung, the reaction can range from something similar to a mild bee sting to severe pain; apply ice at once to prevent swelling. See a doctor if you experience extreme pain, swelling, nausea, or any other severe reaction.

SCORPIONS   Rarely seen, scorpions are found in arid, warm regions; their stings can be serious. Campers in dry areas should always check their boots before putting them on, and shake out sleeping bags and bed rolls. Symptoms of a scorpion sting include shortness of breath, hives, swelling, and nausea. In the unlikely event that you're stung, apply diluted household ammonia and cold compresses to the area of the sting and seek medical attention immediately.

HIKING SAFETY

In addition to taking the appropriate cautions regarding Maui's bug population (see above), hikers should always let someone know where they're heading, when they're going, and when they plan to return; too many hikers get lost on Maui because they don't inform others of their basic plans.

Always check weather conditions with the **National Weather Service** (☎ 808/ 877-5111) before you go. Hike with a pal, never alone. Wear hiking boots, a sun hat, clothes to protect you from the sun and from getting scratches, and high-SPF sunscreen on all exposed areas of skin. Take water. Stay on the trail. Watch your step. It's easy to slip off precipitous trails and into steep canyons, with often disastrous, even fatal, results. Incapacitated hikers are often plucked to safety by fire and rescue squads, who must use helicopters to gain access to remote sites. Many experienced hikers and boaters today pack a cellular phone in case of emergency; just dial ☎ **911.**

VOG

The volcanic haze dubbed "vog" is caused by gases released when molten lava—from the continuous eruption of the volcano on the flank of Kilauea on the Big Island— pours into the ocean. This hazy air, which looks like urban smog, limits viewing from scenic vistas and wreaks havoc with photographers trying to get clear panoramic shots. Some people claim that long-term exposure to vog has even caused bronchial ailments.

There actually is a "vog" season in Hawaii: the fall and winter months, when the trade winds that blow the fumes out to sea die down. The vog is felt not only on the Big Island but as far away as Maui and Oahu.

OCEAN SAFETY

Because most people coming to Maui are unfamiliar with the ocean environment, they're often unaware of the natural hazards it holds. But with just a few precautions, your ocean experience can be a safe and happy one. An excellent book to get is *All Stings Considered: First Aid and Medical Treatment of Hawaii's Marine Injuries* (University of Hawaii Press, 1997), by Craig Thomas (an emergency-medicine doctor) and Susan Scott (a registered nurse). These avid water people have put together the authoritative book on first aid for Hawaii's marine injuries.

SEASICKNESS   The waters off Maui can range from calm as glass to downright frightening (in storm conditions), and they usually fall somewhere in between; in general, expect rougher conditions in winter than in summer.

Some 90% of the population tends toward seasickness. If you've never been out on a boat or if you've gotten seasick in the past, you might want to heed the following suggestions:

- The day before you go out on the boat, avoid alcohol; caffeine; citrus and other acidic juices; and greasy, spicy, or hard-to-digest foods.
- Get a good night's sleep the night before.
- Take or use whatever seasickness prevention works best for you—medication, an acupressure wristband, gingerroot tea or capsules, or any combination—*before* you board; once you set sail, it's generally too late.
- Once you're on the water, stay as low and as near the center of the boat as possible. Avoid the fumes (especially if it's a diesel boat); stay out in the fresh air and watch the horizon. Do not read.
- If you start to feel queasy, drink clear fluids like water, and eat something bland, such as a soda cracker.

STINGS   The most common stings in Hawaii come from jellyfish, particularly Portuguese man-of-war and box jellyfish. Since the poisons they inject are very different, you need to treat each sting differently.

Portuguese Man-of-War   A bluish-purple floating bubble with a long tail, the Portuguese man-of-war causes some 6,500 stings a year on Oahu alone. Stings, although painful and a nuisance, are rarely harmful; fewer than 1 in 1,000 requires medical treatment. The best prevention is to watch for these floating bubbles as you snorkel (look for the hanging tentacles below the surface). Get out of the water if anyone near you spots these jellyfish.

Reactions to stings range from mild burning and redness to severe welts and blisters. *All Stings Considered* recommends the following treatment: First, pick off any visible tentacles with a gloved hand, a stick, or anything handy; rinse the sting with salt or fresh water; and apply ice to prevent swelling and to help control pain.

Hawaii folklore advises using vinegar, meat tenderizer, baking soda, papain, or alcohol, or even urinating on the wound. Studies have shown that these remedies may actually cause further damage. Most Portuguese man-of-war stings will disappear by themselves within 15 to 20 minutes if you do nothing to treat them. Still, be sure to see a doctor if pain persists or if a rash or other symptoms develop.

Box Jellyfish These transparent, square-shaped bell jellyfish are nearly impossible to see in the water. Fortunately, they seem to follow a monthly cycle: 8 to 10 days after the full moon, they appear in the waters on the leeward side of the island and hang around for about 3 days. Also, they seem to sting more in the morning hours, when they're on or near the surface. The best prevention is to get out of the water.

Stings range from no visible marks to red, hivelike welts, blisters, and pain (a burning sensation) lasting from 10 minutes to 8 hours. *All Stings Considered* recommends the following course of treatment: First, pour regular household vinegar on the sting; this may not relieve the pain, but it will stop additional burning. Do not rub the area. Pick off any vinegar-soaked tentacles with a stick. For pain, apply an ice pack. Seek additional medical treatment if you experience shortness of breath, weakness, palpitations, muscle cramps, or any other severe symptoms. Again, ignore any folk remedies. Most box jellyfish stings disappear by themselves without treatment.

PUNCTURES Most sea-related punctures come from stepping on or brushing against the needlelike spines of sea urchins (known locally as *wana*). Be careful when you're in the water; don't put your foot down (even if you have booties or fins on) if you cannot clearly see the bottom. Waves can push you into wana in a surge zone in shallow water (the wana's spines can even puncture a wet suit).

A sea urchin sting can result in burning, aching, swelling, and discoloration (black or purple) around the area where the spines have entered your skin. The best thing to do is to pull any protruding spines out. The body will absorb the spines within 24 hours to 3 weeks, or the remainder of the spines will work themselves out. Again, contrary to popular wisdom, do not urinate or pour vinegar on the embedded spines—this will not help.

CUTS All cuts obtained in the marine environment must be taken seriously, because the high level of bacteria present can quickly cause the cut to become infected. The most common cuts are from coral. Contrary to popular belief, coral cannot grow inside your body. However, bacteria can—and very often does—grow inside a cut. The best way to prevent cuts is to wear a wet suit, gloves, and reef shoes. Never, under any circumstances, should you touch a coral head; not only can you get cut, but you can also damage a living organism that took decades to grow.

The symptoms of a coral cut can range from a slight scratch to severe welts and blisters. *All Stings Considered* recommends gently pulling the edges of the skin open and removing any embedded coral or grains of sand with tweezers, or rinsing well with fresh water. Next, scrub the cut well with fresh water. Never use ocean water to clean a cut. If the wound is bleeding, press a clean cloth against it until it stops. If bleeding continues, or the edges of the injury are jagged or gaping, seek medical treatment.

Don't Get Burned: Smart Tanning Tips

For years, the best souvenir to bring back from Maui was a golden tan. Oh, the look of envy from your friends as your bronzed glow silently told the world that you'd just returned from Hawaii!

Tanning just ain't what it used to be. Nowadays, it can kill you—especially if, in your quest for a tan, you get burned instead. Strong words, but supported by reality: Hawaii's Caucasian population has a higher incidence of deadly skin cancer, malignant melanoma, than anywhere else in the United States. But none of us are safe from the sun's harmful rays: People of all skin types and races can burn when exposed to the sun too long.

To ensure that your vacation won't be ruined by a painful, throbbing sunburn, here are some helpful tips on how to tan safely and painlessly:

- **Wear a strong sunscreen at all times—and use lots of it.** Use a sunscreen with a sun-protection factor (SPF) of 15 or higher; people with a light complexion should use 30. Apply sunscreen as soon as you get out of the shower in the morning, and at least 30 minutes before you're exposed to the sun. You need a tablespoon of lotion per limb; slather it on and rub it in. No matter what the box says—even if the sunscreen is waterproof—reapply it every 2 hours and immediately after swimming.

- **Read the labels.** To prevent developing allergies to sunscreens, avoid those that contain para-aminobenzoic acid (PABA). Look for a sunscreen with zinc oxide, talc, or titanium dioxide, which reduce the risk of developing skin allergies. For the best protection from UVA rays (which can cause wrinkles and premature aging), check the label for zinc oxide, benzophenone, oxybenzone, sulisobenzone, titanium dioxide, or avobenzone (also known as Parsol 1789).

- **Wear a hat and sunglasses.** The hat should have a minimum 4-inch-wide brim (all the way around, to cover not only your face but also the sensitive

7 Getting Married on Maui

Whatever your dreams and your budget, Maui is a great place for a wedding. Not only does the entire island exude romance and natural beauty, but after the ceremony, you're only a few steps away from the perfect honeymoon. And the members of your wedding party will most likely be delighted, since you've given them the perfect excuse for their own island vacation.

It happens every day of the year in Hawaii, where more than 20,000 marriages are performed each year. Nearly half (44.6%) of the couples married here are from somewhere else. This booming business has spawned dozens of companies that can help you organize a long-distance event and stage an unforgettable wedding, Hawaiian style or your style. However, you can also plan your own island wedding, even from afar, and not spend a fortune doing it.

THE PAPERWORK

The state of Hawaii has some very minimal procedures for obtaining a marriage license. The first thing you should do is contact the **Marriage License Office,** State Department of Health Building, 54 S. High St., Wailuku, HI 96793 (☎ **808/ 984-8210;** www.hawaii.gov), open Monday through Friday from 8am to 4pm. The staff will mail you a brochure, *Getting Married,* and direct you to the marriage licensing agent closest to where you'll be staying on Maui.

back of your neck). Make sure that your sunglasses have UV filters to protect your corneas from getting sunburned and to prevent cataracts. To avoid the irritation of sunscreen dripping into your eyes, use a waxy sunscreen stick (available just about everywhere in Maui) to draw half-circles above your eyebrows.

- **Avoid being in the sun between 9am and 3pm.** Seek the shade during these peak hours. Remember that a beach umbrella is not protection enough from the sun's harmful UV rays; in fact, with the reflection from the water, the sand, and even the sidewalk, some 85% of the ultraviolet rays are still bombarding you.

- **Protect children from the sun, and keep infants out of the sun altogether.** Infants under 6 months should not be in the sun at all. Older babies need zinc oxide to protect their fragile skin, and children should be slathered with sunscreen every hour. The burns that children get today predict what their future will be with skin cancer tomorrow.

If you start to turn red, **get out of the sun.** Contrary to popular belief, you don't have to turn red to tan; if your skin is red, it's burned—and that's serious. The redness from a burn may not show until 2 to 8 hours after you get out of the sun, and the full force of that burn may not appear for 24 to 36 hours. During that time, you can look forward to pain, itching, and peeling. The best **remedy** for a sunburn is to get out of the sun immediately and stay out of the sun until all the redness is gone. Aloe vera (straight from the plant or from a commercial preparation), cool compresses, cold baths, and anesthetic benzocaine may also help with the pain of sunburn.

If you've decided to get a head start on your tan by using a self-tanning lotion that dyes your skin a darker shade, remember that this will not protect you from the sun. You'll still need to generously apply sunscreen when you go out.

Once on Maui, the prospective bride and groom must go together to the marriage licensing agent to get a license. A license costs $25 and is good for 30 days; if you don't have the ceremony within the time allotted, you'll have to pay another $25 for another license. The only requirements for a marriage license are that both parties are 15 years of age or older (couples 15 to 17 years old must have proof of age, written consent of both parents, and the written approval of the judge of the family court) and are not more closely related than first cousins. That's it.

Contrary to some reports from the media, gay couples cannot marry in Hawaii. Although the state courts ruled a few years ago that the state of Hawaii had to show a compelling reason why it wouldn't issue a marriage license to gay couples, the issue is still being decided in the courts and debated in the state legislature. Until the issue is decided, the state will not issue marriage licenses to same-sex couples.

PLANNING THE WEDDING

DOING IT YOURSELF   The marriage licensing agents, which range from the governor's satellite office to private individuals, are usually friendly, helpful people who can steer you to a nondenominational minister or marriage performer who's licensed by the state of Hawaii to perform the ceremony. These marriage performers are great sources of information for budget weddings. They usually know great places to have the ceremony for free or for a nominal fee.

If you don't want to use a wedding planner (see below) but want to make arrangements before you arrive on Maui, our best advice is to get a copy of the daily newspaper, the *Maui News,* P.O. Box 550, Wailuku, HI 96793 (☎ **808/244-7691**). People willing and qualified to conduct weddings advertise in the classifieds. They're great sources of information, because they know the best places to have the ceremony and can recommend caterers, florists, and everything else you'll need.

USING A WEDDING PLANNER   Wedding planners, many of whom are marriage licensing agents as well, can arrange everything for you, from a small, private outdoor affair to a full-blown formal ceremony in a tropical setting. They charge anywhere from $450 to a small fortune—it all depends on what you want. Planners on Maui include **A Wedding Made in Paradise,** P.O. Box 986, Kihei, HI 96753 (☎ 800/453-3440 or 808/879-3444; fax 808/874-1278; www.wedinparadise.com; e-mail: wedmaui@ maui.net); **A Dream Wedding: Maui Style,** 143 Dickenson St., Suite 201, Lahaina, HI 96761 (☎ 800/743-2777; fax 808/667-2042; www.maui. net/~dreamwed/dream.html; e-mail: dreamwed@maui.net); **A Romantic Maui Wedding,** P.O. Box 13232, Lahaina, HI 96761 (☎ 800/808-4144 or 808/874-6444; fax 808/879-5525; www.justmauied.com; e-mail: sandy@justmauied.com); **Dolphin Dream Weddings,** P.O. Box 10546, Lahaina, HI 96761 (☎ 800/793-2WED or 808/661-8535; www.maui.net/~dolphin; e-mail: dolphin@maui.net); and **Simply Married,** 2718 Iolani St., Pukalani, HI 96768 (☎ 800/291-0110 or 808/572-7898; fax 800/368-6933 or 808/572-1240; www.maui.net/~married; e-mail: married @maui.net).

8 Tips for Travelers with Special Needs

FOR TRAVELERS WITH DISABILITIES

Travelers with disabilities are made to feel very welcome on Maui. Hotels are usually equipped with wheelchair-accessible rooms, and tour companies provide many special services. The **Commission on Persons with Disabilities,** 919 Ala Moana Blvd., Suite 101, Honolulu, HI 96814 (☎ **808/586-8121**), and the **Hawaii Center for Independent Living,** 414 Kauwili St., Suite 102, Honolulu, HI 96817 (☎ **808/ 522-5400;** fax 808/586-8129; www.hawaii.gov/health/cpd_indx.htm; e-mail: cpdppp@aloha.net), can provide information and send you a copy of the *Aloha Guide to Accessibility* ($15).

A World of Options, a 658-page book of resources for travelers with disabilities, covers everything from biking trips to scuba outfitters. It costs $45 and is available from **Mobility International USA,** P.O. Box 10767, Eugene, OR 97440 (☎ **541/343-1284,** voice and TDD; www.miusa.org). For information on travel destinations, services, accommodations, and transportation, contact **Access/Abilities,** P.O. Box 458, Mill Valley, CA 94942 (☎ **415-388-3250;** www.accessabil.com).

The **Society for the Advancement of Travel for the Handicapped** (SATH), 347 Fifth Ave., Suite 610, New York, NY 10016 (☎ **212/447-7284;** fax 212/725-8253; www.sath.org; e-mail: sathtravel@aol.com), serves as a central clearinghouse for the exchange of information on travel facilities for people with disabilities. Their quarterly magazine, *Open World for Disability and Mature Travel,* is full of good information and resources. **Travelin' Talk Network,** P.O. Box 3534, Clarksville, TN 37043-6670 (☎ **615/552-6670**), has a directory of members willing to share their knowledge of certain areas with travelers with disabilities.

Publications for travelers with disabilities include *Annual Directory of Travel Agencies for the Disabled,* Twin Peaks Press, P.O. Box 129, Vancouver, WA 98666-0129

(☎ 360/694-2462); *Travel Resources for Deaf and Heard of Hearing People,* c/o Gallaudet University, 800 Florida Ave. NE, Washington, DC 20002-3695 (☎ 202/651-5051, or TTY 202/651-5052; www.gallaudet.edu/~nicd); and *The Wheelchair Traveler,* 123 Ball Hill Rd., Milford, NE 03055 (☎ 603/673-4539), which has information on hotels, restaurants, and sightseeing for wheelchair users.

On the Internet, check out **Access-Able Travel Source** (www.access-able.com), which provides information for disabled travelers. **Accessible Vans of Hawaii,** 186 Mehani Circle, Kihei, HI 96753 (☎ 800/303-3750 or 808/879-5521; fax 808/879-0640; www.accessiblevans.com), has details on renting a van in Hawaii.

For travelers with disabilities who want to do their own driving, hand-controlled cars can be rented from **Avis** (☎ 800/331-1212) and **Hertz** (☎ 800/654-3131). The number of hand-controlled cars in Maui is limited, so be sure to book well in advance. Hawaii recognizes other states' windshield placards indicating that the driver of the car has a disability; these can give you access to specially marked handicapped parking spaces, so be sure to bring yours with you.

Vision-impaired travelers who use a Seeing-Eye dog can now travel to Maui without the hassle of quarantine. A recent court decision ruled that visitors with Seeing-Eye dogs need only present documentation that the dog has had rabies shots and that it is a trained Seeing-Eye dog in order to bypass quarantine. Previously, all dogs and cats in Hawaii had to spend 4 months in quarantine, since Hawaii is rabies-free (quarantine has been reduced to 1 month, Seeing-Eye dogs exempted). For more information, contact the **Animal Quarantine Facility** (☎ 808/483-7171; www.hawaii.gov).

FOR GAY & LESBIAN TRAVELERS

Known for its acceptance of all groups, Hawaii welcomes gays and lesbians just as it does any other group.

The best guide for gay and lesbian visitors is travel writer Matthew Link's *Rainbow Handbook Hawaii,* which not only covers travel on every island, but also has information on Hawaii's gay history, gay and lesbian businesses in the state, and interviews with Hawaii residents. The book is available for $14.95 by writing P.O. Box 100, Honaunau, HI 96726 (☎ 800/260-5528; www.rainbowhandbook.com).

To get a sense of the local gay and lesbian community, contact **Both Sides Now,** P.O. Box 5042, Kahului, HI 96733-5042 (☎ 808/244-4566; fax 808/874-6221; www.maui-tech.com/glom; e-mail: gaymaui@maui.net), which publishes a monthly newspaper on news, issues, and events for Maui's gay, lesbian, bisexual, and transgendered community.

For the latest information on the gay marriage issue, contact the **Hawaii Marriage Project** (☎ 808/532-9000).

Pacific Ocean Holidays, P.O. Box 88245, Honolulu, HI 96830 (☎ 800/735-6600 or 808/923-2400; www.gayhawaii.com), offers vacation packages that feature gay-owned and gay-friendly lodgings. It also publishes the *Pocket Guide to Hawaii: A Guide for Gay Visitors & Kamaaina,* a list of gay-owned and gay-friendly businesses throughout the islands. Send $5 for a copy (mail order only; no phone orders, please), or access the online version on the Web site.

FOR SENIORS

Discounts for seniors are available at almost all of Maui's major attractions, and occasionally at hotels and restaurants. Always inquire when making hotel reservations. Members of the **American Association of Retired Persons** (AARP), 601 E St. NW, Washington, DC 20049 (☎ 800/424-3410 or 202/434-2277), are usually eligible for such discounts; AARP also puts together organized tour packages at moderate rates. The **National Council of Senior Citizens,** 8403 Colesville Dr., Suite 1200, Silver Spring, MD 20910 (☎ **301/578-8800**), a nonprofit organization, offers members hotel, condominium, and car-rental discounts, as well as a 24-hour emergency alert service for accident, injury, or illness.

Some great, low-cost trips to Hawaii are offered to people 55 and older through **Elderhostel,** 75 Federal St., Boston, MA 02110 (☎ **617/426-8056;** www.elderhostel.org), a nonprofit group that arranges travel and study programs around the world. You can obtain a complete catalog of offerings by writing to Elderhostel, P.O. Box 1959, Wakefield, MA 01880-5959.

If you're planning to visit Haleakala National Park, you can save sightseeing dollars if you're 62 or older by picking up a **Golden Age Passport** from any national park, recreation area, or monument. This lifetime pass has a one-time fee of $10 and provides free admission to all of the parks in the system, plus a 50% savings on camping and recreation fees. You can pick one up at any park entrance; be sure to have proof of your age with you.

FOR FAMILIES

Maui is paradise for children: beaches to frolic on, water to splash in, unusual sights to see, and a host of new foods to taste. Be sure to check out "Family-Friendly Accommodations," in chapter 4, and "Especially for Kids," in chapter 7.

The larger hotels and resorts have supervised programs for children and can refer you to qualified baby-sitters. You can also contact **People Attentive to Children** (☎ **808/242-9232**), which will refer you to individuals who have taken their training courses on child care.

9 Money-Saving Package Deals

Booking an all-inclusive travel package that includes some combination of airfare, accommodations, rental car, meals, airport and baggage transfers, and sightseeing can be the most cost-effective way to travel to Maui. You can sometimes save so much money by buying all the pieces of your trip through a packager that your transpacific airfare ends up, in effect, being free.

The best place to start looking for a package deal is in the travel section of your local Sunday newspaper. Also check the ads in the back of such national travel magazines as *Travel & Leisure, National Geographic Traveler,* and *Condé Nast Traveller.* **Liberty Travel** (many locations; check your local directory, since there's no central toll-free number), for instance, one of the biggest packagers in the Northeast, usually boasts a full-page ad in Sunday papers. You won't find much in the way of service, but you will get a good deal. **American Express Travel** (☎ 800/AXP-6898; www.americanexpress.com/travel) can also book you a well-priced Hawaiian vacation; it also advertises in many Sunday travel sections.

Hawaii is such an ideal destination for vacation packages that some packagers book Hawaiian vacations as the majority of their business. **Pleasant Hawaiian Holidays** (☎ 800/2-HAWAII or 800/242-9244; www.pleasantholidays.com or www.2hawaii.com) is by far the biggest and most comprehensive packager to Hawaii; it offers an extensive, high-quality collection of 50 condos and hotels in every price range.

Other reliable packagers include the airlines themselves, which often package their flights together with accommodations. Among the airlines offering good-value package deals to Hawaii are **American Airlines FlyAway Vacations** (☎ 800/321-2121; www.2travel.com/americanair/hawaii.html), **Continental Airlines Vacations** (☎ 800/634-5555 or 800/301-3800; www.coolvacations.com), **Delta**

Package-Buying Tip

For one-stop shopping on the Web, go to **www.vacationpackager.com**, a search engine that can link you up to many different package-tour operators, who can then help you plan a custom-tailored trip to Maui. Be sure to look under "Maui," "Hawaii," and the "Hawaiian Islands."

Dream Vacations (☎ 800/872-7786; www.deltavacations.com), **TWA Getaway Vacations** (☎ 800/GETAWAY or 800/438-2929; www.twa.com), and **United Vacations** (☎ 800/328-6877; www.unitedvacations.com). If you're traveling to the islands from Canada, ask your travel agent about package deals through **Air Canada Vacations** (☎ 800/776-3000; www.aircanada.ca).

GREAT DEALS AT HAWAII'S TOP HOTEL CHAINS

Hawaii's three major hotel chains—which together represent nearly 100 hotels, condominiums, resorts, a historic B&B, and even restored plantation homes—have a host of packages that will save you money.

With some 28 properties in Hawaii, including four on Maui, **Outrigger** (☎ **800/OUTRIGGER;** fax 800/622-4852; www.outrigger.com) offers excellent affordable accommodations, all with consistently dependable, clean, and well-appointed rooms. The chain's price structure is based entirely on location, room size, and amenities. You'll be comfortable at any of the chain's outposts: The small rooms at the budget Outriggers are just as tastefully appointed as the larger, more expensive Outrigger rooms right on the beach. Package deals include discounted rates for spring and fall stays, a car package, deals on multinight stays, family plans, cut rates for seniors, and even packages for scuba divers (2 days of two-tank boat dives and a 3-night stay starts at $311 per person, double occupancy).

The **Aston** chain (☎ **800/92-ASTON;** fax 808/922-8785; www.aston-hotels. com), which celebrated 50 years in Hawaii in 1998, has some 29 hotels, condominiums, and resort properties scattered throughout the islands, with eight on Maui. They range dramatically in price and style, from the oceanfront Maui Lu Resort to the economical Aston Maui Islander. Aston offers package deals galore, including family plans; discounted senior rates; car, golf, and shopping packages; and deals on multinight stays, including a wonderful "Island Hopper" deal that allows you to hop from island to island and get 25% off on 7 nights or more at Aston properties.

Marc Resorts Hawaii (☎ **800/535-0085;** fax 800/633-5085; www.marcresorts. com) has 22 properties on every island but Lanai, ranging from the luxury Embassy Suite Resort in Kaanapali to the affordable Molokai Shores condominium on Molokai. The chain offers package deals for seniors, multinight stays, honeymooners, and golfers, as well as corporate discounts and car-rental deals.

10 Getting There

If possible, fly directly to Maui; doing so can save you a 2-hour layover in Honolulu and another plane ride. If you're headed for Molokai or Lanai, you'll have to connect through Honolulu.

If you think of the island of Maui as the shape of a head and shoulders of a person, you'll probably arrive on its neck, at **Kahului Airport.**

At press time, four airlines fly directly from the mainland to Kahului: **United Airlines** (☎ 800/241-6522; www.ual.com) offers daily nonstop flights from San Francisco and

Los Angeles; **Hawaiian Airlines** (☎ 800/367-5320; www.hawaiianair.com) has direct flights from Los Angeles (daily) and Seattle (four times a week); **American Airlines** (☎ 800/433-7300; www.americanair.com) flies direct from Los Angeles; and **Delta Airlines** (☎ 800/221-1212; www.delta-air.com) offers direct flights from San Francisco and Los Angeles. The other carriers fly to Honolulu, where you'll have to pick up an interisland flight to Maui. Both **Aloha Airlines** (☎ 800/367-5250; www.alohaair.com) and **Hawaiian Airlines** (☎ 800/367-5320; www.hawaiianair.com) offer jet service from Honolulu. See "Interisland Flights," below.

For information on airlines serving Hawaii from places other than the U.S. mainland, see chapter 3, "For Foreign Visitors."

LANDING AT KAHULUI AIRPORT   If there's a long wait at baggage claim, step over to the state-operated **Visitor Information Center,** where you can pick up brochures and the latest issue of *This Week Maui,* which features great regional maps of the islands, and ask about island activities. After collecting your bags from the poky, automated carousels, step out, take a deep breath, proceed to the curbside car-rental pickup area, and wait for the appropriate rental-agency shuttle van to take you a half mile away to the car-rental checkout desk. (All major rental companies have branches at Kahului; see "Getting Around," below.)

If you're not renting a car, the cheapest way to get to your hotel is **SpeediShuttle** (☎ 808/875-8070), which can take you between Kahului Airport and all the major resorts between 5am and 9pm daily. Rates vary, but figure on $20 for two passengers to Wailea (one way) and $40 for two to Kapalua (one way). Be sure to call before your flight to arrange pickup.

If you're staying in the Lahaina-Kaanapali area, transportation service is available through **Airporter Shuttle** (☎ 800/533-8765 or 808/661-6667), which runs every half hour from 9am to 4pm; the cost is $13 one way, $19 round-trip.

You'll see taxis outside the airport terminal, but note that they are quite expensive—expect to spend around $60 to $75 for a ride from Kahului to Kaanapali and $50 from the airport to Wailea.

If possible, avoid landing on Maui between 3 and 6pm, when the working stiffs on Maui are "pau work" (finished with work) and a major traffic jam occurs at the first intersection.

AVOIDING KAHULUI   You can avoid Kahului Airport altogether by taking an **Island Air** (☎ 800/323-3345; www.alohaair.com) flight to **Kapalua–West Maui Airport,** which is convenient if you're planning to stay at any of the hotels in Kapalua or at the Kaanapali resorts. If you're staying in Kapalua, it's only a 10- to 15-minute drive to your hotel; it takes 10 to 15 minutes to Kaanapali (as opposed to 35 or 40 minutes from Kahului). Island Air also flies into tiny **Hana Airport,** but you have to make a connection at Kahului to get there.

Agricultural Screening at the Airports

All baggage and passengers bound for the mainland must be screened by agricultural officials before boarding. This takes a little time, but isn't a problem unless you happen to be carrying a football-sized local avocado home to Aunt Emma. Officials will confiscate fresh avocados, bananas, mangoes, and many other kinds of local produce in the name of fruit-fly control. Pineapples, coconuts, and papayas inspected and certified for export, boxed flowers, leis without seeds, and processed foods (macadamia nuts, coffee, jams, dried fruit, and the like) will pass. Call federal or state agricultural officials before leaving for the airport if you're not sure about your trophy.

A newcomer on the interisland commuter scene is Kahului-based **Pacific Wings** (☎ **888/873-0877** or 808/575-4546; fax 808/873-7920; www.pacificwings.com), which flies eight-passenger, twin-engine Cessna 402C aircraft. It currently offers flights from Kahului to Hana, Molokai, and Waimea (on the Big Island), with plans to expand to flights to Kapalua, Lanai, and Honolulu.

INTERISLAND FLIGHTS

Don't expect to jump a ferry between any of the Hawaiian islands. Today, everyone island-hops by plane. In fact, almost every 20 minutes of every day from just before sunrise to well after sunset (usually around 8pm), a plane takes off or lands at the Kahului Airport on the interisland shuttle service. If you miss a flight, don't worry; they're like buses—another one will be along real soon.

Aloha Airlines (☎ **800/367-5250** or 808/244-9071; www.alohaair.com) is the state's largest provider of interisland air transport service. It offers 180 regularly scheduled daily jet flights throughout Hawaii, using an all-jet fleet of Boeing 737 aircraft. Aloha's sibling company, **Island Air** (☎ **800/323-3345** or 808/484-2222; www.alohaair.com), operates deHavilland DASH-8 and DASH-6 turboprop aircraft and serves Hawaii's small interisland airports on Maui, Molokai, and Lanai.

Hawaiian Airlines (☎ **800/367-5320** or 808/871-6132; www.hawaiianair.com), Hawaii's first interisland airline (which also flies daily to Hawaii from the West Coast; see above), has carried more than 100 million passengers to and around the state. It's one of the world's safest airlines, having never had a fatal incident since it began operations in 1929.

MULTI-ISLAND PASSES   At press time, the standard interisland fare was around $100 one way between islands. However, both airlines offer multiple-flight deals that you might want to consider.

Nonresidents of Hawaii can purchase the Aloha Airlines **Visitor Seven-Day Island Pass.** For just $321 per person, including tax, you get unlimited travel on Aloha and Island Air for 7 consecutive days; Aloha also offers a 1-month version for $999. If you're traveling for more than a week but less than a month, you can buy a **Coupon Book** for $315, which contains six blank tickets that you can use—for yourself or any other traveler—any time within 1 year of purchase. This is probably the best deal if you're island-hopping two or three times in the course of your stay.

Hawaiian Airlines offers a variety of discounts based on the number of flights you're taking and the number of passengers flying. The **Hawaiian Island Pass** gives you unlimited interisland flights for $299 per person for 5 consecutive days, $369 for 7 days, and $409 for 2 weeks. Because Hawaiian Airlines also flies to and from the mainland United States, you may also be able to apply your transpacific flight toward discounts on your interisland travel; be sure to inquire when booking.

TRAVEL DEALS FOR NET SURFERS

Grab your mouse and start surfing before you hit the real waves in Maui—you could save a bundle by finding great deals on the Internet.

Several major airlines offer a free e-mail service known as **E-Savers,** via which they'll send you their best bargain airfares on a weekly basis. Once a week, subscribers receive a list of discounted flights to and from various destinations, both international and domestic. Here's the catch: These fares are usually available only if you leave the next Saturday (or sometimes Friday night) and return on the following Monday or Tuesday. Some of the participating airlines include **American Airlines** (www.americanair.com), **Continental Airlines** (www.flycontinental.com), **Northwest Airlines** (www.nwa.com), **TWA** (www.twa.com), and **US Airways** (www.usairways.com).

Internet Airfares (www.air-fare.com) is one of the best sites for searching for low airfares. **Airlines of the Web** (www.itn.net/airlines) has a unique feature: the Low Fare Ticker, which allows you to monitor fares around the clock (particularly useful during fare wars). **AirSaver.com** (www.airsaver.com) specializes in consolidated tickets. **Cheap Fare Finder** (www.cheapfarefinder.com) will search for the cheapest fare, then arrange to have your ticket waiting for you at the airport.

Arthur Frommer's Budget Travel (www.frommers.com) is home of the Encyclopedia of Travel, *Arthur Frommer's Budget Travel* magazine and daily newsletter, and lots of information on Maui.

Travelocity (www.travelocity.com) and **Microsoft Expedia** (www.expedia.com) are multipurpose travel sites. **Epicurious Travel** (travel.epicurious.com) and **Smarter Living** (www.smarterliving.com) allow you to sign up for all the airline e-mail lists at once.

Pleasant Hawaiian Holidays (pleasantholidays.com) now offers its low-cost deals on the Web; check out the site's 360-degree "Surround Video" tours of hotels and destinations. **The Hottest Airfares on Earth** (www.etn.nl/hotfares.htm) is a clearinghouse of information on airfares, packages, and hotel deals from low-cost ticket suppliers, tour operators, and travel agents. **Travel Shop** (www.aonestoptravel.com) has access to consolidated rates on every aspect of travel to Hawaii, and promises to meet or beat any quote you get from a travel agent or airline. Finally, check out the Hawaii package deals at **Travelzoo.com** (www.travelzoo.com).

11 Getting Around

The only way to really see Maui is by rental car. There's no real island-wide public transit.

DRIVING AROUND MAUI

Maui has only a handful of major roads: One follows the coastline around the two volcanoes that form the island, Haleakala and Puu Kukui; one goes up to Haleakala's summit; one goes to Hana; one goes to Wailea; and one goes to Lahaina. It sounds simple, right? Well, it isn't, because the names of the few roads change en route. Study the island map on page 16 or the foldout map in the back of this book before you set out.

The best and most detailed road maps are published by *This Week Magazine,* a free visitor publication available on Maui. For island maps, check out those published by the University of Hawaii Press. Updated periodically, they include a detailed network of island roads, large-scale insets of towns, historical and contemporary points of interest, parks, beaches, and hiking trails. These maps cost about $3 each, or about $15 for a complete set. If you can't find them in a bookstore near you, write to **University of Hawaii Press,** 2840 Kolowalu St., Honolulu, HI 96822. If you seek topographical maps, write the **Hawaii Geographic Society,** P.O. Box 1698, Honolulu, HI 96806 (☎ **808/546-3952;** fax 808/536-5999).

TRAFFIC ADVISORY The road from Central Maui to Kihei and Wailea, Mokulele Highway (Hwy. 311), is a dangerous strip that's often the scene of head-on crashes involving intoxicated and speeding drivers; be careful. Also, be alert on the Honoapiilani Highway (Hwy. 30) en route to Lahaina, since drivers who spot whales in the channel between Maui and Lanai often slam on the brakes and cause major tie-ups and accidents.

If you get into trouble on Maui's highways, look for the flashing blue strobe lights on 12-foot poles; at the base are emergency, solar-powered call boxes (programmed to

The Welcoming Lei

Nothing makes you feel more welcome than a lei. The tropical beauty of the delicate garland, the deliciously sweet fragrance of the blossoms, the sensual way the flowers curl softly around your neck—there's no doubt about it: Getting lei'd in Hawaii is a sensuous experience.

Leis are much more than just a decorative necklace of flowers; they're also one of the nicest ways to say hello, good-bye, congratulations, I salute you, my sympathies are with you, or I love you. The custom of giving leis can be traced back to Hawaii's very roots: According to chants, the first lei was given by Hiiaka, the sister of the volcano goddess, Pele, who presented Pele with a lei of lehua blossoms on a beach in Puna.

During ancient times, leis given to *alii* (royalty) were accompanied by a bow, since it was *kapu* (forbidden) for a commoner to raise his arms higher than the king's head. The presentation of a kiss with a lei didn't come about until World War II; it's generally attributed to an entertainer who kissed an officer on a dare, then quickly presented him with her lei, saying it was an old Hawaiian custom. It wasn't then, but it sure caught on fast.

Lei-making is a tropical art form. All leis are fashioned by hand in a variety of traditional patterns; some are sewn of hundreds of tiny blooms or shells, or bits of ferns and leaves. Some are twisted, some braided, some strung. Every island has its own special flower lei. On Oahu, the choice is *ilima,* a small orange flower. Big Islanders prefer the *lehua,* a large, delicate red puff. Maui likes the *lokelani,* a small rose. On Kauai, it's the *mokihana,* a fragrant green vine and berry. Molokai prefers the *kukui,* the white blossom of a candlenut tree. And Lanai's lei is made of *kaunaoa,* a bright yellow moss, while Niihau uses its abundant seashells to make leis that were once prized by royalty and are now worth a small fortune.

Leis are available at the Kahului Airport, from florists, and even at supermarkets.

Leis are the perfect symbol for Hawaii: They're given in the moment, their fragrance and beauty are enjoyed in the moment, and when they fade, their spirit of aloha lives on. Welcome to the islands!

---

dial 911 as soon as you pick up the handset). There are 29 emergency call boxes on the island's busiest highways and remote areas, including along the Hana and Haleakala highways and on the north end of the island in the remote community of Kahakuloa.

Another traffic note: Buckle up your seat belt—Hawaii has stiff fines for noncompliance.

CAR RENTALS

Maui has one of the lowest car-rental rates in the country. The average nondiscounted, unlimited-mileage rate for a 1-day rental for an intermediate-sized car was $39 in 1999. That's the fourth-lowest rate in the country, compared with the national average of $53.50 a day. Cars are usually plentiful on Maui, except on holiday weekends, which in Hawaii also means King Kamehameha Day, Prince Kuhio Day, and Admission Day (see "When to Go," above). Rental cars are usually at a premium on Molokai and Lanai, so be sure to book well ahead.

All the major car-rental agencies have offices on Maui, usually at both Kahului and West Maui airports. They include: **Alamo** (☎ 800/327-9633; www.goalamo.com),

Avis (☎ 800/321-3712; www.avis.com), **Budget** (☎ 800/935-6878; www. budgetrentacar.com), **Dollar** (☎ 800/800-4000; www.dollarcar.com), **Hertz** (☎ 800/654-3011; www.hertz.com), and **National** (☎ 800/227-7368; www. nationalcar.com).

There are also a few frugal car-rental agencies offering used cars at discount prices. **Word of Mouth Rent-a-Used-Car,** in Kahului (☎ 800/533-5929 or 808/ 877-2436), offers a four-door compact without air-conditioning for $115 a week, plus tax; with air-conditioning, it's $130 a week, plus tax. **AA Rent-a-Dent,** 220 Papa Place, Kahului (☎ 808/893-0057; fax 808/893-0211; www.keysmarketing. com/rentadent), has used cars in good condition; the weekly rate is $129, plus tax. **LTAR,** 1992 S. Kihei Rd., Kihei (☎ 877/874-4800 or 808/874-4800; www.maui.net/~ltar), leases used economy cars at a weekly rate of $99, plus tax, from November through April, and $85, plus tax, from May through October. LTAR provides no airport pickup, however; you'll have to make your own way to Kihei (it's about $20 in the SpeediShuttle van; see "Other Transportation Options," below, for details).

To rent a car in Hawaii, you must be at least 25 years old and have a valid driver's license and a credit card. Your valid home-state license will be recognized here.

MULTI-ISLAND DEALS   If you're going to visit multiple islands, it's usually easiest and cheapest to book with one company and carry your contract through on each island for your entire stay; just drop off your car on the island you're leaving, and there will be one waiting for you on the next island with the same company. By booking your cars this way, as one interisland rental, you can usually take advantage of weekly rates that you'd be excluded from if you treated each rental separately. Both **Avis** (☎ **800/321-3712**; www.avis.com) and **Hertz** (☎ **800/654-3011**; www.hertz.com) can do this for you; inquire about interisland rental arrangements when booking.

INSURANCE   Hawaii is a no-fault state, which means that if you don't have collision-damage insurance, you are required to pay for all damages before you leave the state, whether or not the accident was your fault. Your personal car insurance may provide rental-car coverage; read your policy or call your insurer before you leave home. Bring your insurance identification card if you decline the optional insurance, which usually costs from $12 to $20 a day. Obtain the name of your company's local claim representative before you go. Some credit-card companies also provide collision-damage insurance for their customers; check with yours before you rent.

EASY RIDING AROUND MAUI

Don black denim and motorcycle boots and ride around Maui on a hog, available for $100 to $150 a day at **Island Riders,** 126 Hinau St. (by Pizza Hut), Lahaina (☎ **800/ 529-2925** or 808/661-9966; www.islandriders.com). Forget the greasy Hell's Angels image; latter-day Wild Ones are button-down corporate types, or California Highway Patrol officers on holiday. Whether you blast up Haleakala's grand corniche or haul ass to Hana, it's the most fun you can have on two wheels. This toy store for big boys and girls also rents exotic cars (Dodge Vipers, Cobras, Prowlers, Ferraris, Porches, Corvettes, and Jeeps), which start at about $200 a day and top out around $400. Island Riders offers free pickup from most Maui hotels—convenient if you're throwing caution to the wind for just a day (half-day rentals are available, too).

MOPEDS

Mopeds are available for rent from **Wheels R Us,** at any of their three locations: 741 Wainee St., Lahaina (☎ **808/667-7751**); 75 Kaahumanu Ave., Kahului (☎ **808/ 871-6858**); or in the Rainbow Mall, 2439 S. Kihei Rd., Kihei (☎ **808/875-1221**).

Mopeds, which start at $26 a day (a day being defined as 8am to 4:30pm), are little more than motorized bicycles that get up to around 35 m.p.h. (with a good wind at your back), so we suggest using them only locally (to get to the beach or to go shopping). Don't take them out on the highway, because they can't keep up with the traffic.

OTHER TRANSPORTATION OPTIONS

TAXIS   For island-wide 24-hour service, call **Alii Taxi** (☎ 808/661-3688 or 808/667-2605). You can also try **Kihei Taxi** (☎ 808/879-3000), **Wailea Taxi** (☎ 808/874-5000), or **Yellow Cab of Maui** (☎ 808/877-7000) if you need a ride.

SHUTTLES   SpeediShuttle (☎ **808/875-8070**) can take you between Kahului Airport and all the major resorts from 5am to 9pm daily (for details, see "Landing at Kahului Airport," under "Getting There," above).

Free shuttle vans operate within the resort areas of Kaanapali, Kapalua, and Wailea; if you're staying in those areas, your hotel can fill you in on exact routes and schedules.

12 Tips on Accommodations

Maui offers all kinds of accommodations, from simple rooms in restored plantation homes and quaint cottages on the beach to luxurious ocean-view condo units and opulent suites at palatial resorts. Each has its pluses and minuses—so before you book, make sure you know what you're getting into. Below, we discuss the various options available on Maui, how to get the best possible rate, and when you should consider using a booking agency.

TYPES OF ACCOMMODATIONS

HOTELS   In Hawaii, "hotel" can indicate a wide range of options, from few or no on-site amenities to enough extras to qualify as a miniresort. Generally, a hotel offers daily maid service and has a restaurant, on-site laundry facilities, a pool, and a sundries/convenience-type shop (as opposed to the shopping arcades that most resorts have). Top hotels also provide activities desks, concierge service, business centers, a bar and/or lounge, and perhaps a few more shops. The advantages of staying in a hotel are privacy and convenience; the disadvantage is generally noise: either thin walls between rooms or loud music from a lobby lounge late into the night.

RESORTS   In Hawaii, a resort offers everything a hotel offers and more. What you get varies from property to property, of course, but expect facilities, services, and amenities such as direct beach access, with cabanas and chairs; pools (often more than one) and a Jacuzzi; a spa and fitness center; restaurants, bars, and lounges; a 24-hour front desk; concierge, valet, and bell services; room service (often around the clock); an activities desk; tennis and golf (some of the world's best courses are at Hawaii resorts); ocean activities; a business center; children's programs; and more.

The advantage of staying at a resort is that you have everything you could possibly want in the way of services and things to do; the disadvantage is that the price generally reflects this. Don't be misled by a name—just because a place is called "ABC Resort" doesn't mean it actually *is* a resort. Make sure you're getting what you pay for.

CONDOS   The roominess and convenience of a condo—which is usually a fully equipped multiple-bedroom apartment—makes this a great choice for families. Condominium properties in Hawaii are generally several apartments set in either a single high-rise or a cluster of low-rise units. Condos generally have amenities such as some degree of maid service (ranging from daily to weekly; it may or may not be included

What to Do if Your Dream Hotel Becomes a Nightmare

To avoid any unpleasant surprises, find out when you make your reservation exactly what the accommodation is offering you: the cost, minimum stay, included amenities. Ask if there's a penalty fee for leaving early. Read the small print in the contract—especially that on cancellation fees. Discuss ahead of time with the B&B, vacation rental, condominium agent, or booking agency what their cancellation policy is if the accommodation doesn't meet your expectations. Get this policy in writing (so there are no misunderstandings later).

When you arrive, if the room you're given doesn't meet your expectations, notify the front desk, rental agent, or booking agency immediately. Approach the management in a calm, reasonable manner, and suggest a solution (moving to another unit). Be reasonable and be willing to compromise. Do not make threats or leave; if you leave, it may be harder to get your deposit returned.

---

in your rate, so be sure to ask), a pool, laundry facilities (either in your unit or in a central location), and an on-site front desk or a live-in property manager. The advantages of a condo are privacy, space, and conveniences—which usually include full kitchen facilities, a washer and dryer, a private phone, and more. The downsides include the absence of an on-site restaurant and the density of the units (as opposed to the privacy you get with a single-unit vacation rental).

Condos vary in price according to size, location, and amenities. Many of them are located on or near the beach, and they tend to be clustered in resort areas. While there are some very high-end condos, most tend to be quite affordable, especially if you're traveling in a group that's large enough to require more than one bedroom.

BED-AND-BREAKFASTS   Maui has a wide variety of places that fall under this category: everything from the traditional B&B—several bedrooms in a home (which may or may not share a bathroom), with breakfast served in the morning—to what is essentially a vacation rental on an owner's property that comes with fixings for you to make your own breakfast. Make sure that the B&B you're booking matches your own mental picture. Would you prefer conversation around a big dining-room table as you eat a hearty breakfast, or just a muffin and juice to enjoy in your own private place? Laundry facilities and a private phone are not always available at B&Bs. We've reviewed lots of wonderful places in chapter 4. If you have to share a bathroom, we've spelled it out in the listings; otherwise, you can assume that you will have a private bathroom.

The advantage of a traditional B&B is its individual style and congenial atmosphere. B&Bs are great places to meet other visitors to Maui, and the host is generally very happy to act as your own private concierge, offering tips on where to go and what to do. In addition, B&Bs are usually an affordable way to go (though fancier ones can run $150 or more a night). The disadvantages are lack of privacy, usually a set time for breakfast, few amenities, generally no maid service, and the fact that you'll have to share the quarters beyond your bedroom with others. In addition, B&B owners usually require a minimum stay of 2 or 3 nights, and it's often a drive to the beach.

VACATION RENTALS   This is another great choice for families, as well as for long-term stays. "Vacation rental" usually means there will be no one on the property where you're staying. The actual accommodation can range from an apartment in a condominium building to a two-room cottage on the beach to an entire fully equipped house. Generally, vacation rentals are the kinds of places you can settle into for a while: They have kitchen facilities (which can be either a complete kitchen or just a kitchenette with microwave, fridge, burners, and coffeemaker), on-site laundry facilities, and phone; some also have such extras as TV, VCR, and stereo. The advantages of a vacation rental are complete privacy, your own kitchen (which can save you money on meals), and lots of conveniences. The disadvantages are a lack of an on-site property manager, and generally no maid service; often, a minimum stay is required (sometimes as much as a week). If you book a vacation rental, be sure you have a 24-hour contact so that when the toilet won't flush or you can't figure out how to turn on the air-conditioning, you'll have someone to call.

BARGAINING ON PRICES

Rates can sometimes be bargained down, but it depends on the place. In general, each type of accommodation allows a different amount of latitude in bargaining on their rack (or published) rates.

The best bargaining can be had at **hotels** and **resorts.** Hotels and resorts regularly pay travel agents as much as 30% of the rate they're getting for sending clients their way; if business is slow, some hotels might give you the benefit of at least part of this commission if you book directly instead of going through an airline or travel agent. Most also have *kamaaina* or "local" rates for islanders, which they might extend to visitors during slow periods. It never hurts to ask for a discounted or local rate; a host of special rates are also available for the military, seniors, members of the travel industry, families, corporate travelers, and long-term stays. Ask about package deals, which might include a car rental or free breakfast for the same price as a room. Hotels and resorts offer packages for everyone: golfers, tennis players, families, honeymooners, and more. We've found that it's worth the extra few cents to make a local call to the hotel; sometimes the local reservationist knows about package deals that the toll-free operators are unaware of. If all else fails, try to get the hotel or resort to upgrade you to a better room for the same price as a budget room, or to waive the parking fee or the extra fees for children. Persistence and polite inquiries can pay off.

It's harder to bargain at **bed-and-breakfasts.** You may be able to bargain down the minimum stay, or negotiate a discount if you're staying a week or longer. But generally, a B&B owner has only a few rooms and has already priced the property at a competitive rate; expect to pay what's asked.

You have somewhat more leeway to negotiate on **vacation rentals** and **condos.** In addition to asking for a discount on multinight stays, also ask whether the condo or vacation rental can throw in a rental car to sweeten the deal; believe it or not, they often will.

USING A BOOKING AGENCY VERSUS DOING IT YOURSELF

Sometimes you can save money by making arrangements yourself—not only can you bargain on the phone, but some accommodations may also be willing to pass on a percentage of the commission they would normally have to pay a travel agent or a booking agency.

However, if you don't have the time or money to call several places to make sure they offer the amenities you'd like and to bargain for a price you're comfortable with, then you might consider using a booking agency. The time the agency spends on your behalf might well be worth any fees you'll have to pay.

The top reservations service in the state is **Hawaii's Best Bed & Breakfasts,** P.O. Box 563, Kamuela, HI 96743 (☎ **800/262-9912** or 808/885-4550; fax 808/ 885-0559; www.bestbnb.com; e-mail: bestbnb@aloha.net). This service charges $15 to book the first two locations and $5 for each additional location. Barbara and Susan Campbell personally select the traditional homestays, cottages, and inns, based on each one's hospitality, distinctive charm, and attention to detail. Another great statewide booking agent is **Ann and Bob Babson,** 3371 Keha Dr., Kihei, HI 96753 (☎ **800/824-6409** or 808/874-1166; fax 808/879-7906; www.maui.net/~babson; e-mail: babson@ maui.net), who can steer you in the right direction for both accommodations and car rentals. Not only do they personally inspect the units they recommend, but the Babsons are also impeccably honest and dedicated to matching you up with the place that's right for you.

For vacation rentals, contact **Hawaii Beachfront Vacation Homes** (☎ **808/ 247-3637** or 808/235-2644; www.hotspots.hawaii.com/beachrent1.html; e-mail: hibeach@lava.net). **Hawaii Condo Exchange** (☎ **800/442-0404**; http://wwte.com/ condos) acts as a consolidator for condo and vacation-rental properties.

Fast Facts: Maui

American Express   For 24-hour traveler's check refunds and purchase information, call ☎ **800/221-7282.** Local offices are located in South Maui, at the **Grand Wailea Resort** (☎ 808/875-4526), and in West Maui, at the **Ritz-Carlton Kapalua** (☎ 808/669-6018) and the **Westin Maui** at Kaanapali Beach (☎ 808/661-7155).

Area Code   All of the islands are in the **808** area code. Note that if you're calling one island from another, you must dial 1-808 first, and you'll be billed at long-distance rates (which can be more expensive than calling the mainland).

Business Hours   Most offices are open from 8am to 5pm. The morning commute usually runs from 6 to 8am, and the evening rush is from 4 to 6pm. Bank hours are Monday through Thursday from 8:30am to 3pm, Friday from 8:30am to 6pm; some banks are open on Saturday. Shopping centers are open Monday through Friday from 10am to 9pm, Saturday from 10am to 5:30pm, and Sunday from noon to 5 or 6pm.

Dentist   Emergency dental care is available at **Maui Dental Center,** 162 Alamaha St., Kahului (☎ **808/871-6283**).

Doctor   No appointment is necessary at **West Maui Healthcare Center,** Whalers Village, 2435 Kaanapali Pkwy., Suite H-7 (near Leilani's Restaurant), Kaanapali (☎ **808/667-9721**; fax 808/661-1584), which is open 365 days a year, nightly until 10pm. In Kihei, call **Urgent Care,** 1325 S. Kihei Rd., Suite 103 (at Lipoa Street, across from Star Market), Kihei (☎ **808/879-7781**), open daily from 6am to midnight; doctors are on call 24 hours a day.

Emergencies   Dial ☎ **911** for the police, ambulance, and fire department. District stations are located in Lahaina (☎ **808/661-4441**) and in Hana (☎ **808/ 248-8311**). For the **Poison Control Center,** call ☎ **800/362-3585.**

Hospitals   For medical attention, go to **Maui Memorial Hospital,** in Central Maui at 221 Mahalani, Wailuku (☎ 808/244-9056); East Maui's **Hana Medical Center**, on Hana Highway (☎ 808/248-8924); or **Kula Hospital,** in upcountry Maui at 204 Kula Hwy., Kula (☎ 808/878-1221).

Legal Aid   Call the Legal Aid Society of Hawaii, 2287 Main St., Wailuku (☎ **808/244-3731**).

Liquor Laws   The legal drinking age in Hawaii is 21.

Newspapers   The *Honolulu Advertiser* and the *Honolulu Star Bulletin* are circulated statewide. The *Maui News* is the island's daily paper.

Post Offices   To find the nearest post office, call ☎ **800/ASK-USPS.** In Lahaina, there are branches at the Lahaina Civic Center, 1760 Honoapiilani Hwy., and at the Lahaina Shopping Center, 132 Papalaua St.; in Kahului, there's a branch at 138 S. Puunene Ave.; and in Kihei, there's one at 1254 S. Kihei Rd.

Radio   Honolulu has a score of radio stations that broadcast in English, Hawaiian, Japanese, and Filipino throughout the islands. The most popular stations are KHPR (88.1 or 90.7 FM), the National Public Radio station; KGU (760 AM), for news and talk radio; KUMU (94.7 FM), for easy listening; and KSSK (590 AM), the pop-music station and the top morning-drive DJs.

Safety   Although Hawaii is generally a safe tourist destination, visitors have been crime victims, so stay alert. The most common crime against tourists is rental car break-ins. Never leave any valuables in your car, not even in your trunk. Thieves can be in and out of your trunk faster than you can open it with your own key. Be especially careful at high-risk areas such as beaches and resorts. Never carry large amounts of cash with you. Stay in well-lighted areas after dark. Don't hike on deserted trails alone.

Smoking   It's against the law to smoke in public buildings, including airports, grocery stores, retail shops, movie theaters, banks, and all government buildings and facilities. Hotels have no-smoking rooms available, restaurants have no-smoking sections, and car-rental agencies have smoke-free cars. Most bed-and-breakfasts prohibit smoking indoors.

Taxes   Hawaii's sales tax is 4%. Hotel occupancy tax is 7.25%, and hoteliers are allowed by the state to tack on an additional .001666% excise tax. Thus, expect taxes of about 11.42% to be added to every hotel bill.

Time   Hawaii standard time is in effect year-round. Hawaii is 2 hours behind Pacific standard time and 5 hours behind eastern standard time. In other words, when it's noon in Hawaii, it's 2pm in California and 5pm in New York during standard time on the mainland. There's no daylight-savings time here, so when daylight-savings time is in effect on the mainland, Hawaii is 3 hours behind the West Coast and 6 hours behind the East Coast; in summer, when it's noon in Hawaii, it's 3pm in California and 6pm in New York.

Hawaii is east of the international date line, putting it in the same day as the U.S. mainland and Canada, and a day behind Australia, New Zealand, and Asia.

Weather   For the current weather, call ☎ **808/871-5054;** for Haleakala National Park weather, call ☎ **808/572-9306;** for marine weather and surf and wave conditions, call ☎ **808/877-3477.**

3

For Foreign Visitors

by Jeanette Foster

The pervasiveness of American culture around the world might make the United States feel like familiar territory to foreign visitors, but leaving your own country for the States—especially the unique island state of Hawaii—still requires an additional degree of planning. This chapter will help prepare you for the more common problems, expected and unexpected, that visitors to the islands might encounter.

1 Preparing for Your Trip

ENTRY REQUIREMENTS

Immigration laws are a hot political issue in the United States these days, and the following requirements might have changed somewhat by the time you plan your trip. Check at any U.S. embassy or consulate for current information and requirements. You can also go to the **U.S. State Department's** Web site at **www.state.gov**.

DOCUMENT REGULATIONS   Canadian citizens may enter the United States without visas; they need only proof of residence.

The U.S. State Department has a **Visa Waiver Pilot Program** allowing citizens of certain countries to enter the United States without a visa for stays of up to 90 days. At press time, these included Andorra, Argentina, Australia, Austria, Belgium, Brunei, Denmark, Finland, France, Germany, Iceland, Ireland, Italy, Japan, Liechtenstein, Luxembourg, Monaco, the Netherlands, New Zealand, Norway, San Marino, Slovenia, Spain, Sweden, Switzerland, and the United Kingdom. Citizens of these countries need only a valid passport and a round-trip air or cruise ticket in their possession upon arrival. If they first enter the United States, they may then visit Mexico, Canada, Bermuda, and/or the Caribbean islands and return to the United States without needing a visa. Further information is available from any U.S. embassy or consulate.

Citizens of all other countries must have (1) a valid **passport** with an expiration date at least 6 months later than the scheduled end of their visit to the United States, and (2) a **tourist visa,** which can be obtained without charge from the nearest U.S. consulate.

To obtain a visa, you must submit a completed application form (either in person or by mail) with a 1½-inch-square photo, and you must demonstrate binding ties to a residence abroad. Usually you can obtain a visa at once or within 24 hours, but it may take longer during the summer rush from June to August. If you cannot go in person,

Travel Tip

Be sure to keep a copy of all your travel papers separate from your wallet or purse, and leave a copy with someone at home in case you need it faxed in an emergency.

contact the nearest U.S. embassy or consulate for directions on applying by mail. Your travel agent or airline office may also be able to provide you with visa applications and instructions. The U.S. consulate or embassy that issues your visa will determine whether you will be issued a multiple- or single-entry visa and any restrictions regarding the length of your stay.

British subjects can obtain up-to-date passport and visa information by calling the **U.S. Embassy Visa Information Line** (☎ **0891/200-290**) or the **London Passport Office** (☎ **0990/210-410** for recorded information).

Foreign driver's licenses are recognized in Hawaii, although you might want to get an international driver's license if your home license is not written in English.

MEDICAL REQUIREMENTS Inoculations are not needed to enter the United States unless you are coming from, or have stopped over in, areas known to be suffering from epidemics, particularly cholera or yellow fever.

If you have a disease requiring treatment with medications containing narcotics or drugs requiring a syringe, carry a valid signed prescription from your physician to allay any suspicions that you may be smuggling drugs.

CUSTOMS Every adult visitor may bring in, free of duty, 1 liter of wine or hard liquor, 200 cigarettes or 100 cigars (but no cigars from Cuba) or 3 pounds of smoking tobacco, and $100 worth of gifts. These exemptions are offered to travelers who spend at least 72 hours in the United States and who have not claimed them within the preceding 6 months. It is altogether forbidden to bring into the country foodstuffs (particularly cheese, fruit, cooked meats, and canned goods) and plants (vegetables, seeds, tropical plants, and so on). Foreign tourists may bring in or take out up to $10,000 in U.S. or foreign currency with no formalities; larger sums must be declared to customs on entering or leaving by filing form CM 4790. For more information, contact **U.S. Customs** (☎ **202/927-1770** or www.customs.ustreas.gov).

In addition, you cannot bring fresh fruits and vegetables into Hawaii, even if you're coming from the U.S. mainland and have no need to clear customs. Every passenger is asked shortly before landing to sign a certificate declaring that he or she does not have fresh fruits or vegetables in his or her possession.

INSURANCE There is no nationwide health system in the United States, and the cost of medical care in Hawaii is extremely high. Accordingly, we strongly advise every traveler to secure health insurance coverage before setting out. You may want to take out a comprehensive travel policy that covers (for a relatively low premium) sickness or injury costs (medical, surgical, and hospital); loss or theft of your baggage; trip-cancellation costs; guarantee of bail in case you are arrested; and costs of accident, repatriation, or death. Such packages (such as **Europ Assistance** in Europe) are sold by automobile clubs at attractive rates, as well as by insurance companies and travel agencies. **Worldwide Assistance Services** (☎ **800/821-2828**) is the Europ Assistance agent in the United States.

Insurance for British Travelers Most big travel agents offer their own insurance, and they will probably try to sell you their package when you book a holiday. Think before you sign. Britain's Consumers' Association recommends that you insist on seeing the policy and reading the fine print before buying travel insurance. The **Association of British Insurers** (☎ **0171/600-3333**) gives advice by phone and publishes the free *Holiday Insurance,* a guide to policy provisions and prices. You might also shop around for better deals: try **Columbus Travel Insurance Ltd.** (☎ **0171/375-0011**) or, for students, **Campus Travel** (☎ **0171/730-2101**).

MONEY

CURRENCY   The American monetary system has a decimal base: one U.S. **dollar** ($1) = 100 **cents** (100¢). Dollar bills commonly come in $1 ("a buck"), $5, $10, $20, $50, and $100 denominations (the last two are usually not welcome when paying for small purchases and are not accepted in taxis or movie theaters).

There are six denominations of coins: 1¢ (1 cent or a "penny"), 5¢ (5 cents or a "nickel"), 10¢ (10 cents or a "dime"), 25¢ (25 cents or a "quarter"), 50¢ (50 cents or a "half-dollar"), and the rare $1 piece.

EXCHANGING CURRENCY   Exchanging foreign currency for U.S. dollars can be painless on Maui. Most major banks will exchange your foreign currency for U.S. dollars, and banks generally offer the best rates. Most major hotels also offer exchange services, but the rate of exchange is usually not as good. Aside from desks at banks and hotels, no currency-exchange services on Maui, but there are currency services at the Honolulu International Airport.

TRAVELER'S CHECKS   It's actually cheaper and faster to get cash at an automated teller machine (ATM) than to fuss with traveler's checks. As noted in the "Visitor Information & Money" section in chapter 2, Maui has ATMs almost everywhere. If you do bring traveler's checks, those denominated in U.S. dollars are readily accepted at most hotels, restaurants, and large stores. Do not bring traveler's checks denominated in any currency other than U.S. dollars.

CREDIT CARDS   The method of payment most widely used is the credit card: Visa (BarclayCard in Britain), MasterCard (EuroCard in Europe, Access in Britain, Chargex in Canada), American Express, Diners Club, Discover, and Carte Blanche. You can save yourself trouble by using "plastic money" rather than cash or traveler's checks in most hotels, restaurants, and retail stores (a growing number of food and liquor stores now accept credit cards). You must have a credit card to rent a car on Maui.

SAFETY

GENERAL SAFETY   Although tourist areas are generally safe, crime is on the increase everywhere in the United States, and Maui is no exception. Visitors should always stay alert. It's wise to ask the island tourist office if you're in doubt about which neighborhoods are safe. Avoid deserted areas, especially at night. Generally speaking, you can feel safe in areas where there are many people and open establishments.

Avoid carrying valuables with you on the street, and don't display expensive cameras or electronic equipment. Hold onto your pocketbook, and place your billfold in an inside pocket. In theaters, restaurants, and other public places, keep your possessions in sight. When you go to the beach, do not leave valuables such as your wallet or passport on your beach towel when you go into the water.

Remember also that hotels are open to the public, and in a large hotel, security may not be able to screen everyone entering. Always lock your room door—don't assume that once inside your hotel you are automatically safe and no longer need to be aware of your surroundings.

DRIVING SAFETY   Safety while driving is particularly important. Question your rental agency about personal safety, or ask for a brochure of traveler safety tips when you pick up your car. Ask the agency to provide written directions or a map with the route marked in red showing how to get to your destination.

Recently, more crime has involved burglary of tourist rental cars in hotel parking structures and at beach parking lots. Park in well-lighted and well-traveled areas if possible. Leaving your rental car unlocked and empty of your valuables is probably safer than locking your car with valuables in plain view. Never leave any packages or valuables in sight. If someone attempts to rob you or steal your car, do not try to resist the thief or carjacker—report the incident to the police department immediately.

For more information on driving rules and getting around by car in Maui, see "Getting Around," in chapter 2.

2 Getting to & Around the United States

Airlines serving Hawaii from other than the U.S. mainland include **Air Canada** (☎ 800/776-3000; www.aircanada.ca); **Canada 3000** (☎ 888/CAN-3000; www. canada3000.com); **Canadian Airlines** (☎ 800/426-7000; www.cdnair.ca); **Air New Zealand** (☎ 0800/737-000 in Auckland, 64-3/379-5200 in Christchurch, or 800/ 926-7255 in the U.S.; www.airnz.com), which runs 40 flights per week between Auckland and Hawaii; **Qantas** (☎ 008/177-767 in Australia, or 800/227-4500 in the U.S.; www.qantas.com), which flies between Sydney and Honolulu daily (plus additional flights 4 days a week); **Japan Air Lines** (☎ 03/5489-1111 in Tokyo, 800/ 525-3663 in the U.S.; www.jal.co.jp); **All Nippon Airways** (ANA) (☎ 03/ 5489-1212 in Tokyo, or 800/235-9262 in the U.S.; www.ana.co.jp); **China Airlines** (☎ 02/715-1212 in Taipei, or 800/227-5118 in the U.S.; www.china-airlines.com); **Garuda Indonesian** (☎ 251/2235 in Jakarta, or 800/342-7832 in the U.S.); **Korean Airlines** (☎ 02/656-2000 in Seoul, 800/223-1155 on the East Coast, 800/421-8200 on the West Coast, or 800/438-5000 from Hawaii; www.koreanair.co.kr); and **Philippine Airlines** (☎ 631/816-6691 in Manila, or 800/435-9725 in the U.S.).

Travelers coming from Europe can take advantage of the **APEX** (Advance Purchase Excursion) fares offered by all major U.S. and European carriers. Aside from these, attractive values are offered by **Icelandair** (☎ 354/5050-100 in Reykjavik, 0171/ 388-5599 in London, or 800/223-5500 in the U.S.; www.icelandair.is) on flights from Luxembourg to New York, and by **Virgin Atlantic Airways** (☎ 0293/747-747 in Britain, or 800/862-8621 in the U.S.; www.fly.virgin.com) from London to New York/Newark. You can then catch a connecting domestic flight to Honolulu.

Some large American airlines—such as **American Airlines, Delta, Northwest, TWA,** and **United**—offer travelers on transatlantic or transpacific flights special discount tickets under the name **Visit USA,** allowing travel between any U.S. destinations at reduced rates. These tickets are not on sale in the United States and must, therefore, be purchased before you leave your foreign point of departure. This system is the best, easiest, and fastest way to see the United States at low cost. You should obtain information well in advance from your travel agent or the office of the airline concerned, since the conditions attached to these discount tickets can be changed without advance notice.

The **ETN** (European Travel Network) operates a Web site offering discounts on international airfares to the United States, accommodations, car rentals, and tours: **www.discount-tickets.com**.

Visitors arriving by air should cultivate patience and resignation before setting foot on U.S. soil. Getting through immigration control can take as long as 2 hours on some days, especially during summer weekends. Add the time it takes to clear customs, and you'll see that you should make very generous allowance for delay in planning connections between international and domestic flights—an average of 2 to 3 hours at least.

For further information about travel to Maui, see "Getting There" and "Getting Around," in chapter 2.

Fast Facts: For the Foreign Traveler

Business Hours   See "Fast Facts: Maui," in chapter 2.

Climate   See "When to Go," in chapter 2.

Currency & Currency Exchange   See "Preparing for Your Trip," above.

Electricity   Maui, like the U.S. mainland and Canada, uses 110 to 120 volts AC (60 cycles), compared to 220 to 240 volts AC (50 cycles) in most of Europe, Australia, and New Zealand. In addition to a 100-volt transformer, small appliances of non-American manufacture, such as hair dryers or shavers, will require a plug adapter, with two flat, parallel pins.

Embassies & Consulates   All embassies are located in the nation's capital, Washington, D.C. Some consulates are located in major cities, and most nations have a mission to the United Nations in New York City. If your country isn't listed below, call directory information in Washington, D.C. (☎ **202/555-1212**) for the number of your national embassy.

The embassy of **Australia** is at 1601 Massachusetts Ave. NW, Washington, DC 20036 (☎ 202/797-3000; www.austemb.org). There are consulates in New York, Honolulu, Houston, Los Angeles, and San Francisco.

The embassy of **Canada** is at 501 Pennsylvania Ave. NW, Washington, DC 20001 (☎ 202/682-1740; www.cdnemb-washdc.org). Canadian consulates are in Buffalo (New York), Detroit, Los Angeles, New York, and Seattle.

The embassy of **Ireland** is at 2234 Massachusetts Ave. NW, Washington, DC 20008 (☎ 202/462-3939). Irish consulates are in Boston, Chicago, New York, and San Francisco.

The embassy of **Japan** is at 2520 Massachusetts Ave. NW, Washington, DC 20008 (☎ 202/238-6700; www.embjapan.org). Japanese consulates are located in Atlanta, Kansas City, San Francisco, and Washington, D.C.

The embassy of **New Zealand** is at 37 Observatory Circle NW, Washington, DC 20008 (☎ 202/328-4800; www.emb.com/nzemb). New Zealand consulates are in Los Angeles, Salt Lake City, San Francisco, and Seattle.

The embassy of the **United Kingdom** is at 3100 Massachusetts Ave. NW, Washington, DC 20008 (☎ 202/462-1340). Other British consulates are in Atlanta, Boston, Chicago, Cleveland, Houston, Los Angeles, New York, San Francisco, and Seattle.

Emergencies   Call ☎ **911** to report a fire, call the police, or get an ambulance.

Gasoline (Petrol)   One U.S. gallon equals 3.8 liters, and 1.2 U.S. gallons equals 1 Imperial gallon. You'll notice that several grades (and price levels) of gasoline are available at most gas stations. You'll also notice that their names change from company to company. The ones with the highest octane are the most expensive, but most rental cars take the least expensive "regular" gas with an octane rating of 87.

Holidays   See "When to Go," in chapter 2.

Legal Aid   The ordinary tourist will probably never become involved with the American legal system. If you are pulled over for a minor infraction (for example, driving faster than the speed limit), never attempt to pay the fine directly to a police officer; you might wind up arrested on the much more serious charge of attempted bribery. Pay fines by mail, or directly into the hands of the clerk of the court. If you're accused of a more serious offense, it's wise to say and do nothing before consulting a lawyer. Under U.S. law, an arrested person is allowed one telephone call to a party of his or her choice; call your embassy or consulate.

Mail   If you aren't sure what your address will be in the United States, mail can be sent to you, in your name, c/o **General Delivery** at the main post office of the city or region where you expect to be (call ☎ **800/275-8777** for information on the nearest post office). The addressee must pick up the mail in person and produce proof of identity (driver's license, passport, or the like). Your mail will be held for pickup for up to 1 month.

Mailboxes, generally found at intersections, are blue with a blue-and-white eagle logo and carry the inscription U.S. POSTAL SERVICE. If your mail is addressed to a U.S. destination, don't forget to add the five-figure postal code, or **ZIP code,** after the two-letter abbreviation of the state to which the mail is addressed. The abbreviation for Hawaii is **HI.**

International airmail rates are 60¢ for half-ounce letters (40¢ for letters going to Mexico and 46¢ for letters to Canada) and 50¢ for postcards (35¢ to Mexico and 40¢ to Canada). All domestic first-class mail goes from Hawaii to the U.S. mainland by air, so don't bother paying the extra amount to send a letter back to your grandmother in Michigan.

Taxes   The United States has no VAT (value-added tax) or other indirect taxes at a national level. Every state and city has the right to levy its own local tax on all purchases, including hotel and restaurant checks, airline tickets, and so on. In Hawaii, sales tax is 4%; there's also a 7.25% hotel room tax, so the total tax on your hotel bill will be 11.42%.

Telephone & Fax   The telephone system in the United States is run by private corporations, so rates, particularly for long-distance service and operator-assisted calls, can vary widely—especially on calls made from public phones. Local calls—that is, calls to other locations on Maui—made from public phones cost 35¢.

Generally, hotel surcharges on long-distance and local calls are astronomical. You are usually better off using a **public pay telephone,** which you will find clearly marked in most public buildings and private establishments, as well as on the street.

Most **long-distance and international calls** can be dialed directly from any phone. For calls to Canada and to other parts of the United States, dial 1 followed by the area code and the seven-digit number. For international calls, dial 011 followed by the country code, the city code, and the telephone number of the person you want to call.

In Hawaii, interisland phone calls are considered long-distance and often are as costly as calling the U.S. mainland.

For **reversed-charge or collect calls,** and for **person-to-person calls,** dial 0 (zero, not the letter "O"), followed by the area code and number you want; an operator will then come on the line, and you should specify that you are calling collect, or person-to-person, or both. If your operator-assisted call is international, ask for the overseas operator.

Note that calls to area codes **800, 888,** and **877** are toll-free. However, calls to numbers in area codes **700** and **900** (chat lines, bulletin boards, "dating" services, and so on) can be very expensive—usually a charge of 95¢ to $3 or more per minute.

For **local directory assistance** ("information"), dial ☎ 411; for **long-distance information,** dial 1, then the appropriate area code and 555-1212.

Fax facilities are widely available and can be found in most hotels and many other establishments. Try **Mailboxes Etc., Kinko's,** or any photocopying shop.

There are two kinds of **telephone directories** in the United States. The so-called **White Pages** lists private households and business subscribers in alphabetical order. The inside front cover lists emergency numbers for police, fire, ambulance, the coast guard, poison-control center, crime-victims hot line, and so on. The first few pages are devoted to community-service numbers, including a guide to long-distance and international calling, complete with country codes and area codes. Also in the front are detailed maps of Maui, postal ZIP codes, and a calendar of events. Printed on yellow paper, the **Yellow Pages** lists all local services, businesses, and industries according to activity, with an index in the front. Drugstores (pharmacies) are also listed by geographical location, restaurants by type of cuisine and geographical location, bookstores by special subject and/or language, and places of worship by religious denomination.

Time   See "Fast Facts: Maui," in chapter 2.

Tipping   Tipping is so ingrained in the American way of life that the annual income tax of tip-earning service personnel is based on how much they should have received in light of their employers' gross revenues. Accordingly, they may have to pay tax on a tip you didn't actually give them!

Here are some rules of thumb:

In **hotels,** tip bellhops at least $1 per piece of luggage ($2 to $3 if you have a lot of luggage), and tip the housekeeping staff $1 per person, per day. Tip the doorman or concierge only if he or she has provided you with some specific service (for example, calling a cab for you or obtaining difficult-to-get theater tickets). Tip the valet parking attendant $1 every time you get your car.

In **restaurants, bars,** and **nightclubs,** tip service staff 15% to 20% of the check, tip bartenders 10% to 15%, and tip valet-parking attendants $1 per vehicle. Tip the doorman only if he has provided you with some specific service (such as calling a cab for you). Tipping is not expected in cafeterias and fast-food restaurants.

Tip **cab drivers** 15% of the fare.

As for **other service personnel,** tip skycaps at airports at least $1 per piece ($2 to $3 if you have a lot of luggage), and tip hairdressers and barbers 15% to 20%.

Tipping gas-station attendants and ushers at movies and theaters is not expected.

Toilets   You won't find public toilets or "rest rooms" on the streets in most U.S. cities, but they can be found in bars, fast-food outlets, restaurants, hotels, museums, department stores, or service stations (although the cleanliness of toilets at service stations, parks, and beaches is more open to question). Note, however, that restaurants and bars may reserve their rest rooms for the use of their customers; some establishments display a notice that toilets are for the use of patrons only. You can ignore this sign or, better yet, avoid arguments by paying for a cup of coffee or a soft drink, which will qualify you as a patron.

Accommodations 4

by Jeanette Foster

Maui has accommodations to fit every kind of dream vacation, from luxury oceanfront suites and historic bed-and-breakfasts to reasonably priced condos that will sleep a family of four. Before you book, be sure to read "The Island in Brief," which will help you decide on your ideal location, and "Tips on Accommodations," both in chapter 2.

Remember to consider *when* you will be traveling to the islands. Maui has two seasons: high and low. The highest season, during which rooms are always booked and rates are at the top end, runs from mid-December to March. The second high season, when rates are high but bookings are somewhat easier, is summer, June to September. The low season, with fewer tourists and cheaper rates, is April to June and September to mid-December.

Finally, remember to add Maui's 11.42% accommodations tax to your final bill. Parking is free unless otherwise noted.

1 Central Maui

KAHULUI

If you're arriving late at night or have an early morning flight out, the best choice near Kahului Airport is the **Maui Seaside Hotel,** 100 Kaahumanu Ave. (near Lono Avenue), Kahului, HI 96732 (☎ **800/ 367-7000** or 808/877-3311; www.sand-seaside.com). The rooms are small and somewhat dated, but they're clean and cheap ($90 to $120 double), and some come with kitchenettes. Otherwise, try the **Maui Beach Hotel,** 170 Kaahumanu Ave. (Highway 32, at Highway 340), Kahului, HI 96732 (☎ **800/367-5004** or 808/877-0051; www. castle-group.com), which has nondescript, motel-like rooms ($93 to $120 double) and free airport shuttle service. These places are okay for a night, but don't bother spending more time in Kahului than you have to.

WAILUKU

MODERATE

✪ **Old Wailuku Inn at Ulupono.** 2199 Kahookele St. (at High St., across from the Wailuku School), Wailuku, HI 96732. ☎ **800/305-4899** or 808/244-5897. Fax 808/242-9600. www.aitv.com/ulupono. 7 units. TV TEL. Year-round $120–$180 double. Rates include gourmet breakfast. Extra person $20. AE, CB, DC, DISC, MC, V.

This 1924 former plantation manager's home, lovingly restored by innkeepers Janice and Thomas Fairbanks, offers a genuine old Hawaii experience. Inspired by Hawaii's poet laureate, Don Blanding, the theme is Hawaii of the 1920s and 1930s. Guest rooms are wide and spacious, with exotic ohia-wood floors, high ceilings, and traditional Hawaiian quilts. The mammoth bathrooms (some with claw-foot tubs, some with Jacuzzis) have plush towels and "earth-friendly" toiletries on hand. A full gourmet breakfast is served on the enclosed back lanai or, if you prefer, delivered to your room. You'll feel right at home lounging on the generously sized living-room sofa, or watching the world go by from an old wicker chair on the lanai.

Located in the old historic area of Wailuku, the inn is just a few minutes' walk from the Maui County seat, the state building, the courthouse, and a wonderful stretch of antiques shops. It's fully equipped to handle business travelers, with automated message service, modem jacks, and multiple phones in each room; fax and copy services and computers are available for guest use.

INEXPENSIVE

Backpackers, head for **Banana Bungalow Maui,** a funky Happy Valley hostel at 310 North Market St., Wailuku, HI 96793 (☎ **800/846-7835** or 808/244-5090; fax 808/244-3678; http://home1.gte.net/bungalow), with dorms ($10 per person for the first night, $14 thereafter) and some private rooms ($29 single, $35 double). Dorm-style accommodations ($10 per person for the first night, $14 thereafter) and private rooms ($29.70 single, $40.70 double) are also available at the **Northshore Inn,** in old Wailuku, at 2080 Vineyard St., Wailuku, HI 96793 (☎ **808/242-8999;** fax 808/244-5004). Note, however, that women traveling alone might not feel safe in either of these areas after dark.

2 West Maui

LAHAINA
VERY EXPENSIVE

Puunoa Beach Estates. 45 Kai Pali Pl., Lahaina, HI 96761. ☎ **800/642-6284** or 808/667-1666. Fax 808/661-1025. www.puunoa-beach-estates.com. 10 units. A/C TV TEL. High season $580 two-bedroom (sleeps up to 4), $695 two-bedroom with loft (sleeps up to 6), $730 three-bedroom (sleeps up to 6), $800 three-bedroom with loft (sleeps up to 8); low season $550 two-bedroom, $580 two-bedroom with loft, $605 three-bedroom, $665 three-bedroom with loft. 3-night minimum. Rates include full-size car and grocery package upon arrival. AE, DISC, JCB, MC, V.

Only 10 oceanfront residences dot this tropical 3-acre complex, offering a little corner of heaven in Lahaina. The town house–style units are huge (from the 1,700-square-foot two-bedroom to the 2,100-square-foot three-bedroom with loft), and all have private oceanfront lanais. These elegant homes have everything you can imagine (and at these prices, they should): top-of-the-line kitchen equipment, a separate dining area, two TVs, private bathroom with every bedroom, and a whirlpool tub in the master bedroom. Other extras include daily maid service, resident manager on site, swimming pool with pavilion, whirlpool spa and sauna, barbecue area, and paddle tennis courts.

MODERATE

If you dream of an oceanfront condo but your budget is on the slim side, also consider **Lahaina Roads,** 1403 Front St. (reservations c/o Klahani Travel, 505 Front St., Lahaina, HI 96761; ☎ **800/669-MAUI** or 808/667-2712; fax 808/661-5875; e-mail: robyn@maui.net), which offers small, reasonably priced units in an older building in the quiet part of town ($100 one-bedroom, $180 two-bedroom; 3-night

Lahaina & Kaanapali Accommodations

Aloha Lani Inn 17
Aston Maui Islander 14
Best Western Pioneer Inn 15
Guest House 9
House of Fountains B&B 9
Hyatt Regency Maui 8
Kaanapali Beach Hotel 4
Lahaina Inn 12
Lahaina Roads 10
Lahaina Shores Beach
    Resort 18
Maui Eldorado Resort 2
Maui Marriott Resort 7
Old Lahaina House 16
Plantation Inn 13
Puamana 19
Puunoa Beach Estates 11
Royal Lahaina Resort 1
Sheraton Maui 3
Wai Ola Vacation Paradise 9
Westin Maui 6
The Whaler on Kaanapali
    Beach 5

Golf
Post Office ⊠

Puukolii Rd.

30

LK & P Sugarcane Train

Kekaa St.

Kaanapali North
Golf Course

Honoapiilani Hwy.

Kaanapali Parkway

Royal Kaanapali
Golf Course
Club House

Nohea Kai Dr.

Kaanapali South
Golf Course

Hanakaoo
Beach Park

Police

Wahikuli
Beach Park

Lahaina
Civic Center

Lahaina
Cannery
Mall

Mala Wharf

Kapunakea

Kahoma Stream

Hale Pai,
Lahainaluna
School

Train Depot

Pioneer
Sugar Mill

Lahaina Center

Lahainaluna Rd.

Papalaua St.

Lahaina
Shopping Center

Front St.

Dickenson St.

Wainee St.

30

Lahaina
Small Boat Harbor

Luakini St.

Prison St.

505 Front St.

Shaw St.

0   1 Mile
0   1 Kilometer

N

59

minimum). Another option is **Lahaina Shores Beach Resort**, 475 Front St. (☎ **800/ 628-6699**; www.lahaina-shores.com), a large, oceanfront condo complex with studio and one-bedroom units from $120 to $175.

✪ **Aston Maui Islander.** 660 Wainee St. (between Dickenson and Prison sts.), Lahaina, HI 96761. ☎ **800/92-ASTON,** 800/367-5226, or 808/667-9766. Fax 808/661-3733. www.aston-hotels.com. 372 units. A/C TV TEL. High season $99 double, $125–$135 studio with kitchenette, $155 one-bedroom with kitchen (sleeps up to 4), $220 two-bedroom with kitchen (sleeps up to 6), $299 three-bedroom with kitchen (sleeps up to 8); low season $95 double, $115–$125 studio with kitchenette, $135 one-bedroom with kitchen, $195 two-bedroom with kitchen, $297 three-bedroom with kitchen. Extra rollaway bed $18, cribs free. AE, CB, DC, DISC, JCB, MC, V. Parking $1.

These units are one of Lahaina's great buys, especially those with kitchenettes; the larger ones are perfect for families on a budget. This wooden complex isn't on the beach, but it is on a quiet side street (a rarity in Lahaina) and within walking distance of restaurants, shops, attractions, and, yes, the beach (just 3 blocks away). All of the good-sized rooms, decorated in tropical-island style, are comfortable and quiet. The entire complex is spread across 10 landscaped acres and includes tennis courts (with lights for night play until 10pm), a pool, a sundeck, a barbecue, and a picnic area. The aloha-friendly staff will be happy to take the time to answer all of your questions.

Best Western Pioneer Inn. 658 Wharf St. (in front of Lahaina Pier), Lahaina, HI 96761. ☎ **800/457-5457** or 808/661-3636. Fax 808/667-5708. www.bestwestern.com. 50 units. A/C TV TEL. Year-round $99–$159 double. Extra person $15. AE, CB, DC, DISC, MC, V. Parking $4 in lot 2 blocks away.

This historic hotel has come a long way from its origins as a turn-of-the-century whalers' saloon and inn. Until the 1970s, a room at the Pioneer Inn overlooking Lahaina Harbor went for $20 and included a can of Raid insect repellent; the honky-tonk bar downstairs went until the wee hours of the morning, so no one slept. But those days are long gone—and this old waterfront hotel has never looked better.

This once-rowdy home-away-from-home for sailors and whalers now seems almost respectable, like visiting your great-grandma's house—old but nice, even charming (a word never before associated with this relic). The hotel is a two-story plantation-style structure with big verandas that overlook the streets of Lahaina and the harbor. All rooms have been totally remodeled, with vintage baths and new curtains and carpets; they even have TVs, VCRs, and direct-dial phones now. There's a new outdoor pool, three restaurants, the historic whalers' saloon (without the honky-tonk music), 20 shops, and the Lahaina Harbor just 50 feet away. The quietest rooms face either the garden courtyard—devoted to refined outdoor dining accompanied by live (but quiet) music—or the square-block-sized banyan tree next door. We recommend room no. 47, over the banyan court, with a view of the ocean and the harbor. If you want a front-row seat for all the Front Street action, book no. 48.

House of Fountains Bed & Breakfast. 1579 Lokia St. (off Fleming Rd., north of Lahaina town), Lahaina, HI 96761. ☎ **800/789-6865** or 808/667-2121. Fax 808/667-2120. www.alohahouse.com. 6 units (private bathrooms have shower only). A/C TV. $85–$125 double. Rates include full breakfast. Extra person $15. AE, DISC, MC, V. From Hwy. 30, take the Fleming Rd. exit; turn left on Ainakea; after 2 blocks, turn right on Malanai St.; go 3 blocks, and turn left onto Lokia St.

Talk about escape: A young German couple ran away to Maui for their honeymoon, fell in love with the island, bought a big house above Lahaina, and turned it into one of the area's best B&Bs. Their 7,000-square-foot contemporary home, in a quiet residential subdivision at the north end of town, is popular with visitors from around the world. This place is immaculate (hostess Daniela Clement provides daily maid service). The oversized rooms are fresh and quiet, with white ceramic-tile floors, bright tropical fabrics, and wicker furnishings; the four downstairs rooms all open onto flower-filled private patios. Guests share a pool, Jacuzzi, well-equipped guest kitchen, and barbecue area, and you're welcome to curl up on the living-room sofa facing the fireplace (not really needed in Lahaina) with a book from the library. Breakfast is served in the sunny dining room. Self-service laundry facilities are available for $2. The nearest beach is about 10 minutes away.

✪ **Lahaina Inn.** 127 Lahainaluna Rd. (near Front St.), Lahaina, HI 96761. ☎ **800/ 669-3444** or 808/661-0577. Fax 808/667-9480. www.lahainainn.com. 12 units (most bathrooms have shower only). A/C TEL. $99–$159 double. Rates include continental breakfast. Children under 14 not accepted. AE, DISC, JCB, MC, V. Next-door parking $5.

If the romance of historic Lahaina catches your fancy, a stay here will really underscore the experience. Built in 1938 as a general store, swept by fire in the mid-1960s, and reopened as a hotel in the 1970s, this place deteriorated into a fleabag with an eyesore of a bar at street level. Then, in 1986, rescue came in a classy way: It was saved from extinction by Rick Ralston, the Waikiki airbrush artist who became the Crazy Shirts mogul—and a one-man historic restoration society. About a million dollars of T-shirt money has brought this place back to life as a charming, antique-filled inn right in the heart of Lahaina.

If you like old hotels that have genuine historic touches, you'll love this place. As in many old hotels, some of these Victorian antique–stuffed rooms are small; if that's a problem for you, ask for a larger unit. All come with private bathrooms and lanais. The best room in the house is no. 7 ($99), which overlooks the beach, the town, and the island of Lanai; you can watch the action below or close the door and ignore it. Downstairs is one of Hawaii's finest bistros, David Paul's Lahaina Grill (see chapter 5).

✪ **Plantation Inn.** 174 Lahainaluna Rd. (between Wainee and Luakini sts., 1 block off Hwy. 30), Lahaina, HI 96761. ☎ **800/433-6815** or 808/667-9225. Fax 808/667-9293. www. theplantationinn.com. 18 units (some bathrooms have shower only). A/C TV TEL. Year-round $135–$215 double. Rates include full breakfast. AE, CB, DC, DISC, JCB, MC, V.

Attention, romance-seeking couples: Look no further. This charming inn looks like it's been here 100 years or more, but looks can be deceiving: The Victorian-style hotel is actually of 1990s vintage—an artful deception. The rooms are romantic to the max, tastefully done with period furniture, hardwood floors, stained glass, and ceiling fans; there are four-poster canopy beds and armoires in some rooms, brass beds and wicker in others. All come equipped with soundproofing (a plus in Lahaina), TV, VCR, fridge, private bathroom, and lanai; the suites have kitchenettes. The rooms wrap around the large pool and deck. Also on the property are a spa and an elegantly decorated pavilion lounge, as well as Gerard's, an excellent French restaurant (see chapter 5). It can be pricey, but hotel guests get a discount on dinner (you'll kick yourself if you don't eat here). Breakfast is served around the pool and in the pavilion lounge; ours featured fresh fruit, followed by a choice of Gerard's French toast or his homemade yogurt and granola.

Puamana. Front St., at the extreme southern end of Lahaina, a half mile from downtown (P.O. Box 11108), Lahaina, HI 96760. ☎ **800/669-6284** or 808/667-2712. Fax 808/ 661-5875. E-mail: robyn@maui.com. 40 units. TV TEL. $100–$175 one-bedroom double, $140–$250 two-bedroom, $300–$350 three-bedroom. 3-night minimum. AE, MC, V.

These 28 acres of town houses situated right on the water are the ideal choice for those who want the option of retreating from the crowds and cacophony of downtown Lahaina into the serene quiet of an elegant neighborhood. Private and peaceful are apt descriptions for this complex: Each unit is a privately owned individual home, with no neighbors above or below. Most are exquisitely decorated, and all come with a full kitchen, TV, lanai, barbecue, and at least two bathrooms. There are three pools (one for adults only), a tennis court, table tennis, and on-site laundry facilities (some units have washers and dryers as well). Puamana was once a private estate in the 1920s, part of the sugar plantation that dominated Lahaina; the plantation manager's house has been converted into a clubhouse with oceanfront lanai, library, card room, sauna, and office.

Wai Ola Vacation Paradise on Maui. Kuuipo St. (P.O. Box 12580), Lahaina, HI 96761. ☎ **800/492-4652** or 808/661-7901. Fax 808/661-7901. www.maui.net/~tai/WaiOla.html. 3 units. A/C TV TEL. $95–$115 studio, $100–$120 suite, $115–$135 one-bedroom apt. 5-night minimum high season, 3-night minimum low season. Extra person $15. AE, CB DC DISC, MC, V.

Just 2 blocks from the beach, in a quiet, residential development behind a tall concrete wall, lies Maui's version of Shangri-la: shade trees, sitting areas, gardens, a pool, an ocean mural, and a range of accommodations—a suite inside the 5,000-square-foot home, a separate studio cottage, and a one-bedroom apartment. Hostess Julie Frank owned and operated Julie's Bed-and-Breakfast in Half Moon Bay, California, for years; as a veteran innkeeper, she knows how to provide comfortable accommodations and memorable vacations. The Kuuipo (Sweetheart) Suite comes complete with deck and sweeping views of the Lahaina coastline. Downstairs, just off the pool, hot tub, and deck, is the 1,000-square-foot one-bedroom apartment with full kitchen, queen bed, sofa bed, private phone, TV/VCR, and air-conditioning. The 500-square-foot studio cottage, located in the courtyard, has a full kitchen and tasteful white wicker furniture. Guests have full access to the pool, barbecue facilities, and outdoor wet bar.

INEXPENSIVE

In addition to the following choices, also consider value-priced **Old Lahaina House** (☎ **800/847-0761** or 808/667-4663; fax 808/667-5615; www.mauiweb.com/maui/olhouse), which features comfy twin- and king-bedded doubles for $69 to $95.

Aloha Lani Inn—A Maui Guest House. 13 Kauaula Rd. (at Front St.), Lahaina, HI 96761. ☎ **800/57-ALOHA** or 808/661-8040. Fax 808/661-8045. www.maui.net/~tony/index.html. 3 units (all with shared bathroom). $69 double. 2-night minimum. Extra person $10. AE, MC, V.

If you're on a fixed budget and don't mind sharing a bathroom, this clean, casual B&B, just a block from the beach, is the place for you. Host Melinda Mower, who took over the operation formerly known as Aloha Tony's in June 1996, has livened up the place with tropical and floral interior decor. The entire house is guest-friendly: The living room is stuffed with books on the flora, fauna, history, and marine life of the islands, along with menus from dozens of nearby restaurants; all the drawers and cabinets in the communal kitchen are labeled with their contents; a map of Maui pinpoints great things to do; and loads of brochures are available to help you plan your stay. The guest rooms are small, but the location is dynamite: a stone's throw from the beach and within walking distance of downtown Lahaina (no parking woes), yet in a quiet residential neighborhood. A continental breakfast is available for $3, or you're welcome to fix your own.

✪ Guest House. 1620 Ainakea Rd. (off Fleming Rd., north of Lahaina town), Lahaina, HI 96761. ☎ **800/621-8942** or 808/661-8085. Fax 808/661-1896. www.ourworld. compuserve.com/homepages/guesthouse. 5 units (1 unit shares a bathroom with hosts). A/C TV TEL. $69–$99 double. Rates include full breakfast. Extra person $15. AE, DISC, MC, V. Take Fleming Rd. off Hwy. 30; turn left on Ainakea; the house is 2 blocks down.

This is one of Lahaina's great bed-and-breakfast deals: a charming house with more amenities than the expensive Kaanapali hotels just down the road. The roomy home features parquet floors, floor-to-ceiling windows, and a pool—surrounded by a deck and comfortable lounge chairs—that's larger than some at high-priced condos. Every guest room is air-conditioned and has a ceiling fan, small fridge, TV, and private phone; four of the rooms each have a quiet lanai and a romantic hot tub. The large kitchen (with every gadget imaginable) is available for guests' use. The Guest House also operates Trinity Tours and offers discounts on car rentals and just about every island activity.

KAANAPALI
VERY EXPENSIVE

Other options to consider include the **Royal Lahaina Resort,** 2780 Kekaa Dr., Lahaina, HI 96761 (☎ **800/44-ROYAL** or 808/661-3611; fax 800/432-9752 or 808/661-6150)—but skip the overpriced hotel rooms; stay here only if you can get one of the 122 cottages tucked among the well-manicured grounds ($295 to $385 double). If you aren't looking for something uniquely Hawaiian and you like the Marriott chain's style, consider the **Maui Marriott Resort,** 100 Nohea Kai Dr., Lahaina, HI 96761 (☎ **800/228-9290** or 808/667-1200; fax 808/667-8181; www.marriott. com), where doubles run from $280 to $328.

✪ **Sheraton Maui.** 2605 Kaanapali Pkwy., Lahaina, HI 96761. ☎ **800/STAY-ITT** or 808/661-0031. Fax 808/661-9991. www.sheraton-maui.com. 510 units. A/C TV TEL. $310–$465 double, from $600 suite. Extra person $40; children 17 and under stay free using existing bedding. AE, CB, DC, DISC, MC, V. Valet parking $8, self-parking $5.

Terrific facilities for families and fitness buffs and a premier beach location make this beautiful resort an all-around great place to stay. The first to set up camp in Kaanapali (in 1963), the hoteliers took the best location on the beach: the curving white-sand cove next to Black Rock (a lava formation that rises 80 feet above the beach), where they built into the side of the cliff. The grand dame of Kaanapali Beach reopened in 1997 after a $160 million, 2-year renovation; the resort is virtually new, with six buildings set in well-established tropical gardens. The lobby has been elevated to take advantage of panoramic views, and a new lagoonlike pool features lava-rock waterways, wooden bridges, and an open-air spa.

The new emphasis is on family appeal, with a class of rooms dedicated to those traveling with children (665-square-foot units with two double beds and a pull-down wall bed) and other kid-friendly amenities. Every room is outfitted with all the comforts that make for easy travel—from minifridges and free Kona coffee for the coffeemakers to irons, hair dryers, and even toothbrushes and toothpaste. Other pluses include a "no hassle" check-in policy: The valet takes you and your luggage straight to your room, thus no time wasted standing in line at registration. But not everything has changed, thankfully. Cliff divers still swan-dive off the torch-lit lava-rock headland in a traditional sunset ceremony—a sight to see. And the views of Kaanapali Beach, with Lanai and Molokai in the distance, are some of the best in Kaanapali.

Dining/Diversions: Three restaurants, with cuisine ranging from teppanyaki to steaks and seafood, plus a snack bar and three bars and cocktail lounges.

Amenities: Free summer children's program, in-room dining from 6:30am to 10:30pm, valet laundry, baby-sitting, express checkout, in-house doctors' office. Two pools, three tennis courts, conference facilities, activities desk, fitness center, game center, full beach services, 24-hour coin-op laundry, and hospitality suite for early arrivals or late departures.

ⓗ Family-Friendly Accommodations

If you're traveling with the kids, you'll be welcomed with open arms at many of Maui's accommodations. Our favorites are listed below. Note that by state law, hotels that offer supervised activity programs can accept only children ages 5 to 12.

OUR FAVORITE: Four Seasons Resort Wailea *(see p. 82)*   This is the most kid-friendly hotel on Maui. The *keikis* will feel welcome with such amenities as free milk and cookies on the first day, children's menus in all restaurants (including room service), and complimentary infant needs (crib, stroller, high chair, playpen, car seats) and child-safety features (toilet-seat locks, plug covers, security gates). The resort can also prepurchase a range of necessities (such as diapers and baby food) for you before your arrival. Kids and teens have a huge list of recreational activities and equipment to choose from, including a game room (with Super Nintendo, Sony PlayStation, foosball, and more); a free scuba clinic (for ages 12 and up); children's videos; and a host of sailing, snorkeling, and whale-watching activities.

WEST MAUI

Hale Kai *(see p. 70)*   This small condo complex is ideally located for families: right on the beach, next door to a county park, and a 10-minute drive to Lahaina's attractions. Kids can hang out at the pool, swim in the ocean, or play in the park. There's a TV and VCR in every unit, and the well-equipped kitchens (with dishwasher, microwave, even a blender) allow Mom and Dad to save money on eating out.

Hyatt Regency Maui *(see p. 66)*   The Camp Hyatt program, for hotel guests only, operates daily from 9am to 3pm and offers a range of activities, from "Olympic Games" to a scavenger hunt. The cost is $65, which includes lunch and snacks. The camp also has nightly activities (from 6 to 10pm) such as table games, movies, and video games. The cost is $12 per hour, which includes light snacks.

Kaanapali Beach Hotel *(see p. 67)*   The Kalo Patch Kids Program is offered to hotel guests only, Tuesday through Saturday from 8:30am to 1:30pm. The wide range of activities offered ranges from making Hawaiian crafts to riding on the Kaanapali Train. The cost is $15 per child.

Westin Maui. 2365 Kaanapali Pkwy., Lahaina, HI 96761. ☎ **800/228-3000** or 808/667-2525. Fax 808/661-5831. www.westin.com. 793 units. A/C MINIBAR TV TEL. $265–$495 double, from $800 suite. Extra person $30 ($50 in Royal Beach Club rooms). Special wedding/honeymoon and other packages available. "Resort fee" of $6 for such amenities as free local phone calls, use of fitness center, complimentary coffee and tea, free parking, and free local paper. AE, DC, DISC, ER, JCB, MC, V.

The "Aquatic Playground"—an 87,000-square-foot pool area with five free-form heated pools joined by swim-through grottoes, waterfalls, and a 128-foot-long water slide—sets this resort apart from its peers along Kaanapali Beach. Thanks to mega-hotelier Christopher Hemmeter, who waved his magic wand over the property in the late 1980s, this is the Disney World of water-park resorts—and your kids will be in water-hog heaven. The fantasy theme extends from the estatelike grounds into the interior's public spaces, which are filled with the shrieks of tropical birds and the splash of waterfalls; the oversized architecture, requisite colonnade, and $2 million art collection make a pleasing backdrop for all of the action. Guests seem to love it: The

Maui Park *(see p. 71)*   Located directly across the street from Honokowai Beach Park, the roomy apartments at this three-story complex are a good value for families. Extras include a large swimming pool, a jet spa, and barbecue and picnic areas.

Noelani Condominium Resort *(see p. 72)*   If your kids love to swim, head to this Kahana condo on the ocean. Right next door is great snorkeling at a sandy cove, frequented by spinner dolphins and turtles in summer and humpback whales in winter. On site are two freshwater pools (one heated for night swimming). The units feature complete kitchens and entertainment centers.

Ritz-Carlton Kapalua *(see p. 74)*   The Ritz Kids is a daytime program offering both educational activities (exploring the ecosystems in streams, learning the hula) and sports (from golf to swimming). The cost is $60 for a full day (nonguests pay $75), which includes lunch and a T-shirt, and $40 for a half day (nonguests pay $55).

SOUTH MAUI

Koa Resort *(see p. 78)*   Right across the street from the ocean in Kihei, this deluxe condo complex is great for active families, with its two tennis courts, pool, hot tub, and 18-hole putting green. The spacious, privately owned units are fully equipped and have plenty of room for even a large brood.

Mana Kai Maui Resort *(see p. 80)*   This complex, an unusual combination of hotel and condominium, sits on a beautiful white-sand cove that's one of the best snorkeling beaches on the south coast. Families will like the condo units, which have full kitchens and open living rooms; sliding-glass doors lead to small lanais overlooking the sandy beach and ocean.

UPCOUNTRY MAUI

Nohona Laule'a *(see p. 89)*   If your kids need space to run and you don't want to worry about bothering the neighbors, book this two-bedroom cottage on the slopes of Haleakala. The 700-square-foot cottage has open-beam ceilings, skylights, a complete kitchen, a huge deck with views, and 4 open acres—plenty of room for the kids to play.

---

resort has taken top honors in various readers' surveys, from *Condé Nast Traveller* to *Travel & Leisure*. With lots of indoor and outdoor meeting spaces, it's also a big hit with wedding parties and groups.

The majority of the rooms (refurbished in 1995) in the two 11-story towers overlook the aquatic playground, the ocean, and the island of Lanai in the distance. In addition to the standard features, each comes with a safe, an ironing board and iron, a coffeemaker, and its own lanai. The top-floor Royal Beach Club rooms feature a hospitality lounge and special amenities.

Dining/Diversions: Several outdoor restaurants and lounges, ranging from a sushi bar to a seafood buffet; see chapter 5 for a review of the Villa, a romantic restaurant near waterfalls.

Amenities: Twice-daily maid service, nightly turndown, multilingual staff, American Express and Hertz desks, and secretarial services. Guest Services will help you plan sightseeing and activities. Extensive health club and spa facilities. Extensive supervised kids' program weekdays. Five pools, Jacuzzi, water aerobics classes, scuba lessons for beginners and refresher courses, and guided outdoor adventure hikes. Coin-op laundry, ATM, and hospitality suite for early check-ins and late departures. Beauty salon, retail shops, business center, and conference facilities. Golf, tennis, and shopping are all at hand. A wedding coordinator, known as the director of romance, can help you throw an unforgettable wedding.

EXPENSIVE

Hyatt Regency Maui. 200 Nohea Kai Dr., Lahaina, HI 96761. ☎ **800/233-1234** or 808/661-1234. Fax 808/667-4714. www.hyatt.com. 815 units. A/C MINIBAR TV TEL. $260–$495 double, from $600 suite. Extra person $25 ($45 in Regency Club rooms); children 18 and under stay free using existing bedding. Packages available. AE, DC, DISC, JCB, MC, V. Valet parking $8, free self-parking.

People either absolutely love or hate this fantasy resort. One of several built by Christopher Hemmeter for Hyatt in the 1980s, this hotel—the southernmost of the Kaanapali properties—has lots of imaginative touches: a collection of exotic species (flaming pink flamingos, unhappy-looking penguins, and an assortment of loud parrots and macaws in the lobby), nine waterfalls, and an eclectic Asian and Pacific art collection. This huge place covers some 40 acres; even if you don't stay here, you might want to walk through the expansive tree-filled atrium and the parklike grounds, with their dense riot of plants and fantasy pools with grottoes, slides, and a suspended walking bridge. There's even an artificial beach in case the adjacent public beach is just too crowded.

All the rooms are pleasantly decorated in rich colors, floral prints, and Asian lamps—a welcome change from the typical beiges—and feature separate sitting areas and private lanais. In-room extras include safes, hair dryers, coffeemakers, and irons and ironing boards.

Dining/Diversions: Swan Court is a romantic setting for dinner; the Cascades Grille and Sushi Bar serves steak, seafood, and sushi; and Spats offers Italian fare (see chapter 5 for full reviews). There's also the casual poolside Pavilion, numerous lounges, a swim-up cocktail bar, and the "Drums of the Pacific" dinner show.

Amenities: Twice-daily maid service, concierge, room service, activities desk, and baby-sitting on request. Two Regency Club floors have private concierge, complimentary breakfast, sunset cocktails, and snacks. Camp Hyatt kids' program offers daytime and evening supervised activities for 3- to 12-year-olds. The Great Pool; health club with weight and exercise rooms, Jacuzzi, sauna, and massage studio; six hard-surface tennis courts; three nearby golf courses; game room; and a small lending library. Snorkeling gear, bicycles, kayaks, boogie boards, and video and underwater cameras are available for rent. *Kiele V,* the Hyatt's 55-foot catamaran, sponsors snorkel trips, whale-watching excursions, and evening cruises.

☉ Maui Eldorado Resort. 2661 Kekaa Dr., Lahaina, HI 96761. ☎ **800/688-7444** or 808/661-0021. Fax 808/667-7039. www.outrigger.com. 98 units. AC TV TEL. $175–$200 studio double, $235–$260 one-bedroom (sleeps up to 4), $310–$350 two-bedroom (sleeps up to 6). Numerous packages available, including 7th night free, car packages, senior rates, and more. AE, CB, DC, DISC, JCB, MC, V.

These spacious condominium units—all with full kitchen, washer/dryer, and daily maid service—were built at a time when land in Kaanapali was cheap, contractors took pride in their work, and visitors expected large, spacious rooms with views from every window. You'll find it hard to believe that this was one of Kaanapali's first properties in the late 1960s—this first-class choice still looks like new. The Outrigger chain has managed to keep prices down to reasonable levels, especially if you come in spring or fall. It's a great place for families, with its big units, grassy areas that are perfect for running off excess energy, and beachfront that's usually safe for swimming.

Amenities include daily maid service, travel desk, fax services, personal safe, three pools, beach cabana, barbecue areas, shops, and laundry facilities.

✪ **The Whaler on Kaanapali Beach.** 2481 Kaanapali Pkwy. (next to Whalers Village), Lahaina, HI 96761. ☎ **800/367-7052** or 808/661-4861. Fax 435-655-4844. www. ten-io.com/vri. 360 units; 150 in rental pool. A/C TV TEL. High season $195–$210 studio double, $260–$390 one-bedroom (sleeps up to 4), $430–$510 two-bedroom (sleeps up to 6); low season $195–$205 studio, $235–$355 one-bedroom, $370–$480 two-bedroom. 2-night minimum. Extra person $15; crib $10. Packages available. AE, MC, V.

Location, location, location—in the heart of Kaanapali, right on the world-famous beach, lies this oasis of elegance, privacy, and luxury. The relaxing atmosphere strikes you as soon as you enter the open-air lobby, where light reflects off the dazzling koi in the meditative lily pond. No expense has been spared on these gorgeous accommodations; all have full kitchens, washer/dryers, marble bathrooms, 10-foot beamed ceilings, and blue-tiled lanais. Add to that a rarity in Kaanapali these days: free parking. Every unit boasts spectacular views, which include vistas of both Kaanapali's gentle waves and the humpback peaks of the West Maui Mountains.

Dining/Diversions: Next door is Whalers Village, where you'll find Peter Merriman's terrific Hula Grill (see chapter 5) and a handful of other restaurant and bar choices.

Amenities: Daily maid service, pool and spa, exercise room, five tennis courts. The Kaanapali Golf Club's 36 holes are across the street, and all the ocean activities Maui has to offer are just out back.

MODERATE

Kaanapali Beach Hotel. 2525 Kaanapali Pkwy., Lahaina, HI 96761. ☎ **800/262-8450** or 808/661-0011. Fax 808/667-5978. www.kaanapalibeachhotel.com. 433 units. A/C TV TEL. $150–$250 double, from $210 suite. Extra person $25. Car, bed-and-breakfast, golf, and romance packages available, as well as discount rates for seniors. AE, CB, DC, DISC, JCB, MC, V.

This old beach hotel, set in a garden by the sea, is Maui's most genuinely Hawaiian place to stay—you *live* aloha here. It isn't a luxury property, but it's not bad, either. Three low-rise wings are set around a wide, grassy lawn with coco palms and a whale-shaped pool, bordering a fabulous stretch of beach. The spacious, spotless motel-like rooms are done in wicker and rattan, with Hawaiian-style bedspreads and a lanai that looks toward the courtyard and the beach. The beachfront rooms are separated from the water only by Kaanapali's landscaped walking trail.

The Kaanapali Beach Hotel is older and less high-tech than its upscale neighbors, but it has an irresistible local style and a real Hawaiian warmth that are absent in many other Maui hotels. Old Hawaii values and customs are always close at hand, and in true aloha style, the service is some of the friendliest around. Tiki torches, hula, and Hawaiian music create a festive atmosphere in the expansive open courtyard every night. As part of the hotel's extensive Hawaiiana program, you can learn to cut pineapple, weave lauhala (the leaf of the hala tree), and even dance the *real* hula; there's also an arts-and-crafts fair 3 days a week, a morning welcome reception weekdays, and a Hawaiian library.

The hotel's three restaurants feature native Hawaiian dishes as well as modern Hawaiian cuisine (see chapter 5 for a review of the Tiki Terrace); there's also a poolside bar that fixes a mean piña colada. Amenities include a concierge, baby-sitting, a United Airlines desk, coin-op laundry, in-room movies, convenience shops and salon, conference rooms, beach-equipment rentals, free scuba and snorkeling lessons, access to tennis and Kaanapali golf, and ice, drink, and snack machines.

HONOKOWAI, KAHANA & NAPILI
VERY EXPENSIVE

Embassy Vacation Resort. 104 Kaanapali Shores Pl. (in Honokowai), Lahaina, HI 96761. ☎ **800/669-3155** or 808/661-2000. Fax 808/661-1353. www.maui.net/~embassy. 413 units. A/C TV TEL. $260–$400 one-bedroom suite (sleeps up to 4), $550 two-bedroom suite (sleeps up to 4). Rates include full breakfast and 2-hour cocktail party daily. Extra person $20; children 18 and under stay free using existing bedding. AE, CB, DC, DISC, MC, V. Parking $5. Take the first turn off Hwy. 30 after Kaanapali onto Lower Honoapiilani Rd.; turn left at Kaanapali Shores Place.

Kids will love this place. The all-suite property features a mammoth 1-acre pool with a 24-foot water slide, a great beach for swimming and snorkeling, and complete entertainment centers in every unit that will satisfy even the surliest teenager: 35-inch TV (with HBO), VCR (a vast video library is on site), and stereo. With roomy condolike suites (ranging from 820 to 1,100 square feet) that feature hotel-style amenities, all-you-can-eat breakfasts, and free daily cocktail parties included in the price, Mom and Dad will be happy, too.

You can't miss this place; the shockingly pink pyramid-shaped building is visible from the highway. It's composed of three towers, each set around a central atrium amid tropical gardens with interlocking waterfalls and waterways; a huge wooden deck overlooks the koi-filled ponds and streams. Every unit has a full-sized sofa bed, a good-sized lanai, a minikitchen (microwave, small fridge, wet bar, and coffeemaker with free Kona coffee), two phones, a soaking tub big enough for two, and a second TV in the bedroom.

Dining/Diversions: There are three on-site dining choices: the oceanfront North Beach Grille, the poolside Ohana Bar and Grill, and a sandwich/snack bar, The Deli Planet.

Amenities: Concierge, laundry facilities, dry cleaning, tour desk, children's program (during holidays and in summer). Pool, health club, Jacuzzi, sauna, sundeck, 18-hole minigolf. Kaanapali's shops, golf, tennis, and restaurants are just minutes away.

EXPENSIVE

Families might want to consider the **Sands of Kahana,** 4299 Lower Honoapiilani Rd. (☎ **888/669-0400** or 808/669-1199; fax 808/669-8409; www.sands-of-kahana.com). Despite the austere appearance of the high-rise buildings, these units offer many amenities, including pools and a playground ($165 to $225 one-bedroom, $220 to $280 two-bedroom, $275 to $335 three-bedroom; 5-night minimum).

✪ **Napili Kai Beach Club.** 5900 Honoapiilani Rd. (at the extreme north end of Napili, next door to Kapalua), Lahaina, HI 96761. ☎ **800/367-5030** or 808/669-6271. Fax 808/669-0085. www.napilikai.com. 162 units. TV TEL. $170–$265 studio double, $270–$550 one-bedroom suite (sleeps up to 4), $270–$550 two-bedroom suite (sleeps up to 6). Extra person $10. Packages available. AE, MC, V.

Just south of the Bay Club restaurant in Kapalua, nestled in a small, white-sand cove, lies this comfortable oceanfront complex. Clusters of one- and two-story units with double-hipped Hawaii-style roofs face their very own gold-sand, safe-swimming beach; many have a view of the Pacific, with Molokai and Lanai in the distance. The older beachfront Lahaina Building units—with ceiling fans only—are a good buy at $215. Those who prefer air-conditioning should book into the Honolua Building, where, for the same price, you'll get a fully air-conditioned room set back from the shore around a grassy park-like lawn and pool. All units (except eight hotel rooms) have a fully stocked kitchenette with full-sized fridge, stove, microwave, toaster oven, and coffeemaker; some have dishwashers.

Accommodations from Honokowai to Kapalua

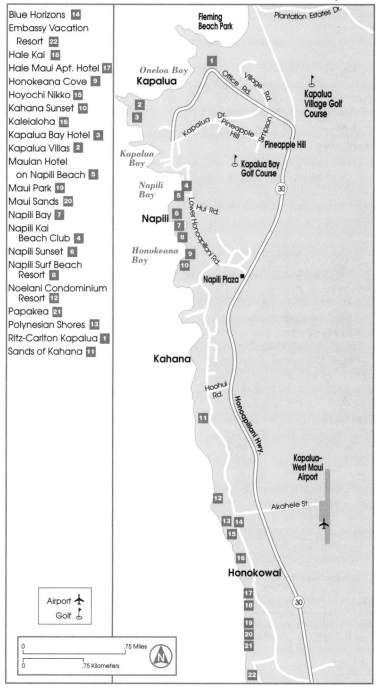

Blue Horizons **14**
Embassy Vacation
  Resort **22**
Hale Kai **18**
Hale Maui Apt. Hotel **17**
Honokeana Cove **9**
Hoyochi Nikko **15**
Kahana Sunset **10**
Kaleialoha **16**
Kapalua Bay Hotel **3**
Kapalua Villas **2**
Mauian Hotel
  on Napili Beach **5**
Maui Park **19**
Maui Sands **20**
Napili Bay **7**
Napili Kai
  Beach Club **4**
Napili Sunset **6**
Napili Surf Beach
  Resort **8**
Noelani Condominium
  Resort **12**
Papakea **21**
Polynesian Shores **13**
Ritz-Carlton Kapalua **1**
Sands of Kahana **11**

Fleming
Beach Park

Plantation Estates Dr.

Oneloa Bay

Kapalua

Office Rd.

Village Rd.

Kapalua
Village Golf
Course

1

2

3

Kapalua Dr.

Pineapple
Hill

Simpson

Pineapple Hill

Kapalua Bay

Kapalua Bay
Golf Course

Napili Bay

4

5

Hui Rd.

Napili

6

Lower Honoapiilani Rd.

7

8

Honokeana Bay

9

10

Napili Plaza ■

Kahana

Hoohui
Rd.

Honoapiilani Hwy.

11

Kapalua–
West Maui
Airport

12

Akahele St.

13 **14**

15

16

Honokowai

17

18

19

20

21

22

Airport ✈

Golf ⛳

0 _____ .75 Miles
0 _____ .75 Kilometers

30

30

69

Dining: The Sea House Restaurant serves three meals (see chapter 5); the Whale Watcher's Bar takes care of cocktails.

Amenities: Daily maid service, laundry facilities, dry cleaning, free children's activities (available Easter, June 15 to August 31, and Christmas), activities desk. Beach pagoda, two shuffleboard courts, barbecue areas, four pools, two 18-hole putting greens, nearby tennis courts, and golf just minutes away. Complimentary beach chairs, mats, swim masks, and snorkels; complimentary tennis rackets and golf putters. Complimentary coffee at the beach pagoda every morning, free tea in the lobby every afternoon, and a free mai tai party once a week.

MODERATE

Another option is **Polynesian Shores,** 3975 Lower Honoapiilani Rd. (near Kahana, and just 2 minutes from the Kapalua–West Maui Airport), Lahaina, HI 96761. (☎ 800/433-6284 or 808/669-6065; fax 808/669-0909; www.maui.net/~polyshor). Every unit (one to three bedrooms, from $100 to $185) has floor-to-ceiling sliding-glass doors which open onto a private lanai with ocean view; there's great snorkeling off the beach out front.

Hale Kai. 3691 Lower Honoapiilani Rd. (in Honokowai), Lahaina, HI 96761. ☎ **800/446-7307** or 808/669-6333. Fax 808/669-7474. www.halekai.com. 40 units. TV TEL. High season $110 one-bedroom double, $140–$145 two-bedroom (sleeps up to 4), $180 three-bedroom (sleeps up to 6); low season $95 one-bedroom, $125–$130 two-bedroom, $180 three-bedroom. 3-night minimum. Extra person $10; children 3 and under stay free. MC, V.

This small, two-story condo complex is ideally located, right on the beach and next door to a county park; shops, restaurants, and ocean activities are all within a 6-mile radius. The units are older but in excellent shape, and come with a full kitchen and TV/VCR. Many guests clamor for the oceanfront pool units, but we find the park-view units cooler, and they still have ocean views (upstairs units also have cathedral ceilings). Book early, because units fill up fast; repeat guests make up most of the clientele.

Honokeana Cove. 5255 Lower Honoapiilani Rd. (in Napili), Lahaina, HI 96761. ☎ **800/237-4948** or 808/669-6441. Fax 808/669-8777. www.honokeana-cove.com. 33 units. A/C TV TEL. $105 one-bedroom double, $147 two-bedroom (sleeps up to 4), $175 three-bedroom (sleeps up to 6). 3-night minimum. Extra person $10–$15. MC, V.

These large, secluded units—cozily set around a pool in a lush tropical setting—have fabulous views of Honokeana Cove. The cobblestone beach is excellent for snorkeling (turtles have been spotted just offshore) and great for whale watching in winter. The well-appointed units all come with a full kitchen, TV (including Spectra Vision at no extra charge), VCR, and lanai. Amenities include laundry, barbecues, deck chairs, and a ramp with railing that leads down to that great beach. All in all, a well-priced option in an expensive neighborhood.

✪ Kahana Sunset. 4909 Lower Honoapiilani Rd. (at the northern end of Kahana, almost in Napili), c/o P.O. Box 10219, Lahaina, HI 96761. ☎ **800/669-1488** or 808/669-8011. Fax 808/669-9170. E-mail: sun2set@maui.net. 49 units; 29 in rental pool. A/C TV TEL. High season $160–$180 one-bedroom (sleeps up to 6), $165–$265 two-bedroom (sleeps up to 6); low season $120–$160 one-bedroom, $140–$200 two-bedroom. 3-night minimum. AE, MC, V. From Hwy. 30, turn *makai* (toward the ocean) at the Napili Plaza (Napilihau St.), then left on Lower Honoapiilani Rd.

Lying in the crook of a sharp horseshoe curve on Lower Honoapiilani Road is this series of wooden condo units, stair-stepping down the slide of a hill to a postcard-perfect white-sand beach. The unique location, nestled between the coastline and the road above, makes Kahana Sunset a very private place to stay. A small pool and Jacuzzi sit in the midst of a grassy lawn; down by the sandy beach are gazebos and picnic areas. The units feature full kitchens, washer/dryers, large lanais with terrific views, and sleeper sofas. This is a great complex for families: The beach out front is safe for swimming, the grassy area is away from traffic, and the units are roomy enough for all. The two-bedroom units have parking just outside, making carrying luggage and groceries that much easier.

Maui Park. 3626 Lower Honoapiilani Rd. (in Honokowai), Lahaina, HI 96761. ☎ **800/367-5004** or 808/669-6622. Fax 800/477-2329 or 808/669-9647. www.castle-group.com. 288 units. A/C TV TEL. High season $114 double, $135–$142 studio double with kitchen, $152–$163 one-bedroom (sleeps up to 4), $198 two-bedroom (sleeps up to 6); low season $99 double, $109–$115 studio double with kitchen, $125–$135 one-bedroom, $169 two-bedroom. Extra person $17. AE, DC, DISC, MC, V.

Directly across the street from Honokowai Beach Park, this three-story, six-building complex offers a haven for families. The property features a large pool, a jet spa, and barbecue and picnic areas; a convenience store is just next door, and coin-op laundry facilities are on site. The large, roomy units all come with balconies and kitchens. There are no elevators, but wheelchair-accessible rooms are available on the ground level.

Maui Sands. Maui Resort Management, 3600 Lower Honoapiilani Rd. (in Honokowai), Lahaina, HI 96761. ☎ **800/367-5037** or 808/669-1902. Fax 808/669-8790. www.mauigetaway.com. 76 units. A/C TV TEL. $85–$140 one-bedroom (sleeps up to 3), $115–$170 two-bedroom (sleeps up to 5). 7-night minimum. Extra person $9. MC, V.

The Maui Sands was built back when property wasn't as expensive and developers took the extra time and money to surround all their condo units with lush landscaping. It's hard to get a unit with a bad view: All face either the ocean (with views of Lanai and Molokai) or tropical gardens blooming with brilliant heliconia and sweet-smelling ginger. Each roomy unit has a big lanai and full kitchen. With two big bedrooms plus space in the living room for a fifth person (or even a sixth), the larger units are good deals for families. There's a narrow beach out front and a pool and laundry facilities on site. In case you have any problems or questions, the management agency is just across the street.

Mauian Hotel on Napili Beach. 5441 Lower Honoapiilani Rd. (in Napili), Lahaina, HI 96761. ☎ **800/367-5034** or 808/669-6205. Fax 808/669-0129. www.mauian.com. 44 units. High season $145–$175 double; low season $125–$155 double. Rates include continental breakfast. Extra third or fourth person $10 each; children under 5 stay free. AE, DISC, MC, V.

The Hawaiian family that built this low-rise hotel in 1961 now owns it again, and they've restored the studio units to their original old Hawaiian style. This is a great place to get away from it all: The Mauian is perched above a beautiful half-mile-long, white-sand beach with great swimming and snorkeling; there's a pool with chaise longues, umbrellas, and tables on the sundeck; and the verdant grounds are bursting with tropical color. The renovated rooms feature hardwood floors, Indonesian-style furniture, and big lanais with great views. Return guests are drawn back by the small touches, such as the fresh flowers in rooms upon arrival (plus chilled champagne for guests celebrating a special occasion). There are no phones and no TVs in the rooms (this place really is about getting away from it all), but the large Ohana (family) room does have a TV with VCR and an extensive library for those who can't bear the solitude, plus complimentary coffee; phones and fax service are available in the business center. Great restaurants are just a 5-minute walk away, Kapalua Resort is up the street, and the nightly sunsets off the beach are spectacular.

Napili Surf Beach Resort. 50 Napili Pl. (off Lower Honoapiilani Rd., in Napili), Lahaina, HI 96761. ☎ **800/541-0638** or 808/669-8002. Fax 808/669-8004. www.napilisurf.com. 53 units (some with shower only). TV TEL. $99–$159 studio (sleeps up to 3), $179–$229 one-bedroom (sleeps up to 4). No credit cards.

This well-maintained, superbly landscaped complex has a great location on Napili Beach. Facilities include two pools, three shuffleboard courts, and three gas barbecue grills. The well-furnished units (all with full kitchen) were renovated in 1997, and free daily maid service—a rarity in condo properties—keeps the units clean. Management encourages socializing: In addition to weekly mai tai parties and coffee socials, the resort hosts annual shuffleboard and golf tournaments, as well as get-togethers on July 4, Thanksgiving, Christmas, and New Year's. Many guests arrange their travel plans around these events at the Napili Surf.

✪ **Noelani Condominium Resort.** 4095 Lower Honoapiilani Rd. (in Kahana), Lahaina, HI 96761. ☎ **800/367-6030** or 808/669-8374. Fax 808/669-7904. www.noelani-condo-resort.com. 50 units. TV TEL. $97–$107 studio double, $127–$135 one-bedroom (sleeps up to 3), $167–$177 two-bedroom (sleeps up to 4), $197–$207 three-bedroom (sleeps up to 6). 3-night minimum. Rates include continental breakfast on first morning. Extra person $10; children under 17 stay free. Packages for honeymooners, seniors, and AAA members available. AE, MC, V.

This oceanfront condo is a great value, whether you stay in a studio or a three-bedroom unit (ideal for large families). The top-notch property is AAA approved and, after extensive exterior and interior renovations, has just been awarded a three-diamond designation. Everything is first class, from the furnishings to the oceanfront location, with a sandy cove next door at the new county park. There's good snorkeling off the cove, which is frequented by spinner dolphins and turtles in the summer and humpback whales in winter. All units feature full kitchens, entertainment centers, and spectacular views. Our favorites are in the Antherium building, where the one-, two-, and three-bedrooms have oceanfront lanais just 20 feet from the water. There are two freshwater swimming pools (one heated for night swimming) and an oceanfront Jacuzzi. Guests are invited to a continental breakfast orientation on their first day and mai tai parties at night.

INEXPENSIVE

Another option is **Hoyochi Nikko,** 3901 Lower Honoapiilani Rd. (in Honokowai), Lahaina, HI 96761 (☎ **800/487-6002** or 808/669-8343; fax 808/669-3937; www.greatrentals.com/HI/Hoyochi/Hoyochi.html), which has just 17 older (but well maintained) one- and two-bedroom units sharing 180 feet of oceanfront ($65 to $115 double; 1-week minimum). Frugal travelers should also consider the **Kaleialoha,** 3785 Lower Honoapiilani Rd. (in Honokowai), Lahaina, HI 96761 (☎ **800/ 222-8688** or 808/669-8197; fax 808/669-2502; e-mail: dwhipple@maui.net), offering recently upgraded one-bedroom condo units ($95 to $105 one-bedroom double; 3-night minimum).

Blue Horizons. 3894 Mahinahina Dr. (2 blocks from the Kapalua–West Maui Airport), Lahaina, HI 96761. ☎ and fax **800/669-1948** or 808/669-1965. www.maui.net/~chips/horizons/horizon.html. 4 units. A/C TV TEL. $79 double; $89–$99 double with kitchenette. 2-night minimum. Rates include breakfast every day but Sun. Extra person $15. AE, MC, V.

The only bed-and-breakfast on the west side outside of Lahaina, Blue Horizons is about a 10-minute drive to Lahaina and about a 5-minute walk to sandy beaches. The four units, in a custom-built home in a subdivision, range from compact to spacious suites with separate bedrooms and a living-room area with sofa bed. Three units have kitchenettes and all four are air-conditioned, which helps not only with the heat of

Mahinahina but also with the noise of the subdivision. A lavish breakfast is served in the screened dining area, where the ocean view may distract you from the banana pancakes. Amenities on site include a tile lap pool, washer/dryer, gas barbecue, and video library.

✪ **Napili Bay.** 33 Hui Dr. (off Lower Honoapiilani Hwy., in Napili), c/o Maui Beachfront Rentals, 256 Papalaua St., Lahaina, HI 96767. ☎ **888/661-7200** or 808/661-3500. Fax 808/661-5210. www.mauibeachfront.com. 33 units. TV TEL. $65–$100 for up to four. 5-night minimum. MC, V.

One of Maui's best secret bargains is this small, two-story complex, located right on Napili's half-mile white-sand beach. It's perfect for a romantic getaway: The atmosphere is comfortable and relaxing, the ocean lulls you to sleep at night, and birdsong wakes you in the morning. The beach here is one of the best on the coast, with great swimming and snorkeling—in fact, it's so beautiful that people staying at much more expensive resorts down the road frequently haul all their beach paraphernalia here for the day. The compact studio apartments have everything you need to feel at home, from a full kitchen (including microwave, coffeemaker, toaster, blender, and more) to a big TV, comfortable queen bed, and roomy lanai that's great for watching the sun set over the Pacific. Louvered windows and ceiling fans keep the units cool during the day. Our favorite is no. 201, a corner unit with fabulous views and a king bed.

Within walking distance of restaurants and a convenience store, the complex is just a mile from a shopping center, 10 minutes from world-class golf and tennis, and 15 minutes from Lahaina. A resident on-site manager is a walking encyclopedia of information on where to go and what to do while you're on Maui. All this for as little as $65 a night—unbelievable! Book early, and tell 'em *Frommer's* sent you.

Napili Sunset. 46 Hui Rd. (in Napili), Lahaina, HI 96761. ☎ **800/447-9229** or 808/669-8083. Fax 808/669-2730. www.napilibay.com. 42 units. TV TEL. High season $95 studio double, $185 one-bedroom double, $265 two-bedroom (sleeps up to 4); low season $75 studio, $159 one-bedroom, $219 two-bedroom. 3-night minimum. Extra person $12; children under 3 stay free. MC, V.

Housed in three buildings (two on the ocean and one across the street) and located just down the street from Napili Bay (see above), these clean, older, but well-maintained units offer good value. At first glance, the plain two-story structures don't look like much, but the location, the bargain prices, and the friendly spirit of the staff are the real hidden treasures here. In addition to daily maid service, the units each have a free in-room safe, full kitchen (with dishwasher), ceiling fans, sofa bed in the living room, small dining room, and small bedrooms. Laundry facilities are on site (you provide the quarters, they provide the free detergent). The beach—one of Maui's best—can get a little crowded, because the public beach access is through this property (and everyone on Maui seems to want to come here). The studio units are all located in the building off the beach and a few steps up a slight hill; they're good-sized, with complete kitchens and either a sofa bed or a queen Murphy bed, and they overlook the small swimming pool and garden. The one- and two-bedroom units are all on the beach (the downstairs units have lanais that lead right to the sand). The staff makes sure each unit has the basics—paper towels, dishwasher soap, coffee filters, condiments—to get your stay off to a good start.

Papakea. Maui Resort Management, 3600 Lower Honoapiilani Rd. (in Honokowai), Lahaina, HI 96761. ☎ **800/367-5037** or 808/669-1902. Fax 808/669-8790. www.mauigetaway.com. 28 units. TV TEL. $80–$100 studio double, $100–$150 one-bedroom (sleeps up to 4), $120–$189 two-bedroom (sleeps up to 6). 7-night minimum. Extra person $9. MC, V.

Just a mile down the beach from Kaanapali lie these low-rise buildings, surrounded by manicured, landscaped grounds and ocean views galore. Palm trees and tropical plants dot the property, a putting green wraps around two kidney-shaped pools, and a foot bridge arches over a lily pond brimming with carp. Each pool has its own private cabana with sauna, Jacuzzi, and barbecue grills; a poolside shop rents snorkel gear for exploring the offshore reefs. As if that weren't enough, there are three private tennis courts on the grounds for guests' use. All units have big lanais, dishwashers, and washer/dryers. The studios have pull-down beds to save space during the day. Definitely a value property.

KAPALUA
VERY EXPENSIVE

Kapalua Bay Hotel & Villas. 1 Bay Dr., Kapalua, HI 96761. ☎ **800/367-8000** or 808/669-5656. Fax 808/669-4694. www.kapaluabayhotel.com. 209 units. A/C MINIBAR TV TEL. $275–$525 double, $375–$525 villa suite, from $800 one- and two-bedroom suites. Extra person $50; children 17 and under stay free using existing bedding. AE, CB, DC, JCB, MC, V.

Few Hawaiian resorts have the luxury of open space like this one. It sits seaward of 23,000 acres of green fields lined by spiky Norfolk pine windbreaks. The 1970s-style rectilinear building sits down by the often windy shore, full of angles that frame stunning views of ocean, mountains, and blue sky. The tastefully designed maze of over-sized rooms fronts a palm-fringed gold-sand beach that's one of the best in Hawaii, as well as an excellent Ben Crenshaw golf course. Each guest room has a sitting area with a sofa, a king or two double beds, and an entertainment center; plantation-style shutter doors open onto private lanais with a view of Molokai across the channel. The renovated bathrooms feature two granite vanities, a large soaking tub, and a glass-enclosed shower.

The one- and two-bedroom villas are situated on the ocean at the very private Oneloa Bay. Each one has several lanais, a full kitchen, a washer/dryer, ceiling fans, an oversized tub, and access to three swimming pools with cabanas and barbecue facilities.

Dining: The most appealing dining spot is the Bay Club (see chapter 5), in its own plantation-style building overlooking the sea, specializing in seafood for lunch and dinner. The casual Gardenia Court serves three meals.

Amenities: 24-hour room service, twice-daily maid service, ice service every afternoon and on request, resort shuttle, complimentary transfer to Kapalua–West Maui Airport, secretarial services, and baby-sitting. Two pools, an exercise facility, a famous trio of golf courses (each with its own pro shop), and 10 Plexi-pave tennis courts for day and night play (villa guests have access to two additional tennis courts). Kamp Kapalua, for kids ages 5 to 12, offers activities ranging from snorkeling and surfing to lei making and cookie baking. Adults can plan similar activities through the hotel's Beach Activity Center. The Kapalua Shops are within easy walking distance.

✪ **Ritz-Carlton Kapalua.** 1 Ritz-Carlton Dr., Kapalua, HI 96761. ☎ **800/262-8440** or 808/669-6200. Fax 808/665-0026. www.kapaluamaui.com. 548 units. A/C MINIBAR TV TEL. $265–$395 double, from $375 suite. Extra person $40 ($80 in Club Floor rooms). Wedding/honeymoon, golf and other packages available. AE, DC, DISC, MC, V. Valet parking $10, free self-parking.

Of all the Ritz-Carltons in the world, this is probably the best. It's in the best place (Hawaii) near the best beach (Kapalua), and it's got a friendly staff who go above and beyond the call of duty to make sure that your vacation is a dream come true. The Ritz is a complete universe, one of those resorts where you can sit by the pool with a book for two whole weeks. It rises proudly on a knoll, in a singularly spectacular setting between the rain forest and the sea. During construction, the remains of hundreds of early Hawaiians were discovered buried in the sand, so the hotel was moved inland to avoid disrupting the graves. The setback improved the hotel's outlook, which now has a commanding view of Molokai.

The style is fancy plantation, elegant but not imposing. The public spaces are open, airy, and graceful, with plenty of tropical foliage and landscapes by artist Sarah Supplee that recall the not-so-long-ago agrarian past. Rooms are up to the usual Ritz standard, outfitted with marble bathrooms, private lanais, in-room fax capability, and voice mail. Hospitality is the keynote here; you'll find the exemplary service you expect from Ritz-Carlton seasoned with good old-fashioned Hawaiian aloha.

Dining/Diversions: Dining is excellent at the Anuenue Room (also great for elegant Sunday brunch), the outdoor Terrace (for breakfast and dinner), and poolside (for lunch). Whether you prefer your gourmet fare regular or macrobiotic, it'll be memorable, thanks to executive chef Patrick Callarec and crew. It's a small hike to the beach, so fortunately the Beach House serves daytime drinks and light fare. Cocktails are served in the Lobby Lounge, which doubles as an espresso bar in the morning. A new pool bar serves drinks by the three pools.

Amenities: 24-hour room service, twice-daily towels, nightly turndowns; private club floors with concierge, continental breakfast, afternoon drinks, private lounge, and other extras. Airport and golf shuttle, secretarial services, daily kids' programs, lei greetings, and multilingual staff. Three top-rated golf courses, a tennis complex, three pools, a nine-hole putting green, a croquet lawn, beach volleyball, a fitness center and salon, guests-only full-day guided backcountry hikes, and a historic plantation-style wedding chapel.

EXPENSIVE

Golfers and families will like the upscale **Kapalua Villas,** 500 Office Rd., Kapalua, HI 96761 (☎ **800/545-0018** or 808/669-8088; fax 808/669-5234; www.kapaluavillas. com), which come fully equipped and can accommodate groups ($185 to $245 one-bedroom condo, $250 to $400 two-bedroom condo, $1,195 three-bedroom home, $2,500 to $3,000 four-bedroom home, $4,000 to $5000 five-bedroom home). Guests have some access to the resort's amenities (some amenities are an additional fee) and enjoy special golf rates.

3 South Maui

MAALAEA

Contact **Maalaea Bay Rentals,** 280 Hauoli St., Wailuku, HI 96793 (☎ **800/367-6084** or 808/244-7012; fax 808/242-7476; e-mail: maalaea@sprynet.com), which has a variety of units in nearly every condominium in Maalaea, ranging from a low of $60 for a one-bedroom garden unit in an older building to $175 for a two-bedroom oceanfront unit. If your stay is shorter than 5 nights, an extra charge will be added for cleaning. Laundry facilities are on site, and all units have full kitchens and complete furnishings down to the TV, phones, linens, and beach towels.

KIHEI

We recommend two booking agencies that represent a host of condominiums and unique homes in the Kihei/Wailea area: **Kihei Maui Vacation,** P.O. Box 1055, Kihei, HI 96753 (☎ **800/541-6284** or 808/879-7581; www.kmvmaui.com), and **Condominium Rentals Hawaii,** 362 Huku Lii Place, Suite 204, Kihei, HI 96753 (☎ **800/ 367-5242** or 808/879-2778; www.crhmaui.com).

EXPENSIVE

In addition to the choices below, also consider **Aston at the Maui Banyan** (☎ 800/ 92-ASTON or 808/875-0004; www.aston-hotels.com), a very nice condo across the street from Kamaole Beach Park II. The one- to three-bedroom units are all nicely done and feature full kitchens (with microwaves), air-conditioning, and washer/dryers, and you'll find a tennis court and a Jacuzzi on site. Rates are $180 to $305 in high season, $145 to $270 in low season; be sure to ask about packages.

Maalaea Surf Resort. 12 S. Kihei Rd. (at S. Kihei Rd. and Hwy. 350), Kihei, HI 96743. ☎ **800/423-7953** or 808/879-1267. Fax 808/874-2884. 34 units in rental pool. A/C TV TEL. $205–$230 one-bedroom double, $277–$307 two-bedroom (sleeps up to 4). Extra person $15. MC, V.

Located at the quiet end of Kihei Road, this two-story condominium complex sprawls over 5 acres of lush tropical gardens. This is the place for people who want a quiet, relaxing vacation on a well-landscaped property, with a beautiful white-sand beach right outside. The large, luxury town houses all have ocean views, big kitchens, air-conditioning, cable TV, VCRs, and phones. Maid service (Monday through Saturday) is included in the price.

✪ **Maui Hill.** 2881 S. Kihei Rd. (across from Kamaole Park III, between Keonekai St. and Kilo-hana Dr.), Kihei, HI 96753. ☎ **800/92-ASTON** or 808/879-6321. Fax 808/879-8945. www.aston-hotels.com. 140 units. A/C TV TEL. High season $205 one-bedroom, $235 two-bedroom, $315 three-bedroom; low season $170 one-bedroom, $200 two-bedroom, $280 three-bedroom. AE, CB, DC, DISC, JCB, MC, V.

If you can't decide between the privacy of a condominium unit and the conveniences a hotel offers, this place will solve your dilemma. Managed by the respected Aston chain, Maui Hill gives you the best of both options. Located on a hill above the heat of Kihei town, this large, Spanish-style resort (with white stucco buildings, red-tile roof, and arched entries) combines all the amenities and activities of a hotel—large pool, hot tub, tennis courts, Hawaiiana classes, and more—with large luxury condos that have full kitchens, lots of space, and plenty of privacy. Nearly all units have ocean views, a dishwasher, a washer/dryer, a queen sofa bed, a big lanai, and daily maid service. Beaches are within easy walking distance. The management here goes out of its way to make sure that your stay is as perfect as you planned it.

Amenities: Daily maid service, concierge service, weekly complimentary continental breakfast, and weekly manager's party. Large pool, hot tub, putting green, tennis courts, shuffleboard, 14 barbecue areas, and classes in Hawaiiana such as lei making and crafts. A variety of restaurants and shops are just a short walk away along South Kihei Road.

MODERATE

The **Kihei Beach Resort,** 36 S. Kihei Rd., Kihei, HI 96753 (☎ **800/367-6034** or 808/879-2744; fax 808/875-0306), has spacious condos right on the beach—the downside is the constant traffic noise from Kihei Road ($110 to $125 one-bedroom, $140 to $160 two-bedroom; 3-night minimum). Another good deal is the **Maui Kamaole,** 2777 S. Kihei Rd., Kihei, HI 96753 (☎ **800/367-5242** or 808/874-5151; fax 808/879-6900; www.crhmaui.com), right across from beautiful Kamaole Beach Park III. The roomy units (high season $135 to $150 one-bedroom, $170 to $190 two-bedroom; 4-night minimum) are great for families.

✪ **Aston Maui Lu Resort.** 575 S. Kihei Rd. (between Kaonoulu and Ohukai sts.), Kihei, HI 96753. ☎ **800/92-ASTON** or 808/879-5881. Fax 808/879-4627. 120 units. A/C TV TEL. High season $120–$185; low season $99–$165. Packages available. AE, DC, DISC, JCB, MC, V.

South Maui Accommodations

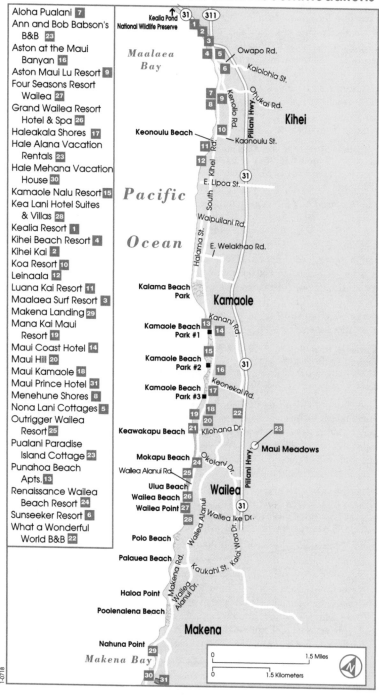

Aloha Pualani 7
Ann and Bob Babson's B&B 23
Aston at the Maui Banyan 16
Aston Maui Lu Resort 9
Four Seasons Resort Wailea 27
Grand Wailea Resort Hotel & Spa 26
Haleakala Shores 17
Hale Alana Vacation Rentals 23
Hale Mehana Vacation House 30
Kamaole Nalu Resort 15
Kea Lani Hotel Suites & Villas 28
Kealia Resort 1
Kihei Beach Resort 4
Kihei Kai 2
Koa Resort 10
Leinaala 12
Luana Kai Resort 11
Maalaea Surf Resort 3
Makena Landing 29
Mana Kai Maui Resort 19
Maui Coast Hotel 14
Maui Hill 20
Maui Kamaole 18
Maui Prince Hotel 31
Menehune Shores 8
Nona Lani Cottages 5
Outrigger Wailea Resort 25
Pualani Paradise Island Cottage 23
Punahoa Beach Apts. 13
Renaissance Wailea Beach Resort 24
Sunseeker Resort 6
What a Wonderful World B&B 22

Kealia Pond National Wildlife Preserve
31 311
1
2
3
Owapo Rd.
4 5
Kaiolohia St.
6
Maalaea Bay
Ohukai Rd.
Kenolio Rd.
7
8
Kihei
Keonoulu Beach
10
Kaonoulu St.
11
12
Pilani Hwy
31
E. Lipoa St.
South Kihei Rd.
Waipuilani Rd.
Pacific
Ocean
Halama St.
E. Welakhao Rd.
Kalama Beach Park
Kamaole
Kamaole Beach Park #1
Kanani Rd.
13
14
15
Kamaole Beach Park #2
16
31
Kamaole Beach Park #3
17
Keonekai Rd.
19 18 22
20
23
21 Kilohana Dr.
Keawakapu Beach
Maui Meadows
Mokapu Beach
24
Okolani Dr.
Wailea Alanui Rd.
25
Pilani Hwy
Ulua Beach
Wailea Beach 26
Wailea Point 27
Wailea
Wailea Ike Dr.
28
Wailea Alanui
Kalai Waa Dr.
Polo Beach
Palauea Beach
Wailea Rd.
Kaukahi St.
Makena Rd.
Haloa Point
Wailea Alanui Dr.
Poolenalena Beach
Makena
Nahuna Point
29
Makena Bay
0   1.5 Miles
0   1.5 Kilometers
30 31
N

I-0718

77

They just don't make them like this anymore. Located at the quieter northern end of Kihei, the Polynesian-style Maui Lu offers a nostalgic old Hawaii atmosphere on its 28 green acres by the sea. Ask for a beach unit if you'd like to be right on the sand; the rest of the resort is across the road and up on a rise, around a pool shaped like the island of Maui. Each big, airy room is outfitted with rattan furniture, ceiling fans, Hawaiian art, two double beds, a coffeemaker, and a small fridge. Tennis and laundry facilities are available. The restaurant, Ukulele Grill, has an inspired local chef and a reasonably priced continental/Hawaiian gourmet menu; it serves breakfast, dinner, and Sunday brunch.

Haleakala Shores. 2619 S. Kihei Rd. (across from Kamaole Park III, at Keonekai St.), Kihei, HI 96753. ☎ **800/869-1097** or 808/879-1218. Fax 808/879-2219. 144 units; 76 in rental pool. TV TEL. High season $120 two-bedroom (sleeps up to 4), 7-night minimum; low season $90 two-bedroom, 5-night minimum. Extra person $10. MC, V.

This is a great buy for frugal travelers and for families on a budget. Each large unit (some 1,200 square feet) sleeps up to six people and comes with two bedrooms, two baths, private lanai, full kitchen with dishwasher, and washer/dryer. The great location, just across the street from Kamaole Park III, makes it an easy walk to restaurants and shopping. Even the parking situation is ideal: There's a free covered garage. Okay, now for the bad news: The units were built in 1974, and most still sport 1970s-style decor. Also, they can be noisy, thanks to traffic on Kihei Road (ask for a unit inside the complex) and thin walls (you can hear your neighbors' TV and conversations quite clearly). If you manage to get a quiet unit and can overlook the nostalgic decor, these units are winners.

Kamaole Nalu Resort. 2450 S. Kihei Rd. (between Kanani and Keonekai rds., next to Kamaole Beach Park II), Kihei, HI 96753. ☎ **800/767-1497** or 808/879-1006. Fax 808/ 879-8693. www.mauigateway.com/~kamaole. 36 units. TV TEL. High season $145–$165 double; low season $100–$130 double. 3-night minimum. Extra person $10–$15. MC, V.

Located between two beach parks, Kamaole I and Kamaole II, this six-story condominium boasts fabulous ocean views. The property, right across the street from a shopping complex, has an ocean-side pool and barbecue facilities that are great for a sunset cookout. The units have large living rooms and private lanais; the kitchens are a bit small but come fully equipped. We recommend no. 306 for its wonderful bird's-eye ocean view. Be warned: Since the building is located on Kihei Road, the units can be noisy.

✪ **Koa Resort.** 811 S. Kihei Rd. (between Kulanihakoi St. and Namauu Place), c/o Bello Realty, P.O. Box 1776, Kihei, HI 96753. ☎ **800/541-3060** or 808/879-3328. Fax 808/ 875-1483. www.bellomaui.com. 54 units. TV TEL. High season $105–$180 double; low season $85–$160 double. No credit cards.

Located just across the street from the ocean, Koa Resort consists of five two-story wooden buildings on more than 5½ acres of landscaped grounds. The spacious, privately owned one-, two-, and three-bedroom units are decorated with care and come fully equipped. Each kitchen comes complete with fridge, dishwasher, disposal, microwave, blender, and coffeemaker. The larger units have both showers and tubs, whereas the smaller units have showers only. All feature large lanais, ceiling fans, and washer/dryers. The property has two tennis courts, a pool, a hot tub, and an 18-hole putting green. For maximum peace and quiet, ask for a unit far from Kihei Road.

Maui Coast Hotel. 2259 S. Kihei Rd. (1 block from Kamaole Beach Park I), Kihei, HI 96753. ☎ **800/895-6284** or 808/874-6284. Fax 808/875-4731. www.maui.net/~mch. 265 units. A/C TV TEL. $129–$139 double, $149–$159 suite, $179 one-bedroom (sleeps up to 4), $225 two-bedroom (sleeps up to 4). Extra person $10. Rental-car packages available. AE, DC, DISC, JCB, MC, V.

Built in 1993, this off-beach midrise stands out as one of the only moderately priced new hotels in Hawaii. That's big news—especially on Maui, where luxury abounds. More great news: For the price of a room (or a one- or two-bedroom apartment), the Maui Coast's Extra Value package gives you a rental car for free. The chief advantages of this hotel are price and location—about a block from Kamaole Beach Park I, with plenty of bars, restaurants, and shopping within walking distance. Rooms are clean and simple; they remind us of college dorms, only with lots of extras: sitting areas, coffee-makers and free coffee, hair dryers, whirlpool tubs, minifridges, safes, ceiling fans, and furnished, private lanais. There's a casual restaurant, a sushi bar, and a poolside bar with nightly entertainment. Additional amenities include room service, an activities desk, laundry, two pools (one for the kids), two Jacuzzis, tennis courts, and a gift shop. This ain't the Ritz, but you'll be very comfortable here—and your wallet will thank you.

INEXPENSIVE

Additional choices include **Aloha Pualani,** 15 Wailana Place, Kihei, HI 96753 (☎ **800/PUALANI** or 808/874-9265; fax 808/874-9127; www.mauigateway. com/~pualani), which offers five suites surrounding a heated pool ($79 to $99 double; 3-night minimum); **Luana Kai Resort,** 940 S. Kihei Rd., Kihei, HI 96753 (☎ **800/ 669-1127** or 808/879-1268; fax 808/879-1455; www.gpsolutions.com/luanakai), an older condo with 113 one- and two-bedroom units ($79 to $149 one-bedroom, $99 to $169 two-bedroom; 4-night minimum); and **Kihei Kai,** 61 N. Kihei Rd., Kihei, HI 96753 (☎ **800/735-2357** or 808/879-2357; fax 808/874-4960; www.maui. net/~kiheikai), which has one-bedroom apartments ($80 to $105) that are ideal for families. Finally, **Sunseeker Resort,** 551 S. Kihei Rd., P.O. Box 276, Kihei, HI 96753 (☎ **800/532-MAUI** or 808/879-1261; fax 808/874-3877; www.maui.net/~sunseekr), offers older, sometimes noisy budget units with great ocean views—somewhat of a rarity on Maui ($55 to $60 studio, $65 to $70 one-bedroom; 3-night minimum).

○ **Ann and Bob Babson's Bed & Breakfast and Sunset Cottage.** 3371 Keha Dr. (in Maui Meadows), Kihei, HI 96753. ☎ **800/824-6409** or 808/874-1166. Fax 808/879-7906. www.mauibnb.com. 4 units. TV TEL. $80–$110 double (including breakfast Mon–Sat), $115–$125 cottage double. 4-night minimum. Extra person $15. MC, V.

In addition to the wonderful accommodations on their property, Ann and Bob Babson also operate a B&B booking service, where they go above and beyond the call of duty to find the ideal place for you. But we highly recommend staying right here on their landscaped half-acre, which boasts 180° views of the islands of Lanai, Kahoolawe, and Molokini, and sunsets not to be missed. Accommodations include two rooms in the house (one with panoramic ocean views, skylights, and a whirlpool tub), a one-bedroom suite downstairs, and a two-bedroom cottage.

Hale Alana Vacation Rentals—Palm & Ginger Cottages. 490 Mikioi Place (Maui Meadows), Kihei, HI 96753. ☎ **800/871-5032** or 808/875-4840. Fax 808/879-3998. www.maui.net/~kstover. 2 units. TV TEL. $80 double. 4-night minimum. Extra person $10. MC, V.

Tucked into the residential neighborhood of Maui Meadows is an oasis of fruit trees, a vegetable garden, and a sundeck with picnic table, chairs, and a hot tub overlooking the ocean. The half-acre lot is home to host Karen Stover's own house and two rental cottages: a two-bedroom and a one-bedroom, each with full kitchen, TV, VCR, CDs, and washer/dryer. The two-bedroom Ginger Cottage is best for families, while the one-bedroom Palm Cottage makes a cozy honeymoon cottage (though it does have a sofa bed). Guests are welcome to pick dinner from the thriving vegetable garden and gather fresh fruits for their breakfast. Occasionally Karen will waive the 4-night minimum for last-minute bookings.

Leinaala. 998 S. Kihei Rd., Kihei, HI 96753. ☎ **800/334-3305** or 808/879-2235. Fax 808/879-8366. www.maui-condo-rentals.com. 24 units. TV TEL. High season $95 one-bedroom double, $115.50 two-bedroom (sleeps up to 4); low season $75 one-bedroom, $100 two-bedroom (7th night free). 4-night minimum. Extra person $10. MC, V.

From Kihei Road, you can't see Leinaala amid the jumble of buildings, but this ocean-front boutique condo offers excellent accommodations at 1980s prices. The building is set back from the water, with a county park—an oasis of green grass and tennis courts—in between. The units are compact, but filled with everything you need: a full kitchen, sofa bed, ocean-view lanai, and hide-a-beds available if you need them. On site are laundry facilities and a freshwater swimming pool.

Kealia Resort. 191 N. Kihei Rd. (north of Hwy. 31, at the Maalaea end of Kihei), Kihei, HI 96753. ☎ **800/265-0686** or 808/879-0952. Fax 808/875-1540. www.apmimaui.com. 51 units. TV TEL. $65–$90 studio double, $85–$130 one-bedroom double, $145–$175 two-bedroom (sleeps up to 4). 4-night minimum. Extra person $10. MC, V.

This oceanfront property at the northern end of Kihei is well maintained and nicely furnished—and the price is excellent. As tempting as the $65 studio units may sound, don't give in: They face noisy Kihei Road and are near a major junction, so big trucks downshifting can be especially noisy at night. Instead, go for one of the ocean-view units, which all have full kitchens, washer/dryers, and private lanais. The grounds, which abut a 5-mile stretch of beach, feature a recently retiled pool with sundeck. The management goes out of its way to provide opportunities for guests to meet; social gatherings include free coffee-and-doughnut get-togethers every Friday morning and pupu parties on Wednesday.

Mana Kai Maui Resort. 2960 S. Kihei Rd. (between Kilohana and Keonekai rds., at the Wailea end of Kihei), Kihei, HI 96753. ☎ **800/367-5242** or 808/879-2778. Fax 808/876-5042. www.crhmaui.com. 132 units. A/C TV TEL. $80–$100 double, $150–$195 one-bedroom (sleeps up to 4), $185–$230 two-bedroom (sleeps up to 6). AE, DC, DISC, MC, V.

This eight-story complex, situated on a beautiful white-sand cove, is an unusual combination of hotel and condominium. The hotel rooms, which constitute half of the total number of units, are small but nicely furnished. The condo units feature full kitchens and open living rooms with sliding-glass doors that lead to small lanais overlooking the sandy beach and ocean. Some units are beginning to show their age, but they're all clean and comfortable. There are laundry facilities on each floor, the open-air restaurant called Five Palms (see chapter 5), a pool on the property, and one of the best snorkeling beaches on the coast just steps away.

Menehune Shores. 760 S. Kihei Rd. (between Kaonoulu and Hoonani sts.), P.O. Box 1327, Kihei, HI 96753. ☎ **800/558-9117** or 808/879-3428. Fax 808/879-5218. www.thesupersites.com/menehune. 70 units. TV TEL. $80–$100 one-bedroom double, $95–$125 two-bedroom double, $110–$140 two-bedroom (sleeps up to 4), $135–$175 three-bedroom (sleeps up to 6). 3-night minimum. Weekly car/condo package $789 one-bedroom double, $905 two-bedroom double, $1,067 two-bedroom (sleeps up to 4), $1,1389 three-bedroom (sleeps up to 6). Extra person $7.50. No credit cards.

If you plan to stay on Maui for a week, you might want to look into the car/condo packages here; they're a real deal, especially for families on a budget. The six-story Menehune Shores is about 30 years old and is showing its age in some places, but all units are well maintained and have ocean views. The design is straight out of the 1970s, but the view from the private lanais is timeless. The kitchens are fully equipped, all units have washer/dryers, and the oceanfront location guarantees a steady breeze that keeps the rooms cool. The U-shaped building sits in front of the ancient Hawaiian fish ponds of Kalepolepo; some Hawaiians still fish them using traditional throw nets, but generally the pond serves as protection from the ocean waves, making it safe for children (and those unsure of their ability) to swim in the relatively calm waters. There's also a heated pool, shuffleboard courts, and a whale-watching platform on the roof garden.

Nona Lani Cottages. 455 S. Kihei Rd. (just south of Hwy. 31), P.O. Box 655, Kihei, HI 96753. ☎ **800/733-2688** or 808/879-2497. Fax 808/891-0273. E-mail: kong_fam@sprynet.com. 11 units. A/C TV. $60 double, $70–$85 cottage. 4-night minimum. Extra person $7–$10 (children 5 and under pay an extra $5). No credit cards.

Picture this: Right across the street from a white-sand beach, a grassy expanse dotted with eight small cottages tucked among palm and fruit trees. Built in 1975, the 400-square-foot cottages are tiny, but they contain all the necessities: a small but complete kitchen, two twin beds that double as couches in the living room, a separate bedroom with queen bed, and a lanai with table and chairs—ideal for watching the ocean waves as you eat your breakfast. The cottages are slightly worn, but the setting and the privacy of your own bungalow make up for it. There are no phones in the cabins (a blessing if you're trying to escape civilization), but there is a public phone near the coin-op laundry.

If the cabins are booked, or if you want a bit more luxury in your accommodations, you might opt for one of the private guest rooms in host David Kong's main house. Each beautiful room features cathedral-like open-beam ceilings, plush carpet, koa bed frames, air-conditioning, and private entrance.

✪ **Pualani Paradise Island Cottage.** 3134 Hoomua Dr. (in Maui Meadows), Kihei, HI 96753. ☎ **808/875-8522.** Fax 808/874-9129. www.maui.net/~mcwebb. 1 cottage. A/C TV TEL. $75 double. 3-night minimum. Rates includes stocked fridge with breakfast fixings. Extra person $10. MC, V.

Tucked away on a quiet street in the residential area above Wailea known as Maui Meadows, you'll find this quaint cottage, surrounded by lush landscaped grounds and a large swimming pool. The cozy cottage, with fully equipped kitchen, is decorated with Balinese works of art. In addition to the queen bed in the separate bedroom, there's also a queen sofa bed in the living room that's great for kids. The immaculate grounds, the charming cottage, and the cool pool regularly draw guests back. If you love animals, the Webbs' two friendly golden retrievers (who regularly show off by diving into the pool) will entertain you for hours.

✪ **Punahoa Beach Apartments.** 2142 Iliili Rd. (off S. Kihei Rd., 100 yards from Kamaole Beach I), Kihei, HI 96753. ☎ **800/564-4380** or 808/879-2720. Fax 808/875-3147. E-mail: pb6110@aol.com. 12 units. TV TEL. High season $93 studio double, $127 one-bedroom double, $130 two-bedroom double; low season $66 studio double, $85 one-bedroom, $94 two-bedroom. 5-night minimum. Extra person $12. AE, MC, V.

Book this place: We can't put it any more simply than that. The location is fabulous: off noisy, traffic-ridden Kihei Road, on a quiet side street with ocean frontage. A grassy lawn rolls about 50 feet down to the beach; there's great snorkeling just offshore and a popular surfing spot next door; and shopping and restaurants are all within walking distance. All of the beautifully decorated units in this small, four-story building have lanais with great ocean views and fully equipped kitchens. Rooms go quickly during the winter months, so book early.

✪ **What a Wonderful World B&B.** 2828 Umalu Place (off Keonakai St., near Hwy. 31), Kihei, HI 96753. ☎ **808/879-9103.** Fax 808/874-9352. E-mail: amauibnb@maui.net. 4 units. A/C TV TEL. $65 double, $75 studio double, $85–$95 one-bedroom apt. Rates include full gourmet breakfast. Children 11 and under stay free. AE, DC, DISC, MC, V.

We couldn't believe what we'd discovered here: an impeccably done B&B with thought and care put into every room, a great location, and excellent rates. Then we met hostess Eva Tantillo, who has not only a full-service travel agency, but also a master's degree—along with several years of experience—in hotel management. The result? One of Maui's finest bed-and-breakfasts, centrally located in Kihei (a half mile to Kamaole II Beach Park, 5 minutes from Wailea golf courses, and convenient to shopping and restaurants). Choose from one of four units: the master suite (with small fridge, coffeemaker, and barbecue grill on the lanai), studio apartment (with fully equipped kitchen), or two one-bedroom apartments (also with fully equipped kitchens). Each comes with private bathroom, phone, and entrance. Guests are welcome to use the barbecue, laundry facilities, and hot tub. Eva serves a gourmet family-style breakfast (eggs Benedict, Alaskan waffles, skillet eggs with mushroom sauce, fruit blintzes, and more) on her lanai, which has views of white-sand beaches, the West Maui Mountains, and Haleakala.

WAILEA

For a complete selection of condominium units throughout Wailea and Makena, contact **Destination Resorts Hawaii,** 3750 Wailea Alanui Dr., Wailea, HI 96753 (☎ **800/367-5246** or 808/879-1595; fax 808/874-3554; www.destinationresortshi. com). The luxury units represented include one-bedroom doubles ($140 to $435), two-bedroom units that sleep up to four ($170 to $510), and three-bedroom units that sleep up to six ($450 to $600; extra person $20). Minimum stays vary by property.

VERY EXPENSIVE

In addition to the choices listed below, consider the Arabian Nights–style fantasy resort, **Kea Lani Hotel Suites & Villas,** 4100 Wailea Alanui Dr., Wailea, HI 96753 (☎ **800/882-4100** or 808/875-4100; fax 808/875-1200; www.kealani.com). Hawaii's only all-suite luxury resort offers either 840-square-foot one-bedroom suites or palatial villas, where movie stars stay, with gourmet kitchens and private plunge pools ($295 to $570 suite, $1,000 to $1,600 one- to three- bedroom villas).

✪ **Four Seasons Resort Wailea.** 3900 Wailea Alanui Dr., Wailea, HI 96753. ☎ **800/ 334-MAUI** or 808/874-8000. Fax 808/874-6449. www.fshr.com. 463 units. A/C MINIBAR TV TEL. $295–$690 double, from $545 suite. Extra person $80 ($140 in Club Floor rooms); children under 18 stay free using existing bedding. Packages available. AE, DC, JCB, MC, V.

All of the luxury hotels in Wailea are fabulous, boasting terrific views and luxurious accommodations. What sets the Four Seasons apart is its relaxing, casual atmosphere, combined with service so great you hardly notice it. If money's not a factor, this is the place to spend it. And bring the kids too: There's a complete activities program designed just for them.

It's hard to beat this modern version of a Hawaiian palace by the sea. Although it sits on the beach between two other hotels, you won't feel like you're on chockablock resort row: The Four Seasons inhabits its own separate world, thanks to an open court-yard of pools and gardens. The spacious (about 600 square feet) rooms feature furnished private lanais (nearly all with ocean views) that are great for watching whales in winter and sunsets year-round. The grand bathrooms have deep marble tubs, showers for two, and lighted French makeup mirrors. Other amenities include safes, irons and ironing boards, hair dryers, and plush terry robes.

Service is attentive but not cloying. At the pool, guests lounge in casbahlike tents, pampered with special touches like iced Evian and chilled towels. And you'll never see a housekeeping cart in the hall: The cleaning staff works in teams, so they're as unobtrusive as possible and in and out of your room in minutes.

This ritzy neighborhood is home to great restaurants and shopping, the Wailea Tennis Center (known as Wimbledon West), and six golf courses—not to mention that great beach, with gentle waves and islands framing the view on either side.

Dining/Diversions: Seasons, the signature restaurant of the resort, recently lost chef George Mavrothalassitis, who was lured back to Honolulu to start his own restaurant—but his Hawaii Regional Cuisine is still served here in a memorable setting. The Seaside Restaurant offers a casual atmosphere by day; at night, it's transformed into Ferraro's at Seaside, serving authentic Italian fare. The poolside Pacific Grill offers lavish breakfast buffets and dinners featuring Hawaii Regional Cuisine (see chapter 5 for a review).

Amenities: Twice-daily maid service, 24-hour room service, same-day dry cleaning and laundry, 1-hour and overnight pressing, free overnight shoe shine or sandal repair, complimentary valet and shuttle around resort, airport limousine service, rental cars at concierge desk, 24-hour medical service, lei greeting and oshibori towel on arrival, and early arrival/late departure facility. Voice mail, safes, hair dryers, irons and ironing boards, and terry robes. Special amenities on Club Floors, including breakfast, afternoon tea and snacks, cocktails, pupus, and open bar. Two pools (one for adults only), 41 pool and beach cabanas, two whirlpools (one for adults only), fitness center with weight room and steam room, tennis (two lighted Plexi-pave courts with rackets and tennis balls provided), putting green, and nearby golf. Beach pavilion with snorkels, boogie boards, kayaks, and other water-sports gear; 1 hour free use of snorkel equipment; complimentary use of bicycles; complimentary exercise and tennis attire on loan. Game room, video library, salon, shops, conference facilities. Year-round kids' program with loads of activities and a complete children's facility, plus a teen recreation center; children's video library and toys.

✪ Grand Wailea Resort Hotel & Spa. 3850 Wailea Alanui Dr., Wailea, HI 96753. ☎ **800/ 888-6100** or 808/875-1234. Fax 808/879-4077. www.grandwailea.com. 814 units. A/C MINIBAR TV TEL. $380–$580 double, from $1,100 suite. Extra person $30 ($50 in Napua Club rooms and suites). AE, DC, DISC, JCB, MC, V.

Here's where grand becomes grandiose. The pinnacle of Hawaii's brief fling with fantasy megaresorts, this monument to excess is extremely popular with families, incentive groups, and conventions; it's the grand prize in Hawaii vacation contests and the dream of many honeymooners.

This hotel really is too much. It has a Japanese restaurant decorated with real rocks hewn from the slopes of Mount Fuji; 10,000 tropical plants in the lobby; an intricate pool system with slides, waterfalls, rapids, and a water-powered elevator to take you up to the top; Hawaii's most elaborate spa (not even the Romans had it this good); Hawaii's most expensive hotel suite, a 5,500-square-foot pad with a 180° view of paradise; a restaurant in an artificial tide pool; a floating New England–style wedding chapel; and nothing but ocean-view rooms, outfitted with every amenity you could ask for. And it's all crowned with a $30 million collection of original art, much of it created expressly for the hotel by Hawaii artists and sculptors. There's also a fantastic beach out front.

Dining/Diversions: Six restaurants and 12 bars range from fine dining to casual poolside snacks, serving everything from Japanese and Italian specialties to local seafood and spa cuisine. See chapter 9 for a description of the Tsunami nightclub. There's also luau grounds for 300.

Amenities: Lei greeting, complimentary valet parking, 24-hour room service, twice-daily towel service, same-day laundry and dry cleaning, multilingual concierge, infant care center, art and hotel tours, Budget Rent-A-Car and American Express tour desks, and 100 Napua Club rooms (with attendants, complimentary continental breakfast, cocktails, and tea service). Hawaii's largest spa, the 50,000-square-foot Spa Grande, with a blend of European-, Japanese-, and American-style techniques; 2,000-foot-long Action Pool, featuring a 10-minute swim/ride through mountains and grottoes; complimentary dive and windsurf lessons; seaside wedding chapel; conference facilities. Kids enjoy a computer center, video game room, arts and crafts, 60-seat children's theater, and outdoor playground. Five golf courses, including two 18-hole championship courses, are nearby.

✪ **Renaissance Wailea Beach Resort.** 3550 Wailea Alanui Dr., Wailea, HI 96753. ☎ **800/9-WAILEA** or 808/879-4900. Fax 808/879-6128. www.renaissancehotels.com. 345 units. A/C TV TEL. $290–$515 double, from $820 suite. Extra person $40; children 18 and under stay free using existing bedding. AE, CB, DC, DISC, MC, V. Parking $3.

This is the place for visitors in search of the luxury of a Wailea hotel, but in a smaller, more intimate setting. Located on 15 acres of rolling lawn and tropical gardens, Renaissance Wailea has the feeling of a small boutique hotel. Perhaps it's the resort's U-shaped design, the series of small coves and beaches, or the spaciousness of the rooms—whatever the reason, it just doesn't feel crowded here.

Each room has a sitting area, large lanai, TV and VCR, three phones (with data ports), fridge, and safe. The bathrooms include such extras as double vanities (one with lighted makeup mirror) and *hapi* coats (Japanese-style cotton robes). Bedspreads, drapes, and towels in all rooms have recently been upgraded. Rooms in the Mokapu Beach Club, an exclusive two-story building just steps from a crescent-shaped beach, feature such extras as private check-in, in-room continental breakfast, and access to a private pool and beach cabanas.

Dining/Diversions: The casual, open-air Palm Court offers buffets and oven-baked pizzas. Hana Gion features a sushi bar and teppanyaki grill. Maui Onion, a casual poolside restaurant surrounded by lush gardens and a cascading waterfall, serves breakfast and lunch. Every Monday, there's a traditional luau at sunset.

Amenities: Room service (from 6am to 11pm), lei greeting, concierge, complimentary in-room coffee and daily newspaper, complimentary video library, traditional Hawaiian craft classes, massage therapy, baby-sitting, Camp Wailea children's program. Complete fitness center, two freshwater swimming pools, two whirlpools, nearby golf and tennis, shopping arcade, hair salon, basketball court, Ping-Pong, and shuffleboard.

EXPENSIVE

Outrigger Wailea Resort. 3700 Wailea Alanui Dr., Wailea, HI 96753. ☎ **800/OUTRIGGER** or 808/879-1922. Fax 800/622-4852. www.outrigger.com. 516 units. A/C TV TEL. $229–$399 double, from $499 suite. Packages available. AE, CB, DC, DISC, JCB, MC, V.

This classic 1970s-style hotel is like a tropical garden by the sea. It was the first resort built in Wailea (in 1976), yet it remains the most Hawaiian of them all. Airy and comfortable, with touches of Hawaiian art throughout and a terrific aquarium that stretches forever behind the front desk, it just feels right.

What's truly special about this hotel is how it fits into its environment without overwhelming it. Eight buildings, all low-rise except for an eight-story tower, are spread along 22 gracious acres of lawns and gardens spiked by coco palms, with lots of open space and a half mile of oceanfront on a point between Wailea and Ulua beaches. The vast, parklike expanses are a luxury on this now-crowded coast.

All of the rooms have private lanais and separate dressing and bathroom areas with marble-topped basins. The Outrigger chain took over management of the hotel in 1999 and plans to make the necessary renovations to restore this once grande dame to her former glory.

Dining/Diversions: At press time, Outrigger had just taken over the hotel and promised to upgrade the dining facilities.

Amenities: Room service (from 6:30am to 11pm), same-day laundry and valet, multilingual concierge. Three pools, gift shop, newsstand, beauty salon, barber shop. Three championship golf courses nearby.

MAKENA
EXPENSIVE

✪ **Hale Mehana Vacation House.** 176 Makena Rd. (by the Keawalai Church in South Makena), Kihei, HI 96753. ☎ **808/879-2957.** Fax 808/877-2046. E-mail: dugal@maui.net. TV TEL. 1 three-bedroom/two-bathroom home. $200 double. 5-night minimum. Extra person $25; maximum 6 people. No credit cards.

Located right on the ocean at Makena (with the waves lapping just a few feet from the magnificent deck), Hale Mehana ("warm-hearted house") consists of the entire upstairs floor of a luxury home. Not a penny has been spared to make this property a dream oceanfront accommodation. A huge deck wraps around the house, offering breathtaking views of Molokini and Kahoolawe in the distance and easy access to swimming, snorkeling, and kayaking. The living area has big picture windows, polished wooden floors, a huge sofa, and a complete entertainment center. The kitchen opens onto the living/dining area, taking advantage of those incredible views; it contains every possible appliance a cook could want. The master bedroom is simply fabulous: a huge bay window looks out on the ocean, and the large master bathroom has a Jacuzzi big enough for two. Two smallish bedrooms share a full bathroom. Makena golf and tennis courts are just 2 minutes away, and Wailea restaurants and shopping are a 5-minute drive.

Maui Prince Hotel. 5400 Makena Alanui, Makena, HI 96753. ☎ **800/321-MAUI** or 808/874-1111. Fax 808/879-8763. www.westin.com. 304 units. A/C MINIBAR TV TEL. $230–$395 double, $440–$840 suite. Packages available. AE, DC, JCB, MC, V.

If you're looking for a vacation in a beautiful, tranquil spot with a golden-sand beach, here's your place. But if you plan to tour Maui, this is definitely out of your way: It's at the end of the road, far, far away from anything else on the island.

When you first see the stark white hotel, it looks like a high-rise motel stuck in the woods—from the outside. Inside, you'll discover an atrium garden with a koi-filled waterfall stream, an ocean view from every room, and a simplicity to the furnishings that makes some people feel uncomfortable and others blissfully clutter-free. Rooms are small but come with private lanais with great views.

Dining/Diversions: Japanese cuisine tops the menu at the elegant Hakone, which also has a sushi bar (see chapter 5). For dinner, the Prince Court specializes in Hawaii Regional Cuisine (see chapter 5), while the casual Cafe Kiowai offers seasonal and international specialties. The Makena Clubhouse Restaurant serves lunch and snacks. The Molokini Lounge has local Hawaiian music nightly.

Amenities: Lei greeting, complimentary early morning coffee and tea, complimentary valet parking, multilingual concierge, same-day dry cleaning and laundry, daily kids' program, early arrival and late departure services. Tennis (six Plexi-pave courts, two lit for night play), 36 holes of Robert Trent Jones–designed golf, separate pools for adults and children, fitness center, six-station fitness trail, conference facilities, library.

INEXPENSIVE

✪ **Makena Landing.** 5100 Makena Rd. (next to the county beach park), Makena, HI 96753. ☎ **808/879-6286.** 2 units. TV TEL. $95 double. 3-night minimum. Extra person $10. No credit cards.

This has to be the most fabulous location for a bed-and-breakfast: right on the ocean at Makena Landing. Once you settle in, you might not want to leave. The view is incredible; the sunsets are to die for; some of the best swimming, snorkeling, diving, and shoreline fishing are within walking distance; and the hosts are the nicest people you'll ever meet. The property has been in the Lu'uwai family for seven generations; hosts Boogie and Vi are both native Hawaiians, and they're brimming with generosity.

To ensure privacy, the two units are at opposite ends of the two-story cedar house. Both have private entrances, full bathrooms, kitchens, and private balconies that overlook the ocean, with Molokini and Kahoolawe off in the distance. The kitchens have everything you can think of, and Vi makes sure that you have all the fixings for breakfast. Outside are a barbecue area and a sundeck; here you'll have the ocean splashing at your feet, and a ringside seat to watch the humpback whales from December to April.

4 Upcountry Maui

MAKAWAO, OLINDA & HALIIMAILE

MODERATE

✪ **Olinda Country Cottages & Inn.** 2660 Olinda Rd. (near the top of Olinda Rd., a 15-min. drive from Makawao), Makawao, HI 96768. ☎ **800/932-3435** or 808/572-1453. Fax 808/573-5326. www.mauibnbcottages.com. 5 units. TV TEL. $95 double (includes continental breakfast), $125 suite double (includes 1st morning's breakfast in fridge), $140–$155 cottage double (sleeps up to 5; includes 1st morning's breakfast in fridge). 2-night minimum for rooms and suite, 3- to 5-night minimum for cottages. Extra person $15. No credit cards.

Set on the slopes of Haleakala in the crisp, clean air of Olinda (just 15 minutes from the restaurants and shops of Makawao), this charming B&B is on an 8½-acre protea farm, surrounded by 35,000 acres of ranch lands (with miles of great hiking trails). The 5,000-square-foot country home, outfitted with a professional eye to detail, has large windows with incredible panoramic views of all of Maui. Upstairs are two guest rooms with antique beds, private full bathrooms, and a separate entryway. Connected to the main house but with its own private entrance, the Pineapple Sweet has a full kitchen, an antique-filled living room, a marble-tiled full bathroom, and a separate bedroom. A separate 1,000-square-foot cottage is the epitome of cozy country luxury, with a fireplace, a bedroom with a queen bed, cushioned window seats (with great sunset views), and open-beam cathedral ceilings. Just added in 1997, the 950-square-foot Hidden Cottage (in a truly secluded spot surrounded by protea flowers) features three decks, 8-foot French glass doors, a full kitchen, a washer/dryer, and a private tub for two on the deck. Beaches are about a half-hour drive away.

INEXPENSIVE

If you'd like your own private cottage, consider **Peace of Maui,** 1290 Haliimaile Rd. (just outside Haliimaile town), Haliimaile, HI 96768 (☎ **808/572-5045;** www.peaceofmaui.com), with full kitchen, bedroom, day bed, and large deck; the cottage goes for $65. Children are welcome.

Banyan Tree House. 3265 Baldwin Ave. (next to Veteran's Cemetery, just 0.8 miles below Makawao), Makawao, HI 96768. ☎ **808/572-9021.** Fax 808/285-5152. www. banyantreehouse.com. 3 units. $85 cottage double, $225 three-bedroom/three-bathroom house (sleeps up to 6). 2- to 3-night minimum for house. MC, V.

Huge monkeypod trees (complete with swing and hammock) extend their branches over this 2½-acre property like a giant green canopy. The restored 1920s plantation manager's house is decorated with Hawaiian furniture from the 1930s; the large guest rooms have big, comfortable beds and private, marble-tiled bathrooms. A fireplace stands at one end of the huge living room, a large lanai runs the entire length of the house, and the hardwood floors shine throughout. The two guest cottages have been totally renovated and also feature hardwood floors and marble bathrooms. The small cottage has a queen bed, private bathroom, microwave, coffeemaker, and access to the fridge in the laundry room. The larger cottage has two beds, private bathroom, small kitchenette, and TV. Guests have use of laundry facilities. The quiet neighborhood and nostalgic old Hawaii ambience give this place a comfortable, easygoing atmosphere. Restaurants and shops are just minutes away in Makawao, and the beach is a 15-minute drive—but this place is so relaxing that you may find yourself wanting to do nothing more than lie in the hammock and watch the clouds float by.

Hale Ho'okipa Inn Makawao. 32 Pakani Place, Makawao, HI 96768. ☎ **808/572-6698.** E-mail: cherie@mauigateway.com. 4 units (2 with shower only). $60–$80 double, $130 suite. Rates include continental breakfast. Extra person $8. No credit cards. From Haleakala Hwy., turn left on Makawao Ave., then turn right on the fifth street on the right off Makawao Ave. (Pakani Place); go to the last house on the right.

Step back in time at this 1924 plantation-style home, rescued by owner Cherie Attix in 1996 and restored to its original charm. Cherie lovingly refurbished the old wooden floors, filled the rooms with antique furniture from the 1920s, and hung works by local artists on the walls. The result is a charming, serene place to stay, just a 5-minute walk from the shops and restaurants of Makawao town, 15 minutes from beaches, and a 1½-hour drive from the top of Haleakala. The guest rooms have separate outside entrances and private bathrooms. The house's front and back porches are both wonderful for sipping tea and watching the sunset. The Kona Wing is a two-bedroom suite with private bathroom and use of the kitchen.

KULA
MODERATE

If you'd like to stay in a former sea captain's cottage, consider **Country Garden Cottage** (☎ **888/878-2858** or 808/878-2859; fax 808/876-1458; www.maui. net/~kulabnb), a meticulously restored 1940s home on the slopes of Haleakala ($100 double; 2-night minimum). Another good choice is the romantic **Bloom Cottage** (☎ and fax **808/878-1425**), with a fireplace and tasteful furnishings ($115 double; 2-night minimum).

✪ **Silver Cloud Ranch.** Old Thompson Rd. (1.2 mi. past Hwy. 37). RR 2, Box 201, Kula, HI 96790. ☎ **800/532-1111** or 808/878-6101. Fax 808/878-2132. www.maui.net/~slvrcld. 12 units. $85–$125 double in main house, $105–$145 studio double in bunkhouse, $150 cottage double. Rates include full breakfast. Extra person $15. AE, DISC, MC, V.

Old Hawaii lives on at Silver Cloud Ranch, founded in 1902 by a sailor who jumped ship when he got to Maui. The former working cattle spread has a commanding view of four islands, the West Maui Mountains, and the valley and beaches below. The Lanai Cottage, a favorite among honeymooners, is nestled in a flower garden and has an ocean-view lanai, claw-foot tub, full kitchen, and wood-burning stove to warm chilly nights; a futon is available if you're traveling with a third person. The best rooms in the main house are on the second floor: the King Kamehameha Suite (with king bed) and the Queen Emma Suite (with queen bed). Each has a royal view, though some prefer Emma's. The Paniolo Bunkhouse, once used by real cowboys, is now fully restored and houses five studios, each with private bathroom, kitchenette, and views of the Pacific or Haleakala (go for the ocean view). All guests are free to use the main house and kitchen.

You'll find it cool and peaceful up here at 2,800 feet (bring a sweater). One-lane Thompson Road makes an ideal morning walk (about 3 miles round-trip), and you can go horseback riding next door at Thompson Ranch. There's a TV available if you feel deprived, but after a few Maui sunsets, you won't even remember why you bothered to ask.

INEXPENSIVE

In addition to the options below, also consider **Gildersleeve's Vacation Rentals,** formerly known as Elaine's Upcountry Guest Rooms (☎ 808/878-6623; fax 808/878-2619); the warm and welcoming hosts let three rooms in their spacious pole house ($65 double), plus a wonderful cottage that sleeps up to four ($110; 3-night minimum). Another good choice is **Halemanu** (☎ 808/878-2729; fax 808/878-2729), a single guest room in a house surrounded by farms and eucalyptus groves—way, way off the usual tourist path ($85 double; 2-night minimum).

✪ **Kili's Cottage.** Kula, c/o Hawaii's Best Bed & Breakfasts, P.O. Box 563, Kamuela, HI 96743. ☎ **800/262-9912** or 808/885-4550. Fax 808/885-0559. www.bestbnb.com. 1 three-bedroom/two-bathroom house. TV TEL. $95 double. 2-night minimum. Rates include breakfast fixings. Extra person $10. DISC.

If you're looking for a quiet getaway in the cool elevation of Kula, this sweet cottage with large lanai, situated on 2 acres, is the perfect place. The amenities are numerous: full kitchen, gas barbecue, washer/dryer, views, even toys for the kids. Hostess Kili Namau'u, who is also the director of a Hawaiian-language immersion school, greets each guest with royal aloha—from the flowers (picked from the garden outside) that fill the house to the welcome basket of with tropical produce grown on the property.

Kula Cottage. 206 Puakea Place (off Lower Kula Rd.), Kula, HI 96790. ☎ **808/878-2043** or 808/871-6230. Fax 808/871-9187. www.gilbertadvertising.com/kulacottage. 1 cottage. TV TEL. $85 double. 2-night minimum. Rates include continental breakfast. No credit cards.

We can't imagine having a less-than-fantastic vacation here. Tucked away on a quiet street amid a half-acre of blooming papaya and banana trees, Cecilia and Larry Gilbert's romantic honeymoon cottage is very private—it even has its own driveway and carport. The 700-square-foot cottage has a full kitchen (complete with dishwasher), washer/dryer, and three huge closets that offer enough storage space for you to move in permanently. An outside lanai has a big gas barbecue and an umbrella table and chairs. Cecilia delivers a continental breakfast daily (visitors rave about her homemade bread in the guest book). If you're an animal lover, Hana, the dog, will be more than happy to be a surrogate pet to you during your vacation; otherwise, Cecilia makes sure that Hana stays out of your way. Groceries and a small take-out lunch counter are within walking distance; it's a 30-minute drive to the beach.

✪ **Kula Lynn Farm Bed & Bath.** 2114 Naalae Rd., Kula, HI 96790. ☎ **800/874-2666,** ext. 300, or 808/878-6176. Fax 808/878-6320. E-mail: captcoon@gte.net. 1 two-bedroom/two-bathroom unit. TV TEL. $85 double. 3-night minimum. Rates include breakfast fixings. Extra person $10. AE, MC, V.

The Coons, the same great family that owns Maui's best sailing adventure, Trilogy, offer this spectacular 1,600-square-foot unit on the ground floor of their custom-built pole house. From its location on the slopes of Haleakala, the panoramic view—across Maui's central valley, with the islands of Lanai and Kahoolawe in the distance—is worth the price alone. Wall-to-wall windows and high ceilings add to the feeling of spaciousness throughout. The two bedrooms, two bathrooms, and two queen sofa beds in the living room make this the perfect place for a family. No expense has been spared in the European-style kitchen, with top appliances and Italian marble floors. This place should appeal to those who enjoy a quiet location and such activities as barbecuing on the lanai and watching the sun set.

✪ **Nohona Laule'a.** 763-2 Kamehameiki Rd. (off Kula Hwy.), Kula, HI 96790. ☎ **808/ 878-6646.** Fax 808/878-6646. 1 two-bedroom cottage. TV TEL. $85 double. 3-night minimum. Extra person $10. No credit cards.

What a deal—an impeccable two-bedroom cottage for $85 for two! Located on a windy road at about 2,500 feet, Nohona Laule'a ("peaceful dwelling") is 4 acres of tropical paradise with the cottage smack-dab in the middle. The 700-square-foot cottage, decorated in Asian style, features open-beam ceilings, skylights, a complete gourmet kitchen, a full bathroom, a living room, a huge deck, and a washer/dryer. The whole cottage has great island views: One bedroom, with Japanese shoji doors and two twin beds, looks out onto Haleakala; the other, with a double bed, has a big picture window overlooking the garden and the north shore beyond. The living room has a comfortable couch, a wooden rocker, and another huge picture window. Owners Brian and Sue Kanegai are congenial hosts; Sue greets guests with her delicious mango or banana bread. True to its name, this place is indeed peaceful. Kick back in a comfortable chair on the big deck and survey the blooming landscape at your feet, and you'll know what it must have been like to experience Eden.

5 East Maui: On the Road to Hana

KUAU

INEXPENSIVE

Kuau Cove Plantation. 2 Wa'a Place (on the ocean side off Hana Hwy., 1 mi. from stoplight in Paia), Paia, HI 96779. ☎ **808/579-8988.** Fax 808/579-8710. www.maui.net/~kuaubnb. 4 units. TV TEL. $85 double, $95 studio apt. 2-night minimum. Rates include continental breakfast. Extra person $10 (a rollaway bed is available). MC, V.

This 1930s plantation doctor's home has been restored and decorated with antiques, wicker, and rattan furniture. An old-fashioned porch greets you upon arrival, and Douglas fir floors run throughout the house. The dining room overlooks a large lawn with two ancient monkeypod trees and lots of exotic blooming plants. Two large bedrooms in the main house each have a queen bed, private bathroom, TV, and phone. Each of the two studios (separate from the main house) has a small kitchenette, bedroom, sitting area, and full bathroom. Our favorite is the upstairs studio, which has its own small lanai with an ocean view. A continental breakfast is served buffet style in the dining room from 7:30 to 9am every day; breakfast is delivered to the two studio apartments.

Quiet accommodations, gorgeous surroundings, and the best part: the private path leading to a secluded ocean cove lined with coconut palms (access is tricky, so you generally have this beach all to yourself). There's world-class windsurfing just a short walk away at Hookipa Beach, restaurants within a 5-minute drive, and great boutiquing a mile away in Paia; it's just 10 minutes to Kahului Airport.

✪ **Mama's Beachfront Cottages.** 799 Poho Place (off the Hana Hwy., in Kuau), Paia, HI 96779. ☎ **800/860-HULA** or 808/579-9764. Fax 808/579-8594. www.maui.net/~mamas. 6 units. TV TEL. $90 one-bedroom apt (sleeps up to 4), $225 two-bedroom apt (sleeps up to 6). 3-night minimum. AE, DC, DISC, MC, V.

The fabulous location (nestled in a coconut grove on the secluded Kuau beach), beautifully decorated interior (with island-style rattan furniture and works by Hawaiian artists), and plenty of extras (Weber gas barbecue, 27-inch TVs, and all the beach toys you can think of) make this place a must-stay for people looking for a centrally located vacation rental. It has everything, even Mama's Fish House next door (where guests get a 20% discount). The one-bedrooms are nestled in a tropical jungle, while the two-bedrooms face the beach. Both have terra-cotta floors, complete kitchens, sofa beds, and laundry facilities. We love Mama's sense of humor: We opened the closet in one unit and found a grass hula skirt complete with a coconut-shell top tacked to the back wall.

HAIKU
MODERATE

Honopo'u Lodge. Haiku, c/o Hawaii's Best Bed & Breakfasts, P.O. Box 563, Kamuela, HI 96743. ☎ **800/262-9912** or 808/885-4550. Fax 808/885-0559. www.bestbnb.com. 3 units. TV TEL. $95–$125 double. Rates include breakfast fixings. 3-night minimum. Extra person $15. DISC.

Hidden on Maui's north shore, next door to a 750-acre ranch, is this upscale vacation retreat: a unique 4,000-square-foot architect-designed octagonal house, with native ohia posts and cedar wood. Two octagonal studios with kitchenette (microwave, small fridge, stove, and coffeemaker), decorated with veteran B&B owner Dr. Fred Fox's impeccable sense of color and design, open up to the spacious atrium. Upstairs is a smaller studio with its own private entrance and small kitchenette. There are ocean views from every room and waterfalls nearby. Amenities include a large (32 feet by 16 feet) pool, Jacuzzi, sundeck, barbecue, laundry facilities, and satellite TV.

✪ **Maui Tradewinds.** Haiku, c/o Hawaii's Best Bed & Breakfasts, P.O. Box 563, Kamuela, HI 96743. ☎ **800/262-9912** or 808/885-4550. Fax 808/885-0559. www.bestbnb.com. 1 unit. TV TEL. $125 double. 2-night minimum. Extra person $10. DISC.

No expense was spared in the construction of this 1,000-square-foot studio apartment, located on the lower level of a custom-built home in the rolling hills of Haiku. Maui Tradewinds distinguishes itself from other accommodations with its floor-to-ceiling windows that capture the ocean view, blonde wood floors, recessed lighting, bamboo furniture, laundry facilities, top-of-the-line kitchen equipment, outdoor Jacuzzi, and full bathroom with dry/steam sauna. With the sofa bed, the unit sleeps up to four adults.

✪ **Pilialoha B&B Cottage.** 2512 Kaupakalua Rd. (0.7 mi. from Kokomo intersection), Haiku, HI 96708. ☎ **808/572-1440.** Fax 808/572-4612. www.pilialoha.com. 1 cottage. TV TEL. $100 double. 3-night minimum. Rates include continental breakfast. Extra person $20. No credit cards.

The minute you arrive at this split-level country cottage, located on 2 acres of eucalyptus trees, you'll see owner Machiko Heyde's artistry at work. Just in front of the cottage is a garden blooming with some 200 varieties of roses. You'll find more of Machiko's handiwork inside the quaint cottage, which is great for couples but can sleep up to five: There's a queen bed in the master bedroom, a twin bed in a small adjoining room, and a queen sleeper sofa in the living room. A large lanai extends from the master bedroom. You'll find a great movie collection for rainy days or cool country nights, a washer/dryer, beach paraphernalia (including snorkel equipment), and a garage. Machiko delivers breakfast daily; if you plan on an early morning ride to the top of Haleakala, she'll make sure you go with a thermos of coffee and her homemade bread. *Pilialoha* translates as "friendship," which is how you will feel about your hostess by the time you leave.

INEXPENSIVE

For a peaceful retreat, try the **Bamboo Mountain Sanctuary,** 1111 Kaupakalua Rd., Haiku, HI 96708 (☎ **808/572-5106**; http://home1.gte.net/zendo1), a 1940s plantation house that has served as a Zen monastery for 17 years; it offers five rooms (all with shared bathroom) on the edge of the Koolau Forest Reserve ($60 double). Conveniently located near Twin Falls and Baldwin Beach is the **Golden Bamboo Ranch,** Kaupakalua Road (at Holokai Road), Haiku (☎ **800/262-9912** or 808/885-4550; fax 808/885-0559; www.bestbnb.com), set on 7 fruit tree–covered acres with wonderful views ($80 to $90 double).

Maui Dream Cottages. 265 W. Kuiaha Rd. (1 block from Pauwela Cafe), Haiku, HI 96708. ☎ **808/575-9079.** Fax 808/575-9477. www.planet-hawaii.com/haiku. 2 cottages (with showers only). TV. $70 for up to four. 7-night minimum. MC, V.

Essentially a vacation rental, this 2-acre country estate is located atop a hill overlooking the ocean. The grounds are dotted with fruit trees (bananas, papayas, and avocados, all free for the picking), and the front lawn is comfortably equipped with a double hammock, chaise longues, and table and chairs. One cottage has two bedrooms, one bathroom, full kitchen (with microwave and coffeemaker), washer/dryer, and entertainment center. The other is basically the same, but with only one bedroom (plus a sofa bed in the living room). They're both very well maintained, comfortably outfitted with furniture that's not only attractive but also casual enough for families with kids. The Haiku location is quiet and restful and offers the opportunity to see how real islanders live. However, you'll have to drive a good 20 to 25 minutes to restaurants in Makawao or Paia for dinner. Hookipa Beach is about a 20-minute drive, and Baldwin Beach (good swimming) is about 25 minutes away.

TWIN FALLS
INEXPENSIVE

Also consider the off-the-beaten-path **Tea House Cottage** (☎ **808/572-5610;** www.maui.net/~teahouse): You park your car and follow a fern-lined path to a secluded hideaway in the jungle, powered by alternative energy (no power poles!). Here's your chance to get away from it all while still having utilities, phone, TV—you can even plug in your laptop ($95 double).

✪ **Maluhia Hale.** P.O. Box 687 (off Hana Hwy., nearly a mile past Twin Falls bridge), Haiku, HI 96708. ☎ **808/572-2959.** Fax 808/572-2959. www.maui.net/~djg/index.html. 2 units. TV. $95 cottage double, $110 suite double. 2-night minimum. Rates include continental breakfast. Extra person $20. No credit cards.

Diane and Robert Garrett design and build homes that are works of art. Here, they've created a private country cottage that has the feeling of a gracious old Hawaiian plantation home. A sense of peace and orderliness reigns in the cottage: You enter through an open and airy screened veranda, which leads to a glassed-in sitting room, a bed in lacy white linen, and a kitchenette. Hand-selected antiques fill the cottage, and Diane's exquisite flower arrangements add splashes of color. A traditional Hawaiian bathhouse is adjacent, with an old claw-foot tub and separate shower. In the main house is a romantic suite complete with a small kitchenette and screened porch. Diane does light housekeeping daily; no matter which accommodation you choose, at the end of the day, you'll return to a softly lit place filled with sweet-smelling tropical flowers. A simply wonderful place.

HUELO
MODERATE

✪ **Huelo Point Flower Farm.** Off Hana Hwy., between mile markers 3 and 4. P.O. Box 1195, Paia, HI 96779. ☎ **808/572-1850.** www.maui.net/~huelopt. 4 units. $120 cottage double, $140 carriage house double, $240 guest house double (rates include continental breakfast). $2,200 per week for main house for 6. Extra person $15. 2-night minimum, except for 7-night minimum in main house. No credit cards.

Here's a little Eden by the sea on a spectacular, remote 300-foot sea cliff near a water-fall stream: a 2-acre estate overlooking Waipio Bay with two guest cottages, a guest house, and a main house available for rent. The studio-sized Gazebo Cottage has a glass-walled ocean front, a koa-wood captain's bed, TV, stereo, kitchenette, private ocean-side patio, private hot tub, and a half-bathroom with outdoor shower. The new 900-square-foot Carriage House apartment sleeps four and has glass walls facing the mountain and sea, plus a kitchen, den, decks, and a loft bedroom. The two-bedroom main house contains an exercise room, fireplace, sunken Roman bathtub, cathedral ceilings, and other extras. There's a natural pool with a waterfall and an oceanfront hot tub. You're welcome to pick fruit, vegetables, and flowers from the extensive garden. Homemade scones, tree-ripened papayas, and fresh-roasted coffee start your day. Despite its seclusion, off the crooked road to Hana, it's just a half hour to Kahului, or about 20 minutes to Paia's shops and restaurants.

✪ **Huelo Point Lookout B&B.** Off Hana Hwy. (between mile markers 3 and 4), c/o Hawaii's Best Bed & Breakfasts, P.O. Box 563, Kamuela, HI 96743. ☎ **800/262-9912** or 808/885-4550. Fax 808/885-0559. www.bestbnb,com. 3 cottages. TV TEL. $95–$275 cottage double. 3-night minimum. Rates include a welcome breakfast on arrival. Extra person $20. DISC.

About a quarter mile from the 300-foot cliffs of Waipio Bay is this lovely B&B, situated on 2 acres of tropical jungle with a hot tub, 40-foot freeform swimming pool, and a view all the way down the coastline to Hana. The main house has pentagonal glass walls that offer sweeping views of the ocean and up the side of Haleakala. It has two private entrances, a large bedroom with king bed, a kitchenette, a big bathroom with a tub for two, and a lotus pond and waterfall outside on the private deck. The Honeymoon Cottage is a totally renovated old fisherman's residence, with an upstairs bedroom, a full kitchen, a sitting room, and a solarium with lots of windows, skylights, and a deck. The bathroom has a Victorian tub and glass all around, with views of Haleakala on one side and the ocean on the other. The Halekala Cottage is smaller but full of amenities, including a full kitchen, king bed, and tiled bathroom that extends outside into the garden so that you can actually take a hot shower under the stars, surrounded by white lattice and tropical flowers. The newest cottage, Rainbow, located next to the swimming pool, features 25-foot-high glass walls with nothing but views. Other unique amenities include a private indoor hot tub, glass-ceilinged bathroom, and work-of-art wooden staircase. The owners, Jeff and Sharyn, also own a video store in Paia, so they can get you the movies of your choice.

INEXPENSIVE

Hale Akua Shangri-la Resort. Star Rte. 1, Box 161 (off Hana Hwy., between mile markers 3 and 4), Haiku, HI 96708. ☎ **888/368-5305** or 808/572-9300. Fax 808/572-6666. www.maui.net/~shangrla/ha.html. 13 units (some with shared bathroom). $50–$140 double, $100–$125 cottage double. Rates include breakfast. Extra person $20. AE, DISC, MC, V.

This place isn't for everyone; the hang-loose atmosphere might or might not be your style. Way off the beaten path, Hale Akua is a collection of eclectic buildings on 2 tropical acres where, at certain times of the year, guests can choose to go "clothing optional" (translation: nude). The main house on the property has breathtaking ocean views and private lanais off most rooms; guests share the living room, bathroom, and kitchen. The Cabana building, next to the 60-foot pool, is a two-story house with five separate rooms, two kitchens, and a dining area. Also on the property is a cottage with two rooms, one pyramid-shaped. Other on-site features include a hot tub, fountain, lily pond, hammock, trampoline, and maze formed by panex trees. Yoga classes are available.

6 At the End of the Road in East Maui: Hana

Picture Shangri-la, Maui style: 66 acres rolling down to the sea in a remote Hawaiian village, with a wellness center, two pools, and access to one of the best beaches in Hana. It all adds up to **Hotel Hana-Maui** (☎ **800/321-HANA** or 808/248-8211; fax 808/248-7202; $395 double, $450 to $495 suite, $525 to $795 cottage). However, this gorgeous luxury resort has been suffering from neglect of late. At press time, welcome rumors were in the wind that a new management team (of impeccable international stature) was in negotiations to acquire the hotel. We hope so, as this gem of a property is in need of massive renovation.

MODERATE

✪ **Ekena.** Off Hana Hwy., above Hana Airport (P.O. Box 728), Hana, HI 96713. ☎ **808/248-7047.** Fax 808/248-7047. www.maui.net/~ekena. 2 two-bedroom units. TV TEL. $150 double, $190–$275 for 4. 3-night minimum. Extra person $15. No credit cards.

Just one glance at the 360° view, and you can see why hosts Robin and Gaylord gave up their careers on the mainland and moved here. This 8½-acre piece of paradise in rural Hana boasts ocean and rain-forest views; the floor-to-ceiling sliding-glass doors in the spacious Hawaiian-style pole house bring the outside in. The elegant two-story home is exquisitely furnished, from the comfortable U-shaped couch that invites you to relax and take in the view to the top-of-the-line mattress on the king bed. The kitchen is fully equipped with every high-tech convenience you can imagine (guests have made complete holiday meals here). Only one floor (and one two-bedroom unit) is rented at any one time to ensure privacy. The grounds are impeccably groomed with tropical plants and fruit trees. Hiking trails into the rain forest start right on the property, and the beaches and waterfalls are just minutes away. Robin places fresh flowers in every room and makes sure you're comfortable; after that, she's available to answer questions about what Hana has to offer, but she also respects your privacy and lets you enjoy your vacation in peace.

✪ **Hamoa Bay Bungalow.** P.O. Box 773, Hana, HI 96713. ☎ **808/248-7884.** Fax 808/248-8642. E-mail: jody@maui.net. 1 cottage. TV TEL. $160 double. 2-night minimum. No credit cards.

Down a country lane guarded by two Balinese statues stands a little bit of Indonesia in Hawaii: a carefully crafted bungalow overlooking Hamoa Bay. Only 2 miles beyond Hasegawa's General Store on the way to Kipahulu, this enchanting retreat sits on 4 verdant acres within walking distance of black-sand Hamoa Beach (which James Michener considered one of the most beautiful in the Pacific). The romantic, 600-square-foot Balinese-style cottage is distinctly tropical, with giant Elephant bamboo furniture from Indonesia, batik prints, a king bed, a full kitchen, and a screened porch with hot tub and shower. Host Jody Baldwin, a lifelong Mauian who lives on the estate, loves to share the secrets of Hana, including the great mountain hiking trail nearby.

Hana Hale Malamalama. Across from the Mormon Church in Hana, c/o Hawaii's Best Bed & Breakfasts, P.O. Box 563, Kamuela, HI 96743. ☎ **800/262-9912** or 808/885-4550. Fax 808/885-0559. www.bestbnb.com. 5 units. TV TEL. $120–$175 double, $250 cottage double.

2-night minimum. Continental breakfast is served to guests at Bamboo Inn. Extra person $15. DISC.

Located on a historic site with ancient fish ponds and a cave mentioned in ancient chants, this place definitely exudes the spirit of old Hawaii. Host John takes excellent care of the ponds (he feeds the fish at 5pm every day, to the delight of his guests) and is fiercely protective of the hidden cave ("it's not a tourist attraction, but a sacred spot"). There's access to a nearby rocky beach, which isn't good for swimming but makes a wonderful place to watch the sun set. All the accommodations include fully equipped kitchens, bathrooms, bedrooms, living/dining areas, and private lanais. The main three-bedroom house is an architectural masterpiece, built entirely of Philippine mahogany with 4-foot-wide skylights the entire length of the house. Entry to the house is down stone steps, so this is not a place for small children or anyone who has trouble climbing steep steps.

The two-level Tree House cottage, nestled between a kamani tree and a coconut palm, contains a Jacuzzi tub for two, a Balinese bamboo bed, a small kitchen/living area, and a small deck. The Pondside Bungalow is a quaint cottage, with full kitchen, living area, and separate bedroom. We strongly recommend staying in the newest building, the Bamboo Inn, where guests are served continental breakfast in the open courtyard. You'll never forget its coconut floors, Indonesian decor, and ocean view from the lanai.

Hana Kai Maui Resort. 1533 Uakea Rd. (P.O. Box 38), Hana, HI 96713. ☎ **800/346-2772** or 808/248-8426. Fax 808/248-7482. www.hanakai.com. 17 units. $125–$145 studio double, $145–$195 one-bedroom (sleeps up to 4). Children under 8 stay free. AE, MC, V.

Hana's only vacation condominium, Hana Kai offers studio and one-bedroom units overlooking Hana Bay. All units have large kitchens and private lanais. The one-bedroom units have a sliding door that separates the bedroom from the living room, plus a sofa bed that sleeps two additional guests. There are no phones or TVs in the units (a pay phone is located on the property), so you can really get away from it all. Ask for a corner unit with wraparound ocean views.

✪ Heavenly Hana Inn. P.O. Box 790, Hana, HI 96713. ☎ and fax **808/248-8442**. www.placestogo.com. 4 units. TV TEL. $100 studio double, $175–$250 suite. 2-night minimum. Rates include a full gourmet breakfast. Children under 15 not accepted. AE, DISC, JCB, MC, V. Located off Hana Hwy., just a stone's throw from the center of Hana town.

Owners Robert Filippi and Sheryl Murray understatedly describe their B&B as a "Japanese-style inn at secluded and beautiful Hana." That's a little like saying a Four Seasons hotel is a big building with rooms. This impeccably thought-out accommodation is a little bit of heaven, where no detail has been overlooked. The suites each have a sitting room with a futon and couch, polished hardwood floors, and a separate bedroom with a raised platform bed (with an excellent, firm mattress). The black-marble bathrooms contain huge tubs and separate glassed-in showers. Flowers are everywhere, ceiling fans keep the rooms cool, and the daily gourmet breakfast (a fruit course and a main entree plus homemade breads and pastries) is not only delicious, but also served in a setting filled with art, including the hand-crafted dining table and matching chairs. The 2 acres of grounds are done in Japanese style with a bamboo fence, tiny bridges over a meandering stream, and Japanese gardens.

Papalani. Star Route 27 (4 mi. past Hasegawa's General Store), Hana, HI 96713. ☎ **808/248-7204**. Fax 808/248-7285. 2 units. TEL. $150 double. 3-night minimum. Extra person $25. No children under 8 accepted. No credit cards.

These luxurious, romantic accommodations are hidden from the road, offering privacy and quiet in a first-class setting. There is only one tiny drawback: mosquitoes—swarms of them, in fact. A stream runs through the property, and although hostess Cybil has done everything possible to eliminate this nuisance (like providing screened-in lanais so that you can enjoy the outdoors without experiencing these biting pests), bring your insect repellent.

Otherwise, Papalani lives up to its name, which means "heaven and all the spiritual powers." The apartment and the cottage, both professionally decorated, have white leather couches, wood floors, and expensive artwork. Everything is first-class, from the appliances in the kitchen to the faucets in the bathroom. The apartment has a kitchenette with minifridge, blender, and coffeemaker, while the separate cottage has a full kitchen. Both units have their own laundry facilities and private hot tubs. This is a TV-free environment, so you can really get in touch with nature. The great location means you're just a 5-minute walk to Waioka Stream (where there's good swimming in the pools), a mile from beautiful Hamoa Beach, and 5 minutes from Hana. Cybil asks that guests not smoke on the property and that meat be cooked on a barbecue outside.

INEXPENSIVE

If you'd like your own cottage, consider the simple but adequately furnished **Aloha Cottages,** 83 Keawa Pl., P.O. Box 205, Hana, HI 96713 (☎ **808/248-8420**), which go for $60 to $92 double.

✪ **Tradewinds Cottage.** 135 Alalele Place (P.O. Box 385), Hana, HI 96713. ☎ **800/ 327-8097** or 808/248-8980. Fax 808/248-7735. www.maui.net/~twt/cottage.html. 2 cottages. TV TEL. $100 studio cottage double, $125 two-bedroom cottage double. 2-night minimum. Extra person $10. MC, V.

Nestled among the ginger and heliconias on a 5-acre flower farm are these two separate cottages, each with complete kitchen, carport, barbecue, hot tub, TV, ceiling fan, and sleeper sofa. The studio cottage sleeps up to four; a bamboo shoji blind separates the sleeping area (with queen bed) from the sofa bed in the living room. The Tradewinds cottage has two bedrooms (with queen bed in one room and two twins in the other), one bathroom (with shower only), sleeper sofa, and huge front porch. The atmosphere is quiet and relaxing, and hosts Mike and Rebecca Buckley, who have been in business for a decade, welcome families (they have two children, a cat, and a very sweet golden retriever). You can use their laundry facilities at no extra charge.

Waianapanapa State Park Cabins. Off Hana Hwy., c/o State Parks Division, 54 S. High St., Rm. 101, Wailuku, HI 96793. ☎ **808/984-8109.** 12 cabins. $45 for 4 (sleeps up to 6). Extra person $5. 5-night maximum. No credit cards.

These 12 rustic cabins are the best lodging deal on Maui. Everyone knows it, too—so make your reservations early (up to 6 months in advance). The cabins are warm and dry and come complete with kitchen, living room, bedroom, and bathroom with hot shower; furnishings include bedding, linen, towels, dishes, and very basic cooking and eating utensils. Don't expect luxury—this is a step above camping, albeit in a beautiful tropical jungle setting unlike any other in the islands. The key attraction at this 120-acre state beach park is the unusual horseshoe-shaped black-sand beach on Pailoa Bay, popular for shore fishing, snorkeling, and swimming. There's a caretaker on site, along with rest rooms, showers, picnic tables, shoreline hiking trails, and historic sites. But bring mosquito protection—this *is* the jungle.

5 Dining

by Jocelyn Fujii

In the past decade, with the ascension of Hawaii Regional Cuisine into national prominence, and with Maui as Hawaii's visitor-industry success story, the islands' best chefs have opened their Maui doors and turned this island into a culinary nexus. Good food here means chefs like David Paul, Beverly Gannon, Eric Leterc (of Maui Prince's Prince Court—not as well known, but still wonderful), Sansei's D. K. Kodama, and other golden-boy arrivals from the outer islands: Peter Merriman (Big Island), Sam Choy (Big Island and Oahu), and Roy Yamaguchi (Oahu). Late 1998 saw the loss of George Mavrothalassitis, who left Seasons at the Four Seasons Resort Wailea to move to Honolulu, and the arrival, in the same season, of Jean-Marie Josselin, another leader in Hawaii Regional Cuisine. The opening of Josselin's A Pacific Cafe Honokowai, in a new shopping complex in West Maui, was his sixth in Hawaii and focused attention on an area that was formerly a no-man's land between Kaanapali and Kapalua. Meanwhile, Peter Merriman still plans to open a restaurant in the Maui Ocean Center and Mark Ellman has closed Avalon in Lahaina, turning his attention to his Maui Tacos franchises across the country.

In this dizzying scenario of musical (dining) chairs, some things haven't changed: You can still dine well at Lahaina's open-air waterfront watering holes, where the view counts for 50% of the dining experience. There are budget eateries here, but not many; Maui's old-fashioned, multigenerational mom-and-pop diners are disappearing by attrition, eclipsed by the flashy newcomers, or clinging to the edge of existence in the older neighborhoods of central Maui. Although you'll have to work harder to find them in the resort areas, you won't have to go far to find creative cuisine, pleasing style, and stellar views in upcountry, south, and west Maui.

In the listings below, reservations are not necessary unless otherwise noted.

1 Central Maui

The **Kaahumanu Center,** the structure that looks like a white *Star Wars* umbrella in the center of Kahului, at 275 Kaahumanu Ave. (5 minutes from Kahului Airport on Highway 32), has a very popular food court with concessions that serve, for the most part, excellent food. The **Juiceland** kiosk offers vitamin-rich (and delicious!) freshly squeezed beet, celery, wheat-grass, carrot, ginger, and creative combinations of vegetable and fruit juices, as well as smoothies made from the legendary fresh fruits of Maui. And busy shoppers seem more than willing to dispense with fine china and other formalities to enjoy a no-nonsense meal on Styrofoam plates that efficiently refreshes them between spurts of shopping. Among the standouts: **Maui Tacos,** one of the string of palate-pleasing Mexican diners sprinkled throughout Maui (see p. 109). (Watch for them on the mainland; founder/chef Mark Ellman has formed a partnership with Blimpie International to open dozens of Maui Tacos outlets nationwide.) The green burritos, painted naturally with spinach, are the best this side of the Rio Grande. **Edo Japan** teppanyaki is a real find, its flat Benihana-like grill dispensing marvelous, flavorful mounds of grilled fresh vegetables and chicken teriyaki for $4.15. **Yummy Korean B-B-Q,** part of a chain well known on Oahu, proffers soups; sesame bean sprouts; potato salad; and many combinations of vegetables, meats, fish, and ribs infused with the assertive flavors of Korea. **Panda Cuisine** serves tasty Chinese food. One spot that's always abuzz is **The Coffee Store** (see p. 113), a no-nonsense java stop that serves sandwiches, salads, pasta, and nearly two dozen different coffee drinks.

When you leave Kaahumanu Center, take a moment to gaze at the West Maui Mountains to your left from the parking lot. They are one of Maui's wonders, a kaleidoscopic show of clouds, sunlight, textured canyons, and deep greens that reflect the mystical qualities of the old mountains.

EXPENSIVE

Sam Choy's Kahului. Kaahumanu Center, 275 Kaahumanu Ave. (5 min. from Kahului Airport on Hwy. 32), Kahului. ☎ 808/893-0366. Reservations recommended. Main courses $4–$10 breakfast, $7–$12 lunch, $25–$30 dinner. AE, DC, DISC, JCB, MC, V. Mon–Thurs 8am–9pm, Fri–Sun 7am–9:15pm. LOCAL/HAWAII REGIONAL.

Sam Choy's cooking, which the *Wall Street Journal* calls "blue-collar chow," has spread from Hawaii to Tokyo, loco moco, poke, and all. But Choy's plans to open a restaurant upstairs in the Kaahumanu Center, where the Sharktooth brewery used to be, haven't yet materialized, keeping his eatery on the first floor of the mall at front row center. It's still poke paradise: His seared poke salad remains a lunchtime staple (vastly overrated, in our opinion), and his seafood laulau, macadamia-nut–crusted ono, and rib-eye steak are some of the evening attractions. At breakfast, locals gather for poke omelets, spinach and shiitake mushroom omelets, the morning's fresh catch, taro cakes, and other regional favorites.

MODERATE

Marco's Grill & Deli. 444 Hana Hwy., Kahului. ☎ **808/877-4446.** Main courses $12.95–$19.95. AE, DC, DISC, JCB, MC, V. Daily 7:30am–10pm (hot entrees from 10am). ITALIAN.

Located in the elbow of central Maui, where the roads to upcountry, west, and south Maui converge, Marco's is popular among area residents for its homemade Italian fare and friendly informality. This is one of those comfortable neighborhood fixtures favored by all generations, who stop here for breakfast, lunch, and dinner, before and after movies, on the way to and from baseball games and concerts. And for business lunches: Readers of the *Maui News* voted Marco's the best place for a business lunch two years in a row. The antipasto salad, vegetarian lasagna, and roasted peppers with garlic, provolone cheese, and anchovies are taste treats, but don't ignore the meatballs and Italian sausage: homemade and robust, they're served on French bread with all the trimmings.

✪ **A Saigon Cafe.** 1792 Main St., Wailuku. ☎ **808/243-9560.** Main courses $6.50–$16.95. DC, MC, V. Mon–Sat 10am–9:30pm, Sun 10am–8:30pm. VIETNAMESE.

Dining Tip

Be sure to take a look at **"A Taste of Maui,"** in the appendix at the back of this book, which includes descriptions of Hawaii Regional Cuisine as well as plate lunches and local food, plus a Hawaiian seafood primer with helpful terms.

How's this for attitude: There's no sign. But Jennifer Nguyen can afford to be elusive, because as difficult as this restaurant is to find, it's always bustling with diners who drive all the way from Kula and points beyond. (The Maui grapevine works overtime.) The menu runs the gamut, from a dozen different soups to cold and hot noodles (including the popular beef noodle soup called *pho*) and chicken and shrimp cooked in a clay pot. Wok-cooked Vietnamese specialties—sautéed with spicy lemongrass and sweet-and-sour sauces—highlight the produce of the season, and the fresh catch (ono, opakapaka) comes whole and crisp or steamed with ginger and garlic. You can create your own Vietnamese "burritos" from a platter of tofu, noodles, and vegetables that you wrap in rice paper and dip in garlic sauce. Among our favorites are the shrimp lemongrass, piquant and refreshing, and the tofu curry, swimming in herbs and vegetables straight from the garden. The Nhung Dam, the Vietnamese version of fondue—a hearty spread of basil, cucumbers, mint, romaine, bean sprouts, pickled carrots, turnips, and vermicelli, wrapped in rice paper and dipped in a legendary sauce—is cooked at your table.

INEXPENSIVE

Class Act. At Maui Community College, 310 Kaahumanu Ave., Wailuku. ☎ **808/984-3480.** Reservations recommended. Five-course lunch $15. No credit cards. Wed and Fri 11am–12:15pm (last seating). Cuisine changes weekly.

Part of a program run by the distinguished Food Service Department of Maui Community College, this restaurant has a growing following. Student chefs show their stuff with a flourish in their "classroom," where they pull out all the stops as if it were their own place. Linen, china, servers in ties and white shirts, and a five-course lunch make this a five-star value. The appetizer, soup, salad, and dessert are set, but you can choose between the regular entree and a heart-healthy entree prepared in the culinary tradition of the week. The filet mignon of French week is popular, and so are the Thai curries; Chinese stir-fries; pastas; and Japanese, Austrian, Moroccan, and other international menus served throughout the months. Tea and soft drinks are offered—and they can get pretty fancy, with fresh fruit and spritzers—but otherwise it's BYOB. Chris Speere, chef instructor, is the owner/chef of the beloved Pauwela Cafe—and we love their food too (see below for a review).

Ichiban. Kahului Shopping Center, 47 Kaahumanu Ave., Kahului. ☎ **808/871-6977.** Main courses $4.25–$5.25 breakfast, from $4.25 lunch (combination plates $8.50), $4.95–$26.95 dinner (combination dinner $11.95, dinner specials from $8.95). DC, MC, V. Mon–Fri 6:30am–2pm and 5–9pm, Sat 10:30am–2pm and 5–9pm. JAPANESE/SUSHI.

What a find: an informal neighborhood restaurant that serves inexpensive, home-cooked Japanese food *and* good sushi at realistic prices. Local residents consider Ichiban a staple for breakfast, lunch, or dinner and a haven of comforts: egg-white omelets, great saimin, chicken yakitori, sushi (everything from unagi and scallop to California rolls), and combination plates—teriyaki chicken, teriyaki meat, *tonkatsu* (pork cutlet), rice, and pickled cabbage. The sushi may not be inexpensive, but like the specials, such as steamed opakapaka for $18.75, it's a good value. *Tip:* We love the tempura, miso soup, and spicy ahi hand roll.

✪ **Maui Bake Shop.** 2092 Vineyard St., Wailuku. ☎ **808/242-0064.** Most items under $5. AE, CB, DISC, MC, V. Mon–Fri 7am–4pm, Sat 7am–2pm. BAKERY/DELI.

Sleepy Vineyard Street has seen many a mom-and-pop business come and go, but Maui Bake Shop is here to stay. Maui native Claire Fujii-Krall and her husband, baker José Krall (who trained in the south of France and throughout Europe), are turning out buttery brioches, healthy nine-grain and two-tone rye breads, focaccia, strudels, sumptuous fresh-fruit gâteaux, puff pastries, and dozens of other baked goods and confections. The breads are baked in one of Maui's oldest brick ovens, installed in 1935; a high-tech European diesel oven handles the rest. The front window displays the more than 100 bakery and deli items, among them salads, a popular eggplant marinara focaccia, homemade quiches, and a moist, inexpensive calzone with chicken-pesto-mushroom-cheese filling. Homemade soups (clam chowder, minestrone, cream of asparagus) team up nicely with sandwiches on freshly baked bread, and they're light enough (well, almost) to justify the Ultimate Dessert: white-chocolate macadamia-nut cheesecake.

Norm's Cafe. 740 Lower Main St., Wailuku. ☎ **808/242-1667**. Main courses $5.35–$6.95. AE, MC, V. Mon–Sat 5am–2pm, Wed–Thurs 5–8pm, Fri–Sat 5–9pm, Sun 6am–2pm. AMERICAN/LOCAL.

The newest rage for the diner crowd, Norm's welcomes you with a plaid yellow concrete-block entrance lined with lava rock—an apt foreshadowing of the old-fashioned, Formica-table celebration that awaits inside. Hot-pink paper menus issue the call for Norm's signature Paukukalo Burger, an 8-ounce hamburger with blue-cheese dressing and all the trimmings; Fran's Club, a turkey-bacon-avocado fantasy on grilled sourdough; and the universal fave, bamboo-steamed ono—at $6.45, a catch. There's always a gaggle of habitués somewhere in the far corner, trying to decide between saimin, dry mein, BLT, and the humongous hamburger, and then winding up with the steamed ono, the dish that put Norm's on the map.

Restaurant Matsu. Maui Mall, 70 E. Kaahumanu Ave., Kahului. ☎ **808/871-0822.** Most items less than $6. No credit cards. Mon–Thurs 9am–6pm, Fri 9am–9pm, Sat 9am–5:30pm, Sun 10am–4pm. JAPANESE/LOCAL.

Customers have come from Hana (more than 50 mi. away) just for Matsu's California rolls, while regulars line up for the cold saimin (julienned cucumber, egg, Chinese-style sweet pork, and red ginger on noodles) and the bento plates, various assemblages of chicken, teriyaki beef, fish, and rice, which make great take-out lunches for working folks and picnickers. The new nigiri sushi items are popular, especially for the don't-dally lunch crowd. The katsu pork and chicken, breaded and deep-fried, are other specialties of this casual Formica-style diner. We love the tempura udon and the saimin, steaming mounds of wide and fine noodles swimming in homemade broths and topped with condiments. The daily specials are a changing lineup of home-cooked classics: ox-tail soup, roast pork with gravy, teriyaki ahi, miso butterfish, and breaded mahimahi.

Sam Sato's. Millyard, 1750 Wili Pa Loop, Wailuku. ☎ **808/244-7124.** Plate lunches $5.25–$5.75. No credit cards. Mon–Sat 7am–2pm. NOODLES/PLATE LUNCHES.

Sam Sato's is a Maui institution, for not only its noodles (saimin, dry noodles, chow fun), but also its flaky baked *manju,* filled with sweetened lima beans or azuki. Sam opened his family eatery in 1933, and his daughter, Lynne Toma, still makes the broth the old-fashioned way: from scratch. The saimin and the dry noodles, with broth that comes in a separate bowl, are big sellers. One regular comes to the counter, with its wooden stools and homemade salt and pepper shakers, for his "usual": two barbecued meat sticks, two scoops of rice, and three macaroni salads. The peach, apple, coconut, and pineapple turnovers fly out the door, too, as do take-out noodles by the tray for large Maui gatherings. *Tip:* If you want them to hold the MSG, be sure to make your request early.

Wei Wei BBQ and Noodle House. Millyard Plaza, 210 Imi Kala St., Wailuku. ☎ **808/ 242-7928.** Combination plates $4.95–$6.95, main courses $3–$8.50. No credit cards. Daily 10am–9pm. CHINESE/NOODLES.

Noodles are rapidly gaining on Big Macs as the fast-food choice of Hawaii these days, and Wei Wei is a good example. Open only a couple of years, it's the darling of the on-the-go, no-nonsense, noodle-loving Maui crowd. You order at the counter, fast-food style, from a menu that includes Chinese classics: saimin with roast duck, shrimp-vegetable chow mein, dim sum, and the extremely popular house fried noodles. American favorites—hamburger, teriyaki chicken burger, turkey sandwich, and the popular chicken katsu burger—are winning fans, too. The hot-and-sour soup is a Szechuan touch, and the combination plates (steak, chicken, katsu, ahi, sweet-and-sour spareribs) are gaining the attention of budget-conscious diners.

2 West Maui

LAHAINA

Maui's branch of the **Hard Rock Cafe** is in the Lahaina Center at 900 Front St. (☎ **808/667-7400**). You'll find **Planet Hollywood** down the street at 744 Front St. (☎ **808 /667-7877**).

EXPENSIVE

Chart House. 1450 Front St., at Honoapiilani Hwy. (Hwy. 30). ☎ **808/661-0937.** Main courses $16.95–$36.95. AE, CB, DC, DISC, MC, V. Daily 5–10pm, lounge until midnight. AMERICAN.

Chart House restaurants have a knack for finding locations with drop-dead-gorgeous views, and Lahaina has one of the best. Location is its strongest suit: Perched at the north end of Front Street, removed from congested Lahaina proper and elevated for optimal view, the restaurant offers a singular look at Lanai, Molokai, the ocean, and the sunset. At this writing renovations are planned, as well as menu changes (most welcome) to include more Hawaii regional flavors and presentations. Otherwise, expect the formula fare that marks all Chart Houses: prime rib; East-West prawns and garlic steak; and an assortment of fresh fish in teriyaki, garlic-herb, and mayonnaise sauces. Especially indulgent is the mud pie, a weighty dessert of Kona coffee ice cream, Oreo cookie crust, fudge, almonds, and whipped cream.

Other Chart House locations are at 100 Wailea Ike Dr. in Wailea (☎ 808/637-8005), and 500 N. Puunene in Kahului (☎ 808/877-2476).

✪ **David Paul's Lahaina Grill.** 127 Lahainaluna Rd. ☎ **808/667-5117.** Reservations required. Main courses $19–$38. AE, CB, DC, DISC, MC, V. Daily 5:30–10pm. Bar daily 5:30pm–midnight. NEW AMERICAN.

Nationally applauded and a recipient of numerous culinary awards, David Paul's is most people's favorite Maui restaurant. On an island where excellent dining is as ubiquitous as ocean views, that's saying a lot. A special custom-designed chef's table can be arranged with 48-hour notice for parties of six to eight, but the daily menu is enticement enough: tequila shrimp with firecracker rice, Kona lobster-crab cakes in a sesame-Dijon sauce, Kona coffee–roasted rack of lamb, kalua duck in a plum wine reduction, seared ahi encrusted in Maui onion, and many other seductions. The bar

Lahaina & Kaanapali Dining

Aloha Mixed Plate 7

Beachside Grill and Leilani's on the Beach 2

Cascades Grille & Sushi Bar 4

Chart House 5

Cheeseburger in Paradise 10

Compadres Bar & Grill 6

David Paul's Lahaina Grill 11

Gerard's 12

Groovy Smoothies 14

Hard Rock Cafe 8

Hula Grill 2

Kimo's 9

Lahaina Coolers 15

Lahaina Fish Company 10

Maui Brews/Island Bistro 8

Pacific'o Restaurant 17

Pizza Paradiso Express 2

Planet Hollywood 13

Sam Choy's Lahaina Restaurant and Big Aloha Brewery 8

Spats 4

Swan Court 4

Swiss Cafe 16

Tiki Terrace 1

The Villa 3

Village Pizzeria 17

Golf
Post Office

Puukolii Rd.

Kekaa St.

LK & P Sugarcane Train

Kaanapali North Golf Course

Whalers Village

Kaanapali Parkway

Honoapiilani Hwy.

Royal Kaanapali Golf Course Club House

Nohea Kai Dr.

Kaanapali South Golf Course

Hanakaoo Beach Park

Police

Wahikuli Beach Park

Lahaina Civic Center

Lahaina Cannery Mall

Kapunakea

Mala Wharf

Kahoma Stream

Hale Pai, Lahainaluna School

Train Depot

Pioneer Sugar Mill

Lahaina Center

Papalaua St.

Lahainaluna Rd.

Lahaina Shopping Center

Dickerson St.

Wainee St.

Lahaina Small Boat Harbor

Luakini St.

Prison St.

505 Front St.

Shaw St.

0   1 Mile

0   1 Kilometer

N

is the busiest spot in Lahaina, and the ambience—black-and-white tile floors, pressed tin ceilings, eclectic 1890s decor—is a good match for the cuisine, set in a historic building next to the faithfully restored Lahaina Inn.

Gerard's. Plantation Inn, 174 Lahainaluna Rd. ☎ **808/661-8939.** Reservations recommended. Main courses $26.50–$32.50. AE, CB, DC, DISC, JCB, MC, V. Daily 6–10pm. FRENCH.

Winner of the *Wine Spectator* Award of Excellence for 1994, 1995, and 1997, Gerard's Gallic offerings still score high in this competitive culinary atmosphere. The rave-drawing starters: the oyster and shiitake mushroom appetizer, savory and steaming in puff pastry, and the ahi tartare with taro chips, followed by Gerard's famous roasted Hawaiian snapper in a spicy orange and ginger-butter sauce. Gerard Reversade specializes in fresh seafood, which he buys daily from the fishermen at the harbor, then transforms into haute cuisine. Choices for game lovers include duck confit with garlic petals, venison with peppered sauce and ohelo-berry compote, and a legendary grilled rack of lamb with mint crust and poached garlic. Vegetarians, take note: Gerard's also has a reputation for its willingness to accommodate vegetarian requests.

Pacific'o Restaurant. 505 Front St. ☎ **808/667-4341.** Reservations recommended. Main courses $9–$14 lunch, $19–$26 dinner. AE, CB, DC, MC, V. Daily 11am–4pm and 5:30–10pm. PACIFIC RIM/CONTEMPORARY PACIFIC.

You can't get any closer to the ocean than the tables here, which are literally on the beach. With good food complementing this sensational setting, plus live jazz in the evenings, foodies and aesthetes have little to complain about. The split-level dining starts at the top, near the entrance, with a long, cordial bar (where you can also order lunch or dinner) and a few tables along the railing. Steps lead to the outdoor tables, where the award-winning seafood dishes come to you with the backdrop of Lanai across the channel. We love the Asian gravlax, a marvel of house-cured salmon on sweet potato applejack, topped with wasabi-chive sour cream and caviar. The shrimp and basil wontons, and the ahi and ono tempura wrapped in nori and fried tempura style, are winners as well. Fresh fish comes grilled, steamed in bamboo, and bathed in exotic Asian spices. Vegetarians love Pacific'o, too, for the marvelous quinoa-lentil-shiitake–Maui onion entree with roasted tofu steak; with the spicy jalapeño roll, it's heaven.

Sam Choy's Lahaina Restaurant and Big Aloha Brewery. Lahaina Center, 900 Front St. ☎ **808/661-3800.** Reservations recommended for dinner. Main courses $22–$32. AE, DC, DISC, JCB, MC, V. Daily 10:30am–3pm, appetizer menu 3–5pm, dinner 5–9:30pm. HAWAII REGIONAL/SEAFOOD.

The chef especially known for his love of food has opened his second restaurant on Maui and his fifth in Hawaii, featuring a marine motif, a garden terrace, and an open kitchen for the 210-seat dining room. Choy offers an extensive appetizer menu, including barbecued spareribs, fried poke, steamed clams with miso-sake sauce, crab cakes with ginger pesto, and crab nachos. Lunches of fish-and-chips, noodles, burgers and sandwiches, and the signature rib-eye steak and fresh fish with shiitake mushroom sauce will bring on the siesta big-time. Choy's dinner fare comes in his customarily huge servings (there's a keiki menu too) and include his well-known seafood laulau, king crab legs, and misoyaki-plum salmon with wasabi mashed potatoes. All dinner items come with soup and salad, and when the brewery is ready, five beers brewed on the premises.

MODERATE

Compadres Bar & Grill. Lahaina Cannery Mall, 1221 Honoapiilani Hwy. ☎ **808/661-7189.** Main courses $12–$18.50. DC, JCB, MC, V. Daily 8am–11:30pm. MEXICAN.

Despite its concrete floor and high industrial ceilings, Compadres exudes an upbeat spirit and good cheer. The food is classic Tex-Mex, good any time of the day, beginning with huevos rancheros, egg burritos, hotcakes, and omelets (the Acapulco is heroic) and progressing to enchiladas and appetizers for the margarita-happy crowd. Stay spare (vegetable enchilada in fresh spinach tortilla) or get hefty (Texas T-bone and enchiladas); it's a carefree place with a large capacity for merrymaking.

✪ **Kimo's.** 845 Front St. ☎ **808/661-4811.** Reservations recommended for dinner. Main courses $5.95–$10.95 lunch, $12.95–$23.95 dinner. AE, DC, DISC, MC, V. Daily 11am–3pm and 5–10:30pm. STEAK/SEAFOOD.

Kimo's has a loyal following that keeps it from falling into the faceless morass of waterfront restaurants serving surf-and-turf with great sunset views. It's a formula restaurant (sibling to Leilani's and the Hula Grill) that works not only because of its oceanfront patio and upstairs dining room, but because, for the price, there are some satisfying choices. It's always crowded, buzzing with people having fun on a deck that takes in Molokai, Lanai, and Kahoolawe. Burgers and sandwiches are affordable and reliable, and the fresh catch in garlic-lemon and a sweet-basil glaze is a top seller, rivaling the hefty prime rib complete with salad, carrot muffins, herb rolls, and herb rice. Keep in mind that the waistline-defying hula pie—macadamia-nut ice cream in a chocolate-wafer crust with fudge and whipped cream—originated here.

Lahaina Fish Company. 831 Front St. ☎ **808/661-3472.** Main courses $7.95–$22.95. AE, JCB, MC, V. Daily 11am–midnight. SEAFOOD.

The open-air dining room is literally over the water, with flickering torches after sunset and an affordable menu that covers the seafood-pasta basics. Before 3pm, head to an ocean-side table and order a cheeseburger, chickenburger, fishburger, a generous basket of peel-and-eat shrimp, or sashimi; lingering is highly recommended. From noon to 5pm, cocktails are reduced and the big attraction is the appetizer-happy menu. Nightly specials range from island fish-and-chips to several pastas; standard steak-and-seafood combos; and four types of fresh island fish prepared in Asian, American, and European styles.

Maui Brews/Island Bistro. Lahaina Center, 900 Front St. ☎ **808/667-7794.** Reservations recommended. Burgers $6.40–$8.90, dinner main courses $13.90–$17.90. AE, DC, DISC, MC, V. Daily 11:30am–2am. AMERICAN/ECLECTIC.

Open for lunch, dinner, and late-night appetizers, Maui Brews is an all-purpose dining and entertainment center in one corner of the Lahaina Center. Appetizers, burgers, and sandwiches are the biggest draw here, with a few basic pies for the pizza-and-beer crowd. Nachos, baby back ribs, pasta, garlic chicken, and ahi carpaccio are some of the other offerings on the eclectic menu. You can dine outdoors, cafe-style (it gets very hot in summer), or indoors, where a large nightclub features live music regularly (see chapter 9).

INEXPENSIVE

Aloha Mixed Plate. 1285 Front St. ☎ **808/661-3322.** Main courses $3.50–$9.95. MC, V. Daily 7:30am–10pm, Thurs–Sat 10:30am–1am. PLATE LUNCHES/BEACHSIDE GRILL.

The operators of the Old Lahaina Luau have moved north in a big way. Recently, they opened this eatery in a charming, freestanding, plantation-style building directly across from the Lahaina Cannery Mall, next to the site of the luau. You can sit on an open deck under umbrellas and tuck into inexpensive mahimahi, kalua pig and cabbage, shoyu chicken, teriyaki beef, and other local plate-lunch specials, all at budget-friendly prices. Gardenburgers and hamburgers cost even less. In pricey Lahaina, a find.

Cheeseburger in Paradise. 811 Front St. ☎ **808/661-4855.** Main courses $5.95–$9.95. AE, DISC, MC, V. Daily 8am–11pm. AMERICAN.

Wildly successful, always crowded, highly visible, and very noisy with its live music in the evenings, Cheeseburger is a shrine to the American classic. The home of three-napkin cheeseburgers with attitude, this is burger country, tropical style, with everything from tofu and gardenburgers to the biggest, juiciest beef and chicken burgers, served on whole-wheat and sesame buns baked fresh daily. There are good reasons why the two-story green-and-white building next to the seawall is always packed: good value, good grinds, and a great ocean view. The Cheeseburger in Paradise—a hefty hunk with Jack and cheddar cheeses, sautéed onions, lettuce, fresh tomatoes, and Thousand Island dressing—is a paean to the basics. You can build your own burger by adding sautéed mushrooms, bacon, grilled ortega chiles, and other condiments for an extra charge. Onion rings, chili-cheese fries, and cold beer complete the carefree fantasy.

Groovy Smoothies. 708 Front St. ☎ **808/661-8219.** Smoothies under $4.50. No credit cards. Daily 9am–9:30pm. SMOOTHIES.

This closet-size take-out stand makes the best smoothies in Lahaina. But if they're too pure for you, there's always muffins, espresso, and Danishes. We love the mango-and-banana smoothie, but others may pine for the piña colada, the Elvis Peachly, or any of the berry delights. Protein powders, bee pollen, and other nutritious ingredients can be blended into these tasty, healthful treats.

Lahaina Coolers. 180 Dickenson St. ☎ **808/661-7082.** Main courses $7.50–$9.95 lunch, $9.50–$18.95 dinner. AE, DC, DISC, MC, V. Daily 8am–midnight, bar until 2am. ECLECTIC.

The newly renovated Coolers has shed its rubber zoris for a more upscale menu and look—wood floors, teak chairs, tablecloths, umbrellas, a new bar that looks like a surfboard—but it's still casual in the true Maui way. A huge marlin still hangs above the bar, a big TV shows continuous surf videos, and open windows on three sides create a cordial, cheerful atmosphere. Hot tips: steak or skillet-roasted clams with garlic, served sizzling hot on a cast-iron skillet; house-made pasta, a special touch for a place more Beach Boys than Puccini; and fresh fish dinner specials at $18.95. The cuisine's gone international with peel-and-eat shrimp, artichoke hearts on pizza or crostini, burgers, fresh fish tacos, shrimp tempura, and Moroccan chicken. The Evil Jungle Pizza, grilled chicken in a spicy Thai peanut sauce, and the Evil Jungle Pasta are menu staples. A big plus: Everything can be prepared vegetarian upon request.

Swiss Cafe. 640 Front St. ☎ **808/661-6776.** Seven-inch pizza $6.95–$7.95, lunch specials $5, sandwiches $5.95–$6.95. No credit cards. Daily 9am–6pm. SANDWICHES/PIZZA.

This tiny cafe, a take-out stand with a few outdoor tables just off Lahaina's main drag, serves a Swiss breakfast, but it's mainly a sandwich and pizza shop. It's cheap and popular for ice cream—$2 for two scoops of Maui-made Roselani pineapple, coconut, or macadamia nut!—and sandwiches, including Boboli, spicy roast beef, Mexican garden, and other vegetarian choices. People also line up for the Italian Lavazza espresso, cappuccino, and coffee drinks, and hot sandwiches such as turkey broccoli melt and spicy chicken with mushrooms, onions, and melted cheese. There aren't many places on Maui where you can find a $5 lunch.

Village Pizzeria. 505 Front St. ☎ **808/661-8112.** Salad and pizza $3.95, main courses and special pizzas $6.95–$24.50. AE, DC, DISC, MC, V. Daily 11am–9:30pm. PIZZA.

With thin or thick crust, more than a dozen toppings, and the signature clam-and-garlic pizza that you can smell from around the corner, this pizzeria is a corner landmark at the 505 Front St. shopping complex. Appetizers, sandwiches, and pasta round out the offerings.

KAANAPALI
EXPENSIVE

Cascades Grille and Sushi Bar. Hyatt Regency Maui, 200 Nohea Kai Dr. ☎ **808/661-1234**. Reservations not accepted at sushi bar. Grille main courses $16–$32, sushi rolls $4.50–$15. AE, CB, DC, DISC, JCB, MC. V. Daily 5:45–10pm. STEAK/SEAFOOD/SUSHI.

It was a great idea to open the tiny sushi bar just outside the Cascades Grille, where Lahaina Provisions Company used to be. Although you can order traditional nigiri sushi and sashimi, trendy fusion sushi is the main attraction here, à la the highly successful Sansei in Kapalua. The Paia maki is a vegetarian's bonanza, a hand roll of burdock, red ginger, cucumber, avocado, and other vegetables. Eel and avocado, salmon-skin roll, the spider (soft-shell crab with avocado and vegetables), and the Philadelphia (cream cheese, smoked salmon, and cucumber) are some of the unorthodox offerings. We recommend the Rainbow California, an inside-out roll with ahi, salmon, and avocado—both creative and scrumptious. Inside, the Grille offers fresh island fish in five different preparations, top-grade steaks, and wide-ranging appetizers with ethnic influences.

Spats. Hyatt Regency Maui, 200 Nohea Kai Dr. ☎ **808/661-1234.** Reservations recommended. Main courses $20–$30. AE, DISC, MC, V. Daily 6–10pm. ITALIAN.

Descend the stairs to the Italianate entrance and behold the chandeliers, Titian reds, and sensory stimuli straight out of a Coppola film. When we visited, the dining room was filled with the aroma of garlic and tomato and an Italian aria floated through the sound system. It used to be a lot more uptight than it is today; one female server even wore a visor during dinner. The Spats salad was notable, a celebration of simplicity and freshness. We also loved the puttanesca and the tiramisu, lighter and cakier than most, and delicious without being frothy.

Swan Court. Hyatt Regency Maui, 200 Nohea Kai Dr. ☎ **808/661-1234.** Reservations recommended for dinner. Main courses $28–$38. AE, DC, DISC, JCB, MC, V. Daily 6:30–11:30am and 6–10pm. CONTINENTAL.

Even as a resort restaurant, Swan Court is hard to resist. Recent refurbishments have added a dance floor and new furnishings to this romantic restaurant. Come here as a splurge or on a bottomless expense account, and enjoy the continental menu in incomparable surroundings. The combination of waterfalls, ocean view, Japanese gardens, and swans and flamingos serenely gliding by is irresistible, especially with alfresco dining and appropriately extravagant fare. The menu changes frequently, but some basics remain: fresh opakapaka with ginger-citrus vinaigrette, broiled rack of lamb with Maui onion marmalade, basil-scented prawns with pepper-seared bison. One diner raved about the fresh Hawaiian spiny tail lobster, available in season. It was caught off the north shore of Kauai and presented on a bed of artichoke mashed potatoes.

The Villa. Westin Maui, 2365 Kaanapali Pkwy. ☎ **808/667-2525.** Reservations recommended. Main courses $18–$32, fixed-price menu $28. AE, DC, DISC, JCB, MC. V. Daily 6–9pm. HAWAII REGIONAL.

The Westin's signature restaurant offers a romantic ambience with tables encircling a man-made lagoon near waterfalls and a large banyan tree. The dining room is surrounded by water, and even with its soaring ceilings and enormous visual scale, it's an informal, comfortable place, with dishes that range from good to excellent. The fixed-price menu might offer black turtle bean soup or smoked ahi risotto; grilled marinated chicken and wild-mushroom pasta; and the pièce de résistance, the ahi poke martini. Served in a martini glass, the fresh, finely cubed ahi comes topped with seaweed, shiso (a savory flat leaf used as an accompaniment in sushi), tobiko (flying-fish roe), finely cubed cucumber, green onions, and a daringly spicy garlic sauce. Vegetarian specials, such as eggplant terrine, are gourmet fare.

MODERATE

Beachside Grill and Leilani's on the Beach. Whalers Village, 2435 Kaanapali Pkwy. ☎ **808/661-4495.** Reservations suggested for dinner. Lunch and dinner (Beachside Grill) $5.95–$9.95; dinner (Leilani's) from $14.95. AE, DC, DISC, MC, V. Beachside Grill daily 11am–11pm (bar daily until 12:30am); Leilani's daily 5–10pm. STEAK/SEAFOOD.

The Beachside Grill is the informal, less expensive room downstairs on the beach, where folks wander in off the sand for a frothy beer and a beachside burger. Leilani's is the dinner-only room, with more expensive but still not outrageously priced steak and seafood offerings. At Leilani's, you can order everything from affordable spinach, cheese, and mushroom ravioli to lobster and steak at the higher market price. Still, children can order a quarter-pound hamburger for under $5 or a broiled chicken breast for a couple dollars more—a value for sure. Pasta, rack of lamb, filet mignon, and Alaskan king crab at market price are among the temptations in the upstairs room. Although the steak-and-lobster combinations can be pricey, the good thing about Leilani's is the strong middle range of entree prices, especially the fresh fish for around $20. All of this, of course, comes with an ocean view. There's live Hawaiian music every afternoon except Friday, when the rock 'n' roll Aloha Friday set gets those decibels climbing. Free concerts are usually offered on a stage outside the restaurant from 2pm to sunset on the last Sunday of the month. The popular program, Music on the Beach, is always a big draw—and another big reason to love Leilani's. Any way you cut it, the view, food, prices, and location make this a hard-to-beat Kaanapali staple.

✪ **Hula Grill.** Whalers Village, 2435 Kaanapali Pkwy. ☎ **808/667-6636.** Reservations recommended for dinner. Lunch and Barefoot Bar menus $5.95–$11.95, dinner main courses from $12.95. AE, CB, DC, DISC, MC, V. Daily 11am–12:30am. HAWAII REGIONAL/SEAFOOD.

Who wouldn't want to be tucking into poisson cru, crab and corn cakes, or ahi poke rolls under a thatched umbrella, with a sand floor and palm trees at arm's length and a view of Lanai across the channel? What a cheerful place this is, a Kaanapali magnet, *the* place to dine while watching swimmers and catamarans bobbing in the sea. Peter Merriman, a culinary guru and one of the originators of Hawaii Regional Cuisine, segued seamlessly from his smallish, Big Island upcountry enclave to this large, high-volume dining room on the beach. He has redefined chain-restaurant cuisine with this 300-seat, open-air restaurant in the style of a 1930s kamaaina beach house.

Hula Grill is one of those dining rooms with a wide range of prices and choices; although it can be expensive, it doesn't have to be. The superb menu includes Merriman's signature wok-charred ahi; seafood pot stickers; and several different fresh-fish preparations, including his famous ahi poke rolls, lightly sautéed rare ahi wrapped in rice paper with Maui onions. Lunchtime burgers are de rigueur, or order gourmet appetizers from the Barefoot Bar menu (sandwiches, crab wontons, fresh fish-and-chips, pizza, smoked-turkey sandwiches). There's happy-hour entertainment and Hawaiian music daily.

INEXPENSIVE

Pizza Paradiso Express. Whalers Village, 2435 Kaanapali Pkwy. ☎ **808/667-0333.** Gourmet pizza $3.35–$3.95 (by the slice), whole pizzas $16.95–$22.95. No credit cards. Daily 11am–10pm. PIZZA.

Great Hawaiian Grinds: From Poi to Pohole Ferns

Bravo to the **Tiki Terrace** restaurant at the Kaanapali Beach Hotel, 2525 Kaana-pali Parkway (☎ **808/661-0011**), for its low-salt, employee-tested Native Hawaiian diet. Titled Kulaiwi Cuisine, the menu features the healthy, traditional Hawaiian diet of fresh fish and taro greens, flavored with herbs and spices. The use of salt is kept to a minimum, but you can always add your own. The Kulaiwi menu consists of pohole fern shoots from Keanae Valley (on the way to Hana), marinated with onions and seaweed and served with ginger-tomato dressing. (We think that with their freshness, pleasing crunch, and mild flavor, fern shoots are one of the most under-utilized greens of Hawaii.) Entrée choices, priced from $5.95 to $29, might be oven-poached breast of chicken or fresh catch, served with pureed taro tops (like spinach, but better), grilled bananas, steamed sweet potato, taro, and fresh poi made on the premises. The seafood can be ordered with shrimp, scallops, spinach, and sweet potatoes, cooked in ti leaves laulau style, or in a Hawaiian seafood stew. The vegetable laulau is another stroke of genius: fresh vegetables with tofu and sweet potato, with the coconut sauce prudently served on the side. If this is too tame for you, the à la carte menu proffers baked prawns stuffed with crab and mushrooms, chicken baked or filled with shiitake mushrooms and fresh spinach, and many other choices—fish grilled, sauteed, steamed, baked, or poached in roasted garlic, ginger teriyaki, sherried peppercorn, shallot, and other sauces. The dining room is old-fashioned Hawaii, not fancy, with tables on a terrace ringed with plumeria and palm trees. Dinner is offered daily from 5:30 to 9pm; reservations are recommended.

At the buffet-style **Mixed Plate** on the same property, the Hawaiian Friday lunch is widely touted among residents, who voted this the best Hawaiian food in the *Maui News:* fresh poi, lomi salmon, laulau, kalua pig, ahi poke, and pohole fern salad, $8.95 for the works. The hotel also sponsors Aunty Aloha's Breakfast Luau at 8am weekdays, with live music, hula, breakfast (scrambled eggs, Portuguese sausage, and rice), and the inimitable and hilarious Aunty Aloha, who does a fire-knife dance with cigarette lighters and will tell you how to save money on your Maui vacation. Her slide show of Maui activities lasts about an hour and a half.

Word's out that the pastas are selling as fast as the pizzas. From the Veg Wedge to the Maui Wowie (with ham and Maui pineapple), the Jimmy Hoffa (pepperoni and mozzarella), and the God Father (roasted chicken, artichoke hearts, sun-dried tomatoes, the works), these pizzas are always described in superlatives, even by jaded New Yorkers. Pizza Paradiso has hit upon a simple but effective formula: good crust, uncompromising sauces, and toppings loyal to tradition but with an edge for those who want it. Create your own pizza with a long menu of possibilities, and enjoy it in this mallish fast-food atmosphere—or take it to Kaanapali Beach, just a few steps away.

The new **Pizza Paradiso** location in Honokowai is also garnering rave reviews (see below).

HONOKOWAI, KAHANA & NAPILI
EXPENSIVE

A Pacific Cafe Honokowai. Honokowai Marketplace, 3350 Lower Honoapiilani Rd. ☎ **808/669-2724.** Reservations recommended. Main courses $19–$30. AE, DC, JCB, MC, V. Daily 5–10pm. HAWAII REGIONAL.

Anchored by Star Market's flagship store, the new Honokowai Marketplace is a mix of everyday good things for the neighborhood: a supermarket, dry cleaner, ice cream, pizza, health foods, and this, Jean-Marie Josselin's sixth restaurant in Hawaii. How does he do it? A large rotisserie with an open, U-shaped kitchen, a 1,000-square-foot lanai, and a menu that has earned him star status among Maui foodies. The offerings change daily, but you can count on fresh island ingredients: innovative soups, such as the "creamless" asparagus soup with seared sea scallops and white truffle oil; grilled items (ahi steak au poivre, Mongolian rack of lamb); house specialties (wok-charred mahimahi with sesame-garlic crust, pan-seared ono with soba noodles), and meats and pizzas baked in the tandoor oven.

✪ **Roy's Kahana Bar & Grill/Roy's Nicolina Restaurant.** Kahana Gateway, 4405 Honoapiilani Hwy. ☎ **808/669-6999.** Reservations strongly recommended. Main courses $13–$26. AE, CB, DC, DISC, JCB, MC, V. Roy's Kahana daily 5:30–10pm; Roy's Nicolina, daily 5:30–10pm. EUROASIAN.

These two sibling restaurants are next door to each other, have the same menu, and are busy, busy, busy. They bustle with young, hip servers impeccably trained to deliver blackened ahi or perfectly seared lemongrass shutome (broadbill swordfish) hot to your table, in rooms that sizzle with cross-cultural tastings. Both are known for their rack of lamb and fresh seafood (usually eight or nine choices), and for the large, open kitchens that turn out everything from pizza to sake-grilled New York steak and roasted half-chickens in garlic and orange, glistening in cabernet sauce. If pot stickers are on the menu, don't resist. Large picture windows open up Roy's Kahana but don't quell the noise, another tireless trait long ago established by Roy's Restaurant in Honolulu, the flagship of Roy Yamaguchi's burgeoning empire. Roy's Nicolina now features dining on the lanai.

Sea House Restaurant. Napili Kai Beach Club, 5900 Honoapiilani Hwy. ☎ **808/ 669-1500.** Reservations required for dinner. Main courses $15–$26, appetizers $4–$13. AE, MC, V. Sat–Thurs 8–11am, noon–2pm (pupu menu 2–9pm), and 5:30–9pm (6–9pm in summer); Fri Polynesian Show 6–9pm. STEAK/SEAFOOD.

The Sea House is not glamorous, famous, or hip, and its food is not always terrific, but it's worth mentioning for its view of Napili Bay, one of the two most gorgeous in West Maui. The Napili Kai Beach Club, where Sea House is located, is a charming throwback to the days when hotels blended in with their surroundings, had lush tropical foliage, and were sprawling rather than vertical. Dinner entrees come complete with soup or salad, vegetables, and rice or potato. The lighter appetizer menu is a delight—more than a dozen choices range from sautéed or blackened crab cake to crisp Pacific Rim sushi of ahi wrapped in nori and cooked tempura style. The top attraction here, however, is the million-dollar view. On Friday nights, a Polynesian dinner show features the children of the Napili Kai Foundation, an organization devoted to supporting Hawaiian culture.

MODERATE

Fish & Game Brewing Co. & Rotisserie. Kahana Gateway, 4405 Honoapiilani Hwy. ☎ **808/669-3474.** Reservations recommended for dinner. Main courses $6.95–$12.95 lunch, $13.95–$25.95 dinner. AE, CB, DC, DISC, JCB, MC, V. Daily 11am–3pm, happy hour 3–5:30pm, dinner 6–10pm, late-night menu 10:30pm–2am. SEAFOOD.

Large microbrew vats have been installed to one side of what used to be Fish & Game Sports Grill, a popular spot in Kahana notable for its overabundance of testosterone and ubiquitous TVs. The restaurant consists of an oyster bar, deli counter and retail section, and tables. The small retail section sells fresh seafood, while the sit-down menu covers basic tastes: salads (Caesar, Oriental chicken with wontons), fish-and-chips, fresh fish sandwiches ($10.95), cheeseburgers ($7.95), and beer—lots of it. At dinner, count on heavier meats and the fresh catch of the day (ahi, mahimahi, ono), with rotisserie items such as grilled chicken, steaks, and duck. The special late-night menu offers shrimp, cheese fries, quesadillas, and other lighter fare.

INEXPENSIVE

Hawaiian Moons Community Market & Deli. Honokowai Marketplace, 3636 Lower Honoapiilani Rd. ☎ **808/665-1339.** Menu items $5.50–$14.95. AE, DC, JCB, MC, V. Mon–Sat 7am–5pm (health-food store until 9pm), Sun 7am–6pm; hot foods served Mon–Sat 10:30am–5pm, Sun 10:30am–6pm. NATURAL FOODS.

Our favorite south Maui health-food store has set out its shingle in west Maui with this natural-foods deli that also offers fresh fish specials, chili, soups, sushi, a salad bar, and sandwiches (not to mention an ATM!). The ingredients are wholesome: eggless mayonnaise, grain mustard, free-range turkey, "mock chicken" made of seasoned tofu, gardenburgers, whole-wheat bread, and a gourmet tuna sandwich with capers, red peppers, fresh dill, celery, and seasonings. This is an all-purpose natural-foods market and deli with a large selection of Maui products and produce; area health foodies are rejoicing.

Maui Tacos. Napili Plaza, 5095 Napili Hau St. ☎ **808/665-0222.** Most items under $6.95. No credit cards. Mon–Sat 9:30am–9pm, Sun 9:30am–8pm. MEXICAN.

Lahaina's Avalon is now dust, but Mark Ellman's Maui Tacos chain is growing faster than you can say "Haleakala." Ellman put gourmet Mexican on paper plates and on the island's culinary map. Barely more than a take-out counter with a few tables, this and the other three Maui Tacos on the island are all the rage among hungry surfers, discerning diners, burrito buffs, and Hollywood glitterati, like Sharon Stone, whose picture adorns a wall or two. We like the excellent fresh-fish tacos, chimichangas, searing salsas, and mouth-breaking compositions such as the Hookipa, a "surf burrito" of fresh fish, black beans, and salsa. The green-spinach burrito contains four kinds of beans, rice, and potatoes. Hard tacos, soft tacos, vegetarian burritos, regular burritos, quesadillas, nachos, enchiladas—no chihuahua's asking for Taco Bell.

Additional locations are in Kaahumanu Center, Kahului (☎ 808/871-7726); Lahaina Square, Lahaina (☎ 808/661-8883); and Kamaole Beach Center, Kihei (☎ 808/665-0222).

Pizza Paradiso Italian Caffe. Honokowai Marketplace, 3350 Lower Honoapiilani Rd. ☎ **808/667-2929.** Pizzas $11.95–$22.95, pastas $5.95–$8.95. MC, V. Daily 7:30am–10pm. PIZZA/ITALIAN.

Owner Paris Nabavi had such success with his Pizza Paradiso in Whalers Village that he opened up in the new marketplace—and keeps expanding to keep up with demand. The pastas—marinara, pescatore, Alfredo, Florentine, and pesto, with options and add-ons on top of that—are selling as fast as the pizzas and panini sandwiches. Take-out or dine in, this is a hot spot in the neighborhood, with free delivery.

KAPALUA
EXPENSIVE

The Bay Club. Kapalua Bay Hotel & Villas, 1 Bay Dr. ☎ **808/669-5656.** Reservations recommended for dinner. Dress code at dinner: evening resort wear for women, long slacks for men. Main courses $24–$38. AE, CB, JCB, MC, V. Daily 11:30am–2pm and 6–9:30pm. SEAFOOD.

Tried and true, the Bay Club is one of Maui's lasting pleasures. The classic enjoyments— a stellar view, beatific sunsets, attentive service from bow-tied servers—are matched by a seafood menu that has lost none of its luster with the years. The Caesar salad is still tossed tableside, the seafood is fresh, the peppered steak just so, the vegetarian dishes quite elegant. A perfect lunch: onion leek soup ($7.50) and the seafood Cobb ($14), a peerless untossed salad of shrimp, scallops, calamari, vegetables, and walnuts. (The grilled ahi on poi bread looked enticing, too.) Duck, rack of lamb, bouillabaisse, salads, fresh catches, sandwiches and pasta for lunch, and a host of simple delights can be relished in this open-air dining room. The view changes as the sun moves south, eventually to set behind Lanai in the winter months.

Plantation House. 200 Plantation Club Dr. (at Kapalua Plantation Golf Course). ☎ **808/ 669-6299.** Reservations recommended. Main courses $18–$24. AE, MC, V. Daily 8am–3pm and 5:30–10pm. SEAFOOD/ISLAND REGIONAL.

With its teak tables, fireplace, and open sides, Plantation House gets high marks for ambience: the 360° view from high among the resort's pine-studded hills takes in Molokai and Lanai, the ocean, the rolling fairways and greens, the northwestern flanks of the West Maui Mountains, and the daily sunset spectacular. Readers of the *Maui News* have deemed this the island's "Best Ambience"—a big honor on this island of ubiquitous views. Choices include fresh fish prepared seven ways—among them, Mediterranean (seared), Upcountry (sautéed with Maui onions and vegetable stew), Island (pan-seared in sweet sake and chile-sesame sauce), Asian Pacific (charred with Asian mushrooms and sake sauce), and Rich Forest (with roasted wild mushrooms), the top seller.

MODERATE

Jameson's Grill & Bar at Kapalua. 200 Kapalua Dr. (at the 18th hole of the Kapalua Golf Course). ☎ **808/669-5653.** Reservations recommended for dinner. Lunch $5.95–$11.95; cafe menu (3–10pm) $6.95–$12.95; dinner main courses $15.95–$39.95. AE, DC, DISC, JCB, MC, V. Daily 8am–1pm. AMERICAN.

This is the quintessential country-club restaurant, open-air with mountain and ocean views. The glass-enclosed room is across the hall from the Kapalua pro shop, a short lob from the tennis courts and golf course. The familiar Jameson's mix of fresh fish (sautéed, wok-seared, or grilled), stuffed shrimp, prawns, rack of lamb, ahi steak, and other basic surf-and turf selections prevail at dinner. At lunch, for duffers dashing to make tee time, inexpensive "golf sandwiches" (roast beef, turkey, tuna salad) are a pleasing alternative if you're not in the mood for the other, richer, choices: fish-and-chips, patty melt, crab cakes, and an affordable cafe menu of gourmet appetizers. A swell start to a Kapalua day: eggs Benedict, eggs Elizabeth (marlin on a muffin with all the trimmings), or eggs Kapalua (crab cakes topped with poached egg and wild-mushroom sauce), for just under $10. With the view of Lanai across the channel and the charming bonsai on every table, it's hard to beat.

✪ Sansei Seafood Restaurant and Sushi Bar. Kapalua Shops, 115 Bay Dr. ☎ **808/ 669-6286.** Reservations recommended. Main courses $15–$19.75. AE, DC, DISC, MC, V. Sat–Wed 5:30–10pm, sushi bar until 11pm; Thurs–Fri 5:30pm–1am. PACIFIC RIM.

People drive from central Maui to dine here, and that's a long drive. Why do they come? Furiously fusion, part Hawaii Regional Cuisine, and all parts sushi, Sansei is tirelessly creative, with a menu that scores higher with the adventurous than the purists. Maki is the mantra here: Paia maki, asparagus maki, and so on, and if you don't like cilantro, watch out for those complex spicy crab rolls. Also on the menu: panko-crusted ahi sashimi, ahi carpaccio, udon and ramen, lobster tail, traditional shrimp and vegetable tempura, Asian rock-shrimp cake in ginger-lime chili butter and cilantro pesto. But there's simpler fare as well, such as pasta and wok-tossed upcountry vegetables. And don't forget the desserts: tempura fried ice cream with chocolate sauce, crème brûlée, and an autumn phenom, persimmon crème brûlée, made with Kula persimmons.

3 South Maui

MAALAEA & KIHEI
EXPENSIVE

✪ **A Pacific Cafe Maui.** Azeka Place II, 1279 S. Kihei Rd. ☎ **808/879-0069.** Reservations recommended. Main courses $24.75–$32. AE, CB, DC, MC, V. Daily 5:30–10pm. HAWAII REGIONAL.

This restaurant is busy every night of the week, so make your reservations as early as possible. You'll dine on rattan chairs at hammered-copper tables under very high ceilings, in a room bordered with windows overlooking the parking lot (but you'll be so busy enjoying the food, you won't notice the lack of view). From the open kitchen and a menu that changes daily comes a stream of marvels: the signature tiger-eye ahi sushi tempura, light and delectable; garlic-sesame, pan-seared mahimahi, a Pacific Cafe staple; salmon firecracker rolls; pan-seared sea scallops; and the recently introduced hormone-free, Hawaii-grown specialty meats—lamb, elk, veal, and Kobe beef.

Carelli's on the Beach. 2980 S. Kihei Rd. ☎ **808/875-0001.** Reservations recommended. Main courses $22–$38. MC, V. Daily 6–10pm, bar until 11pm. ITALIAN/SEAFOOD.

Kihei's well-tanned, chicly attired trendies come here for pasta, seafood, and the view. It is stupendous: With its prime on-the-sand location at Keawakapu Beach, you can watch the sunset in ravishing surroundings over cioppino (the most popular item, at a pricey $36), fresh fish specials, seafood ravioli, carpaccio, rack of lamb in Asiago cheese crust with truffle sauce, and other Italian favorites. The wood-burning brick oven turns out great pizzas, and the food is top-drawer. To sit at a table on the dining floor, though, a $25 minimum order is required—a policy that lacks aloha.

Five Palms. Mana Kai Maui Resort, 2960 S. Kihei Rd. ☎ **808/879-2607.** Reservations recommended for dinner. Main courses $17.95–$49. AE, DC, JCB, MC, V. Daily 8am–2:30pm and 5–9pm. ECLECTIC.

This is the best lunch spot in Kihei—open-air, with tables a few feet from Keawakapu Beach and million-dollar views of Kahoolawe and Molokini. The white-sand beach with lava outcroppings is Kihei's finest feature, and this unpretentious dining room is the front-row seat for diners. At lunch, the hot items include Kula greens, burgers, sandwiches on homemade focaccia, a perfectly grilled vegetable platter, and capellini with shiitake mushrooms, sun-dried tomatoes, and white-wine sauce. At dinner, with the torches lit on the beach and the main dining room open, the ambience shifts to evening romantic, but it's still casual.

Steve Amaral's Cucina Pacifica. Upstairs in the Rainbow Mall, 2439 S. Kihei Rd., no. 201A. ☎ **808/875-7831.** Reservations recommended. Main courses $19–$32. AE, DC, DISC, MC, V. Sun–Thurs 5:30–10pm, Fri–Sat 5:30pm–1am. MEDITERRANEAN/SEAFOOD.

If you're willing to pay these prices for dinner in a room without a view—in Kihei, no less—then Cucina may appeal to you. The menu features Mediterranean culinary traditions and fresh Maui seafood and vegetables; the restaurant has an air of pretension, but there's no doubting Amaral's culinary skill. The menu changes seasonally to highlight fresh seasonal produce. What you might find during winter: Italian winter truffle and potato soup; wild-mushroom risotto; spanakopita of pan-seared diver scallops; and a Spanish stew of clams, meaty mussels, whole shrimp, and scallops. In the spring:

seared ahi Genovese, in an herb crust with Maui basil pesto; skillet-crisped snapper with watercress and caramelized Maui onions; and Maui onion and tiger prawn risotto. There's live music Wednesday, Friday, and Saturday evenings, with dancing into the wee hours.

The Waterfront at Maalaea. Maalaea Harbor, 50 Hauoli St. ☎ **808/244-9028.** Reservations recommended. Main courses $18–$38. AE, DC, DISC, JCB, MC, V. Daily 5–8:30pm (last seating). SEAFOOD.

The Waterfront has won awards for wine excellence, service, and seafood, but its biggest boost is word of mouth. Loyal diners rave about the friendly staff and seafood, served in simple surroundings with a bay and harbor view. You have nine choices of preparations for the several varieties of fresh Hawaiian fish, ranging from en papillote (baked in buttered parchment) to light cuisine (broiled or poached, then topped with steamed, fresh vegetables). Other choices: Kula onion soup, an excellent Caesar salad, lobster chowder, and grilled eggplant layered with Maui onions, tomatoes, and spinach, served with red-pepper coulis and Big Island goat cheese.

MODERATE

Buzz's Wharf. Maalaea Harbor, 50 Hauoli St. ☎ **808/244-5426.** Reservations suggested. Main courses $10.95–$24.95. AE, CB, DC, DISC, JCB, MC, V. Daily 11am–10pm. AMERICAN.

Buzz's is another formula restaurant that offers a superb view, substantial sandwiches, meaty french fries, and surf-and-turf fare—in a word, satisfying but not sensational. Still, this bright, airy dining room is a fine way station for whale watching over a cold beer and a fresh mahimahi sandwich with fries, or, if you're feeling extravagant, the house specialty, Prawns Tahitian. Some diners opt for several appetizers (stuffed mushrooms, steamer clams, clam chowder, onion soup) and a salad (there are three different types of Caesar), then splurge on dessert. Buzz's prize-winning Tahitian Baked Papaya is a warm, fragrant melding of fresh papaya with vanilla and coconut—the pride of the house.

The Greek Bistro. 2511 S. Kihei Rd. ☎ **808/879-9330.** Reservations recommended. Combination and family style dinners $14.95–$21.95 per person; family style platter $35 for two. Children's portions also available for considerably less. AE, DC, CB, JCB, MC, V. Daily 5–10pm. GREEK.

The banana trees, yellow ginger, and hibiscus that surround the tile-floored terrace add a lot of character to the dining experience at this indoor/outdoor bistro, especially in chaotic Kihei. Homemade pita bread, quality feta and spices, classic spanakopita and chicken and lamb souvlaki (the Greek version of shish kebab) are some of the authentic and popular Mediterranean offerings. The family style combination platters include lamb souvlaki and the fresh fish of the day. Also popular are the Greek lasagna; chopped lamb and beef with cinnamon and cheeses; and the Mediterranean chicken breast, an elaborate platter of mushroom-and-wine–infused organic skinless chicken, served with linguine and vegetables.

Hapa's Brew Haus & Restaurant. Lipoa Shopping Center, 41 E. Lipoa St. ☎ **808/ 879-9001.** Reservations recommended. Main courses $8–$18.95. AE, DISC, JCB, MC, V. Daily 4pm–2am. BREW HOUSE/INTERNATIONAL.

Food, beer, and music are the primary offerings here, but the best news is the weekly Wednesday night appearance of guitarist and singer nonpareil Willie K. Besides being a nightclub, Hapa's is also a microbrewery with lagers to accompany the appetizers (chicken wings, poke, spring rolls, lumpia), starters (baked artichoke hearts, nachos, Caesar salad), sandwiches (beef burger, grilled chicken), pizzas, calzones, plate lunches (mahimahi, teriyaki beef, beef broccoli), and noodles. From 4 to 6pm daily, pupus are reduced to half price and draft beer goes for $2. The pizzas come heaped with grilled chicken, pesto shrimp, clams, garlic sauce, vegetables, and any number of combinations, on thin or thick crust. On Sundays from 2 to 6pm, members of the Maui Symphony Orchestra Band (MSO) take over the stage and play swing music—and after that, the teen disco starts spinning. (See also chapter 9.)

La Pastaria. Lipoa Shopping Center, 41 E. Lipoa St. ☎ **808/891-1555.** Reservations recommended. Main courses $9–$26. AE, DISC, MC, V. Mon–Sat 5–10pm. ITALIAN/SEAFOOD.

La Pastaria was a Kihei fixture that disappeared when the owners opened Hapa's instead. But La Pastaria is back, a tiny bistro with only 32 seats and every dish made to order, resurrected where Hapa's pool tables used to be. On the menu: frutti di mare, mushroom penne (with portobello and shiitake), linguine carbonara, filet mignon, double breast of chicken in rosemary, and fresh catch sautéed or grilled, served in one of four sauces. Diners at La Pastaria can duck next door to Hapa's for late-night entertainment without a cover charge.

Stella Blues Cafe & Deli. Long's Center, 1215 S. Kihei Rd. ☎ **808/874-3779.** Main courses $9.95–$17.95. DISC, MC, V. Daily 8am–9pm. AMERICAN.

Stella Blues gets going at breakfast and continues through to dinner with something for everyone—vegetarians, children, pasta and sandwich lovers, hefty steak eaters, and sensible diners who'll spring for the inexpensive fresh Kula green salad. Grateful Dead posters line the walls, and a covey of gleaming motorcycles is invariably parked outside. It's loud and lively, casual, irreverent, and unpretentious. Sandwiches are the highlight, two dozen selections ranging from Tofu Extraordinaire to Mom's egg salad on croissant to gardenburgers and grilled chicken. Tofu wraps and the mountain-size Cobb salads are popular, and for the carefree, large coffee shakes with mounds of whipped cream. Daily specials include fresh seafood and other surprises—all homestyle cooking, made from scratch, down to the pesto mayonnaise and homemade herb bread. At dinner, selections are geared toward good-value family dining, from affordable full dinners to pastas and burgers.

INEXPENSIVE

✪ **Alexander's Fish & Chicken & Chips.** 1913 S. Kihei Rd. ☎ **808/874-0788.** Fish-and-chips $6.75–$9.50. MC, V. Daily 11am–9pm. FISH-AND-CHIPS/SEAFOOD.

Look for the ocean mural in front, Kalama Park across the street, and a marketplace next door: This is Alexander's, a friendly neighborhood take-out stand with patio seating outside and a very busy kitchen (beachwear is welcome here). Fresh ono, mahimahi, and ahi, broiled or fried, fly out of the kitchen with baskets of french fries or rice. Equally popular are the 13-piece shrimp, chicken, oyster, calamari, rib, or fish baskets for $16.50 to $19.95. Other offerings: fresh fish, Cajun chicken, calamari, teriyaki chicken, barbecued beef, and shrimp sandwiches, along with onion rings, corn bread, chicken wings, and other side orders in a light and tasty batter. This may be the most popular restaurant on the south shore—and they use canola oil.

The Coffee Store. Azeka Place II, 1279 Kihei Rd. ☎ **808/875-4244.** All items under $8.50. AE, CB, DC, DISC, MC, V. Sun–Thurs 6am–10pm, Fri–Sat 6am–11pm. COFFEEHOUSE.

This simple, classic coffeehouse for caffeine connoisseurs serves two dozen different types of coffee and coffee drinks, from mochas, lattes, and frappes to cappuccino, espresso, and toddies. Breakfast items include smoothies, lox and bagels, quiches, granola, and assorted pastries. Pizza, salads, vegetarian lasagna, veggie-and-shrimp quesadillas, and sandwiches (gardenburger, tuna, turkey, ham, grilled veggie panini) also move briskly from the take-out counter. If that's too tame, the turkey and veggie tortilla-wrapped sandwiches are a local legend. There are only a few small tables and they fill up fast, often with musicians and artists who spent the previous evening entertaining at the Wailea and Kihei resorts.

Peggy Sue's. Azeka Place II, 1279 S. Kihei Rd. ☎ **808/875-8944.** Burgers $6–$11, plate lunches $5–$10. DC, MC, V. Sun–Thurs 11am–9pm, Fri–Sat 11am–10pm. AMERICAN.

Just for a moment, forget that diet and take a leap. Peggy Sue's, a 1950s-style diner with oodles of charm, is a swell place to spring for a chocolate malt and french fries. You'll find the best malt on the island here, as well as sodas, shakes, floats, and egg creams. Old-fashioned soda-shop stools, an Elvis Presley Boulevard sign, and jukeboxes on every Formica table serve as backdrop for the famous burgers, brushed with teriyaki sauce and served with all the goodies, as well as plate lunches and gardenburgers.

Shaka Sandwich & Pizza. 1295 S. Kihei Rd. ☎ **808/874-0331.** Sandwiches $3.75–$8, pizzas up to $25.95. Sun–Thurs 10:30am–9pm, Fri–Sat 10:30am–10pm (deliveries daily 10:30am–9pm). PIZZA.

How many "best pizzas" are there on Maui? It depends on which shore you're on, the west or the south. At this south-shore old-timer, award-winning pizzas share the limelight with New York–style hoagies and Philly cheese steaks, calzones and salads, homemade garlic bread, and homemade meatball sandwiches. Shaka uses fresh Maui produce, homemade sauces, and homemade Italian bread. Choose thin or Sicilian thick crust with gourmet toppings: Maui onions, spinach, anchovies, jalapeño peppers, and a spate of other vegetables. Don't be misled by the whiteness of the white pizza; with the perfectly balanced flavors of olive oil, garlic, and cheese, you won't even miss the tomato sauce. Clam-and-garlic pizza, spinach pizza (with olive oil, spinach, garlic, and mozzarella), and the Shaka Supreme (with at least 10 toppings!) will satisfy even the insatiable.

WAILEA
EXPENSIVE

Joe's Bar & Grill. Wailea Tennis Club, 131 Wailea Ike Place. ☎ **808/875-7767.** Reservations recommended. Main courses $17–$30. AE, DC, MC, V. Daily 5:30–10:30pm. AMERICAN GRILL.

Beverly Gannon's style of American home-cooking with a regional twist is inspiring and inimitable, with hearty staples you're not likely to forget: Molokai mashed potatoes, perhaps the best you'll have on Maui; slipper lobster and filet mignon; and our favorite, an appetizer of ahi tartare in a sesame-caper sauce. We also recommend the crisp calamari with spicy Thai fish sauce and the ahi with farfalle in basil, garlic, and tomato. Others have lauded the lamb chops and grill items; whatever you order, save room for the chocolate cake. The 360° view spans the golf course, tennis courts, ocean, and Haleakala. At night, the interior theater lighting highlights the 43-foot copper bar, high ceilings, plank floors, and informal ambience.

✪ **Nick's Fishmarket Maui.** Kea Lani Hotel, 4100 Wailea Alanui Dr. ☎ **808/879-7224.** Reservations recommended. Main courses $23.95–$38. AE, CB, DC, DISC, JCB, MC, V. Daily 5:30–10pm, bar until 11pm. SEAFOOD.

Hawaii's newest Nick's has the perfect balance of visual sizzle and memorable food. What a dining room! The private space with attractive murals seats 50, and the round bar, where you can sit facing the ocean, is highlighted by unobtrusive, minimalist, dangling amber lights that are one of the friendliest touches in the hotel. Stefanotis vines are rapidly creating shade on the terrace, where the sunset views reveal the best of Wailea. We love the onion vichyssoise with taro swirl and a hint of tobiko (flying-fish roe); Maui Wowie Greek salad with hearts of palm, Kula tomatoes, avocados, feta cheese, Maui onions, and rock shrimp; and the mahimahi, done to perfection. Bow-tied waiters and almond-scented cold towels add an extra touch to this ocean-side phenomenon—not to mention the torch lighting at sunset and the lavish wine list.

Pacific Grill. Four Seasons Resort Wailea, 3900 Wailea Alanui Dr. ☎ **808/874-8000.** Main courses $9.25–$24.50 breakfast, $23–$28.50 dinner. AE, CB, DC, DISC, JCB, MC, V. Daily 6–11:30am and 6–9:30pm. HAWAII REGIONAL.

This is a good alternative for those wanting something between very casual and super-luxe. Open for lunch only occasionally, Pacific Grill is the hotel's almost full-service restaurant, serving gourmet breakfasts and smashing dinners ranging from Asian-style steamed snapper to lemongrass mahimahi baked in parchment paper with shiitake mushrooms and spinach. One could dine happily on the starters alone, from the limu kohu ahi poke (cubed ahi with seasonings that include a pungent variety of seaweed) with watercress and fried taro to the scallop and goat cheese wonton.

MODERATE

Caffé Ciao. Kea Lani Hotel, 4100 Wailea Alanui Dr. ☎ **808/875-4100.** Reservations recommended. Main courses $14.95–29.95, pizzas $15–$21. AE, CB, DC, DISC, JCB, MC, V. Daily 11am–10pm, bar until 11pm. ITALIAN.

There are two parts to this charming trattoria: the deli/take-out section and the tables under the trees, next to the bar. Rare and wonderful wines are sold in the deli, along with ultraluxe rose soaps and other bath products, assorted pastas, roasted potatoes, vegetable panini, vegetable lasagna, abundant salads, and an appealing selection of microwavable and take-out goodies for those nights when room service or going out won't do. A standout: chef Massimo's special Italian salsa, made with premium tomatoes and olive oil. On the terrace under the trees, the tables are cheerfully accented with Italian herbs growing in cachepots; there's friendly service to go with the pizzas and pastas. A fave: the linguine pomodoro with fresh tomatoes, spinach-tomato sauce, and a dollop of mascarpone.

SeaWatch. 100 Wailea Golf Club Dr. ☎ **808/875-8080.** Reservations required for dinner. Main courses $4.50–$12 lunch, from $21 dinner. AE, DC, MC, V. Daily 8am–10pm. ISLAND.

SeaWatch's use of fresh Maui produce, Big Island goat cheese, and island fish in ethnic preparations sets it apart from most other upscale clubhouse restaurants, and it's one of the more affordable stops in tony Wailea. Lunchtime sandwiches, pastas, salads, crab cakes, and soups are moderately priced, and you get 360° views to go with them. You'll dine on the terrace or in a high-ceilinged room, on a menu that carries the tee-off-to-19th-hole crowd with ease. Smoked salmon Benedict, Pacific crab cakes, and the fresh-catch sandwich are some of the breakfast and lunchtime stars. At dinner, the nightly fresh catch, which can be ordered in one of three preparations, is a SeaWatch staple. Miso-chili-glazed tiger prawns and rack of lamb in a mango-mustard crust are temptations, but save room for the warm chocolate soufflé and cinnamon ice cream.

MAKENA
EXPENSIVE

✪ **Hakone.** Maui Prince Hotel, 5400 Makena Alanui. ☎ **808/874-1111.** Reservations recommended. Complete dinners $22–$42; Mon night buffet $38, Sun sushi buffet $45; Kaiseki (multicourse Kyoto-style dinners, requiring 24-hr. advance notice) $85. AE, JCB, MC, V. Sun 6–9pm, Mon–Sat 6–9:30pm. JAPANESE.

The Prince Hotels know Japanese cuisine and spared no effort to create a slice of Kyoto in Makena, complete with sandalwood walls and pillars assembled by Japanese craftsmen. Hakone offers Japanese fare, very haute-Kyoto, gorgeously presented, and pricey. The popular Sunday-night sushi buffet and Monday-night Japanese dinner buffet offer a sampling of this elegant cuisine. The Japanese dinner buffet includes sushi, broiled miso butterfish, shrimp tempura, and several salads, as well as pupus, miso soup, and rice. Sashimi, tempura, broiled fish, and other traditional Japanese delicacies are offered on the regular menu.

✪ **Prince Court.** Maui Prince Hotel, 5400 Makena Alanui. ☎ **808/874-1111.** Reservations recommended. Main courses $27–29, Sun brunch $34. AE, JCB, MC, V. Sun 9:30am–1pm, Thurs–Mon 6–9:30pm. HAWAII REGIONAL.

Half of the Sunday brunch experience is the head-turning view of Makena Beach, the crescent-shaped islet called Molokini, and Kahoolawe island. The other half is the lavish buffet, spread over several tables: pasta, omelets, cheeses, pastries, sashimi, crab legs, smoked salmon, fresh Maui produce, and a smashing array of ethnic and continental foods. The dinner menu changes regularly, and although we miss the guava-glazed baby back ribs, the chef's special, which changes weekly, could offer up some pleasant surprises. Chef Greg Gaspar and assistant Eric Leterc are a formidable team, having fun with their Pacific Rim offerings with Mediterranean flavors. If the seafood risotto with poi is on the menu, don't miss it.

4 Upcountry Maui

MAKAWAO
MODERATE

Casanova Italian Restaurant. 1188 Makawao Ave. ☎ **808/572-0220.** Reservations recommended for dinner. Main courses $8–$23, 12-inch pizzas from $10. DC, MC, V. Mon–Sat 11:30am–2pm and 5:30–9pm, Sun 5:30–9pm. Lounge daily 5:30pm–12:30 or 1am. Deli daily 8am–6:30pm. ITALIAN.

Look for the tiny veranda with a few stools, always full, in front of a deli at Makawao's busiest intersection—that's the most visible part of Casanova's restaurant and lounge. Makawao's center of nightlife consists of a stage and dance floor, restaurant, and bar in the split-level dining room next to the deli. This is pasta heaven: spaghetti fra diavolo (seafood in a caper, Greek olive, and tomato sauce), spinach gnocchi in a fresh tomato-Gorgonzola sauce; a huge pizza selection; grilled lamb chops in balsamic vinegar; several types of fresh fish; and luscious desserts. Our personal picks on a stellar menu: garlic spinach topped with Parmesan and pine nuts, polenta with radicchio (the mushrooms and cream sauce are fabulous!), and tiramisu, the best on the island.

Polli's Mexican Restaurant. 1202 Makawao Ave. ☎ **808/572-7808.** Main courses $6–$15. AE, DC, DISC, MC, V. Daily from about 9am (call to see if they're open) to 10pm. MEXICAN.

Sizzling fajitas are the house special, featuring fish, shrimp, chicken, tofu, or steak in a dramatic entrance, on a crackling hot platter with vegetables and spices, six flour tortillas, sour cream, and guacamole—a gargantuan group endeavor. Expect the usual south-of-the-border favorites, from tamales, tacos, and burritos to cheese-, mushroom-, and Mexi-burgers, laced with jalapeños and pepper Jack cheese.

INEXPENSIVE

✪ **Café 'O Lei.** Paniolo Courtyard, 3673 Baldwin Ave. ☎ **808/573-9065.** Sandwiches and salads $4.50–$5.95. No credit cards. Mon–Sat 11am–4pm. AMERICAN/ISLAND.

Dana Pastula managed restaurants at Lanai's Manele Bay Hotel and the Four Seasons Resort Wailea before opening her tiny, charming outdoor cafe in this sunlit sliver of

Makawao. And the alfresco dining is just part of it: From the sandwiches (roast chicken breast, turkey breast, prosciutto) and salads to the soup of the day, the offerings are homemade and excellent. The chic Makawao shopkeepers lunch here daily and never tire of the quinoa salad, the ginger chicken soup, the roasted-beet-and-potato soup, and the talk of the town—a towering Asian salad of Oriental vegetables, tofu, and baby greens, tossed in a sesame vinaigrette with fresh mint, ginger, and lemongrass, and served over Chinese noodles.

Kitada's Kau Kau Corner. 3617 Baldwin Ave. ☎ **808/572-7241.** Lunch plates $3.75–$7.25. No credit cards. Mon–Sat 6am–1:30pm. AMERICAN/JAPANESE.

This is saimin central, a combination of Grandma's kitchen and a cowboy diner known for its paniolo-size servings and tasty saimin. Kitada's plate lunches are legendary, and the dry mein, a heap of noodles, is a cross between saimin and Chinese fried noodles. You'll see everyone from upcountry ranch hands to expensively dressed Makawao ladies digging in. It's a tiny diner, with lots of local color and cheap eats.

HALIIMAILE & PUKALANI

✪ **Haliimaile General Store.** Haliimaile Rd., Haliimaile. ☎ **808/572-2666.** Reservations recommended. Lunch $6–$14, dinner $14–$28. DC, MC, V. Mon–Fri 11am–2:30pm and 5:30–9:30pm, Sat 5:30–9:30pm, Sun 10am–2:30pm (brunch) and 5:30–9:30pm. AMERICAN.

Ten years after opening her foodie haven in the pineapple fields, Bev Gannon, one of the 12 original Hawaii Regional Cuisine chefs, is still going strong. You'll dine at tables set on old wood floors under high ceilings (sound ricochets fiercely here), in a peach-colored room emblazoned with works by local artists. The food, a blend of eclectic American with ethnic touches, manages to avoid the usual pitfalls of Hawaii Regional Cuisine: the same-old, same-old, I'm-bored-with-seared-ahi syndrome. Even the fresh-catch sandwich on the lunch menu is anything but prosaic. The house salad, island greens with Mandarin oranges, onions, toasted walnuts, and blue cheese, is a touch of genius, and the sashimi napoleon (crisp wonton layered with smoked salmon, ahi tartare, and sashimi, served with wasabi vinaigrette) is every bit as delicious as it sounds. Dinner splurges include the Szechuan salmon, Bev's Boboli topped with crab dip, and her famous paniolo ribs in tangy barbecue sauce.

Upcountry Cafe. Andrade Building, 7–2 Aewa Place (just off Haleakala Hwy.), Pukalani. ☎ **808/572-2395.** Lunch $5.95–$8.95, most dinner items under $14.95. MC, V. Mon 6:30am–3pm, Wed–Thurs 6:30am–3pm and 5:30–8:30pm, Fri–Sat 6:30am–3pm and 5:30–9pm, Sun 6:30am–1pm. AMERICAN/LOCAL.

Pukalani's inexpensive, casual, and very popular cafe features cows everywhere: on the walls, chairs, menus, aprons, even the exterior. But the food is the draw: simple, home-cooked comfort food such as meat loaf, roast pork, and humongous hamburgers, plus home-baked bread, oven-fresh muffins, and local faves such as saimin and Chinese chicken salad. Soups and salads (homemade cream of mushroom, Cobb and Caesar salads) and shrimp scampi with bow-tie pasta are among the cafe's other pleasures. The signature dessert is the cow pie, a naughty pile of chocolate cream cheese with macadamia nuts in a cookie crust, shaped like you-know-what.

KULA
EXPENSIVE

Kula Lodge. Haleakala Hwy. (Hwy. 377). ☎ **808/878-2517.** Reservations recommended for dinner. Main courses $7.25–$14 lunch, $18–$26 dinner. MC, V. Daily 6:30am–9pm. HAWAII REGIONAL/AMERICAN.

Don't let the dinner prices scare you, because the Kula Lodge is equally enjoyable, if not more so, for breakfast and lunch, when the prices are lower and the views through the picture windows have an eye-popping intensity. The outdoor dining area with its wood-burning oven is a recent addition, open from 11am daily for as long as the weather permits. The million-dollar view through the large picture windows spans the flanks of Haleakala, rolling 3,200 feet down to central Maui, the ocean, and the West Maui Mountains. If possible, go for sunset cocktails and watch the colors change. When darkness descends, a roaring fire and lodge atmosphere turn the attention to the coziness of the room. At breakfast, the lodge is famous for its banana–macadamia nut pancakes. For lunch, choices include smoked-turkey sandwiches, garden- and mahimahi burgers, soups, salads, seared ahi, and pizza.

INEXPENSIVE

Cafe 808. Lower Kula Rd., past Holy Ghost Church, across Morihara St. ☎ **808/878-6874.** Burgers from $3.50, main courses $4.50–$7.50. No credit cards. Daily 6am–8pm. AMERICAN/ LOCAL.

The owners of the popular Upcountry Cafe opened this Formica-table haven on a quiet road in Kula, and word spread quickly. Despite its out-of-the-way location (or perhaps because of it), Cafe 808 has become the universal favorite among residents of all ages for its tasty, straightforward home-style cooking: chicken lasagna, smoked-salmon omelet, taro burger, beef burrito, roast pork, and a huge selection of local-style specials. Regulars rave about the roast pork, chicken katsu, saimin, and beef stew. The few tables are sprinkled around a room with linoleum tile floors, hardwood benches, plastic patio chairs, and old-fashioned booths.

Grandma's Coffee House. At the end of Hwy. 37, Keokea. ☎ **808/878-2140.** Most items under $8.95. MC, V. Daily 7am–5pm. COFFEEHOUSE/AMERICAN.

Alfred Franco's grandmother started what is now a fifth-generation coffee business back in 1918, when she was 16 years old. Today, the tiny wooden coffeehouse he named after her, still fueled by homegrown Haleakala coffee beans, is the quintessential roadside oasis. About 6 miles before the Tedeschi Vineyards in Ulupalakua, Grandma's is a gathering place for hot and cold espresso drinks, home-baked pastries, inexpensive pasta, sandwiches (including sensational avocado and gardenburgers), homemade soups, fresh juices, and local plate-lunch specials. Aside from the coffee cake, muffins, and cinnamon rolls (all baked fresh daily), rotating specials include Hawaiian beef stew, ginger chicken, saimin, lentil soup, and sandwiches piled high with Kula vegetables.

Kula Sandalwoods Restaurant. Haleakala Hwy. (Hwy. 377). ☎ **808/878-3523.** Most items under $8.75. DISC, MC, V. Mon–Sat 6:30–2pm, Sun 6:30am–noon (brunch). AMERICAN.

The chef, Eleanor Loui, a graduate of the Culinary Institute of America, makes hollandaise sauce every morning from fresh upcountry egg yolks, sweet butter, and Myers lemons, which her family grows in the yard above the restaurant. This is Kula cuisine, with produce from the backyard and everything made from scratch: French toast with home-baked Portuguese sweetbread, crab cakes, hotcakes or Belgian waffles with fresh fruit, French baguettes, grilled teriyaki chicken breast, and an outstanding veggie burger. The Kula Sandalwoods salad features grilled chicken breast with crimson Kula tomatoes and onions and, when the garden allows, just-picked red-oak, curly green, and red-leaf lettuces. The Kula Sandalwoods omelet is an open-faced marvel with cheddar and Jack cheeses, tomatoes, and green onions, served with cottage potatoes— a gourmet treat. And Sunday brunchers will be happy to know that a goat-cheese omelet and crab-cake Benedict have been added to the menu. You'll dine in one of two separate rooms, in the gazebo, or on the terrace, with dazzling views in all directions, including, in the spring, a yard dusted with lavender jacaranda flowers and a hillside ablaze with fields of orange akulikuli blossoms.

5 East Maui: On the Road to Hana

KUAU & PAIA

EXPENSIVE

✪ Mama's Fish House. 799 Poho Place (off the Hana Hwy.), Kuau. ☎ **808/579-8488**. Reservations recommended. Main courses $22.95–$45. AE, CB, DC, JCB, MC, V. Daily 11am–9:30pm.

The restaurant's entrance, a cove with windsurfers, tide pools, white sand, and a canoe resting under palm trees, is a South Seas fantasy reminiscent of Gauguin. The menu and interior complement the setting splendidly, with curved lauhala-lined ceilings, split bamboo on the walls, lavish arrangements of tropical blooms, and picture windows to capture the view. Waiters in ultracool aloha shirts and waitresses with flowers behind their ears serve mai tais and seafood in a sea of pareu prints; for a moment, it feels like Tahiti. But it's Hawaii, which means mahimahi laulau with Kula spinach, baked in ti leaves, with kalua pig and lemongrass rice; mahimahi baked in roasted macadamia nuts, stuffed with shrimp and crab; and several types of fresh catch (monchong, onaga, ahi), offered in four preparations. Sashimi comes in several forms and is an appropriate start to the fish feast. *Hint:* We loved fisherman Mark Hobson's onaga, baked in a mustard crust with Maui onion and herbs.

MODERATE

Jacques Bistro. 89 Hana Hwy. ☎ **808/579-6255.** Reservations recommended. Main courses $8–$19. MC, V. Daily 5–10pm, bar until later. FRENCH/AMERICAN/ISLAND.

Fresh local seafood with a French touch, served in Paia by a chef named Jacques in a room with a 42-foot monkeypod bar and arches, columns, and a garden lanai lush with palms, bromeliads, and towering banyan trees—that's Paia's newest bistro. The owners transformed this site with fresh ideas and a likable chef who whips up diverse, affordable delights: catch of the day (from Paia fishermen), ahi poke, bouillabaisse, sashimi, seviche, steak, duck, and special touches such as seasoned purple potatoes and lightly steamed Kula vegetables. (For light eaters, the gargantuan Greek salad and perfect seviche are starters that equal an entree.) With this setting and menu, they could have jacked up the prices and injected some attitude—but they haven't. When lit up at night, Jacques is an oasis of serenity at Paia's busiest corner.

INEXPENSIVE

Milagros Food Company. Hana Hwy. and Baldwin Ave. ☎ **808/579-8755**. Breakfast about $7, lunch $3–$8, dinner $7–$16. DC, DISC, MC, V. Daily 8am–9:30pm. SOUTHWESTERN/SEAFOOD.

Milagros has gained a following with its great food, upbeat atmosphere, and highly touted margaritas. Although there are fabulous fish tacos, this is much more than Mexican food. Regulars anticipate the fresh ahi creation of the evening, a combination of Southwestern and Pacific Rim styles and flavors accompanied by fresh veggies and Kula greens. Blackened ahi taquitos and pepper-crusted ono pasta are among the new offerings at this Paia hot spot. The bountiful chile rellenos plate comes with grilled ahi, beans, rice, and Kula greens—a sensation, and generous. The daily happy hour features $2.50 margaritas ($12 for a pitcher) from 3 to 6pm. Outdoor seating at this nexus of Paia makes this a great spot for people watching, too.

A Worthy Stop

To find the **Nahiku Coffee Shop, Smoked Fish Stand,** and **Ti Gallery,** watch for mile marker 28 on the Hana Highway (no phone). Pick up locally made baked goods at the small coffee shop, then move on to the main attraction: the cast-iron smoker, which puts out smoked and grilled chicken, beef, and fresh local fish. The teriyaki-based marinade, made by the owner, adds a special touch to the fish (ono, ahi, marlin) and meats, sold for $3 a skewer. These are not jerky-like smoked meats; the process keeps the kebabs moist while retaining the smoke flavor. The bread-fruit—sliced, wrapped in banana leaf, and baked—can be bland and starchy (like a baked potato), but it's a stroke of genius to give visitors a taste of this important Polynesian staple. There are a few roadside picnic tables, or you can take your lunch on to Hana for a beachside picnic. Hours for the coffee shop are daily from 6:30am to 4:30pm; for the fish stand, daily from 10am to 5pm; and for the gallery, daily from 9:30am to 4:30pm.

Paia Fish Market. 110 Hana Hwy. ☎ **808/579-8030.** Lunch and dinner plates $6.95–$18.95. DC, MC, V. Daily 11am–9:30pm. SEAFOOD.

This really is a fish market, with fresh fish to take home and cooked seafood, salads, pastas, fajitas, and quesadillas to take out or enjoy at the few picnic tables inside the restaurant. It's an appealing and budget-friendly selection: Cajun-style fresh catch, fresh fish specials (ahi, salmon), fish tacos and quesadillas, and seafood and chicken pastas. You can also order hamburgers, cheeseburgers, and fish-and-chips (shrimp-and-chips, too), and wonderful lunch and dinner plates, cheap and tasty. Peppering the walls are photos of the number-one sport here, windsurfing.

Pic-nics. 30 Baldwin Ave. ☎ **808/579-8021.** Most items under $6.95. JCB, MC, V. Daily 7am–7pm. SANDWICHES/PICNIC LUNCHES.

Breakfast is terrific here—omelets, eggs to order, Maui Portuguese sausage, Hawaiian pancakes—and so is lunch. Pic-nics is famous for many things, among them the spinach-nut burger, an ingenious vegetarian blend topped with vegetables and cheddar cheese. Stop here to fill your picnic basket for the drive to Hana or upcountry Maui. These are gourmet sandwiches (Kula vegetables, home-baked breast of turkey, Cajun fish) worthy of the most idyllic picnic spot. The rosemary herb–roasted chicken can be ordered as a plate lunch (two scoops of rice and Haiku greens) or as part of the Hana Bay picnic, which includes sandwiches, meats, Maui-style chips, and home-baked cookies and muffins. You can also order old-fashioned fish-and-chips, shrimp-and-chips, or pastries baked fresh daily. Fresh breads from the Maui Bake Shop add to the appeal, and several coffee drinks made with Maui-blend coffee may give you the jolt you need for the drive ahead.

Raw Experience. 42 Baldwin Ave. ☎ **808/579-9729.** Main courses $5.95–$10. MC, V. Mon–Thurs 10am–6pm, Fri–Sun 10am–8pm. VEGAN/JUICE BAR.

Raw Experience gets top marks in our book. This juice bar/restaurant has dispelled most myths about raw food, organic food, and raw organic food—that it's healthful but boring—with a tirelessly creative menu and food that's good for you, visually appealing, and exciting to the palate. You don't have to be a tofu addict to love the hummus made of sprouted chickpeas and herbs, angel-hair pasta made of carrots and beets with a sun-dried tomato–vegetable marinara, and soups ranging from spicy Thai coconut to creamy carrot-ginger broth. For sushi lovers: carrot-almond pâté and sunflower-seed cheese rolled with vegetables and avocado in sun-dried nori. The salads—mounds of

In case you want to be welcomed there.

We're here to see that you're always welcomed at establishments everywhere. That's why millions of people carry the American Express® Card – for peace of mind, confidence, and security, around the world or just around the corner.

do more

Cards

And in case you'd rather be safe than sorry.

We're here with American Express® Travelers Cheques. They're the safe way to carry money on your vacation, because if they're ever lost or stolen you can get a refund, practically anywhere or anytime. To find the nearest place to buy Travelers Cheques, call 1 800 495-1153. Another way we help you do more.

do more **AMERICAN EXPRESS**

Travelers Cheques

fresh and marinated vegetables with zesty dressings—include sprouts, seaweeds, and exotic fruit. The desserts (coconut custard made of coconut-date pudding, carob cake with walnut-lemon crème) and smoothies are anything but boring. Besides the usual roster of fresh-squeezed juices (carrot, beet, ginger, orange), they also serve mango, chirimoya, sapote, sapodilla, jackfruit, and other exotic fruit in season, whipped up into creamy smoothies. Ginger lemonade and coconut water are among the health drinks we love, but others may prefer the "live chai" made from apples and ginger or the Elvis Parsley, made from parsley, cayenne, and orange juice.

The Vegan. 115 Baldwin Ave. ☎ **808/579-9144.** Main courses $4.95–$8.95. MC, V. Daily noon–9pm. GOURMET VEGETARIAN/VEGAN.

Wholesome foods with ingenious soy substitutes and satisfying flavors appear on a menu that dares you to feel deprived. Not here! Pad Thai garlic noodles are the best-selling item, cooked in a creamy coconut sauce and generously seasoned with garlic and spices. Curries, grilled polenta, pepper steak made of seitan (a meat substitute), and organic hummus are among the items that draw vegetarians from around the island. Proving that desserts are justly deserved, the Vegan offers a carob cake and coconut milk–flavored tapioca pudding that hints of Thailand yet doesn't contain dairy milk.

HAIKU

✪ **Pauwela Cafe.** 375 W. Kuiaha Rd. ☎ **808/575-9242.** Most items under $6. No credit cards. Mon–Sat 7am–3pm, Sun 8am–2pm. INTERNATIONAL.

It's a long drive from anywhere, but the kalua turkey sandwich is reason enough for the journey. Because it's located in an industrial center of sailboard and surfboard manufacturers, you may find a surf legend dining at the next table. For many reasons, the tiny cafe with concrete floors and six tables has a strong local following. Becky Speere, a gifted chef, and her husband, Chris, a food-service instructor at Maui Community College and a former sous chef at the Maui Prince Hotel, infuse every sandwich, salad, and muffin with a high degree of culinary finesse. We never dreamed we could dine so well with such pleasing informality. The scene-stealing kalua turkey is one success layered upon another: warm, smoky, moist shredded turkey, served with cheese on home-baked French bread and covered with a green-chile and cilantro sauce. It gets our vote as the best sandwich on the island. The salads, too, are fresh and uncomplicated, served with homemade dressings. For breakfast, eggs chilaquile are a good starter, with layers of corn tortillas, pinto beans, chiles, cheese, and herbs, topped with egg custard and served hot with salsa and sour cream—the works, for an unbelievable $5.50. All the breads are baked on the premises—French baguette, Scottish oat, whole wheat, English muffins—and served in broke-the-mouth sandwiches, such as the roasted eggplant with aged provolone.

6 At the End of the Road in East Maui: Hana

Hana Ranch Restaurant. Hana Hwy. ☎ **808/248-8255.** Reservations required Fri–Sat. Main courses $16.95–$34.95. AE, DC, DISC, JCB, MC, V. Restaurant daily 7am–10am and 11am–3pm, Fri–Sat 6–8pm. Take-out counter daily 6:30–10am and 11am–4pm. AMERICAN.

Part of the Hotel Hana-Maui operation, the Hana Ranch Restaurant is the informal alternative to the hotel's dining room. In fact, it's the only other dining room in Hana. Dinner choices include New York steak; prawns and pasta; and a few Pacific Rim options, such as spicy shrimp wontons and the predictable fresh-fish poke. Aside from the weekly, warmly received Wednesday Pizza Night, the luncheon buffet is a more affordable prospect: baked mahimahi, pocket pita sandwiches ($7.95 to $10.95), chicken stir-fry, club and fresh catch sandwiches, and cheeseburgers. It's not an inspired menu, and the service can be nonexistent—especially when the tour buses descend during the lunch rush. There are indoor tables as well as two outdoor pavilions that offer ocean views. At the take-out stand adjoining the restaurant, the fast-food classics prevail: teriyaki plate lunch, mahimahi sandwich, cheeseburgers, hot dogs, and ice cream.

Fun in the Surf & Sun

6

by Jeanette Foster

This is why you have come to Maui—the sun, the sand, the surf. In this chapter, we'll tell you about the best beaches, from where to go to soak up the rays to the best place to plunge beneath the waves for a fish's-eye view of the underwater world. We've covered a range of ocean activities on Maui, as well as our favorite places and operators for these marine adventures. Also in this chapter are things to do on dry land: the best spots for hiking and camping, the greatest golf courses, and the lowdown on other outdoor activities.

1 Beaches

Maui has more than 80 accessible beaches of every conceivable description, from rocky black-sand beaches to powdery golden sands; there's even a rare red-sand beach. What follows is a selection of the finest of Maui's beaches, carefully chosen to suit a variety of needs, tastes, and interests.

For beach toys and equipment, contact **Rental Warehouse,** in Lahaina at 578 Front St., near Prison Street (☎ **808/661-1970**), or in Kihei at Azeka Place II, on the mountain side of Kihei Road near Lipoa Street (☎ **808/875-4050**). Beach chairs rent for $2 a day, coolers (with ice!) for $2 a day, and a host of toys (Frisbees, volleyballs, and more) for $1 a day.

WEST MAUI
✪ D. T. FLEMING BEACH PARK

This quiet, out-of-the-way beach cove, named after the man who started the commercial growing of pineapple on the Valley Isle, is a great place to take the family. The crescent-shaped beach, located north of the Ritz-Carlton Hotel, starts at the 16th hole of the Kapalua golf course (Makaluapuna Point) and rolls around to the sea cliffs at the other side. Ironwood trees provide shade on the land side. Offshore, a shallow sandbar extends to the edge of the surf. The waters are generally good for swimming and snorkeling; sometimes, off on the right side near the sea cliffs, the waves build enough for bodyboarders and surfers to get a few good rides in. This park has lots of facilities: rest rooms, showers, picnic tables, barbecue grills, and a paved parking lot.

Beaches & Outdoor Pursuits

Cabins & Campgrounds
Holua Cabin & Campground ⑬
Hosmer Grove ⑫
Kapalaoa Cabin ⑮
Oheo Campground ⑱
Paliku Cabin & Campground ⑯
Polipoli Springs State Recreation Area Campground ⑩
Polipoli State Park ⑩
Waianapanapa State Park Cabins & Campground ㉑

Golf Courses
Kaanapali Courses ②
Kapalua Resort Courses ①
Makena Courses ⑥
Pukalani Country Club ⑦
Silversword Golf Club ④
Waiehu Municipal Golf Course ③
Wailea Courses ⑤

Hikes
Fagan's Cross ⑲
Halemauu Trail ⑭
Hana-Waianapanapa Coastal Trail ⑳
Hosmer Grove Nature Trail ⑫
Kaupo Gap ⑰
Polipoli Loop ⑨
Skyline Trail ⑧
Sliding Sands Trail ⑪

✪ Kapalua Beach

The beach cove that fronts the Kapalua Bay Hotel is the stuff of dreams: a golden crescent bordered by two palm-studded points. The sandy bottom slopes gently to deep water at the bay mouth; the water is so clear that you can see where the gold sands turn to green, and then deep blue. Protected from strong winds and currents by the lava-rock promontories, Kapalua's calm waters are great for snorkelers and swimmers of all ages and abilities, and the bay is big enough to paddle a kayak around without getting into the more challenging channel that separates Maui from Molokai. Waves come in just right for riding. Fish hang out by the rocks, making it great for snorkeling. The beach is accessible from the hotel on one end, which provides sun chairs with shades and a beach-activities center for its guests, and a public access way on the other. It isn't so wide that you'll burn your feet getting in or out of the water, and the inland side is edged by a shady path and cool lawns. Outdoor showers are stationed at both ends. Parking is limited to about 30 spaces in a small lot off Lower Honoapiilani Road, by Napili Kai Beach Club, so arrive early; next door is a nice but somewhat pricey oceanfront restaurant, Kapalua's Bay Club (see chapter 5 for a review). Facilities include showers, rest rooms, lifeguards, rental shack, and plenty of shade.

✪ Kaanapali Beach

Four-mile-long Kaanapali is one of Maui's best beaches, with grainy gold sand as far as the eye can see. The beach parallels the sea channel through most of its length, and a paved beach walk links hotels and condos, open-air restaurants, and Whalers Village shopping center. Because Kaanapali is so long and most hotels have adjacent swimming pools, the beach is crowded only in pockets—there's plenty of room to find seclusion. Summertime swimming is excellent. The best snorkeling is around Black Rock, in front of the Sheraton; the water is clear, calm, and populated with clouds of tropical fish. Facilities include outdoor showers; you can use the rest rooms at the hotel pools. Various beach-activity vendors line up in front of the hotels, offering nearly every type of water activity and equipment. Parking is a problem, though. There are two public entrances: At the south end, turn off Honoapiilani Highway into the Kaanapali Resort, and pay for parking there; or continue on Honoapiilani Highway, turn off at the last Kaanapali exit at the stoplight near the Maui Kaanapali Villas, and park next to the beach signs indicating public access.

Wahikuli County Wayside Park

This small stretch of beach, adjacent to Honoapiilani Highway between Lahaina and Kaanapali, is one of Lahaina's most popular beach parks. It's packed on weekends, but during the week it's a great place for swimming, snorkeling, sunbathing, and picnics. Offshore, the bottom is composed of rocks and sand, gradually sloping down to deeper water. Facilities include paved parking, rest rooms, showers, and small covered pavilions with picnic tables and barbecue grills.

Launiupoko County Wayside Park

Families with children will love this small park off Honoapiilani Highway, just south of Lahaina. A large artificial wading pool for kids fronts the shady park, with giant boulders protecting the wading area from the surf outside. Just to the left is a small sandy beach with good swimming when conditions are right. Offshore, the waves are occasionally big enough for surfing. The view from the park is one of the best: You can see the islands of Kahoolawe, Lanai, and Molokai in the distance. Facilities include paved parking lot, rest rooms, showers, picnic tables, and barbecue grills. It's crowded on weekends.

SOUTH MAUI
KAMAOLE III BEACH PARK

Three beach parks—Kamaole I, II, and III—stand like golden jewels in the front yard of the funky seaside town of Kihei, which all of a sudden is sprawling like suburban blight. The beaches are the best thing about Kihei (if you don't count A Pacific Cafe Maui—see chapter 5 for a review). All three are popular with local residents and visitors because they're easily accessible. On weekends they're jam-packed with fishers, picnickers, swimmers, and snorkelers. The most popular is Kamaole III, or "Kam-3," as locals say. The biggest of the three beaches, with wide pockets of golden sand, it's the only one with a playground for children and a grassy lawn that meets the sand. Swimming is safe here, but scattered lava rocks are toe stubbers at the water line, and parents should watch to make sure that kids don't venture too far out, because the bottom slopes off quickly. Both the north and south shores are rocky fingers with a surge big enough to attract fish and snorkelers, and the winter waves attract body-surfers. Kam-3 is also a wonderful place to watch the sunset. Facilities include rest rooms, showers, picnic tables, barbecue grills, and lifeguards. There's also plenty of parking on South Kihei Road, across from the Maui Parkshore condos.

✪ WAILEA BEACH

Wailea, which means "water of Lea," the Hawaiian goddess of canoe makers, is the best golden-sand crescent on Maui's sunbaked southwestern coast. One of five beaches within Wailea Resort, Wailea is big, wide, and protected on both sides by black lava points. It's the front yard of the Four Seasons Wailea and the Grand Wailea Resort Hotel and Spa, respectively Maui's most elegant and outrageous beach hotels. From the beach, the view out to sea is magnificent, framed by neighboring Kahoolawe and Lanai and the tiny crescent of Molokini, probably the most popular snorkel spot in these parts. The clear waters tumble to shore in waves just the right size for gentle riding, with or without a board. From shore, you can see Pacific humpback whales in season (December through April), and unreal sunsets nightly. Facilities include rest rooms, outdoor showers, and limited free parking at the blue SHORELINE ACCESS sign, on Wailea Alanui Drive, the main drag of this resort. Wailea Resort's beaches might seem off-limits, hidden from plain view by an intimidating wall of luxury resorts, but they're all open to the public.

ULUA BEACH

One of the most popular beaches in Wailea, Ulua is a long, wide, crescent-shaped gold-sand beach between two rocky points. When the ocean is calm, Ulua offers Wailea's best snorkeling; when it's rough, the waves are excellent for bodysurfers. The ocean bottom is shallow and gently slopes down to deeper waters, making swimming generally safe. The beach is usually occupied by guests of nearby resorts; in high season (from Christmas to March and June to August), it's carpeted with beach towels and packed with sunbathers like sardines in cocoa butter. Facilities include showers and rest rooms. A variety of equipment is available for rent at the nearby Wailea Ocean Activity Center. To find Ulua, look for the new blue SHORELINE ACCESS sign on South Kihei Road, near Stouffer Wailea Beach Resort. A tiny parking lot is nearby.

✪ MALUAKA BEACH (MAKENA BEACH)

On the southern end of Maui's resort coast, development falls off dramatically, leaving a wild, dry countryside of green kiawe trees. The Maui Prince sits in isolated splendor, sharing Makena Resort's 1,800 acres with only a couple of first-rate golf courses and a necklace of perfect beaches. The strand nearest the hotel is Maluaka Beach, often called Makena, notable for its beauty and its views of Molokini Crater, the offshore islet, and Kahoolawe, the so-called "target" island. It's a short, wide, palm-fringed crescent of golden, grainy sand set between two black-lava points and bounded by big sand dunes topped by a grassy knoll. Swimming in this mostly calm bay is considered the best on Makena Bay, which is bordered on the south by Puu Olai cinder cone and historic Keawala'i Congregational Church. Facilities include rest rooms, showers, a landscaped park, lifeguards, and roadside parking. Along Makena Alanui, look for the SHORELINE ACCESS sign near the hotel, turn right, and head down to the shore.

ONELOA BEACH (BIG BEACH)
Oneloa, which means "long sand" in Hawaiian, is one of the most popular beaches on Maui. Locals call it Big Beach—it's 3,300 feet long and more than 100 feet wide. Mauians come here to swim, fish, sunbathe, surf, and enjoy the view of Kahoolawe and Lanai. Snorkeling is good around the north end at the foot of Puu Olai, a 360-foot cinder cone. During storms, however, big waves lash the shore and a strong rip current sweeps the sharp drop-off, posing a danger for inexperienced open-ocean swimmers. There are no facilities except portable toilets, but there's plenty of parking. To get here, drive past the Maui Prince Hotel to the second dirt road, which leads through a kiawe thicket to the beach.

On the other side of Puu Olai is **Little Beach,** a small pocket beach where assorted nudists work on their all-over tans, to the chagrin of uptight authorities who take a dim view of public nudity. You can get a real nasty sunburn and a lewd-conduct ticket, too.

EAST MAUI
BALDWIN PARK
Located off the Hana Highway between Sprecklesville and Paia, this popular beach park is well used by Maui residents, especially bodyboard enthusiasts. Named after Harry Baldwin, who was a delegate to Congress, the park was originally developed for the employees of Hawaiian Commercial & Sugar Co., who lived in the nearby area. In 1963, the company turned the park over to the county. It's easy to see why this place is so popular: The surf breaks along the entire length of the white-sand beach, creating perfect conditions for bodyboarding. On occasion, the waves get big enough for surfing. A couple of swimming areas are safe enough for children: one in the lee of the beach rocks near the large pavilion, and another at the opposite end of the beach, where beach rocks protect a small swimming area. There's a large pavilion with picnic tables and kitchen facilities, barbecue grills, additional picnic tables on the grassy area, rest rooms, showers, a semipaved parking area, a baseball diamond, and a soccer field. The park is well used on weekends; weekdays are much quieter.

HOOKIPA BEACH PARK
Two miles past Paia, on the Hana Highway, you'll find one of the most famous windsurfing sites in the world. Due to constant wind and endless waves, Hookipa attracts top windsurfers and wave jumpers from around the globe. Surfers and fishermen also enjoy this small, gold-sand beach at the foot of a grassy cliff, which provides a natural amphitheater for spectators. Except when international competitions are being held, weekdays are the best time to watch the daredevils fly over the waves. When the water is flat, snorkelers and divers explore the reef. Facilities include rest rooms, showers, pavilions, picnic tables, barbecue grills, and a parking lot.

✪ WAIANAPANAPA STATE PARK
Four miles before Hana, off the Hana Highway, is this beach park, which takes its name from the legend of the Waianapanapa Cave, where Chief Kaakea, a jealous and

---

Safety Tip

Be sure to see the section "Staying Healthy," in chapter 2, before setting out on your Maui adventures. It includes useful information on hiking, camping, and ocean safety, plus how to avoid seasickness. Even if you just plan to lie on the beach, take a look at our tips on tanning—and what to do should you get stung by a jellyfish.

---

cruel man, suspected his wife, Popoalaea, of having an affair. Popoalaea left her husband and hid herself in a chamber of the Waianapanapa Cave. She and her attendant ventured out only at night, for food. Nevertheless, a few days later, Kaakea was passing by the area and saw the shadow of the servant. Knowing he had found his wife's hiding place, Kaakea entered the cave and killed her. During certain times of the year, the water in the tide pool turns red as a tribute to Popoalaea, commemorating her death. Scientists claim, however, that the change in color is due to the presence of small red shrimp.

Waianapanapa State Park's 120 acres have 12 cabins, a caretaker's residence, a beach park, picnic tables, barbecue grills, rest rooms, showers, a parking lot, a shoreline hiking trail, and a black-sand beach (it's actually small black pebbles). This is a wonderful area for both shoreline hikes (bring insect repellent, as the mosquitoes are plentiful) and picnicking. Swimming is generally unsafe, though, due to powerful rip currents and strong waves breaking offshore, which roll into the beach unchecked. Because Waianapanapa is crowded on weekends with local residents and their families, as well as tourists, weekdays are generally a better bet.

✪ HAMOA BEACH

This half moon–shaped, gray-sand beach (a mix of coral and lava) in a truly tropical setting is a favorite among sunbathers seeking rest and refuge. The Hotel Hana-Maui maintains the beach and acts as though it's private, which it isn't—so just march down those lava-rock steps and grab a spot on the sand. James Michener said of Hamoa, "Paradoxically, the only beach I have ever seen that looks like the South Pacific was in the North Pacific—Hamoa Beach . . . a beach so perfectly formed that I wonder at its comparative obscurity." The 100-foot-wide beach is three football fields long and sits below 30-foot black-lava sea cliffs. An unprotected beach open to the ocean, Hamoa is often swept by powerful rip currents. Surf breaks offshore and rolls ashore, making this a popular surfing and bodysurfing area. The calm left side is best for snorkeling in summer. The hotel has numerous facilities for guests; there's an outdoor shower and rest rooms for nonguests. Parking is limited. Look for the Hamoa Beach turnoff from Hana Highway.

---

2 Hitting the Water

Maui is a haven for every type of water activity for enthusiasts of all kinds, from windsurfers twirling in the ocean breezes to beginners donning a mask and snorkel for the first time to view the dazzling array of underwater life. You can skim across the water on a fast-moving sailing boat, plunge beneath the waves in a high-tech submarine, or soar above the water in a parasail. Whatever your interest, you'll find it on Maui.

BOATING & SAILING

To really appreciate Maui, you need to get off the land and get on the sea. Trade winds off the Lahaina Coast and the strong wind that rips through Maui's isthmus make sailing around the island exciting. Many different boats, from a three-masted schooner to spacious trimarans, offer day cruises from Maui.

For fishing charters, see "Sportfishing," below. For trips that combine snorkeling with whale watching, see "Whale-Watching Cruises," below.

You can experience the thrill of competition sailing with **World Class Yacht Charters,** 107 Kahului Heliport, Kahului, HI 96732 (☎ **800/600-0959** or 808/ 667-7733). There's nothing like it, especially when all you have to do is hold on and cheer. *World Class,* a 65-foot custom yacht designed for Maui waters, takes 24 passengers for a variety of sailing adventures: 2-hour whale-watching tours for $25; 4-hour morning snorkel sails for $59; high-performance sails for $35; and a 2-hour trade-winds sunset sail for $45. The 2pm high-performance sailing tour is the most exciting. Be prepared to get wet: The captain and crews of this cutter-rigged, high-tech yacht are serious about sailing. All trips leave from Kaanapali Beach.

You can also take a ride on *America II,* Lahaina Harbor, slip 5 (☎ **888/667-2133** or 808/667-2195), a U.S. contender in the America's Cup. It's a true racing boat: no snorkeling, just the thrill of racing the wind. Trips include a morning whale-watching sail, an afternoon sail, and a sunset sail. Each trip lasts 2 hours and costs $29.95 to $32.95 for adults, $14.95 to $16.48 for children ages 6 to 12; free for children 5 and under.

SNORKEL CRUISES TO MOLOKINI

If you'd like take a snorkel boat to Molokini (see "Snorkeling" and "An Expert Shares His Secrets: Maui's Best Dives," below), call the **Ocean Activities Center,** 1847 S. Kihei Rd., Kihei (☎ **800/798-0652** or 808/879-4485), which also operates out of a number of hotels and condos. The best deal is the Maka Kai cruise, which includes continental breakfast, deli lunch, snorkel gear, and instruction; it's $55 for adults, $35 for children ages 3 to 12. The 5-hour cruise departs from Maalaea Harbor, slip 62, at 7am.

You can also try **Maui Classic Charters** (☎ **800/736-5740** or 808/879-8188; www.mauicharters.com). Its snorkel-sail cruises on the 63-foot *Lavengro* leave Maalaea, slip 80, at 7am for a 6-hour journey that includes continental breakfast and deli lunch; it costs $59 for adults and $40 for children under 12. This outfitter also has a new boat, *Four Winds II,* a 55-foot glass-bottom catamaran, which offers both 5-hour snorkel trips ($69 for adults, $45 for children ages 3 to 12) and 3½- hour trips ($40 for adults, $30 for children) with a naturalist on board during whale season.

For an action-packed snorkel-sail experience, check out *Pride of Maui,* which operates out of Maalaea Harbor (☎ **808/875-0955**). The 5½-hour cruises not only go to Molokini, but also stop at Turtle Bay, off the cost of the Maui Prince Hotel, and in Makena, for more snorkeling. Continental breakfast, barbecue lunch, gear, and instruction are included in the price: $76 for adults, $69 for kids 13 to 17, $49 for kids 3 to 12, and free for kids under 3.

DAY CRUISES TO MOLOKAI

The *Lahaina Princess,* Lahaina Harbor, slip 3 (☎ **800/275-6969** or 808/667-6165; fax 808/661-5792; www.maui.net/~ismarine), a 65-foot, 149-passenger yacht, sails from Lahaina to Kaunakakai, Molokai, offering visitors four different options: the Walking Tour (boat passage only), the Cruise Drive Tour (boat passage and rental car), the Alii Tour (boat passage, guided van tour, and lunch), and the Overnight Trip (boat passage and overnight stay at Kaluakoi Resort). Prices range from $73 for the Walking Tour ($37 for children ages 3 to 12) to $169 per person for the Overnight Trip, double occupancy. Trips are offered on Tuesday and Thursday from April to mid-December, and on Saturday only from mid-December to April.

A Sightseeing Tip

Check out **"The Natural World: An Environmental Guide to Maui,"** in the appendix at the back of this book, to learn about the many varieties of flowers, fruit trees, birds, and animals you may spot during your vacation on Maui.

DAY CRUISES TO LANAI

Hop aboard ✪ **Trilogy Excursions'** 50-foot catamaran for a 90-minute sail to Lanai and a fun-filled day of sailing, snorkeling, swimming, and whale watching. This is the only cruise that offers a personalized ground tour of the island. Breakfast (homemade cinnamon buns and freshly brewed Kona coffee) and lunch (a Hawaiian barbecue) are included. The trip is $159 for adults, $79.50 for children ages 3 to 12, and free for children under 3—we think it's worth every penny. Call ☎ **800/874-2666** or 808/661-4743, or point your browser to www.sailtrilogy.com.

The ✪ **Expeditions Lahaina/Lanai Passenger Ferry** (☎ **808/661-3756**) will take you from Maui to Lanai and back for $50 round-trip. The ferry services run daily, five times a day. Before you go, contact **Red Rover** (☎ **87-RED ROVER or** 808/565-7722; www.onlanai.com/rover.htm) or **Lanai City Service** (☎ **800/800-4000** or 808/ 565-7227) to arrange vehicle and equipment rentals or rides (see chapter 11).

A day with **Club Lanai** (☎ **808/871-1144**) consists of a catamaran trip departing from Lahaina Harbor, slip 4, at 7:30am to Lanai's eastern shore, where you can spend the day snorkeling, kayaking, bicycling, and relaxing in a hammock at an 8-acre beachfront estate. An all-you-can-eat buffet lunch and an open bar are included in the cost: $89 for adults, $69 for children ages 13 to 20, $29 for children ages 4 to 12, and free for children 3 and under.

Scotch Mist (☎ **808/661-0386**), a 50-foot Santa Cruz sailboat anchored in Lahaina Harbor, slip 9, offers half-day sail-snorkel cruises to Lanai; you won't actually set foot on Lanai, but you'll swim with the fish in its sparkling offshore waters. The price—$70 for adults, $49 for children ages 5 to 11, and free for kids under 4—includes snorkel gear, fruit juice, fresh pineapple spears, Maui chips, beer, wine, and soda.

For an amazingly smooth, stable, and swift ride, call *Maui Nui Explorer* (☎ **800/ 852-4183** or 808/873-3475). This 48-foot, 49-passenger adventure craft leaves Lahaina Harbor for a 4-hour journey along the coast of Lanai, where you'll be able to swim and snorkel in remote coves and bays. Coffee, juice, and a deli-style lunch (sandwiches, Maui chips, fresh fruit, and cookies) are included, along with snacks, snorkel gear, and whale watching (in season). There's always a Hawaiian cultural specialist/marine-life expert on board to answer questions about the islands and their surrounding waters. The cost is $65 for adults and $45.50 for children ages 5 to 11.

BODYBOARDING (BOOGIE BOARDING) & BODYSURFING

Bodysurfing—riding the waves without a board, becoming one with the rolling water—is a way of life in Hawaii. Some bodysurfers just rely on their outstretched hands (or hands at their sides) to ride the waves; others use handboards (flat, paddle-like gloves).

For additional maneuverability, try a boogie or bodyboard (also known as belly boards or *paipo* boards). These 3-foot-long vehicles, which support the upper part of your body, are easy to carry and very maneuverable in the water. Both bodysurfing and bodyboarding require a pair of open-heeled swim fins to help propel you through the water. Both kinds of wave riding are very popular in the islands because the equipment is inexpensive and easy to carry, and both sports can be practiced in the small, gentle waves.

You can rent boogie boards and fins for $6.50 a day or $26 a week from **Snorkel Bob's** (www.snorkelbob.com), open from 8am to 5pm daily at two locations: Napili Village Hotel, 5425 Lower Honoapiilani Rd., Napili (☎ **808/669-9603**); and 161 Lahainaluna Rd., Lahaina (☎ **808/661-4421**). They're also available for rent from **West Hawaii Surfing Academy,** 658 Front St. (in front of the Wharf Cinema Center and across the street from the Banyan Tree), Lahaina (☎ **808/667-5399**), for $5 for 2 hours. The cheapest place to rent boogie boards is **Rental Warehouse,** in Lahaina at 578 Front St., near Prison Street (☎ **808/661-1970**), or in Kihei at Azeka Place II, on the mountain side of Kihei Road, near Lipoa Street (☎ **808/875-4050**), where they go for as little as $2 a day.

Baldwin Beach, just outside of Paia, has great bodysurfing waves nearly year-round. In winter, Maui's best bodysurfing spot is **Mokuleia Beach,** known locally as Slaughterhouse because of the cattle slaughterhouse that once stood here, not because of the waves—although they are definitely for expert bodysurfers only. To get to Mokuleia, take Honoapiilani Highway just past Kapalua Bay Resort; various hiking trails will take you down to the pocket beach.

Storms from the south bring fair bodysurfing conditions and great boogie boarding to the lee side of Maui: **Oneloa** (Big Beach) in Makena, **Ulua** and **Kamaole III** in Kihei, and **Kapalua** beaches are all good choices.

OCEAN KAYAKING

Gliding silently over the water, propelled by a paddle, seeing Maui from the sea the way the early Hawaiians did—that's what ocean kayaking is all about. One of Maui's best kayak routes is along the Kihei Coast, where there's easy access to calm water. Mornings are always best, because the wind comes up around 11am, making seas choppy and paddling difficult.

Kayak rentals are available for $15 per hour from **West Hawaii Surfing Academy,** 658 Front St. (in front of the Wharf Cinema Center and across the street from the Banyan Tree), Lahaina (☎ **808/667-5399**). The island's cheapest kayak rentals are at **Rental Warehouse,** in Lahaina at 578 Front St., near Prison Street (☎ **808/ 661-1970**), or in Kihei at Azeka Place II, on the mountain side of Kihei Road, near Lipoa Street (☎ **808/875-4050**), where one-person kayaks are $10 a day and two-person kayaks are $15 a day.

For the uninitiated, our favorite kayak-tour operator is **Makena Kayak Tours** (☎ **808/879-8426**). Professional guide Dino leads the 2½-hour tour from Makena Landing and loves taking first-time kayakers over the secluded coral reefs and into remote coves. His wonderful tour will be the highlight of your trip; it costs $55 per person, including refreshments and snorkel and kayak equipment.

Gordon Godfrey, Suzanne Simmons, and the expert guides of **South Pacific Kayaks,** 2439 S. Kihei Rd., Kihei, HI 96753 (☎ **800/776-2326** or 808/875-4848; fax 808/875-4691; www.maui.net/~kayak), are Maui's oldest kayak-tour company. They offer ocean kayak tours that include lessons, a guided tour, and snorkeling. Tours run from 2½ to 5 hours and range in price from $59 to $89. Kayak rentals start at $20 a day.

In Hana, **Hana Bay Kayak and Snorkel Tours** (☎ **808/248-7711**) runs 2½-hour tours of Hana's coastline on wide, stable "no roll" kayaks (plus snorkeling) for $59 per person. You can also spend a day learning how to kayak-surf with an instructor for $79 for 7 hours—or rent your own kayak for $27.50 per hour.

OCEAN RAFTING

If you're semiadventurous and looking for a more intimate experience with the sea, try ocean rafting. The inflatable rafts hold 6 to 24 passengers, and tours usually include snorkeling and coastal cruising. One of the best (and most reasonable) outfitters is **Hawaiian Ocean Raft,** P.O. Box 381, Lahaina, HI 96761 (☎ **888/677-RAFT** or 808/667-2191; fax 808/878-3574; www.ocean-rafting.com), which operates out of the Lahaina Harbor. The best deal here is the 5-hour morning tour, which heads over to Lanai, goes searching for dolphins, and includes two snorkeling stops; it costs $69 for adults, $49 for children ages 5 to 12 (children under 5 ride free). The all-day (8am to 4pm) tour with eight snorkel stops and lunch costs $109 for adults and $79 for children ages 5 to 12.

PARASAILING

Soar high above the crowds (at around 400 feet) for a bird's-eye view of Maui. This ocean adventure sport, which is something of a cross between skydiving and water-skiing, involves sailing through the air, suspended under a large parachute attached by a tow line to a speedboat. Keep in mind, though, that parasailing tours don't run during whale season, which is roughly December through May.

We recommend **UFO Parasail** (☎ **800/FLY-4-UFO** or 808/661-7UFO; www.ufoparasail.com), which picks you up at Kaanapali Beach. The Early Bird Special (arrive by 7am) costs $37 (as opposed to $42) for a 7-minute ride. During whale season, the company converts its 37-foot speedboat into a whale-watching machine, and offers 1½-hour whale-watching trips for $25 per person.

SCUBA DIVING

Some people come to Maui for the sole purpose of plunging into the tropical Pacific and exploring the underwater world. You can see the great variety of tropical marine life (more than 100 endemic species found nowhere else on the planet), explore sea caves, and swim with sea turtles and monk seals in the clear tropical waters off the island.

We recommend going early in the morning. Trade winds often rough up the seas in the afternoon, so most dive operators schedule early morning dives that end at noon, and then take the rest of the day off.

Unsure about scuba diving? Take an introductory dive; most operators offer no-experience-necessary dives, ranging from $70 to $95. You can learn from this glimpse into the sea world whether diving is for you.

Everyone dives **Molokini,** a marine-life park and one of Hawaii's top dive spots. This crescent-shaped crater has three tiers of diving: a 35-foot plateau inside the crater basin (used by beginning divers and snorkelers), a wall sloping to 70 feet just beyond the inside plateau, and a sheer wall on the outside and backside of the crater that plunges 350 feet. This underwater park is very popular thanks to calm, clear, protected waters and an abundance of marine life, from manta rays to clouds of yellow butterfly fish.

If you're interested in the marine environment and natural history, call **Mike Severns Diving,** P.O. Box 627, Kihei (☎ **808/879-6596;** www.severns.maui.hi.us), for small (12-person maximum, divided into two groups of six people each), personal diving tours on his 38-foot Munson/Hammerhead boat with freshwater shower. Mike and his wife, Pauline Fiene-Severns, are both biologists who make diving not only fun, but also educational (they have a spectacular underwater photography book called *Molokini Island*). In their 20-plus years of operation, they have been accident-free. Two-tank dives are $100 without equipment ($109 with equipment).

If the Severns are booked, contact **Ed Robinson's Diving Adventures** (☎ **800/635-1273** or 808/879-3584; fax 808/874-1939; www.mauiscuba.com), another great dive operator. Ed is a widely published underwater photographer who offers specialized

An Expert Shares His Secrets: Maui's Best Dives

Ed Robinson, of Ed Robinson's Diving Adventures (see above), knows what makes a great dive. Here are some of his favorites on Maui—and he'll be happy to take you to any or all of them:

Hawaiian Reef   This area off the Kihei-Wailea coast is so named because it hosts a good cross-section of topography and marine life typical of Hawaiian waters. Diving to depths of 85 feet, you'll see everything from lava formations and coral reef to sand and rubble, plus a diverse range of both shallow and deepwater creatures. You'll see for yourself why this area was so popular with ancient Hawaiian fishermen: Large helmet shells, a healthy garden of large antler coral heads, and large schools of snapper are common.

❸Third Tank   Located off Makena Beach at 80 feet, this World War II tank is one of the most picturesque artificial reefs you're likely to see around Maui. It acts like a fish magnet: Because it's the only large solid object in the area, any fish or invertebrate looking for a safe home comes here. Surrounding the tank is a cloak of schooling snapper and goat fish just waiting for a photographer with a wide-angle lens. For its small size, the Third Tank is loaded with more marine life per square inch than any other site off Maui.

Molokini Crater   The backside is always done as a live boat drift dive. The vertical wall plummets from over 150 feet above sea level to around 250 feet below. Looking down to unseen depths gives you some idea of the vastness of the open ocean. Pelagic fish and sharks are often sighted, and living coral perches on the wall, which is home to lobsters, crabs, and a number of photogenic black coral trees at 50 feet.

There are actually two great dive sites around Molokini crater. Named after common chub or rudder fish, **Enenue Side** gently slopes from the surface to

charters for small groups. Most of his business comes from repeat customers. Ed offers two-tank dives for $104 ($10 extra for equipment); his dive boats depart from Kihei boat ramp.

Maui's largest diving retailer, with everything from rentals to scuba-diving instruction to dive-boat charters, is **Maui Dive Shop** (www.mauidiveshop.com or www.scubasales.com), which can be found all over the island: in Kihei at Azeka Place II Shopping Center (☎ **808/879-1919**), Kamaole Shopping Center (☎ **808/879-1533**), and 1455 S. Kihei Road ☎ **808/879-3388**); in Lahaina at Lahaina Cannery Mall (☎ **808/661-5388**); and in the Honokowai Market Place (☎ **808/661-6166**). Other locations include Wailea Shopping Village (☎ **808/879-3166**); Whalers Village, Kaanapali (☎ **808/661-5117**); and Kahana Gateway, Kahana (☎ **808/669-3800**).

SNORKELING

Snorkeling is the main attraction in Maui—and almost anyone can do it. All you need are a mask, a snorkel, fins, and some basic swimming skills. Floating over underwater worlds through colorful clouds of tropical fish is like a dream. In many places, all you have to do is wade into the water and look down.

If you've never snorkeled before, you can take advantage of the snorkeling equipment and lessons offered by most resorts and excursion boats. However, you won't really need lessons; it's plenty easy to figure out for yourself, especially once you're at the beach—everybody around you will be doing it.

about 60 feet, then drops rapidly to deeper waters. The shallower area is an easy dive, with lots of tame butterfly fish. It's also the home of Morgan Bentjaw, one of our friendliest moray eels. Enenue Side is often done as a live boat drift dive to extend the range of the tour. Diving depths vary. Divers usually do a 50-foot dive, but on occasion advanced divers drop to the 130-foot level to visit the rare boar fish and the shark condos.

Almost every kind of fish found in Hawaii can be seen in the crystalline waters of **Reef's End.** Reef's End is an extension of the rim of Molokini crater, which runs for about 200 yards underwater, barely breaking the surface. Reef's End is shallow enough for novice snorkelers and exciting enough for experienced divers. The end and outside of this shoal drop off in dramatic terraces to beyond diving range. In deeper waters, there are shark ledges at varying depths, and dozens of eels, some of which are tame, including moray, dragon, snowflake, and garden eels. The shallower inner side is home to Garbanzo, one of the largest and first eels to be tamed. The reef is covered with cauliflower coral; in bright sunlight, it's one of the most dramatic underwater scenes in Hawaii.

✪**La Pérouse Pinnacle** In the middle of scenic La Pérouse Bay, site of Haleakala's most recent lava flow, is a pinnacle rising from the 60-foot bottom to about 10 feet below the surface. Getting to the dive site is half the fun: The scenery above water is as exciting as that below the surface. Underwater, you'll enjoy a very diversified dive. Clouds of damselfish and triggerfish will greet you on the surface. Divers can approach even the timid bird wrasse. We find more porcupine puffers here than anywhere else, as well as schools of goatfish and fields of healthy finger coral. La Pérouse is good for snorkeling and long, shallow second dives.

Some snorkel tips: Always go with a buddy. Look up every once in a while to see where you are, how far offshore you are, and whether there's any boat traffic. Don't touch anything; not only can you damage coral, but camouflaged fish and shells with poisonous spines might surprise you. Always check with a dive shop, lifeguards, and others on the beach about the area in which you plan to snorkel: Are there any dangerous conditions you should know about? What are the current surf, tide, and weather conditions?

Snorkel Bob's (www.snorkelbob.com) can rent everything you need at their three Maui locations: 161 Lahainaluna Rd., Lahaina (☎ **808/661-4421**); Napili Village, 5425-C Lower Honapiilani Hwy., Napili (☎ **808/669-9603**); and Kihei Market Place, 34 Keala St. (just off S. Kihei Road), Kihei (☎ **808/879-7449**). Snorkel gear (fins, mask, and snorkel) rent for $2.50 to $6.50 a day, or $9 to $39 a week.

Rental Warehouse, in Lahaina at 578 Front St., near Prison Street (☎ **808/ 661-1970**), and in Kihei at Azeka Place II, on the mountain side of Kihei Road, near Lipoa Street (☎ **808/875-4050**), also has everything you need to experience the underwater world. The snorkel sets include mask, fins, snorkel, gear bag, map of great snorkeling areas, no-fog lotion (for your mask), and fish identification chart—just add water and you're ready to go.

Maui's best snorkeling beaches include **Kapalua Beach; Black Rock,** at Kaanapali Beach; along the Kihei coastline, especially at **Kamaole III Beach Park;** and along the Wailea coastline, particularly at **Ulua Beach.** Mornings are best, because local winds don't kick in until around noon. If you'd like to head over to Lanai for a pristine day of snorkeling, see "Day Cruises to Lanai" under "Boating & Sailing," above.

Two truly terrific places require more effort to get to but are worth it, because they're home to Maui's tropical marine life at its best:

✪ **MOLOKINI**   Like a crescent moon fallen from the sky, this sunken crater sits almost midway between Maui and the uninhabited island of Kahoolawe. Tilted so that only the thin rim of its southern side shows above water in a perfect semicircle, Molokini stands like a scoop against the tide, and it serves, on its concave side, as a natural sanctuary for tropical fish and snorkelers, who commute daily in a fleet of dive boats to this marine-life preserve. See "Snorkel Cruises to Molokini" under "Boating & Sailing," above, for details on getting here.

AHIHI-KINAU NATURAL PRESERVE   You can't miss in Ahihi Bay, a 2,000-acre state natural area reserve in the lee of Cape Kinau, on Maui's rugged south coast, where Haleakala spilled red-hot lava that ran to the sea in 1790. Fishing is strictly *kapu* here, and the fish know it; they're everywhere in this series of rocky coves and black-lava tide pools. The black, barren, lunar-like land stands in stark contrast to the green-blue water. After snorkeling, check out La Pérouse Bay on the south side of Cape Kinau, where the French admiral La Pérouse became the first European to set foot on Maui. A lava-rock pyramid known as Pérouse Monument marks the spot. To get here, drive south of Makena past Puu Olai to Ahihi Bay, where the road turns to gravel and sometimes seems like it'll disappear under the waves. At Cape Kinau, there are three four-wheel-drive trails that lead across the lava flow; take the shortest one, nearest La Pérouse Bay.

SPORTFISHING

The largest blue marlin taken on a rod and reel in the waters around Maui tipped the scale at more than 1,200 pounds. Marlin, tuna, ono, and mahimahi await the baited hook in Maui's coastal and channel waters. No license is required; just book a sport-fishing vessel out of Lahaina or Maalaea harbors. Most charter boats that troll for big-game fish carry a maximum of six passengers. You can walk the docks, inspecting boats and talking to captains and crews, or book through an activities desk or one of the out-fitters recommended below.

Shop around: Prices vary widely according to the boat, the crowd, and the captain. A shared boat for a half-day of fishing starts at $100; a shared full day of fishing starts at around $140. A half-day exclusive (you get the entire boat) is around $300 to $535; a full-day exclusive boat can range from $450 to $900. Also, many boat captains tag and release marlin or keep the fish for themselves (sorry, that's Hawaii style). If you want to eat your mahimahi for dinner or have your marlin mounted, tell the captain before you go.

If you want to fish out of Maalaea, you can spend the day with **Capt. Joe Yurkanin** and **Capt. Ermin Fergerstrom** on their 37-foot Tollycraft, the *No Ka Oi III* (☎ 800/798-0652 or 808/879-4485). For other ideas, try the **Maalaea Activities** desk at the harbor (☎ 808/242-6982).

At Lahaina Harbor, go for one of the following charter companies: **Hinatea Sport-fishing,** slip 27 (☎ 808/667-7548); **Lucky Strike Charters,** slips 50 and 51 (☎ 808/661-4606); or **Aerial Sportfishing Charters,** slip 2 (☎ 808/667-9089).

SURFING

The ancient Hawaiian sport of *hee nalu* ("wave sliding") is probably the sport most people picture when they think of the islands. You, too, can be doing some wave sliding—just sign up at any one of the recommended surfing schools listed below.

Always wanted to learn to surf, but didn't know who to ask? Contact the **Nancy Emerson School of Surfing,** P.O. Box 463, Lahaina, HI 96767 (☎ **808/244-SURF** or 808/874-1183; fax 808/874-2581; www.maui.net/~ncesurf/ncesurf.html). Nancy has been surfing since 1961—she was a stunt performer for various movies, including *Waterworld.* She has pioneered a new instructional technique called "Learn to Surf in One Lesson." It's $70 per person for 2 hours with a group; private classes run $115 for 2 hours.

Even if you've never seen a surfboard before, Andrea Thomas claims she can teach you the art of riding the waves. She has instructed thousands at **Maui Surfing School,** P.O. Box 424, Puunene, HI 96784 (☎ **800/851-0543** or 808/875-0625; www.mauisurf.com), including students as young as 3 and as "chronologically gifted" as 70. She backs her classes with a guarantee that she'll get you surfing, or you'll get 110% of your money back. Two-hour lessons are $60, available by appointment.

Steve and Ava McNanie, owners of the **West Maui Surfing Academy,** 658 Front St. (in front of the Wharf Cinema Center, across the street from the Banyan Tree), Lahaina (☎ **808/667-5399**), offer 2½-hour lessons for $65; surfboards are $10 for 2 hours. Surfboards are also available for rent from **Hunt Hawaii Surf and Sail** in Paia (☎ **808/575-2300**), starting at $20 a day.

Surfers on a budget will find the lowest rates on rental boards at **Rental Warehouse,** in Lahaina at 578 Front St., near Prison Street (☎ **808/661-1970**), and in Kihei at Azeka Place II, on the mountain side of Kihei Road, near Lipoa Street (☎ **808/ 875-4050**). "Goober's" boards rent for $10 a day and "shredder's" boards go for $19 a day.

Expert surfers visit Maui in winter when the surf's really up. The best surfing beaches include **Honolua Bay, Lahaina Harbor** (in summer, there'll be waves just off the channel entrance with a south swell), **Maalaea** (a clean, world-class left), and **Hookipa Beach,** where surfers get the waves until noon; after that—in a carefully worked-out compromise to share this prized surf spot—the windsurfers take over.

WHALE WATCHING

Every winter, pods of Pacific humpback whales make the 3,000-mile swim from the chilly waters of Alaska to bask in Maui's summery shallows, fluking, spy hopping, spouting, and having an all-around swell time.

The humpback whale is a cottage industry here. No creature on earth is celebrated in so many ways: You'll see whale posters, T-shirts, jewelry, and art, some of it quite awful. Don't waste your money on whale stuff; go see the real thing. The humpback is the star of the annual whale-watching season, which usually begins in January and lasts, sometimes, until May. About 1,500 to 3,000 humpback whales appear in Hawaii waters each year.

Humpbacks are one of the world's oldest, most impressive inhabitants. Adults grow to be about 45 feet long and weigh a hefty 40 tons; when they splash, it looks as though a 747 has hit the drink. Humpbacks are officially an endangered species; in 1997, some of the waters around the state were designated the Hawaiian Islands Humpback Whale National Marine Sanctuary, the country's only federal single-species sanctuary.

WHALE WATCHING FROM SHORE

The best time to whale watch is between mid-December and April: Just look out to sea. There's no best time of day for whale watching, but the whales seem to appear when the sea is glassy and the wind calm. Once you see one, keep watching in the same vicinity; they might stay down for 20 minutes. Bring a book—and binoculars, if you can. You can rent binoculars for $2 a day at **Rental Warehouse,** in Lahaina at 578 Front St., near Prison Street (☎ **808/661-1970**), and in Kihei at Azeka Place II, on the mountain side of Kihei Road, near Lipoa Street (☎ **808/875-4050**).

Some good whale-watching points on Maui are:

McGregor Point On the way to Lahaina, there's a scenic lookout at mile marker 9 (just before you get to the Lahaina Tunnel); it's a good viewpoint to scan for whales.

Outrigger Wailea Resort On the Wailea coastal walk, stop at this resort (formerly the Aston Wailea Resort) to look for whales through the telescope installed as a public service by the Hawaiian Island Humpback Whale National Marine Sanctuary.

Olowalu Reef Along the straight part of Honoapiilani Highway, between McGregor Point and Olowalu, you'll see whales leap out of the water. Sometimes, their appearance brings traffic to a screeching halt: People abandon their cars and run down to the sea to watch, causing a major traffic jam. If you stop, pull off the road so that others can pass.

Puu Olai It's a tough climb up this coastal landmark near the Maui Prince Hotel, but you're likely to be well rewarded: This is the island's best spot for offshore whale watching. On the 360-foot cinder cone overlooking Makena Beach, you'll be at the right elevation to see Pacific humpbacks as they dodge Molokini and cruise up Alalakeiki Channel between Maui and Kahoolawe. If you don't see one, you'll at least have a whale of a view.

WHALE-WATCHING CRUISES

For a closer look, take a whale-watching cruise. The **Pacific Whale Foundation,** 101 N. Kihei Rd., Kihei, HI 96753 (☎ **800/942-5311** or 808/879-8811; www. pacificwhale.org), is a nonprofit foundation in Kihei that supports its whale research by offering cruises and snorkel tours, some to Molokini and Lanai. They operate a 65-foot power catamaran called *Ocean Spirit,* a 50-foot sailing catamaran called *Manute'a,* and a sea kayak. They have 15 daily trips to choose from, and their rates for a 2-hour whale-watch cruise would make Moby Dick smile (starting at $19.80 for adults, $14.90 for children). Cruises are offered from December through May, out of both Lahaina and Maalaea harbors.

The **Ocean Activities Center** (☎ **800/798-0652** or 808/879-4485) runs three 2-hour whale-watching cruises on its spacious 65-foot catamaran, which leaves out of Maalaea Harbor; trips are $30 for adults and $18 for children 3 to 12. Bring a towel and your swimsuit; everything else—fins, mask, snorkel, and usually whales—is provided.

If you want to combine ocean activities, then a snorkel or dive cruise to Molokini, the sunken crater off Maui's south coast, might be just the ticket. You can see whales on the way there, at no extra charge. See "Scuba Diving" and "Boating & Sailing," above.

WHALE WATCHING BY KAYAK & RAFT

Seeing a humpback whale from an ocean kayak or raft is awesome. The best budget deal for rafting is **Capt. Steve's Rafting Excursions,** P.O. Box 12492, Lahaina, HI 96761 (☎ **808/667-5565**), which offers 2-hour whale-watching excursions out of Lahaina Harbor. Take the early bird trip at 7:30am and spot some whales for only $35 per person (regular rates are $55 for adults, $35 for children 12 and under).

Kayakers should call **South Pacific Kayaks,** 2439 S. Kihei Rd., Kihei (☎ **800/ 776-2326** or 808/875-4848; www.maui.net/~kayak), which leads small groups on 3-hour trips in the calm waters off Maui for $59 per person.

In your excitement at seeing a whale or a school of dolphins, don't get too close—both are protected under the Marine Mammals Protection Act. Swimmers, kayakers, and windsurfers must stay at least 100 yards away from all whales, dolphins, and other marine mammals. And yes, they have prosecuted visitors for swimming with dolphins! If you have any questions, call the **National Marine Fisheries Service** (☎ **808/541-2727**) or the **Hawaiian Islands Humpback Whale National Marine Sanctuary** (☎ **800/831-4888**).

WINDSURFING

Maui has Hawaii's best windsurfing beaches. In winter, windsurfers from around the world flock to the town of **Paia** to ride the waves. **Hookipa Beach,** known all over the globe for its brisk winds and excellent waves, is the site of several world-championship contests. **Kanaha,** west of Kahului Airport, also has dependable winds; when conditions are right, it's packed with colorful butterfly-like sails. When the winds turn northerly, **Kihei** is the spot to be; some days, you can spot whales in the distance behind the windsurfers.

Hawaiian Island Surf and Sport, 415 Dairy Rd., Kahului (☎ **800/231-6958** or 808/871-4981; fax 808/871-4624; www.hawaiianisland.com), offers lessons, rentals, and repairs. Other shops offering rentals and lessons are **Hawaiian Sailboarding Techniques,** 444 Hana Hwy., Kahului (☎ **808/871-5423**); and **Maui Windsurf Co.,** 520 Keolani Place, Kahului (☎ **800/872-0999** or 808/877-4816). Complete equipment rental (board, sail, rig harness, and roof rack) is available from $45 a day and $295 a week. Lessons, from beginner to advanced, range in price from $50 to $75 for 2 hours.

For daily reports on wind and surf conditions, call the **Wind and Surf Report** at ☎ **808/877-3611.**

3 Hiking & Camping

In the past 2 decades, Maui has grown from a rural island to a fast-paced resort destination, but its natural beauty remains largely inviolate; there are still many places that can be explored only on foot. Those interested in seeing the backcountry—complete with virgin waterfalls, remote wilderness trails, and quiet meditative settings—should head for Haleakala's upcountry or the tropical Hana coast.

Camping on Maui can be extreme (inside a volcano) or benign (by the sea in Hana). It can be wet, cold, and rainy, or hot, dry, and windy—often all on the same day. If you're heading for Haleakala, remember that U.S. astronauts trained for the moon inside the volcano; bring survival gear. Don't forget both your swimsuit and rain gear if you're bound for Waianapanapa. Rental equipment (as well as gear for sale) is available from **The Base Camp,** 3619 Baldwin Ave. (on the way to Haleakala), Makawao (☎ 808/573-2267). If you need to buy equipment, check out **Gaspro,** 365 Hanakai, Kahului (☎ 808/877-0056), or **Maui Sporting Goods,** 92 N. Market, Wailuku (☎ 808/244-0011).

For more information on Maui camping and hiking trails and to obtain free maps, contact **Haleakala National Park,** P.O. Box 369, Makawao, HI 96768 (☎ 808/ 572-9306; www.nps.gov/hale), and the **State Division of Forestry and Wildlife,** 54 S. High St., Wailuku, HI 96793 (☎ 808/984-8100; www.hawaii.gov). For information on trails, hikes, and camping, and permits for state parks, contact the **Hawaii**

State Department of Land and Natural Resources, State Parks Division, 54 S. High St., Rm. 101, Wailuku, HI 96793 (☎ 808/984-8109; www.hawaii.gov). For information on Maui County Parks, contact **Maui County Parks and Recreation,** 1580-C Kaahumanu Ave., Wailuku, HI 96793 (☎ 808/243-7380; www.mauimapp.com).

TIPS ON SAFE HIKING & CAMPING   Water might be everywhere in Hawaii, but it more than likely isn't safe to drink. Most stream water must be treated because cattle, pigs, and goats have probably contaminated the water upstream. The department of health continually warns campers of bacterium leptospirosis, which is found in freshwater streams throughout the state and enters the body through breaks in the skin or through the mucous membranes. It produces flulike symptoms and can be fatal. Make sure that your drinking water is safe by vigorously boiling it, or if boiling is not an option, use tablets with hydroperiodide; portable water filters will not screen out the bacterium leptospirosis.

Since firewood isn't always available, it's a good idea to carry a small, light backpacking stove, which you can use both to boil water and to cook meals for your hiking and camping adventures.

Remember, there is crime in paradise: Never leave your valuables (wallet, airline ticket, and so on) unprotected. Carry a day pack if you have a campsite, and never camp alone.

Some more do's and don'ts: Do bury personal waste away from streams, don't eat unknown fruit, do carry your trash out, and don't forget there is very little twilight in Maui when the sun sets—it gets dark quickly.

GUIDED HIKES   If you would like a knowledgeable guide to accompany you on a hike, contact **Maui Hiking Safaris,** P.O. Box 11198, Lahaina, HI 96761 (☎ **888/ 445-3963** or 808/573-0168; fax 808/572-3037; www.maui.net/~mhs). Owner Randy Warner takes visitors on half-day (4 to 5 hours) and full-day (8 to 10 hours) hikes into valleys, rain forests, and coastal areas. Randy has been hiking around Maui for more than 10 years and is wise in the ways of Hawaiian history, native flora and fauna, and volcanology. His rates are $49 for a half day, $89 for a full day (children 13 and under get 10% off on all hikes), and include day packs, rain parkas, snacks, water, and, on full-day hikes, sandwiches.

Maui's oldest hiking-guide company is **Hike Maui,** P.O. Box 330969, Kahului, HI 96733 (☎ **808/879-5270;** www.hikemaui.com), headed by Ken Schmitt, who pioneered guided hikes on the Valley Isle. Hike Maui offers five different hikes a day, ranging from an easy 3½-mile stroll through the rain forest to a waterfall ($75 for adults, $55 for children 15 and under) to a strenuous, full-day hike in the rain forest and along a mountain ridge ($115 for adults, $90 for children 15 and under). Rates include equipment and transportation.

An all-day hike to the lush rain forests and waterfall pools of the West Maui Mountains is offered exclusively by **Kapalua Nature Society** (☎ **800/KAPALUA** or 808/669-0244). Groups of up to nine can go on guided hiking tours, which include a picnic lunch and transportation to and from the trails. Two exclusive hikes are offered: the easy, 1¾-mile Maunalei Arboretum/Puu Kaeo Nature Walk, which starts at 1,200 feet above sea level and goes to the 1,635-foot summit of Puu Kaeo; and the breathtaking, 4-mile Manienie Ridge Hike, a more strenuous hike with moderate slope, some uneven footing, and close vegetation. Kapalua Nature Society is a not-for-profit organization dedicated to preserving the island's natural and cultural heritage. Proceeds go toward the preservation of Puu Kukui rain forest. The cost is $59; children must be 12 or older.

A Word of Warning About the Weather

The weather at nearly 10,000 feet can change suddenly and without warning. Come prepared for cold, high winds, rain, and even snow in winter. Temperatures can range from 77°F down to 26°F (which feels even lower when you factor in the wind chill), and high winds are frequent. Rainfall varies from 40 inches a year on the west end of the crater to more than 200 inches on the eastern side. Bring boots, waterproof gear, warm clothes, extra layers, and lots of sunscreen—the sun shines very brightly up here.

HALEAKALA NATIONAL PARK

For complete coverage of the national park, see "House of the Sun: Haleakala National Park," in chapter 7.

INTO THE WILDERNESS: SLIDING SANDS & HALEMAUU TRAILS

Hiking into Maui's dormant volcano is really the best way to see it. The terrain inside the wilderness area of the volcano, which ranges from burnt-red cinder cones to ebony-black lava flows, is simply spectacular. Inside the crater, there are some 27 miles of hiking trails, two camping sites, and three cabins.

The best route takes in two trails: into the crater along **Sliding Sands Trail,** which begins on the rim at 9,800 feet and descends into the belly of the beast, to the valley floor at 6,600 feet; and back out along **Halemauu Trail.** Hardy hikers can consider making the 11.3-mile one-way descent, which takes 9 hours, and the equally long return ascent in one day. The rest of us will need to extend this steep but wonderful hike to 2 days. The descending and ascending trails aren't loops; the trailheads are miles (and several thousand feet in elevation) apart, so you'll need to make transportation arrangements in advance. Arrange to stay at least 1 night in the park; 2 or 3 nights will allow you more time to actually explore the fascinating interior of the volcano. See below for details on the cabins and campgrounds in the wilderness area in the valley.

Before you set out, stop at park headquarters to get camping and hiking updates. There is no registration for day hikers.

The trailhead for Sliding Sands is well marked and the trail easy to follow over lava flows and cinders. As you descend, look around: The view is breathtaking. In the afternoon, waves of clouds flow into the Kaupo and Koolau gaps. Vegetation is sparse to nonexistent at the top, but the closer you get to the valley floor, the more vegetation you'll see: bracken ferns, pili grass, shrubs, even flowers. On the floor, the trail travels across rough lava flows, passing rare silversword plants, volcanic vents, and multicolored cinder cones.

The Halemauu Trail goes over red and black lava and past vegetation, such as evening primrose, as it begins its ascent up the valley wall. Occasionally, riders on horseback use this trail as an entry and exit from the park. The proper etiquette is to step aside and stand quietly next to the trail as the horses pass.

SOME SHORTER & EASIER OPTIONS   Take a half-mile walk down the **Hosmer Grove Nature Trail,** or start down **Sliding Sands Trail** for a mile or two to get a hint of what lies ahead. Even this short hike can be exhausting at the high altitude. A good day hike is **Halemauu Trail** to Holua Cabin and back, an 8-mile, half-day trip.

GUIDED HIKES   A 20-minute orientation presentation is given daily in the Summit Building at 9:30, 10:30, and 11:30am. The park rangers offer two guided hikes. The 2-hour, 2-mile **Cinder Desert Hike** takes place Tuesday and Friday at 10am and starts from the Sliding Sands Trailhead at the end of the Haleakala Visitor Center parking lot. The 3-hour, 3-mile **Waikamoi Cloud Forest Hike** leaves every Monday and Thursday at 9am; it starts at the Hosmer Grove, just inside the park entrance, and traverses through the Nature Conservancy's Waikamoi Preserve.

STAYING IN THE WILDERNESS AREA   Most people stay at one of two tent campgrounds, unless they get lucky and win the lottery—the lottery, that is, for one of the three wilderness cabins. For more information, contact **Haleakala National Park,** P.O. Box 369, Makawao, HI 96768 (☎ **808/572-9306;** www.nps.gov/hale).

Cabins   It can get really cold and windy down in the valley (see "A Word of Warning About the Weather," above), so try for a cabin. They're warm, protected from the elements, and reasonably priced. Each has 12 padded bunks (but no bedding; bring your own), a table, chairs, cooking utensils, a two-burner propane stove, and a wood-burning stove with firewood (you might also have a few cockroaches). The cabins are spaced so that each one is an easy walk from the other: Holua cabin is on the Halemauu Trail, Kapalaoa cabin on Sliding Sands Trail, and Paliku cabin on the eastern end by the Kaupo Gap. The rates are $40 a night for groups of one to six and $80 a night for groups of seven to 12.

The cabins are so popular that the National Park Service has a lottery system for reservations. Requests for cabins must be made 3 months in advance (be sure to request alternate dates). You can request all three cabins at once; you're limited to no more than 2 nights in one cabin and no more than 3 nights within the wilderness per month.

Campgrounds   If you don't win the cabin lottery, all is not lost, as there are three tent-camping sites that can accommodate you: two in the wilderness, and one just outside at Hosmer Grove. There is no charge for tent camping.

Hosmer Grove, located at 6,800 feet, is a small, open grassy area surrounded by a forest. Trees protect campers from the winds, but nights still get quite cold. Hard to believe, but sometimes there's ice on the ground up here. This is the best place to spend the night in a tent if you want to see the Haleakala sunrise. Come up the day before, enjoy the park, take a day hike, and then turn in early. The enclosed-glass summit building opens at sunrise for those who come to greet the dawn—a welcome windbreak. Facilities include a covered pavilion with picnic tables and grills, chemical toilets, and drinking water. No permits are needed at Hosmer Grove, and there's no charge—but you can stay for only 3 nights in a 30-day period.

The two tent-camping areas inside the volcano are **Holua,** just off Halemauu at 6,920 feet; and **Paliku,** just before the Kaupo Gap at the eastern end of the valley, at 6,380 feet. Facilities at both campgrounds are limited to pit toilets and nonpotable catchment water. Water at Holua is limited, especially in summer. No open fires are allowed inside the volcano, so bring a stove if you plan to cook. Tent camping is restricted to the signed area. No camping is allowed in the horse pasture. The inviting grassy lawn in front of the cabin is *kapu.* Camping is free, but limited to 2 consecutive nights, and no more than 3 nights a month inside the volcano. Permits are issued daily at Park Headquarters on a first-come, first-served basis. Occupancy is limited to 25 people in each campground.

HIKING & CAMPING AT KIPAHULU (NEAR HANA)

In the East Maui section of Haleakala National Park, you can set up at **Oheo Campground,** a first-come, first-served, drive-in campground with tent sites for 100 near the ocean, a few tables, barbecue grills, and chemical toilets. No permit is required, but there's a 3-night limit. No food or drinking water is available, so bring your own. Bring a tent as well—it rains 75 inches a year here. Contact **Kipahulu Ranger Station,** Haleakala National Park, HI 96713 (☎ **808/248-7375;** www.nps.gov/hale).

HIKING FROM THE SUMMIT   If you hike from the crater rim down **Kaupo Gap** to the ocean, more than 20 miles away, you'll pass through climate zones ranging from arctic to tropical. On a clear day, you can see every island except Kauai on the trip down.

APPROACHING KIPAHULU FROM HANA   If you drive to Kipahulu, you'll have to approach it from the Hana Highway, as it's not accessible from the summit. Always check in at the ranger station before you begin your hike; the staff can inform you of current conditions and share their wonderful stories about the history, culture, flora, and fauna of the area.

There are two hikes you can take here. The first is a short, easy half-mile loop along the **Kaloa Point Trail** (Kaloa Point is a windy bluff overlooking **Oheo Gulch**), which leads toward the ocean along pools and waterfalls and back to the ranger station. The clearly marked path leaves the parking area and rambles along the flat, grassy peninsula. Crashing surf and views of the Island of Hawaii are a 5-minute walk from the ranger station. Along the way you'll see the remnants of an ancient fishing shrine, a house site, and a lauhala-thatched building depicting an earlier time. The loop stops at the bridge you drove over when you entered the park; this is the best place for a photo opportunity. The pools are above and below the bridge; the best for swimming are usually above the bridge.

The second hike is for the more hardy. Although just a 4-mile round-trip, the trail is steep and you'll want to stop and swim in the pools, so allow 3 hours. Wear hiking boots, as you'll be climbing over rocks and up steep trails. Take water, snacks, swim gear, and insect repellent (to ward off the swarms of mosquitoes). Always be on the lookout for flash-flood conditions. This walk will pass two magnificent waterfalls, the 181-foot **Makahiku Falls** and the even bigger 400-foot ✪ **Waimoku Falls.** The trail starts at the ranger station, where you'll walk uphill for a half mile to a fence overlook at the thundering Makahiku Falls. The tired can turn around here, but the true adventurers will press on.

Behind the lookout, the well-worn trail picks up again and goes directly to a pool on the top of the Makahiku Falls. The pool is safe to swim in as long as the waters aren't rising; if they are, get out and head back to the ranger station. Back on the trail, you'll cross a meadow and then a creek, where you'll scramble up the rocky bank and head into a bamboo forest jungle. At the edge of the jungle is another creek, but the trail doesn't cross this one. A few minutes more, and the vertical Waimoku Falls will be in sight.

GUIDED HIKES   The rangers at Kipahulu conduct a 1-mile hike to the **Bamboo Forest** at 9am daily; half-mile hikes or orientation talks are given at noon, 1:30, 2:30, and 3:30pm daily; and a 4-mile round-trip hike to **Waimoku Falls** takes place on Saturday at 9:30am. All programs and hikes begin at the ranger station.

SKYLINE TRAIL, POLIPOLI SPRINGS STATE RECREATION AREA

This is some hike—strenuous but worth every step if you like seeing the big picture. It's 8 miles, all downhill, with a dazzling 100-mile view of the islands dotting the blue Pacific, plus the West Maui Mountains, which seem like a separate island.

The trail is located just outside Haleakala National Park at Polipoli Springs National Recreation Area; however, you access it by going through the national park to the summit. The Skyline Trail starts just beyond the Puu Ulaula summit building on the south side of Science City and follows the southwest rift zone of Haleakala from its lunarlike cinder cones to a cool redwood grove. The trail drops 3,800 feet on a 4-hour hike to the recreation area, in the 12,000-acre Kahikinui Forest Reserve. If you'd rather drive, you'll need a four-wheel-drive vehicle to access the trail.

There's a campground at the recreation area, at 6,300 feet. No fee or reservations are required, but your stay must be limited to five nights. Tent camping is free, but you'll need a permit. One 10-bunk cabin is available for $45 a night for one to four guests ($5 for each additional guest); it has a cold shower, a gas stove, and no electricity. There is no drinking water available, so bring your own. To reserve, contact the State Parks Division, 54 S. High St., Rm. 101, Wailuku, HI 96793 (☎ **808/984-8109** between 8am and 4pm Monday through Friday; www.hawaii.gov).

POLIPOLI STATE PARK

One of the most unusual hiking experiences in the state can be found at Polipoli State Park, part of the 21,000-acre Kula and Kahikinui Forest Reserve on the slope of Haleakala. At Polipoli, it's hard to believe that you're in Hawaii. First of all, it's cold, even in summer, because the loop is up at 5,300 to 6,200 feet. Second, this former forest of native koa, ohia, and mamane trees, which was overlogged in the 1800s, was reforested in the 1930s with introduced species: pine, Monterey cypress, ash, sugi, red adler, redwood, and several varieties of eucalyptus. The result is a cool area, with muted sunlight filtered by towering trees.

The **Polipoli Loop** is an easy, 5-mile hike that takes about 3 hours; dress warmly for it. To get here, take the Haleakala Highway (Highway 37) to Keokea and turn right onto Highway 337; after less than a half mile, turn on Waipoli Road, which climbs swiftly. After 10 miles, Waipoli Road ends at the Polipoli State Park campgrounds. The well-marked trailhead is next to the parking lot, near a stand of Monterey cypress; the tree-lined trail offers the best view of the island.

Polipoli Loop is really a network of three trails: Haleakala Ridge, Plum Trail, and Redwood Trail. After a half mile of meandering through groves of eucalyptus, blackwood, swamp mahogany, and hybrid cypress, you'll join the Haleakala Ridge Trail, which, about a mile into the trail, joins with the Plum Trail (named for the plums that ripen in June and July). It passes through massive redwoods and by an old Conservation Corps bunkhouse and a rundown cabin before joining up with the Redwood Trail, which climbs through Mexican pine, tropical ash, Port Orford cedar, and, of course, redwood.

Camping is allowed in the park with a permit from the **Division of State Parks,** 54 S. High St., Rm. 101, Wailuku, HI 96793 (☎ **808/984-8109;** www.hawaii.gov). There's one cabin, available by reservation.

KANAHA BEACH PARK CAMPING

The only Maui County camping facility on the island is Kanaha Beach Park, located next to the Kahului Airport. The county has two separate areas for camping: seven tent sites on the beach and an additional ten tent sites inland. This well-used park is a favorite of windsurfers, who take advantage of the strong winds that roar across this end of the island. Facilities include a paved parking lot, portable toilets, outdoor showers, barbecue grills, and picnic tables. Camping is limited to no more than 3 consecutive days; the permit fee is $3 per person, per night, and can be obtained from the **Maui County Parks and Recreation Department,** 1580-C Kaahumanu Ave., Wailuku, HI 96793 (☎ **808/243-7380;** www.mauimapp.com). Since this is Maui's only county camping facility, the 17 sites book up quickly; reserve your dates far in advance (the county will accept reservations a year in advance).

WAIANAPANAPA STATE PARK

Tucked in a tropical jungle, on the outskirts of the little coastal town of Hana, is Waianapanapa State Park, a black-sand beach set in an emerald forest.

HANA-WAIANAPANAPA COAST TRAIL   This is an easy, 6-mile hike that takes you back in time. Allow 4 hours to walk along this relatively flat trail, which parallels the sea, along lava cliffs and a forest of lauhala trees. The best time of day is in either the early morning or the late evening, when the light on the lava and surf makes for great photos. Midday is the worst time; not only is it hot (lava intensifies the heat), but there's no shade or potable water available.

There's no formal trailhead; join the route at any point along the Waianapanapa Campground and go in either direction. Along the trail, you'll see remains of an ancient *heiau* (temple), stands of lauhala trees, caves, a blowhole, and a remarkable plant, *naupaka,* that flourishes along the beach. Upon close inspection, you'll see that the naupaka has only half-blossoms; according to Hawaiian legend, a similar plant living in the mountains has the other half of the blossoms. One ancient explanation is that the two plants represent never-to-be-reunited lovers: As the story goes, the two lovers bickered so much that the gods, fed up with their incessant quarreling, banished one lover to the mountain and the other to the sea.

CAMPING   Waianapanapa has 12 cabins and a tent campground. Go for the cabins, as it rains torrentially here, sometimes turning the campground into a mud-wrestling arena. If you opt to tent-camp, it's free, but limited to 5 nights in a 30-day period. Permits are available from the **State Parks Division,** 54 S. High St., Rm. 101, Wailuku, HI 96793 (☎ **808/984-8109;** fax 808/989-8111; www.hawaii.gov). Facilities include rest rooms, outdoor showers, drinking water, and picnic tables.

HANA: THE HIKE TO FAGAN'S CROSS

This 3-mile hike to the cross erected in the memory of Hana Ranch and Hotel Hana-Maui founder Paul Fagan offers spectacular views of the Hana coast, particularly at sunset. The uphill trail starts across Hana Highway from the Hotel Hana-Maui. Enter the pastures at your own risk; they're often occupied by glaring bulls with sharp horns and cows with new calves, so beware the bulls, avoid the nursing cows, and don't wear red. Watch your step as you ascend this steep hill on a Jeep trail across open pastures; you'll be rewarded at the cross with the breathtaking view.

KEANAE ARBORETUM

About 47 miles from Kahului, along the Hana Highway and just after the Keanae YMCA Camp (and just before the turnoff to the Keanae Peninsula), is an easy family walk through the Keanae Arboretum, which is maintained by the State Department of Land and Natural Resources, Division of Forestry and Wildlife. The walk, which is just over 2 miles, passes through a forest with both native and introduced plants. Allow 1 to 2 hours; swimming is available, so you might want to stay longer. Take rain gear and mosquito repellent.

Park at the Keanae Arboretum and pass through the turnstile. Walk along the fairly flat Jeep road to the entrance. For a half mile, you will pass by plants introduced to Hawaii (ornamental timber, pummelo, banana, papaya, hibiscus, and more), all with identifying tags. At the end of this section is a taro patch showing the different varieties that Hawaiians used as their staple crop. After the taro, a 1-mile trail leads through a Hawaiian rain forest. The trail crisscrosses a stream as it meanders through the forest. Our favorite swimming hole is just to the left of the first stream crossing, at about 100 yards.

WAIHEE RIDGE

This 3- to 4-mile strenuous hike, with a 1,500-foot climb, offers spectacular views of the valleys of the West Maui Mountains. Allow 3 to 4 hours for the round-trip hike. Pack a lunch, carry water, and pick a dry day, as this area is very wet. There's a picnic table at the summit with great views.

To get here from Wailuku, turn north on Market Street, which becomes the Kahekilii Highway (Highway 340) and passes through Waihee. Go just over 2½ miles from the Waihee Elementary School and look for the turnoff to the Boy Scouts' Camp Maluhia on the left. Turn into the camp and drive nearly a mile to the trailhead on the left side of the road. Park at the trailhead.

Pass through the turnstile and walk on the Jeep road. About a third of a mile in, there will be another gate, marking the entrance to the West Maui Forest Reserve. A foot trail, kept in good shape by the State Department of Land and Natural Resources, begins here. The trail climbs to the top of the ridge, offering great views of the various valleys. The trail is marked by a number of switchbacks and can be extremely muddy and wet. In some areas, it's so steep that you have to grab onto the trees and bushes for support. There's temporary relief to this climb after about 1½ miles, when the trail crosses a flat area (which can be so wet that it's impassable). After the swampy area, the trail ascends again for about a mile to **Lanilili Peak,** where a picnic table and magnificent views await.

4 Great Golf

In some circles, Maui is synonymous with golf. The island's world-famous golf courses start at the very northern tip of the island and roll right around to Kaanapali, jumping down to Kihei and Wailea in the south. There are also some lesser-known municipal courses that offer challenging play for less than $100. Golfers new to Maui should know that it's windy here, especially between 10am and 2pm, when winds of 10 to 15 m.p.h. are the norm. Play two to three clubs up or down to compensate for the wind factor. We also recommend bringing extra balls—the rough is thicker here and the wind will pick your ball up and drop it in very unappealing places (like water hazards). If your heart is set on playing on a resort course, book at least a week in advance. For the ardent golfer on a tight budget: Play in the afternoon, when discounted twilight rates are in effect. There's no guarantee you'll get 18 holes in, especially in winter when it's dark by 6pm, but you'll have an opportunity to experience these world-famous courses at half the usual fee.

If you don't bring your own, rent clubs from **Rental Warehouse,** in Lahaina at 578 Front St., near Prison Street (☎ 808/661-1970), or in Kihei at Azeka Place II, on the mountain side of Kihei Road, near Lipoa Street (☎ 808/875-4050), where top-quality clubs go for $15 a day, not-so-top-quality for $10 a day. **Golf Club Rentals** (☎ 808/665-0800; www.maui.net/~rentgolf) offers custom-built clubs for men, women, and juniors in both right- and left-handed versions. Their rates are just $15 a day and they offer delivery island-wide.

For last-minute and discount tee times, call **Stand-by Golf** (☎ 888/645-BOOK in Hawaii, or 808/874-0600 from the mainland) between 7am and 11pm, Hawaii standard time. Stand-by offers discounted (by 10% to 40%) and guaranteed tee times for same-day or next-day golfing.

CENTRAL MAUI

Waiehu Municipal Golf Course. P.O. Box 507, Wailuku, HI 96793. ☎ **808/244-5934.** From the Kahului Airport, turn right on the Hana Hwy. (Hwy. 36), which becomes Kaahumanu

Ave. (Hwy. 32). Turn right at the stoplight at the junction of Waiehu Beach Rd. (Hwy. 340). Go another 1½ miles, and you'll see the entrance on your right.

This public, ocean-side, par-72 golf course is like playing two different courses: The first nine holes, built in 1930, are set along the dramatic coastline, whereas the back nine holes, added in 1966, head toward the mountains. It's a fun playing course that probably won't challenge your handicap. The only hazard here is the wind, which can rip off the ocean and play havoc with your ball. Basically, this is a flat and straight course. The only hole that can raise your blood pressure is the 511-yard, par 5, 4th hole, which is very narrow and very long. To par here, you have to hit a long accurate drive, then another long and accurate fairway drive, and finally a perfect pitch over the hazards to the greens (yeah, right).

Facilities include a snack bar, driving range, practice greens, golf-club rental, and clubhouse. Since this is a public course, the greens fees are low—$25 Monday through Friday, $30 Saturday and Sunday—but getting a tee time is tough.

WEST MAUI

✪ **Kaanapali Courses.** Off Hwy. 30, Kaanapali. ☎ **808/661-3691.** At the first stoplight in Kaanapali, turn onto Kaanapali Pkwy.; the first building on your right is the clubhouse.

Both courses at the Kaanapali Resort offer a challenge to all golfers, from high hand-icappers to near-pros. The par-72, 6,305-yard **North Course** (originally called the Royal Lahaina Golf Course) is a true Robert Trent Jones design: an abundance of wide bunkers; several long, stretched-out tees; and the largest, most contoured greens on Maui. It has a tricky 18th hole (par 4; 435 yd.) with a water hazard on the approach to the green. The par-72, 6,250-yard **South Course** is an Arthur Jack Snyder design; although shorter than the North Course, it requires more accuracy on the narrow, hilly fairways. It, too, has a water hazard on its final hole, so don't tally up your score card until the final putt is sunk.

Facilities include a driving range, putting course, and clubhouse with dining. Greens fees are $130, $65 after 2pm (for resort guests, $105, $65 after 2pm); weekday tee times are best.

✪ **Kapalua Resort Courses.** Off Hwy. 30, Kapalua.

The views from these three championship courses are worth the greens fees alone. The first to open was the **Bay Course** (☎ **808/669-8044**), a par-72, 6,761-yard course inaugurated in 1975. Designed by Arnold Palmer and Ed Seay, this course is a bit forgiving with its wide fairways; the greens, however, are difficult to read. The well-photographed 5th overlooks a small ocean cove; even the pros have trouble with this rocky par-3, 205-yard hole. The par-71, 6,632-yard **Village Course** (☎ **808/ 669-8044**), another Palmer/Seay design, is the most scenic of the three courses; the hole with the best vista is definitely the 6th, which overlooks a lake with the ocean in the distance. But don't get distracted by the view—the tee is between two rows of Cook pines.

The **Plantation Course** (☎ **808/669-8044**), scene of the PGA Kapalua Mercedes Championship, was designed by Ben Crenshaw and Bill Coore. A 6,547-yard, par-73 course on a rolling hillside of the West Maui Mountains, this one is excellent for developing your low shots and precise chipping. Facilities for the three courses include locker rooms, a driving range, and an excellent restaurant. Greens fees are $140 ($70 after 2pm) at the Village and Bay courses, $150 at the Plantation Course (at all times). Weekdays are your best bet for tee times.

SOUTH MAUI

✪ **Makena Courses.** On Makena Alanui Dr., just past the Maui Prince Hotel. ☎ **808/879-3344.**

Here you'll find 36 holes of "Mr. Hawaii Golf"—Robert Trent Jones Jr.—at its best. Add to that spectacular views: Molokini islet looms in the background, humpback whales gambol offshore in winter, and the tropical sunsets are spectacular. This is golf not to be missed; the par-72, 6,876-yard **South Course** has a couple of holes you'll never forget. The view from the par-4 15th hole, which shoots from an elevated tee 183 yards downhill to the Pacific, is magnificent. The 16th hole has a two-tiered green that's blind from the tee 383 yards away (that is, if you make it past the gully off the fairway). The par-72, 6,823-yard **North Course** is more difficult and more spectacular. The 13th hole, located partway up the mountain, has a view that makes most golfers stop and stare. The next hole is even more memorable: a 200-foot drop between tee and green.

Facilities include clubhouse, driving range, two putting greens, pro shop, lockers, and lessons. Beware of crowded conditions on weekends. Greens fees are $85 for Makena Resort guests, $140 for nonguests.

Silversword Golf Club. 1345 Piilani Hwy. (near the Lipoa St. turnoff), Kihei. ☎ **808/874-0777.**

Sitting in the foothills of Haleakala, just high enough to afford spectacular ocean views from every hole, this course is for golfers who love the views as much as the fairways and greens. It's very forgiving, especially for duffers and high handicappers. Just one caveat: Go in the morning. Not only is it cooler, but, more important, it's less windy. In the afternoon, the winds really pick up, blustering down Haleakala with great gusto. Silversword is a fun course to play, with some challenging holes (the par-5 no. 2 is a virtual minefield of bunkers, and the par-5 no. 8 shoots over a swale and then up a hill).

Greens fees vary with the season; from April 1 to October 31, they're $59, with twilight rates of $42. The rest of the year, they're $70, with twilight rates of $48. You can play nine holes after 3:30pm, year-round, for $23.

✪ Wailea Courses. Wailea Alanui Dr. (off Wailea Iki Dr.), Wailea. ☎ **888/328-MAUI** or 808/879-2966.

There are three courses to choose from at Wailea. The **Blue Course,** a par-72, 6,700-yard flat, open course designed by Arthur Jack Snyder and dotted with bunkers and water hazards, is for duffers and pros alike. The wide fairways appeal to beginners, and the undulating terrain makes it a course everyone can enjoy. A little more difficult is the par-72, 7,073-yard championship **Gold Course,** with narrow fairways, several tricky dogleg holes, and the classic Robert Trent Jones Jr. challenges: natural hazards, like lava-rock walls, and native Hawaiian grasses. The **Emerald Course,** originally an Arthur Jack Snyder design, was renovated by Robert Trent Jones Jr. into a more challenging course.

With 54 holes to play, getting a tee time is slightly easier here on weekends than at other resorts, but weekdays are best (the Gold Course is usually the toughest to book). Facilities include a pro shop, a restaurant, locker rooms, and a complete golf training facility. Greens fees are $80 to $140, depending on the season and where you're staying. Twilight rates range from $60 to $75. Special deals are available April through December.

UPCOUNTRY MAUI

Pukalani Country Club. 360 Pukalani St., Pukalani. ☎ **808/572-1314.** Take the Hana Hwy. (Hwy. 36) to Haleakala Hwy. (Hwy. 37) to the Pukalani exit; turn right onto Pukalani St. and go 2 blocks.

This cool course at 1,100 feet offers a break from the resorts' high greens fees, and it's really fun to play. The par-72, 6,962-yard course has 19 greens. There's an extra green because the third hole offers golfers two different options: a tough iron shot from the tee (especially into the wind), across a gully (yuck!) to the green; or a shot down the side of the gully across a second green into sand traps below. (Most people choose to shoot down the side of the gully; it's actually easier than shooting across a ravine.) High handicappers will love this course; more experienced players can make it more challenging by playing from the back tees. Facilities include club and shoe rentals, practice areas, lockers, a pro shop, and a restaurant. Greens fees, which include the cart fee, are only $20.

5 Bicycling, Horseback Riding & Other Outdoor Pursuits

BICYCLING

It's not even close to dawn, but here you are, rubbing your eyes awake, riding in a van up the long, dark road to the top of Maui's sleeping volcano. It's colder than you ever thought possible for a tropical island. The air is thin. You stomp your chilly feet while you wait, sipping hot coffee. Then comes the sun, exploding over the yawning Haleakala Crater, which is big enough to swallow Manhattan whole—a mystic moment you won't soon forget, imprinted on a palette of dawn colors. Now you know why Hawaiians named it the House of the Sun. But there's no time to linger: Decked out in your screaming yellow parka, you mount your special steed and test its most important feature, the brakes—because you're about to coast 37 miles down a 10,000-foot volcano.

Cruising down Haleakala, from the lunarlike landscape at the top, past flower farms, pineapple fields, and eucalyptus groves, is quite an experience—and you don't have to be an expert cyclist to do it; you just have to be able to ride a bike. This is a safe, comfortable, no-strain bicycle trip, although it requires some stamina in the colder, wetter months between November and March. Wear layers of warm clothing, as there may be a 30° change in temperature from the top of the mountain to the ocean. Generally, tour groups will not take riders under 12, but younger children can ride along in the van that accompanies the groups, as can pregnant women. The trip usually costs between $100 and $120, which includes hotel pickup, transport to the top, bicycle and safety equipment, and meals.

Maui's oldest downhill company is **Maui Downhill,** 199 Dairy Rd., Kahului, HI 96732 (☎ **800/535-BIKE** or 808/871-2155; e-mail: mauidown@gte.net), which has a sunrise-safari bike tour, including continental breakfast and brunch, starting at $100. Haleakala rides for $120 are offered by both **Maui Mountain Chasers** in Makawao (☎ **800/232-6284** or 808/871-6014) and **Mountain Riders Bike Tours** in Kahului (☎ **800/706-7700** or 808/242-9739).

For bike excursions on other parts of Maui, contact **Chris' Adventures,** P.O. Box 869, Kula, HI 96790 (☎ **800/224-5344** or 808/871-2453). Chris offers various bike tours, with costs ranging from $49 to $110. We recommend the Waihee-Kahakuloa Coastal Adventure ($59), which involves hiking the Waihee Valley or Ridge and then biking along the spectacular northwestern coast, which feels like old Hawaii.

If you want to venture out on your own, cheap rentals—$10 a day for cruisers and $20 a day for mountain bikes—are available from **Rental Warehouse,** in Lahaina at 578 Front St., near Prison Street (☎ **808/661-1970**), and in Kihei at Azeka Place II, on the mountain side of Kihei Road, near Lipoa Street (☎ **808/875-4050**).

For maps and information on bikeways, contact Walter Enomoto, chair of the **Mayor's Advisory Committee on Bicycling** (☎ **808/871-6886**). A great book for mountain bikers who want to venture out on their own is John Alford's *Mountain Biking the Hawaiian Islands,* published by Ohana Publishing, P.O. Box 240170, Honolulu, HI 96824-0170 (www.bikehawaii.com).

HORSEBACK RIDING

Maui offers spectacular adventure rides through rugged ranch lands, into tropical forests, and to remote swimming holes. For a 5½-hour tour on horseback—complete with swimming and lunch—call **Adventure on Horseback,** P.O. Box 1419, Makawao, HI 96768 (☎ **808/242-7445** or 808/572-6211); the cost is $175 per person. The day begins over coffee and pastries, while owner Frank Levinson matches the horses to the riders, in terms of both skill and personality. Frank leads small groups across pastures, through thick rain forests, alongside streams, and up to waterfalls and pools. After a hearty lunch, the group retraces its route back.

If you're out in Hana, **Oheo Stables,** Kipahulu Ranch, Start Route 1, Box 151 A, on Highway 31 (1 mi. past Oheo Gulch), Kipahulu (☎ **808/667-2222;** www.maui.net/~ray/index.html), offers two daily rides through the mountains above Oheo Gulch (Seven Sacred Pools). The best deal is the 11:30am ride ($139), which includes brunch and snacks during the 4-hour adventure (2½ hours in the saddle). The ride ventures into the Haleakala National Park, stopping at scenic spots like the Pipiwai lookout, where you can glimpse the 400-foot Waimoku Falls.

If you enjoy your ride, remember to kiss your horse and tip your guide.

HALEAKALA ON HORSEBACK If you'd like to ride down into Haleakala's crater, contact **Pony Express Tours,** P.O. Box 535, Kula, HI 96790 (☎ **808/667-2200** or 808/878-6698; fax 808/878-3581), which offers half-day rides down to the crater floor and back up, from $80 to $130 per person. Gentler 1- and 2-hour rides are also offered at Haleakala Ranch, located on the beautiful lower slopes of the volcano, for $40 and $65. Pony Express provides well-trained horses and experienced guides, and accommodates all riding levels. In order to ride, you must be at least 10 years old, weigh no more than 230 pounds, and wear long pants and closed-toe shoes.

WAY OUT WEST ON MAUI: RANCH RIDES We recommend riding with **Mendes Ranch & Trail Rides,** on Kahekili Highway, 4 miles past Wailuku (☎ **808/871-5222**). The 300-acre Mendes Ranch is a real-life working cowboy ranch that has all the essential elements of an earthly paradise—rainbows, waterfalls, palm trees, coral-sand beaches, lagoons, tide pools, a rain forest, and its own volcanic peak. Allan Mendes, a third-generation wrangler, will take you from the edge of the rain forest out to the sea. On the way, you'll cross tree-studded meadows where Texas longhorns sit in the shade like surreal lawn statues, and past a dusty corral where Allan's father, Ernest, a champion roper, may be breaking in a wild horse. All the while, Allan keeps close watch, turning often in his saddle on his pinto, Pride, to make sure that everyone is happy. He points out flora and fauna and fields questions, but generally just lets you soak up Maui's natural splendor in golden silence. The morning ride, which lasts 3 hours and ends with a barbecue back at the corral (the perfect ranch-style lunch after a morning in the saddle), is $130; the 2½-hour afternoon ride is $85, including snacks.

SPELUNKING

Most people come to Maui to get outdoors and soak up some Hawaiian sunshine, but don't miss the opportunity to see how the islands were made by exploring a million-year-old underground lava tube/cave. Chuck and Deborah Thorne of ✪ **Maui Cave Adventures,** P.O. Box 40, Hana, HI 96713 (☎ **808/248-7308;** www.maui.net/~hanacave), offer several tours of this unique geological feature. After more than

10 years of leading scuba tours through underwater caves around Hawaii, Chuck discovered some caves on land that he wanted to show visitors. When the land surrounding the largest cave on Maui went on the market in 1996, Chuck snapped it up and started his own tour company. He'll take you hiking into enormous subterranean passages of a huge, extinct lava tube with 40-foot ceilings. This a geology lesson you won't soon forget—Chuck is a long-time student of the science of volcano-speleology and can discuss every little formation in the cave, how it came to be, and what its purpose is. All the equipment you'll need (lights, hard hats, gloves, water bottles) is supplied on the tours, which cost $50 for 2 hours (no children under 9), $100 for 4 hours (no children under 18) and $150 for 6 hours (no children under 18). All tours by appointment only. Wear long pants and closed shoes, and bring your camera.

If you want to combine caving with a tour of Hana, contact **Temptation Tours** (☎ **808/877-8888**), which offers not only a 2-hour cave tour, but also an air-conditioned van tour from your hotel to Hana; the $159 cost includes continental breakfast, beachside picnic lunch, and a stop for a swim.

TENNIS

Maui County has excellent tennis courts located all over the island. All are free and available from daylight to sunset; a few are even lit for night play until 10pm. The courts are available on a first-come, first-served basis; when someone's waiting for a court, please limit your play to no more than 45 minutes. For a complete list of all public tennis courts, contact **Maui County of Parks and Recreation,** 1580-C Kaahumanu Ave., Wailuku, HI 96793 (☎ **808/243-7389**).

Private tennis courts are available at most resorts and hotels on the island. The **Kapalua Tennis Garden and Village Tennis Center,** Kapalua Resort (☎ **808/ 669-5677;** www.kapaluamaui.com), is home to the Kapalua Open, featuring the largest purse in the state. Kapalua also provides matchmaking services for those traveling without a tennis partner. Court rentals are $10 an hour for resort guests, $15 for nonguests. In Wailea, the **Wailea Tennis Club,** 131 Wailea Iki Place, Wailea (☎ **808/ 879-1958**), has 11 Plexi-pave courts. Court rentals are $25 per day for Wailea resort guests, $30 an hour for players not staying in Wailea.

7

Seeing the Sights

by Jeanette Foster

After a few days of just relaxing on the beach, the itch to explore the rest of Maui sets in: What's on top of Haleakala, looming in the distance? Is the road to Hana really the tropical jungle everyone raves about? What does the inside of a 19th-century whaling boat look like?

There is far more to the Valley Isle than just sun, sand, and surf. Get out and see for yourself the other-worldly interior of a 10,000-foot volcanic crater; watch endangered sea turtles make their way to nesting sites in a wildlife sanctuary; wander back in time to the days when whalers and missionaries fought for the soul of Lahaina; and feel the energy of a thundering waterfall cascade into a serene mountain pool.

1 By Air, Land & Sea: Guided Island Adventures

Admittedly, the adventures below aren't cheap. However, each one offers such a wonderful opportunity to see Maui from a unique perspective that, depending on your interests, you might make one of them the highlight of your trip—it'll be worth every penny.

FLYING HIGH: HELICOPTER RIDES

Only a helicopter can bring you face-to-face with remote sites like Maui's little-known Wall of Tears, up near the summit of Puu Kukui in the West Maui Mountains. A helicopter ride on Maui isn't a wild ride; it's more like a gentle gee-whiz zip into a seldom-seen Eden. You'll glide through canyons etched with 1,000-foot waterfalls, and over dense rain forests; you'll climb to 10,000 feet, high enough to glimpse the summit of Haleakala, and fly by the dramatic vistas at Molokai.

The first chopper pilots in Hawaii were good ol' boys on their way back from Vietnam—hard-flying, hard-drinking cowboys who cared more about the ride than the scenery. But not anymore. Today, pilots, like the ones at Blue Hawaiian (see below), are an interesting hybrid: part Hawaiian historian, part DJ, part tour guide, and part amusement-ride operator. As you soar through the clouds, absorbing Maui's scenic terrain, you'll learn about the island's flora and fauna, history, and culture.

Among the many helicopter-tour operators on Maui, the best is **Blue Hawaiian,** at Kahului Airport (☎ **800/745-BLUE** or

Especially for Kids

A Submarine Ride   Atlantis Submarines (☎ **800/548-6262**) takes the whole family down into the shallow coastal waters off Lahaina in a real sub. The kids will love seeing all the fish—maybe even a shark!—and you'll stay dry the entire time. See "Going Under: Submarine Rides," below, for details.

The Sugarcane Train   This ride will appeal to small kids as well as train buffs of all ages. A steam engine pulls open passenger cars of the Lahaina/Kaanapali & Pacific Railroad on a 30-minute, 12-mile round-trip through sugarcane fields between Lahaina and Kaanapali. The conductor sings and calls out the landmarks, and along the way, you can see Molokai, Lanai, and the backside of Kaanapali. Tickets are $14 for grown-ups, $7.50 for kids ages 3 to 12; call ☎ **808/661-0089.**

Star Searches   The stars over Kaanapali shine big and bright because the tropical sky is almost entirely free of both pollutants and the interference of big-city lights. Amateur astronomers can probe the Milky Way, see the rings of Saturn's and Jupiter's moons, and scan the Sea of Tranquillity in a 60-minute star search on the world's first recreational computer-driven telescope. It costs $20 for adults, $15 for children (ages 12 and under). Contact the Hyatt Regency Maui, 200 Nohea Kai Dr., Kaanapali Beach (☎ **808/661-1234**).

In-Line Skating   Bring your own skates and roll, glide, and skid around the free, newly constructed rink in Kihei's Kalama Park. It's open daylight hours, with the occasional Maui In-Line Hockey Association game scheduled. For information, call ☎ **808/879-4364.**

Sharks, Stingrays & Starfish   Hawaii's largest aquarium, the Maui Ocean Center (☎ **808/875-1962**), has a range of sea critters—from tiger sharks to tiny starfish—that are sure to fascinate kids of all ages. At this 5-acre facility in Maalaea, visitors can take a virtual walk from the beach down to the ocean depths via the three dozen tanks, countless exhibits, and 100-foot-long, 600,000-gallon main oceanarium.

A Dragonfly's View   Kids will think this is too much fun to be educational. Don a face mask and get the dizzying perspective of what a dragonfly sees as it flies over a mountain stream, or watch the tiny *oopu* fish climb up a stream at the Hawaii Nature Center (☎ **808/244-6500**) in beautiful Iao Valley, where you'll find some 30 hands-on, interactive exhibits and displays of Hawaii's natural history.

808/871-8844; www.bluehawaiian.com), which not only takes you on the ride of your life, but also entertains, educates, and leaves you with an experience you'll never forget. Flights vary from 45 minutes to a half-day affair and range from $130 to $220. A keepsake video of your flight is available for $19.95 (so your friends at home can ooh and aah).

If Blue Hawaiian is booked, try **Sunshine Helicopters** (☎ **800/544-2520** or 808/ 871-0722; www.sunshinehelicopters.com), which offers a variety of flights from short hops around the West Maui Mountains to island tours. Prices range from $99 to $179.

GOING UNDER: SUBMARINE RIDES

This is the stuff dreams are made of: Plunge 100 feet under the sea in a state-of-the-art, high-tech submarine and experience swarms of vibrant tropical fish up close and personal as they flutter through the deep blue waters off Lahaina. ✪ **Atlantis**

Submarines, 665 Front St., Lahaina, HI 96761 (☎ **800/548-6262** or **808/ 667-7816**), offers trips out of Lahaina Harbor, every hour on the hour from 8am to 3pm. Tickets are $79. Allow 2 hours for your underwater adventure.

ECOTOURING

Venture into the lush West Maui Mountains with an experienced guide on one of the **Ritz-Carlton Kapalua's Eco-Tours** (☎ **808/669-6200**). After a continental break-fast, you'll hike by streams and waterfalls, through native trees and plants, and on to breathtaking vistas. The tour takes breaks for a picnic lunch, dips in secluded pools, and memorable photo opportunities. The 2- to 3-mile, 4-hour excursion is classified as "easy"; it's offered Saturday through Monday and costs $65. The 4- to 5-mile, 6-hour hike, classified as "easy-moderate," is offered Tuesday through Friday; it costs $110 for adults, $90 for children 13 to 18. Wear comfortable walking or hiking shoes and bring a swimsuit, sunscreen, and a camera. The tour company supplies the meals, a fanny pack with bottled water, and rain gear if necessary. No children under 13 are allowed.

About 1,500 years ago, the verdant Kahakuloa Valley was a thriving Hawaiian vil-lage. Today, only a few hundred people live in this secluded hamlet, but old Hawaii still lives on here. Explore the valley with **Ekahi Tours** (☎ **808/877-9775**). Your guide, a Kahakuloa resident and a Hawaiiana expert, walks you through a taro farm, explains the mystical legends of the valley, and gives you a peek into ancient Hawaii. The Kahakuloa Valley Tour is $60 for adults, $50 for children under 12. It starts at 7am daily and lasts 7½ hours. A snack, beverages, and hotel pickup are included in the price.

2 Central Maui

Central Maui isn't exactly tourist central; this is where real people live. You'll most likely land here and head directly to the beach. However, there are a few sights worth checking out if you need a respite from the sun 'n' surf.

KAHULUI

Under the airport flight path, next to Maui's busiest intersection and across from Costco and K-Mart in Kahului's new business park, is the most unlikely place: **Kanaha Wildlife Sanctuary,** Haleakala Highway Extension and Hana Highway (☎ **808/984-8100**). Look for a parking area off Haleakala Highway Extension (behind the mall, across the Hana Highway from Cutter Automotive), and you'll find a 50-yard trail that meanders along the shore to a shade shelter and lookout. Watch for the sign proclaiming this the permanent home of the endangered black-neck Hawaiian stilt, whose population is now down to between 1,000 and 1,500. Natural-ists say this is a good place to see endangered Hawaiian Koloa ducks, stilts, coots, and other migrating shorebirds. For a quieter, more natural-looking wildlife preserve, try the **Kealia Pond National Wildlife Preserve** in Kihei (see "South Maui," below).

PUUNENE

This town, located in the middle of the Central Maui plains, is nearly gone. Once a thriving sugar-plantation town with hundreds of homes, a school, a shopping area, and a community center, today Puunene is little more than the sugar mill, a post office, and a museum. The Hawaiian Commercial & Sugar Co., owners of the land

and the mill, has slowly phased out the rental plantation housing to open up more land to plant sugar.

The **Alexander & Baldwin Sugar Museum,** at Puunene Avenue (Highway 350) and Hansen Road (☎ **808/871-8058**), is a former sugar-mill superintendent's home converted into a museum that tells the story of sugar in Hawaii. Exhibits explain how sugar is grown, harvested, and milled. An eye-opening display shows how Samuel Alexander and Henry Baldwin managed to acquire huge chunks of land from the Kingdom of Hawaii and how they ruthlessly fought to gain access to water on the other side of the island, making sugarcane an economically viable crop. Hours are Monday through Saturday from 9:30am to 4:30pm; admission is $4 for adults, $2 for children 6 to 17, and free for children under 5.

WAIKAPU

Across the sugarcane fields from Puunene, and about 3 miles south of Wailuku on the Honoapiilani Highway, lies the tiny, one-street village of Waikapu, which has two attractions that are worth a peek, especially if you're trying to kill time before your flight out.

Relive Maui's past by taking a 40-minute narrated tram ride around fields of pineapple, sugarcane, and papaya trees at **Maui Tropical Plantation,** 1670 Honoapiilani Hwy., Waikapu (☎ **800/451-6805** or 808/244-7643). A shop sells fresh and dried fruit. The working plantation is open daily from 9am to 5pm. Admission is free; the tour is $8.50 for adults and $3.50 for kids 5 to 12.

Marilyn Monroe and Frank Lloyd Wright meet for dinner every night at **Waikapu Golf and Country Club,** 2500 Honoapiilani Hwy. (☎ **808/244-2011;** fax 808/242-8089), one of Maui's most unusual buildings. Neither actually visited Maui in real life, but these icons of architecture and glamour who traded on the curvilinear live on in this paradise setting. Wright designed the place for a Pennsylvania family in 1949, but it was never actually constructed. In 1957, Marilyn Monroe and husband Arthur Miller wanted it built for them in Connecticut, but they separated the following year. When Tokyo billionaire Takeshi Sekiguchi went shopping at Taliesen West for a signature building to adorn his 18-hole golf course, he found the blueprints, and he had Marilyn's Wright House cleverly redesigned as a clubhouse. A horizontal in a vertical landscape, it doesn't quite fit the setting, but it's still the best-looking building on Maui today. You can walk in and look around at Wright's architecture and the portraits of Marilyn in Monroe's, the restaurant.

WAILUKU

This historic gateway to Iao Valley (see below) is worth a visit, if only for a brief stop at the **Bailey House Museum,** 2375-A Main St. (☎ **808/244-3326;** fax 808/244-3920). Missionary and sugar planter Edward Bailey's 1833 home—an architectural hybrid of stones laid by Hawaiian craftsmen and timbers joined in a display of Yankee ingenuity—is a treasure trove of Hawaiiana. Inside, you'll find an eclectic collection, from precontact artifacts like scary temple images, dog-tooth necklaces, and a rare lei made of tree-snail shells to latter-day relics like Duke Kahanamoku's 1919 redwood surfboard and a koa-wood table given to President Ulysses S. Grant, who had to refuse it because he couldn't accept gifts from foreign countries. There's also a gallery devoted to a few of Bailey's landscapes, painted from 1866 to 1896, which capture on canvas a Maui we can only imagine today. Hours are daily from 10am to 4pm. Admission is $4 for adults, $3.50 for seniors, and $1 for children 6 to 12.

Walking Tour
Historic Wailuku

The historic town of Wailuku, which most visitors merely whiz by on their way to Iao Valley, has played a significant role in Maui's history over the past 200 years. One of Hawaii's bloodiest battles took place here in 1790, when Kamehameha I fought the Maui chiefs in his bid to unite the Hawaiian Islands. Wailuku, which means "bloody waters," took its name from that battle, in which the carnage was so intense that the 4-mile Iao Stream turned red from the slaughter.

Wailuku was also where the missionaries landed in the mid-1800s to "save" the natives and convert them to Christianity. You can still see the New England architectural influences they brought to this quaint community.

Sugar came to Wailuku in 1860, when the Wailuku Sugar Co. housed its operations in the old town. The industry drew immigrants from China, Japan, Okinawa, Korea, the Philippines, and Europe, each contributing aspects of its culture to the local way of life.

In 1905, Wailuku became the county seat of Maui's government; soon the small town became the center not only of government, but also of finance, commerce, and entertainment. Vaudeville thrived, movie houses were packed, and Wailuku was in its heyday.

In the 1970s, however, sugar lost its sweetness, and sugar planters began to cut back operations due to economic conditions. Wailuku began to shrink. As modern subdivisions popped up in nearby Kahului and retail shops moved to shopping centers there, Wailuku became frozen in history.

Today, visitors can experience the past 200 years of Maui's history by spending an hour wandering through Wailuku.

Getting There: From Lahaina and Kihei, take Honoapiilani Highway (Highway 30) north across the central plains of the island. The Honoapiilani Highway becomes High Street in Wailuku.

Start: Wailuku Elementary School, High Street.

Finish: Same location.

Time: About an hour, depending on how much time you spend in the shops.

Best Times: When the shops are open, Monday through Saturday from 9am to 4pm.

Begin your walk at the:

1. **Wailuku Elementary School.** This old stone building has housed Maui schoolchildren since 1904. It was designed by C. W. Dickey, one of Wailuku's most prolific architects in his day, known for developing a Hawaiian style of architecture characterized by a distinctive double-hipped roof.

Right next door is the:

2. **Wailuku Union Church,** a brick structure built in 1911 that still holds church services every Sunday at 10am.

Continue down High Street to Apuni Street; on the corner is the:

3. **Wailuku Public Library.** When the white-columned library (also designed by C. W. Dickey) was built in 1928, no one ever imagined that computers would be used to locate the books within the arched doorways and that children would line up to communicate over the Internet.

Now cross Apuni Street to the:

4. **Territorial Building,** yet another C. W. Dickey design. Built in 1930, it was once home to the business of the Territory of Hawaii, but now the thick white concrete walls house the State District Court and traffic court.

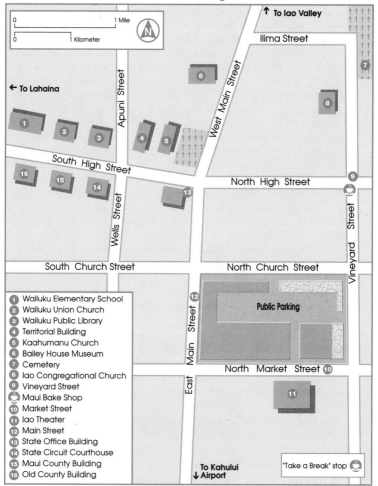

0   1 Mile
0   1 Kilometer

↑ To Iao Valley

Ilima Street

← To Lahaina

Apuni Street

West Main Street

South High Street

North High Street

Wells Street

Vineyard Street

South Church Street

North Church Street

1. Wailuku Elementary School
2. Wailuku Union Church
3. Wailuku Public Library
4. Territorial Building
5. Kaahumanu Church
6. Bailey House Museum
7. Cemetery
8. Iao Congregational Church
9. Vineyard Street
   Maui Bake Shop
10. Market Street
11. Iao Theater
12. Main Street
13. State Office Building
14. State Circuit Courthouse
15. Maui County Building
16. Old County Building

Main Street

East Main Street

Public Parking

North Market Street

"Take a Break" stop

To Kahului
↓ Airport

Next door, on the spreading lawns beneath a huge monkeypod tree, is the:

5. Kaahumanu Church, one of the most important churches on the island. Named after Queen Kaahumanu, the monarch whose conversion to Christianity prompted thousands of her subjects to follow her lead, this was one of Maui's first stone churches. It was originally a grass-hut chapel until 1832, when missionaries built an adobe-type church that the frequent rains of Wailuku eventually washed away. In 1837, the adobe structure was replaced by a stone church, designed by Edward Bailey (see below). In 1876, the stone church we see today replaced the existing stone structure. When the steeple needed repairing in 1984, the company hired was Skyline Engineers, from Massachusetts, the same place the missionaries came from some 150 years earlier. A small cemetery on the far side of the church property contains graves of the first missionaries and their families. Services are held at 9:30am on Sundays; the congregation sings hymns in Hawaiian.

Now turn left on Main Street and head up the hill toward the West Maui Mountains; on the left is the:

6. Bailey House Museum, built in 1833. In the 1840s, the building was used as Hawaii's first boarding school for girls, the Wailuku Female Seminary, with Edward Bailey serving as principal. Bailey, who went on to manage the Wailuku Sugar Co., is also widely known as a prolific landscape painter. (See description of museum, above.) The Maui Historical Society has its offices here.

Continue up Main Street and turn right at Ilima Street, where at the bend in the road you'll see the:

7. Cemetery. At the elbow in the road where Ilima and Vineyard streets meet is a cemetery that reflects Wailuku's history. The various ethnic groups who flocked to Maui during the sugar-boom years buried their dead in this quiet area with breathtaking views of Iao Valley and the West Maui Mountains.

Continue down Vineyard; on your right is the:

8. Iao Congregational Church, built in 1895 and still an active part of the surrounding community, offering day-care facilities and Sunday services at 9:30am. Various community groups use the church for meetings.

Turn left upon leaving the church and continue down:

9. Vineyard Street, an eclectic combination of old plantation houses, now-defunct stores, and a modern high-rise condominium plopped down in the middle. The next 2 blocks consist of boarded-up stores beside thriving businesses, and renovated old buildings alongside dilapidated shacks.

🍴TAKE A BREAK On the corner of Vineyard and High streets is **Maui Bake Shop** (☎ 808/242-0064), a world-class European bakery offering more than 100 bakery and deli items and breads baked in one of Maui's oldest brick ovens. You won't be able to resist the white-chocolate macadamia-nut cheesecake here. (See chapter 5 for a complete review.)

Walk further down Vineyard and turn right onto:

10. Market Street. Local residents call this street Antique Row for the curios, collectibles, memorabilia, and antiques shops that line the street.

In the middle of the block is the:

11. Iao Theater. This restored art-deco building, constructed in 1928, has had numerous lives. It first housed vaudeville, then became a movie theater, and finally fell into disrepair. In the 1970s, it reopened as a movie theater, showing art-house flicks, and was eventually fully restored to its former glory. It now hosts plays performed by the Maui Community Theater.

Turn right at the corner of Market and Main streets and continue up:

12. Main Street, where the collection of small shops offers everything from knick-knacks to antiques from Asia.

Continue up Main Street and turn left on High Street, where on the corner is the:

13. State Office Building. One of the few modern buildings in old Wailuku town, it houses most of the state agencies, including the Department of Land and Natural Resources, which offers information on state parks and camping permits.

Continue down High Street and cross Wells Street, and on the corner you'll see the:

14. State Circuit Courthouse. Built in 1907, trials are still being heard in this stately old building today.

Next door on High Street is the:

15. Maui County Building. The modern, nine-story structure stands out among the historic buildings surrounding it. When it was being built in the early 1970s, the mayor at the time said he wanted it to be the biggest building in Wailuku. He got his wish.

Next door is the:

16. Old County Building. When it was built in 1925, this old stone edifice was large enough to serve all the needs of Maui County. Fifty years later, a nine-story building was needed to serve the same purpose. This historic site is now home to the County Department of Planning's Land Use and Codes.

If you continue down High Street, you'll be back at your car in front of the Wailuku Elementary School.

IAO VALLEY

A couple of miles north of Wailuku, past the Bailey House Museum where the little plantation houses stop and the road climbs ever higher, Maui's true nature begins to reveal itself. The transition between suburban sprawl and raw nature is so abrupt that most people who drive up into the valley don't realize they're suddenly in a rain forest. The walls of the canyon begin to close around them, and a 2,250-foot needle pricks gray clouds scudding across the blue sky. After the hot tropic sun, the air is moist and cool, and the shade a welcome comfort. This is Iao Valley, a 6.2-acre state park whose great nature, history, and beauty have been enjoyed by millions of people from around the world for more than a century.

Iao ("Supreme Light") Valley, 10 miles long and encompassing 4,000 acres, is the eroded volcanic caldera of the West Maui Mountains. The head of the Iao Valley is a broad circular amphitheater where four major streams converge into Iao Stream. At the back of the amphitheater is rain-drenched Puu Kukui, the West Maui Mountains' highest point. No other Hawaiian valley lets you go from seacoast to rain forest so easily. This peaceful valley, full of tropical plants, rainbows, waterfalls, swimming holes, and hiking trails, is a place of solitude, reflection, and escape for residents and visitors alike.

Just the Facts

WHEN TO GO   The park is open daily from 7am to 7pm. Go early in the morning or late in the afternoon, when the sun's rays slant into the valley and create a mystical atmosphere. You can bring a picnic and spend the day, but be prepared at any time for a tropical cloudburst, which often soaks the valley and swells both waterfalls and streams.

ACCESS POINTS   From Wailuku, take Main Street, then turn right on Iao Valley Road to the entrance to the state park.

INFORMATION & VISITOR CENTERS   For information, contact **Iao Valley State Park,** State Parks and Recreation, 54 S. High St., Rm. 101, Wailuku, HI 96793 (☎ **808/984-8109;** fax 808/984-8111; www.hawaii.gov). The ✪ **Hawaii Nature Center,** 875 Iao Valley Rd. (☎ **808/244-6500**), home of the Iao Valley Nature Center, features hands-on, interactive exhibits and displays relating the story of Hawaiian natural history; it's an important stop for all who want to explore Iao Valley. Hours are daily from 10am to 4pm; admission is $5 for adults and $3 for children under 12.

Seeing the Highlights

Two paved walkways loop into the massive green amphitheater, across the bridge of Iao Valley Stream, and along the stream itself. The one-third–mile loop on a paved trail is Maui's easiest hike—you can even take your grandmother on this one. The leisurely walk will allow you to enjoy lovely views of the Iao Needle and the lush vegetation. Others often proceed beyond the state park border and take two trails deeper into the valley, but the trails enter private land, and NO TRESPASSING signs are posted.

The feature known as **Iao Needle** is an erosional remnant composed of basalt dikes. The phallic rock juts an impressive 2,250 feet above sea level. Youngsters play in **Iao Stream,** a peaceful brook that belies its bloody history. In 1790, King Kamehameha the Great and his men engaged in the bloody battle of Iao Valley to gain control of Maui. When the battle ended, so many bodies blocked Iao Stream that the battle site was named Kepaniwai, or "damning of the waters." An architectural heritage park of Hawaiian, Japanese, Chinese, Filipino, and New England–style houses stands in harmony by Iao Stream at **Kepaniwai Heritage Garden.** This is a good picnic spot, as there are plenty of picnic tables and benches. You can see ferns, banana trees, and other native and exotic plants in the **Iao Valley Botanic Garden** along the stream.

3 Lahaina & West Maui

THE SCENIC ROUTE TO WEST MAUI: KAHEKILI HIGHWAY

The usual road to West Maui from Wailuku is the Honoapiilani Highway, which takes you across the isthmus to Maalaea and around to Lahaina, Kaapanali, and Kapalua. But those in search of a back-to-nature driving experience should go the other way, along the ✪ **Kahekili Highway** (Highway 340). ("Highway" is a bit of a euphemism for this paved but somewhat precarious narrow road; check your rental-car agreement before you head out.) It was named after the great chief Kahekili, who built houses from the skulls of his enemies.

On the way, stop at the **Halekii and Pihanakalani Heiau,** which most visitors rarely see. To get here from Wailuku, turn north from Main Street onto Market Street. Turn right onto Mill Street and follow it until it ends; then make a left on Lower Main Street. Follow Lower Main until it ends at Waiehu Beach Road (Highway 340), and turn left. Turn left on Kuhio Street and again at the first left onto Hea Place, and drive through the gates and look for the Hawaii Visitor's Bureau marker.

These two heiau, built in 1240 from stones carried up from the Iao Stream below, sit on a hill with a commanding view of central Maui and Haleakala. Kahekili, the last chief of Maui, lived here. After the bloody battle at Iao Stream, Kamehameha I reportedly came to the temple here to pay homage to the war god, Ku, with a human sacrifice. Halekii ("House of Images") is made of stone walls with a flat grassy top, whereas Pihanakalani ("gathering place of supernatural beings") is a pyramid-shaped mount of stones. If you sit quietly nearby (never walk on any heiau, because that's considered disrespectful), the view alone explains why this spot was chosen.

Go back to Waiehu Beach Road (Highway 340), turn left, head for the tiny town of Waiehu, and then on to the true wild nature of Maui: a narrow and winding road that weaves for 20 miles along an ancient Hawaiian coastal footpath.

If you want views, these are photo opportunities from heaven: steep ravines, rolling pastoral hills, tumbling waterfalls, exploding blowholes, crashing surf, jagged lava coastlines, and a tiny Hawaiian village straight off a postcard.

Along the route, nestled in a crevice between two steep hills, is the picturesque village of **Kahakuloa** ("the tall hau tree"), with a dozen weather-worn houses, a church with a red-tile roof, and vivid green taro patches. From the northern side of the village, you can look back at the great view of Kahakuloa, the dark boulder beach, and the 636-foot Kahakuloa Head rising in the background.

A couple of miles down the road, just past the 16-mile marker, look for the **POHAKU KANI** sign, marking the huge, 6-foot-by-6-foot, bell-shaped stone. To "ring" the bell, look on the side facing Kahakuloa for the deep indentations, and strike the stone with another rock.

A little farther down the road (less than a half mile), you'll come to a wide turnoff providing a great photo op: a view of the jagged coastline down to the crashing surf.

Just past the 20-mile mark, after a sharp turn in the road, look for a small turnoff on the mauka side of the road (just after the guardrail ends). Park here and walk across the road, and on your left you'll see a spouting **blow hole.** In winter, this is an excellent spot to look for whales.

As the road rounds the point, the island of Molokai comes into view. At Honokohau, the road becomes Honoapiilani Highway (Highway 30). At the next valley, you'll come to the twin bays, **Honolua** and **Mokuleia,** which have been designated as Marine Life Conservation Areas (the taking of fish, shells, or anything else is prohibited).

KAPALUA

If you're taking the Kahekili Highway (Highway 340), Kapalua is the first resort area you'll see in West Hawaii.

For generations, West Maui meant one thing: pineapple. Hawaii's only pineapple cannery today, **Maui Pineapple Co.,** offers tours of its pineapple plantation through the Kapalua Resort Activity Center (☎ **808/669-8088**). Real plantation workers lead the 2½-hour tours, which feature the history of West Maui, facts about growing and harvesting pineapple, and lots of trivia about plantation life. Participants are even allowed to pick and harvest their own pineapple. The tours, which depart from the Kapalua Shops (next door to the Kapalua Bay Hotel), are given twice daily Monday through Friday; fees are $26 per person, and children must be at least 12 years old. Before or after the tour, you might want to take some time to wander through the Kapalua Bay Hotel (see chapters 4 and 6).

A WHALE OF A PLACE IN KAANAPALI

Heading south from Kapalua, the next resort area you'll come to is Kaanapali. If you haven't seen a real whale yet, go to **Whalers Village,** 2435 Kaanapali Pkwy., a shopping center that has adopted the whale as its mascot. You can't miss it: a huge, almost life-size metal sculpture of a mother whale and two nursing calves greets you. A few more steps, and you're met by the looming, bleached-white bony skeleton of a 40-foot sperm whale; it's pretty impressive.

On the second floor of the mall is the **Whale Center of the Pacific** (www. mauimapp.com/museums/whalecenter.htm), which features two museums. **Whalers Village Museum** (☎ **808/661-5992**) centers around the "Golden Era of Whaling" (1825–60) from the whaler's point of view, depicting the long voyages, the dangers of the hunt, and the whalers' constant longing for home. Harpoons and scrimshaw are on display, and the museum has even re-created the cramped quarters of a whaler's seagoing vessel.

Across the way, **Hale Kohola, House of the Whale** (☎ **808/661-6752**) tells the story from the whale's point of view, as it were. The museum houses exhibits on 70 species of whales and more whale lore than you could hope to absorb. Venture into the Bone Room, where volunteers scrape and identify the bones of marine mammals that wash ashore in Hawaiian waters to use in future exhibits. Pick up the free *Whale Watch Guide* that points you out the door and toward the ocean.

Both museums are open during mall hours, daily from 9:30am to 10pm; admission is free. For tips on seeing the real thing, see "Whale Watching" under "Hitting the Water," in chapter 6.

HISTORIC LAHAINA

Located between the waving green sugarcane blanketing the West Maui Mountains and the deep azure ocean offshore, Lahaina stands out as one of the few places in Hawaii that has managed to preserve its 19th-century heritage while still accommodating 20th-century guests.

In ancient times, powerful chiefs and kings ruled this hot, dry ocean-side village. At the turn of the 19th century, after King Kamehameha united the Hawaiian Islands, he made Lahaina the royal capital—which it remained until 1845, when Kamehameha III moved the capital to the larger port of Honolulu.

In the 1840s, the whaling industry was at its peak: Hundreds of ships called into Lahaina every year. The streets were filled with sailors 24 hours a day. Even Herman Melville, who later wrote *Moby Dick,* was among the throngs of whalers in Lahaina.

Just 20 years later, the whaling industry was waning, and sugar had taken over the town. The Pioneer Sugar Mill Co., which still exists today, reigned over Lahaina for the next 100 years.

Today, the drunken and derelict whalers who wandered through Lahaina's streets in search of bars, dance halls, and brothels have been replaced by hordes of tourists crowding into the small mile-long main section of town in search of boutiques, art galleries, and chic gourmet eateries. Lahaina's colorful past continues to have a profound influence today. This is no quiet seaside village, but a vibrant, cutting-edge kind of place, filled with a sense of history—but definitely with its mind on the future.

Baldwin Home Museum. 696 Front St. (at Dickenson St.). ☎ **808/661-3262.** Admission $3 adults, $2 seniors, $1 children, $5 family. Daily 10am–4:30pm.

The oldest house in Lahaina, this coral-and-rock structure was built in 1834 by Rev. Dwight Baldwin, a doctor with the fourth company of American missionaries to sail around the Horn to Hawaii. Like many missionaries, he came to Hawaii to do good—and did very well for himself. After 17 years of service, Baldwin was granted 2,600 acres for farming and grazing in Kapalua. His ranch manager experimented with what Hawaiians called *hala-kahiki,* or pineapple, on a 4-acre plot; the rest is history. Open for guided tours, the house looks as though Baldwin had just stepped out for a minute to tend a sick neighbor down the street.

Next door is the **Masters' Reading Room,** Maui's oldest building. This became visiting sea captains' favorite hangout once the missionaries closed down all of Lahaina's grog shops and banned prostitution; but by 1844, once hotels and bars started reopening, it lost its appeal. It's now the headquarters of the **Lahaina Restoration Foundation,** a plucky band of historians who try to keep this town alive and antique at the same time. Stop in and pick up a self-guided walking-tour map. You'll learn the stories of those who lived Lahaina's colorful past, from the missionary doctor who single-handedly kept a cholera epidemic from wiping out Maui's people to the boy king who lived on his very own island.

Banyan Tree. At the Courthouse Building, 649 Wharf St.

Of all the banyan trees in Hawaii, this is the biggest, most sheltering of all—so big that you can't get it in your camera's viewfinder. It was only 8 feet tall when it was planted in 1873 by Maui Sheriff William O. Smith to mark the 50th anniversary of Lahaina's first Christian mission; the big old banyan from India is now more than 50 feet tall, has 12 major trunks, and shades two-thirds of an acre in the courthouse square.

Where to Park for Free—or Next to Free—in Lahaina

Lahaina is the worst place on Maui for parking. The town was created and filled with shops, restaurants, and historic sites before the throngs of tourists (and their cars) invaded. Street parking is hit-or-miss. You can either drive around the block for hours looking for a free place to park on the street or park in one of the nearly 20 parking lots. We've divided the lots into four classes: free; free for customers; discount with validation; and pay.

Free: Of the free lots, the best is the public lot on the south side of Prison Street, between Front and Luakini streets (the lot across the street is pay), which offers 3 hours of free parking. Another free lot is on the corner of Front and Shaw streets, for the users of Maluuluolele Park.

Free for Customers: The three lots on Papalaua Street are all free for customers. The largest is the Lahaina Shopping Center lot, with 2 free hours. Next in size is the Lahaina Center, across the street (which allows 4 hours free, but you must get validation from a store in the Lahaina Center); the smallest is the Lahaina Square lot on Papalaua and Wainee streets, which offers 2 free hours for customers.

Discount with Validation: Customers of the Wharf Cinema Center, located on Front Street, can get a discount by parking at either of the theater's two lots: one on Wainee Street, between Dickenson and Prison streets; and the other on Luakini Street, between Dickenson and Prison streets.

Pay: Lahaina is filled with pay lots ranging from 50¢ for a half hour to all-day parking for $8 to $10. Pay lots on Front Street are located between Papalaua Street and Lahainaluna Road, on the corner of Dickenson Street, and underground at the 505 Front Street shopping center. Pay lots on Luakini Street are located near the Prison Street intersection and near the Lahainaluna Road intersection. Lahainaluna Road has several pay lots between Wainee and Front streets. Dickenson Street has three pay lots between Wainee and Luakini streets.

The Brig *Carthaginian II*. Lahaina Harbor. ☎ **808/661-8527.** Admission $3 adults, $2 seniors, $5 family. Daily 10am–4:30pm.

This authentically restored square-rigged brigantine is an authentic replica of a 19th-century whaling ship, the kind that brought the first missionaries to Hawaii. This floating museum features exhibits on whales and 19th-century whaling life. You won't believe how cramped the living quarters were—they make today's cruise-ship cabins look downright roomy.

Hale Pai. Lahainaluna High School Campus, 980 Lahainaluna Rd. (at the top of the mountain). ☎ **808/661-3262.** Free admission. Mon–Fri by appointment only.

When the missionaries arrived in Hawaii to spread the word of God, they found the Hawaiians had no written language. They quickly rectified the situation by converting the Hawaiian sounds into a written language. They then built the first printing press in order to print educational materials that would assist them on their mission. Hale Pai was the printing house for the Lahainaluna Seminary, the oldest American school west of the Rockies. Today Lahainaluna is the public high school for the children of West Maui.

Lahaina Jodo Mission. 12 Ala Moana St. (off Front St., near the Mala Wharf). ☎ **808/ 661-4304.** Free admission. Daily during daylight hours.

Lahaina

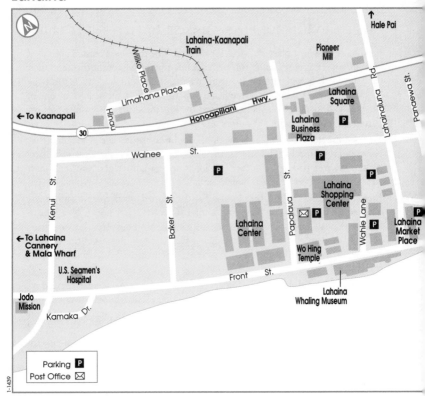

This site has long been held sacred. The Hawaiians called it Puunoa Point, which means "the hill freed from taboo." Once a small village named "Mala" ("garden"), Japanese immigrants, who came to Hawaii in 1868 as laborers for the sugarcane plantations, loved to spend time in this peaceful place and eventually built a small wooden temple to worship here. In 1968, on the 100th anniversary of the Japanese in Hawaii, a Great Buddha statue, the largest outside of Japan (some 12 feet high and weighing 3½ tons) was brought here from Japan. The immaculate grounds also contain a replica of the original wooden temple and 90-foot-tall pagoda.

Lahaina Whaling Museum. At Crazy Shirts, 865 Front St. (near Papalaua St.). ☎ **808/ 661-4775.** Free admission. Daily 9:30am–9pm.

Yankee whalers came to Lahaina to reprovision ships' stores, get drunk, and raise hell with "the girls of old Mowee." Everything was fine and dandy until 1819, when Congregational missionaries arrived and declared the port town "one of the breathing holes of hell." They tried to curb drinking and prostitution, but failed; Lahaina grew ever more lawless until the whaling era came to an end with the discovery of oil in Pennsylvania and the birth of the petroleum industry. That rambunctious era is recalled in this small museum full of art and relics from Lahaina's glory days.

Maluuluolele Park. Front and Shaw sts.

At first glance, this Front Street park appears to be only a hot, dry, dusty softball field. But under home plate is the edge of Mokuula, where a royal compound once stood more than 100 years ago, now buried under tons of red dirt and sand. Here, Prince

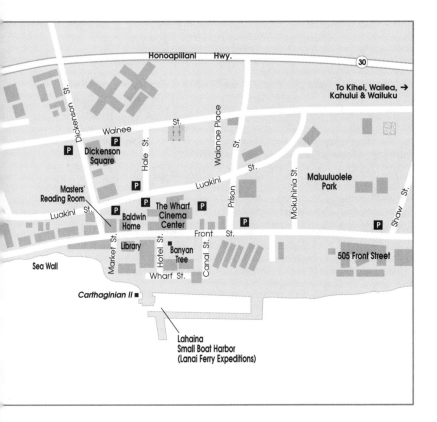

Kauikeaolui, who ascended the throne as King Kamehameha III when he was only 10, lived with the love of his life, his sister Princess Nahienaena. Missionaries took a dim view of incest, which was acceptable to Hawaiian nobles in order to preserve the royal bloodlines. Torn between love for her brother and the new Christian morality, Nahienaena grew despondent and died at the age of 21. King Kamehameha III, who reigned for 29 years—longer than any other Hawaiian monarch—presided over Hawaii as it went from kingdom to constitutional monarchy, and absolute power over the islands began to transfer from island nobles to missionaries, merchants, and sugar planters. Kamehameha died in 1854 at the age of 39. In 1918, his royal compound, containing a mausoleum and artifacts of the kingdom, was demolished and covered with dirt to create a public park. The baseball team from Lahainaluna School now plays games on the site of this royal place, still considered sacred to many Hawaiians.

Wo Hing Temple. Front St. (between Wahie Lane and Papalaua St.). ☎ **808/661-3262.** Admission by donation. Daily 10am–4pm.

The Chinese were among the various immigrants brought to Hawaii to work in the sugarcane fields. In 1909, several Chinese workers formed the Wo Hing society, a chapter of the Chee Kun Tong society, which dates from the 17th century. In 1912, they built this social hall for the Chinese community. Completely restored, the Wo Hing Temple contains displays and artifacts on the history of the Chinese in Lahaina; next door in the old cookhouse is a theater with movies of Hawaii taken by Thomas Edison in 1898 and 1903.

Walking Tour
Historic Lahaina

Back when "there was no God west of the Horn," Lahaina was the capital of Hawaii and the Pacific's wildest port. Today, it's a mild, mollified version of its old self—mostly a hustle-bustle of whale art, timeshares, and "Just Got Lei'd" T-shirts. We're not sure the rowdy whalers would have been pleased. But, if you look hard, you'll still find the historic port town they loved, filled with the kind of history that inspired James Michener to write his best-selling epic novel *Hawaii*.

Members of the Lahaina Restoration Foundation have worked for three decades to preserve Lahaina's past. They have marked a number of historical sites with brown-and-white markers; below, we've provided explanations of the significance of each site as you walk through Lahaina's historic past.

Getting There: From the Kahului Airport, take the Kuihelani Highway (Highway 38) to the intersection of Honoapiilani Highway (Highway 30), where you turn left. Follow Honoapiilani Highway to Lahaina and turn left on Lahainaluna Road. When Lahainaluna Road ends, make a left on Front Street. Dickenson Street is a block down (see the box on parking, above).

Start: Front and Dickenson streets.

Finish: Same location.

Time: About an hour.

Best Time: Daylight hours.

Worst Time: After 4pm, when everything is closed.

1. **Masters' Reading Room.** This coral-and-stone building looks just as it did in 1834, when Rev. William Richards and Rev. E. Spaulding convinced the whaling-ship captains that they needed a place for the ships' masters and captains, many of whom traveled with their families, to stay while they were ashore. The bottom floor was used as a storage area for the mission; the top floor, from which you could see the ships at anchor in the harbor, was for the visiting ships' officers.

   Next door is the:

2. **Baldwin Home.** Harvard-educated physician Rev. Dwight Baldwin, with his wife of just a few weeks, sailed to Hawaii from New England in 1830. Baldwin was first assigned to a church in Waimea, on the Big Island, and then to Lahaina's Wainee Church in 1838. He and his family lived in this house until 1871. The Baldwin Home and the Masters' Reading Room are the oldest standing buildings in Lahaina, made from thick walls of coral and hand-milled timber. Baldwin also ran his medical office and his missionary activities out of this house. (See the Baldwin Home Museum, above, for information on hours and admission.)

   On the other side of the Baldwin Home is the former site of the:

3. **Richards House.** The open field is empty today, but it represents the former home of Lahaina's first Protestant missionary, Rev. William Richards, who had quite an influence on the Kingdom of Hawaii. Richards went on to become the chaplain, teacher, and translator to Kamehameha III. He was also instrumental in drafting Hawaii's constitution and acted as the king's envoy to the United States and England, seeking recognition of Hawaii as an independent nation. After his death in 1847, he was buried in the Wainee Churchyard.

   From here, cross Front Street and walk toward the ocean, with the Lahaina Public Library on your right and the green Pioneer Inn on your left, until you see the:

Walking Tour–Historic Lahaina

← To Kaanapali

Honoapiilani Hwy.

To Kihei, Wailea, →
Kahului & Wailuku

Wainee St.

Dickenson Square

Waianae Place

Luakini St.

The Wharf Cinema Center

Prison St.

Mokuhinia St.

Maluuluolele Park

Luakini St.

Library

Front St.

Sea Wall

Wharf St.

505 Front Street

Lahaina Small Boat Harbor
(Lanai Ferry Expeditions)

- ❶ Masters' Reading Room
- ❷ Baldwin Home
- ❸ Richards House
- ❹ Taro Patch
- ❺ Hauola Stone
- ❻ Brick Palace
- ❼ *Carthaginian II*
- ❽ Pioneer Inn
- ❾ Banyan Tree
- ❿ Courthouse
- ⓫ Fort
- ⓬ Canal
- ⓭ Government Market
- ⓮ Holy Innocents Episcopal Church
- ⓯ Hale Piula
- ⓰ Maluuluolele Park
- ⓱ Wainee Church
- ⓲ Waihee Cemetery
- ⓳ Hongwanji Mission
- ⓴ David Malo's Home
- ㉑ Old Prison
- ㉒ Episcopal Cemetery
- ㉓ Hale Aloha
- ㉔ Buddhist Church
- ㉕ Luakini Street

4. Taro Patch. The lawn in front of the Lahaina Library was once a taro patch stretching back to the Baldwin Home. The taro plant was a staple of the Hawaiian diet: The root was used to make poi, and the leaves were used in cooking. At one time, Lahaina looked like Venice of the tropics, with streams, ponds, and waterways flooding the taro fields. As the population of the town grew, the water was siphoned off for drinking water.

Walk away from the Lahaina Harbor toward the edge of the lawn, where you'll see the:

5. Hauola Stone. Hawaiians believed that certain stones placed in sacred places had the power to heal. Kahunas of medicine used stones like this to help cure illnesses.

Turn around and walk back toward the Pioneer Inn; look for the concrete depression in the ground, which is all that's left of the:

6. Brick Palace, begun in 1798 as the first Western-style building in Hawaii. King Kamehameha I had this 20-by-40-foot, two-story brick structure built for his wife, Queen Kaahumanu (who is said to have preferred a grass thatched house nearby). Inside, the walls were constructed of wood and the windows were glazed glass. Kamehameha I lived here from 1801 to 1802, when he was building his war canoe, *Peleleu,* and preparing to invade Kauai. A handmade stone seawall surrounded the palace to protect it from the surf. Amazingly, the building stood for 70 years; in addition to being a royal compound, it was also used as a meeting house, storeroom, and warehouse.

Behind you, dockside of the loading pier of the Lahaina Harbor, is the:

7. *Carthaginian,* a replica of a 19th-century brig, which carried commerce back and forth to Hawaii. It also serves as a museum and exhibit of 19th-century boating and whaling. (For details on hours and fees, see the listing for the Brig *Carthaginian II,* above.)

Directly opposite the Carthaginian is the:

8. Pioneer Inn, Lahaina's first hotel and the scene of some wild parties at the turn of the century. George Freeland, of the Royal Canadian Mounted Police, tracked a criminal to Lahaina and then fell in love with the town. He built the hotel in 1901 but soon discovered that Lahaina wasn't the tourist mecca it is today. To make ends meet, Freeland built a movie theater, which was wildly successful. The Pioneer Inn remained the only hotel in all of West Maui until the 1950s. You can stay at this restored building today (see chapter 4).

From the Pioneer Inn, cross Hotel Street and walk along Wharf Street, which borders the harbor. On your left is the:

9. Banyan Tree, which has witnessed decades of luaus, dances, concerts, private chats, public rallies, and resting sojourners under its mighty boughs. Hard to believe that this huge tree was once only 8 feet tall. (See complete listing, above.)

Continue along Wharf Street; near the edge of the park is the:

10. Courthouse. In 1858, a violent windstorm destroyed about 20 buildings in Lahaina, including Hale Piula, which served as the courthouse and palace of King Kamehameha III. It was rebuilt immediately, using the stones from the previous building; it served not only as courthouse, but also as custom house, post office, tax collector's office, and government offices.

Continue down Wharf Street to Canal Street. On the corner are the remains of the:

11. Fort, which covered 1-acre and had 20-foot-high walls. In 1830, some whalers fired a few cannonballs into Lahaina in protest of Rev. William Richards's meddling in their affairs. (Richards had convinced Governor Hoapili to create a law forbidding the women of Lahaina from swimming out to greet the whaling ships.) The fort was constructed from 1831 to 1832 with coral blocks taken from the ocean where the Lahaina Harbor sits today. As a further show of strength, cannons were placed along the waterfront, where they remain today. Historical accounts seem to scoff at the "fort," saying it appeared to be more for show than for force. It was later used as a prison, until it was finally torn down in the 1850s; its stones were used for construction of the new prison, Hale Paahao (see no. 21, below).

Cross Canal Street to the:

12. Canal. Unlike Honolulu with its natural deep-water harbor, Lahaina was merely a roadstead with no easy access to the shore. Whalers would anchor in deep water offshore, then board smaller boats (which they used to chase down and harpoon whales) to make the passage over the reef to shore. If the surf were up, coming ashore could be dangerous. In the 1840s, the U.S. consular representative recommended digging a canal from one of the freshwater streams that ran through Lahaina and charging a fee to the whalers who wanted to obtain fresh water. In 1913, the canal was filled in to construct Canal Street.

Next door is the:

13. Government Market. A few years after the Canal was built, the government built a thatched marketplace with stalls for Hawaiians to sell goods to the sailors. Merchants quickly took advantage of this marketplace and erected drinking establishments, grog shops, and other pastimes of interest nearby. Within a few years, this entire area became known as "Rotten Row."

Make a right onto Front Street and continue down the street, past Kamehameha III Elementary School. Across from the park is:

14. Holy Innocents Episcopal Church. When the Episcopal missionaries first came to Lahaina in 1862, they built a church across the street from the current structure. In 1909, the church moved to its present site, which was once a thatched house built for the daughter of King Kamehameha I. The present structure, built in 1927, features unique paintings of a Hawaiian Madonna and endemic birds and plants to Hawaii, executed by DeLos Blackmar in 1940.

Continue down Front Street, and at the next open field look for the white stones by the ocean, marking the former site of:

15. Hale Piula, the "iron-roofed house." In the 1830s, the two-story stone building with a large surrounding courtyard was built for King Kamehameha III. However, the king preferred sleeping in a small thatched hut nearby, so the structure was never really completed. In the 1840s, Kamehameha moved his capital to Honolulu and wasn't using Hale Piula, so it became the local courthouse. The wind storm of 1858, which destroyed the Courthouse on Wharf Street (see no. 10, above), also destroyed the iron-roofed house. The stones from Hale Piula were used to rebuild the Courthouse on Wharf Street.

Continue down Front Street; across from the 505 Front St. complex is:

16. Maluuluolele Park, a sacred spot to Hawaiians and now site of a park and ball field. This used to be a village, Mokuhinia, with a sacred pond that was the home of a *moo* (a spirit in the form of a lizard), which the royal family honored as their personal guardian spirit. In the middle of the pond was a small island, Mokuula, home to Maui's top chiefs. After conquering Maui, Kamehameha I claimed this sacred spot as his own; he and his two sons, Kamehameha II and III, lived here when they were in Lahaina. In 1918, in the spirit of progress, the pond was drained and the ground leveled for a park.

Make a left onto Shaw Street and then another left onto Wainee Street; on the left side, just past the cemetery, is:

17. Wainee Church, the first stone church built in Hawaii (between 1828 and 1832). At one time the church could sit some 3,000 people, albeit tightly packed together, complete with "calabash spittoons" for the tobacco-chewing Hawaiian chiefs and the ship captains. That structure didn't last long—the 1858 wind storm that destroyed several buildings in Lahaina also blew the roof off the original church, knocked over the belfry, and picked up the church's bell and deposited it 100 feet away. The structure was rebuilt, but that too was destroyed—this time by Hawaiians protesting the 1894 overthrow of the monarchy. Again the church was rebuilt, and again it was destroyed—by fire, in 1947. The next incarnation of the church was destroyed by yet another windstorm, in 1951. The current church has been standing since 1953, and so far, so good. Be sure to walk around to the back of the church: The row of palm trees on the ocean side are among the oldest in Lahaina.

Wander next door to the:

18. Waihee Cemetery, the first Christian cemetery in Hawaii. Established in 1823, it tells a fascinating story of old Hawaii, with graves of Hawaiian chiefs, commoners, missionaries and their families (infant mortality was high then), and sailors. Enter this ground with respect, because Hawaiians consider it sacred—many members of the royal family were buried here, including Queen Keopuolani, who was wife of King Kamehameha I, mother of Kings Kamehameha II and III, and the first Hawaiian baptized as a Protestant. Among the other graves are Rev. William Richards (the first missionary in Lahaina) and Princess Nahienaena (sister of Kings Kamehameha II and III).

Continue down Waihee Street to the corner of Luakini Street and the:

19. Hongwanji Mission. The temple was originally built in 1910 by members of Lahaina's Buddhist sect. The current building was constructed in 1927, housing a temple and language school. The public is welcome to attend the New Year's Eve celebration, Buddha's birthday in April (see the calendar in chapter 2), and O Bon Memorial Services in August.

Continue down Wainee Street; just before the intersection with Prison Street, look for the historical marker for:

20. David Malo's Home. Although no longer standing, the house that once stood here was the home of Hawaii's first scholar, philosopher, and well-known author. Educated at Lahainaluna School, his book on ancient Hawaiian culture, *Hawaiian Antiquities,* is considered *the* source on Hawaiiana today. His alma mater celebrates David Malo Day every year on April 24, in recognition of his contributions to Hawaii.

Cross Prison Street; on the corner of Prison and Waihee is the:

21. Old Prison, which the Hawaiians called Hale Paahao ("stuck in irons house"). Sailors who refused to return to their boats at sunset used to be arrested and taken to the old fort (see no. 11, above). In 1851, however, the fort physician told the government that sleeping on the ground at night made the prisoners ill, costing the government quite a bit of money to treat them—so the Kingdom of Hawaii used the prisoners to build a prison from the coral block of the old fort. Most prisoners here had terms of a year or less (those with longer terms were shipped off to Honolulu) and were convicted of crimes like deserting ship, being drunk, or working on Sunday. Today the grounds of the prison have a much more congenial atmosphere, as they are rented out to community groups for parties.

Continue down Waihee Street, just past Waianae Place, to the small:

22. Episcopal Cemetery, which tells another story in Hawaii's history. During the reign of King Kamehameha IV, his wife, Queen Emma, formed close ties with the British Royalty. She encouraged Hawaiians to join the Anglican Church after asking the Archbishop of Canterbury to form a church in Hawaii. This cemetery contains the burial sites of many of those early Anglicans.

Next door is:

23. Hale Aloha. This "house of love" was built in 1858 by Hawaiians in "commemoration of God's causing Lahaina to escape the small pox, while it desolated Oahu in 1853, carrying off 5,000 to 6,000 of its population." The building served as a church and school until the turn of the century, when it fell into disrepair.

Turn left onto Hale Street and then right onto Luakini Street to the:

24. Buddhist Church. This green, wooden Shingon Buddhist temple is very typical of the myriad of Buddhist churches that sprang up all over the island when the Japanese laborers were brought to work in the sugarcane fields. Some of the churches were little more than elaborate false "temple" fronts on existing buildings.

On the side of Village Galleries, on the corner of Luakini and Dickenson streets, is the historical marker for:

25. Luakini Street. *Luakini* translates as a *heiau* or temple where the ruling chiefs prayed and where human sacrifices were made. This street received its unforgettable name after serving as the route for the funeral procession of Princess Harriet Naiehaena, sister of King Kamehameha III. The princess was a victim of the rapid changes in Hawaiian culture. A convert to Protestantism, she had fallen in love with her brother at an early age. Just 20 years earlier, their relationship would have been nurtured in order to preserve the purity of the royal bloodlines. The missionaries, however, frowned on brother and sister marrying. In August 1836, the couple had a son, who only lived a few short hours. Nahienaena never recovered and died in December of that same year (the king was said to mourn her death for years, frequently visiting her grave at the Waihee Cemetery; see no. 18, above). The route of her funeral procession through the breadfruit and koa trees to the cemetery became known as "Luakini," in reference to the gods "sacrificing" the beloved princess.

Turn left on Dickenson and walk down to Front Street, where you'll be back at the starting point.

OLOWALU

Most people drive right by ✪ **Olowalu,** 5 miles down Honoapiilani Highway from Lahaina; there's little to mark the spot but a small general store and Chez Paul, an expensive, but not very good, French restaurant. Olowalu ("many hills") was the scene of a bloody massacre in 1790. The Hawaiians, fascinated with iron nails and fittings, stole a skiff from the U.S. ship *Eleanora,* took it back to shore here, and burned it for the iron parts. The captain of the ship, Simon Metcalf, was furious and tricked the Hawaiians into sailing out in their canoes to trade with the ship. As the canoes approached, he mowed them down with his cannons, killing a hundred people and wounding many others.

Olowalu has great snorkeling around the 14-mile marker, where there is a turtle-cleaning station about 50 to 75 yards out from shore. Turtles line up here to have cleaner wrasses pick small parasites off.

4 South Maui

MAALAEA

At the bend in the Honopiilani Highway (Highway 30), Maalaea Bay runs along the south side of the isthmus between the West Maui Mountains and Haleakala. This is the windiest area on Maui: Trade winds blowing between the two mountains are funneled across the isthmus, and by the time they reach Maalaea, gusts of 25 to 30 m.p.h. are not uncommon.

This creates ideal conditions for windsurfers out in Maalaea Bay. Surfers are also seen just outside the small boat harbor in Maalaea, which has one of the fastest breaks in the state.

✪ **Maui Ocean Center.** Maalaea Harbor Village, at the triangle between Honoapiilani Hwy. and Maalaea Rd. ☎ **808/875-1962.** www.coralworld.com/moc. Admission $17 adults, $12 children 3–12, free for children under 3. Daily 9am–5pm.

This 5-acre facility, which opened in early 1998, houses the largest aquarium in the state and features regional marine life, including one of Hawaii's largest predators: the tiger shark. As you walk past some three dozen tanks and countless exhibits, you'll slowly descend from the "beach" to the deepest part of the ocean, without ever getting wet. Start at the surge pool, where you'll see shallow-water creatures like spiny urchins and cauliflower coral, then move on to the reef tanks, turtle pool, "touch" pool (with starfish and sea urchins), and eagle-ray pool before reaching the star of the show: the 100-foot-long, 600,000-gallon main tank, featuring tiger, gray, and white-tip sharks, as well as tuna, surgeonfish, triggerfish, and numerous other tropicals. The most phenomenal thing about this tank is that the walkway goes right through it—so you'll be surrounded on three sides by marine creatures.

KIHEI

Capt. George Vancouver "discovered" Kihei in 1778, when it was only a collection of fisherman's grass shacks on the hot, dry, dusty coast (hard to believe, eh?). A **totem pole** stands today where he's believed to have landed, across from Aston Maui Lu Resort, 575 S. Kihei Rd. Vancouver sailed on to discover British Columbia, where a great international city and harbor now bear his name.

West of the junction of Piilani Highway (Highway 31) and Mokulele Highway (Highway 350) is **Kealia Pond National Wildlife Preserve** (☎ **808/875-1582**), a 700-acre U.S. Fish and Wildlife wetland preserve where endangered Hawaiian stilts, coots, and ducks hang out and splash. These ponds work two ways: as bird preserves and as sedimentation basins that keep the coral reefs from silting from runoff. You can take a self-guided tour along a boardwalk dotted with interpretive signs and shade shelters, through sand dunes, and around ponds to Maalaea Harbor. The boardwalk starts at the outlet of Kealia Pond on the ocean side of North Kihei Road (near mile marker 2 on Piilani Highway). Among the Hawaiian waterbirds seen here are the black-crowned high heron, Hawaiian coot, Hawaiian duck, and Hawaiian stilt. There are also shorebirds like sanderling, Pacific golden plover, ruddy turnstone, and wandering tattler. From July to December, the hawksbill turtle comes ashore here to lay her eggs.

If you're interested in going to one of the many beaches along Kihei's 6-mile coast, eating in one of the dozens of restaurants, or taking in some shopping, the South Kihei Road borders the ocean and goes through the heart of town. If you're bypassing Kihei, take the Piilani Highway (Highway 31), which parallels the South Kihei Road, and avoid the hassle of stoplights and traffic.

WAILEA

The dividing line between arid Kihei and artificially green Wailea is distinct. Wailea once had the same kiawe-strewn, dusty landscape as Kihei until Alexander & Baldwin Inc. (of sugarcane fame) began developing a resort here in the 1970s (after piping water from the other side of the island to the desert terrain of Wailea). Today, the manicured 1,450 acres of this affluent resort stand out like an oasis along the normally dry leeward coast.

The best way to explore this golden resort coast is to rise with the sun and head for Wailea's 1½-mile **coastal nature trail,** stretching between the Kea Lani Hotel and the kiawe thicket just beyond the Renaissance Wailea. It's a great morning walk on Maui, a serpentine path that meanders uphill and down past native plants, old Hawaiian habitats, and a billion dollars' worth of luxury hotels. You can pick up the trail at any of the resorts or from clearly marked SHORELINE ACCESS points along the coast. The best time to go is when you first wake up; by midmorning, the coastal trail is too often clogged with joggers, and it grows crowded with beachgoers as the day wears on. As the path crosses several bold black-lava points, it affords new vistas of islands and ocean; benches allow you to pause and contemplate the view across Alalakeiki Channel, which jumps with whales in season. Sunset is another good time to hit the trail.

MAKENA

A few miles south of Wailea, the manicured coast turns to wilderness; now you're in Makena ("abundance").

In the 1800s, cattle were driven down the slope from upland ranches, lashed to rafts, and sent into the water to swim to boats that waited to take them to market. Now, **Makena Landing** is a beach park with boat-launching facilities, showers, toilets, and picnic tables. It's great for snorkeling and for launching kayaks bound for Pérouse Bay and Ahihi-Kinau preserve.

From the landing, go south on Makena Road; on the right is **Keawali Congregational Church** (☎ 808/879-5557), built in 1855 with walls 3 feet thick. Surrounded by ti leaves, which by Hawaiian custom provides protection, and built of lava rock with coral used as mortar, this Protestant church sits on its own cove with a gold-sand beach. It always attracts a Sunday crowd for its 9:30am Hawaiian-language service. Take some time to wander through the cemetery; you'll see great examples of the old custom of having a ceramic picture of the deceased on the tombstone.

A little farther south on the coast is **La Pérouse Monument,** a pyramid of lava rocks that marks the spot where French explorer Admiral Comte de la Pérouse set foot on Maui in 1786. The first Westerner to "discover" the island, he described the "burning climate" of the leeward coast, observed several fishing villages near Kihei, and sailed on into oblivion, never to be seen again; some believe he may have been eaten by cannibals in what is now Vanuatu. To get here, drive south past Puu Olai to Ahihi Bay, where the road turns to gravel. Go another 2 miles along the coast to La Pérouse Bay; the monument sits amid a clearing in black lava at the end of the dirt road.

The rocky coastline and sometimes rough seas contribute to the lack of appeal for water activities here; hiking opportunities, however, are excellent. Bring plenty of water and sun protection, and wear hiking boots that can withstand walking on lava. From La Pérouse Bay, you can pick up the old King's Highway trail, which at one time circled the island. Walk along the sandy beach at La Pérouse and look for the trail indentation in the lava, which leads down to the lighthouse at the tip of Cape Hanamanioa, about a three-quarter–mile round-trip. Or you can continue on the trail as it climbs up the hill for 2 miles, then ventures back toward the ocean, where there are quite a few old Hawaiian home foundations and rocky/coral beaches.

5 House of the Sun: Haleakala National Park

At once forbidding and compelling, ✪ **Haleakala National Park** ("House of the Sun") is Maui's main natural attraction. More than 1.3 million people a year go up the 10,023-foot-high mountain to peer down into the crater of the world's largest dormant volcano. (Haleakala is officially considered to be "active, but not currently erupting," even though it has not rumbled or spewed lava since 1790.) That hole would hold Manhattan: 3,000 feet deep, 7½ miles long by 2½ miles wide, and encompassing 19 square miles.

But there's more to do here than simply stare in a big black hole: Just going up the mountain is an experience in itself. Where else on the planet can you climb from sea level to 10,000 feet in just 37 miles, or a 2-hour drive, without ever leaving the ground? The snaky road passes through big puffy cumulus clouds to offer magnificent views of the isthmus of Maui, the West Maui Mountains, and the Pacific Ocean.

The Hawaiians recognized the mountain as a sacred site. Ancient chants tell of Pele, the volcano goddess, and one of her siblings doing battle on the crater floor where Kawilinau ("Bottomless Pit") now stands. Commoners in ancient Hawaii didn't spend much time here, though. The only people allowed into this sacred area were the kahunas, who took their apprentices to live for periods of time in this intensely spiritual place. Today, New Agers also revere Haleakala as one of the earth's powerful energy points, and even the Air Force has a not-very-well-explained presence here.

Many drive up to the summit in predawn darkness to watch the sunrise over Haleakala; writer Mark Twain called it "the sublimest spectacle" of his life. Others take a trail ride inside the bleak lunar landscape of the wilderness inside the crater, or coast down the 37-mile road from the summit on a bicycle with special brakes (see "Horseback Riding" and "Bicycling," in chapter 6, section 5). Hardy adventurers hike and camp inside the crater's wilderness (see "Hiking & Camping," in chapter 6, section 3). Those bound for the interior bring their survival gear, because the terrain is raw, rugged, and punishing—not unlike the moon. However you choose to experience Haleakala National Park, it will prove memorable—guaranteed.

JUST THE FACTS

Haleakala National Park extends from the summit of Mount Haleakala into the crater, down the volcano's southeast flank to Maui's eastern coast, beyond Hana. There are actually two separate and distinct destinations within the park: **Haleakala Summit** and the **Kipahulu** coast (See "Just Beyond Hana" in section 8, below). The summit gets all the publicity, but Kipahulu draws crowds, too—it's lush, green, and tropical, and home to Oheo Gulch (also known as Seven Sacred Pools). No road links the summit and the coast; you have to approach them separately, and you need at least a day to see each place.

WHEN TO GO At the 10,023-foot summit, weather changes fast. With wind chill, temperatures can be below freezing any time of year. Summer can be dry and warm, winters wet, windy, and cold. Before you go, get current weather conditions from the park (☎ **808/572-9306**) or the **National Weather Service** (☎ **808/871-5054**).

From sunrise to noon, the light is weak, but the view is usually free of clouds. The best time for photos is in the afternoon, when the sun lights the crater and clouds are few. Go on full-moon nights for spectacular viewing.

ACCESS POINTS **Haleakala Summit** is 37 miles, or about a 2-hour drive, from Kahului. To get here, take Highway 37 to Highway 377 to Highway 378. For details on the drive, see "The Drive to the Summit," below. Pukalani is the last town for water, food, and gas.

The **Kipahulu** section of the national park is on Maui's east end near Hana, 60 miles from Kahului on Highway 36 (the Hana Highway). Due to traffic and rough road conditions, plan on 4 hours for the drive, one way (see "Driving the Road to Hana" in section 7, below). Hana is the only nearby town for services, water, gas, food, and overnight lodging; some facilities may not be open after dark.

INFORMATION, VISITOR CENTERS & RANGER PROGRAMS For information before you go, contact **Haleakala National Park,** Box 369, Makawao, HI 96768 (☎ **808/572-9306;** www.nps.gov.hale).

One mile from the park entrance, at 7,000 feet, is **Haleakala National Park Headquarters** (☎ **808/572-9306**), open daily from 7am to 4pm. You can pick up information on park programs and activities, get camping permits, and, occasionally, see a Hawaiian nene (goose)—one or more are often here to greet visitors. Rest rooms, a pay phone, and drinking water are available.

The **Haleakala Visitor Center,** open daily from sunrise to 3pm, is near the summit, 11 miles from the park entrance. It offers a panoramic view of the volcanic landscape, with photos identifying the various features, and exhibits that explain its history, ecology, geology, and volcanology. Park staff members are often handy to answer questions. The only facilities are rest rooms and water.

Rangers offer excellent, informative, and free **naturalist talks** at 9:30, 10:30, and 11:30am daily in the summit building. For information on **hiking** (including guided

Haleakala National Park

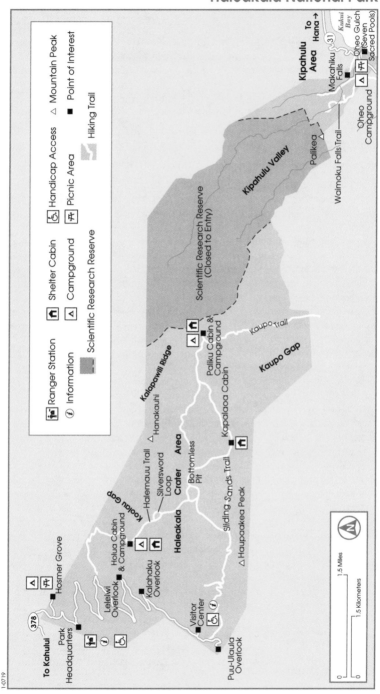

hikes) and **camping,** including cabins and campgrounds in the wilderness itself, see "Hiking & Camping," in chapter 6.

THE DRIVE TO THE SUMMIT

If you look on a Maui map, almost in the middle of the part that resembles a torso, there's a black wiggly line that looks like this: WWWWW. That's **Highway 378,** also known as **Haleakala Crater Road**—one of the few roads in the world that climbs from sea level to 10,000 feet in just 37 miles. This grand corniche has at least 33 switchbacks; passes through numerous climate zones; goes under, in, and out of clouds; takes you past rare silversword plants and endangered Hawaiian geese sailing through the clear, thin air; and offers a view that extends for more than 100 miles.

Going to the summit takes about 2 hours from Kahului. No matter where you start out, you'll follow Highway 37 (Haleakala Highway) to Pukalani, where you'll pick up Highway 377 (which is also Haleakala Highway), which you'll take to Highway 378. Along the way, expect fog, rain, and wind. You might encounter stray cattle and down-hill bicyclists. Fill up your gas tank before you go—the only gas available is 27 miles below the summit at Pukalani. There are no facilities beyond the ranger stations. Bring your own food and water.

Remember, you're entering a high-altitude wilderness area. Some people get dizzy due to the lack of oxygen; you might also suffer lightheadedness, shortness of breath, nausea, or worse: severe headaches, flatulence, and dehydration. People with asthma, pregnant women, heavy smokers, and those with heart conditions should be especially careful in the rarefied air. Bring water and a jacket or a blanket, especially if you go up for sunrise. Or you might want to go up to the summit for sunset instead.

At the **park entrance,** you'll pay an entrance fee of $10 per car (or $2 for a bicycle). About a mile from the entrance is **Park Headquarters,** where an endangered **nene,** or Hawaiian goose, might greet you with its unique call. With its black face, buff cheeks, and partially webbed feet, the gray-brown bird looks like a small Canada goose with zebra stripes; it brays out "nay-nay" (thus its name), doesn't migrate, and prefers lava beds to lakes. The unusual goose clings to a precarious existence on these alpine slopes. Vast populations of more than 25,000 once inhabited Hawaii, but hunters, pigs, feral cats and dogs, and mongooses preyed on the nene; coupled with habitat destruction, these predators nearly caused its extinction. By 1951, there were only 30 left. Now protected as Hawaii's state bird, the wild nene on Haleakala numbers fewer than 250—and the species remains endangered.

Beyond headquarters are **two scenic overlooks** on the way to the summit. Stop at Leleiwi on the way up and Kalahaku on the way back down, if only to get out, stretch, and get accustomed to the heights. Take a deep breath, look around, and pop your ears. If you feel dizzy or drowsy, or get a sudden headache, consider turning around and going back down.

Leleiwi Overlook is just beyond mile marker 17. From the parking area, a short trail leads you to a panoramic view of the lunar-like crater. When the clouds are low and the sun is in the right place, usually around sunset, you can experience a

The Legend of the House of the Sun

According to ancient legend, Haleakala got its name from a very clever trick that the demigod Maui pulled on the sun. Maui's mother, the goddess Hina, complained one day that the sun sped across the sky so quickly that her tapa cloth couldn't dry.

Maui, known as a trickster, devised a plan. The next morning, he went to the top of the great mountain and waited for the sun to poke its head above the horizon. Quickly, Maui lassoed the sun, bringing its path across the sky to an abrupt halt.

The sun begged Maui to let go, and Maui said he would on one condition: that the sun slow its trip across the sky to give the island more sunlight. The sun assented. In honor of this agreement, the Hawaiians call the mountain Haleakala, or "House of the Sun."

To this day, the top of Haleakala has about 15 minutes more sunlight than the communities on the coastline below.

---

phenomenon known as the "Specter of the Brocken"—you can see a reflection of your shadow, ringed by a rainbow, in the clouds below. It's an optical illusion caused by a rare combination of sun, shadow, and fog that occurs in only three places on the planet: Haleakala, Scotland, and Germany.

Two miles farther along is **Kalahaku Overlook,** the best place to see a rare **silversword.** You can turn into this overlook only when you are descending from the top. The silversword is the punker of the plant world, its silvery bayonets displaying tiny purple bouquets—like a spacey artichoke with attitude. This botanical wonder proved irresistible to humans, who gathered them in gunnysacks for Chinese potions, for British specimen collections, and just for the sheer thrill of having something so rare. Silverswords grow only in Hawaii, take from 4 to 50 years to bloom, and then, usually between May and October, send up a 1- to 6-foot stalk with a purple bouquet of sunflower-like blooms. They're now very rare, so don't even think about taking one home.

Continue on, and you'll quickly reach the **Haleakala Visitor Center,** which offers spectacular views. You'll feel as if you're at the edge of the earth. But don't turn around here; the actual summit's a little farther on, at **Puu Ulaula Overlook** (also known as Red Hill), the volcano's highest point, where you'll find a mysterious cluster of buildings officially known as Haleakala Observatories, but unofficially called **Science City.** If you do go up for sunrise, the building at Puu Ulaula Overlook, a triangle of glass that serves as a windbreak, is the best viewing spot. After the daily miracle of sunrise—the sun seems to rise out of the vast crater (hence the name "House of the Sun")—you can see all the way across Alenuihaha Channel to the often snowcapped summit of Mauna Kea on the Big Island.

MAKING YOUR DESCENT   Put your car in low gear; that way, you won't suddenly see smoke coming from your brakes, and you won't destroy your brakes by riding them the whole way down.

6 More in Upcountry Maui

Come upcountry and discover a different side of Maui: On the slopes of Haleakala, cowboys, planters, and other country people make their homes in serene, neighborly communities like **Makawao** and **Kula,** a world away from the bustling beach resorts.

Even if you can't spare a day or two in the cool upcountry air, there are some sights that are worth a look on your way to or from the crater. Shoppers and gallery hoppers might really want to make the effort; see chapter 8, "Shops & Galleries," for details.

On the slopes of Haleakala, Maui's breadbasket has been producing vegetables since the 1800s. In fact, during the gold rush in California, the Hawaiian farmers in Kula shipped so many potatoes that it was nicked named Nu Kaleponi, a sort of pidgin Hawaiian pronunciation of "New California." In the late 1800s, Portuguese and Chinese immigrants, who had fulfilled their labor contracts with the sugarcane companies, moved to this area, drawn by the rural agricultural lifestyle. That lifestyle continues today, among the fancy gentlemen's farms that have sprung up in the past two decades. Kula continues to grow the well-known onions, lettuce, tomatoes, carrots, cauliflower, and cabbage. It is also a major source of cut flowers for the state: Most of Hawaii's proteas, as well as nearly all the carnations used in leis, come from Kula.

To experience a bit of the history of Kula, turn off the Kula Highway (Highway 37) onto Lower Kula Road. Well before the turnoff, you'll see a white octagonal building with a silver roof, the **Holy Ghost Catholic Church** (☎ **808/878-1091**). Hawaii's only eight-sided church, it was built between 1884 and 1897 by Portuguese immigrants. The church resembles something out of Portugal; it's worth a stop to see the hand-carved altar and works of art for the stations of the cross, with inscriptions in Portuguese.

✪ **Kula Botanical Garden.** Hwy. 377, south of Haleakala Crater Rd. (Hwy. 378), $^7/_{10}$ mile from Hwy. 37. ☎ **808/878-1715**. Admission $4 adults, $1 children 6–12. Daily 9am–4pm.

This 5-acre garden offers a good overview of Hawaii's exotic flora in one small, cool place. You can take a self-guided, informative, leisurely stroll through more than 700 native and exotic plants, including three unique collections of orchids, proteas, and bromeliads.

Tedeschi Vineyards and Winery. Off Hwy. 37 (Kula Hwy.); P.O. Box 953, Ulupalakua. ☎ **808/878-6058**. Free tastings. Winery tours daily 9am–5pm.

On the southern shoulder of Haleakala, you'll enter cattle country and the **Ulupalakua Ranch,** more than 20,000 acres once owned by legendary sea captain James Makee, celebrated in the Hawaiian song and dance *Hula O Makee*. Wounded in a Honolulu waterfront brawl in 1843, Captain Makee moved to Maui and bought Ulupalakua. He renamed it Rose Ranch and planted sugar as a cash crop. He grew rich and toasted life until his death, in 1879. Still in operation, the ranch is now home to Maui's only winery, established in 1974 by Napa vintner Emil Tedeschi, who began growing California and European grapes here and producing serious still and sparkling wines, plus a silly wine made of pineapple juice. The rustic grounds are the perfect place for a picnic. Pack a basket before you go, but don't BYOB: There's plenty of great wine to enjoy at Tedeschi. Spread your picnic lunch under the sprawling camphor tree, pop the cork on a Blanc du Blanc, and toast your good fortune in being here.

Across from the winery are the remains of the three smokestacks of the **Makee Sugar Mill,** built in 1878. This is home to Maui artist Reems Mitchell, who carved the mannequins on the front porch of the Ulupakalua Ranch Store: a Filipino with his fighting cock, a cowboy, a farmhand, and a sea captain, all representing the people of Maui's history.

7 Driving the Road to Hana

Top down, sunscreen on, radio tuned to a little Hawaiian music on a Maui morning: It's time to head out to Hana along the Hana Highway (Highway 36), a wiggle of a

Road Closures on the Road to Hana

Around mile marker 14 on the Hana Highway, just Hana side of Honomanu Bay, the road has slowly been falling into the ocean for years. The good news is the state is finally repairing the road by carving into the hillside. The bad news is that until mid-2000, the road will be closed at the repair site (just beyond mile marker 14—at 14.39 to be exact) Monday through Friday from 6 to 8:30am and 11am to 3pm. Your choices: Drive the Hana Highway when this portion is open, from 8:30 to 11am and 3pm to 6am the following day; take the "back road" to Hana through Ulupalakua and Kaupo (see "Even Farther Around the Bend," at the end of this chapter); or go on a weekend. Call ☎ **808/874-6871** for recorded information.

road that runs along Maui's northeastern shore. The drive takes at least 3 hours—but take all day. Going to Hana is about the journey, not the destination.

There are wilder roads and steeper roads and even more dangerous roads, but in all of Hawaii no road is more celebrated than this one. It winds for 50 miles past taro patches, magnificent seascapes, waterfall pools, botanical gardens, and verdant rain forests, and it ends at one of Hawaii's most beautiful tropical places.

The outside world discovered the little village of Hana in 1926, when the narrow coastal road, carved by pickax-wielding convicts, opened with 56 bridges and 600 hairpin switchbacks. The mud-and-gravel road, often subject to landslides and washouts, was paved in 1962, when tourist traffic began to increase; it now sees more than 1,000 cars and dozens of vans a day, according to storekeeper Harry Hasegawa. That equals about 500,000 people a year on this road, which is way too many. Go at the wrong time, and you'll be stuck in a bumper-to-bumper rental-car parade—peak traffic hours are midmorning and midafternoon year-round, especially on weekends.

In the rush to "do" Hana in a day, most visitors spin around town in 10 minutes flat and wonder what all the fuss is about. It takes time to take in Hana, play in the waterfalls, sniff the tropical flowers, hike to bamboo forests, and take in the spectacular scenery; stay overnight if you can, and meander back in a day or two.

However, if you really must do the Hana Highway in a day, go just before sunrise and return after sunset: On a full-moon night, you'll believe in magic when you see the sea and the waterfalls glowing in soft white light, with mysterious shadows appearing in the jungle. And you'll have the road almost to yourself on the way back.

Akamai tips: Forget your mainland road manners. Practice aloha: Give way at the one-lane bridges, wave at oncoming motorists, let the big guys in four-by-fours with pig-hunting dogs in the back have the right of way—it's just common sense, brah. If the guy behind you blinks his lights, let him pass. Oh, yeah, and don't honk your horn—in Hawaii, it's considered rude.

THE JOURNEY BEGINS IN PAIA   Before you even start out, fill up your gas tank. Gas in Paia is mucho expensive ($2-plus a gallon), and it's the last place for gas until you get to Hana, some 42 miles, 54 bridges, and 600 hairpin turns down the road.

The former plantation village of Paia was once a thriving sugar-mill town. The mill is still here, but the population shifted to Kahului in the 1950s when subdivisions opened there, leaving Paia to shrivel up and die. But the town refused to give up, and it has proven its ability to adapt to the times. Now chic eateries and trendy shops stand next door to the ma-and-pa establishments that have been serving generations of Paia customers.

Plan to be here early, around 7am, when **Charley's,** 142 Hana Hwy. (☎ **808/579-9453**), opens. Enjoy a big, hearty breakfast for a reasonable price. After your

The Road to Hana

meal, head up Baldwin Avenue; about a half block from the intersection of the Hana Highway and Baldwin Avenue, stop by **Pic-nics,** 30 Baldwin Ave. (☎ **808/ 579-8021**), to stock up for a picnic lunch for the road (see chapter 5).

As you leave Paia, on your right you'll see acres of sugarcane fields, the crop that kept Maui alive for more than a century. Just before the bend in the road, you'll pass the Kuau Mart on your left; a small general store, it's the only reminder of the once-thriving community of **Kuau.** The road then bends into an S-turn; in the middle of the S is the entrance to **Mama's Fish House,** depicted by a restored 1935 panel truck with Mama's logo on the side. Just past the truck on the ocean side is the entrance to Mama's parking lot and adjacent small sandy cove in front of the restaurant. Mainly surfers use this treacherous ocean access over very slippery rocks into strong surf, but the beach is a great place to sit and soak up some sun.

WINDSURFING MECCA   A mile from Mama's, just before mile marker 9, is a place known around the world as one of the greatest windsurfing spots on the planet, **Hookipa Beach Park.** Hookipa ("hospitality") is where the top-ranked windsurfers come to test themselves against the forces of nature: thunderous surf and forceful wind. World-championship contests are held here (see "Maui Calendar of Events," in chapter 2), but on nearly every windy day after noon (the board surfers have the waves in the morning), you can watch dozens of windsurfers twirling and dancing in the wind like colored butterflies. To watch the windsurfers, do not stop on the highway, but go past the park and turn left at the entrance on the far side of the beach. You can either park on the high grassy bluff or drive down to the sandy beach and park along-side the pavilion. The park also has rest rooms, a shower, picnic tables, and a barbecue area.

INTO THE COUNTRY   Past Hookipa Beach, the road winds down into **Maliko** ("Budding") **Gulch** at mile marker 10. At the bottom of the gulch, look for the road

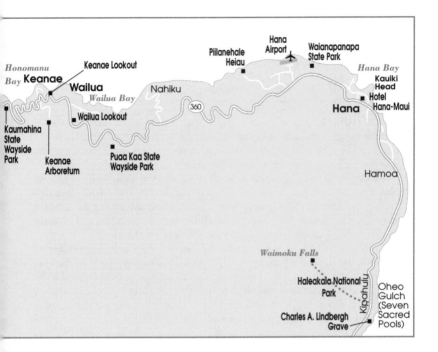

on your right, which will take you out to **Maliko Bay.** Take the first right, which goes under the bridge and past a rodeo arena (scene of competitions by the Maliko Roping Club in summer) and on to the rocky beach. There are no facilities here except a boat-launch ramp. In the 1940s, Maliko had a thriving community at the mouth of the bay, but its residents rebuilt farther inland after a strong tidal wave wiped it out.

Back on the Hana Highway, as you leave Maliko Gulch, you'll see acres of pineapple fields on your right around mile marker 11. Don't be tempted to stop and pick pineapples, because they're the private property of Maui Land & Pineapple Co.; picking is considered stealing. For the next few miles, you'll pass through the rural area of **Haiku,** with banana patches, glimpses of farms, cane grass blowing in the wind, and forests of guava trees, avocados, kukui trees, palms, and Christmas berry. Just before mile marker 15 is the **Maui Grown Market and Deli** (☎ **808/572-1693**), a good stop for drinks or snacks for the ride.

At mile marker 16, the curves begin, one right after another. Slow down and enjoy the view of bucolic rolling hills, mango trees, and vibrant ferns. After mile marker 16, the road is still called the Hana Highway, but the number changes from Highway 36 to Highway 360, and the mile markers go back to 0.

A GREAT PLUNGE ALONG THE WAY A dip in a waterfall pool is everybody's tropical-island fantasy. The first great place to stop is **Twin Falls,** at mile marker 2. Just before the wide, concrete bridge, pull over on the mountain side and park (but not in front of the sign that says DO NOT BLOCK DRIVEWAY). Keep in mind that there have been thefts in this area, and remember that a good thief can get into your locked trunk faster than you can with your key. Hop over the ladder on the right side of the red gate and walk about 3 to 5 minutes to the waterfall and pool off to your left, or continue on another 10 to 15 minutes to the second, larger waterfall and pool (do not go in if it has been raining recently). What a way to start the trip to Hana.

Travel Tip ──

If you'd like to know exactly what you're seeing as you head down the road to Hana, we suggest renting a cassette tour, available from **Rental Warehouse,** in Lahaina at 578 Front St., near Prison Street (☎ **808/661-1970**), or in Kihei at Azeka Place II, on the mountain side of Kihei Road near Lipoa Street (☎ **808/875-4050**), for $10 a day.

HIDDEN HUELO   Just before mile marker 4 on a blind curve, look for a double row of mailboxes overseen by a fading HAWAII VISITORS BUREAU sign. Down the road lies a hidden Hawaii: a Hawaii of an earlier time, where ocean waves pummel soaring lava cliffs and where an indescribable sense of serenity prevails.

Protruding out of Maui's tumultuous northern coastline, hemmed in by Waipo and Hoalua Bays, is the remote, rural community of **Huelo.** Once, this fertile area supported a population of 75,000; today, only a few hundred live among the scattered homes on this windswept land, where a handful of bed-and-breakfasts and exquisite vacation rentals are known only to a select few travelers (see chapter 4).

The only reason Huelo is even marked is the historic 1853 **Kaulanapueo Church,** which sits in the center of a putting-green–perfect lawn, bordered with hog-wire fence and accessible through a squeaky, metal turnstile. Reminiscent of New England architecture, this coral-and-cement church, topped with a plantation-green steeple and a cloudy gray tin roof, is still in use, although services are held just once or twice a month. It still has the same austere, stark interior of 1853: straight-backed benches, a no-nonsense platform for the minister, and no distractions on the walls to tempt you from paying attention to the sermon.

Next to the church is a small graveyard, a personal history of this village in concrete and stone. The graves, facing the setting sun and bleached white over the decades, are the community's garden of memories, each well tended and oft-visited.

KOOLAU FOREST RESERVE   After Huelo, the vegetation seems lusher, as though Mother Nature had poured Miracle-Gro on everything. This is the edge of the **Koolau Forest Reserve.** Koolau means "windward," and this certainly is one of the greatest examples of a lush windward area: The coastline here gets about 60 to 80 inches of rain a year, and farther up the mountain, the rainfall is 200 to 300 inches a year.

Here you will see 20- to 30-foot-tall guava trees, their branches laden with green (not ripe) and yellow (ripe) fruit. The skin is peeled and the fruit inside of the guava eaten raw, squeezed for juice, or cooked for jams or jellies. Also in this prolific area are mangos, java plums, and avocados the size of softballs. The spiny, long-leafed plants you see are hala trees, which the Hawaiians used for roofing material and for weaving baskets, mats, and even canoe sails. The very tall trees, up to 200 feet tall, are eucalyptus, brought to Hawaii from Australia to supply the sugarcane mills with power for the wood-burning engines. Unfortunately, in the nearly 100 years since the fast-growing tree was first introduced, it has quickly taken over Hawaiian forests, forcing out native plants and trees.

The 200 to 300 inches of rainfall up the mountain means a waterfall (and one-lane bridge) around nearly every turn in the road from here on out, so drive slowly and be prepared to stop and yield to oncoming cars.

DANGEROUS CURVES   About a half mile after mile marker 6, there's a sharp U-curve in the road, going uphill. The road is practically one lane here, with a brick wall on one side and virtually no maneuvering room. Sound your horn at the start of the U-curve to let approaching cars know you are coming. Take this curve, as well as the few more coming up in the next several miles, very slowly.

Just before mile marker 7 is a forest of waving **bamboo.** The sight is so spectacular that drivers are often tempted to take their eyes off the road. Be very cautious. Wait until just after mile marker 7, at the **Kaaiea** ("breathtaking") **Bridge** and stream below, to pull over and take a closer look at the hand-hewn stone walls. Then turn around to see the vista of bamboo, a photo opportunity that certainly qualifies as "breathtaking."

A GREAT FAMILY HIKE   At mile marker 9, there's a small state wayside area with rest rooms, a pavilion, picnic tables, and a barbecue area. The sign says Koolau Forest Reserve, but the real attraction here is the **Waikamoi Ridge Trail,** an easy ¾-mile loop that the entire family can do. The start of the trail is just behind the QUIET TREES AT WORK sign. The well-marked trail meanders through eucalyptus (including the unusual paper-bark eucalyptus), ferns, and hala trees.

THE GARDEN OF EDEN   Just past mile marker 10 is the **Garden of Eden Arboretum and Botanical Garden** (☎ **808/572-6453**), some 26 acres of nature trails, picnic areas, and more than 500 exotic plants and trees from around the Pacific (wild ginger, an assortment of ti plants, and an impressive palm collection). The Garden of Eden is the dream of arborist/landscape designer Alan Bradbury; he and his staff have been helping to restore a natural ecosystem and promote Hawaii's native and indigenous species since 1991. Don't be surprised if this place looks familiar—it's in the opening sequence of *Jurassic Park.* Hours are daily from 9am to 2pm; admission is $3 per person.

MORE GREAT PLUNGES   Another great waterfall is **Puohokamoa Falls,** a 30-foot falls that spills into an idyllic pool in a fern-filled amphitheater. Naturalist Ken Schmidt says that its name, loosely translated, means "valley of the chickens bursting into flight"—which is what hot, sweaty hikers look like as they take the plunge. Park at the bridge at mile marker 11 and take the short walk up the trail, which is lined with stone walls. The spectacular waterfall and deep swimming pool are surrounded by banana trees, colorful heliconias, and sweet-smelling ginger. Bring mosquito repellent. There's a picnic table at the pool.

Back at your car, be sure to check out the view toward the ocean from the bridge: Dozens of varieties of heliconias blanket the valley below.

CAN'T-MISS PHOTO OPPORTUNITIES   Just past mile marker 12 is the **Kaumahina** ("moonrise") **State Wayside Park.** Not only is this a good pit stop (rest rooms are available here) and a wonderful place for a picnic under the tall eucalyptus trees (with tables and barbecue area), but it's also a great vista point. The view of the rugged coastline makes an excellent photo—you can see all the way down to the jutting Keanae Peninsula. Just past the park on the ocean side, there's another scenic turnoff (be careful crossing the oncoming traffic) and great photo opportunity.

Another mile and a couple of bends in the road, and you'll enter the Honomanu Valley ("valley of the bird"), with its beautiful bay. To get down to the **Honomanu Bay County Beach Park,** look for the turnoff on your left, just after mile marker 14, as you begin your ascent up the other side of the valley. The rutted dirt-and-cinder road takes you down to the rocky black-sand beach. There are no facilities here, except for a stone fire pit someone has made in the sand. This is a popular site among surfers and net fishermen. There are strong rip currents offshore, so swimming is best in the stream inland from the ocean. You'll consider the drive down worthwhile as you stand on the beach, well away from the ocean, and turn to look back on the steep cliffs covered with vegetation.

THE ROAD CLOSURE   Back on the Hana Highway, just beyond mile marker 14, the state highway crews will be at work. See "Road Closures on the Road to Hana," above.

MAUI'S BOTANICAL WORLD Farther along the winding road, between mile markers 16 and 17, is a cluster of bunkhouses composing the YMCA Camp Keanae. A quarter-mile down is the **Keanae Arboretum,** where the region's botany is divided into three parts: native forest; introduced forest; and traditional Hawaiian plants, food, and medicine. You can swim in the pools of Piinaau Stream, or press on along a mile-long trail into Keanae Valley, where a lovely tropical rain forest waits at the end (see "Hiking & Camping," in chapter 6).

KEANAE PENINSULA The old Hawaiian village of **Keanae** stands out against the Pacific like a place time forgot. Here, on an old lava flow graced by an 1860 stone church and swaying palms, is one of the last coastal enclaves of native Hawaiians. They still grow taro in patches and pound it into poi, the staple of the old Hawaiian diet; they still pluck *opihi* (shellfish) from tide pools along the jagged coast and cast throw-nets at schools of fish.

The turnoff to the Keanae Peninsula is on the left, just after the arboretum. The road passes by farms and banana bunches as it hugs the peninsula. Where the road bends, there's a small beach where fishers gather to catch dinner. A quarter-mile farther is the **Keanae Congregational Church** (☎ **808/248-8040**), built in 1860 of lava rocks and coral mortar, standing out in stark contrast to the green fields surrounding it. Beside the church is a small beach-front park, with false kamani trees against a backdrop of black lava and a roiling turquoise sea.

For an experience in an untouched Hawaii, follow the road until it ends. Park by the white fence and take the short, 5-minute walk along the shoreline over the black lava. Continue along the footpath through the tall California grass to the black rocky beach, separating the freshwater stream, **Pinaau,** which winds back into the Keanae Peninsula, nearly cutting it off from the rest of Maui. This is an excellent place for a picnic and a swim in the cool waters of the stream. There are no facilities here, so be sure you leave no evidence that you were here (carry everything out with you and use rest room facilities before you arrive). As you make your way back, notice the white PVC pipes sticking out of the rocks—they're fishing-pole holders for fishermen, usually hoping to catch ulua.

ANOTHER PHOTO OP: KEANAE LOOKOUT Just past mile marker 17 is a wide spot on the ocean side of the road, where you can see the entire Keanae Peninsula's checkerboard pattern of green taro fields and its ocean boundary etched in black lava. Keanae was the result of a postscript eruption of Haleakala, which flowed through the Koolau Gap and down Keanae Valley and added this geological punctuation to the rugged coastline.

FRUIT & FLOWER STANDS Around mile marker 18, the road widens; you'll start to see numerous small stands selling fruits or flowers. Many of these stands work on the honor system: You leave your money in the basket and select your purchase. We recommend stopping at **Uncle Harry's,** which you'll find just after the Keanae School around mile marker 18. Native Hawaiian Harry Kunihi Mitchell was a legend in his time. An expert in native plants and herbs, he devoted his life to the Hawaiian-rights and nuclear-free movements. Mitchell's family sells a variety of fruit and juices here, Monday through Saturday from 9am to 4pm.

WAILUA Just after Uncle Harry's, look for the Wailua Road off on the left. This will take you through the hamlet of homes and churches of Wailua, which also contains a shrine depicting what the community calls a "miracle." Behind the pink **St. Gabriel's Church** is the smaller blue-and-white **Coral Miracle Church,** home of the **Our Lady of Fatima Shrine.** According to the story, in 1860, the men of this village were building a church by diving for coral to make the stone. But the coral offshore was in deep water and the men could only come up with a few pieces at a time, making the construction of the church an arduous project. A freak storm hit the area and deposited the coral from the deep on a nearby beach. The Hawaiians gathered what they needed and completed the church. This would make a nice enough miracle story, but there's more—after the church was completed, another freak storm hit the area and swept all the remaining coral on the beach back out to sea.

If you look back at Haleakala from here, on your left you can see the spectacular, near-vertical **Waikani Falls.** On the remainder of the dead-end road is an eclectic collection of old and modern homes. Turning around at the road's end is very difficult, so we suggest you just turn around at the church and head back for the Hana Highway.

Back on the Hana Highway, just before mile marker 19, is the **Wailua Valley State Wayside Park,** on the right side of the road. Climb up the stairs for a view of the Keanae Valley, waterfalls, and Wailua Peninsula. On a really clear day, you can see up the mountain to the Koolau Gap.

For a better view of the Wailua Peninsula, continue down the road about a quarter mile; on the ocean side, there will be a pull-off area with parking.

PUAA KAA STATE WAYSIDE PARK   You'll hear this park long before you see it, about halfway between mile markers 22 and 23. The sound of waterfalls provides the background music for this small park area with rest rooms, a phone, and a picnic area. There's a well-marked path to the falls and to a swimming hole. Ginger plants are everywhere: Pick some flowers and put them in your car so that you can travel with that sweet smell.

OLD NAHIKU   Just after mile marker 25 is a narrow 3-mile road leading from the highway, at about 1,000 feet elevation, down to sea level—and to the remains of the old Hawaiian community of **Nahiku.** At one time, this was a thriving village of thousands; today, the population has dwindled to fewer than a hundred—including a few Hawaiian families, but mostly extremely wealthy mainland residents who jet in for a few weeks at a time to their luxurious vacation homes. At the turn of the century, this site saw brief commercial activity as home of the Nahiku Rubber Co., the only commercial rubber plantation in the United States. You can still see rubber trees along the Nahiku Road. However, the amount of rainfall, coupled with the damp conditions, could not support the commercial crop; the plantation closed in 1912, and Nahiku was forgotten until the 1980s, when multimillionaires "discovered" the remote and stunningly beautiful area.

At the end of the road, you can see the remains of the old wharf from the rubber-plantation days. Local residents come down here to shoreline fish; there's a small picnic area off to the side. Dolphins are frequently seen in the bay.

HANA AIRPORT   After mile marker 31, a small sign points to the Hana Airport, down Alalele Road on the left. **Island Air** (☎ **800/323-3345** from the mainland, or 800/652-6541 in Hawaii) has two flights a day to Kahului with connections to other islands. Newly formed commuter airline **Pacific Wings** (☎ **888/575-4546**) offers three flights daily to and from Hana, with connecting flights from Kahului as well. There is no public transportation in Hana. Car rentals are available through **Dollar Rent A Car** (☎ **800/800-4000** or 808/248-8237).

WAIANAPANAPA STATE PARK   At mile marker 32, just on the outskirts of Hana, shiny black-sand Waianapanapa Beach appears like a vivid dream, with bright-green jungle foliage on three sides and cobalt blue water lapping at its feet. The 120-acre park on an ancient lava flow includes sea cliffs, lava tubes, arches, and the beach, plus 12 cabins, tent camping, picnic pavilions, rest rooms, showers, drinking water, and hiking trails. If you're interested in staying here, see chapter 4; also see "Beaches" and "Hiking & Camping," in chapter 6.

8 The End of the Road: Heavenly Hana

Green, tropical Hana is a destination all its own, a small coastal village that's probably what you came to Maui in search of.

Here you'll find a rain forest dotted with cascading waterfalls and sparkling blue pools, skirted by red- and black-sand beaches. Beautiful Hana enjoys more than 90 inches of rain a year—more than enough to keep the scenery lush. Banyans, bamboo, breadfruit trees—everything seems larger than life in this small town, especially the flowers, such as wild ginger and plumeria. Several roadside stands offer exotic blooms for $1 a bunch. Just "put money in box." It's the Hana honor system.

A LOOK AT THE PAST

The Hana coast is rich in Hawaiian history and the scene of many turning points in Hawaiian culture. The ancient chants tell of rulers like the 15th-century **Piilani,** who united the island of Maui and built fish ponds, irrigation fields, paved roads, and the massive **Piilanihale Heiau,** which still stands today. It was Piilani's sons and grandson who finished the heiau and built the first road to Hana from West Maui, not only along the coast, but also up the Kaupo Gap and through the Haleakala Crater.

In 1849, the cantankerous sea captain **George Wilfong** brought commerce to this isolated village when he started the first sugar plantation on some 60 acres. Because his harsh personality and set demands for plantation work did not sit well with the Hawaiians, Wilfong brought in the first Chinese immigrants to work his fields. In 1864, two Danish brothers, **August and Oscar Unna,** contributed to the growth of the local sugar industry when they established the Hana Plantation. Four years later, they brought in Japanese immigrants to labor in the fields.

By the turn of the century, sugar wasn't the only crop booming in Hana (there were some six plantations in the area): Rubber was being commercially grown in Nahiku, wheat in Kaupo, pineapple in Kipahulu, and tobacco in Ulupalakua. In the 1920s and 1930s, several self-sufficient towns lined the coast, each with its own general store, school, and churches; some had movie theaters as well. Hana has all of the above plus some 15 stores, a pool hall, and several restaurants.

We can only guess what those towns would have been like today if tragedy hadn't struck. On April 1, 1946, a huge tidal wave hit the state. The damage along the Hana coast was catastrophic: The Keanae Peninsula was swept clear (only the stone church remained), Hamoa was totally wiped out, and entire villages completely disappeared.

After World War II, the labor movement became a powerful force in Hawaii. **C. Brewer,** owner of the largest sugar plantation in Hana, decided to shut down his operation instead of fighting the labor union. The closure of the plantation meant not only the loss of thousands of jobs, but also the loss of plantation-supplied homes and the entire plantation lifestyle. Thankfully, **Paul I. Fagan,** an entrepreneur from San Francisco who had purchased the Hana Sugar Co. from the Unna Brothers in the 1930s, became the town's guardian angel.

Fagan wanted to retire here, so he focused his business acumen on the tiny town with big problems. Recognizing that sugar in isolated Hana was no longer economically feasible, he looked at the community and saw other opportunities. He bought

14,000 acres of land in Hana, stripped it of sugarcane, planted grass, and shipped in cattle from his ranch on Molokai.

Next, he did something that was years ahead of his time: He thought tourism might have a future in Hana, so he established an inn in 1946 that later became the **Hotel Hana-Maui.** Fagan also pulled off a public-relations coup: He brought the entire San Francisco Seals baseball team (which he happened to own) to Hana for spring training, and, more important, he brought out the sportswriters as well. The writers loved Hana and wrote glowing reports about the town; one even gave the town a nickname that stuck: "Heavenly Hana."

In 1962, the state paved the Hana Highway. By the 1970s, tourists had not only "discovered" Maui, but they also were willing to make the long trek out to Hana. The biggest change to the local lifestyle came in December 1977, when television finally arrived—after a local cable operator spent 6 months laying cable over cinder cones, mountain streams, and cavernous gulches from one side of the island to the other. Some 125 homes tuned in to the tube—and the rural Hawaiian community was never the same. Today, Hana is inhabited by 2,500 people, many part Hawaiian.

SEEING THE SIGHTS

Most visitors will zip through Hana, perhaps taking a quick look out their car windows at a few sights before buzzing on down the road. They might think they've "seen" Hana, but they definitely haven't "experienced" Hana. Allow at least 2 or 3 days to really let this land of legends show you its breathtaking beauty and quiet serenity.

As you enter Hana, the road splits about a half mile past mile marker 33, at the police station. Both roads will take you to Hana, but the lower road, Uakea Road, is more scenic. Just before you get to Hana Bay, you'll see the old wood-frame **Hana District Police Station and Courthouse.** Next door is the **Hana Museum Cultural Center,** on Uakea Road (☎ **808/248-8622;** fax 808/248-8620; www.planet-hawaii.com/hana), open daily from 10am to 4pm (most of the time). This small building has an excellent collection of Hawaiian quilts, artifacts, books, and photos. Also on the grounds are Kauhala O Hana, composed of four *hale* (houses) for living, meeting, cooking, and canoe building or canoe storage

Catercorner from the cultural center is the entrance to **Hana Bay.** You can drive right down to the pier and park. There are rest rooms, showers, picnic tables, barbecue areas, and even a snack bar here. The 386-foot, red-faced cinder cone beside the bay is **Kauiki Hill,** the scene of numerous fierce battles in ancient Hawaii and the birthplace of Queen Kaahumanu in 1768. A short, 5-minute walk will take you to the spot. Look for the trail along the hill on the wharf side, and follow the path through the ironwood trees; the lighthouse on the point will come into view, and you'll see pocket beaches of red cinder below. Grab onto the ironwood trees for support, because the trail has eroded in some areas. This is a perfect place for a secluded picnic, or you can continue on the path out to the lighthouse. To get to the lighthouse, which sits on a small island, watch the water for about 10 minutes to get a sense of how often and from which direction the waves are coming. Between wave sets, either swim or wade in the shallow, sandy bottom channel or hop across the rocks to the island.

To get to the center of town, leave Hana Bay, cross Uakea Road, and drive up Keawa Place; turn left on Hana Highway, and on the corner will be the **Hotel Hana-Maui,** the luxurious hotel established by Paul Fagan in 1946 (for a review, see chapter 4). On the green hills above Hotel Hana-Maui stands a 30-foot-high white cross made of lava rock. Citizens erected the cross in memory of Paul Fagan, who founded the Hana Ranch as well as the hotel, and helped keep the town alive. The hike up to **Fagan's Cross** provides a gorgeous view of the Hana coast, especially at sunset, when

Fagan himself liked to climb this hill. See "Hiking & Camping," in chapter 6, for details.

Back on the Hana Highway, just past Hauoli Road, is the majestic **Wananalua Congregation Church.** It's on the National Historic Register not only because of its age (it was built from 1838 to 1842 from coral stones), but also because of its location, atop an old Hawaiian heiau.

Just past the church on the right side of the Hana Highway is the turnoff to the **Hana Ranch Center,** the commercial center for Hana, with a post office, bank, general store, the Hana Ranch Stables, and a restaurant and snack bar (see chapter 5). But the real shopping experience is across the Hana Highway at the **Hasegawa General Store,** a Maui institution (see chapter 8), which carries oodles of merchandise from soda and fine French wines to fishing line to name-brand clothing, plus everything you need for a picnic or a gourmet meal. This is also the place to find out what's going on in Hana: The bulletin board at the entrance has fliers and hand-written notes advertising everything from fund-raising activities to classes to community-wide activities. You cannot make a trip to Hana without a stop at this unique store.

If you need gas before heading back, note that the two service stations, **Chevron** and **Hasegawa's Hana Geko Gas,** sit nearly side by side on the right side of the Hana Highway as you leave town.

OUTDOOR PURSUITS

Most day-trippers to Hana can't imagine what there is to do in this tiny community. The answer is: everything. One of the best areas on Maui for ocean activities, it also boasts a wealth of incredible nature hikes, remote places to explore on horseback, waterfalls to discover, and even lava tube caves to investigate.

For more information on the lava tubes, see **Maui Cave Adventures** (☎ 808/ 248-7308) on page 150. For details on horseback riding, see **Oheo Stables** (☎ 808/667-2222) on page 150. If you're a tennis player, you can take advantage of the free public courts located next to the Hotel Hana-Maui, available on a first-come, first-served basis.

BEACHES & OCEAN ACTIVITIES

Hana's beaches come in numerous varieties: white, black, gray, or red sand; perfectly shaped coves, crescents, or long stretches; and excellent for just about every kind of ocean activity you can think of. Call **Hana Kayak and Snorkel Tours** (☎ 808/ 248-7711) if you'd like to snorkel or kayak (see "Ocean Kayaking" under "Hitting the Water," in chapter 6), or venture out on your own at our favorite beaches:

HANA The waters in the Hana Bay are calm most of the time and great for swimming. There's excellent snorkeling and diving by the lighthouse. Strong currents can run through here, so don't venture farther than the lighthouse. See Hana Bay, under "Seeing the Sights," above, for more details on the facilities and hikes here.

RED SAND BEACH The Hawaiian name for this beach is Kaihalulu Beach, which means "roaring sea," and it's easy to understand why: The beach is as red as a Ferrari at a five-alarm fire. It's truly a sight to see. The beach is on the ocean side of Kauiki Hill, just south of Hana Bay, in a wild, natural setting on a pocket cove, where the volcanic cinder cone lost its seaward wall to erosion and spilled red cinders everywhere to create the red sands. Before you put on your bathing suit, there are two things to know about this beach: You have to trespass to get here (trespassing is against the law and you could face charges), and nudity (also illegal in Hawaii—arrests have been made) is common here.

Fagan's Cross ❷
Hamoa Beach ❶❹
Hana Beach Park ❹
Hana Cultural Center ❸
Hana Ranch Center ❾
Hana Ranch Restaurant ❶❶
Hana Ranch Stables ❶❷
Hasegawa General Store ❶⓿
Hotel Hana-Maui ❼
Koki Beach ❶❹
Oheo Gulch (Seven Sacred Pools) ❶❸
Queen Kaahumanu Plaque ❺
Red Sand Beach ❻
Wananalua Church ❽
Waianapanapa State Park ❶

Beach
Church
Gas Station
Post Office

0   .5 Miles
0   .5 Kilometers

To reach the beach, put on solid walking shoes (no flip-flops) and walk south on Uakea Road, past Haoli Street and the Hotel Hana-Maui, to the parking lot for the hotel's Sea Ranch Cottages. Turn left and cross the open field next to the Hana Community Center. Look for the dirt trail and follow it to the huge ironwood tree, where you turn right (do not go ahead to the old Japanese cemetery). If it's wet, do not attempt to go down the treacherous trail. Use the ironwood trees to maintain your balance as you follow the ever-eroding cinder footpath a short distance along the shoreline, down the narrow cliff trail. The trail suddenly turns the corner, and into view comes the burnt-red beach, set off by the turquoise waters, black lava, and vivid green ironwood trees.

The lava outcropping protects the bay and makes it safe for swimming. Snorkeling is excellent and there's a natural whirlpool area on the Hana Bay side of the cove. Stay away from the surge area where the ocean enters the cove.

KOKI BEACH One of the best surfing and boogie-boarding beaches on the Hana Coast lies just a couple of miles from the Hasegawa General Store in the Oheo Gulch direction. There is a very strong rip current here, so unless it is dead calm and you are a strong swimmer, do not attempt swimming here. In fact, a sign on the emergency call box—installed after a drowning in 1996—warns of the strong currents. It's a great place, though, to sit on the white sand and watch the surfers. The only facility is a big parking area. To get here, drive toward Oheo Gulch from Hana, where Highway 36 changes to Highway 31. About 1½ miles outside of Hana, turn left at Haneoo Road.

HAMOA BEACH   For one of Hana's best beaches—great for swimming, boogie boarding, and lying out—continue another half mile down the Haneoo Road loop to Hamoa Beach. There is easy access from the road down to the sandy beach, and facilities include a small rest room and an outdoor shower. The large pavilion and beach accessories are for the guests of the Hotel Hana-Maui.

WAIOKA POND   Locally, this swimming hole in a series of waterfalls and pools is called Venus Pool, and the rumor is that in ancient Hawaii, only royalty was allowed to use this exquisite site. The freshwater swimming area is a great place to spend a secluded day. Only two warnings here: Don't go to the pond if it has been raining (flash floods), and don't go near the surf at the ocean end of the stream (strong undertow). To get here, park your car well off the Hana Highway at mile marker 48, before the bridge. Hop over the fence on the ocean side of the bridge, and follow the well-worn footpath that parallels the stream. At the stream, turn to your right to take the path down to the smooth rocks above the stream. There's a huge pond just off the white-rock waterfall with a little island you can swim to in the middle.

Hiking

Hana is woven with hiking trails along the shoreline, through the rain forest, and up in the mountains. See "Hiking & Camping," in chapter 6, for a discussion of hiking in Waianapanapa and up to Fagan's Cross.

Another excellent hike leads you to **Blue Pool** and **Piilanihale Heiau.** This easy, 3-mile round-trip takes you to a freshwater, ocean-side waterfall and swimming pool at the halfway point. On the way back, you can tour a tropical botanical garden and see the largest heiau in the state. The hike is on a Jeep trail with some climbing over boulders, so wear good hiking boots or tennis shoes (no flip-flops) and bring a swimsuit and mosquito repellent. Go in the morning, when the sun lights up the ocean-side pool, and you'll have plenty of time for a picnic lunch before seeing the garden and heiau in the afternoon.

Turn toward the ocean on Ulaino Road, by mile marker 31. Drive down the paved road (which turns into a dirt road but is still drivable) to the first stream (about 1½ miles). If the stream is flooded, turn around and go back. If you can forge the stream, cross it and park on the right side of the road by the huge breadfruit trees. The trees are part of the 122-acre **Kahanu Garden** (☎ **808/248-8912**), owned and operated by the National Tropical Botanical Garden (www.ntbg.org), which also has two gardens on Kauai. Call before you go to reserve a spot on the guided tours of the garden and heiau. Tours (limited to 15) are given Monday through Friday from 1 to 3pm; they cost $10 for adults and are free for children 12 and under.

After you park your car, walk down the Jeep road that parallels the Kahanu Gardens. You'll have to forge two more streams before the road ends at the beach. Cross the rock-and-gravel beach. If it has been dry, you can just walk along the shoreline. If there has been rain, you will need to cross over the big boulders in the stream. Continue walking down the beach to the 100-foot waterfall on your left with its deep freshwater pool, known locally as **Blue Pool.** After a dip in the bracing spring water, you can sun yourself and eat a picnic lunch on the large boulders.

If you've made reservations for the tour of Kahanu Garden, be back at your car before the 1pm tour begins. The tour offers a history of Hawaii through a discussion of its native plants, plus the history of the Piilanihale Heiau and a chance to see the rugged coastline of this remote area. The 122 acres encompass plant collections from the Pacific Islands, concentrating on plants of value to the people of Polynesia, Micronesia, and Melanesia. Fringed by a vast native pandanus forest, Kahanu

Garden contains the largest known collection of breadfruit cultivars. This collection serves as a germplasm repository for this important South Pacific food crop, housing cultivars from more than 17 Pacific Island groups and Indonesia, the Philippines, and the Seychelles.

The real draw here is the **Piilanihale Heiau** ("House of Piilani," one of Maui's greatest chiefs—see "A Look at the Past," above). Believed to be the largest in the state, it measures 340 feet by 415 feet, and it was built in a unique terrace design not seen anywhere else in Hawaii. The walls are some 50 feet tall and 8 to 10 feet thick. Historians believe that Piilani's two sons and his grandson built the mammoth temple, which was dedicated to war, sometime in the 1500s.

JUST BEYOND HANA
TROPICAL HALEAKALA: OHEO GULCH AT KIPAHULU

If you're thinking about heading out to the so-called Seven Sacred Pools, out past Hana at the Kipahulu end of Haleakala National Park, let's clear this up right now: There are more than seven pools—about 24, actually—and *all* water in Hawaii is considered sacred. It's all a PR scam that has spun out of control into contemporary myth. Folks here call the attraction by its rightful name, **Oheo Gulch,** and visitors sometimes refer to it as Kipahulu, which is actually the name of the area where Oheo Gulch is located. No matter what you call it, it's a beautiful sight. The dazzling series of waterfall pools and cataracts cascading into the sea is so popular that it now has its own roadside parking lot.

ACCESS POINTS   Even though Oheo is part of Haleakala National Park, you cannot drive from the summit. Even hiking from Halekala to Oheo is tricky: The access trail out of Haleakala is down Kaupo Gap, which ends at the ocean, a good 6 miles down the coast from Oheo. To drive to Oheo, head for Hana, some 60 miles from Kahului on the Hana Highway (Highway 36). Oheo is about 30 to 50 minutes beyond Hana, along Highway 31. The Highway 31 bridge passes over pools near the ocean; the other pools, plus magnificent 400-foot Waimoku falls, are reachable via an often-muddy but rewarding, hour-long uphill hike (see "Hiking & Camping," in chapter 6). Expect showers on the Kipahulu coast.

VISITOR CENTER   The **Kipahulu Ranger Station** (☎ **808/248-7375**) is staffed from 9am to 5pm daily. Rest rooms are available, but no drinking water. Kipahulu rangers offer safety information, exhibits, books, and a variety of walks and hikes year-round; check at the station for current activities.

HIKING & CAMPING   There are a number of hikes in the park, and tent camping is allowed. See "Hiking & Camping," in chapter 6, for details.

Check with the Haleakala Park rangers before hiking up to or swimming in the pools, and always keep one eye on the water in the streams; the sky can be sunny near the coast, but flood waters travel 6 miles down from 8,000 acres of Kipahulu Valley and can rise 4 feet in less than 10 minutes.

LINDBERGH'S GRAVE

A mile past Oheo Gulch on the ocean side of the road is **Lindbergh's Grave.** First to fly across the Atlantic Ocean, Charles A. Lindbergh (1902–74) found peace in the Pacific; he settled in Hana, where he died of cancer in 1974. The famous aviator is buried under river stones in a seaside graveyard behind the 1857 **Palapala Hoomau Congregational Church,** where his tombstone is engraved with his own words: "If I take the wings of the morning and dwell in the uttermost parts of the sea. . . ."

EVEN FARTHER AROUND THE BEND

Those of you who are continuing on around Maui to the fishing village of **Kaupo** and beyond should be warned that Kaupo Road, or Old Piilani Highway (Highway 31), is rough and unpaved in parts, often full of potholes and ruts. About 2½ miles past Oheo Gulch, the pavement ends for about 5 miles—5 very rough miles as the narrow road becomes one lane around blind bends hugging the ocean cliffs, wandering in and out of valleys with sharp rock walls lining the single-car road. You may encounter wild pigs and stray cows. There are no phones or services until you reach **Ulupalakua Ranch** (see "More in Upcountry Maui," above), where there's a winery, general store, and gas station, which is likely to be closed. Before you attempt it, ask around about road conditions, or call the **Maui Public Works Department** (☎ 808/248-8254) or the **Police Department** (☎ 808/248-8311). This road frequently washes out in the rain. You'd really be better off retracing your route through Hana.

About 6 miles and about 60 minutes from Oheo Gulch, you'll see the restored **Huialoha Congregationalist "Circuit" Church,** originally constructed in 1859. Across from the church and down the road a bit is the **Kaupo Store** (☎ 808/248-8054), which marks the center of the ranching community of Kaupo. Store hours are officially Monday through Friday from 7:30am to 4:30pm, but in this arid cattle country, posted store hours often prove meaningless. The Kaupo Store is the last of the Soon family stores, which at one time stretched from Kaupo to Keanae.

From the Kaupo Store, the landscape turns into barren, dry desert. In the lee of Haleakala, this area gets little rain. Between mile markers 29 and 30, look for the ancient lava flow that created an arch as it rolled down Haleakala. Keep an eye peeled for cattle, because this is open range country. Eventually the road will wind uphill, and suddenly the forest and greenery of Ulupalakula come into sight. The upcountry town is about 45 minutes from Kahului.

Shops & Galleries   8

by Jocelyn Fujii

So, what do you do on Maui when it's too late for a Haleakala sunrise, not quite happy hour, and not sunny enough for the beach? Go shopping, of course—a major activity on this particular island. And why not? You can leapfrog from one shopping center to the next simply by following the main road—and enjoy the views of Haleakala or the West Maui Mountains in between. Maui is also an arts center of the islands, with a large number of resident artists who show their works in dozens of galleries and countless gift shops.

From Kula to Hana, Maui is also the queen of specialty products, an agricultural cornucopia that includes Kula onions, upcountry protea, Kaanapali coffee, world-renowned potato chips, and many other treats that are shipped worldwide.

As with any popular visitor destination, you'll have to wade through oceans of bad art and mountains of trinkets, particularly in Lahaina and Kihei, where touristy boutiques line the streets between rare pockets of treasures. If you shop in South or West Maui, expect to pay resort prices, clear down to a bottle of Evian or sunscreen. But Maui's gorgeous finds are particularly rewarding. Residents work, live, and shop for everyday needs in Central Maui, and it's home to first-rate boutiques for specialized tastes as well: Historic Wailuku has its own antiques alleys (N. Market and Main streets), and the Kaahumanu Center in neighboring Kahului is becoming more fashionable by the month. Also in Kahului is the $28 million Maui Arts and Cultural Center, a dream venue for the performing and visual arts, with two theaters and a 3,500-square-foot gallery. Upcountry, Makawao's boutiques are worth seeking out, despite some attitude and high prices. Finally, the big news on the Maui shopping scene is the imminent expansion of cultural and retail icon Sig Zane Designs to Wailuku. When the Hilo-based Zane moved his shop to east Hawaii's Hilo Bayfront, the whole area perked up, and we predict the same for this central Maui town.

1 Central Maui

KAHULUI

Kahului's best shopping is concentrated in two places. Almost all of the shops listed below are at one of the following centers:

Kaahumanu Center, 275 Kaahumanu Ave. (☎ **808/877-3369**), a commercial hub only 5 minutes from the Kahului Airport on

Highway 32, has more than 100 shops, restaurants, and theaters. With a thoughtful selection of food and retail shops, Kaahumanu covers all the bases, from the arts and crafts to a **Foodland Supermarket,** with everything in between: a thriving food court; the island's best beauty supply, **Lisa's Beauty Supply & Salon** (☎ 808/877-6463), and its sister store for cosmetics, **Madison Avenue Day Spa and Boutique** (☎ 808/873-0880); mall standards like **Sunglass Hut, Radio Shack,** and **Local Motion** (surf and beach wear—including the current fad, women's board shorts, a combination of hot pants and men's surf trunks); department stores **Liberty House** and **Shirokiya;** and attractive boutique/galleries such as **Ki'i** and **Maui Hands.** From 11:30am to 1:30pm on the last Friday of every month, there are food demonstrations and samplings, fashion shows, and live entertainment in the center's **Queen's Market Food Court.**

Rough around the edges and dramatically eclipsed by the Kaahumanu Center down the street, **Maui Mall,** 70 E. Kaahumanu Ave. (☎ 808/877-7559), is still a source for everyday good things, from **Long's Drugs,** which anchors the modest mall, to **Star Market.**

Caswell-Massey. Kaahumanu Center. ☎ **808/877-7761.**

Although part of a worldwide chain, this Caswell-Massey is unique for its selection of Maui-made soaps and bath products that use tropical fragrances and botanicals. As America's oldest perfume company, established in 1752, Caswell-Massey triple-mills all of its soaps (so they last three times longer), scents them with natural oils, and uses old-fashioned, tried-and-true methods and ingredients. Choose from hundreds of specialty products, from decadent bath salts with 23-karat gold flakes to Damask rose shampoo and bath gels, eye creams, body lotions, sachets, candles, perfume bottles, room mists, and more. They prepare handsome, custom-designed baskets at no extra charge.

Cost Less Imports. Maui Mall. ☎ **808/877-0300.**

Natural fibers are everywhere in this tiny corner of the mall. You'll find lauhala, bamboo blinds, grassy floor and window coverings, shoji-style lamps, burlap yardage, baskets, tactile Balinese cushions—Asian, Indonesian, and Polynesian imports, as well as top-of-the-line, made-on-Maui soaps and handicrafts. This is Hawaii's only direct importer of Chinese seagrass-rush mats and a good source for tropical and Asian home decor.

Hoaloha Heirlooms. Kaahumanu Center. ☎ **808/873-0461.**

Lavish koa ukuleles by Maui Ukulele and leis made of kukui nuts, wiliwili seeds, and Job's tears are part of the Hawaiian offerings at this wonderful gift shop. Paintings, koa tables, small Hawaiian quilts, children's clothes, muumuus and dresses, hair ornaments, handmade paper, fiber baskets, and hundreds of gift items from Hawaii, Indonesia, and the South Pacific are part of Hoaloha's offerings. We love this Hawaiian/Polynesian touch in the middle of the mall.

✪ Ki'i Gallery. Kaahumanu Center. ☎ **808/871-4557.**

The eclectic collection includes glass art and black pearls, as well as a wide assortment of made-on-Maui crafts. Chinese porcelains, clay teapots, jewelry, hand-painted maple-wood bowls, perfume bottles, and an occasional esoteric item (such as the Yiking clay forms from Shanghai) keep regulars returning. But it's the glass vases that dominate the room with their brilliance and luminosity. All handcrafted, of high quality, the glass reflects excellent craftsmanship and design, from Venetian and Czech glass to Pizzo from Maui and Vandemark Merritt from New Jersey.

Ki'i also has shops in the Grand Wailea Resort, Sheraton Maui, and the Hyatt Regency Maui.

Lightning Bolt Maui Inc. 55 Kaahumanu Ave. ☎ **808/877-3484.**

Here's an excellent selection of women's board shorts, aloha shirts, swimwear, sandals and shoes, beach towels, and all necessary accoutrements for fun in the sun. Quality labels such as Patagonia and high-tech, state-of-the-art outdoor gear and moccasins attract adventurers heading for the chilly hinterlands as well as the sun-drenched shores.

Manikin. 55 Kaahumanu Ave. ☎ **808/877-1473.**

Women who like washable, flowing clothing in silks, rayons, and natural fibers will love Manikin. If you don't find what you want on the racks of simple bias-cut designs, you can have it made from the bolts of stupendous washable fabrics lining the shop. Except for a few hand-painted silks, everything in the shop is washable.

Maui Hands. Kaahumanu Center. ☎ **808/877-0368.**

Maui hands have made most of the items in this tiny store. Because it's a consignment shop, you'll find Hawaii-made handicrafts and prices that aren't inflated. The selection includes jewelry, glass marbles, native-wood bowls, tchotchkes for every budget, and paintings and prints aplenty, in all price ranges. This is an ideal stop for made-on-Maui products and crafts of good quality; 90% of what's sold here was made on the island.

The original Maui Hands remains in Makawao at The Courtyard, 3620 Baldwin Ave. (☎ 808/572-5194).

Maui Swap Meet. S. Puunene Ave. (next to the Kahului Post Office). ☎ **808/877-3100.**

Throughout the year, there are more than 100 vendors here, which makes Maui Swap Meet, the pioneer of neighbor-island markets, a large and popular event. After Thanksgiving and throughout December, the number of booths nearly doubles and the activity reaches fever pitch. The colorful Maui specialties include vegetables from Kula and Keanae, fresh taro, plants, proteas, crafts, household items, homemade ethnic foods, and baked goods, including fabulous fruit breads. On Saturday from 5:30am to noon, vendors spread out their wares in booths, under tarps, in a festival-like atmosphere that is pure Maui with a touch of kitsch. Between the cheap Balinese imports and New Age crystals and incense, you may find some vintage John Kelly prints and 1930s collectibles. Admission is 50¢, and if you go early while the vendors are setting up, no one will turn you away.

✪ **Summerhouse.** In the Dairy Center, 385 Dairy Rd. ☎ **808/871-1320.**

Sleek, chic, tiny Summerhouse is big on style: linens by Russ Berens, FLAX, Kiko, and Tencel jeans by Signature—the best. We adore the hats, accessories, easy-care clothing, and up-to-the-minute evening dresses that Summerhouse carries in abundance. The high-quality T-shirts, always a cut above, can take you from day to evening. The casual selection is well suited to the island lifestyle.

WAILUKU

Wailuku's attractive vintage architecture, numerous antiques shops, and mom-and-pop eateries imbue the town with a charm noticeably absent in the resort areas of west, south, and upcountry Maui. There is no plastic aloha in Wailuku. Of course there's junk, but a stroll along Main and Market streets usually turns up a treasure or two. It's a mixed bag, but a treasure hunt too.

Hilo-based **Sig Zane Designs** plans a summer 1999 opening on Wailuku's Market Street, near Iao Theater. Zane and his partner, Punawai Rice, have redefined Hawaiian wear; their aloha shirts, women's clothing, and furnishings evoke a gracious Hawaii of an earlier time. Sig Zane Designs in Wailuku will likely become a cultural outpost.

✪ **Bailey House Gift Shop.** At the Bailey House Museum, 2375-A Main St. ☎ **808/244-3920.**

If you're shopping for made-in-Hawaii items and have time for only one stop in Wailuku, make it Bailey House. The small space contains a choice selection of remarkable gift items, from Hawaiian music albums to exquisite woods, traditional Hawaiian games to pareus and books. Koa-framed prints by the legendary Hawaii artist Madge Tennent, lauhala hats hanging in mid-air, hand-sewn pheasant hatbands, jams and jellies, Maui cookbooks, and an occasional Hawaiian quilt are some of the treasures to be found here. Hawaiian music often wafts in from a neighboring room, where a slack-key guitar class may be in session. Classes range from lauhala weaving to gourd-making, slack-key guitar, and ukulele. This is a thoroughly enjoyable browse through authoritative Hawaiiana in a museum that's one of the finest examples of missionary architecture, dating from 1833.

✪ **Bird of Paradise Unique Antiques.** 56 N. Market St. ☎ **808/242-7699.**

Owner Joe Myhand loves furniture, old Matson liner menus, blue willow china, kimonos for children, and anything nostalgic that happens to be Hawaiian. The furniture ranges from 1940s rattan to wicker and old koa—those items tailor-made for informal island living and leisurely moments on the lanai. Myhand also collects bottles and mails his license plates all over the world. The collection ebbs and flows with his finds, keeping buyers waiting in the wings for his Depression glass, California pottery from the 1930s and 1940s (Bauer, Metlox, Vernon, Franciscan Ware, the occasional precious Roseville), old dinnerware, perfume bottles, vintage aloha shirts, and vintage Hawaiian music on cassettes.

✪ **Brown-Kobayashi.** 160-A N. Market St. ☎ **808/242-0804.**

From self-adornment to interior design, graceful living is the theme here. Prices range from a few dollars to the thousands in this 750-square-foot treasure trove. Asian antiques mingle quietly with old and new French, European, and Hawaiian objects. Japanese kimono and obi, Bakelite and Peking glass beads, breathtaking Japanese lacquerware, cricket carriers, cloisonné, and a lotus-leaf basket carved of bamboo are among the many treasures here. Exotic and precious Chinese woods (purple sandalwood and huanghauali) glow discreetly from quiet corners, and an occasional monarchy-style lidded milo bowl comes in and flies out.

Memory Lane. 130 N. Market St. ☎ **808/244-4196.**

This 1,500-square-foot showroom is filled with art, Hawaiian collectibles, Asian antiques, kitsch, vintage textiles and aloha shirts, English crystal from the 1700s, Depression glass, antique silver, and furniture "from the very old to the 1950s and Federal," says the owner. Like all shop owners in Wailuku, Joe Ransberger, a painter, finds that old koa furniture is a rarity much in demand. Some things he can't part with, such as the curly koa chest made in the 1800s, and some of the one-of-a-kind wood-pulp rayon textiles. Prices range from $1 to $30,000, with many pieces over $1,000. You may even find the needle in the haystack: A man searching for a needle for his antiquated 78-rpm phonograph miraculously found one here.

CENTRAL MAUI EDIBLES

The **Star Market,** in the Maui Mall; **Foodland,** in the Kaahumanu Center; and **Safeway,** at 170 E. Kamehameha Ave., will satisfy your ordinary grocery needs. On Saturday, you may want to check out the **Maui Swap Meet** (see above).

With a move from Wailuku to Kahului, both the service and the selection have improved at **Down to Earth Natural Foods,** 305 Dairy Rd. (☎ **808/877-2661**). Fresh organic Maui produce, a bountiful salad bar, sandwiches and smoothies, vitamins and supplements, freshly baked goods, chips and snacks, whole grains, and several packed aisles of vegetarian and health foods have made Down to Earth a health-food staple for many years.

Established in 1941, the **Ooka Super Market,** 1870 Main St., Wailuku (☎ **808/244-3931**), Maui's ultimate home-grown supermarket, is a mom-and-pop business that has grown by leaps and bounds but still manages to keep its neighborhood flavor. Ooka sells inexpensive produce (fresh Maui mushrooms for a song), fresh island seafood, certified Angus beef, and Maui specialties such as manju and mochi. Proteas cut the same day, freesias in season, hydrangeas, fresh leis, torch gingers from Hana, upcountry calla lilies in season, and multicolored anthuriums compose what is one of Maui's finest and most affordable retail flower selections. Prepared foods are also a hit: bentos and plate lunches, roast chicken and lau lau, and specialties from all the islands. The fish is fresh, and the seaweed, poi, Kula persimmons in the fall, fresh Haiku mushrooms, and dried marlin from Kona are among the local delicacies that make Ooka a Maui favorite.

Most of the space at **Shirokiya,** in the Kaahumanu Center (☎ **808/877-5551**), is devoted to food, with a well-stocked prepared-foods section, but check out the fresh produce (bananas, papayas), juices, health-food supplements, home appliances, and audio-video equipment as well. The Dee Lite Bakery has a small corner, with its famous haupia cake and other white-and-bright pastries, but most of the other foods are local or Japanese plate-lunch fare offered in neatly packaged bento boxes or hot from the counter. Specialties such as Maui manju and Maui mochi are also available.

Maui's produce has long been a source of pride for islanders, and **Ohana Farmers Market,** Kahului Shopping Center, next to Ah Fook's Super Market (☎ **808/878-3189**), is where you'll find a fresh, inexpensive selection of Maui-grown fruit, vegetables, flowers, and plants in season. Crafts and gourmet foods add to the event, and the large monkeypod trees provide welcome shade.

Located in the northern section of Wailuku, **Takamiya Market,** 359 N. Market St. (☎ **808/244-3404**), is much loved by local folks and visitors, who often drive all the way from Kihei to stock up on picnic fare and mouth-watering ethnic foods for sunset gatherings and beach parties. This is for adventurous palates, local all the way. Unpretentious home-cooked foods from East and West are prepared daily and served on Styrofoam plates from an ethnic smorgasbord. From the chilled-fish counter come fresh sashimi and poke, and in the renowned assortment of prepared foods are mounds of shoyu chicken, tender fried squid, roast pork, kalua pork, lau lau, Chinese noodles, fiddlehead ferns, and Western comfort foods, such as corn bread and potato salad. Fresh produce and paper products are also available, but it's the prepared foods, and fresh fish counter, that have made Takamiya's a household name in central Maui.

2 West Maui

LAHAINA

Lahaina's merchants and art galleries go all out from 6:30 to 9pm on Fridays, when **Art Night** brings an extra measure of hospitality and community spirit. The Art Night openings are usually marked with live entertainment and refreshments and a livelier-than-usual street scene.

If you're in Lahaina on the second or last Thursday of the month, stroll by the front lawn of the **Baldwin Home,** 696 Front St. (at Dickenson Street), for a splendid look at lei making and an opportunity to meet the gregarious senior citizens of Lahaina. In a program sponsored by the American Association of Retired Persons, they gather from 10am to 4pm to demonstrate lei making, to sell their floral creations, and equally important, to socialize.

What was formerly a big, belching pineapple cannery is now a maze of shops and restaurants at the northern end of Lahaina town known as the **Lahaina Cannery Mall,** 1221 Honoapiilani Hwy. (☎ **808/661-5304**). Find your way through the T-shirt and sportswear shops to **Lahaina Printsellers,** home of rare maps, antique originals, prints, paintings, and wonderful 18th- to 20th-century cartography representing the largest collection of engravings and antique maps in Hawaii. Follow the scent of coffee to **Sir Wilfred's Coffee House,** where you can unwind with espresso and croissants, or head for **Compadres Bar & Grill,** where the margaritas flow freely and the Mexican food is tasty (see chapter 5 for a review). At **Enseres,** the Balinese home accessories include woven mats, coconut earrings and utensils, and carved coconut candle holders. For coconut of the edible kind, and more important, chocolate to go with it, the **Maui Chocolate Company** has a dangerously decadent selection of fudge and all things chocolate, which they will ship to the unsuspecting. In the central mall area, **Gertrude Mahi** sells gorgeous feather lei and lauhala hats of a fine weave. Other crafts, including some handsome hand-turned woods of koa, milo, and tamarind, are displayed in the **Simon-Jon Art and Design Gallery** in the same center. Half of the gallery displays the landscapes, still lifes, and seascapes of **Julie Taylor Ellingboe.** For necessities (film, water, aspirin, sunscreen), **Long's Drugs** and **Safeway** are two old standbys that anchor the cannery.

The **Lahaina Center,** 900 Front St. (☎ **808/667-9216**), is north of Lahaina's most congested strip, where Front Street begins. Across the street from the center, the seawall is a much-sought-after front-row seat to the sunset. There's plenty of free validated parking with easy access to more than 30 shops, a hair salon, restaurants, a nightclub, and a movie theater. Chef Sam Choy opened **Sam Choy's Lahaina** in January 1999 (see chapter 5), not long after **Ruth's Chris Steak House** opened its doors in the same center. **Maui Brews** (see chapter 5) serves lunch and dinner and offers live music nightly except weekends. Among the shopping stops: **Banana Republic,** the **Hilo Hattie Fashion Center** (a dizzying emporium of aloha wear), **McInerny** (wonderfully discounted designer clothes), and **ABC Discount Store**.

The conversion of 10,000 square feet of parking space into the re-creation of a traditional Hawaiian village is a welcome touch of Hawaiiana at Lahaina Center. With the commercialization of modern Lahaina, it's easy to forget that it was once the capital of the Hawaiian kingdom and a significant historic site. The village, called **Hale Kahiko,** features three main houses, called *hale:* a sleeping house; the men's dining house; and the crafts house, where women pounded lauhala for mats and baskets. Construction of the houses consumed 10,000 feet of ohia wood from the island, 20 tons of pili grass, and more than 4 miles of handwoven coconut sennit for the lashings. Artifacts, weapons, a canoe, and indigenous trees are among the authentic touches in this village, which can be toured privately or with a guide.

David Lee Galleries. 712 Front St. ☎ **808/667-7740.**

This gallery is devoted to the works of David Lee, who uses natural powder colors to paint on silk. The pigments and technique create a luminous, ethereal quality.

Foreign Intrigue Imports. 505 Front St. ☎ **808/667-4004.**

The intriguing selection of interior accents here puts a new spin on the often-tired world of Indian and Balinese imports: gorgeous hand-painted wooden trays, gilded Buddhas, cat benches, chests and armoires of all sizes, and sturdy hemp pouches and accessories. Hundreds of functional and decorative accessories line the shop and reflect Balinese artists' mastery of detail. Although hand-painted cabinets, trunks, and household accessories from India are a hit, there are items in all price ranges—and intrepid shoppers may find some deals among the vast and colorful selection, including one-of-a-kind, made-on-Maui necklaces of antique beads and jades.

Lahaina Body & Bath. 713 Front St. ☎ **808/661-1076.**

Lei Spa Maui. 505 Front St. ☎ **808/661-1178**.

The new Front Street location is an extension of Lei Spa, and both stores are worth a stop. It's a good sign that 95% of the beauty and bath products sold here are made on Maui, and that includes Hawaiian Botanical Pikake shower gel; kukui and macadamia-nut oils; Hawaiian potpourris; mud masks with Hawaiian seaweed; and a spate of rejuvenating, cleansing, skin-soothing potions for hair and skin. Aromatherapy body oils and perfumes are popular, as are the handmade Hawaiian soaps and fragrances of torch ginger, plumeria, coconut, tuberose, and sandalwood. Scented candles in coconut shells, inexpensive and fragrant, make great gifts.

Martin Lawrence Galleries. In the Lahaina Market Place, 126 Lahainaluna Rd. ☎ **808/661-1788.**

The front is garish, with pop art, kinetic sculptures, and bright, carnivalesque glass objects. Toward the back of the gallery, however, there's a sizable inventory of two-dimensional art and some plausible choices for collectors of Keith Haring, Andy Warhol, and other pop artists. The focus is on national and international artists, with very little art from Maui.

Miki's. 762 Front St. ☎ **808/661-8991.**

See why aloha shirts are so fab: Tiny, busy, and bursting with color, Miki's has a tasteful assortment of aloha wear, from Tommy Bahama shirts and coordinates to Honu Bay T-shirts, Jams, surf shorts, and beach slippers.

Totally Hawaiian Gift Gallery. Lahaina Cannery Mall, 1221 Honoapiilani Hwy. ☎ **808/667-2558.**

A good browse for its selection of Niihau shell jewelry, excellent Hawaiian CDs, Norfolk pine bowls, and Hawaiian quilt kits. Hawaiian quilt patterns sewn in Asia (at least they're honest about it) are labor-intensive, less expensive, and attractive, although not totally Hawaiian.

✪ **Village Galleries in Lahaina.** 120 and 180 Dickenson St. ☎ **808/661-4402** or 808/661-5559.

The 28-year-old Village Galleries is the oldest continuously running gallery on Maui, and it's highly esteemed as one of the few galleries with consistently high standards. Art collectors know this as a respectable showcase for regional artists; the selection of mostly original two- and three-dimensional art offers a good look at the quality of work originating on the island. The newer contemporary gallery offers colorful gift items and jewelry.

There's another location in the Ritz-Carlton Kapalua, 1 Ritz-Carlton Dr. (☎ 808/669-1800).

Westside Natural Foods. 193 Lahainaluna Rd. ☎ 808/667-2855.

A longtime Lahaina staple, Westside is serious about providing tasty food that's healthy and affordable. A healthy clientele is attracted to its excellent food bar, with vegetarian lasagna, marinated tofu strips, vegetarian pot pie, crisp salads, grains, curries, and gorgeous organic produce.

KAANAPALI

Whalers Village, 2435 Kaanapali Pkwy. (☎ **808/661-4567**), has gone shockingly upscale, but there are some new additions that ease the pain somewhat. Our favorite shoe store, **Sandal Tree,** has moved here from the Hyatt Regency (see below). Another welcome addition is **Martin & MacArthur** and its Hawaii crafts: Larry DeLuz lidded koa bowls, Hawaiian-quilt cushion covers, ceramic anthurium bowls, jewelry, boxes, soaps, books, and a stunning selection of woodworks. You can also find award-winning **Kimo Bean** coffee at a kiosk, and an expanded **Reyn's** for aloha wear. **Cinnamon Girl,** a hit in Honolulu with its matching mother-daughter clothing and accessories, opened its third Hawaii store in Whalers Village. Once you've stood under the authentic whale skeleton or squeezed the plastic whale blubber at the **Whale Center of the Pacific,** you can blow a bundle at **Tiffany, Prada, Chanel, Ferragamo, Dolce & Gabbana,** or any of the 70 shops and restaurants that have sprouted up in this beachfront shopping center. The posh Euro trend doesn't bode well; even with the newcomers, there's too little here that's Hawaiian. Some of the village's mainstream possibilities: The **Body Shop** has the best and most globally conscious products for bath and home. **The Eyecatcher** has one of the most extensive selections of sunglasses on the island, located just across from the busiest **ABC** store in the state. The most comforting stop of all is the **Maui Yogurt Company,** where Maui-made Roselani ice cream is sold in mouth-watering flavors, including a bracing mint chocolate chip. The Whalers Village is open daily from 9:30am to 10pm.

Rhonda's Quilts. In the Hyatt Regency Maui, 210 Nohea Kai Dr. ☎ **808/667-7660.**

Rhonda's has increased its made-in-Hawaii selection. Some T-shirts, tote bags, mouse pads, and Hawaiian quilt designs are designed in house, but there are also dolls, children's and women's clothing, locally made tiles in Hawaiian quilt patterns, books, stuffed animals, and other eclectic goods in this cheerful store. The Hawaiian quilts are made both here and, much less expensively, in the Philippines, and all are of high quality. Quilt pillows, supplies, patterns, and kits are sold here, and quilting classes, which include all supplies, are offered on Friday.

✪ **Sandal Tree.** Whalers Village, 2435 Kaanapali Pkwy. ☎ **808/667-5330.**

It's unusual for a resort shop to draw local customers on a regular basis (add time and parking costs to that pair of sandals), but the Sandal Tree attracts a flock of footwear fanatics who come here from throughout the islands for rubber thongs and topsiders, sandals and dressy pumps, athletic shoes and hats, Arche comfort footwear, and much more. Accessories range from fashionable knapsacks to indulgences such as avant-garde geometric handbags. Prices are realistic, too.

Another Maui location is at the Grand Wailea Resort, 3850 Wailea Alanui Dr.

KAHANA

Those driving north of Kaanapali toward Kapalua will notice the spanking-new **Honokowai Marketplace** on Lower Honoapiilani Road, only minutes before the Kapalua Airport. The splashy new A Pacific Cafe is only one of its welcome features (see chapter 5); there's also the flagship **Star Market, Hula Scoops** for ice cream, **Hawaiian Moons** for natural foods, a gas station, copy shop, the first One-Hour Martinizing dry cleaner in Hawaii, a few clothing stores, and the sprawling **Hawaiian Interiorz**.

Nearby **Kahana Gateway** is an unimpressive mall built to serve the condominium community that sprawls along the coastline between Honokowai and Kapalua. If you need women's swimsuits, however, **Rainbow Beach Swimwear** is a find. It carries a wide selection of suits for all shapes, at lower-than-resort prices, slashed even further during the frequent (and welcome) sales. **Hutton's Fine Jewelry** offers high-end pieces from designers around the country (lots of platinum and diamonds), reflecting discerning taste for those who can afford it. Tahitian black pearls and jade (some hundreds of years old, all certified) are among Hutton's specialties, but we love the Carleton Kinkade oil paintings hanging on the walls.

KAPALUA

Honolua Store. 502 Office Rd. (next to the Ritz-Carlton Kapalua). ☎ **808/669-6128.**

Walk on the old wood floors peppered with holes from golf shoes and find your everyday essentials: bottled water, stationery, mailing tape, jackets, chips, wine, soft drinks, paper products, fresh fruit and produce, and aisles of notions and necessities. One corner is dedicated to the Kapalua Nature Society, which leads hikes into the West Maui Mountains. There are always long lines of customers for the take-out counter offering deli items, more than a dozen types of sandwiches, salads, and the budget-friendly breakfast of eggs, biscuits, and gravy—and there are picnic tables on the veranda. Golfers and surfers love to come here for the morning paper and coffee.

Kapalua Shops. At the Kapalua Bay Hotel and Villas, 1 Bay Dr. ☎ **808/669-1029.**

Shops have come and gone in this small, exclusive, and once-chic shopping center, now much quieter than in days past. Tiny **Mandalay** still sells East-West luxe with its silk clothing and handful of interior accents. Mostly, though, it's logo wear, jewelry, and real-estate offices.

Village Galleries. In the Ritz-Carlton Kapalua, 1 Ritz-Carlton Dr. ☎ **808/669-1800.**

Maui's finest exhibit their works here and in the other two Village Galleries in Lahaina. Take heart, art lovers: There's no clichéd marine art here. Translucent, delicately turned bowls of Norfolk pine gleam in the light, and George Allan, Betty Hay Freeland, Joyce Clark, Diana Lehr, and Pamela Andelin are included in the pantheon of respected artists represented in the tiny gallery. Watercolors, oils, sculptures, hand-blown glass, Niihau shell leis, jewelry, and all media are represented. The Ritz-Carlton's monthly Artist-in-Residence program features Village Gallery artists in demonstrations and special hands-on workshops—free, including materials.

3 South Maui

KIHEI

Kihei is one long strip of strip malls. Most of the shopping here is concentrated in the **Azeka Place Shopping Center** on South Kihei Road. Fast foods abound—Taco Bell, Pizza Hut, Baskin Robbins—as do tourist-oriented clothing shops like **Crazy Shirts** and the overly tropical **Tropical Tantrum.** Across the street, **Azeka Place II** houses several prominent attractions, including the popular restaurant called A Pacific Cafe, **General Nutrition Center,** the **Coffee Store,** and a cluster of specialty shops with everything from children's clothes to sunglasses, beauty services, and swimwear. Also on South Kihei Road is the **Kukui Mall,** with its movie theaters, **Waldenbooks,** and **Whaler's General Store.**

A Creative Way to Spend the Day

Make a bowl from clay or paint a premade one, then fire it and take it home. The **Art School at Kapalua** (☎ **808/665-0007**), in a charming 1920s plantation building that was part of an old cannery operation, features local and visiting instructors and is open daily for people of all ages and skill levels. Programs, classes, and workshops at this not-for-profit organization highlight creativity in all forms, including photography, figure drawing, landscape painting, painting on silk, and the performing arts (ballet, yoga, creative movement, Pilates). Classes are inexpensive; call the school to see what's scheduled while you're on Maui.

Aloha Books. In the Kamaole Beach Center, 2411 S. Kihei Rd. ☎ **808/874-8070.**

Thanks go to Tom Holland for adding an espresso bar with indoor-outdoor seating and live music, poetry, and theatrical performances. This is a community bookstore with character, and it has only gotten better with the years. Holland is a collector and dealer in Hawaiian antiques, collectibles, and art, and his bookstore reflects his passion: The shelves are stocked with books on Hawaii, and the walls are covered with vintage Hawaiian and Polynesian art. There are new, used, and rare books, and although this isn't a big bookstore, the titles cover a range of tastes, from popular fiction and historic novels to health, music, travel, and Dick Francis whodunits. A sampling: old copies of *Rolling Stone, Bullfinch's Mythology,* William Saroyan's *The Human Comedy,* and a shelf full of old LPs, including most of the Beatles albums. If there's an out-of-print Don Blanding or an old John Kelly print to be found in the neighborhood, it's likely to be here.

✪ Hawaiian Moons Natural Foods. 2411 S. Kihei Rd. ☎ **808/875-4356.**

Hawaiian Moons is a health-food store, and a great one, but it's also a mini-supermarket with one of the best selections of made-on-Maui products we've encountered on the island, plus a salad bar. The Mexican tortillas are made on Maui (and good!), and much of the produce here, such as organic vine-ripened tomatoes and organic onions, is grown in the fertile upcountry soil of Kula. There's locally grown organic coffee, Maui teas, gourmet salsas, Maui shiitake mushrooms, organic lemongrass and okra, Maui Crunch bread, free-range Big Island turkeys and chickens (no antibiotics or artificial nasties), and fresh Maui juices. Cosmetics are also top-of-the-line: sunblocks, fragrant floral oils, kukui-nut oil from Waialua on Oahu, and the Island Essence made-on-Maui mango-coconut and vanilla-papaya skin lotions, the ultimate in body pampering.

Maui Sports & Cycle. In Dolphin Plaza, 2395 S. Kihei Rd. ☎ **808/875-2882.** Also at Long's Center, 1215 S. Kihei Rd. ☎ 808/875-8448.

These upbeat water-sports retail and rental shops are a hit among beachgoers and water-sports enthusiasts. Plans call for the addition of golf clubs, tennis racquets, and binoculars to the rental department, which is good news for golfers heading for the greens. A friendly, knowledgeable staff helps you choose from the mind-boggling selection of snorkel gear, boogie boards, kayaks, beach umbrellas, coolers, and view boards for "snorkeling lying down." You'll find swimwear and mountain bikes, too, and gear for riding on land or sea. The selection of good-quality snorkel equipment is so extensive you can tailor your choice to your budget as well as your fit. Prescription masks are available, as are underwater cameras, sunscreens and lotions, jewelry, T-shirts, postcards, and hats and visors by the bushel.

✪ **Old Daze.** In Azeka I, 1280 S. Kihei Rd. ☎ **808/875-7566.**

Nineteenth-century Americana and Hawaiian collectibles are nicely wedded in this charming shop. Some recent finds: an 1850s German sideboard, a Don Blanding teapot, an old Noritake tea set, Royal Worcester china, 1940s head vases, a turn-of-the-century pie safe, antique kimonos, framed vintage music sheets, and Hawaiian silver collectible spoons. The collection features a modest furniture selection, Hawaiian pictures, 1960s ashtrays, Depression glass, old washboards, souvenir plates from county fairs, and an eclectic assortment of items for table and home. Choices range from hokey to rustic to pleasantly nostalgic, with many items for the kitchen.

Tuna Luna. Kihei Kalama Village, 1941 S. Kihei Rd. ☎ **808/874-9482.**

There are treasures to be found in this small cluster of tables and booths where Maui artists display their work. Ceramics, exotic wood photo albums, jewelry, candles and soaps, handmade paper, and fiber accessories are functional and not, and make great gifts to go.

WAILEA

Wailea consists largely of upscale resort shops that sell expensive souvenirs, gift items, clothing, and accessories for a life of perpetual vacations. **Sandal Tree** (see "Kaanapali," above), with its affordable-and-up designer wear, raises the footwear banner at the Grand Wailea Resort, while stores like **Mandalay,** in the Grand Wailea Shops and the Four Seasons Resort Maui, specialize in sumptuous Thai silks and Asian imports, from resort wear to the very dressy. **Lahaina Printsellers** has moved to the Grand Wailea from the Wailea Shopping Village, now under new ownership and soon to become The Shops at Wailea. **Banana Republic, Louis Vuitton,** and **Tiffany** are among the new tenants at the yet-to-open Shops.

Grand Wailea Shops. At the Grand Wailea Resort, 3850 Wailea Alanui Dr. ☎ **808/875-1234.**

The sprawling Grand Wailea Resort is known for its long arcade of shops and galleries tailored to hefty pocketbooks. However, gift items in all price ranges can be found at **Lahaina Printsellers** (the premier store for old maps and prints), **Dolphin Galleries, H. F. Wichman, Sandal Tree,** and **Napua Gallery,** which houses the private collection of the resort owner. The sleek **Ki'i Gallery** is luminous with studio glass and the warm glow of exquisitely turned woods.

4 Upcountry Maui

MAKAWAO

Besides being a shopper's paradise, Makawao is the home of the island's most prominent arts organization, the ✪ **Hui No'eau Visual Arts Center,** 2841 Baldwin Ave. (☎ **808/572-6560**). Designed in 1917 by C. W. Dickey, one of Hawaii's most prominent architects, the two-story, Mediterranean-style stucco home that houses the center is located on a sprawling, manicured, 9-acre estate called Kaluanui. Its tree-lined driveway features two of Maui's largest hybrid Cook and Norfolk Island pines. A legacy of Maui's prominent kamaaina (native-born, longtime residents), Harry and Ethel Baldwin, the estate became an art center in 1976. Visiting artists offer lectures, classes, and demonstrations, all at reasonable prices, in basketry, jewelry making, ceramics, painting, and diverse media. Half-day classes on Hawaiian art, culture, and history are also available. Call ahead for schedules and details. Hui No'eau's exhibits are drawn from a wide range of disciplines and multicultural sources, and include both contemporary and traditional art from established and emerging artists. Maui artists long to exhibit here, considering it the most prestigious of venues. There's also a unique gift shop worth a special stop, featuring many one-of-a-kind works by local artists and artisans. Hours are Monday through Saturday from 10am to 4pm.

✪ Collections. 3677 Baldwin Ave. ☎ **808/572-0781.**

This longtime Makawao attraction is showing renewed vigor after more than 2 decades on Baldwin Avenue. Its selection of sportswear, soaps, jewelry, candles, and marvelous miscellany reflects good sense and style. Dresses, separates, sweaters, home and bath accessories, and a shop full of good things make this a Makawao must.

Cuckoo for Coconuts. 1158 Makawao Ave. ☎ **808/573-6887.**

The owner's quirky sense of humor pervades every inch of this tiny shop, barely bigger than a large walk-in closet and brimming with vintage collectibles, gag gifts, silly coconuts, 1960s and '70s aloha wear, tutus, sequined dresses, vintage wedding gowns, and all sorts of oddities, arranged around an old claw-foot bathtub in the middle of the shop. Things we've seen here: an Elvira wig, very convincing; a raffia hat looking suspiciously like a nest, with blue eggs on top; and some vintage aloha shirts that would make a collector drool. The new services—singing telegrams, costumes, make-up, and gag gifts—keep the laughs coming.

Gecko Trading Co. Boutique. 3621 Baldwin Ave. ☎ **808/572-0249.**

The selection here is eclectic and always changing: One day it's St. John's Wort body lotion and mesh T-shirts in a dragon motif, the next day it's soaps from Provence and antique lapis jewelry. You never know what you'll find in this tiny boutique; we've seen everything from hair scrunchies to handmade crocheted bags from New York, clothing from Spain and France, collectible bottles, T-shirts, toys, shawls, and Mexican hammered-tin candle holders. The prices are reasonable, the service is friendly, and it's not self-consciously stylish in the way that some other local boutiques are.

Holiday & Co. 3681 Baldwin Ave. ☎ **808/572-1470.**

Attractive women's clothing in natural fibers hangs from racks, while jewelry to go with it beckons from the counter. Recent finds include lotus-fiber bags from Bali and sumptuous Ambre bubble bath, expensive and French and worth it. The Holiday signature: the latest in comfortable clothing and interchangeable styles in easy-care fabrics. Classic linen dresses, cotton and chenille sweaters, tasteful T-shirts, and silks in all weaves fill this understated store.

Hot Island Glassblowing Studio & Gallery. 3620 Baldwin Ave. ☎ **808/572-4527.**

You can watch the artist transform molten glass into works of art and utility in this cordial studio in Makawao's Courtyard, where an award-winning family of glass-blowers built its own furnaces. It's fascinating to watch the shapes emerge from glass melted at 2,000°F. The colorful works displayed in the studio range from small paperweights to large vessels, and they're shipped around the world. Four to five artists participate in the demonstrations, which begin when the furnace is heated, about half an hour before the studio opens at 10am.

Hurricane. 3639 Baldwin Ave. ☎ **808/572-5076.**

This chic boutique carries clothing, gifts, accessories, and books that are two steps ahead of the competition. Tommy Bahama silk piqué aloha shirts and aloha print dresses, Sigrid Olsen's line of clothing (knit shells, Tencel jeans and skirts, cardigans, extraordinary silk tank dresses—morning-to-evening attire that's expensive but wonderful), hats, art by local artists, and hard-to-find, eccentric books and home accessories are part of the Hurricane appeal.

The Mercantile. 3673 Baldwin Ave. ☎ **808/572-1407.**

The jewelry, home accessories (especially the Tiffany-style glass-and-shell lamps), dinnerware, Italian linens, plantation-style furniture, and clothing are tastefully selected, a salute to the good life. Soothing eye pillows filled with flaxseeds, handmade designer dolls, hand-carved armoires, down-filled furniture and slipcovers, and a large selection of Kiehl's products will make it easy to part with your time and money. The clothing—comfortable cottons and upscale European linens—is for men and women, as are the soaps, including Maui Herbal Soap products and some unusual finds from Provence.

✪ **Ola's Makawao.** In the Paniolo Building, 1156 Makawao Ave. ☎ **808/573-1334.**

You'll always find a Doug Britt painting or two, which is reason enough to stop by Ola's. Britt's scintillating paintings and furniture assemblages (vanities and lockers of found wood!) are among the great art finds of Hawaii. Owners and sisters Cindy Heacock and Shari O'Brien add a personal touch to the delightful environment they've created in this bright, thoughtfully designed space. Handmade American art by more than 160 artists includes Hawaii's best in glassware, ceramics, wood, jewelry, paper, and other media. Enjoy the studio glass, porcelain vases, koa chopsticks, outrageous martini glasses, seed lei, toys, letter openers, dolls, silks, and sumptuous bath products, but don't forget Bella's at Ola's, a line of fourth-generation handmade chocolates from Brooklyn, offered in 12 pricey but irresistible varieties.

Silk Angel. Corner of Baldwin and Makawao aves. ☎ **808/573-1124.**

This tiny corner boutique is filled with all things silk and angelic, gathered from the owner's Asian and Indonesian travels: hand-painted sarongs, batiks, scarves from India, capes, and a gorgeous selection of sarongs made from Indian sari material.

Tropo. 3643 Baldwin Ave. ☎ **808/573-0356.**

Tropo, the sister store of Hurricane (see above), gives men equal shopping time and an equally delectable selection. This magnet for stylish, sensitive, *and* rugged men carries books, clothing, hats, and Crabtree & Evelyn products. Find the latest in shirts and the literary tomes to go with them, as well as Tommy Bahama silk pique trousers and shorts; tasteful T-shirts; Western shirts (with snap buttons, made by Rockmount, whose clothes Robert Redford wore in *The Horse Whisperer*); stylish winter wovens by Toes on the Nose; great aloha shirts by Que and Kahala; and an intoxicating selection of fragrance and bath products for men and women.

✪ **Viewpoints Gallery.** 3620 Baldwin Ave. ☎ **808/572-5979.**

The island's only fine-arts cooperative showcases the work of dozens of Maui artists in an airy, attractive gallery located in a restored theater with a courtyard, glassblowing studio, and restaurants. The delightful gallery features two-dimensional art, jewelry, fiber art, stained glass, papermaking, sculpture, and other media. The cooperative maintains a high degree of professionalism, as the artists involved (all full-time professionals) have passed a rigorous screening. A fine example of what can happen in a collectively supportive artistic environment.

UPCOUNTRY EDIBLES

Working folks in Makawao who long to eat in arrive at the **Rodeo General Store,** 3661 Baldwin Ave. (☎ **808/572-7841**), to pick up their spaghetti and lasagna, sandwiches, salads, and specials from the deli. Even in their plastic-wrapped paper trays, the pastas are tasty, as if they came straight from a neighborhood trattoria in Little Italy. You can get all the necessary accompaniments here—fresh produce, wine, soft drinks, paper products, baked goods, and sweets.

Down to Earth Natural Foods, 1169 Makawao Ave. (☎ 808/572-1488), always has fresh salads and sandwiches, a full section of organic produce (Kula onions, strawberry papayas, mangos, and litchis in season), bulk grains, vitamins and supplements, beauty aids, herbs, juices, snacks, condiments, tofu, seaweed, soy products, and aisles of vegetarian and health foods—canned, packaged, prepared, and fresh. Whether it's a smoothie, a Ginger Blast, or a burrito, it's Down to Earth territory.

In the more than 6 decades that the **T. Komoda Store and Bakery,** 3674 Baldwin Ave. (☎ 808/572-7261), has spent in this spot, untold numbers have creaked over the wooden floors to pick up the famous cream puffs. Old-timers know to come early, or they'll be sold out. Then the cinnamon rolls, doughnuts, pies, and chocolate cake take over, keeping the aromas of fresh baking wafting through the old store. Pastries are just the beginning; poi, macadamia-nut candies and cookies, and small bunches of local fruit keep the customers coming.

FRESH FLOWERS IN KULA

Like anthuriums on the Big Island, proteas are a Maui trademark and an abundant crop on Haleakala's rich volcanic slopes. They also travel well, dry beautifully, and can be shipped worldwide with ease. Among Maui's most prominent sources is **Sunrise Protea** (☎ 808/876-0200), in Kula at the base of Haleakala National Park. Sunrise offers a walk-through garden and gift shops, friendly service, and a larger-than-usual selection. If you want the freshly cut flowers, they arrive from the fields on Tuesday and Friday afternoons. You can order individual blooms, baskets, arrangements, or wreaths for shipping all over the world. (Next door, the Sunrise Country Market proffers fresh local fruits, snacks, and sandwiches, with picnic tables for lingering.) **Proteas of Hawaii** (☎ 808/878-2533), another reliable source, offers regular walking tours of the University of Hawaii Extension Service gardens across the street in Kula.

For flower shopping in other parts of Maui, **Ooka Super Market** (see "Central Maui Edibles," above) and the Saturday-morning **Maui Swap Meet** (see "Kahului," above) are among the best and least expensive places for tropical flowers of every stripe.

5 East Maui: On the Road to Hana

PAIA

Biasa Rose Boutique. 104 Hana Hwy. ☎ 808/579-8602.

Unusual gift items and clothing with a tropical flair are the Biasa Rose specialties: capri pants in bark cloth, floating plumeria candles, retro fabrics, dinnerware, children's clothes, stylish FLAX wrap skirts in a vintage wallpaper pattern. If the aloha shirts don't get you, the candles in the shape of nude males and females will surely catch your eye. Eighty percent of the items are locally made, and you can custom-order clothing from the selection of washable rayons.

Big Bugga Sportswear. 18 Baldwin Ave. ☎ 808/579-6216.

Someone decided to take care of the Little Buggas (6 months to size 4) and the Big Buggas (up to size 10X), and this wonderful store in Paia was born. You have to be microsized or ultrahuge to shop here. Togs for tots are a small part of the inventory of T-shirts and surf wear; the rest begins at XL and goes up to 10X, with aloha shirts as large as 7X. Sorry, mediums and larges, there's nothing for you here. The great selection of sportswear goes from shorts for 40-inch to 60-inch waistlines to T-shirts for the ultra-ample girth. They'll even take special orders for sweatpants and sweatshirts up to size 10X.

Katie's Place Gifts & Collectibles. At Baldwin Ave. and Hana Hwy. ☎ **808/579-8660.**

Hula dolls galore! Find the wiggling collectibles here in all price ranges, a good match for the Don Blanding dinnerware (popular and hard to find), Depression glass, salt and pepper shakers, Matson liner menus, music sheets, vintage 1940s bark-cloth curtains, and countless other snippets of the past, in prices that won't break the bank. As with all collectibles shops, there are things for both serious and whimsical collectors, and the selection changes constantly.

Maui Crafts Guild. 43 Hana Hwy. ☎ **808/579-9697.**

The old wooden storefront at the gateway to Paia houses local crafts of high quality and in all price ranges, from pit-fired raku to bowls of Norfolk pine and other Maui woods fashioned by Maui hands. Basketry, fabrics, glass, musical instruments, Hawaiian quilts, handmade paper, ceramics, jewelry, bamboo flutes, hand-turned bowls, koa accessories, prints, pressed flowers, and hundreds of items are displayed in the rustic two-story gift gallery. They ship anywhere, and all artists are selectively screened. **Aloha Bead Company** (☎ **808/579-9709**) in the back of the gallery is a treasure trove of beads.

Moonbow Tropics. 36 Baldwin Ave. ☎ **808/579-8592**.

If you're looking for a tasteful aloha shirt, Moonbow has one of the best selections in town—not exhaustive, but a few carefully culled racks of the top labels in aloha wear. There are shorts, a few purses, and a small jewelry selection, but mostly it's shirts, in good-quality fabrics.

EDIBLES ON THE ROAD TO HANA

Nahiku Coffee Shop, Smoked Fish Stand, and Ti Gallery. Hana Hwy., mile marker 28, Nahiku. No phone.

What a delight to stumble across this trio of comforts on the long drive to Hana! The small coffee shop, open daily from 6:30am to 4:30pm, serves locally made baked goods, while the Ti Gallery, open daily from 9:30am to 4:30pm, sells locally made crafts. The cast-iron smoker (our favorite part of the operation) puts out smoked and grilled chicken, beef, and fresh local fish, sending seductive smoky aromas wafting through the moist Nahiku air, daily from 10am to 5pm. The teriyaki-based marinade, made by the owner, adds a special touch. These are not jerkylike smoked meats; the process keeps the kebabs moist while retaining the smoke flavor. The breadfruit—sliced, wrapped in banana leaf, and baked—can be bland and starchy (like a baked potato), but it's a stroke of genius to give visitors a taste of this important Polynesian staple. There are a few roadside picnic tables, or you can take your lunch on to Hana for a beachside picnic.

6 At the End of the Road in East Maui: Hana

✪ **Hana Coast Gallery.** Hotel Hana-Maui. ☎ **808/248-8636.**

This gallery is known for its high level of curatorship and commitment to the cultural art of Hawaii. There are no jumping whales or dolphins here—and except for a section of European and Asian masters (Renoir, Japanese woodblock prints), the 3,000-square-foot space is devoted to Hawaii artists. Dozens of well-established local artists display their sculptures, paintings, prints, feather work, stone work, carvings, and three-dimensional works in displays that are so natural they could well exist in someone's home.

Hasegawa General Store. Hana Hwy. ☎ **808/248-8231.**

Established in 1910, immortalized in song since 1961, burned to the ground in 1990, and back in business in 1991, this legendary store is indefatigable and more colorful than ever in its third generation in business. The aisles are choked with merchandise: Hana-blend coffee specially roasted and blended for the store, Ono Farms organic dried fruit, fishing equipment, every tape and CD that mentions Hana, the best books on Hana to be found, T-shirts, beach and garden essentials, mugs, baseball caps, film, baby food, napkins, and other necessities for the Hana life.

Maui After Dark

9

by Jocelyn Fujii

The island's most prestigious entertainment venue is the $28-million **Maui Arts and Cultural Center** in Kahului (☎ **808/242-7469**), a first-class center for the visual and performing arts. It has proved to be a great success, a Maui star: Since its 1994 opening, the state-of-the-art facilities have attracted first-rate performers and sold-out shows. Bonnie Raitt has performed here, as have Hiroshima, Pearl Jam, Ziggy Marley, and Tony Bennett, not to mention the finest in local and Hawaii talent. It has booked world-class cultural exhibits, rock and reggae, the Lakota Sioux Indian Dance Theatre, Carlos Santana, the Maui Symphony Orchestra, the stars of the Moscow Ballet, John Mayall, Kenny Loggins, magic shows, top Hawaiian performers, the Hawaii International Film Festival, and many other notable acts. The center is as precious to Maui as the Met is to New York, with a visual-arts gallery, an outdoor amphitheater, offices, rehearsal space, a 300-seat theater for experimental performances, and a 1,200-seat main theater. Whether it's hula, the Iona Pear Dance Company, Willie Nelson, or Hawaiian-music icon Keali'i Reichel, only the best will appear at the Maui Arts and Cultural Center. The center's activities are well publicized locally, so check the *Maui News* or ask your hotel concierge what's going on during your visit.

HAWAIIAN MUSIC

Except for Casanova in Makawao, Hapa's in Kihei, Tsunami in Wailea, and Maui Brews in Lahaina, nightlife options on this island are limited. The major hotels generally have lobby lounges offering regular Hawaiian music, soft jazz, or hula shows beginning at sunset. If the duo called **Hapa, Willie K and Amy Gilliom,** or the soloist **Keali'i Reichel** are playing anywhere on their native island, don't miss them; they're a Hawaiian music bonanza, among the finest Hawaiian musicians around today.

JAZZ & BLUES

To find out what's happening in jazz or blues, look in at **Hapa's Brew Haus** (☎ **808/879-9001**) in Kihei (see "South Maui," below). It seems to be the nightlife nexus for this genre, with quality music and overflow crowds that linger into the wee hours. The thriving blues scene throughout Hawaii can be credited to the efforts of Louie Wolfenson, his partner Kurt Kangas, and the **Maui Blues Association** (☎ **808/879-6123**), which books sold-out events at clubs throughout

It Begins with Sunset. . .

Nightlife in Maui begins at sunset, when all eyes turn westward to see how the day will end. Like spotting the same whale or school of spinner dolphins, sunset viewers seem to bond in the mutual enjoyment of a natural spectacle. And what better way to take it all in than over cocktails? Maui is a haven for lovers of both. With its view of Molokai to the northwest and Lanai to the west, Kaanapali and the west Maui destinations are graced with panoramic vistas unique to this island. In south Maui's Wailea and Makena, tiny Kahoolawe and the crescent-shaped Molokini islet are visible as familiar forms on the horizon, and the West Maui Mountains look like an entirely separate island. No matter what your vantage point, you are likely to be treated to an astonishing view.

Sunset viewers along south and west Maui shorelines need only head for the ocean and find a seat. Our favorite sunset watering holes begin with **The Bay Club at Kapalua** (☎ 808/669-5656), where a pianist plays nightly and the northwesterly view of Molokai and Lanai is enhanced by the elegant surroundings. It's quiet here, removed from the hubbub that prevails in the more populated Kaanapali Beach Resort to the south.

In Kaanapali, park in Whalers Village and head for **Leilani's** (☎ 808/661-4495) or **Hula Grill** (☎ 808/667-6636), next to each other on the beach. Both have busy, upbeat bars and tables bordering the sand. These are happy places for great people watching, gazing at the lump of Lanai that looks to be a stone's throw away, and enjoying end-of-day rituals like mai tais and margaritas. Hula Grill's Barefoot Bar appetizer menu is a cut above, offering such treats as macadamia-nut/crab wontons, fresh fish-and-chips, and pizza. Leilani's has live music daily from 2:30 to 6pm, while Hula Grill offers hula from 3 to 5pm and at 6:30pm.

Now, Lahaina: It's a sunset-lover's nirvana, lined with restaurants that hang over the ocean and offer fresh fish in a multitude of preparations—and mai tais elevated to an art form. If you love loud rock, head for **Cheeseburger in**

the state. Check the papers to see what's on while you're on Maui. Their annual Islands Blues Mele, a festival around Memorial Day, grows by the year and has assumed a life of its own.

MOVIES

Film buffs can check the local newspapers to see what's playing at the few theaters around town: the **Kaahumanu Theatres** in the Kaahumanu Center in Kahului (☎ 808/873-3133); the **Maui Theatre** in the Kahului Shopping Center (☎ 808/877-3560); the **Kukui Mall Theater** at 1819 S. Kihei Rd. in Kihei (☎ 808/875-4533); and the **Wallace Theatres** in Lahaina (☎ 808/661-3347), at the Wharf Cinema Center, 658 Front St., and the Front Street Theatres at the Lahaina Center, 900 Front St.

1 West Maui: Lahaina

Maui Brews, 900 Front St. (☎ 808/667-7794), opens daily from 11:30am, with happy hour from 3 to 6pm; it turns into a nightclub from 9pm to 1:30am. Swing, salsa, reggae, and late-night jams draw a crowd to this corner of the Lahaina Center. There's live music every night except weekends, and Ladies' Night is on Thursday.

Paradise (☎ 808/661-4855). A few doors away, **Lahaina Fish Company** (☎ 808/661-3472) and **Kimo's** (☎ 808/661-4811) are magnets all day long and especially at sunset, when their open decks fill up with revelers. These three restaurants occupy the section of Front Street between Lahainaluna Road and Papalaua Street.

At the southern end of Lahaina, in the 505 Front Street complex, **Pacific'o** (☎ 808/667-4341) is a solid hit, with a raised bar, seating on the ocean, and a backdrop of Lanai across the channel. Besides the view and the friendly service, the food is notable, having won many awards for seafood.

Moving south toward Wailea, the harbor stop called Maalaea is famous for its whale sightings during the winter months. Year-round, **Buzz's Wharf** (☎ 808/244-5426) is a formula restaurant with a superb ocean view and continuous service between lunch and dinner. Those are the basic makings of a sunset-viewing way station. Add an ice-cold beer or mai tai and a steaming order of fish-and-chips, and the sunset package is complete.

In Wailea, our favorite stop is the **Hula Moons** outdoor terrace at Outrigger Wailea Resort (☎ 808/879-1922)—for the ambience, if not the food. It's more open than its fancier neighbors and, in a corny but romantic touch, live Hawaiian music with a hula dancer is offered daily from 5:30 to 9:30pm. In Makena resort further south, you can't beat the Maui Prince's **Molokini Lounge** (☎ 808/874-1111), with its casual elegance and unequalled view of Molokini islet on the ocean side and, on the mauka side, a graceful, serene courtyard with ponds, rock gardens, and lush foliage. Adding to the setting is the appetizer menu, which comes from the esteemed Prince Court kitchen. From 5:30pm nightly, the pupu menu features a Molokini sampler platter (Thai-style spring rolls, shrimp summer rolls, ahi sashimi), a seared ahi seaweed salad on a tortilla shell, and panfried tiger shrimp. There's live Hawaiian entertainment nightly from 6 to 6:45pm.

At **Longhi's,** 888 Front St. (☎ 808/667-2288), live music spills out into the streets from 9:30pm to midnight on some weekends. Usually it's salsa or jazz, but call ahead to confirm. Other special gigs can be expected if rock 'n' rollers or jazz musicians who are friends of the owner happen to be passing through. It wouldn't hurt to ask what's happening here.

You won't have to ask what's going on at **Cheeseburger in Paradise,** 811 Front St. (☎ 808/661-4855), the two-story green-and-white building at the corner of Front and Lahainaluna streets. Just go outside and you'll hear it: loud, live, and lively tropical rock blasting into the streets and out to sea daily from 4:30 to 11pm. There's no cover.

AN INTIMATE AFFAIR: LUAU, MAUI STYLE

Most of the larger hotels in Maui's major resorts offer luaus and Polynesian entertainment on a regular basis. You'll pay about $65 to attend one. To protect yourself from disappointment, don't expect it to be a home-grown affair prepared in the traditional Hawaiian way; the labor-intensive nature of this feast makes achieving that an impossible endeavor for large-scale commercial operations offered on a regular basis. There are, however, commercial luaus that capture the romance and spirit of the affair with quality food and entertainment in outdoor settings.

The Green Flash

The green flash is a common sight in Maui at sunset (and no, we don't mean you have to down a couple of mai tais to see it). As the last sliver of sun sinks into the ocean, the atmosphere works like a prism and bends the last rays of light, scattering the blue end of the spectrum, so just for a second you see an emerald green "flash." If you're up early enough, and looking out over the ocean, you can see the flash at sunrise, too.

Maui's best luau is indisputably the nightly **Old Lahaina Luau,** (☎ 808/ 667-1998), an even bigger hit at its new 1-acre site just ocean side of the Lahaina Cannery. We thought it couldn't get better, but it did. Local craftspeople display their wares only a few feet from the ocean. Seating is provided on lauhala mats for those wishing to dine as the traditional Hawaiians did, but there are tables for everyone else. Although there is no fire dancing in the program, you won't even miss it. Thatched buildings, amphitheater seating, excellent food and entertainment, and the backdrop of a Lahaina sunset are among its unforgettable features. This is the consummate luau, with a healthy balance of entertainment, showmanship, authentic high-quality food, educational value, and sheer romantic beauty. (No watered-down mai tais, either; these are the real thing.)

The luau begins at sunset and features Tahitian and Hawaiian entertainment, including ancient hula, hula from the missionary era, modern hula, and an intelligent narrative on the dance's rocky course of survival into modern times. The entertainment is riveting, even for jaded locals, and the food is as much Pacific Rim as authentically Hawaiian, served from an open-air thatched structure: imu-roasted kalua pig, baked mahimahi in Maui onion–cream sauce, guava chicken, teriyaki sirloin steak, lomi salmon, poi, dried fish, poke, Hawaiian sweet potato, sautéed vegetables, seafood salad, and the ultimate taste treat, taro leaves with coconut milk. The cost is $65 for adults, $30 for children, plus tax.

The **Maui Marriott Luau** (☎ 808/667-1200) is beachside in Kaanapali and costs $65 for adults and $26 for children, free for those under 5. An open bar, outdoor stage, Hawaiian games, and after-dinner show appeal to those with Las Vegas tastes, with fire dancers and hula. The luau is offered from 5 to 8pm nightly.

2 South Maui

KIHEI

Hapa's Brew Haus, Lipoa Shopping Center, 41 E. Lipoa St. (☎ 808/879-9001), is the liveliest game in town, with local icon **Willie K.** packing them in every Wednesday night. He is a powerful musical presence who is worth the drive to Kihei. The intimate environment, tiered seating, and state-of-the-art sound and lighting show off his virtuoso guitar playing and unmistakable vocals to great advantage. Call the hot line (☎ 808/875-1990) to find out whether jazz, blues, rock, reggae, funk, Jawaiian (a fusion of Jamaican and Hawaiian), the Maui Symphony Orchestra band (MSO), or the duo named Hapa will be filling the house.

WAILEA

The Grand Wailea Resort's **Tsunami,** 3850 Wailea Alanui Dr. (☎ 808/875-1234), Maui's most high-tech club, happens to be south Maui's only nightspot for dancing. But what a club: 10,000 square feet, with marble, laser lights, huge video screens, futuristic decor, and well-dressed revelers. It's all disco, no live music, and is open Thursday, Friday, and Saturday from 9pm to 2am with a $5 cover. The DJ plays everything from 1980s hits to Top 40 on weekends. Thursday is ladies' night: no cover charge for women, drink specials, and a flower or other memento for the wily females who turn out to "dress and impress." On Friday, "Flashback Fever" (music from the '70s and '80s) takes over.

3 Upcountry Maui

Upcountry in Makawao, the partying never ends at **Casanova,** 1188 Makawao Ave. (☎ **808/572-0220**), the popular Italian ristorante (see chapter 5 for a review) where the good times roll with the pasta. This is a restaurant, nightclub, bar, and dance spot all in one. If a big-name mainland band is resting up on Maui following a sold-out concert on Oahu, you may find its members setting up for an impromptu night here. On Maui, word spreads quickly. DJs take over on Wednesday (ladies' night) and Thursday nights. Every other Thursday is a fundraiser for the Maui AIDS Society, and on Friday and Saturday, live entertainment draws fun-lovers from even the most remote reaches of the island. Entertainment starts at 9:45pm and continues to 1:30am. Expect good blues, rock 'n' roll, reggae, jazz, Hawaiian, and the top names in local and visiting entertainment. Elvin Bishop, the local duo Hapa, Los Lobos, and many others have filled Casanova's stage. The cover charge is usually $5.

10

Molokai, the Most Hawaiian Isle

by Jeanette Foster & Jocelyn Fujii

Born of volcanic eruptions 1½ million years ago, Molokai remains a time capsule on the eve of the 21st century. It has no deluxe resorts, no fancy restaurants, no stoplights, and no buildings taller than a coconut tree. Less is definitely more on this languid island—and, fortunately for adventure travelers, Molokai is the least developed, most "Hawaiian" of all the islands.

The cradle of Hawaiian dance (the hula was born here), the ancient science of aquaculture, and sacred rites, Molokai lives up to its reputation as the most Hawaiian place chiefly through its lineage; there are, in fact, more people here of Hawaiian blood than anywhere else. An aura of ancient mysticism clings to the slipper-shaped island, and the old ways still govern life here. The residents survive by taking fish from the sea and hunting wild pigs and axis deer on the range. Some folks still catch reef fish in throw nets and troll the reef for squid, a traditional Hawaiian delicacy. Families are important, friendship ties are cherished, and the Hawaiian concept of taking care of the land remains a priority. Modern Hawaii's high-rise hotels, shopping centers, and other trappings of tourism haven't been able to gain a foothold here—one lone low-rise resort, Kaluakoi, built more than 25 years ago, is Molokai's token attempt at contemporary tourism.

The only "new" development since Kaluakoi is the Molokai Ranch's ecotourism project of upscale "camping" in semipermanent "tentalows" (a combination of a bungalow and a tent) on the 53,000-acre ranch. The focus here is on outdoor recreation and adventure with a comfortable place to sleep in the wilderness.

The slow-paced, simple life of the people and the absence of contemporary landmarks are what attracts those in search of the "real" Hawaii. But what makes them stand in awe is this little island's diverse natural wonders: Hawaii's highest waterfall and greatest collection of fishponds, the world's tallest sea cliffs, and sand dunes, coral reefs, rain forests, hidden coves—and empty, gloriously empty, beaches.

EXPLORING THE "MOST HAWAIIAN" ISLE   Only 38 miles from end to end and just 10 miles wide, Molokai stands like a big green wedge in the blue Pacific. It has an east side, a west side, a backside, and a topside. Formed by three volcanic eruptions, the long, narrow island is like yin and yang: One side is a flat, austere, arid desert; the other is a lush, green, steepled tropical Eden. But the volcanic gods weren't done with Molokai until a third eruption produced

Molokai

PACIFIC OCEAN

Pali Coast

THE EAST END

THE NORTH COAST

THE WEST END

Paiolo Channel

Kalohi Channel

Kaiwi Channel

Cape Halawa
Mokuhooniki Island
Kikipua Point
Halawa
Halawa Valley
Waialua
450
Pukoo
15
16
17
18
19
Kamalo
Kamehameha V Hwy.
Kawela
Kamiloloa
1
460
2
KAUNAKAKAI
Kaunakakai Wharf
Mokapo Is.
Kahiu Point
13
Kalaupapa
11
12
Kalae
470
9 10
8
3
Hoolehua
4
Kualapuu
Pali Ave.
Limi St.
Paualaia Point
Mokio Point
Illo Point
7
Hoolehua Airport
460
Maunahui Rd.
Kaluakoi Rd.
Kaluakoi Resort
Wahilauhue
Laau Point
Maunaloa
5
6
Halena
Kolo
Hale o Lono

Airport ✈
Lighthouse ⚓

1-0723

Ancient Fishponds (from Kaunakakai to Waialua) **17**
Coffees of Hawaii Plantation Store **3**
Illiliopae Heiau **15**
Kalaupapa Lookout **10**
Kalaupapa National Historic Park **13**
Kamakou Preserve **14**
Kapuaiwa Coconut Grove/Kiowea Park **2**

Kaunakakai Wharf **1**
Mapulehu Glass House **11**
Molokai Mule Ride **16**
Molokai Museum and Cultural Center **12**
Molokai Ranch Outfitters Center **6**
Molokai Rodeo Arena **5**
Moomomi Dunes **7**

Palaau State Park **8**
Phallic Rock **9**
Purdy's All-Natural Macadamia Nut Farm **4**
R. W. Meyer Sugar Mill **12**
St. Joseph's Catholic Church **19**
Smith Bronte Landing Site **18**

the island's "thumb"—a peninsula jutting out of the steep cliffs of the north shore, like a punctuation mark on the island's geological story.

The few tourists who come here are separated from the adventurers at Hoolehua, home to Molokai's tin-roofed, lava-rock airport. Those who deplane in boots—hiking or cowboy—are going one place, and those in tasseled loafers or white tennies are heading for quite another. Most everyone ends up barefoot on the beach, though.

On the red-dirt southern plain, where most of the island's 6,000 residents live, the rustic village of Kaunakakai looks like the set of an old Hollywood Western, with sun-faded clapboard houses and horses tethered in tall grass on the side of the road. At mile marker 0, in the center of town, the island is divided into east and west so dramatically that an arid cactus desert lies on one side, and a lush coco-palm jungle on the other.

Eastbound, along the coastal highway named for King Kamehameha V, are Gauguin-like, palm-shaded cottages set on small coves or near fishponds; spectacular vistas that take in Maui, Lanai, and Kahoolawe; and a fringing coral reef visible through the crystal-clear waves.

Out on the sun-scorched west end is the island's lone destination resort, Kaluakoi, overlooking a gold-sand beach too big to fit on a postcard with water usually too rough to swim. A few old-timers inhabit the old hilltop plantation town of Maunaloa, now being remade into an upscale version of itself. Cowboys ride the range on Molokai Ranch, a 53,000-acre spread. Adventure travelers and outdoor recreation buffs stay at the tentalows on the ranch property and spend their days mountain biking, kayaking, horseback riding, sailing, hiking, snorkeling, and just vegetating on the endless white-sand beaches.

Elsewhere around the island, in hamlets like Kualapuu, old farmhouses with pickup trucks in the yards and sleepy dogs under the shade trees stand amid row crops of papaya, coffee, and corn—just like farm towns in Anywhere, USA.

But that's not all there is. The "backside" of Molokai is a rugged wilderness of spectacular beauty. On the outskirts of Kaunakakai, the land rises gradually from sea-level fishponds to cool uplands and the Molokai Forest, long ago stripped of sandalwood for the China trade. All that remains is an indentation in the earth that natives shaped like a ship's hull, a crude matrix that gave them a rough idea of when they'd cut enough sandalwood to fill a ship (it's identified on good maps as Luanamokuiliahi, or Sandalwood Boat).

The land inclines sharply to the lofty mountains and the nearly mile-high summit of Mount Kamakou, then ends abruptly with emerald-green cliffs, which plunge into a lurid aquamarine sea dotted with tiny deserted islets. These breathtaking 3,250-foot sea cliffs, the highest in the world, stretch 14 majestic miles along Molokai's north shore, laced by waterfalls and creased by five valleys—Halawa, Papalaua, Wailau, Pelekunu, and Waikolu—once occupied by early Hawaiians who built stone terraces and used waterfalls to irrigate taro patches.

Long after the sea cliffs were formed, a tiny volcano erupted out of the sea at their feet and spread lava into a flat, leaflike peninsula called Kalaupapa—the infamous 1860s leper exile where Father Damien de Veuster of Belgium devoted his life, caring for the afflicted. A few people remain in the remote colony by choice, keeping it tidy for the daily company that arrives on mules and small planes.

WHAT A VISIT TO MOLOKAI IS *REALLY* LIKE   There's plenty of aloha on Molokai, but the so-called "friendly island" remains ambivalent about vacationers. One of the least visited Hawaiian islands, Molokai welcomes travelers on its own take-it-or-leave-it terms and makes few concessions beyond that of gracious host; it never wants to attract too big of a crowd, anyway. A sign at the airport offers the first clue: SLOW DOWN, YOU ON MOLOKAI NOW—a caveat to heed on this island, where life proceeds at its own pace.

Rugged, red-dirt Molokai isn't for everyone, but those who like to explore remote places and seek their own adventures should love it. The best of the island can be seen only on foot, mule, or horse, or via kayak or sailboat. The sea cliffs are accessible only by sea in the summer, when the Pacific is calm, or via a 10-mile trek through the Wailau Valley—an adventure only a handful of hardy hikers attempt each year. The great Kamakou Preserve is open just once a month, by special arrangement with the Nature Conservancy. Even Moomomi, which holds bony relics of prehistoric flightless birds and other *Lost World* creatures, requires a guide to divulge the secrets of the dunes.

Those in search of nightlife have come to the wrong place; Molokai shuts down after sunset. The only public diversions are softball games under the lights of Mitchell Pauole Field, movies at Maunaloa, and the few restaurants that stay open after dark, serving everything from local brew to pizza.

The "friendly" island may captivate you—on the other hand, you may leave with your head shaking, never to return. It all depends on how you approach Molokai. Boots or loafers. Either way, take it slow.

1 Orientation

ARRIVING

BY PLANE   Molokai has two airports, but you'll most likely fly into **Hoolehua Airport,** which everyone calls "the Molokai Airport"; it's on a dusty plain about 6 miles from Kaunakakai town. From Maui, **Island Air** (☎ **800/323-3345** from the mainland, or 800/652-6541 from Maui; www.alohaair.com) offers four direct flights a day. A new Maui-based carrier, **Pacific Wings** (☎ **888/575-4546** from the mainland, or 808/873-0877 from Maui; www.pacificwings.com), has begun offering flights from Kahului to both Molokai airports, in eight-passenger, twin-engine Cessna 402-C aircraft.

Molokai Air Shuttle (☎ **808/545-4988**) and **Hawaiian Airlines** (☎ **800/367-5320** or 808/553-3644; www.hawaiianair.com) both have direct daily flights from Honolulu to Molokai.

BY BOAT   You can cross the seas from Lahaina Harbor on Maui to the Kaunakakai Wharf on Molokai via the ***Lahaina Princess,*** Lahaina Harbor, slip 3 (☎ **800/275-6969** or 808/667-6165; fax 808/661-5792; www.maui.net/~ismarine). The 65-foot yacht (certified for 149 passengers) makes the journey twice a week from April to December (once a week during whale season, December 19 to mid-April). Cost of the round-trip boat ride is $73 for adults, $37 for children 3 to 12, and free for children under 3. The boat departs Lahaina at 6:15am, arrives in Molokai at 8am, departs Molokai for the return trip at 2pm, and arrives in Lahaina at 3:30pm. Day tours of Molokai are also available: The Cruise Drive Tour, which covers boat passage and rental car, costs $105 per person. The Alii Tour, which includes boat passage, guided van tour of Molokai, and lunch, is $137 for adults, $84 for children 3 to 12, and free for children under 3. Finally, the Overnight Trip includes boat passage and an overnight stay at Kaluakoi Resort, $169 per person, double occupancy.

VISITOR INFORMATION

Look for a sun-faded yellow building on the main drag, Kamehameha V Highway (Highway 460), on the right just past the town's first stop sign, at mile marker 0; it's the **Molokai Visitors Association,** P.O. Box 960, Kaunakakai, HI 96748 (☎ **800/ 800-6367,** 808/553-3876 from the U.S. mainland and Canada, or 800/553-0404 or 808/553-3876 interisland; www.molokai-hawai.com). The staff can give you all the information you need on what to see and do while you're on Molokai.

THE ISLAND IN BRIEF

KAUNAKAKAI   Dusty cars are parked diagonally along Ala Malama Street. The family car is a pickup truck. It could be any small town, except it's Kaunakakai, Molokai, where Friendly Isle Realty and Friendly Isle Travel offer islanders dream homes and impossible vacations; Rabang's Filipino Food posts bad checks in the window; antlered deer-head trophies guard the grocery aisles at Misaki's Market; and Kanemitsu's, the town's legendary bakery, churns out fresh loaves of onion-cheese bread daily.

Once an ancient canoe landing, Kaunakakai was the royal summer place of King Kamehameha V. The port town bustled when pineapple and sugar were king, but those days, too, are gone. With Old West–style storefronts laid out in a 3-block grid on a flat, dusty plain, Kaunakakai is a town from the past. Molokai's main settlement might appear rustic, but the spirit of aloha still reigns. At the end of Wharf Road is **Kaunakakai Wharf,** a rather picturesque place to fish, photograph, and just hang out.

THE NORTH COAST   Upland from Kaunakakai, the land tilts skyward and turns green with scented plumeria in yards and glossy coffee trees all in a row until it blooms into a true forest—then abruptly ends at a great precipice, falling 3,250 feet to the sea. The green cliffs are creased with five V-shaped cliffs so deep that light in the crevices is seldom seen (to paraphrase a Hawaii poet).

The north coast is the wild coast, a remote, forbidding place with a solitary penin-sula, **Kalaupapa,** once the home for exiled lepers (it's now a national historical park). Easy on the eyes, difficult to visit.

THE WEST END   This end of the island, home to **Molokai Ranch,** is miles of stark, minimal desert terrain, bordered by some of the most beautiful white-sand beaches in Hawaii. The rugged rolling terrain slopes down to Molokai's only destina-tion resort, **Kaluakoi,** a cul-de-sac of condos clustered around a 20-year-old seafront hotel near 3-mile-long Papohaku, the island's biggest beach. On the way to Kalu-akoi—where everyone shows up at least once, if only to wait in line to eat dinner at Ohia Lodge—you'll find **Maunaloa,** a 1920s-era pineapple-plantation town that, in Molokai's first and only urban renewal project, is in the midst of being transformed into a master-planned community, Maunaloa Village.

THE EAST END   The area east of Kaunakakai becomes lush, green, and tropical, with golden pocket beaches and a handful of cottages and condos that are popular with thrifty travelers. Beyond Kaunakakai, the two-lane road curves along the coast past piggeries, palm groves, and a 20-mile string of fishponds, as well as an ancient heiau, Damien-built churches, and a few contemporary condos by the sea. It ends in the earthly paradise of **Halawa Valley,** one of Hawaii's most beautiful valleys.

2 Getting Around

Getting around Molokai isn't easy if you don't have a rental car, and rental cars are often hard to find on this island. On holiday weekends—and remember, Hawaii cel-ebrates different holidays than the rest of the United States (see "When to Go," in chapter 2)—car-rental agencies simply run out of cars. Book before you go. There's no municipal transit or shuttle service, but a 24-hour taxi service is available.

CAR-RENTAL AGENCIES Rental cars are available from **Budget** (☎ **808/ 567-6877**) and **Dollar** (☎ **808/567-6156**); both agencies are located at the Molokai Airport. We recommend trying **Island Kine** (☎ **808/553-5242;** fax 808/553-3880; e-mail: cars@molokai-aloha.com); not only are the cars cheaper, but Barbara Shonely and her son, Steve, also give personalized service. They'll meet you at the Molokai Airport, take you to their office in Kaunakakai, and recommend which outfitters to choose for your activities. The used cars are in perfect condition ("I would drive every one of them with my grandkids") and are air-conditioned. Vans and pickup trucks are also available.

TAXI & TOUR SERVICES Regular taxi service and island tours are offered by **Molokai Off-Road Tours & Taxi** (☎ **808/552-2218**). **Kukui Tours & Limousines** (☎ **808/552-2282**) has air-conditioned limos available for tours, airport shuttle, and 24-hour taxi service.

Fast Facts: Molokai

Molokai, like Lanai, is part of Maui County. For **local emergencies,** call ☎ **911.** For nonemergencies, call the **police** at ☎ 808/553-5355, the **fire department** at ☎ 808/553-5601, and **Molokai General Hospital,** in Kaunakakai, at ☎ 808/553-5331.

Downtown Kaunakakai also has a **post office** (☎ **808/553-5845**) and several banks, including the **Bank of Hawaii** (☎ **808/553-3273**), which has a 24-hour ATM.

Rawlins Chevron Service, mile marker 0, Kaunakakai (☎ **808/553-3214**), is the "last stop to the airport from Kaunakakai"—where you'll rush to fill up your rental car with 87-octane at the self-serve pump. Or wish you had. It's open Monday through Thursday from 6:30am to 8:30pm, Friday and Saturday until 9pm, and Sunday from 7am to 6pm.

3 Accommodations

Molokai is Hawaii's most affordable island; in fact, hotel prices here are lower than those on any other island. Plus, because Molokai's restaurants are few, most hotel rooms and condos come with kitchens, which can save you a bundle on dining costs.

There aren't a ton of accommodations options on Molokai—mostly B&Bs, condos, and a handful of funky hotels that are really more like motels. Camping on Molokai involves two options: the upscale "tentalows" offered by Molokai Ranch, along with a host of activities; or, for hardy souls, camping with your own tent at the beach or in the cool upland forest (see "Hiking & Camping," below). We've listed our top picks below; you may want to contact **Destination Molokai Association** (☎ **800/ 800-6367;** fax 808/553-5288) for additional options.

Note: Taxes of 11.42% will be added to your hotel bill. Parking is free, unless noted.

KAUNAKAKAI
MODERATE

Molokai Shores Suites. Kamehameha V Hwy. (P.O. Box 1037), Kaunakakai, HI 96748. ☎ **800/535-0085** or 808/553-5954. Fax 808/553-5954. www.marcresorts.com. 100 units. TV. $144 one-bedroom apt (sleeps up to 4), $180 two-bedroom apt (sleeps up to 6). Discounted rates for weekly and extended stays, plus corporate, military, and senior discounts. AE, DC, JCB, MC, V.

Bright, clean, basic units with kitchens and large lanais face a small gold-sand beach and the ocean beyond in this quiet complex of three-story Polynesian-style buildings, less than a mile from Kaunakakai. Alas, the beach is mostly for show (offshore, it's shallow mud flats underfoot), fishing, or launching kayaks, but the swimming pool comes with an ocean view. Well-tended gardens, spreading lawns, and palms frame a restful view of fishponds, offshore reefs, and neighbor islands. The central location can be a plus, minimizing driving time from the airport or town, and it's convenient to the mule ride, as well as the lush East End countryside.

INEXPENSIVE

Hotel Molokai. Kamehameha V Hwy. (P.O. Box 1020), Kaunakakai, HI 96748. ☎ **800/ 367-5004** from the mainland and Canada, 800/272-5275 from Hawaii, or 808/553-5347. Fax 800/477-2329. www.castle-group.com. 45 units. TV TEL. $75–$125 double, $130 suite with kitchenette (sleeps up to 4). Extra bed/crib $17. AE, CB, DC, DISC, JCB, MC, V.

Once one of Molokai's prized oceanfront hotels, this cluster of old swayback Polynesian chiefs' huts had fallen into disrepair. In 1998, the 32-year-old hotel was sold and underwent extensive renovation, reopening in early 1999. The complex is composed of a series of modified A-frame units, nestled under coco palms along a gray-sand beach with a great view of Lanai. The rooms are basic (be sure to ask for one with a ceiling fan), with phone, TV, tub/shower combo, fridge, and lanai. On-site facilities include a freshwater swimming pool, an activities desk, laundry, a gift shop, a restaurant serving three meals, and a cocktail lounge. Not the Ritz, but more along the lines of a nostalgic Hawaiian hideaway.

Kahale Mala Bed & Breakfast. 7 Kamakana Place (P.O. Box 1582), Kaunakakai, HI 96748. ☎ and fax **808/553-9001.** www.molokai-aloha.com/kahalemala. 1 unit. TV. $60 double. Breakfast $5 extra. Extra person $10. No credit cards.

In a subdivision just outside town (off Kamehameha V Highway, before mile marker 5), you'll find the home of Jack Pugh and Cheryl Corbeil. When they moved here from western Canada, Jack and Cheryl loved the property but thought it was too big for two—so they bought the house and started a one-room B&B. The large unit has a private entrance through the garden, with a Jacuzzi just outside. Inside, the decor consists of white rattan furnishings, including two twin beds, and a full kitchen— Cheryl will happily share her home-grown, organic produce. Although you'll pay less if you make your own breakfast, we recommend Cheryl's: taro pancakes, sourdough waffles, or a vegetable-egg pie, along with fresh fruit, homemade bread, muffins, and cinnamon buns.

THE WEST END
MODERATE

Also consider **Kaluakoi Villas,** Kaluakoi Resort, 1131 Kaluakoi Rd., Maunaloa, HI 96770 (☎ **800/367-5004** or 808/552-2721; fax 800/477-2329 or 808/552-2201). The aging, Polynesian-style units are comfortable but could definitely use some work ($125 to $150 studio, $150 to $180 one-bedroom apartment, $200 cottage). Another option is the **Kaluakoi Hotel and Golf Club,** Kaluakoi Resort (P.O. Box 1977), Kepuhi Beach, HI 96770 (☎ **888/552-2550** or 808/552-2555; fax 808/552-2821), the only resort hotel on the island, with a faultless location—but we still consider it way overpriced and in need of dire renovations. If you stay here, book a condo with kitchen ($105 to $130 double, $205 to $275 suite, $155 to $170 studio, $185 to $195 one-bedroom condo, $220 one-bedroom cottage).

And don't forget about the upscale camping at the ۞ **Great Molokai Ranch Trail** (see "Hiking & Camping," below).

⓯ Family-Friendly Accommodations: From Tentalows to Condos

✪ **Great Molokai Ranch Trail** *(see p. 235)*   The upscale, luxurious "camping" at the Panaolo Camp (on Molokai Ranch property, just outside Maunalao) features comfortable "tentalows" (tent-bungalows) and lots of outdoor fun, including special activities for children. Prices ($215 for adults, $75 for kids) include three all-you-can-eat meals and snacks every day, two activities, transportation (including airport pickup), and daily maid services.

Ke Nani Kai Resort *(see p. 221)*   Located in Kaluakoi Resort, these one- and two-bedroom condo units offer families lots of space, with full kitchens, washer/dryers, VCRs, and breezy lanais. For active families, there's a huge pool, a volleyball court, tennis courts, and golf at neighboring Kaluakoi.

Molokai Shores Suites *(see p. 219)*   At this great central location, just outside Kaunakakai, families can choose from large one- and two-bedroom units in a tropical garden complex with great views of the fishponds, offshore reefs, and neighbor islands. Facilities include a pool and laundry; shopping is nearby.

✪ **Puunana/Pauwalu Beachfront Cottages** *(see p. 223)*   Private two-bedroom cottages, located on the beach in the lush East End, make this the perfect spot for a family getaway. Each cottage sits on its own secluded beach and has a full kitchen, washer/dryer, VCR, large deck, and breathtaking views (great for watching whales in winter).

Ke Nani Kai Resort. Kaluakoi Resort, Kaluakoi Rd., off Hwy. 460 (P.O. Box 289), Maunaloa, HI 96770. ☎ **800/535-0085** or 808/552-2761. Fax 808/552-0045. www.marcresorts.com. 100 units. TV TEL. $149–$159 one-bedroom apt (sleeps up to 4), $179–$199 two-bedroom apt (sleeps up to 6). AE, CB, DISC, DC, JCB, MC, V.

A home away from home, especially for families that will like the space and quiet. These large apartments are set up for full-time living with real kitchens, washer/dryers, VCRs, attractive furnishings, and breezy lanais. There's a huge pool, a volleyball court, tennis courts, and golf on the neighboring Kaluakoi course. These condos are the farthest from the sea of those at Kaluakoi Resort, but it's just a brief walk down to the hotel facilities and the beach beyond. The two-story buildings are surrounded by parking and garden areas.

✪ **Paniolo Hale.** Next door to Kaluakoi Resort, Lio Place (P.O. Box 190), Maunaloa, HI 96770. ☎ **800/367-2984** or 808/552-2731. Fax 808/552-2288. www.lava.net/paniolo. 77 units. TV. $95–$155 studio double, $115–$180 one-bedroom apt (sleeps up to 4), $145–$215 two-bedroom apt (sleeps up to 6). 2-night minimum; 1-week minimum Dec 20–Jan 5. Extra person $10. AE, MC, V.

This is far and away Molokai's most charming lodging, and probably its best value—be sure to ask about discounted weekly rates and special condo/car packages when making your reservations here. Paniolo Hale's two-story, old Hawaii ranch-house design is airy and homey, with oak floors and walls of folding-glass doors that open to huge screened verandas, doubling your living space. The one- and two-bedrooms come with two baths, so they accommodate three or four easily. Some have hot tubs on the lanai. Units are spacious and well equipped, with full kitchens and washer/dryers. They're comfortably furnished by the owners, who run their own rental operation.

The whole place overlooks the Kaluakoi Golf Course, a green barrier that separates these condos from the rest of Kaluakoi Resort. Hotel shops, a restaurant, and a lounge are just across the fairway, as is Kepuhi Beach (these are the closest units to the beach); it's a scenic place to walk and beachcomb, but the seas are too hazardous for most swimmers. There's a pool, paddle tennis, and barbecue facilities on the property, which adjoins open grassland countryside.

THE EAST END
MODERATE

Wavecrest Resort. Kamehameha V Hwy. (P.O. Box 1037), Kaunakakai, HI 96748. ☎ **800/535-0085** or 808/558-8103. Fax 800/633-5085 or 808/558-8206. www.marcresorts.com. 126 units. TV. $119–$149 one-bedroom apt (sleeps up to 4), $149–$189 two-bedroom apt (sleeps up to 6). AE, MC, V.

If you want to get away and pull up the drawbridge, this is a good place to go. The condos—some of them newly remodeled, some in need of remodeling—are in three-story tropical structures surrounded by lawns, palms, mountainous inland slopes, and the solitude of the island's lush East End. The units, individually decorated by the owners, come with full kitchens, large lanais, and either garden or ocean views. If the complex is full, it can be noisy. Wavecrest is more remote than Molokai Shores—it's about 12 miles of leisurely driving to Kaunakakai (translation: 30-plus minutes), 7 more to the airport, and a substantial drive to West End activities—but more appropriately tropical than West End properties. Fortunately, there's a small store on the property for snacks, drinks, and video rentals, as well as two lighted tennis courts and a pool. The haunting views of the three neighboring islands provide a truly unique sense of place, but the shoreline here isn't Molokai's best for swimming.

INEXPENSIVE

Country Cottage at Puu O Hoku Ranch. Kamehameha V Hwy., at mile marker 25 (HC-01, Box 900), Kaunakakai, HI 96748. ☎ **808/558-8109.** Fax 808/558-8100. 1 two-bedroom cottage (sleeps up to 5). $85 double. 2-night minimum. Extra person $10. No credit cards.

Escape to a working cattle ranch! Ranch manager Jack Spruance welcomes visitors to *Puu o Hoku* ("Star Hill") Ranch, which spreads across the East End of Molokai. The ranch, on 14,000 acres of pasture and forests, is the last place to stay before Halawa Valley—it's at least an hour's drive from Kaunakai along the shoreline. Two acres of tropically landscaped property circle the ranch's rustic wooden cottage, which has breathtaking views of rolling hills and the Pacific ocean. It contains comfortable country furniture, a fully equipped kitchen, two bedrooms (one with double bed, one with two twins), two bathrooms, a big living area, and a separate dining room on the enclosed lanai. TVs and VCRs are available on request. We recommend stargazing at night, watching the sunrise in the morning, and playing in the afternoon: croquet, hiking, swimming, or just roaming the grounds.

Honomuni House. Kamehameha V Hwy., just after mile marker 17 (HC-01, Box 700), Kaunakakai, HI 96748. ☎ **808/558-8383.** 1 one-bedroom cottage. TV. $80 double. Extra person $10 adult, $5 child. No credit cards.

Old stonework taro terraces and house foundations testify that Honomuni Valley was popular with early Hawaiians, whose groves of breadfruit, coconut, fruit, ginger, and coffee still flourish in the wilderness. Modern folks can sample this miniparadise at a remote cottage—17½ miles from Kaunakakai, a mile or more from the nearest public beach area—set in the forest along the foot of the East End upslope. Freshwater prawns and native fish hide out in the stream that carved the valley. Experienced hikers will enjoy exploring upstream, where they'll find pools for swimming and watching (or catching) prawns and, farther up, a waterfall of their very own. The small cottage has a full kitchen, separate bedroom, bathroom, and an outside shower for rinsing off the sand from the beach. You're welcome to enjoy the tropical fruits growing right on the premises, which are dominated by a huge monkeypod tree. The cottage does sit right on the road, but there's generally little traffic after dark.

✪ **Kamalo Plantation Bed & Breakfast.** Kamehameha V Hwy., just past mile marker 10 (HC01, Box 300), Kaunakakai, HI 96748. ☎ and fax **808/558-8236.** www.molokai.com/kamalo. 2 units. TV. $75 double, $85 cottage double (with shower only; sleeps up to 4). 2-night minimum in cottage. Rates include continental breakfast. Extra person $10. No credit cards.

Glenn and Akiko Foster's 5-acre spread includes an ancient heiau ruin in the front yard, plus leafy tropical gardens and a working fruit orchard. The genial Fosters have lived and sailed in the islands for many years and are full of island lore. The Eden-like property, which they bought in 1992, is easy to find: It's right across the East End road from Father Damien's historic St. Joseph church. The plantation-style cottage is tucked under flower trees and surrounded by swaying palms; it has its own lanai, a big living room with a queen-size sofa bed, and a separate bedroom with king bed, so it can sleep four comfortably. The kitchen is fully equipped (including spices), and there's a barbecue outside. The room in the home has a separate entrance, private lanai, bathroom, coffeemaker, microwave, and fridge. Guests are provided with beach mats and towels. A breakfast of fruit and freshly baked bread is served every morning.

✪ **Puunana/Pauwalu Beachfront Cottages.** Kamehameha V Hwy., past mile marker 18. Reservations c/o Kip and Leslie Dunbar, HC 01 Box 901, Kaunakakai, HI 96748. ☎ **800/673-0520** or 808/558-8153. Fax 808/558-8153. www.molokai-aloha.com/kainalu. 2 two-bedroom cottages (each sleeps up to 4). TV. $115 cottage; $690 per week. 3-night minimum. No credit cards.

As clichéd as it sounds, these two five-star cottages by the sea really are the stuff that dreams are made of. Some 18 miles from Kaunakakai, this is one of the most peaceful, comfortable, and elegant properties on Molokai's East End, and the setting is simply stunning. Built in 1996, each of the green-and-white plantation-style cottages sits on its own secluded beach—you'll feel like you're on your own private island. The Puunana Cottage has a king bed and two twins, while the Pauwalu has a queen, a double, and a sofa bed. Both have full kitchens, VCRs, washer/dryers, ceiling fans, comfortable tropical furniture, large furnished decks, and views of Maui, Lanai, and Kahoolawe across the channel; in the winter, the deck is a perfect place for whale watching. Your hosts, whose family has held this property for generations, live nearby.

4 Dining

A few new eateries have opened up recently on this traditionally slow-moving island. Most of them are fast-food or take-out places, but a few of them have a home-cooked touch. Even with these new developments, one of the best things about Molokai is its glacial pace of change. Lovers of the fast lane might consider this aspect of the island's personality a con rather than a pro, but they wouldn't choose to come here, anyway. Sybarites, foodies, and pampered oenophiles had best lower their expectations upon arrival, or turn around and leave the island's natural beauty to nature lovers.

Personally, we like the unpretentiousness of the island; it's an oasis in a state where plastic aloha abounds. Most Molokai residents fish, collect seaweed, grow potatoes and tomatoes, and prepare for backyard luaus; if you happen to be walking past on the beach (as we were on a first trip to the island many years ago), they may invite you in with a broad, generous wave of the arm, hollering, "Come eat, come eat! Got plenty food."

Unlike Lanai (see chapter 11), which is small and rural but offers some of the finest dining in the islands, Molokai provides no such mix of innocence and sophistication. You must meet this island on its own terms: It doesn't pretend to be anything more than a combination of old ways and an informal lifestyle, a lifestyle closer to the land than to a chef's toque.

You'll even find a certain defiant stance against the trappings of modernity. Although some of the best produce in Hawaii is grown on this island, you're not likely to find much of it served in its restaurants, other than in the take-out items at Outpost Natural Foods, or at the Molokai Pizza Cafe, which is one of the most pleasing eateries on the island. The rest of the time, content yourself with ethnic or diner fare, or fresh fish from the Molokai Ice House—or by cooking for yourself. The many visitors who stay in condos find that it doesn't take long to sniff out the best sources of produce, groceries, and fresh fish to fire up at home when the island's other dining options are exhausted. The "Edibles" sections in "Shops & Galleries," later in this chapter, will point you to the shops and markets where you can pick up foodstuffs for your own island-style feast.

Except for the Ohia Lodge at Kaluakoi Resort, Molokai's restaurants are inexpensive or moderately priced, and several of them do not accept credit cards. At press time, Hotel Molokai, under new ownership, was poised to reopen the doors of its ocean-side restaurant, at one time the most pleasing restaurant on the island. It's too early to include it in this edition, but be sure to check it out. Reservations are not accepted unless otherwise noted, and regardless of where you are, you certainly won't have to dress up. In most cases, we've listed just the town rather than the street address, because as you'll see, street addresses are as meaningless on this island as fancy cars and sequins.

KAUNAKAKAI

Codi's Lunch Wagon. 90 Makaena Place, Kaunakakai. ☎ **808/553-3443.** $4.25–$5. No credit cards. Mon–Fri 10:30am–1:30pm. LOCAL.

Only days after its opening in March 1998, residents were touting the spareribs, oxtail soup, and pork adobo served up at this tiny lunch wagon. "A welcome addition to Kaunakakai" is how Codi's is commonly described. The four different plate lunches are served with rice, macaroni salad, and kimchi—a good value. The rotating menu includes chicken broccoli, chicken papaya, roast pork, meat loaf, shrimp curry, and other ethnic fare, served with a smile.

Kamoi Snack-N-Go. Kamoi Professional Center. ☎ **808/553-3742.** Ice cream $1.65–$3.40. No credit cards. Mon–Sat 9am–9pm, Sun noon–9pm. ICE CREAM/SNACKS.

The Kamoi specialty: sweets and icy treats. Ice cream made by Dave's on Oahu comes in flavors such as green tea, litchi sherbet, and many other tropical and traditional flavors. Schoolchildren and their parents line up for the ice-cream cones, shakes, floats, sundaes, and the popular Icee floats served at this tiny snack shop. No tables, but there are aisles of candies.

Kanemitsu's Bakery & Restaurant. 79 Ala Malama St., Kaunakakai. ☎ **808/553-5855.** Most items under $5.50. No credit cards. Restaurant Wed–Sat 5:30am–1pm, Sun 5:30–11am. Bakery Wed–Mon 5:30am–6:30pm. BAKERY/DELI.

Morning, noon, and night, this local legend fills the Kaunakakai air with the sweet smells of baking. Taro lavosh is the hot new seller, joining Molokai bread—developed in 1935 in a cast-iron, kiawe-fired oven—as a Kanemitsu signature. Flavors range from apricot-pineapple to mango (in season), but the classics remain the regular white, wheat, cheese, sweet, and onion-cheese breads. For those who like their bread warm, the bread mixes (regular, sweet, and macadamia-nut) offer a way to take Molokai home.

In the adjoining coffee shop/deli, all sandwiches come on their own freshly baked buns and breads. The hamburgers, egg-salad sandwiches, mahi burgers, and honey-dipped fried chicken are all popular.

Not many people know about Kanemitsu's other life as a late-night institution for die-hard bread lovers. Those in the know line up at the bakery's back door at 10:30pm, when the bread is whisked hot out of the oven and into waiting hands. You can order your fresh bread with butter, jelly, cinnamon, or cream cheese, and the bakers will cut the hot loaves down the middle and slather on the works so it melts in the bread.

Molokai Drive-Inn. Kaunakakai. ☎ **808/553-5655.** Most items under $6. No credit cards. Mon–Fri 5:30am–10pm, Sat–Sun 6am–10:30pm. AMERICAN/TAKE-OUT.

The $6 plate-lunch prices are a bit steep at this greasy spoon, but it's one of the rare drive-up places with fresh *akule* (mackerel) and ahi (when available), plus fried saimin at budget-friendly prices. The honey-dipped fried chicken is a favorite among residents, who also come here for the floats, shakes, and other artery-clogging choices. But don't expect much in terms of ambience: This is a fast-food take-out counter with the smells of frying in the surrounding air—and it doesn't pretend to be otherwise.

Molokai Mango. 93-D Ala Malama St. ☎ **808/553-3981.** Sandwiches $1.99–$3.59. MC, V. Mon–Sat 9am–8:30pm, Sun noon–8:30pm. DELI/AMERICAN.

The former owner of JoJo's restaurant in Maunaloa opened this video store and popular sandwich shop in downtown Kaunakakai, where he sells sandwiches and nachos from the take-out counter. Turkey, ham, and roast beef (Angus beef) are served on five different breads, and all are popular. The inexpensive nachos are a big hit, too, for those evenings at home with an old rented movie. Molokai Mango also rents and sells videos, games, and equipment, including TV sets.

✪ Molokai Pizza Cafe. Kahua Center, on the old Wharf Rd. ☎ **808/553-3288.** Large pizzas $12.60–$22.15. No credit cards. Sun 11am–10pm, Mon–Thurs 8am–10pm, Fri–Sat 8am–11pm. PIZZA.

Molokai's favorite eatery is now open for breakfast, serving made-to-order omelets, breakfast pizzas (egg, cheese, bacon, sausage), cereal, waffles, and other wake-up wonders. This place was the talk of the town when it opened—"Molokai has pizza now," locals announced proudly—and its excellent pizzas and sandwiches have made it a Kaunakakai staple as well as our favorite on the island. There are seven different pizzas, each named after a Hawaiian island (Niihau has yet to arrive in the Kaunakakai pizza pantheon). The best-selling pizzas: the Molokai (pepperoni and cheese), the Big Island (pepperoni, ham, mushroom, Italian sausage, bacon, and vegetables), and the Molokini (plain cheese slices). Pasta, sandwiches, and specials round out the menu. Coin-operated cars and a toy airplane follow the children's theme, but adults should feel equally at home with the very popular barbecued baby-back rib plate and the fresh fish dinners. Children's art and letters in the tiled dining room add an entertaining and charming touch. "Dear Uncle Sean," reads one of them. "Thank you from the bottom of our tummies."

✪ Outpost Natural Foods. 70 Makaena, Kaunakakai. ☎ **808/553-3377.** Most items under $5. No credit cards. Sun–Fri 10am–3pm. VEGETARIAN.

The most healthful and freshest food on the island is served at the lunch counter of this health-food store, around the corner from the main drag on the makai (ocean) side of Kaunakakai town. The tiny store abounds in Molokai papayas, bananas, herbs, potatoes, watermelon, and other produce, complementing its selection of vitamins, cosmetics, and health aids. But the real star is the closet-size lunch counter. The salads, burritos, tempeh sandwiches, tofu-spinach lasagna specials, and mock chicken, turkey, lamb, and meat loaf (made from oats, sprouts, seeds, and seasonings) will likely dispel the notion most folks have about vegetarian food being boring. Not so! Outpost serves hearty, creative lunches using no animal or unwholesome products.

Rabang's. Kaunakakai. ☎ **808/553-5841.** Most items under $4.50; combination plate $6. No credit cards. Daily 7am–9pm. FILIPINO.

Specialties here include sweet-and-sour turkey tail prepared Ilocano style (as opposed to Tagalog) and a Filipino dish called *pinat bet*—a mixture of eggplant, string beans, pumpkin, lima beans, and other vegetables, with a smidgen of pork and some assertive seasonings. The diner is a bit more in the thick of things and more inviting than Oviedo's down the street, but it's still extremely casual, with only a few tables that are always full at lunchtime. The Friday Hawaiian plate, barbecued-chicken plate, and sweet-and-sour pork are among the Molokai favorites.

Sundown Deli. 145 Puali St. ☎ **808/553-3713.** Sandwiches and salads $3–$5.95. No credit cards. Mon–Fri 10:30am–6pm, Sat 10:30am–2pm. DELI.

Across the street from Veteran's Memorial Park, Sundown is another Molokai new-comer serving sandwiches and food-to-go with a home-cooked flavor. Eight types of sandwiches (smoked turkey, chicken salad) and several salads (Caesar, Oriental, stuffed tomato) are served daily, with a soup that changes by the day (it might be clam chowder, Portuguese bean, or cream of broccoli); saimin is $3.50. There are a couple of tables for those who want to eat in.

EN ROUTE TO THE NORTH COAST
Kualapuu Cook House. Kualapuu. ☎ **808/567-6185.** Main courses $7.50–$17.95. No credit cards. Daily 7am–9pm, except 7am–4pm on first Sun of the month. AMERICAN.

The rusting wagon frame in front of the old plantation house marks this popular diner and breakfast spot where local farmers and cowboys gather to chitchat over coffee and the renowned omelets (humongous), steak and eggs (more humongous!), and other American dishes with a local twist. The mahimahi omelet goes for $7.75, the veggie omelet for less, and at lunch and dinner, burgers, chili, fresh fish, and surf-and-turf items are the norm. Thursday is prime-rib night, when you can order a sizable dinner for less than $15. You can dine indoors or out. Unsolicited advice: Save room for the chocolate–macadamia-nut pie.

THE WEST END
Ohia Lodge. Kaluakoi Hotel and Golf Club, Maunaloa. ☎ **808/552-2555.** Reservations rec-ommended for dinner. Main courses $12–$22. AE, DC, DISC, MC, V. Daily 6:30–10:30am and 6–9pm. CONTINENTAL/HAWAII REGIONAL.

The view of Kepuhi Beach has always been the best thing about this room, well posi-tioned for spectacular sunsets and close enough to hear the waves. On a clear day, diners can even see the Makapuu Lighthouse on Oahu, and whales are in full view during the height of the winter season. This is the only full-service restaurant serving the West End.

The last year has seen much improvement in the food. The fresh fish served with basmati rice is broiled and served with pineapple-papaya salsa and shoyu-mustard beurre blanc. Sautéed, the fresh catch comes in lemon beurre blanc, macadamia nuts, and capers; when seared in the wok, with Asian black beans and beurre blanc. The choices and preparations vary, and if nothing on the fresh catch list appeals to you, the herb-roasted chicken is popular.

The Village Grill. Maunaloa. ☎ **808/552-0012.** Reservations recommended for lunch and dinner. Main courses $5.25–$8.50 lunch, $8–$18.95 dinner. AE, MC, V. Daily 11am–2pm and 6–9pm. AMERICAN.

The plantation architecture of the original building remains, with a wraparound veranda and indoor dining room around an antique bar from the 1800s. (Owners say the bar sailed here on a ship from the East Coast.) On a clear day, you can see Oahu from the deck—the backside of Diamond Head is a surprising sight from Molokai. The Grill is busy at sunset, when diners gather on the cool veranda over platters of seafood, ethnic specialties, nachos, ribs, and other appetizer fare.

The menu is basically American steak house, featuring Molokai vegetables and fresh fish, such as Cactus Charley's Big Catch of the Day, usually pink snapper, mahimahi, or ono. Heavier tastes may go for Pistol Pete's Prime Rib; the 10-ounce New York steak, called the Mare Cut; or the Stallion T-bone steak. Also popular are the jumbo prawns, shrimp-and-scallop stir-fry, and vegetable tempura, featuring Molokai sweet potatoes.

THE EAST END
Neighborhood Store 'N Counter. Pukoo. ☎ **808/558-8498.** Most items under $7. No credit cards. Daily 8am–6pm. AMERICAN.

The store/lunch counter appears like a mirage near mile marker 16 in the Pukoo area en route to the East End. Picnic tables under a royal poinciana tree are a cordial sight, and the food does not disappoint. The Mexican plate is excellent, the chicken laulau a local legend. The food stop serves omelets, Portuguese sausage, and other breakfast specials, then segues into sandwiches, salads, mahimahi plates, and varied over-the-counter lunch offerings. There are daily specials, ethnic dishes, and some vegetarian dishes. The Neighborhood Store is nothing fancy, and that's what we love about it: its Molokai-style informality, its rural charm, and the good grinds to go with them. (Also see "Shops & Galleries," later in this chapter.)

5 Beaches

With imposing sea cliffs on one side and lazy fishponds on the other, Molokai has little room for beaches along its 106-mile coast. Still, a big gold-sand beach flourishes on the West End, and you'll find tiny pocket beaches on the East End. The emptiness of Molokai's beaches is both a blessing and a curse: The welcome seclusion means no lifeguards, and nobody to rely on except yourself.

KAUNAKAKAI'S BEACH
ONE ALII BEACH PARK
This thin strip of sand, once reserved for the *alii* (chiefs), is the oldest public beach park on Molokai. You'll find One Alii Beach Park (pronounced *o-nay*, not *won*) by a coconut grove on the outskirts of Kaunakakai. Safe for swimmers of all ages and abilities, it's often crowded with splashy families on weekends, but it can be all yours on weekdays. Facilities include outdoor showers, rest rooms, and free parking.

WEST END BEACHES
✪ PAPOHAKU BEACH
Nearly 3 miles long and 100 yards wide, gold-sand Papohaku Beach is one of the biggest in Hawaii (17-mile-long Polihale Beach on Kauai is the biggest). The big surf and rip currents make swimming risky except in summer, when the calm waters make

it hospitable. Papohaku is great for walking, beachcombing, picnicking, and sunset watching year-round. Go early in the day when the tropic sun is less fierce and the wind calm. The beach is so big that you might never see another soul except at sunset, when a few people gather on the shore to watch the sun sink into the Pacific in hopes of spotting the elusive green flash, a daily natural wonder when the horizon is cloud-free. Facilities include outdoor showers, rest rooms, picnic grounds, and free parking.

Kepuhi Beach

Duffers see this picturesque golden strand in front of the Kaluakoi Resort and Golf Course as just another sand trap, but sunbathers like the semiprivate grassy dunes; they're seldom, if ever, crowded. Beachcombers often find what they're looking for here, but swimmers won't: They'll have to dodge lava rocks and risk rip tides to survive. Oh, yes—look out for errant golf balls. There are no facilities or lifeguards, but cold drinks and rest rooms are handy at the resort.

EAST END BEACHES
✪ Sandy Beach

Molokai's most popular swimming beach—ideal for families with small kids—is a roadside pocket of gold sand protected by a reef with a great view of Maui and Lanai. You'll find it off the King Kamehameha V Highway (Highway 450) at mile marker 20. There are no facilities—just you, the sun, the sand, and the surf.

Murphy Beach Park (Kumimi Beach Park)

In 1970, the Molokai Jaycees wanted to create a sandy beach park with a good swimming area for the children of the East End. They chose a section known as Kumimi Beach, which was owned by the Puu o Hoku Ranch. The beach was a dump, literally. The ranch owner, George Murphy, immediately gave his permission to use the site as a park; the Jaycees cleaned it up and built three small pavilions, plus picnic tables and barbecue grills. Officially, the park is called the George Murphy Beach Park (shortened to Murphy Beach Park over the years), but some old-timers still call it Kumimi Beach, and, just to make things real confusing, some people call it Jaycees Park.

No matter what you call it, this small park is shaded by ironwood trees that line a white-sand beach. Generally, it's a very safe swimming area. On calm days, snorkeling and diving are great outside the reef. Fishermen are also frequently spotted here looking for papio and other island fish.

Halawa Beach Park

At the foot of scenic Halawa Valley is this beautiful black-sand beach with a palm-fringed lagoon, a wave-lashed island offshore, and a distant view of the West Maui Mountains across the Pailolo Channel. The swimming is safe in the shallows close to shore, but where the waterfall stream meets the sea, the ocean is often murky and unnerving. A winter swell creases the mouth of Halawa Valley on the north side of the bay and attracts a crowd of local surfers. Facilities are minimal; bring your own water. To get here, take the King Kamehameha V Highway (Highway 450) east to the end.

6 Hitting the Water

Molokai Fish & Dive, Kaunakakai (☎ 808/553-5926), is a mind-boggling store filled with outdoor gear. You can rent snorkeling gear, fishing gear, and even ice chests here. This is also the hot spot for fishing news and tips on what's running where.

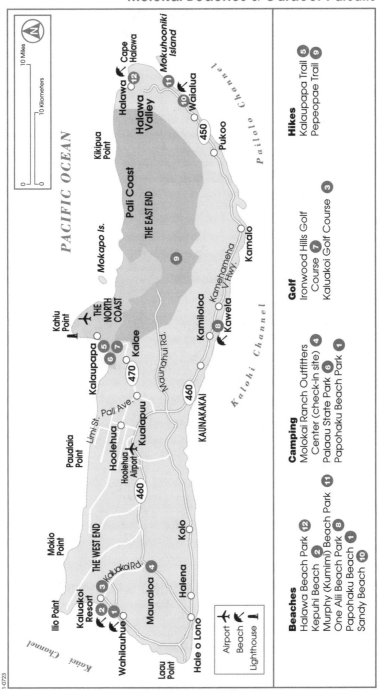

Molokai Beaches & Outdoor Pursuits

PACIFIC OCEAN

Kaiwi Channel

Kalohi Channel

Pailolo Channel

THE WEST END

THE EAST END

THE NORTH COAST

Pali Coast

Halawa Valley

Mokapo Is.

Mokuhooniki Island

Illo Point
Mokio Point
Paualaia Point
Kahiu Point
Kikipua Point
Cape Halawa
Wahilauhue
Maunaloa
Halena
Kolo
Hale o Lono
Laau Point
Kaluakoi Resort
Kaluakoi Rd.
Hoolehua
Hoolehua Airport
Limi St.
Pali Ave.
Kualapuu
KAUNAKAKAI
Kalaupapa
Kalae
Maunahui Rd.
Kamiloloa
Kamaloa
Kamehameha V Hwy.
Kawela
Kamalo
Pukoo
Waialua
Halawa

450
460
460
470

Beaches
Halawa Beach Park **12**
Kepuhi Beach **2**
Murphy (Kumimi) Beach Park **11**
One Alii Beach Park **8**
Papohaku Beach **1**
Sandy Beach **10**

Camping
Molokai Ranch Outfitters Center (check-in site) **4**
Palaau State Park **6**
Papohaku Beach Park **1**

Golf
Ironwood Hills Golf Course **7**
Kaluakoi Golf Course **3**

Hikes
Kalaupapa Trail **5**
Pepeopae Trail **9**

Airport ✈
Beach ⤦
Lighthouse ⍓

N ⌖

10 Miles
10 Kilometers

1-0723

✪ Frommer's Favorite Molokai Experiences

Travel Back in Time on the Pepeopae Trail. This awesome hike takes you through the Molokai Forest Reserve and back a few million years to a time before any creature set foot on the island. Along the misty trail, expect close encounters of the botanical kind: mosses, sedges, violets, lichens, and knee-high ancient ohias.

Stroll the Sands at Papohaku. Go early, when the tropic sun isn't so fierce, and stroll this 3-mile stretch of unspoiled golden sand—it's one of the longest in Hawaii. The big surf and rip tides make swimming somewhat risky, but Papohaku is perfect for walking, beachcombing, and, in the evening, sunset watching.

Soak in the Warm Waters off Sandy Beach. On the East End, about 20 miles outside Kaunakakai—just before the road starts to climb to Halawa Valley—lies a small pocket of white sand known as Sandy Beach. Submerging yourself in the warm, calm waters (an outer reef protects the cove) is a sensual experience par excellence.

Snorkel Among Clouds of Butterfly Fish. You don't have to pay for a boat ride or an expensive guide to explore the calm waters at Kumimi Beach. Just don a snorkel, a mask, and fins, and head to the reef, where you'll find lots of exotic tropical fish, including long-nosed butterfly fish, saddle wrasses, and convict tang.

Venture into the Garden of Eden. Drive the 30 miles along Molokai's East End. Take your time. Stop to smell the flowers and pick guavas by the side of the road. Pull over for a swim. Wave at every car you pass and every person you see. At the end of the road, stand on the beach at Halawa Valley and see Hawaii as it must have looked in A.D. 650, when the first people arrived in the islands.

Celebrate the Ancient Hula. Hula is the heartbeat of Hawaiian culture, and Molokai is the birthplace of the hula. Although most visitors never get to see the real thing, it's possible to see it here—once a year, on the third Saturday in May, when Molokai celebrates the birth of the hula at its Ka Hula Pikoi Festival. The daylong affair at Papohaku Beach Park includes dance, music, food, and crafts.

Ride a Mule into Kalaupapa. Don't pass up the opportunity to see this hauntingly beautiful peninsula. Buzzy Sproats's mules go up and down the 3-mile trail (with 26 switchbacks) to Molokai's famous leper colony, a once-in-a-lifetime ride. The views are breathtaking: You'll see the world's highest sea cliffs (taller than a 300-story skyscraper) and waterfalls plunging thousands of feet into the ocean. If you're afraid of heights, catch the views from the Kalaupapa Lookout.

BODYBOARDING (BOOGIE BOARDING) & BODYSURFING

Molokai only has three beaches that offer ridable waves for bodyboarding and bodysurfing: Papohaku, Kepuhi, and Halawa. Even these beaches are only for experienced bodysurfers, due to the strength of the rip currents and undertows. Bring your own boogie boards, as no one rents them on Molokai. However, **Molokai Ranch & Fun Hogs** (☎ **808/552-2791**; www.molokai-ranch.com) offers surfing or bodyboarding excursions on Monday, Wednesday, Friday, and Sunday afternoons for $60 for 3 hours, including lesson, equipment, and transportation.

Kayak Along the North Shore. This is the Hawaii of your dreams: waterfalls thundering down sheer cliffs, remote sand beaches, miles of tropical vegetation, and the sounds of the sea splashing on your kayak and the wind whispering in your ear. Best times to go are the brief window in early spring, around March to April, or in summer, especially August to September, when the normally galloping ocean lies down flat.

Sample the Local Brew. Saunter up to the Espresso Bar at the Coffees of Hawaii Plantation Store in Kualapuu for a fresh cup of java made from beans that were grown, processed, and packed on this 450-acre plantation. Afterward (or while you sip), survey the vast collection of native crafts.

Taste Aloha at a Macadamia Nut Farm. It could be owner Tuddie Purdy and his friendly disposition that make the macadamia nuts here taste so good. Or it could be his years of practice in growing, harvesting, and shelling them on his 1½-acre farm. Either way, Purdy produces a perfect crop. See how he does it on a short, free tour of Purdy's All-Natural Macadamia Nut Farm in Hoolehua, just a nut's throw from the airport.

Talk Story with the Locals. The number-one favorite pastime of most islanders is "talking story," or exchanging experiences and knowledge. It's an old Hawaiian custom that brings people, and generations, closer together. You can probably find residents more than willing to share their wisdom with you while fishing from the wharf at Kaunakakai, hanging out at Molokai Fish & Dive, or having coffee at any of the island's restaurants.

Post a Nut. Why send a picturesque postcard to your friends and family back home when you can send a fresh coconut? The Hoolelua Post Office will supply the free coconuts, if you'll supply the $3 postage fee.

Watch the Sunset from a Coconut Grove. Kapuaiwa Coconut Beach Park, off Maunaloa Highway (Highway 460), is a perfect place to watch the sunset: The sky behind the coconut trees fills with a kaleidoscope of colors as the sun sinks into the Pacific. Be careful where you sit, though: Falling coconuts could have you seeing stars well before dusk.

Stay at the Beach for Just $3. You can sleep under the stars at the West End's Papohaku Beach Park, the island's largest beach. All the facilities you need are here: rest rooms, drinking water, showers, barbecue grills. Just bring your own tent or sleeping bag and $3—and you'll have the best oceanfront accommodations on the island.

OCEAN KAYAKING

During the summer months, when the waters on the north shore are calm, Molokai offers some of the most spectacular kayaking in Hawaii. You can paddle from remote valley to remote valley, spending a week or more exploring the exotic terrain. However, Molokai is for experienced kayakers only, especially those adept in open ocean swells and through rough waves. Kayak tours are available through **Molokai Ranch & Fun Hogs** (☎ **808/552-2791;** www.molokai-ranch.com); during the winter, this is a great way to whale-watch. The escorted tours cost $60 per person (you must be at least 10 years old) and are available on Saturday only, from 1 to 4pm.

SAILING

Molokai Charters (☎ 808/553-5852) offers a variety of sailing trips on *Satan's Doll,* a 42-foot sloop: 2-hour sunset sails for $40 per person, a half day of sailing and whale watching for $50, and a full-day sail to Lanai with swimming and snorkeling for $90 (which includes lunch, cold drinks, snacks, and all equipment). Owners Richard and Doris Reed have been sailing visitors around Molokai's waters since 1975.

Molokai Ranch & Fun Hogs (☎ 808/552-2791; www.molokai-ranch.com) offers catamaran sailing by expert sailor/diver/kayaker Mike Holmes in his 28-foot boat, *Nanea,* every Tuesday, Thursday, and Saturday afternoon, at a cost of $60 per person.

SCUBA DIVING

Want to see turtles or manta rays up close? How about sharks? Molokai resident Bill Kapuni has been diving the waters around Molokai his entire life; he'll be happy to show you whatever you're brave enough to encounter. **Bill Kapuni's Snorkel & Dive,** Kaunakakai (☎ 808/553-9867; www.molokai-aloha.com/kapuni), can provide everything you need: gear, boat, even instruction. Two tank dives are $85 in his 22-foot Boston whaler, and include Bill's voluminous knowledge of the legends and lore of Hawaii.

SNORKELING

When the waters are calm, Molokai offers excellent snorkeling; you'll see a wide range of butterfly fish, tangs, and angelfish. Good snorkeling can be found—when conditions are right—at many of Molokai's beaches (see box, below). Snorkeling gear can be rented for $8.95 a day from **Molokai Fish & Dive** in Kaunakakai (☎ 808/553-5926); staffers will also point out that day's best snorkeling spots. Snorkeling tours are available for $45 from **Bill Kapuni's Snorkel & Dive** (☎ 808/553-9867), which also rents snorkeling gear for $25 a day (see "Scuba Diving," above).

Walter Naki of **Molokai Action Adventures** (☎ 808/558-8184) offers snorkeling, diving, and swimming trips in his 21-foot Boston whaler for $75 per person for a 4- to 6-hour custom tour.

Molokai Ranch & Fun Hogs (☎ 808/552-2791; www.molokai-ranch.com) offers snorkeling excursions in a 25-foot hard-bottom inflatable boat (certified for 18 passengers) daily from 9am to noon, for $60 per person, which includes lunch and all snorkeling equipment.

SPORTFISHING

Molokai's waters can provide prime sporting opportunities, whether you're looking for big-game sportfishing or bottom fishing. When customers are scarce, Captain Joe Reich, who has been fishing the waters around Molokai for 2 decades, goes commercial fishing, so he always knows where the fish are biting. He runs *Alyce C* Sportfishing out of Kaunakakai Harbor (☎ 808/558-8377). A full day of fishing for up to six people is $400, three-quarters of a day is $350, and a half day is $300. You can persuade him to do a whale-watching cruise during the winter months.

For fly-fishing or for light-tackle reef-fish trolling, contact Walter Naki at **Molokai Action Adventures** (☎ 808/558-8184). Walter has been fishing his entire life and loves to share his "secret spots" with visiting fishermen—he knows *the* place for bonefishing on the flats. A half-day trip in his 21-foot Boston whaler is $50 per person (minimum two people), $100 per person for a full day.

For light-tackle/deep-sea fishing, **Molokai Ranch & Fun Hogs** (☎ 808/552-2791; www.molokai-ranch.com) has afternoon (from 1 to 4pm) fishing excursions on Tuesday,

Molokai's Best Snorkel Spots

Most Molokai beaches are too dangerous to snorkel in winter, when big waves and strong currents are generated by storms that sweep down from Alaska. Stick to Murphy (Kumimi) Beach on the East End in winter. In summer, roughly May to mid-September, when the Pacific Ocean takes a holiday and turns into a flat lake, the whole west coast of Molokai opens up for snorkeling. "Fun Hog" Mike Holmes's favorite snorkel spots are:

Kawakiu Nui, Ilio Point, and Pohaku Moiliili (West End)   These are all special places seldom seen by even those who live on Molokai. You can reach Kawakiu Nui and Pohaku Moiliili on foot after a long, hot, dusty ride in a four-wheel-drive vehicle, but it's much easier and quicker to go by sea.

Kapukahehu (Dixie Maru) Beach (West End)   This is a good, gold-sand family beach, because the cove is well protected and the reef is close and shallow. The name Dixie Maru comes from a 1920s Japanese fishing boat, stranded off the rocky shore. One of the Molokai Ranch cowboys hung the wrecked boat's nameplate on a gate by Kapukahehu Beach, and the name Dixie Maru stuck. To get here, take Kaluakoi Road to the end of the pavement, and then take the footpath 100 yards to the beach.

Murphy (Kumimi) Beach Park (East End)   Located at mile marker 20–21, off Kamehameha V Highway, the reef here is easily reachable, and the waters are calm year-round.

Thursday, and Saturday on a 25-foot hard-bottom inflatable boat. The cost is $250 for one to four passengers.

WHALE WATCHING

The humpback whales that frequent the waters around Molokai from mid-December to mid-March can be seen up-close-and-personal with **Molokai Charters,** Kaunakakai (☎ **808/553-5852**), which has a 42-foot sloop, *Satan's Doll* (see "Sailing," above).

Also contact **Molokai Ranch & Fun Hogs** (☎ **808/552-2791;** www.molokai-ranch.com), which offers a variety of whale-watching charters during the winter months.

7 Hiking & Camping

HIKING MOLOKAI'S PEPEOPAE TRAIL

Molokai's most awesome hike is the ✪ **Pepeopae Trail;** it takes you back a few million years to a time before any human or creature set foot on the island. On the cloud-draped trail (actually a boardwalk across the bog), you'll see mosses, sedges, native violets, knee-high ancient ohias, and lichens that evolved in total isolation over eons. Eerie intermittent mists blowing in and out will give you an idea of this island at its creation.

The narrow boardwalk, built by volunteers, protects the bog and keeps you out of the primal ooze. Don't venture off of it; you could damage this fragile environment or get lost. The 3-mile round-trip takes about 90 minutes to hike—after you drive about 20 miles from Kaunakakai, deep into the Molokai Forest Preserve on a four-wheel-drive road. Plan a full day for this outing. Better yet, go on a guided nature hike with the **Nature Conservancy of Hawaii,** which guards this unusual ecosystem. For

---

A Tip for the Adventurous

If it's action you crave, call **Molokai Action Adventures** (☎ **808/558-8184**). Island guide Walter Naki will take you skin diving, reef trolling, kayaking, hunting, or hiking into remote hidden valleys. Hiking tours are $50 per person for 4 hours, and he limits the number of participants to no more than four. Not only does Walter know Molokai like the back of his hand, but he also loves being outdoors and talking story with visitors; he'll tell you about the island, the people, the politics, the myths, and anything else you want to know.

---

information, contact the Nature Conservancy of Hawaii, 1116 Smith St., Suite 201, Honolulu, HI 96817 (www.tnc.org/hawaii). No permit is required for this easy hike. You should call ahead (☎ **808/537-4508**, or 808/553-5236 on Molokai) to check on the condition of the ungraded, four-wheel-drive red-dirt road that leads to the trailhead and to let people know that you'll be up here.

To get here, take Highway 460 west from Kaunakakai for 3½ miles, and turn right before the Maunawainui Bridge onto the unmarked Molokai Forest Reserve Road (sorry, there aren't any road signs). The pavement ends at the cemetery; continue on the dirt road. After about 2 to 2½ miles, you'll see a sign telling you that you are now in the Molokai Forest Reserve. At the Waikolu Lookout and picnic area, which is just over 9 miles on the Molokai Forest Reserve Road, sign in at the box near the entrance. Continue on the road for another 5 miles to a fork in the road with the sign PUU KOLEKOLE pointing to the right side of the fork. Do not turn right; instead, continue straight at the fork, which will lead to the clearly marked trailhead.

HIKING TO KALAUPAPA

This hike is like going down a switchback staircase with what seems like a million steps. You don't always see the breathtaking view, because you're too busy watching your step. It's easier going down—you go from 2,000 feet to sea level in 2½ miles—which takes about an hour; it sometimes takes twice as long on the way up. The trailhead starts on the mauka (toward the mountains) side of Highway 470, just past the Mule Barn (you can't miss it). Check in here at 7:30am, get a permit, and go before the mule train departs. You must be 16 or older (it's an old state law that kept kids out of the leper colony) and should be in good shape. Wear good hiking boots or sneakers; you won't make it past the first turn in sandals.

HIKING THROUGH HALAWA VALLEY

Once the agricultural center of Molokai, Halawa Valley was planted in taro as far as the eye could see as recently as the 19th century. In 1946, a tidal wave scoured the valley and turned the "velvet taro in sweet mud"—salty ponds of brittle leaf. A second tsunami doomed agriculture here in 1957, and the valley became a natural garden of earthly delights, including escaped mango, papaya, and bananas.

The beach is still open for swimming and picnicking (see "Beaches," above), but the only way to see the falls and the magnificent valley, with its 11 heiau ruins and fish shrines dating from A.D. 650, is via **Pilipo's Halawa Falls and Cultural Hike**, P.O. Box 863, Kaunakakai, HI 96749 (☎ **808/553-4355**; www.molokai-hawaii.com). You must reserve in advance for the 4-hour hike. Forget your white tennies and shorts. Beautiful from a distance for its variety of shades of green, the valley up close is a fecund jungle of primal ooze; it's like being in a heady perfumed steam bath full of voracious mosquitoes. The trail is always wet and often sloppy; sometimes you may be in ankle-deep muck, but the reward for the tough 2-hour slog is an icy cold 40-foot-wide pool refreshed by the splashy tail of Moaula Falls. Bring a lunch, drinks, mosquito repellent, and a swimsuit. Cost is $25 per person, $15 for children under 12.

CAMPING
AT THE BEACH

One of the best year-round places to camp on Molokai is **Papohaku Beach Park** on the island's West End, a drive-up seaside site that's a great getaway. The island's largest beach is ideal for rest and relaxation. Facilities include rest rooms, drinking water, outdoor showers, barbecue grills, and picnic tables. Groceries and gas are available in Maunaloa, 6 miles away. Kaluakoi Resort is a mile away. Obtain camping permits by contacting **Maui County Parks Department,** P.O. Box 526, Kaunakakai, HI 96748 (☎ **808/553-3204;** www.mauimapp.com). Camping is limited to 3 days, but if nobody has applied, the time limit is waived. Cost is $3 a person per night.

IN AN IRONWOOD FOREST

At the end of Highway 470 is the 234-acre piney woods known as **Palaau State Park,** home to the Kalaupapa Lookout (the best vantage point for seeing the historic leper colony if you're not hiking or riding a mule in). It's airy and cool in the park's ironwood forest, where many love to camp at the designated state campground. Camping is free here, but you'll need a permit from the **State Division of Parks** (☎ **808/567-6618;** www.hawaii.gov). For more on the park, see "Seeing the Sights," below.

ON MOLOKAI RANCH

For a unique experience, the **Molokai Ranch Outfitters Center,** P.O. Box 259, Maunaloa, HI 96770 (☎ **800/254-8871** or 808/552-2791; www.molokai-ranch.com), offers an ecoadventure called the ✪ **Great Molokai Ranch Trail.** It features upscale, "comfortable" camping in a tent/bungalow called a "tentalow," plus lots of outdoor activities. Paniolo Camp, the first camp to open in 1997, is located just south of Molokai Ranch headquarters in Maunaloa. The camp is a collection of 40 comfortable tents mounted on wooden platforms. All tents have queen-size beds, ceiling fans, private bathrooms with self-composting toilets, hot-water showers, and solar-powered lights. Each individual campsite is located on a footpath that meanders through ironwood trees.

Within the Paniolo Camp is an open-air dining pavilion, a swimming pool, a fire pit, nature trails, mountain-bike paths, and volleyball and horseshoe areas. Rates are $128 per person (children under 12 stay free with a paying adult) and include meals, snacks, transportation (including airport pickup), daily maid service, and two major adventures per day (mountain biking, hiking, cultural experiences, children's program, and other activities). Equestrian and ocean adventures are available for an additional charge.

The Paniolo Camp is set up for families with children. Another camp, Kalo Camp, which features 20 yurts (circular canvas shelters on platforms) down by the beach, is for adults only. Rates are $138 per person and include the same great meal/adventure amenities.

The newest camp, Kaupoa Beach Camp, is located on a crescent, white-sand beach, close to ocean activities. Rates for Kaupoa are $148 per person and also include the meals and activities program. No matter which camp you decide on, don't miss the mountain-biking adventures, conducted by Bob Ward of Hairbrain Adventures; he offers the best tours on the best mountain-bike trails in the state.

Even if you aren't a "camping" fan, don't miss this fabulous opportunity to experience a comfortable yet adventurous side of Molokai.

8 Golf, Horseback Riding & Tennis

GOLF

Golf is one of Molokai's best-kept secrets; it's challenging and fun, tee times are open, and the rates are lower than your score will be. Most popular is the par-72, 6,564-yard **Kaluakoi Golf Course,** which designer Ted Robinson calls "the most spectacular and unusual course in the islands." The course is cut along the ocean (six holes are along the shoreline) and through the woods (pheasants, axis deer, and wild turkeys freely roam the fairways); it offers hilly, wooded fairways bisected by ravines, and a grand finish, beginning at the par-3, 16th hole. Called "The Gorge," the 16th plays 190 yards over a deep ravine to a two-tiered green. When you finish that, both the 17th and the 18th holes are very long par-4s, with greens blind from the tee. Facilities include a driving range, putting green, pro shop, and restaurant. It's rarely crowded; greens fees are $45 for Kaluakoi Resort guests and $65 for nonguests, and twilight rates are $38 for nonguests and $27 for guests. Call ☎ **808/552-2739.**

The real find in golf courses is the **Ironwood Hills Golf Course,** off Kalae Highway (☎ **808/567-6000**). It's located just before the Molokai Mule Ride mule barn, on the road to the Lookout. One of the oldest golf courses in the state, Ironwood Hills (named after the two predominant features of the course, ironwood trees and hills) was built in 1929 by Del Monte Plantation for its executives. This unusual course, which sits in the cool air at 1,200 feet, delights with its rich foliage, open fairways, and spectacular views of the rest of the island. Surrounded by bushes, the third hole—a par-3, 158-yard shot from the tee over a gully—could qualify as the signature hole. If you play here, use a trick developed by the local residents: After teeing off on the 6th hole, just take whatever clubs you need to finish playing the hole, and a driver for the 7th hole, and park your bag under a tree. The climb to the 7th hole is steep—you'll be glad that you're carrying only a few clubs. Greens fees are $10 for 9 holes, $14 for 18 holes. Cart fees are $7 for 9 holes, $14 for 18. You can also rent a hand cart for just $2.50, and club rentals are $7 for 9 holes and $12 for 18.

HORSEBACK RIDING

One of the most scenic places to go horseback riding on Molokai is **Pu'u-O-Hoku Ranch** (☎ 808/558-8109; e-mail: hoku@aloha.net), located about 25 miles outside of Kaunakakai on the East End. Guided trail rides lead through green pastures on one of the largest working ranches on the island, then up into the high mountain forest. Don't forget your camera, as you'll want to capture the many scenic views of waterfalls, the Pacific Ocean, and the islands of Maui and Lanai in the distance. Rates are $55 for a 2-hour ride and $75 for a 4-hour ride.

TENNIS

Maui County has only two tennis courts on Molokai. Both are located at the **Mitchell Pauole Center** in Kaunakakai (☎ 808/553-5141). Both courts have night lights and are available on a first-come, first-served basis.

9 Seeing the Sights

IN & AROUND KAUNAKAKAI

Kapuaiwa Coconut Grove/Kiowea Park. Along Maunaloa Hwy. (Hwy. 460), 2 mi. west of Kaunakakai.

This royal grove—a thousand coconut trees on 10 acres planted in 1863 by the island's high chief Kapua'iwa (later King Kamehameha V)—is a major roadside attraction in

Molokai. The shoreline park is a favorite subject of sunset photographers and visitors who delight in a hand-lettered sign that warns: DANGER: FALLING COCONUTS. In its backyard, across the highway, stands Church Row: seven churches, each a different denomination, stark evidence of the missionary impact on Hawaii.

Post-A-Nut. Hoolehua Post Office, Puu Peelua Ave., near Maunaloa Hwy. (Hwy. 460). ☎ **808/567-6144**. Mon–Fri 7:30–11:30am and 12:30–4:30pm.

Postmaster Margaret Keahi-Leary will help you say "Aloha" with a dried Molokai coconut: Write a message on the coconut with a felt-tip pen, and she'll send it via U.S. mail over the sea. Coconuts are free, but postage is $3 for a mainland-bound 2-pound coconut.

Purdy's All-Natural Macadamia Nut Farm. Lihipali Ave. (behind Molokai High School), Hoolehua. ☎ **808/567-6601**. www.visitmolokai.com. Mon–Fri 9:30am–3:30pm, Sat 10am–2pm. Free admission.

The Purdys have made macadamia nut–buying an entertainment event, offering tours of the 1½-acre homestead and lively demonstrations of nutshell-cracking in the shade of their towering trees. The tour of the 70-year-old nut farm explains the growth, bearing, harvesting, and shelling processes, so that by the time you crunch into the luxurious macadamia nut, you'll have more than a passing knowledge of its entire life cycle.

Tuddie Purdy has invented a rubber holding device that has conquered the otherwise slippery (and hazardous) shelling process. The nuts sold here are grown on Molokai and the Big Island and packaged on the farm—they make great, affordable souvenirs.

THE NORTH COAST

Most people never get a chance to see Hawaii's most dramatic coast in its entirety, but nobody should miss the opportunity to glimpse it from the Kalaupapa Lookout at Palaau State Park. On the way, there are a few diversions (arranged here in geographical order).

EN ROUTE TO THE NORTH COAST

Coffees of Hawaii Plantation Store. Hwy. 480 (near the junction of Hwy. 470), Kualapuu. ☎ **800/709-BEAN** or 808/567-9023. Fax 808/567-9270.

The defunct Del Monte pineapple town of Kualapuu is rising again—only this time coffee is the catch, not pineapple. Located in the cool foothills, Coffees of Hawaii has planted coffee beans on 600 acres of former pineapple land. The plantation is irrigating the plants with a high-tech, continuous water and fertilizer drip system (using the world's largest rubber-lined reservoir, which holds 1.4 billion gallons of water). Stop by the Espresso Bar for a Mocha Mama (Molokai coffee, ice, chocolate, chocolate ice cream, chocolate syrup, whipped cream, and chocolate shavings on top). It'll keep you going all day, maybe even all night.

Molokai Museum and Cultural Center. At the old R. W. Meyer Sugar Mill, Hwy. 470 (just after the turnoff for the Ironwood Hills Golf Course, and 2 mi. below Kalaupapa Overlook), Kalae. ☎ **808/567-6436**. Admission $2.50 adults, $1 students. Mon–Sat 10am–2pm.

En route to the California Gold Rush in 1849, Rudolph W. Meyer, a German professor, came to Molokai, married the high chiefess Kalama, and, after planting corn, wheat, and potatoes, began to operate a small sugar plantation near his home. Now on the National Register of Historic Places, the restored 1878 sugar mill, with its century-old steam engine, mule-driven cane crusher, copper clarifiers, and redwood evaporating pans—all in working order—is the last of its kind in Hawaii. The mill also

Especially for Kids

Flying a Kite *(see p. 246)* Not only can you get a guaranteed-to-fly kite at the **Big Wind Kite Factory** (☎ **808/552-2634**) in Maunaloa, but kite designer Jonathan Socher also offers free kite-flying classes to kids, who will learn how to make their kites soar, swoop, and, most important, stay in the air for more than 5 minutes.

Spending the Day at Murphy (Kumimi) Beach Park *(see p. 228)* Just beyond Wailua on the East End is this small wayside park that's perfect for kids. There's safe swimming conditions for children, plenty of shade from the ironwood trees, and small pavilions with picnic tables and barbecue grills.

Riding a Wagon *(see p. 242)* Kids will love being in a wagon drawn by two horses as it traverses a dirt trail through a mango grove, bound for an ancient temple of sacrifice. After the ride, the whole family is treated to a beachside lunch and an old-fashioned ukulele songfest.

Watching Whales *(see p. 233)* From mid-December to mid-March, whale watching for kids of all ages on Molokai Charters's 42-foot sloop, *Satan's Doll,* offers a variety of ways to spot these leviathans that visit Hawaiian waters in the winter.

Visiting the Past *(see p. 237)* The Molokai Museum and Cultural Center lets kids step into the past and see how sugar was made (with a restored 1878 sugar mill, complete with old steam engine, mule-driven cane crusher, and redwood evaporating pans).

houses a museum that traces the history of sugar growing on Molokai and features special events such as wine tastings every 2 months, taro festivals, an annual music festival, and occasional classes in ukulele making, loom weaving, and sewing; call for schedule.

Palaau State Park. At the end of Hwy. 470.

This 234-acre piney woods park 8 miles out of Kaunakakai is a sleeper. It doesn't look like much until you get out of the car and take a hike, which literally puts you between a rock and a hard place: Go right, and you end up on the edge of Molokai's magnificent sea cliffs, with its panoramic view of the infamous Kalaupapa leper colony; go left, and you come face-to-face with a stone phallus.

If you have no plans to scale the cliffs on mule or foot (see "Hiking & Camping," above), the ✪ **Kalaupapa Lookout** is the only place from which to see the former place of exile. The trail is marked, and historic photos and interpretive signs will explain what you're seeing.

It's airy and cool in the ironwood forest, where camping is free at the designated state campground. You'll need a permit from the **State Division of Parks** (☎ 808/567-6618; www.hawaii.gov). Not many people seem to camp here, probably because of the legend associated with the **Phallic Rock.** Six feet high, pointed at an angle that means business, Molokai's famous Phallic Rock is a legendary fertility tool that appears to be working today. According to Hawaiian legend, a woman who wishes to become pregnant need only spend the night near the rock and . . . voilà! It's probably just a coincidence, of course, but Molokai does have a growing population of young, pregnant women. If you want to avoid an unwanted pregnancy, it might be wise to avoid camping in the rock's vicinity.

Phallic Rock is at the end of a well-worn uphill path, through an ironwood grove past other rocks that vaguely resemble sexual body parts. No mistaking the big guy, though—it's definitely a giant, erect male penis. Supposedly, it belonged to Nanahoa, a demigod who quarreled with his wife, Kawahuna, over a pretty girl. In the tussle, Kawahuna was thrown over the cliff, and both husband and wife were turned to stone.

Of all the phallic rocks in Hawaii and the Pacific, this is the one to see. It's so famous, it's featured on a postcard with a tiny, awe-struck Japanese woman standing next to it.

THE LEGACY OF FATHER DAMIEN: KALAUPAPA NATIONAL HISTORIC PARK

An old tongue of lava that sticks out to form a peninsula, Kalaupapa became infamous because of man's inhumanity to victims of a formerly incurable contagious disease.

King Kamehameha V sent the first lepers—nine men and three women—into exile on this lonely shore, at the base of ramparts that rise like temples against the unbroken Pacific, on January 6, 1866. More than 11,000 lepers arrived between 1865 and 1874, dispatched to disfigure and die in one of the world's most beautiful, and lonely, places. They called Kalaupapa "The Place of the Living Dead."

One of the world's least contagious diseases, leprosy is caused by a germ, *Mycobacterium leprae,* that attacks the nerves, skin, and eyes. It's transmitted by direct, repetitive, person-to-person contact over a long period of time. American scientists found a cure for the disease, sulfone, in the 1940s.

Before science intervened, there was Father Damien. Born to wealth in Belgium, Joseph de Veuster traded a life of excess for exile among lepers; he devoted himself to caring for the afflicted at Kalaupapa. Father Damien, as he became known, volunteered to go out to the Pacific in place of his ailing brother when he was 33. Horrified at the conditions in the leper colony, Father Damien worked at Kalaupapa for 16 years, building houses, schools, and churches, and giving patients hope of redemption. He died on April 15, 1889, in Kalaupapa, of leprosy. He was 49.

A hero nominated for Catholic sainthood, Father Damien is buried not in his tomb next to St. Philomena Church, but in his native Belgium. His hand was recently returned to Molokai, however, and was reinterred at Kalaupapa as a relic of his martyrdom.

This small peninsula is probably the final resting place of more than 11,000 souls. The sand dunes are littered with grave markers, sorted by the religious affiliation—Catholic, Protestant, Lutheran, Buddhist—of those who died here. But so many are buried in unmarked graves that no census of the dead is believed to be either accurate or complete.

Kalaupapa is now a National Historic Park (☎ **808/567-6802;** www.nps.gov/kala) and one of Hawaii's richest archaeological preserves, with sites that date from A.D. 1000. About 60 former patients chose to remain in the tidy village of whitewashed houses with tombstones on the coast and statues of angels in their yards. The original name for their former affliction, "leprosy," was officially banned in Hawaii by the state legislature in 1981. The correct name now is "Hansen's Disease," for Dr. Gerhard Hansen of Norway, who discovered the germ in 1873. The few residents of Kalaupapa still call their disease leprosy, although they aren't too keen on being called lepers.

Kalaupapa welcomes visitors who arrive on foot, by mule, or by small plane. You can visit Father Damien's St. Philomena church, built in 1872. Once off-limits, the quiet village is now open to visitors, who can see it from a yellow school bus driven by resident tour guide Richard Marks, an ex-seaman and sheriff who survived the disease. You won't be able to roam freely, and you'll be allowed to enter only the museum, the craft shop, and the church.

In the chronicle of man there is perhaps no more melancholy landing than this. . . .
　　　　　　　　　　　　　　　　—Robert Louis Stevenson, on Kalaupapa

Smile. It No Broke Your Face.
　　　　　　　　　　　　　　　　　　　　　　　　　—sign at Kalaupapa

○ **MULE RIDES TO KALAUPAPA**   The first turn's a gasp, and it's all downhill from there. You can close your eyes and hold on for dear life, or slip the reins over the pommel and sit back, letting the mule do the walking down the precipitous path to Kalaupapa National Historic Park.

Even if you have only 1 day to spend on Molokai, spend it on a mule. It's a once-in-a-lifetime ride for most—the cliffs are taller than a 300-story skyscraper—but Buzzy Sproat's mules go up and down the narrow 3-mile trail daily, rain or shine, without ever losing a rider or mount on 26 switchbacks. From 1,600 feet on the nearly perpendicular ridge, the sure-footed mules step down the muddy trail, pausing often to calculate their next move—and always, it seems to us, veering a little too close to the edge. Each switchback is numbered; by the time you get to number four, you'll catch your breath, put the mule on cruise control, and begin to enjoy Hawaii's most awesome trail ride.

The mule tours are offered once daily starting at 8am, and they last until about 3:30pm. The cost is $135 per person for the all-day adventure, which includes the round-trip mule ride, a guided tour of the settlement, a visit to Father Damien's church and grave, lunch at Kalawao, and souvenirs. To go, you must be at least 16 years old and physically fit. Contact ○ **Molokai Mule Ride,** 100 Kalae Hwy., Suite 104, on Highway 470, 6 miles north of Highway 460 (☎ **800/567-7550,** 808/567-6088, or 808/567-6400 between 8 and 10pm; fax 808/567-6244; www.muleride. com). Advance reservations are required.

SEEING KALAUPAPA BY PLANE   Father Damien Tours, P.O. Box 1, Kalaupapa, HI 96742 (☎ and fax **808/567-6171**), picks you up at the Kalaupapa airport and takes you to some of the area's most scenic spots, including Kalawao, where Father Damien's church still stands, and the town of Kalaupapa. The $30 fee includes the tour of Kalaupapa and the permit to enter this secluded area. Airfare is additional. **Molokai-Lanai Air Shuttle** (☎ **808/567-6847**) charges $49.90 round-trip from Molokai Airport (in Hoolelua); **Island Air** (☎ **800/652-6541**) charges $180 round-trip from either Honolulu or Molokai Airport (AAA members get a special fare of $136); and Maui-based **Paragon Air** (☎ **808/244-3356**) offers a package deal of airfare from Kahului Airport (on Maui) to Kalaupapa, the 4½-hour tour, and lunch and drinks for $199. All visitors must be at least 16 years old.

THE WEST END
MAUNALOA

"Eleven hundred feet above the ocean in the rolling hills of west Molokai, something wonderful is happening," the real-estate prospectus reads. "A classic island town is becoming new again."

In the first and only urban renewal on Molokai, the 1920s-era pineapple-plantation town of Maunaloa is coming down. The termite-filled houses built by Libby, McNeil, and Libby are being scrapped by bulldozers; in their place is rising a new tract of $125,000 houses. Streets are being widened and paved, and curbs and sidewalks are going in. Historic Maunaloa is being transformed into Maunaloa Village, and already there's a movie theater and a Kentucky Fried Chicken outlet.

The only master-planned village on Molokai will have a museum, a bed-and-breakfast lodge, a town park with a playing field, new restaurants, artisans' studios, and tidy new plantation-style houses with steel rafters, solar water heaters, and low-flow fixtures and toilets—uptown stuff for Molokai. And with the newly opened Molokai Ranch Outfitters Center, the old plantation town is moving up in the world as a destination for both cowboys and those who dream of being cowboys. All this gentrification is unsettling to longtime residents, who resisted the change—and the end of an era of cheap rents. Only Jonathan Socher's Big Wind Kite Factory (see "Shops & Galleries," below), the town's main attraction, remains in place for now, his kites and books wrapped in cellophane against constant clouds of red dust raised by construction crews. Even the Cooke Island pines of Maunaloa need a bath.

Unfortunately, the very popular Molokai Ranch Wildlife Conservation Park, which offered entertaining tours of the collection of exotic African and Indian animals in the wild, has closed. Tours are no longer available.

KALUAKOI

At the end of the stark desert of the West End lies an oasis: spectacular beaches; a cluster of seacoast condos that hug an 18-hole, par-72 golf course; and the island's only resort hotel, Kaluakoi Hotel and Golf Club.

Kaluakoi is Hawaiian for "adz quarry"; many have been found on the rocky West End. This area is riddled with historical sites: heiau (temples), ancient Hawaiian house sites, calendar rock fields (similar to Stonehenge), huge stone boulders marking district boundaries, and even an enchanted forest. At the 110-foot Puu o Kaiaka, a crumbly cinder cone that separates Kepuhi and Papohaku beaches, San Francisco hotelier Ben Swig once planned to build a Fairmount Hotel, but his plans were defeated by islanders—so the coast is clear, just as it was more than 200 years ago.

ON THE NORTHWEST SHORE: MOOMOMI DUNES

Undisturbed for centuries, the Moomomi Dunes, on Molokai's northwest shore, are a unique treasure chest of great scientific value. It may look like just a pile of sand to you as you fly over on the final approach to Hoolehua Airport, but Moomomi Dunes is much more than that. Archaeologists have found adz quarries, ancient burial sites, and shelter caves; botanists have identified five endangered plant species; and marine biologists are finding evidence that endangered green sea turtles are hauling out from the waters once again to lay eggs here. The greatest discovery, however, belongs to Smithsonian Institute ornithologists, who have found bones of prehistoric birds, some of them flightless, that existed nowhere else on earth.

Accessible by Jeep trails that thread downhill to the shore, this wild coast is buffeted by strong afternoon breezes. It's hot, dry, and windy, so take water, sunscreen, and a windbreaker. At Kawaaloa Bay, a 20-minute walk to the west, there's a broad golden beach that you can have all to yourself. Stay on the trails, out of the water, and along the beach.

This 920-acre preserve is open to guided nature tours once a month. Contact the **Nature Conservancy of Hawaii** (☎ **808/553-5236** or 808/524-0779; www.tnc. org/hawaii) for an exact schedule and details.

To get to Moomomi Dunes, take Highway 460 (Maunaloa Highway) from Kaunakakai; turn right onto Highway 470, and follow it to Kualapuu. At Kualapuu, turn left on Highway 480 and go through Hoolehua Village; it's 3 miles to the bay.

THE EAST END

The East End is a cool and inviting green place that's worth a drive to the end of King Kamehameha V Highway (Highway 450), even if one of the island's greatest natural attractions, Halawa Valley, is now essentially off-limits.

AN ADVENTURE FOR EVERYONE: A WAGON RIDE TO ILIILIOPAE HEIAU

In a wagon drawn by two horses, you bump along a dirt trail through an incredible mango grove, bound for an ancient temple of human sacrifice. The temple of doom—right out of *Indiana Jones*—is Iliiliopae, a huge rectangle of stone made of 90 million rocks, overlooking the once-important village of Mapulehu and four ancient fish-ponds. The wagon glides under the perfumed mangoes, then heads uphill through a kiawe forest filled with Java plums to the heiau, which stands across a dry stream bed under cloud-spiked Kaunolu, the 4,970-foot island summit.

Hawaii's most powerful heiau attracted kahunas from all over the islands, who came to learn the rules of human sacrifice at this university of sacred rites. Contrary to Hollywood's version, historians say the victims here were always men, not young virgins, and they were strangled, not thrown into a volcano, while priests sat on lauhala mats watching silently. Spooky, eh?

This is the biggest, oldest, and most famous heiau on Molokai. It's a massive 22-foot-high stone altar, dedicated to Lono, the Hawaiian god of fertility. The heiau resonates with *mana* (power) strong enough to lean on. Legend says Iliiliopae was built in a single night by a thousand men, who passed rocks hand over hand through the Wailau Valley from the other side of the island; each received a shrimp (*'opae*) in exchange for the rock (*ili'ili*). Others say it was built by *menehunes*, the mythic elves who accomplished Herculean feats.

After the visit to the awesome temple, the horse-drawn wagon takes you back to the mango grove for a beachside lunch and an old-fashioned backyard ukulele songfest. Popular with families, this little adventure might sound too down-home for some, but the search for the "real" Molokai begins here.

Contact **Molokai Wagon Rides,** P.O. Box 1528, King Kamehameha V Highway (Highway 450), at mile marker 15, Kaunakakai, HI 96748 (☎ **808/558-8132**). The adventure via the wagon ride is $35 per person and includes lunch; it begins daily at 10am and lasts at least a couple of hours, sometimes longer. The company also offers a tour to the heiau on horseback for $40 per person (no lunch). The hour-long ride goes up to the heiau, then beyond it to the top of the mountain for those breathtaking views, and finally back down to the beach.

KAMAKOU PRESERVE

It's hard to believe, but close to the nearly mile-high summit, it rains more than 80 inches a year—enough to qualify as a rain forest. The Molokai Forest, as it was historically known, is the source of 60% of Molokai's water. Nearly 3,000 acres from the summit to the lowland forests of eucalyptus and pine are now held in preserve by the Nature Conservancy, which has identified 219 Hawaiian plants that grow here exclusively. The preserve is also the last stand of the endangered Molokai thrush (*olomao*) and Molokai creeper (*kawawahie*).

To get to this Nature Conservancy preserve, take the Forest Reserve Jeep road from Kaunakakai. It's a 45-minute, four-wheel-drive journey on a dirt trail to Waikolu Lookout Campground; from here, you can venture into the wilderness preserve on foot across a boardwalk on a 1½-hour hike (see "Hiking Molokai's Pepeopae Trail," above). For more information, contact the **Nature Conservancy** (☎ **808/553-5236;** www.tnc.org/hawaii).

EN ROUTE TO HALAWA VALLEY

No visit to Molokai is complete without at least a passing glance at the island's **ancient fishponds,** a singular achievement in Pacific aquaculture. With a hunger for fresh fish and a lack of ice or refrigeration, Hawaiians perfected aquaculture in 1400, before Christopher Columbus "discovered" America. They built gated, U-shaped stone and coral walls on the shore to catch fish on the incoming tide; they would then raise them in captivity. The result: a constant, ready supply of fresh fish.

The ponds stretch for 20 miles along Molokai's south shore and are visible from Kamehameha V Highway (Highway 450). Molokai's fishponds offer a clue to the island's ancient population. It took something like a thousand people to tend a single fishpond, and more than 60 ponds once existed on this coast. All of the fishponds are named; a few are privately owned. Some are silted in by red-dirt runoff from south coast gulches. Others have been revived by folks who raise fish and seaweed.

The largest, 54-acre **Keawa Nui Pond,** is surrounded by a 3-foot-high, 2,000-foot-long stone wall. **Alii Fishpond,** reserved for kings, is visible through the coconut groves at One Alii Beach Park (see "Beaches," above). You can see **Kalokoeli Pond,** 6 miles east of Kaunakakai on the highway, from the road.

Our Lady of Sorrows Catholic Church, one of five churches built by Father Damien on Molokai and the first outside Kalaupapa, sits across the highway from a fishpond. Park in the church lot (except on Sunday) for a closer look.

St. Joseph's Catholic Church. King Kamehameha V Hwy. (Hwy. 450), just after mile marker 10.

The afternoon sun strikes St. Joseph's Church with such a bold ray of light that it's as though God were about to perform a miracle. The stunning brightness compels you to stop and visit the little 1876 wood-frame church, one of four that Father Damien built "topside" on Molokai. Restored in 1971, the church stands beside a seaside cemetery, where feral cats play under the gaze of a Damien statue amid gravestones decorated with flower leis.

Smith Bronte Landing Site. King Kamehameha V Hwy. (Hwy. 450), at mile marker 11, on the makai (ocean) side.

In 1927, Charles Lindbergh soloed the Atlantic Ocean in a plane called *The Spirit of St. Louis* and became an American hero. That same year, Ernie Smith and Emory B. Bronte took off from Oakland, California, on July 14 in a single-engine Travelair aircraft named *The City of Oakland,* setting out 2,397 miles across the Pacific Ocean for Honolulu. The next day, after running out of fuel, they crash-landed upside-down in a kiawe thicket on Molokai, but emerged unhurt to become the first civilians to fly to Hawaii from the U.S. mainland. The 25-hour, 2-minute flight landed Smith and Bronte a place in aviation history—and on a roadside marker on Molokai.

Mapulehu Glass House. King Kamehameha V Hwy. (Hwy. 450), at mile marker 15. ☎ **808/558-8160.** Mon–Fri 7am–noon, or by appointment. Free guided tour at 10:30am.

This 1920s-era glass house, the biggest in Hawaii, stands in a garden that in itself is worth a visit, to see the exotic tropicals that Ellen Osborne ships to the mainland (see "Shops & Galleries," below). The tour takes in both the house and the 9-acre cut-flower farm.

HALAWA VALLEY

Of the five great valleys of Molokai, only Halawa, with its two waterfalls, golden beach, sleepy lagoon, great surf, and offshore island, is easily accessible. Access to Molokai's most popular hike through Halawa Valley, a fertile valley that was inhabited for centuries, and to 250-foot Moaula Falls, is once again open to the public through **Pilipo's Halawa Falls and Cultural Hike**, P.O. Box 863, Kaunakakai, HI 96748 (☎ 808/553-4355; www.molokai-hawaii.com; see page 234 for details). However, do *not* venture into the valley on your own. In a kind of 20th-century kapu, the private landowner, worried about slip-and-fall lawsuits, has, on the advice of lawyers, closed the trail to the falls. NO TRESPASSING signs are posted, and folks have been turned away by security guards.

To get to Halawa Valley, drive north from Kaunakakai on Highway 450 for 30 miles along the coast to the end of the road, which descends into the valley past Jersalema Hou Church, where the trail begins. If you'd just like a glimpse of the valley on your way to the beach, there's a scenic overlook along the road: After Puuo Hoku Ranch at mile marker 25, the narrow two-lane road widens at a hairpin curve, and you'll find the overlook on your right; it's 2 miles more to the valley floor.

10 Shops & Galleries

KAUNAKAKAI

Molokai Surf, Molokai Island Creations, Molokai Imports (which has great, inexpensive lauhala bags and local lemons), and **Lourdes** are clothing and gift shops in close proximity to one another in downtown Kaunakakai, where most of the retail shops sell T-shirts, muumuus, surf wear, and informal apparel. For food shopping, there are several good alternatives. Since many visitors to the island stay in condos, knowing where the grocery stores are is especially important. Other than that, serious shoppers will be disappointed, unless they love kites or native wood vessels. The following are Kaunakakai's notables.

Imamura Store. ☎ 808/553-5615.

Wilfred Imamura, whose mother founded the store (she died in 1992 at age 97), recalls the old railroad track that stretched from the pier to a spot across the street. "We brought our household things from the pier on a hand-pumped vehicle," he recalls. His store, appropriately, is a leap into the past, a marvelous amalgam of precious old-fashioned things. Rubber boots, Hawaiian-print tablecloths, Japanese tea plates, ukulele cases, plastic slippers, and even coconut bikini tops line the shelves. But it's not all nostalgia: The Molokai T-shirts, jeans, and palaka shorts are of good quality and inexpensive, and the pareu fabrics are a find.

Molokai Drugs. In the Kamoi Professional Center. ☎ 808/553-5790.

David Mikami, whose father-in-law founded the pharmacy in 1935, has made this more than a drugstore: It's a gleaming, friendly stop full of life's basic necessities, with generous amenities such as a phone and a rest room for passersby (!). You'll find the best selection of guidebooks, books about Molokai, and maps here, as well as greeting cards, paperbacks, party favors, cassette players, flip-flops, and every imaginable essential.

When Mikami's daughter, Kelly, became a pharmacist in 1995, she was the fourth in the family. The Mikamis are a household name on the island not only because of their pharmacy, but also because the family has shown exceptional kindness to the often economically strapped Molokaians.

Molokai Fish & Dive. ☎ 808/553-5926.

The island's largest selection of T-shirts and souvenirs shares space with fishing, snorkeling, and outdoor gear for rent and sale. Wend your way among the fishnets, boogie boards, diving equipment, bamboo rakes, juices and soft drinks, disposable cameras, and the other miscellany of this chockablock store. One entire wall is lined with T-shirts, and the Molokai book selection is extensive.

Take's Variety Store. ☎ 808/553-5442.

If you need luggage tags, buzz saws, toys, candy, cloth dolls, canned goods, canteens, camping equipment, hardware, signs, batteries, candles, paints, pipe fittings, fishing supplies—whew!—and other products for work and play, this 51-year-old variety store is the answer. You may suffer from claustrophobia in the crowded, dusty aisles, but Take's carries everything—if you can find it. If you can't, the staff is friendly and helpful.

EDIBLES

Friendly Market Center. ☎ 808/553-5595.

You can't miss this salmon-colored wooden storefront on the main drag of "downtown" Kaunakakai, where multigenerational stores are the norm rather than the exception. It's friendly! We like all the old mom-and-pop stores, but Friendly's has an especially good selection of produce and healthful foods. (Another is Outpost Natural Foods.) Blue-corn tortilla chips, soy milk, organic brown rice, a good selection of pasta sauces, and Kumu Farms macadamia-nut pesto, the island's stellar gourmet food, are among the items that surpass standard grocery-store fare.

Misaki's Grocery and Dry Goods. ☎ 808/553-5505.

Established in 1922, this third-generation local legend is one of Kaunakakai's two grocery stores, as essential as the Molokai air. Some of the notable items: chopped garlic from Gilroy, California (the garlic capital of the world), fresh luau leaves (taro greens), fresh okra, Boca Burgers, large Korean chestnuts in season, and gorgeous bananas. The fish section includes akule and ahi, fresh and dried, but the stock mostly consists of meats, produce, baking products, and a humongous array of soft drinks. Liquor, stationery, candies, and paper products round out the selection.

Molokai Ice House. At the end of Kaunakakai Wharf Rd. ☎ 808/553-3054.

A fishermen's co-op established in 1988 opened its retail doors as a fish market in 1994—and it's a find. Gathered daily from the fishing boats at the wharf, the seafood comes in all forms—sashimi, poke (the seasoned, raw fish), lomi (mixed, seasoned, and worked with the fingers) salmon and squid, oysters, seaweed, and teriyaki marlin fillets. It can't come any fresher, and it's all skillfully seasoned and reasonably priced. Locals come here for their fresh fish, whole or in fillets. The lomi 'o'io and the lomi ahi (yellowfin tuna) may look like mashed raw fish, but with perfectly balanced seasonings of green onions, a pungent type of seaweed (limukohu), and roasted kukui nut (inamona), they're delicacies much appreciated by Molokaians and neighbor islanders. Various seasoned shrimp and octopus dishes, and frequent surprise catches that catch the fancy of the chef, make this an ever-changing adventure. The prepared foods are perfect for no-fuss cooking or a quiet lunch at the wharf. In true Hawaiian spirit, they sell poi to go with the fish.

Molokai Wines & Spirits. ☎ 808/553-5009.

This is your best bet on the island for a decent bottle of wine. The shop offers more than 200 labels, including Caymus, Silver Oak, Joseph Phelps, Heitz, Bonny Doon, and a carefully culled European selection. *Wine Spectator* reviews are tacked to some of the selections, which always helps, and the snack selection shows at least some glimmers of mercy: Cambozola gourmet cheeses, salami, and Carr's biscuits. For those who like the effortless frozen burritos, canned tuna, chips, and prepackaged nibbles, they're on the shelves, too.

EN ROUTE TO THE NORTH COAST

Coffees of Hawaii Plantation Store. Hwy. 480 (near the junction of Hwy. 470), Kualapuu. ☎ **800/709-BEAN** or 808/567-9023.

This is a fairly slick—for Molokai—combination coffee bar, store, and gallery for more than 30 artists and craftspeople from Molokai, Maui, and the Big Island. Sold here are the Malulani Estate and Muleskinner coffees that are grown, processed, and packed on the 500-acre plantation surrounding the shop. (A tour of the plantation is offered weekdays at 10am and 1pm and, upon special request, Saturdays at 10am; the cost is $14 for adults and $7 for kids.) You may find better prices on coffee at other retail outlets, but the gift items are worth a look: pikake and plumeria soaps from Kauai; perfumes and pure beeswax candles from Maui; koa bookmarks and hair sticks; and pottery, woods, and baskets.

Molokai Museum Gift Shop. At the old R. W. Meyer Sugar Mill, Hwy. 470 (just after the turnoff for the Ironwood Hills Golf Course, and 2 mi. below Kalaupapa Overlook), Kalae. ☎ **808/567-6436.**

The restored 1878 sugar mill sits 1,500 feet above the town of Kualapuu (see "Seeing the Sights," earlier in this chapter). It's a drive from town, definitely, but a good cause for those who'd like to support the museum and the handful of local artisans who sell their crafts, fabrics, cookbooks, quilt sets, and other gift items in its tiny shop. A modest selection of cards, T-shirts, coloring books, and, at Christmas, handmade ornaments of lauhala and koa, are sprinkled throughout.

EDIBLES

Kualapuu Market. Kualapuu. ☎ **808/567-6243.**

This market, in its third generation, is a stone's throw from the new Coffees of Hawaii store. It's a scaled-down, one-stop shop with wine, food, and necessities—and a surprisingly presentable, albeit small, assortment of produce, from Molokai sweet potatoes to Kau navel oranges in season. The shelves are filled with canned goods, propane, rope, hoses, paper products, and baking goods, reflecting the uncomplicated, rural lifestyle of the area.

THE WEST END

Big Wind Kite Factory & the Plantation Gallery. Maunaloa. ☎ **808/552-2634.**

Jonathan and Daphne Socher, kite designers and inveterate Bali-philes, have combined their interests in a kite factory/import shop that dominates the commercial landscape of Maunaloa, the reconstituted plantation town. Maunaloa's naturally windy conditions make it ideal for kite-flying classes, which are offered free when conditions are right. The adjoining Plantation Gallery features local handicrafts such as milo-wood bowls, locally made T-shirts, Hawaii-themed sandblasted glassware, baskets of lauhala and other fibers, and Hawaiian-music CDs. There are many Balinese handicrafts, from jewelry to clothing and fabrics, and an occasional Fiji cannibal fork.

Maunaloa General Store. ☎ **808/552-2346.**

Maunaloa's only general store sells everything from paper products to batteries, dairy products, frozen and fresh meats, wine, canned goods, and a cross-section of necessities.

Molokai Ranch Outfitters Provisions. ☎ **808/552-2791**.

Located next to the ranch's bike rentals in a newly renovated wooden building, this shop could, indeed, outfit you for life's great adventures. North Face parkas, Bullfrog sunscreens, saddle blankets, socks, Teva sandals, bicycle helmets, swimwear, T-shirts, kites, walking sticks, and camping gear for all kinds of conditions line the shelves. The food items and souvenirs are also diverse: mugs, magnets, CDs and cassettes, Buckeye corn bread, pasta, Molokai Ranch toffees, mobiles, toys, plastic buckets, lidded koa boxes, Dr. Bronner's soaps, coconut-shell soap dishes, picture frames, and other gifts and survival gear.

A Touch of Molokai. Kaluakoi Hotel and Golf Club. ☎ **808/552-0133.**

We were pleasantly surprised by the selection of gift items in this hotel shop. The surf shorts and aloha shirts are better than the norm, with attractive, up-to-date choices by Quiksilver and other name brands. Tencel dresses, South Pacific shell necklaces (up to $200), visors, and a magnificent hand-turned milo-wood bowl also caught our attention. Most impressive were the wiliwili, kamani, and soapberry leis and a handsome array of lauhala bags, all made on Molokai.

THE EAST END
EDIBLES
The Neighborhood Store 'N Counter. Pukoo. ☎ **808/554-8498.**

The Neighborhood Store, the only grocery on the East End, sells batteries, film, aspirin, cookies, beer, Molokai produce, candies, paper products, and other sundries. There's good food pouring out of the kitchen for the breakfast and lunch counter, too.

11 Molokai After Dark

The big news is that the movies have come to Molokai. **Maunaloa Cinemas** (☎ **808/552-2707**) is a triplex theater that shows first-run movies in the middle of Maunaloa town—four screenings a day at each of the three theaters, beginning with the matinee. Otherwise, Molokai nightlife is an oxymoron. The **Ohia Lodge** at the Kaluakoi Resort, which features live entertainment on Friday and Saturday nights, is the only other spot for after-dark socializing. Keep an eye out for the Hotel Molokai, soon to open as of this writing. Hopes are up that it will help fill the void left by the closing of Pau Hana Inn, for many years Kaunakakai's liveliest nightspot.

11

Lanai: A Different Kind of Paradise

by Jeanette Foster & Jocelyn Fujii

Lanai is not an easy place to get to. There are no direct flights from the mainland, and most air carriers route flights onto the island from Honolulu. It is almost as if this quiet, gentle oasis that's known, paradoxically, for both its small-town feel and its celebrity appeal, demands that its visitors go to great lengths to get here to ensure that those who come will appreciate it.

Lanai (pronounced lah-*nigh*-ee), Hawaii's sixth largest island and the nation's biggest defunct pineapple patch, now claims to be one of the world's top tropical destinations. It's a bold claim, since so little is here: no stoplights, barely 30 miles of paved road, no fast-food joints, no strip malls, no taxis—in short, none of what you usually find in a vacation destination. Instead, what you have here is something quite rare: an almost virgin island, unspoiled by what passes for progress, except for a tiny 1920s-era plantation village—and, of course, its fancy new neighbors, two first-class luxury hotels where room rates hover around $400 a night.

As soon as you arrive, you'll feel the blanket of coziness of a small town: People wave to every car, residents stop to "talk story" with their friends, taking time to fish or work in the garden is considered a priority in life, and leaving the keys in your car's ignition is standard practice.

For generations, Lanai was little more than a small village, owned and operated by the pineapple company, surrounded by acres of pineapple fields. The few visitors to the island were either relatives of the mainly Filipino residents or occasional weekend hunters. Life in the 1960s was pretty much the same as in the 1930s.

But all that changed in 1990, when the Lodge at Koele, a 102-room hotel resembling an opulent English Tudor mansion, opened its doors, followed a year later by the 250-room Manele Bay Hotel, a Mediterranean-style luxury resort overlooking Hulopoe Bay. Overnight, the isolated island was transformed: Corporate jets streamed into the tiny Lanai Airport, former pineapple-plantation workers were retrained in the art of serving gourmet meals, and the population of 2,500 swelled with transient visitors and outsiders coming to work in the island's new hospitality industry. Microsoft multibillionaire Bill Gates chose the island for his lavish wedding, buying up all of its hotel rooms to fend off the press—and uncomplicated Lanai went on the map as a place where the rich and powerful vacation.

But it's also a place where people come looking for dramatic beauty, quiet, solitude, and an experience with nature away from the bright

Lanai

Kalohi Channel

Polihua Beach

Kaena Point

Shipwreck Beach

Kiolohia Bay

Hawaiilanui Gulch

Kahua Gulch

Keomuku Hwy.

Keomuku Hwy.

① Garden of the Gods

② Kanepuu Preserve

Kanepuu Hwy.

▲ Mt. Kaapahu

▲ Mt. Kanepuu

Koele ③

Keomuku ⑩

Honopu Gulch

⑤ ④

Naboko Gulch

Makaiwa Point

Honopu Bay

Lanai City ⑥

Kaumalapau Hwy.

Lanai Airport

Manele Rd.

▲ Mt. Lanaihale

Lopa Gulch

Awehi Gulch

⑨

(440)

Kaumalapau

(440)

Kapua Gulch

Lopa Beach

⑦

Manele Rd.

Kamaiki Point

⑧

Palaea Point

Manele Bay

Hulopoe Beach

Hulopoe Bay

Kealaikahiki Channel

Airport ✈
Beach ⚑
Mountain ▲

Accommodations
Dreams Come True ⑥
Hotel Lanai ⑥
The Lodge at Koele ③
Manele Bay Hotel ⑧

Attractions
Garden of the Gods ①
Kanepuu Preserve ②
Kaunolu Village ⑦
Keomuku Village ⑩
Luahiwa Petroglyph Field ⑨
Munro Trail ④

Golf Courses
Cavendish Golf Course ⑤
The Challenge at Manele ⑧
The Experience at Koele ③

1-0726

lights of Waikiki, the publicity of Maui, and the hoopla surrounding most resorts. The sojourners who find their way to Lanai come seeking the melodramatic views, the tropical fusion of stars at night, and the chance to be alone with the elements.

They also come for the wealth of activities: snorkeling and swimming in the sapphire waters of the marine preserve known as Hulopoe Bay; hiking on 100 miles of remote trails that canvass the 141-square-mile island; talking story with the friendly locals; and beachcombing and whale watching along a stretch of otherwise deserted sand. For the adventurous, there's horseback riding in the mist of the forest, scuba diving in caves, playing golf next to scenic ocean views, or renting a four-wheel-drive vehicle for the day and discovering wild plains where spotted deer run free and a rich cultural history comes alive in the ruins of a once-vibrant village.

In a single decade, a plain red-dirt pineapple patch has become one of Hawaii's most unusual fantasy destinations. They cultivate vacationers here now, not pineapples. But the real Lanai is a multifaceted place that's so much more than its newfound status as a luxury resort—and it's the traveler who comes to discover the island's natural wonders, local lifestyle, and other inherent joys who's bound to have the most genuine island experience.

THE PINEAPPLE ISLAND'S UNUSUAL PAST This old shield volcano in the rain shadow of Maui has a history of resisting change in a big way. Early Polynesians, fierce Hawaiian kings, European explorers, 20th-century farmers—the island has seen them all and sent most of them packing, empty-handed and broken. The ancient Hawaiians believed that the island was haunted by spirits so wily and vicious that no human could survive here. The "cannibal spirits" were finally driven off around A.D. 1400, and people settled in.

But those spirits never really went away, it seems. In 1778, just before Captain Cook "discovered" Hawaii, the king of the Big Island invaded Lanai in what was called "the war of loose bowels." His men slaughtered every warrior, cut down trees, and set fire to all that was left except a bitter fern whose roots gave them all dysentery.

In 1802, Wu Tsin made the first attempt to harvest on the island, but he ultimately abandoned his cane fields and went away. Charles Gay acquired 600 acres at public auction to experiment with pineapple as a crop, but a 3-year drought left him bankrupt. Others tried in vain to grow cotton, sisal, and sugar beets; they started a dairy and a piggery, and raised sheep for wool. But all enterprises failed, mostly for lack of water.

Harry Baldwin, a missionary's grandson and Massachusetts Institute of Technology grad, was the first to do okay for himself. He bought Lanai for $588,000 in 1917, developed a 20-mile water pipeline between Koele and Manele, and sold the island 5 years later to Jim Dole for $1.1 million.

Dole planted and irrigated 18,000 acres of pineapple, built Lanai City, blasted out a harbor, and turned the island into a fancy fruit plantation. For a half century, he enjoyed great success. Even Dole was ultimately vanquished, however; cheaper pineapple production in Asia brought an end to Lanai's heyday.

The island still resembles old photographs taken in the glory days of Dole. Any minute now, you half expect to look up and see old Jim Dole himself rattling up the road in a Model-T truck with a load of fresh-picked pineapples. Only now, there's a new lord of the manor, and his name is David Murdock.

A NEW KING—AND A REINVENTED ISLAND Of all who have looked at Lanai with a gleam in their eye, nobody has succeeded quite like David Murdock, a self-made billionaire who acquired the island in a merger more than a decade ago. About 97% of it is now his private holding.

After declaring Lanai's plantation era over, Murdock spent $400 million to build two grand hotels on the island: the Lodge at Koele, which resembles an English country retreat, and the Manele Bay Hotel, a green tile–roofed Mediterranean palazzo by the sea. Murdock recycled the former field hands into wait staff, even summoning a London butler to school the natives in the fine art of service, and carved a pair of daunting golf courses out of the island's interior and along the wave-lashed coast. He then set out to attract tourists by touting Lanai as "the private island."

Murdock is now trying to make all this pay for itself by selling vacation homes and condos next door to the two resorts. Hardly Thoreau's cabin in the woods, the homes and condos start at around $500,000 and carry an upward price tag of $3 million.

The redevelopment of this tiny rock should have been a pushover for the big-time tycoon, but island-style politics have continually thwarted his schemes. GO SLOW, a sun-faded sign at Dole's old maintenance shed once said. Murdock might have heeded the warning, because his grandiose plans are taking twice as long to accomplish as he had expected. Every permit he's sought has stuck in the tropic heat like a damp cotton shirt. Lanai is under the political thumb of many who believe that the island's precious water supply shouldn't all be diverted to championship golf courses and Jacuzzis, and there remains opposition from Lanaians for Sensible Growth, who advocate affordable housing, alternative water systems, and civic improvements that benefit residents.

Lanai residents, who might have lived in a rural setting, certainly haven't been isolated. Having watched the other islands in Hawaii attempt the balancing act of economic growth and the maintenance of an island lifestyle, the residents of Lanai are cautiously welcoming visitors, but at a pace that is still easy for this former plantation community to digest.

1 Orientation

ARRIVING

BY PLANE   From Maui, you'll have to make a connection in Honolulu, where you can easily catch a small plane for the 25-minute flight to Lanai's new $4 million airport. Jet service to Lanai is now available, but only on **Hawaiian Airlines** (☎ 800/367-5320 or 808/565-6977; www.hawaiianair.com), which offers two flights a day. Twin-engine planes take longer and are sometimes bumpier, but they offer great views since they fly lower. **Island Air** (☎ 800/652-6541 or 808/565-6744; www.alohaair.com) offers 9 to 12 flights a day. For more details on these airlines, including details on how to get the cheapest fares, see "Money-Saving Package Deals" and "Getting There," in chapter 2.

Prop or jet, you'll touch down in Puuwai Basin, once the world's largest pineapple plantation; it's about 10 minutes by car to Lanai City and 25 minutes to Manele Bay.

BY BOAT   A round-trip on **Expeditions Lahaina/Lanai Passenger Ferry** (☎ 808/661-3756) takes you between Maui and Lanai for $50. The ferry service runs five times a day, 365 days a year. It leaves Lahaina at 6:45am, 9:15am, 12:45pm, 3:15pm, and 5:45pm; the return ferry from Lanai's Manele Bay Harbor leaves at 8am, 10:30am, 2pm, 4:30pm, and 6:45pm. The 9-mile channel crossing takes 45 minutes to an hour, depending on sea conditions. Reservations are strongly recommended. Baggage is limited to two checked bags and one carry-on.

VISITOR INFORMATION

Destination Lanai (☎ 800/947-4774 or 808/565-7600; fax 808/565-9316) and the **Hawaii Visitors and Convention Bureau** (☎ 800/GO-HAWAII or 808/923-1811; www.gohawaii.com) will both provide you with brochures, maps, and island guides. For a free *Road and Site Map* of hikes, archaeological sites, and other sights, contact **The Lanai Company,** P.O. Box 310, Lanai, HI 96763 (☎ **808/565-3812;** www.lanai-resorts.com).

THE ISLAND IN BRIEF

Inhabited Lanai is divided into three parts—Lanai City, Koele, and Manele—and two distinct climate zones: hot and dry, and cool and misty.

Lanai City (population 2,800) sits at the heart of the island at 1,645 feet above sea level. This is the only place on the island where you'll find services. Built in 1924, this plantation village is a tidy grid of quaint tin-roofed cottages in bright pastels, with roosters penned in tropical gardens of banana, lilikoi, and papaya. Many of the residents are Filipino immigrants who worked the pineapple fields and imported the art, culture, language, food, and lifestyle of the Philippines. Their clapboard homes, now worth $250,000 or more, are an excellent example of historic preservation; the whole town looks like it's been preserved under a bell jar, or like a Guy Buffet painting of an upscale Southern Philippines *barangay* (village) come to life.

Around Dole Park Square, a charming village square lined with towering Norfolk and Cook Island pines, plantation buildings house general stores with basic necessities: a U.S. post office (where people stop to chat), two banks, and a police station with a jail that consists of three bright, blue-and-white wooden outhouse-sized cells with padlocks.

In the nearby cool upland district of **Koele** is the Lodge at Koele, standing by itself on a knoll overlooking pastures and the sea at the edge of a pine forest, like a grand European manor or a British colonial hill station. The other bastion of indulgence, the Manele Bay Hotel, is on the sunny southwestern tip of the island at **Manele.** You'll get more of what you expect from Hawaii here—beaches, swaying palms, mai tais, and the like.

2 Getting Around

With so few paved roads, you'll need a four-wheel-drive vehicle if you plan on exploring the island's remote shores, its interior, or the summit of Mount Lanaihale. Even if you only have one day on Lanai, rent one and see the island. You can contact one of the following two car-rental firms, or call **Lanai Ecoadventure Centre** to arrange a 4x4 adventure tour (see "Seeing the Sights," below).

Both cars and four-wheel-drive vehicles are available at the **Dollar Rent A Car** desk at **Lanai City Service,** 1036 Lanai Ave. (☎ **800/800-4000** for Dollar reservations; 808/565-7227 for Lanai City Service). Expect to pay about $60 a day for the cheapest car, a Nissan Sentra, and $129 to $145 a day for a four-wheel-drive vehicle; for both types of vehicles, the rate drops 10% if you rent for a week or more.

A small fleet of Land Rovers is available from ✪ **Red Rover,** P.O. Box 464 (located at the Hotel Lanai), Lanai City, HI 96763 (☎ **87-RED-ROVER** or 808/565-7722; fax 808/565-6450; www.onlanai.com/rover.htm). Their Land Rovers carry from two to nine passengers each and are available for $100 a day to guests of the Hotel Lanai, $175 for nonguests. Each vehicle comes equipped with a CB radio (in case you get stuck, they'll come and get you), as well as a winch and tool kit. In addition, as part of the rental fee, they will supply you with all the beach gear you'll need (masks, fins, snorkels, towels, sunscreen, boogie boards, even fishing rods and reels), provide a map of the best off-road trips, and, on request, even throw in a cell phone.

Be warned: Gas is expensive on Lanai. At press time, it was $2.09 a gallon (versus $1.84 in Kona and $1.55 in Honolulu)—and those Jeeps don't get good gas mileage. Since everything in Lanai City is within walking distance, it makes sense to just rent a Jeep for the day (or days) that you want to explore the island. (The two big resort hotels run shuttle vans around the island, but you can use them only if you're staying at one of the hotels.) **Lanai City Service** (☎ **808/565-7227**) will provide taxi service from the airport to Lanai City for $5 per person and will also transport you from Lanai City to Hulopoe Beach for $10 per person one way.

Fast Facts: Lanai

Lanai is part of Maui County. For **local emergencies,** call ☎ **911** for the police, fire station, and ambulance, or the **Poison Control Center** at ☎ **800/362-3585.** For nonemergencies, call the **police** at ☎ **808/565-6428.**

For emergency dental care, call **Dr. Nick's Family Dentistry** (☎ **808/ 565-7801**). If you need a doctor, contact the **Lanai Family Health Center** (☎ **808/565-6423**) or the **Lanai Community Hospital** (☎ **808/565-6411**).

Whether or not you rent a car, sooner or later you'll find yourself at **Lanai City Service,** 1036 Lanai Ave. (☎ **808/565-7227**), the glorified name for the only gas station in town. The all-in-one grocery store, coffee bar, rental-car agency, and souvenir shop serves as the island's Grand Central Station; you can pick up information, directions, maps, and all the local gossip.

For a weather report, call the **National Weather Service** at ☎ **808/565-6033.**

3 Accommodations

The majority of the accommodations are located "in the village," as residents call Lanai City. Above the village is the luxurious Lodge at Koele, while down the hill at Huelopoe Bay are two options: the equally luxurious Manele Bay Hotel, or tent camping under the stars at the park.

In addition to the choices listed below, also consider the B&B accommodations offered by **Delores Fabrao** (☎ **808/565-6134**), who has two guest rooms in her home: a double with a shared bathroom, and a family room with private bathroom that sleeps up to six ($55 double, $100 for four); she doesn't provide breakfast, but you'll have the run of the entire house, including the kitchen. At **Hale Moe** (☎ **808/ 565-9520**), host and Lanai native Momi Suzuki makes two bedrooms in her Lanai City home available to guests; both have private bathrooms, and guests are welcome to use the entertainment center, large deck, and Momi's two bicycles ($60 to $70 double). For a fully equipped, two-bedroom vacation rental that sleeps up to six, call **Hale O Lanai** in Lanai City (☎ **808/247-3637;** www.hotspots.hawaii.com/ beachrent1.html); rates range from $95 to $125.

Don't forget to add 11.42% in taxes to all accommodations bills. Parking is free.

VERY EXPENSIVE

The Lodge at Koele. P.O. Box 310, Lanai City, HI 96793. ☎ **800/321-4666** or 808/ 565-7300. Fax 808/565-3868. www.lanai-resorts.com. 107 units. A/C MINIBAR TV TEL. Year-round $325–$495 double, $625–$1,600 suite. Extra person $45. AE, CB, DC, MC, V. Airport shuttle $10.

Although the Lodge at Koele has earned a long list of kudos from magazines naming it the best of this and that, on our last trip here we noticed some signs of a formerly first-class resort on the decline: Employee cutbacks have left some areas (such as the fitness center) unstaffed, the waiters in the main dining room were either surly or undertrained, and some bicycles had torn seats and needed to be cleaned. Not the end of the world, but not the shining resort it once was. We hope that management will bring this grand resort back up to its usual high standards.

That said, this has always been the place to stay for a quiet, relaxing vacation in the cool mist of the mountains. The atmosphere is informal during the day, more formal after sunset (jackets are required in the main dining room). The Lodge, as folks here call it, stands in a 21-acre grove of Norfolk Island pines at 1,700 feet above sea level, 8 miles inland from any beach—a locus that flies in the face of conventional wisdom, which dictated for more than a century that the beach was the only place for a Hawaii vacation hotel.

The 102-room resort resembles a grand English country estate. Inside, heavy timbers, beamed ceilings, and the two huge stone fireplaces of the Great Hall complete the look. Overstuffed furniture sits invitingly around the fireplaces, and all the coffee-table books on Hawaii that you've ever wanted to read are scattered on tables around you. Richly patterned rugs adorn the floor, while museum-quality art hangs on the walls. Cushioned wicker chairs on the long porches are perfect for a long afternoon with a good book.

Guest rooms continue the English theme with four-poster beds, sitting areas (complete with window seats for reading), flowery wallpaper, formal writing desks, and luxury bathrooms with oversized tubs and just about every amenity imaginable.

There are plenty of activities here and at Manele Bay, the sister resort down the hill, so you'll have the best of both hotels. Most guests who stay at the Lodge are looking for a slightly less frenzied vacation: relaxing out on the porch, reading or watching the turkeys mosey across the manicured lawns; strolling through the Japanese hillside garden; or watching the sun sink into the Pacific and the stars light up at night.

Dining/Diversions: A formal dining room serves dinner (see "Dining," below); a less formal interior terrace is open all day. Both use local island ingredients. Entertainment is limited to quiet live music, hula, and periodic guest appearances by celebrities who chat informally in a drawing-room setting about their work (see "'Talk Story' with the Greats" under "Lanai After Dark," below).

Amenities: Complimentary shuttle service to the golf courses, beach, and Manele Bay Hotel. Complimentary coffee and tea in the lobby, and formal tea every afternoon. Twice-daily maid service, turndowns, some rooms with butler service. Golf at the 18-hole championship Greg Norman/Ted Robinson–designed course, the Experience at Koele. Croquet lawns, stables, tennis courts, bicycles, rental jeeps, an executive putting green, a pool, upcountry hiking trails, extensive lawns, and garden walks. Library, game room, bar, and music room. Guests have access to the Manele Bay facilities as well.

✪ **Manele Bay Hotel.** P.O. Box 310, Lanai City, HI 96793. ☎ **800/321-4666** or 808/565-7700. www.lanai-resorts.com. 250 units. A/C MINIBAR TV TEL. $295–$575 double, $600–$2,000 suite. Extra person $45. AE, CB, DC, MC, V. Airport shuttle $10.

If you want to stay at the beach, come to this sun-washed southern bluff overlooking Hulopoe Beach, one of Hawaii's best stretches of golden sand. The U-shaped hotel steps down the hillside to the pool and that great beach, then fans out in oceanfront wings separated by gardens with lush flora, man-made waterfalls, lotus ponds, and streams. Bordered on the other side by golf greens on a hillside of dry land scrub, the hotel is a real oasis against the dry Arizona-like heat of Lanai's arid south coast.

This is a traditional luxury beachfront hotel: open, airy, and situated so that every room has a peek of the big blue Pacific. The lobby is filled with murals depicting scenes from Hawaiian history, sea charts, potted palms, soft camel-hued club chairs, and hand-woven kilim rugs. The oversized guest rooms resemble an English country house on the beach: sunny chintz fabrics, mahogany furniture, Audubon prints, huge marble bathrooms, and semiprivate lanais.

This resort is much less formal than the Lodge up the hill. Its proximity to the beach attracts more families, and because it's warmer here, people wander through the lobby in shorts and T-shirts. This is perfect for a beach vacation, with a few forays up to the Lodge and Lanai City to enjoy the mountain activities.

Dining/Diversions: Hulopoe Court features innovative Hawaii Regional Cuisine and ocean views; do not miss chef Edwin Goto's creations in the Ihilani, the specialty dining room (see "Dining," below, for reviews of both). Entertainment is limited to quiet live music, hula, and periodic guest-lecture appearances by celebrities (see "'Talk Story' with the Greats," below).

Amenities: Complimentary shuttle service to the golf courses, the Lodge at Koele, and Manele Boat Harbor. Twice-daily maid service, turndowns, and 13 butlered suites. The Jack Nicklaus–designed Challenge at Manele adds 18 more holes to play, a seaside layout in nice contrast to the upland Experience (see "The Lodge at Koele," above). Water sports at the neighboring beach, plus pool, tennis courts, bicycling, game room, library, spa, historic tours, and Jeep tours. Guests can also enjoy the amenities at the Lodge at Koele.

MODERATE

✪ **Hotel Lanai.** 828 Lanai Ave. (P.O. Box 520), Lanai City, HI 96763. ☎ **800/795-7211** or 808/565-7211. Fax 808/565-6450. www.onlanai.com. 11 units. $95–$105 double, $140 cottage double. Nearby two-bedroom house (sleeps up to 6) $200. Rates include continental breakfast. Extra person $10. AE, MC, V. Airport shuttle $10.

This is the perfect place for families and other vacationers who can't afford to spend $300 to $400 a night for a hotel room but still want to enjoy the atmosphere and activities of Lanai. Just a few years ago, the Hotel Lanai, on a rise overlooking Lanai City, was the only place to stay and eat unless you knew someone who lived on the island. Built in the 1920s for VIP plantation guests, this clapboard plantation-era relic has retained its quaint character and lives on as a country lodge. Soon after the resorts opened, the owners of the Hotel Lanai gave their rustic hotel a $450,000 facelift and repositioned it as a B&B. In August 1996, a well-known chef from Maui, Henry Clay Richardson (formerly of the Kapalua Bay Hotel & Villas, David Paul's Lahaina Grill, and Gerard's Restaurant), became the inn's new owner and executive chef in the dining room. Richardson has transformed this quaint inn into a real center for ecoadventure tourists. Every morning at breakfast, the activity director meets with you to help set up activities for the day. The hotel has a range of options, including four-wheel-drive Land Rover rentals (a deal at $100 a day), off-road tours in Richardson's comfy Hummer, mountain biking, guided hikes, golf carts for nearby Cavendish Golf Course, and marine activities.

The Hotel Lanai's one-story wooden building is bordered by a verdant lawn, bright flowers, and a stalwart stand of pines. The guest rooms are small, clean, and newly decorated, plantation style, with Hawaiian quilts and wood furniture. The standard hotel rooms are extremely small, with private bathrooms, a double bed or two twin beds, and little else. The garden rooms, which are the largest, have king beds. The most popular are the lanai rooms, which feature a shared lanai with the room next door. They're smaller than the garden rooms and have queen beds, but the lanai is a great spot to sit and watch the sunset. All rooms have phones, ceiling fans, and private bathrooms with shower only. Only the small one-bedroom cottage on the property has a TV and bathtub; it's perfect for a family of three or four adults.

The hotel serves as a down-home crossroads where total strangers meet local folks on the lanai to drink iced beer and "talk story," or play the ukulele and sing into the dark tropic night. Often, a curious visitor in search of an authentic experience will join the party and discover Lanai's very Hawaiian heart. A restaurant serves continental breakfast to guests only, then opens to the public for dinner nightly (see "Dining," below, for a review).

INEXPENSIVE

Dreams Come True. 547 12th St. (P.O. Box 525), Lanai City, HI 96763. ☎ **800/565-6961** or 808/565-6961. www.go-native.com/Inns/0117.html. E-mail: hunters@aloha.net. 3 units. $75 double. Rates include continental breakfast. Extra person $20. AE, DC, DISC, MC, V.

Your dreams just may come true in this quaint plantation house, tucked away among papaya, banana, lemon, and avocado trees in the heart of Lanai City, at 1,620 feet.

Hosts Susan and Michael Hunter have filled their house with Southeast Asian antiques collected on their travels. Both are jewelers, and they operate a working studio on the premises. All three bedrooms have private bathrooms; two come with a four-poster canopied bed, with an additional single bed (perfect for a small family), while the third room has just one queen bed. The common area looks out on the garden and is equipped with both TV and VCR. Breakfast usually consists of freshly baked bread with homemade jellies and jams, tropical fruit, juice, and coffee. The Hunters rent a nearby three-bedroom/two-bathroom house to families for $190 a night.

4 Dining

Dining on Lanai is uncomplicated and extreme. On this island of three hotels, a handful of stores, and fewer than 3,000 residents, you can go from a greasy-spoon breakfast to a five-star dinner in less than a mile and a few hundred feet in altitude. When the Lodge at Koele and the Manele Bay Hotel opened their doors in 1990 and 1991, respectively, Lanai went from "Pineapple Island" to luxury resort—and it did so with a vengeance, quickly transforming its agricultural renown into a fine-dining cachet that immediately won top placement in the diner-rated Zagat Hawaii Restaurant Survey.

You can dine like a sultan on this island, but be prepared for high prices. The tony hotel restaurants require deep pockets (or bottomless expense accounts), and there are only a handful of other options.

EXPENSIVE

Formal Dining Room. The Lodge at Koele. ☎ **808/565-4580.** Reservations required. Jackets required for men. Main courses $36–$40. AE, DC, JCB, MC, V. Daily 6–9:30pm. AMERICAN.

Changes, changes, changes. Not only does the menu at this dining room change with the seasons, but since we last visited, chef Edwin Goto has departed for Manele Bay Hotel, Koele's oceanfront sister. Although recent service has been less than impressive, we hope the Lodge will maintain the impeccable standards that have won it numerous national awards and accolades. The octagonal-shaped dining room is elegant and intimate, with a menu that has earned its rightful place in Hawaii's culinary hierarchy. The roaring fire and the bountiful sprays of orchids add up to an atmosphere befitting the hotel's grandly soaring ceilings.

Foie gras is a menu staple, with renewed emphasis on stews, braised meats, and short ribs cooked in a pot. During fall and winter months, expect to see pumpkins, beans, ragouts, and braised items offered in creative seasonal preparations. Roast loin of lamb and Lanai venison top the list for game lovers, and the fish au courant, moi, is a year-round attraction. The Dining Room is known for its use of fresh herbs, vegetables, and fruit grown on the island, harvested just minutes away, and for its lodge-friendly cuisine—soups both hearty and elegant, and wintry delights of wild mushrooms, buttery squashes, local game, and elegant meats.

Hulopoe Court. Manele Bay Hotel. ☎ **808/565-7700.** Reservations recommended. Collared shirt required for men. Main courses $26–$32. AE, DC, JCB, MC, V. Daily 6–9:30am and 7–11pm. HAWAII REGIONAL.

Hulopoe is casual compared to the hotel's fine dining room, Ihilani, but formal compared to the Pool Grille, the lunchtime oasis for Manele Bay guests. The 17th-century palanquin in the adjoining lower lobby, the Asian accents, the tropical murals by gifted Lanai artists, and the high vaulted ceilings add up to an eclectic ambience. Some of the offerings: fresh fish preparations using taro and shiitake mushrooms, guava-glazed chicken with Molokai sweet potatoes, and breakfasts highlighted by Molokai sweet-potato pancakes and local produce.

Ihilani. Manele Bay Hotel. ☎ **808/565-2290.** Reservations required. Jackets recommended for men. Main courses $40–$48; set menu $105 without wine, $145 with wine. AE, DC, JCB, MC, V. Daily 6–9:30pm. FRENCH/MEDITERRANEAN.

The Manele Bay's formal dining room sits across the lobby from Hulopoe Court; its lower ceilings (beautifully painted with bird-of-paradise murals) and pleasing design permit an ocean view and a clubby, darker, more intimate ambience. There are three sections to the split-level dining room: the terrace, overlooking the ocean and pool; the indoor middle area next to the terrace; and the elevated dining area with banquettes and private niches. The recent arrival of award-winning chef Edwin Goto from the Lodge at Koele bodes well for Ihilani and its menu of Mediterranean marvels. Some standouts: New Zealand langoustine chowder with fresh corn, saffron, and Molokai sweet potatoes; Muscovy duck with sautéed figs; and poached Maine lobster on butternut-squash risotto with assorted wild mushrooms, with discreet dabs of vanilla-infused olive oil. Pastry chef Niel Koep is a firm believer that "dessert is important." Witness the paradise chocolate cake, crème brûlée with a hint of citrus, and the rotating repertoire of 20 different sorbets.

The Terrace. The Lodge at Koele. ☎ **808/565-4580.** Reservations recommended. Main courses $7.25–$14.50 breakfast, $9.75–$14 lunch, $16–$27 dinner. AE, DC, JCB, MC, V. Daily 6am–9:30pm. AMERICAN.

Located next to the Formal Dining Room, between the 35-foot-high Great Hall and a wall of glass overlooking prim English gardens, the Terrace is far from your typical hotel dining room. Hearty breakfasts of wild-rice waffles, warm cinnamon-bread pudding, artichoke and asparagus frittata, and eggs Polihua (on blue crab cakes with watercress-tomato hollandaise) are a grand start to the day. At dinner, the choices include polenta "pizza" topped with eggplant, portobello mushrooms, and goat cheese; skillet-roasted chicken; grilled and roasted vegetables; and seafood, venison, and pork entrees.

MODERATE

Henry Clay's Rotisserie. Hotel Lanai, 828 Lanai Ave. ☎ **808/565-7211.** Main courses $8.50–$17.95. JCB, MC, V. Daily 5:30–9pm. COUNTRY CUISINE.

Henry Clay Richardson, a New Orleans native, has made some welcome changes to Lanai's dining landscape. The menu focuses on American country cuisine: fresh meats, seafood, and local produce. The meats, which could be rabbit, quail, venison, osso bucco, beef, or chicken, are spit-roasted on the rotisserie. Appetizers and entrees reflect Cajun, regional, and international influences. From the rotisserie come herb-marinated chicken and Louisiana-style pork ribs, while gourmet pizzas and salads occupy the lighter end of the menu. The two fireplaces and pine-paneled walls add to the coziness of this old Lanai favorite.

Manele Bay Clubhouse. The Challenge at Manele Clubhouse. ☎ **808/565-7700**. Reservations recommended. Main courses $12–$15. AE, DC, JCB, MC, V. Sun–Mon 11am–5pm, Tues–Sat 11am–4pm and 5–9pm. PACIFIC RIM.

The view may be the best on the island, high on a bluff on the famous Challenge at Manele golf course. Dine alfresco and marvel at the vista of Kahoolawe, Haleakala on Maui and, on an especially clear day, the peaks of Mauna Kea and Mauna Loa on the Big Island. This is a casual restaurant, serving only chilled and warm pupus: sashimi, rock shrimp cocktail with green papaya salad, mushroom ravioli, dim sum, fresh fish or shrimp tacos, and grilled Thai fish cakes. At lunch, lighter fare prevails: Peking duck salad, Caesar with chicken, herbed chicken sandwich on sourdough, burgers, and fish-and-chips.

Pool Grille. Manele Bay Hotel. ☎ **808/565-7700.** Main courses $6–$16. AE, DC, JCB, MC, V. Daily 11am–5pm. ECLECTIC.

At this, the most casual of the hotel's restaurants, you'll dine on double-digit hamburgers (homemade buns, of course) and gourmet salads poolside under beach umbrellas, in weather that can be sweltering during the summer and fall months. The salads are perfect for the weather and location. Marinated grilled vegetables with Big Island goat cheese, spicy chicken, Caesar salad with shrimp, grilled ahi, and tuna pita are among the popular sandwich choices.

INEXPENSIVE

Blue Ginger Cafe. 409 Seventh St. ☎ **808/565-7016.** Most items under $12. No credit cards. Daily 6am–9pm. COFFEE SHOP.

This is a very local, very casual, and affordable alternative to Lanai's fancy hotel restaurants. The four tables on the front porch face the cool Norfolk pines of Dole Park and are always filled with locals who "talk story" from morning to night. The tiny cafe is often jammed from 6 to 7am with construction workers on their way to work. The offerings are solid, no-nonsense, everyday fare: fried saimin (no MSG, a plus), the very popular hamburgers on homemade buns, and the mahimahi with capers in a white-wine sauce. Blue Ginger also serves a tasty French toast of homemade bread, a vegetable lumpia (the Filipino version of a spring roll), and inexpensive homemade omelets.

Pele's Other Garden. Dole Park, 811 Houston St. ☎ **808/565-9628.** Most items under $6. AE, DC, DISC, JCB, MC, V. Mon–Thurs 11am–7pm, Fri–Sat 11am–9pm. DELI/PIZZERIA/JUICE BAR.

Healthful, tasty eats come streaming across the counter at this New York–style deli. It breaks all the rules: It's healthful *and* delicious, and it's not expensive. Sandwiches, daily soup and menu specials, salads, pizzas, fresh organic produce, fresh juices, and special touches such as top-quality black-bean burritos, roasted red peppers, and stuffed grape leaves are some of the features that make Pele's Other Garden a Lanai City must. Our vegetarian pizza, with fresh shiitake mushrooms and vegetarian pepperoni, was excellent. Sandwiches are made with whole-wheat bread delivered fresh daily, and the turkey is free-range. All menu items are made from natural and organic ingredients, and there is no sacrifice in flavor. It's mostly take-out, but there are a couple of tables on the veranda, facing the tree-shaded square.

Tanigawa's. 419 Seventh St. ☎ **808/565-6537.** Reservations not accepted. Breakfasts under $7. No credit cards. Thurs–Tues 6:30am–1pm. HAMBURGERS/LOCAL.

Formerly S. T. Properties, famous for its hamburgers, Tanigawa's has changed its name but remains the landmark that it's been since the 1920s. In those days, the tiny storefront sold canned goods and cigarettes; the 10 tables, hamburgers, and Filipino food came later. Jerry Tanigawa has kept his hole-in-the-wall a local institution, whose homemade hamburgers and bento lunches (rice with meat or fish, a plantation legacy) have fed two generations of Lanai residents. The fare—saimin, plate lunches, beef stew, and omelets—is a nod to sentiment, more greasy spoon than gourmet, and friendliest above all to the pocketbook.

5 Beaches

If you like big, wide, empty golden sands and crystal-clear, cobalt-blue water full of bright tropical fish—and who doesn't?—go to Lanai. With 18 miles of sandy shoreline, Lanai has some of Hawaii's least crowded and most interesting beaches. One spot in particular is perfect for swimming, snorkeling, and watching spinner dolphins play: Hulopoe Beach, Lanai's best.

✪ HULOPOE BEACH

In 1997, Stephen Leatherman, of the University of Maryland, ranked Hulopoe the best beach in the United States. Leatherman, who compiles an annual ranking, considers 50 standards (including sand and waves, water quality, human use, lifeguard protection, noise) in judging some 650 public beaches every year. It's easy to see why he said this is the best: The bay at the foot of the Manele Bay Hotel is a protected marine preserve, and the schools of colorful fish know it. So do the spinner dolphins who come here to play, as well as the Pacific humpback whales who cruise by in winter (that's when the mercury drops below 80°). This palm-fringed, gold-sand beach is bordered by black-lava fingers, protecting swimmers from the serious ocean currents that sweep around Lanai. In summer, Hulopoe is perfect for swimming, snorkeling, or just lolling about; the water temperature is usually in the mid-70s. The protected bay is usually safe, except when swells kick up in the winter. Hulopoe is also Lanai's premier beach park, with a grassy lawn, picnic tables, barbecue grills, rest rooms, showers, and ample parking.

HULOPOE'S TIDE POOLS   Some of the best lava-rock tide pools in Hawaii are found along the south shore of Hulopoe Bay. These miniature Sea Worlds are full of strange creatures: asteroids (sea stars) and holothurians (sea cucumbers), not to mention spaghetti worms, Barber Pole shrimp, and Hawaii's favorite local delicacy, the opihi, a tasty morsel also known as the limpet. Youngsters enjoy swimming in the enlarged tide pool at the eastern edge of the bay.

When you explore tide pools, do so at low tide. Never turn your back on the waves. Wear tennis shoes or reef walkers, as wet rocks are slippery. There's a kapu (taboo) against collecting specimens in this marine preserve, so don't take any souvenirs home.

SHIPWRECK BEACH

Named for the rusty ship, *Liberty*, stuck on the coral reef, this 8-mile-long windswept strand along the northeastern shore, from Polihua Beach to Kahokunui, is a sailor's nightmare and a beachcomber's dream. It's a great place to dig up treasures of the sea, or perhaps to pick up a new pair of slippers: You might notice that some Lanai residents wear two different slippers, usually because they've found a perfectly good, though unmatched, pair on a recent beachcombing trip.

The strong currents yield all sorts of flotsam, from rare pelagic paper nautilus shells to lots of junk. Occasionally, a handblown-glass ball from a Japanese fishing boat will float in—in Hawaii, this is considered the greatest beachcombing treasure you can find. Shipwreck Beach is also a great place to spot whales from December to April, when the Pacific humpbacks cruise in from Alaska to winter in the calm offshore waters. The road to the beach is paved most of the way, but you really need a four-wheel-drive vehicle to get down here.

POLIHUA BEACH

So many sea turtles once hauled themselves out of the water to lay their eggs in the sunbaked sand on Lanai's northwestern shore that Hawaiians named the beach there

Polihua, or "egg nest." Although Hawaii's endangered green sea turtles are making a comeback, they're seldom seen here now. You're more likely to spot an offshore whale (in season) or the perennial litter that washes up onto this deserted north shore beach, at the end of Polihua Road, a 4-mile jeep trail. There are no facilities except fishermen's huts and driftwood shelters. Bring water and sunscreen. Beware the strong currents, which make the water unsafe for swimming. This strand's really ideal for beach-combing (those little green-glass Japanese fishing-net floats often show up here), fishing, or just being alone.

6 Hitting the Water

Lanai actually has Hawaii's best water clarity, because it lacks major development and has low rainfall and runoff, and its coast is washed clean daily by the sea current known as "The Way to Tahiti." But the strong sea currents pose a threat to swimmers, and there are few good surf breaks. Most of the aquatic adventures—swimming, snor-keling, and scuba diving—are centered on the somewhat protected south shore, around Hulopoe Bay.

BODYBOARDING (BOOGIE BOARDING), BODYSURFING & BOARD SURFING

When the surf's up on Lanai, it's a real treat. Under the right conditions, Hulopoe and Polihua are both great for catching waves. Bring your own board, as the beach shack at Hulopoe Beach provides complimentary boogie boards for hotel guests (Manele Bay and the Lodge at Koele) only. Or, if you rent a four-wheel Land Rover from **Red Rover,** P.O. Box 464 (located at the Hotel Lanai), Lanai City, HI 96763 (☎ **87-RED-ROVER** or 808/565-7722; fax 808/6322), they'll provide free boogie boards and other beach gear.

OCEAN KAYAKING

Lanai Ecoadventure Centre, P.O. Box 1394, Lanai City, HI 96763 (☎ **808/ 565-7737** or 808/565-7373; www.kayakhawaii.com), offers half-day sea kayak/ snorkeling adventures aimed at introducing beginners to the world of ocean kayaking. They provide state-of-the-art kayaks (with lightweight graphite paddles), back-support seats, life vests, the latest in snorkel equipment, dry bags, towels, water, and snacks. After receiving instruction on how to kayak, your group will set off to explore the waters around Lanai with stops for snorkeling, snacks, and beachcombing. The 4-hour trip costs $69 to $89. Kayaks are also available for rent, starting at $20 a day.

SCUBA DIVING

Two of Hawaii's best-known dive spots are found in Lanai's clear waters, just off the south shore: **Cathedrals I** and **II,** so named because the sun lights up the underwater grotto like a magnificent church. **Trilogy Charters** (☎ **800/874-2666** or 808/ 565-9303; www.sailtrilogy.com) offers sailing, diving, and snorkeling trips on their catamarans. The cost is $95 for snorkelers and $130 for certified scuba divers for a one-tank dive. The trip, from 8:45am to 1pm, includes continental breakfast, lunch, and all snorkeling and diving equipment.

   Lanai Ecoadventure Centre, P.O. Box 1394, Lanai City, HI 96763 (☎ **808/ 565-7737** or 565-7373; www.kayakhawaii.com), offers kayak-scuba adventures from $69 to $89 for one-tank dives.

✪ Frommer's Favorite Lanai Experiences

Snorkel Hulopoe Beach. Crystal-clear water teems with brilliant tropical fish off a postcard-perfect beach that's one of Hawaii's best. There are tide pools to explore, waves to play in, and other surprises—like a pod of spinner dolphins that often makes a splashy entrance.

Explore the Garden of the Gods. Eroded by wind, rain, and time, this geologic badlands is worth visiting at sunrise or sunset, when the low light plays tricks on the land—and your mind.

Hike the Munro Trail. The 11-mile Munro Trail is a lofty, rigorous hike along the rim of an old volcano, across a razorback ridge through a cloud forest, that offers big views of the nearby islands. Some hike the ridge to see the rain forest; others take a four-wheel-drive vehicle to spend more time on top of the island, where you might catch a rare five-island view.

Four-Wheel It. Four-wheeling is a way of life on Lanai, since there's only 30 miles of pavement. Plenty of rugged trails lead to deserted beaches, abandoned villages, and wild game–filled valleys. No other island offers off-road adventures like this one.

Camp under the Stars. The campsites at Hulopoe Beach Park are about as close to the heavens as you can get. The sound of the crashing surf will lull you to sleep at night, while the chirping of the birds will wake you in the morning. If you're into roughing it, this is the most affordable way to experience Lanai.

Watch the Whales at Polihua Beach. Located on the northern coast, this beach—which gets its name from the turtles that nest here—is a great place to spend the day scanning the ocean for whales during the winter months.

SNORKELING

Hulopoe is Lanai's best snorkeling spot. Fish are abundant and friendly in the marine-life conservation area. Try the lava-rock points at either end of the beach and around the lava pools. Snorkel gear is free to guests of the two resorts, or can be rented from **Lanai Ecoadventure Centre,** P.O. Box 1394, Lanai City, HI 96763 (☎ 808/565-7737 or 808/565-7373; www.kayakhawaii.com), for $9.95 a day. (Also see "Ocean Kayaking," above, for their sea kayak/snorkel trips.) **Red Rover,** P.O. Box 464 (at the Hotel Lanai), Lanai City, HI 96763 (☎ 87-RED ROVER or 808/565-7722; fax 808/6322), provides free snorkeling gear with each four-wheel Land Rover rental.

SPORTFISHING

Jeff Menze, a Lanai resident, will take you out on the 28-foot Omega boat *Spinning Dolphin* (☎ 808/565-6613). His 4-hour fishing charters cost $400 for six people, or $600 for six people for 8 hours. He also offers exclusive 3-hour whale-watching charters, which are $300 for six passengers.

WHALE WATCHING

From late December to March, **Trilogy Charters** (☎ 800/874-2666 or 808/565-9303; www.sailtrilogy.com), offer 3-hour whale-watching adventures either on their 50-plus-foot catamarans or on a 34-foot, 26-passenger rigid-hulled inflatable boat. Rates are $75, which includes snacks.

7 Hiking & Camping

HIKING

A LEISURELY MORNING HIKE

The 3-hour **Koele Nature Hike** starts by the reflecting pool in the backyard of the Lodge at Koele and takes you on a 5-mile loop trail through a cathedral of Norfolk Island pines, into Hulopoe Valley, past wild ginger, and up to Koloiki Ridge, with its panoramic view of Maunalei Valley and Molokai and Maui in the distance. You're welcome to take the hike even if you're not a guest at the Lodge. The trailhead isn't obvious—just keep going toward the trees—and the path isn't clearly marked, but the concierge will give you a free map.

THE CHALLENGING MUNRO TRAIL

This tough, 11-mile (round-trip) uphill climb through the groves of Norfolk pines is a lung-buster, but you'll get a bonus if you reach the top: that breathtaking view of Molokai, Maui, Kahoolawe, the peaks of the Big Island, and, on a really clear day, Oahu in the distance. Figure on 7 hours. The trail begins at Lanai Cemetery along Keomoku Road (Highway 44) and follows Lanai's ancient caldera rim, ending up at the island's highest point, Lanaihale. Go in the morning for the best visibility. After 4 miles, you'll get a view of Lanai City. The weary retrace their steps from here, whereas those determined to see "the view" go the last 1⅓ miles to the top. Diehards go down Lanai's steep south crater rim to join the highway to Manele Bay.

For more details on the Munro Trail, including details on four-wheel-driving it to the top, see "Seeing the Sights," below.

A SELF-GUIDED NATURE TRAIL

In 1997, with the help of some 40 volunteers, the Nature Conservancy of Hawaii completed a self-guided nature trail open to the public in the Kanepuu Preserve. The trailhead is clearly marked on the Polihua Road on the way to the Garden of the Gods. The trail is about a 10- to 15-minute walk through eight stations, with interpretive signs explaining the natural or cultural significance of the area. Kanepuu is one of the last remaining examples of the type of forest that once covered the dry lowlands throughout the state. Here there are some 49 plant species that are found only in Hawaii (such as sandalwood and Hawaiian gardenia, both listed as endangered species). The Nature Conservancy conducts guided hikes every month; call ☎ 808/565-7430 for details.

GUIDED HIKES

Lanai Ecoadventure Centre, P.O. Box 1394, Lanai City, HI 96763 (☎ 808/565-7737 or 808/565-7373; www.kayakhawaii.com), offer 4x4 adventure treks that combine hiking and four-wheeling. The trips include such destinations as the Munro Trail, Poiaiwa Gulch, and Garden of the Gods. The cost is $69 to $89 per person, which includes fruit, drinks, snacks, and transportation. Also available are guided overnight hiking/camping trips; call for details.

CAMPING AT HULOPOE BEACH PARK

There is only one place to "legally" camp on Lanai: Hulopoe Beach Park, which is owned by the Lanai Company. To camp in this exquisite beach park, with its crescent-shaped, white-sand beach bordered by kiawe trees, contact the **Lanai Company,** P.O. Box 310, Lanai City, HI 96763 (☎ 808/565-3982; www.lanai-resorts.com). There's a $5 registration fee, plus a charge of $5 per person, per night. Hulopoe has six campsites, each of which can accommodate up to six people. Facilities include rest rooms, running water, showers, barbecue areas, and picnic tables.

The Lanai Company recommends bringing a tent (expect rain year-round), a cooking stove or hibachi (the number of barbecues is limited), and insect repellent (mosquitoes are plentiful). You can rent equipment from **Lanai Ecoadventure Centre,** P.O. Box 1394, Lanai City, HI 96763 (☎ **808/565-7737**; www.kayakhawaii.com), which has everything from backpacks to tents; a set of camping gear starts at $25 per day.

8 Other Outdoor Pursuits

BICYCLING

Downhill road-bike treks are available through **Lanai Ecoadventure Centre,** P.O. Box 1394, Lanai City, HI 96763 (☎ **808/565-7737** or 808/565-7373; www.kayakhawaii.com), for $69 to $89 per person. The 3½-hour tours are perfect for beginners as they're all downhill, with a 4X4 van meeting you at the bottom with snacks and a tour of the petroglyphs, then a ride back up to the top. They also offer trips for more advanced riders, as well as 21-speed suspension mountain bikes for rent, starting at $20 a day.

For general information about bicycling trails, point your Web browser to **www.bikehawaii.com**.

GOLF

✪ **The Challenge at Manele.** P.O. Box 310, Lanai City, HI 96763. ☎ **808/565-2222.** Located next to the Manele Bay Hotel in Hulopoe Bay.

This target-style, desert-links course, designed by Jack Nicklaus, is one of the most "challenging" courses in the state. First of all, check out the local rules: "No retrieving golf balls from the 150-foot cliffs on the ocean holes 12, 13, or 17," and "All whales, axis deer, and other wild animals are considered immovable obstructions." That's just a hint of the uniqueness of this course, which is routed among lava outcroppings, archaeological sites, kiawe groves, and ilima trees. Two of the more challenging holes of the 7,039-yard, par-72 course are the signature 12th hole, where you simply tee off a couple of hundred yards across the Pacific Ocean 150 yards below (bring extra balls), and the par-4 17th, where you tee off on the ocean cliff across a ravine to a sloping, narrow, downhill fairway (shoot long). The five sets of staggered tees give a challenging game to everyone from the casual golfer to the pro. Rates are $125 for guests of Manele Bay Hotel, the Lodge at Koele, or Hotel Lanai, and $175 for nonguests. You can get a rate for play at both this course and the Experience at Koele: $150 for hotel guests and $225 for nonguests, plus $25 for the cart rental for the second round. Facilities include clubhouse, pro shop, rentals, practice area, lockers, and showers.

✪ **The Experience at Koele.** P.O. Box 310, Lanai City, HI 96763. ☎ **808/565-4653** (808/565-GOLF). Located next to the Lodge at Koele in Lanai City.

When this par-72 uplands course opened in 1991, it was voted "Best New Golf Course" by *Fortune* magazine and one of 1991's "Top 10 New Resort Courses" by *Golf* magazine. This traditional course, designed by Greg Norman with fairway architecture by Ted Robinson, has a very different front and back nine holes. You start off on a high plateau at nearly 2,000 feet, where Mother Nature reigns: Cook Island and Norfolk pines, indigenous plants, and water—lots of water, including seven lakes, flowing streams, cascading waterfalls, and one green (the 17th) completely surrounded by a lake. All goes well until you hit the signature hole, number 8, where you tee off from a 250-foot elevated tee to a fairway bordered by a lake on the right and trees and dense shrubs on the left. After you have recovered, the back nine holes drop dramatically through ravines filled with pine, koa, and eucalyptus trees. The grand finale, the 18th, a par 5, features a green rimmed by waterfalls that flow into a lake on the left side. To give golfers a break, Norman and Robinson have added four different sets of tees to level the playing field. Rates are $125 for guests of Manele Bay Hotel, the Lodge at Koele, or Hotel Lanai, and $175 for nonguests. You can get a rate for play at both this course and the Challenge at Manele: $150 for hotel guests and $225 for nonguests, plus $25 for the cart rental for the second round. Facilities include clubhouse, pro shop, rentals, practice area, lockers, and showers.

Cavendish Golf Course. No phone. Located next to the Lodge at Koele in Lanai City.

It's a quirky par-36, nine-hole public course with not only no clubhouse or club pros, but also no tee times, score cards, or club rentals. To play, just show up, put a donation ($5 to $10 would be nice) into the little wooden box next to the first tee, and hit away. The 3,071-yard, E. B. Cavendish–designed course was built by the Dole plantation in 1947 for its employees. The greens are a bit bumpy—nothing will roll straight here— but the views of Lanai are great, and the temperatures are usually quite mild.

HORSEBACK RIDING

A great way to explore Lanai's unique landscape is by horse. You can venture up wooded upland areas that are impossible to get to, even in a four-wheel-drive vehicle. **The Stables at Koele** (☎ **808/565-4424**) offers various rides, starting at $35 for a 1-hour trip. We recommend the 2-hour **Paniolo Trail Ride,** which gives you an escape into the hills surrounding Koele. Meander through guava groves and patches of ironwood trees, with glimpses of axis deer, quail, wild turkeys, and Santa Getrudis cattle, and end with panoramic views of Maui and Lanai. The cost is $65. Long pants and shoes are required; safety helmets are provided. Bring a jacket, as the weather is chilly and rain frequent. Children must be at least 9 years old and 4 feet tall. The maximum weight limit is 250 pounds.

TENNIS

Public courts, lit for night play as well as day, are available in Lanai City at no charge; call ☎ **808/565-6979** for reservations. Guests staying at the Lodge at Koele or the Manele Bay Hotel have complimentary tennis privileges either at the Tennis Center at Manele, with its six Plexi-pave courts, a fully equipped pro shop, and tournament facilities, or at the courts at Koele. Instruction is available for a fee. For information, call ☎ **808/565-2072.**

9 Seeing the Sights

You'll need a four-wheel-drive vehicle to reach all of the sights listed below. Renting a Jeep is an expensive proposition on Lanai, so we suggest that you rent one just for the day (or days) you plan on sightseeing; otherwise, it's easy enough to get to the beach and around Lanai City without your own wheels. For details on how to rent a Jeep, see "Getting Around," above.

For a guided 4x4 tour, contact either **Lanai Ecoadventure Centre,** P.O. Box 1394, Lanai City, HI 96763 (☎ **808/565-7737** or 808/565-7373; www.kayakhawaii.com), which offers 3- to 4-hour off-road tours at $69 to $89 per person, or the **Hotel Lanai** (☎ **800/795-7211** or 808/565-7211; www.onlanai.com), which gives custom tours in a Hummer, starting at $150 for the 2-hour tour for up to three people.

Adventures for Kids—and Kids at Heart

Explore Hulopoe Tide Pools *(see p. 259)*   An entire world of marine life lives in the tide pools on the eastern side of Hulopoe Bay. Not only are there tiny fish swimming around, but everything in the waters is small—kid-size. After examining the wonders of the tide pool, check out the larger swimming holes in the lava rock, perfect for keiki swimming.

Hunt for Petroglyphs *(see p. 266)*   The Luahiwa Petroglyphs Field, located just outside Lanai City, is spread out over a 3-acre site. Make it a game: Whoever finds the most petroglyphs gets ice cream from the Pine Isle Market.

Listen to Storytellers   Check with the Lanai Library, Fraser Avenue, near Fifth Street, Lanai City (☎ **808/565-6996**), to see if any storytelling or other activities for children are scheduled. The events are usually free and open to everyone.

Run with the Wind   Play hide-and-seek or any other game in the town square, Dole Park (bordered by Fraser Avenue, Lanai Avenue, Seventh Street, and Eighth Street), which has plenty of room for active children to run to their heart's content.

✪ GARDEN OF THE GODS

A dirt Jeep road leads out of Lanai City, through the now-uncultivated pineapple fields, and past the Kanepuu Preserve (a dry-land forest preserve teeming with rare plant and animal life) to the so-called Garden of the Gods, out on Lanai's north shore. This place has little to do with gods, Hawaiian or otherwise. It is, however, the ultimate rock garden: a rugged, barren, beautiful place full of rocks strewn by volcanic forces and shaped by the elements into an infinite variety of shapes and colors—brilliant reds, oranges, ochers, and yellows.

Scientists have numerous explanations for how these boulders got here. Some claim it's an "ongoing posterosional event," while others say it's a "plain and simple badlands." However, ancient Hawaiians considered this desolate, windswept place an entirely supernatural phenomenon. Take a four-wheel-drive ride out here and decide for yourself which explanation you accept.

Go early in the morning or just before sunset, when the light casts eerie shadows on the mysterious lava formations that dot the amber- and ocher-colored ground. Drive west from the Lodge on Polihua Road; in about 2 miles, you'll see a hand-painted sign that will point you in the right direction, left down a one-lane, red-dirt road through a kiawe forest and past sisal and scrub to the site.

✪ FIVE ISLANDS AT A SINGLE GLANCE: THE MUNRO TRAIL

In the first golden rays of dawn, when lone owls swoop low over abandoned pineapple fields, hop into your rented Jeep and head out on the two-lane blacktop toward Mount Lanaihale, the 3,370-foot summit of Lanai. Your destination is the Munro Trail, the narrow winding ridge trail that runs across Lanai's razorback spine to the summit. From here, it is hoped you'll be able to see a rare Hawaii treat: five islands at once. On a clear day, you can see all of the main islands in the Hawaiian chain except Kauai.

Lanai's chief arboreal feature isn't the palm tree, the usual tropical icon of Hawaii, but two other interesting Pacific trees: the Norfolk Island and the Cook Island pines, so symmetrical that they look like artificial silk trees made in China. They're everywhere—on ridge lines, in the town square, and on the summit, where they do more than look picturesque: Moisture-laden clouds get snagged on the sharp boughs of the summit trees and shed welcome rain on the island, which receives a precious 37 inches a year. (Oahu's Manoa Valley, by comparison, gets 158 inches a year.) New Zealander George Campbell Munro, who came to Hawaii in 1909 to collect birds, was the first to figure out this rainmaking technique, which involves hydraulics far too complex to be explained fully here. He planted the pines on horseback, dropping seeds wherever he went to both promote rain and check erosion. The summit trail is named in his memory.

When it rains, the Munro Trail becomes slick and boggy with major washouts. Rainy-day excursions often end with a rental Jeep on the hook of the island's lone tow truck—and a $250 tow charge. You could even slide off into a major gulch and never be found, so don't try it. But in late August and September, when trade winds stop and the air over the islands stalls in what is called a *kona* condition, Mount Lanaihale's suddenly visible peak becomes an irresistible attraction.

When you're on Lanai, look to the summit. If it's clear in the morning, get a four-wheel-drive vehicle and take the Munro Trail to the top. (*Note:* Lanai City Service/ Dollar Rent A Car does not allow their four-wheel-drive vehicles to venture up the Munro Trail.) Look for a red-dirt road off Manele Road (Highway 440), about 5 miles south of Lanai City; turn left and head up the ridge line. No sign marks the peak. Nothing says "Summit 3,370 feet," so you'll have to keep an eye out. Look for a wide spot in the road and a clearing that falls sharply to the sea.

The islands stand in order on the flat blue sea, just like a real-life topographic map: Kahoolawe, Maui, The Big Island of Hawaii, Molokini's tiny crescent. Even the summits show. You can see the silver domes of Space City on Haleakala; Puu Moaulanui, the tongue-twisting summit of Kahoolawe; and, looming like the mighty sea mountain it is, Mauna Kea peering above the clouds. At another clearing further along the thickly forested ridge, all of Molokai, including the 4,961-foot summit of Kamakou, and the faint outline of Oahu (more than 30 miles across the sea) are visible. You actually can't see all five in a single glance anymore, because George Munro's thriving pine forest blocks the view. The old forester would have been delighted.

For details on hiking the trail, see "Hiking & Camping," above.

LUAHIWA PETROGLYPH FIELD

With more than 450 known petroglyphs in Hawaii at 23 sites, Lanai is second only to the Big Island in its wealth of prehistoric rock art, but you'll have to search a little to find it. Some of the best examples are on the outskirts of Lanai City, on a hillside site known as Luahiwa Petroglyph Field. The characters you'll see incised on 13 boulders on this grassy 3-acre knoll include a running man, a deer, a turtle, a bird, a goat, and even a rare, curly tailed Polynesian dog (some latter-day wag has put a leash on him—some joke).

To find Luahiwa from the road to Hulopoe Beach, look to the left about 2 miles out of Lanai City, up on the slopes of the crater, for a cluster of reddish-tan boulders (which ancients believed formed a rain heiau, or shrine, where people called up the gods Ku and Hina to nourish their crops). A cluster of spiky century plants marks the spot. Take any dirt road that veers across the abandoned pineapple fields to the boulders. Go between 3pm and sunset for ideal viewing and photo ops.

KAUNOLU VILLAGE

Out on Lanai's nearly vertical Gibraltar-like sea cliffs is an old royal compound and fishing village. Now a national historic landmark and one of Hawaii's most treasured ruins, it's believed to have been inhabited by King Kamehameha the Great and hundreds of his closest followers about 200 years ago.

Ruins of 86 house platforms and 35 stone shelters have been identified on both sides of Kaunolu Gulch. The residential complex also includes the Halulu Heiau temple, named after a mythical man-eating bird. His Majesty's royal retreat is thought to have stood on the eastern edge of Kaunolu Gulch, overlooking the rocky shore facing Kahekili's Leap, a 62-foot-high bluff named for the mighty Maui chief who leaped off cliffs as a show of bravado. Nearby are burial caves, a fishing shrine, a lookout tower, and many warriorlike stick figures carved on boulders. Just offshore stands the telltale fin of little Shark Island, a popular dive spot that teems with bright tropical fish and, frequently, sharks.

Excavations are underway to discover more about how ancient Hawaiians lived, worked, and worshipped on Lanai's leeward coast. Who knows? The royal fishing village might yet yield the bones of King Kamehameha. His burial site, according to legend, is known only to the moon and the stars.

It's a hot, dry, dusty, slow-going 3-mile Jeep drive from Lanai City to Kaunolu, but the miniexpedition is worth it. Take plenty of water, don a hat to protect yourself from the sun, and wear sturdy shoes.

KANEPUU PRESERVE

Don't expect giant sequoias big enough to drive a car through; this ancient forest on the island's western plateau is so fragile, you can visit only once a month. Kanepuu, which has 48 species of plants unique to Hawaii, including the endangered Hawaiian gardenia (*na'u*) and the once-plentiful sandalwood (*iliahi*), survives under the Nature Conservancy's protective wing. Botanists say the 590-acre forest is the last dry lowland forest in Hawaii; the others have all vanished, trashed by axis deer, agriculture, or "progress."

Among the botanical marvels of this dry forest are the remains of *olopua* (native olive), *lama* (native ebony), *mau hau hele* (a native hibiscus), and the rare *'aiea* trees, which were used for canoe parts.

Due to the forest's fragile nature, guided hikes are led only 12 times a year, on a monthly, reservations-only basis. Contact the **Nature Conservancy Oahu Land Preserve** manager at 1116 Smith St., Suite 201, Honolulu, HI 96817 (☎ **808/ 537-4508;** www.tnc.org/hawaii), to reserve.

OFF THE TOURIST TRAIL: KEOMOKU VILLAGE

If you have absolutely nothing better to do, are sunburned lobster red, have read all the books you brought, and are starting to get island fever, take a little drive to Keomoku Village, on Lanai's east coast.

You're really off the tourist trail now. All that's in Keomoku, a ghost town since the mid-1950s, is a 1903 clapboard church in disrepair, an overgrown graveyard, an excellent view across the 9-mile Auau Channel to Maui's crowded Kaanapali Beach, and some really empty beaches that are perfect for a picnic or a snorkel. This former ranching and fishing village of 2,000 was the first non-Hawaiian settlement on Lanai, but it dried up after drought killed off the Maunalei Sugar Company. The village, such as it is, is a great little escape from Lanai City. Follow Keomoku Road for 8 miles to the coast, turn right on the sandy road, and keep going for 5.7 miles.

10 Shops & Galleries

Akamai Trading. 408 Eighth St. ☎ **808/565-6587.**

Located between Richard's and Pine Isle on Dole Park, Akamai sells newspapers and magazines, coffee mugs, seed lei, bagels, cappuccino, soft-serve ice cream, fresh pastries,

Lanai T-shirts, parkas, jeans, sunglasses, a small selection of aloha shirts, inexpensive island gifts, and souvenirs. Same-day film processing also appeals to visitors.

Gifts with Aloha. Dole Park, at Eighth and Houston sts. ☎ **808/565-6589.**

Phoenix and Kimberly Dupree decided to open a store with their favorite things, and that means gift items by Hawaii artists, children's books and toys, select jams and jellies, and Hawaiian quilt pillows and kits. And sarongs and aloha shirts, too. Handmade earrings, raku vessels, gourmet teas, hand-poured candles, and made-on-Maui body lotions serve equally well as souvenirs to go or items for life on Lanai. Recent finds: a lidded milo bowl, crafted on Lanai, and rounded earrings made of beach glass gathered from Lanai's shores.

International Food & Clothing. 833 Ilima Ave. ☎ **808/565-6433.**

Old-timers still call it the "Dela Cruz" store, after the family that opened it in 1952. Again, the basics: groceries, a few housewares, T-shirts, hunting and fishing supplies, over-the-counter drugs, paper goods, and hardware. We were pleasantly surprised by the extraordinary candy and bubble-gum section, the luscious local bananas in the small produce section, and the best knife sharpener we've seen—handy for rural Lanai life.

Lanai Art Program. 339 Seventh St. ☎ **808/565-7503.**

This is the retail space for a not-for-profit arts program that supports and showcases Lanai artists and shares their work in adult and children's classes. Located between the Laundromat and the community college office, Lanai Art Program displays and sells jewelry, ceramics, scarves, watercolors, woodworks, and other two- and three-dimensional pieces. All artists in the program are from Lanai. Classes are offered in the schools and at this center, where the artists share their skills in a pottery barn, glass shop, and wood shop, and lead classes in painting, wood crafts, and sculpting.

Lanai Marketplace. Dole Square.

Everyone on Lanai, it seems, is a backyard farmer; from 8am to noon on Saturday, they all flock to the square to sell their dewy-fresh produce, home-baked breads, plate lunches, and handicrafts. This is Lanai's version of the green market: petite in scale (like the island) but charming and unpretentious, especially in the shade of the sky-high pine trees that line the park.

Dolores Fabrao's jams and jellies, under the Fabrao House label (☎ **808/ 565-6134,** if you want to special-order), are a big seller at the market and at the resort gift shops where they're sold. The exotic flavors include pineapple-coconut, pineapple-mango, papaya, guaivi (strawberry guava), poha (gooseberry) in season, passion fruit, Surinam cherry, and the very tart karamay jelly. All fruits are grown on the island; gift packs and bags are available.

Pele's Garden. 811 Houston St. ☎ **808/565-9629.**

Even if nothing ails you, Beverly Zigmond's store is *the* destination on Lanai for products promoting health of body, mind, and spirit. Shop here for health-related reference books, vitamins, herbs, homeopathics, greeting cards and magazines, natural and organic groceries, baby food, natural pet products, organic seeds, and natural health and beauty aids. With the addition of Pele's Other Garden (Zigmond's brother's deli) serving up guiltless gourmet fare in the front section of the store, this corner of Lanai is a place you'll want to be.

Pine Isle Market. 356 Eighth St. ☎ **808/565-6047.**

"Talk Story" with the Greats:
Lanai's Visiting Artists Program

Not so very long ago, before CNN, e-mail, faxes, and modems, the word spread in person, on the lips of those who chanced by these remote islands, the most distant populated place on earth. Visitors were always welcome, especially if they had a good story to tell. The *hai mo'olelo*, or storyteller, was always held in high regard; Hawaii's kings invited them to the grass palace to discuss topics of contemporary life. Maybe you've seen the pictures in history books: King Kalakaua and Robert Louis Stevenson sitting on the beach at Waikiki, the famous author regaling His Majesty with bons mots. Or jaunty Jack London describing the voyage of his Snark to Queen Liliuokalani. In Hawaiian pidgin, it's called "talk story."

Hawaii grew up with this grand tradition of welcoming performing artists from every corner of the globe. Sooner or later, everyone from Kwame Ture to Tab Hunter seems to wash ashore like a note in a bottle. It's amazing, really. You never know who's going to drop in on Hawaii. Islanders might live apart from the continental drift of history, but such brief intense visits illuminate the lives of these insular folks. Joan Didion once remarked that Honolulu without visitors "would be Racine, Wisconsin, Saturday night," a fate presumably worse than death.

It doesn't just happen in Honolulu. When the Lodge at Koele opened, David Murdock invited a few friends over. The "friends" just happened to be Henry Mancini, Sidney Sheldon, and Michael York, and they all had a fabulous time in the Great Hall, singing, playing the piano, and reciting poetry. Kurt Matsumoto, general manager at the Lodge, liked what he saw and scheduled more informal gatherings of creative people. "We never had anything like this on this island before," said Matsumoto, born and reared on Lanai, where the only "live" entertainment in plantation days was chicken fights.

In December 1992, the two resorts began the Lanai Visiting Artists Program. To this former black hole of art and culture come the literati of America, in a new version of talk story. On any given weekend, you may find yourself in the company of poets, musicians, writers, actors, filmmakers, chefs, and other creative types. You can plan your vacation with, say, classical pianist Andre Watts, humorist Calvin Trillin, author John McPhee, "A Prairie Home Companion" host Garrison Keillor, jazz legend Cleo Laine, chef Larry Forgione (of New York's An American Place), *In the Name of the Father* screenwriter Terry George, award-winning short-story author David Wong Louie, best-selling novelist and screenwriter Susan Isaacs, or who knows which Pulitzer Prize or Academy Award winner, each sharing his or her talent and insights in a casual living-room atmosphere.

Now, with the Lanai Visiting Artists Program, even this little island is no Racine, Wisconsin.

The program is free and open to everyone, so contact the Lodge at Koele (☎ **808/565-7300;** www.lanai-resorts.com), to see who's visiting while you're on Lanai.

A two-generation local landmark, Pine Isle specializes in locally caught fresh fish when it's available. You can also shop here for fresh herbs and spices from Pete Felipe's garden, canned goods, electronic games, ice cream, toys, zoris, diapers, paint, cigars, and the basic essentials of work and play. The fishing section is outstanding, with every lure imaginable.

The Tamashiros' family business has been on the square since 1946, and except for the merchandise, not much has changed. The "shopping center" is, in fact, a general store with a small grocery section, paper products, ethnic foods, meats (mostly frozen), liquor, toys, tatami zoris, film, cosmetics, fishing gear, sunscreens, clothing, kitchen utensils, and other miscellany. A nice touch: gourmet breads from the Lanai Bake Shop.

11 Lanai After Dark

Once, when we inquired about nightlife on Lanai, an island woman we'd just met raised her eyebrows in mock umbrage. "Oh," she said, "that's personal."

Except for special programs such as the annual **Pineapple Festival** in May, when some of Hawaii's best musicians arrive to show their support for Lanai (see "Maui Calendar of Events," in chapter 2), the only regular nightlife venues are the Lanai Playhouse, at the corner of Seventh and Lanai avenues, and the two resorts, the Lodge at Koele and Manele Bay Hotel.

The **Lanai Playhouse** is a historic 1920s building that has received awards for its renovations. When it opened in 1993, the 150-seat venue stunned residents by offering first-run movies with Dolby sound—quite contemporary for anachronistic Lanai. Except for epics (such as *Titanic*), when only one screening is given, Lanai Playhouse usually shows two movies each evening from Friday to Monday, at 6:30 and 8:30pm. Tickets are $6 for adults and $3.50 for kids, and five "movie bucks" accumulated on Sundays get you one free ticket. On Tuesday and Wednesday nights, the only show, at 7pm, costs $3.50. The playhouse is also the venue for occasional special events.

The Hotel Lanai has discontinued its weekend program of live music, but the Lodge at Koele has stepped up its live entertainment. In the **Lodge's Great Hall,** in front of its manorial fireplaces, visiting artists bring contemporary Hawaiian, jazz, Broadway, classical, and other genres to listeners who sip port and fine liqueurs while sinking into plush chairs. The special programs are on weekends, but throughout the week, some form of nightly entertainment takes place in the Great Hall from 7 to 10pm. In the lounge area near the main lobby of the **Manele Bay Hotel,** above Ihilani, a pianist plays nightly from 7 to 10pm.

Both the Lodge at Koele and Manele Bay Hotel are known for their Visiting Artists Program (see "'Talk Story' with the Greats," above), which brings acclaimed literary and performing artists from across the country to this tiny island. These are scheduled throughout the year, usually on a monthly or bimonthly basis.

Other than that, what happens after dark is really up to you. You can linger over your evening meal, letting dinner become leisurely extended entertainment. You can repair to your room with that book you've been meaning to read. You can find an after-dinner crowd in the Tea Room at Koele or a game of billiards at Manele. The local folks out on the veranda of the Hotel Lanai will be happy to welcome you, and there's always a TV set somewhere to remind you of the great world beyond.

Appendix: Maui in Depth

by Jeanette Foster & Jocelyn Fujii

Maui is the only island in the Hawaiian chain named after a god—well, actually a demigod (half man, half god). Hawaiian legends are filled with the escapades of Maui, who had a reputation as a trickster. In one story, Maui is credited with causing the birth of the Hawaiian Islands when he threw his "magic" fish hook down to the ocean floor and pulled the islands up from the bottom of the sea. Another legend tells how Maui lassoed the sun to make it travel more slowly across the sky—so that his mother could more easily dry her clothes. Maui's status as the only island to carry the name of a deity seems fitting, considering its reputation as the perfect tropical paradise, or as Hawaiians say, *Maui no ka oi* ("Maui is the best").

1 Maui Today

Following the U.S. overthrow of the Hawaiian monarchy in 1893, the first years of the 20th century saw Maui in a state of confusion. Island life was thrown into upheaval with a massive influx of immigrants, drawn to Maui by the sugar and pineapple plantations. World War II and a series of postwar labor-union skirmishes created still more conflict on the island; as soon as that settled down, a new change emerged: the rapid increase in the number of visitors to this sleepy, agrarian community, which found itself suddenly designated the "in" place to visit.

The islanders spent the 1970s trying to adjust not only to this sudden influx of visitors, but also to the fact that the visitors liked what they saw and wanted to stay. Seemingly overnight, a massive building campaign began, with condominiums mushrooming along the coastline. By the 1980s, the furious pace of building had slowed, but the new visitors to the island were no longer content to just sit on the beach: They wanted snorkeling and sailing trips, bike rides down Haleakala, and guided tours to Hana. A new industry developed to service these action-oriented vacationers.

In the 1990s, Hawaii's state economy went into a tailspin following a series of events: First, the Gulf War severely curtailed air travel to the island; then, Hurricane Iniki slammed into Kauai, crippling its infrastructure; and finally, sugarcane companies across the state began shutting down, laying off thousands of workers. Maui, however, seemed to be able to weather this turbulent economic storm. As the rest of the state struggled with the stormy economy, the outlook remained sunny and clear on Maui.

What did Maui have that the other islands didn't? According to experts, the farsightedness to build up the island's name recognition in the fickle tourism industry, coupled with a diversified economy. Not only had Maui started planning "destination resort areas" in the 1960s, with Kaanapali the first planned resort area outside of Waikiki, but the island's tourism industry also knew that a reputation for the ability to deliver was the key calling card to success. Or as one expert put it: "Maui has been unbelievably successful at name recognition. You'd be hard-pressed to find someone in the U.S. or Canada over 20 years old who has not heard of Maui."

In addition, Maui did not put all its eggs into the visitor-industry basket. Instead, island leaders continued to nurture Maui's agricultural roots, but instead of wooing giant agribusiness, they courted small niche farming: organic farmers, the flower industry, herb growers. The island also branched out into various high-tech fields, including the rapidly growing Internet industry. It's no coincidence that just as the World Wide Web was starting to become a household word, Maui's visitor industry—from tiny, two-bedroom B&Bs to megaresorts—had one of the highest rates of Web sites per capita in the United States.

Maui has seen centuries of change since Captain Cook first cruised by. The island, once populated only by Hawaiians, is today home to a diverse mix of Asians, Pacific Islanders, Caucasians, and African Americans. The population continues to learn lessons in balance: how to nurture the visitor industry without destroying the very product that visitors come to see.

2 Life & Language

Plantations brought so many different people to Hawaii that the state is now a rainbow of ethnic groups. No one group is a majority; everyone's a minority. Living here are Caucasians, African Americans, American Indians, Eskimos, Aleuts, Japanese, Chinese, Filipinos, Koreans, Tahitians, Asian Indians, Vietnamese, Hawaiians, Samoans, Tongans, and other Asian and Pacific Islanders. Add to that a few Canadians, Dutch, English, French, German, Irish, Italians, Portuguese, Scottish, Puerto Ricans, and Spanish.

More than a century ago, W. Somerset Maugham noted: "All these strange people live close to each other, with different languages and different thoughts; they believe in different gods and they have different values; two passions alone they share: love and hunger." More recently, noted travel journalist Jan Morris said of Hawaii's population: "Half the world's races seem to be represented and interbred here, and between them they have created an improbable microcosm of human society as a whole."

In combination, it's a remarkable potpourri. Many people seem to retain an element of the traditions of their homeland. Some Japanese Americans of Hawaii, even three and four generations removed from the homeland, are more traditional than the Japanese of Tokyo. And the same is true of many Chinese, Koreans, Filipinos, and the rest of the 25 or so ethnic groups that make Hawaii a kind of living museum of various Asian and Pacific cultures.

THE HAWAIIAN LANGUAGE

Almost everyone here speaks English, so except for pronouncing place names, you should have no trouble communicating on Maui. Many folks in Hawaii now speak Hawaiian, for the ancient language is making a comeback. Everybody who visits Hawaii, in fact, will hear the words *aloha* and *mahalo* (thank you). If you've just arrived, you're a *malihini*. Someone who's been here a long

> ## ❷ Did You Know?
>
> - Maui has more miles of swimming beaches than any of the other Hawaiian islands.
> - Haleakala is the largest dormant volcano in the world, rising some 30,000 feet from the ocean floor.
> - Maui has the largest *heiau* (temple) in the state, Piilanihale, in Hana.
> - Maui has the only paved road in the world that goes from sea level to 10,000 feet in just 37 miles.
> - Haleakala Crater is so big that the entire island of Manhattan could easily fit inside it.
> - Kamehameha chose Lahaina as the capital of Hawaii after he united all the islands.
> - Puu Kukui, the highest point in the West Maui Mountains, gets some 40 feet (500 inches) of rain a year.
> - The lowest temperature ever recorded in Hawaii was atop Haleakala, when the thermometer dropped to 11°F in 1961.

time is a *kamaaina*. When you finish a job or your meal, you are *pau* (over). On Friday it's *pau hana* (work over). When you go *pau hana,* you put *pupus* in your mouth (that's Hawaii's version of hors d'oeuvres).

The Hawaiian alphabet, created by the New England missionaries, has only 12 letters—the five regular vowels (*a, e, i, o,* and *u*) and seven consonants (*h, k, l, m, n, p,* and *w*). The vowels are pronounced in the Roman fashion, that is, *ah, ay, ee, oh,* and *oo* (as in "too")—not *ay, ee, eye, oh,* and *you,* as they are in English. For example, *huhu* is pronounced *who-who.* Almost all vowels are sounded separately, although some are pronounced together, as in *Kalakaua: Kah-lah-cow-ah.*

WHAT *HAOLE* MEANS   When Hawaiians first saw Western visitors, they called the pale-skinned, frail men *haole,* because they looked so out of breath. In Hawaiian, *ha* means breath, while *ole* means an absence of what precedes it. In other words, a lifeless-looking person. Today, the term *haole* is generally a synonym for Caucasian or foreigner and is used casually without intending any disrespect. However, if uttered by an angry stranger who adds certain adjectives like stupid or dumb, the term *haole* can be construed as a mild racial slur.

SOME HAWAIIAN WORDS   Here are some basic Hawaiian words that you'll often hear in Hawaii and see throughout this book. For a more complete list of Hawaiian words, point your Web browser to **www.volcanoalley.com/lang.html**.

akamai   smart
alii   Hawaiian royalty
aloha   greeting or farewell
ewa   in the direction of Ewa, an Oahu town; generally meaning west ("drive *ewa* 5 miles")
halau   school
hale   house or building
heiau   Hawaiian temple or place of worship
hui   club, assembly
kahuna   priest or expert

kamaaina   old-timer
kapa   tapa, bark cloth
kapu   taboo, forbidden
keiki   child
lanai   porch or verandah
lomilomi   massage
mahalo   thank you
makai   a direction, toward the sea
malihini   stranger, newcomer
mana   spirit power
mauka   a direction, toward the mountains
muumuu   loose-fitting gown or dress
nene   official state bird, a goose
ono   delicious
pali   cliff
wiki   quick

PIDGIN: 'EH FO'REAL, BRAH

If you venture beyond the tourist areas, you might hear another local tongue: pidgin English. A conglomeration of slang and words from the Hawaiian language, pidgin was developed by sugar planters as a method to communicate with their Chinese laborers in the 1800s. Today it's used by people who grew up in Hawaii to talk with their peers.

"Broke da mouth" (tastes really good) is the favorite pidgin phrase and one you might hear; "'Eh fo'real, brah" means "It's true, brother." You could be invited to hear an elder "talk story" (relating myths and memories), or to enjoy local treats like "shave ice" (a tropical snow cone) and "crack seed" (highly seasoned preserved fruit). But since pidgin is really the province of the locals, your visit to Maui is likely to pass without your hearing much pidgin at all.

3 A Taste of Maui

A decade ago, visitors could expect to find frozen mahimahi beurre blanc with frozen or canned vegetables as the premium dish on a fine-dining menu in the islands. But not anymore. It's a whole new world in Maui's restaurant kitchens.

THE NEW GUARD: HAWAII REGIONAL CUISINE

Since the mid-1980s, when Hawaii regional cuisine (HRC) ignited a culinary revolution, Hawaii has elevated its standing on the global epicurean map to bona-fide star status. Fresh ideas and sophisticated menus have made the islands a culinary destination, applauded and emulated nationwide. (In a tip of the toque to island tradition, *ahi*—a word ubiquitous in Hawaii—has replaced *tuna* on many chic New York menus.) And options have proliferated at all levels of the local dining spectrum: Waves of new Asian residents have planted the food traditions of their homelands in the fertile soil of Hawaii, resulting in unforgettable taste treats true to their Thai, Vietnamese, Japanese, Chinese, and Indo-Pacific roots. Like the peoples of Hawaii, traditions are mixed and matched—and when combined with the fresh harvests from sea and land for which Hawaii is known, these ethnic and culinary traditions take on renewed vigor and a cross-cultural, uniquely Hawaiian quality.

This is good news for the eager palate. From the five-star restaurant to the informal neighborhood gathering place, from the totally eclectic to the purely

Japanese to the multiethnic plate lunch, dining in Hawaii is one great culinary joyride.

Expect to encounter Indonesian sates, Polynesian imu-baked foods, and guava-smoked meats in sophisticated presentations in the finest dining rooms on Maui. If there's pasta or risotto or rack of lamb on the menu, it could be *nori* (seaweed) linguine with *opihi* (limpet sauce), or risotto with local seafood served in taro cups, or a rack of lamb in cabernet and *hoisin* sauce (fermented soybean, garlic, and spices), or with macadamia nuts and coconut. Watch for *ponzu* sauce, too; it's lemony and zesty, much more flavorful than the soy sauce it resembles, and a welcome new staple on local menus.

While on Maui, you'll encounter many labels that embrace the fundamentals of HRC and the sophistication, informality, and nostalgia it encompasses. Euro-Asian, Pacific Rim, Pacific Edge, Euro-Pacific, fusion cuisine, hapa cuisine—by whatever name, Hawaii regional cuisine has evolved as Hawaii's singular cooking style, what some say is this country's current gastronomic, as well as geographic, frontier. It highlights the fresh seafood and produce of Hawaii's rich waters and volcanic soil, the cultural traditions of Hawaii's ethnic groups, and the skills of well-trained chefs—such as Beverly Gannon (Haliimaile General Store), Roy Yamaguchi (Roy's on Oahu, Maui, Hawaii, and Kauai), Peter Merriman (Merriman's on the Big Island and Hula Grill on Maui), George Mavrothalassitis (Chef Mavro Restaurant in Honolulu), and Jean-Marie Josselin (A Pacific Cafe on Kauai, Maui, and Oahu)—who broke ranks with their European predecessors to forge new ground in the 50th state. Some of Hawaii's most prominent chefs, such as David Paul (David Paul's Lahaina Grill and David Paul's Diamond Head Grill), were not original HRC members but have gone ahead to form their own strong culinary identities.

Fresh ingredients are foremost, and farmers and fishers work together to provide steady supplies of just-harvested seafood, seaweed, fern shoots, vine-ripened tomatoes, goat cheese, lamb, herbs, taro, gourmet lettuces, and countless harvests from land and sea that wind up in myriad forms on ever-changing menus, prepared in Asian and Western culinary styles. Exotic fruits introduced by recent Southeast Asian immigrants, such as sapodilla, mangosteen, soursop, and rambutan, are beginning to appear regularly in Chinatown markets. Aquacultured seafood, from seaweed to salmon to lobster, is a staple on many menus. Additionally, fresh-fruit salsas and sauces (mango, litchi, papaya, pineapple, guava), ginger-sesame-wasabi flavorings, corn cakes with sake sauces, tamarind and fish sauces, coconut-chile accents, tropical-fruit vinaigrettes, and other local and newly arrived seasonings from Southeast Asia and the Pacific impart unique qualities to the preparations.

Here's a sampling of what you can expect to find on a Hawaii Regional menu: seared Hawaiian fish with lilikoi shrimp butter; taro-crab cakes; Molokai sweet-potato or breadfruit vichyssoise; Ka'u orange sauce and Kahua Ranch lamb; fern shoots from Waipio Valley; Hawaiian bouillabaisse with fresh snapper, Kona crab, and fresh aquacultured shrimp; blackened ahi summer rolls; and gourmet Waimanalo or Kula greens, picked that day. With menus that often change daily, and the unquenchable appetites the leading chefs have for cooking on the edge, the possibilities for once-in-a-lifetime dining adventures are more available than ever on Maui.

PLATE LUNCHES & MORE: LOCAL FOOD

At the other end of the spectrum is the vast and endearing world of "local food." By that we mean plate lunches and poke, shave ice and saimin, bento lunches and manapua—cultural hybrids all.

Ahi, Ono & Opakapaka: A Hawaiian Seafood Primer

The fresh seafood in Hawaii has been described as the best in the world. In the pivotal book *The New Cuisine of Hawaii*, by Janice Wald Henderson, acclaimed chef Nobuyuki Matsuhisa (chef/owner of Matsuhisa in Beverly Hills and Nobu in Manhattan and London) writes, "As a chef who specializes in fresh seafood, I am in awe of the quality of Hawaii's fish; it is unparalleled anywhere else in the world." And why not? Without a doubt, the islands' surrounding waters, the waters of the remote northwestern Hawaiian Islands, and a growing aquaculture industry are fertile grounds for this most important of Hawaii's food resources.

The reputable restaurants in Hawaii buy fresh fish daily at predawn auctions or from local fishers. Some chefs even spear-fish their ingredients themselves. "Still wiggling" is the ultimate term for freshness in Hawaii. The fish can then be grilled over *kiawe* (mesquite) or prepared in innumerable ways.

Although most menus include the Western description for the fresh fish used, most often the local nomenclature is listed, turning dinner for the uninitiated into a confusing, quasi-foreign experience. To help familiarize you with the menu language of Hawaii, here's a basic glossary of island fish:

ahi   yellowfin or bigeye tuna, important for its use in sashimi and poke, at sushi bars, and in Hawaii Regional Cuisine

aku   skipjack tuna, heavily utilized by local families in home cooking and poke

ehu   red snapper, delicate and sumptuous, yet lesser known than opakapaka (see below)

hapuupuu   grouper, a sea bass whose use is expanding from ethnic to nonethnic restaurants

hebi   spearfish, mildly flavored and frequently featured as the "catch of the day" in upscale restaurants

Reflecting a polyglot population of many styles and ethnicities, Hawaii's idiosyncratic dining scene is eminently inclusive. Consider Surfer Chic: barefoot in the sand, in a swimsuit, you chow down on a plate lunch ordered from a lunch wagon, consisting of fried mahimahi, "two scoops rice," macaroni salad, and a few leaves of green, typically julienned cabbage or iceberg lettuce. (Generally, teriyaki beef or shoyu chicken are options.) Heavy gravy is often the accompaniment of choice, accompanied by a soft drink in a paper cup. Like saimin—the local version of noodles in broth topped with scrambled egg, green onions, and, sometimes, pork—the plate lunch is Hawaii's version of high camp.

Because this is Hawaii, at least a few licks of *poi*—the Hawaiian staple of cooked, pounded taro (the local tuber)—and the other examples of indigenous cuisine are de rigueur, if not at a corny luau, then at least in a Hawaiian plate lunch. The native samplers include foods from before and after Western contact, such as *laulau* (pork, chicken, or fish steamed in ti leaves), *kalua* pork (pork cooked in a Polynesian underground oven known here as an *imu*), *lomi* salmon (salted salmon with tomatoes and green onions), squid *luau* (octopus cooked in coconut milk and taro tops), *poke* (cubed raw fish seasoned with onions and seaweed, and the occasional sprinkling of roasted *kukui* nuts),

kajiki Pacific blue marlin, also called *au*, with a firm flesh and high fat content that make it a plausible substitute for tuna in some raw fish dishes, and as a grilled item on menus

kumu goatfish, a luxury item on Chinese and upscale menus, served en papillote or steamed whole, Oriental style, with sesame oil, scallions, ginger, and garlic

mahimahi dolphin fish (the game fish, not the mammal) or dorado, a classic sweet, white-fleshed fish requiring vigilance among purists because it is often disguised as fresh when it's actually "fresh-frozen"—a big difference

monchong bigscale or sickle pomfret, an exotic, tasty fish, scarce but gaining a higher profile on Hawaiian Island menus

nairagi striped marlin, also called *au;* good as sashimi and in poke, and often substituted for ahi in raw-fish products

onaga ruby snapper, a luxury fish, versatile, moist, and flaky; top-of-the-line

ono wahoo, firmer and drier than the snappers, often served grilled and in sandwiches

opah moonfish, rich and fatty, and versatile—cooked, raw, smoked, and broiled

opakapaka pink snapper, light, flaky, and luxurious, suited for sashimi, poaching, sautéing, and baking; the best-known upscale fish

papio jack fish, light, firm, and flavorful, and favored in island cookery

shutome broadbill swordfish, of beeflike texture and rich flavor

tombo albacore tuna, with a high fat content, suitable for grilling and sautéing

uhu parrot fish, most often encountered steamed, Chinese style

uku gray snapper of clear, pale-pink flesh, delicately flavored and moist

ulua large jack fish, firm-fleshed and versatile

haupia (creamy coconut pudding), and *kulolo* (steamed pudding of coconut, brown sugar, and taro).

Bento, another popular choice for the dine-and-dash set, is also available throughout Hawaii. The compact, boxed assortment of picnic fare usually consists of neatly arranged sections of rice, pickled vegetables, and fried chicken, beef, or pork. Increasingly, however, the bento is becoming more streamlined and health-conscious, as in macrobiotic bento lunches or vegetarian brown-rice bentos. A derivative of the modest lunch box for Japanese immigrants who once labored in the sugar and pineapple fields, bentos are dispensed ubiquitously throughout Hawaii, from department stores like Daiei and Shirokiya (bento bonanzas) to corner delis and supermarkets.

Also from the plantations come *manapua,* a bready, doughy round with tasty fillings of sweetened pork or sweet beans. In the old days, the Chinese "manapua man" would make his rounds with bamboo containers balanced on a rod over his shoulders. Today, you'll find white or whole-wheat manapua containing chicken, vegetables, curry, and other savory fillings.

The daintier Chinese delicacy, dim sum, is made of translucent wrappers filled with fresh seafood, pork hash, and vegetables, served for breakfast and lunch in Chinatown restaurants. The Hong Kong–style dumplings are ordered fresh and hot from bamboo steamers from invariably brusque servers who move their carts from table to table. Much like hailing a taxi in Manhattan, you have to be quick and loud for dim sum.

TASTY TREATS: SHAVE ICE & MALASSADAS

For dessert or a snack, the prevailing choice is shave ice, the island version of a snow cone. Particularly on hot, humid days, long lines gather for the rainbow-colored cones heaped with finely shaved ice and topped with sweet tropical syrups. (The sweet-sour *li hing mui* flavor is a current rage.) The fast-melting mounds requiring prompt, efficient consumption are quite the local summer ritual for those with a sweet tooth. Aficionados order shave ice with ice cream and sweetened adzuki beans plopped in the middle.

You might also encounter *malassadas,* the Portuguese version of doughnuts, and if you do, it's best to eat them immediately. A leftover malassada has all the appeal of a heavy, lumpen, cold doughnut. When fresh and hot, however, as at school carnivals (where they attract the longest lines) or at bakeries and roadside stands, the sugary, yeasty doughnut-without-a-hole is enjoyed by many as one of the enduring legacies of the Portuguese in Hawaii.

PINEAPPLES, PAPAYAS & OTHER ISLAND FRUITS

Lanai isn't growing pineapples commercially anymore, but low-acid, white-fleshed, wondrously sweet Hawaiian Sugar Loaf pineapples are being commercially grown, on a small scale, on Kauai as well as the Big Island. That's just one of the developments in the rapidly changing agricultural landscape in Hawaii, where the litchilike Southeast Asian *rambutan; longan* (Chinese dragon's-eye litchis); 80-pound Indian jackfruits; the starfruit; the luscious, custardy mangosteen; and the usual mangoes, papayas, guava, and *lilikoi* (passion fruit) make up the dazzling parade of fresh island fruits that come and go with the seasons.

Papayas, bananas, and **pineapples** grow year-round, but pineapples are always sweetest, juiciest, and most yellow in the summer. Although new papaya hybrids are making their way into the marketplace, the classic bests include the fleshy, firm-textured Kahuku papayas, the queen of them all; the Big Island's sweet Kapoho and Puna papayas; and the fragile, juicy, and reddish-orange Sunrise papayas from Kauai. Those who have transferred their allegiance from Puna to Sunrise claim they're sweeter, juicier, and more elegant than all others. Also called strawberry papayas, the Sunrise variety is easily misjudged and often served overripe; delicate inside and out, these papayas are easily bruised and fragile in texture, yet robust in flavor. Apple bananas are smaller, firmer, and tarter than the standard, and they are a local specialty that flourish throughout the islands.

Litchis and **mangoes** are long-awaited summer fruit. Mangoes begin appearing in late spring or early summer and can be found at roadside fruit stands, markets, and health-food stores (where the high prices may shock you). Our favorite is the white pirie—rare and resinous, fiberless, and so sweet and juicy it makes the high-profile Hayden seem prosaic. A popular newcomer is the Rapoza mango, only a few years in the islands yet already earning raves for its sweetness, resilience, and fiberless, 2-pound fruit.

Watermelons are a summer hit and a signature of Molokai and Oahu. The state of Hawaii, which consumes more watermelons per capita than any other in the country, also produces top-notch fruit for its loyal clientele. Kahuku watermelons, available in the summer months, give the popular Molokai variety a run for its money. Juicy, fleshy, and sweet, Kahuku watermelons are now grown primarily in Waialua on Oahu's north shore, while production of the Molokai variety has expanded to central Oahu. Most markets sell these bulging orbs of refreshment throughout summer and early fall.

In the competitive world of **oranges,** the Kau Gold navel oranges from the southern Big Island put Sunkist to shame. Grown in the volcanic soil and sunny conditions of the South Point region (the southernmost point in the United States), the "Ugly Orange" is brown, rough, and anything but pretty. But the browner and uglier they are, the sweeter and juicier. Because the thin-skinned oranges are tree-ripened, they're fleshy and heavy with liquid, and they will spoil you for life. Although these oranges have traditionally been a winter fruit, they're appearing more abundantly year-round.

4 The Natural World: An Environmental Guide to Maui

Born of violent volcanic eruptions from deep beneath the ocean's surface, the first Hawaiian islands emerged about 70 million years ago—more than 200 million years after the major continental land masses formed. Two thousand miles from the nearest continent, Mother Nature's fury began to carve beauty from barren rock. Untiring volcanoes spewed forth curtains of fire that cooled into stone, while severe tropical storms, some with hurricane-force winds, battered and blasted the cooling lava rock into a series of shapes. Ferocious earthquakes flattened, shattered, and reshaped the islands into precipitous valleys, jagged cliffs, and recumbent flatlands. Monstrous surf and gigantic tidal waves rearranged and polished the lands above and below the reaches of the tide.

It took millions upon millions of years for nature to chisel the familiar form of Maui's majestic Haleakala peak, to create the waterfalls on Molokai's northern side, to shape the reefs of Hulopoe Bay on Lanai, and to establish the lush rain forests of the Hana coastline. The result is an island-chain-within-a-chain like no other on the planet—rich in unique flora and fauna, surrounded by a vibrant underwater world that will haunt you forever.

THE ISLAND LANDSCAPES

Maui sits in the midst of a remote fleet of islands, isolated from the nearest land mass by some 2,500 miles. At one time, Maui, Molokai, and Lanai most likely composed one land mass, but today Molokai and Lanai, along with Kahoolawe, are satellite islands just off Maui's coast. Each island in Maui County has its own particular climate and topography.

MAUI The 728-square-mile island is the result of the marriage of two volcanoes, Puu Kukui, in the West Maui Mountains, and 10,000-foot-high Haleakala, in the east, which spilled enough lava between them to create a valley—thus inspiring the island's nickname, the Valley Isle. Thanks to this unusual makeup, Maui is the only place in the world where you can drive from sea level to 10,000 feet in just 37 miles, passing through tropical beaches, sugar and pineapple plantations, and rolling grassy hills; past the timber line; and up to the lunarlike surface of the top of Haleakala. In addition to 33 miles of public beaches on the south and west shores, Maui is home to the swampy bogs of the West Maui Mountains, the lush breadbasket of upcountry, the verdant rain forest of the Hana coast, and the arid desert of Kaupo.

KAHOOLAWE Just 7 miles southwest of Maui lies Kahoolawe, the smallest of the main Hawaiian islands. This arid island has some beautiful white-sand

For me, its balmy airs are always blowing, its summer seas flashing in the sun, the pulsing of its surf beat is in my ears. . . . [Hawaii is] the loveliest fleet of islands anchored in any ocean.

—Mark Twain (1866)

beaches and a unique topography: Years of overgrazing by ranchers coupled with the island's use as a bombing target by the U.S. military from 1945 to 1994 caused the fairly flat island to lose most of its topsoil. Native Hawaiians, who recently reclaimed the island from the federal government, are attempting to restore, reforest, and replant the island. Access to Kahoolawe is restricted.

LANAI   This small, kidney bean–shaped island—only 13 miles wide by 17 miles long—rises out of the ocean like the shell of a turtle, with cliffs on the west side that rise to a high point of 3,370 feet. Lanai slopes down to sea level on the east and south sides; the only town on the island, Lanai City, sits at 1,600 feet. The high point of the island is covered with Norfolk pines and is usually shrouded in clouds, whereas the arid beaches survive on minimal rainfall. One area in particular stands out: the Garden of the Gods, just 7 miles from Lanai City. Here, oddly strewn boulders lie in the amber- and ocher-colored dirt, and bizarre stone formations dot the landscape. The ancient Hawaiians formed romantic legends explaining the enigma, but modern-day scientists are still debating this mystery.

MOLOKAI   Roughly the shape of Manhattan, Molokai is 37 miles long and 10 miles wide, with a thumb protruding from the north shore. The north shore begins on the west, with miles of white-sand beaches that fringe a desert-like landscape. The protruding thumb—the Kalaupapa Peninsula—is cut off by a fence of cliffs, some 2,000 feet tall, that line the remainder of the north side. Molokai can be divided into two areas: the dry west end, where the high point is 1,381 feet; and the rainy, tropical east and north ends, where the high point is Mount Kamakou, at 4,970 feet.

THE FLORA OF MAUI

Maui radiates with the sweet smell of flowers, lush vegetation, and exotic plant life.

AFRICAN TULIP TREES   Even from afar, you can see the flaming red flowers on these large trees, which can grow to be more than 50 feet tall. Children in Hawaii love them because the buds hold water—they use the flowers as water pistols.

ANGEL'S TRUMPETS   These small trees can grow up to 20 feet tall, with an abundance of large (up to 10 inches in diameter) pendants—white or pink flowers that resemble, well, trumpets. The Hawaiians call them *nana-honua,* which means "earth gazing." The flowers, which bloom continually from early spring to late fall, have a musky scent. However, beware: All parts of the plant are poisonous and contain a strong narcotic.

ANTHURIUMS   One of Hawaii's most popular cut flowers, anthuriums originally came from the tropical Americas and the Caribbean islands. There are more than 550 species, but the most popular in Hawaii are the heart-shaped red, orange, pink, white, and even purple flowers with tail-like spathes. Look for the heart-shaped green leaves in shaded areas. These exotic plants have no scent but will last several weeks as cut flowers.

BIRDS OF PARADISE These natives of Africa have become something of a trademark of Hawaii. They're easily recognizable by the orange and blue flowers nestled in gray-green bracts, looking somewhat like birds in flight.

BOUGAINVILLEA Originally from Brazil and named for the 18th-century French explorer Louis Antoine de Bougainville, these colorful, tissue-thin bracts (ranging in color from majestic purple to fiery orange) hide tiny white flowers.

BROMELIADS The pineapple plant is the best-known bromeliad; native to tropical South America and the islands of the Caribbean, bromeliads comprise more than 1,400 species. "Bromes," as they're affectionately called, are generally spiky plants ranging in size from a few inches to several feet in diameter. They are popular not only for their unusual foliage but also for their strange and wonderful flowers, which range from colorful spikes to delicate blossoms resembling orchids. Bromeliads are widely used in landscaping and as interior decoration, especially in resort areas.

COFFEE Hawaii is the only state that commercially produces coffee. Coffee is an evergreen shrub with shiny, waxy, dark-green, pointed leaves. The flower is a small, fragrant white blossom that develops into half-inch berries that turn bright red when ripe. Look for coffee plants in Kaanapali on Maui and in Kualapuu on Molokai.

GINGER Some of the most fragrant flowers in Hawaii are white and yellow ginger. Usually found in clumps, and growing 4 to 7 feet tall in areas blessed by rain, these sweet-smelling, 3-inch-wide flowers are composed of three dainty petal-like stamens and three long, thin petals. Both white and yellow ginger are so prolific that many people assume they are native to Hawaii; actually, they were introduced in the 19th century from the Indonesia-Malaysia area. Look for white and yellow ginger from late spring to fall. If you see them on the side of the road (especially on the Hana Highway), stop and pick a few blossoms—your car will be filled with a divine fragrance for the rest of the day. The only downside is that, once picked, the flowers will live only briefly.

Other members of the ginger family frequently seen in Hawaii (there are some 700 species) include red, shell, and torch gingers. Red ginger consists of tall, green stalks with foot-long red "flower heads." The red "petals" are actually bracts; inch-long white flowers are protected by the bracts and can be seen if you look down into the red head. Red ginger, which does not share the heavenly smell of white ginger, will last a week or longer when cut. Look for red ginger from spring through late fall. Cool, wet mountain forests are ideal conditions for shell ginger; natives of India and Burma, these plants, with their pearly white, clamshell-like blossoms, bloom from spring to fall.

Perhaps the most exotic ginger is the red or pink torch ginger. Cultivated in Malaysia as seasoning (the young flower shoots are used in curries), torch ginger rises directly out of the ground; the flower stalks, which are about 5 to 8 inches in length, resemble the fire of a lighted torch. This is one of the few types of ginger that can bloom year-round.

HELICONIA Some 80 species of the colorful heliconia family came to Hawaii from the Caribbean and Central and South America. The bright yellow, red, green, and orange bracts overlap and appear to unfold like origami birds. The most obvious heliconia to spot is the lobster claw, which resembles a string of boiled crustacean pincers—the brilliant crimson bracts alternate on the stem. Another prolific heliconia is the parrot's beak; growing to about hip height, it's composed of bright-orange flower bracts with black tips, not unlike the beak of a parrot. Look for parrot's beak in the spring and summer, when it blooms in profusion.

HIBISCUS One variety of this year-round blossom, the yellow hibiscus, is the official state flower. The 4- to 6-inch hibiscus flowers come in a range of colors, from lily white to lipstick red. The flowers resemble crepe paper, with stamens and pistils protruding spire-like from the center. Hibiscus hedges can grow up to 15 feet tall. Once plucked, the flowers wither quickly.

JACARANDA Beginning around March and sometimes lasting until early May, these huge, lacy-leafed trees metamorphose into large clusters of spectacular lavender-blue sprays. The bell-shaped flowers drop quickly, leaving a majestic purple carpet beneath the tree.

NIGHT-BLOOMING CEREUS Look along rock walls for this spectacular night-blooming flower. Originally from Central America, this vinelike member of the cactus family has green scalloped edges and produces foot-long white flowers that open as darkness falls and wither as the sun rises. The plant also bears a red fruit that is edible.

ORCHIDS To many minds, nothing says Hawaii more than orchids. The orchid family is the largest in the entire plant kingdom. The most widely grown variety—and the major source of flowers for leis and garnish for tropical libations—is the vanda orchid. The vandas used in Hawaii's commercial flower industry are generally lavender or white, but they grow in a rainbow of colors, shapes, and sizes. The orchids used for corsages are the large, delicate cattleya; the ones used in floral arrangements—you'll probably see them in your hotel lobby—are usually dendrobiums.

PLUMERIA Also known as frangipani, this sweet-smelling, five-petal flower, found in clusters on trees, is the most popular choice of lei makers. The Singapore plumeria has five creamy-white petals, with a touch of yellow in the center. Another popular variety, ruba—with flowers from soft pink to flaming red—is also used in leis. When picking plumeria, be careful of the sap from the flower, as it is poisonous and can stain clothes.

PROTEAS Originally from South Africa, this unusual plant comes in more than 40 varieties. Proteas are shrubs that bloom into a range of flower types. Different species of proteas range from those resembling pincushions to a species that looks just like a bouquet of feathers. Proteas are long-lasting cut flowers; once dried, they will last for years.

FRUIT TREES

BANANA Edible bananas are among the oldest of the world's food crops. By the time Europeans arrived in the islands, the Hawaiians had planted more than 40 types of bananas. Most banana plants have long green leaves hanging from the tree, with the flowers giving way to fruit in clusters.

BREADFRUIT A large tree, more than 60 feet tall, with broad, sculpted, dark-green leaves, the famous breadfruit produces a round, head-size green fruit that is a staple in the diets of all Polynesians. When roasted or baked, the whitish-yellow meat tastes somewhat like a sweet potato.

LITCHI This evergreen tree, which can grow to well over 30 feet across, originated in China. Small flowers grow into panicles about a foot long in June and July. The round, red-skinned fruit appears shortly afterward.

MACADAMIA A transplant from Australia, macadamia nuts have become a commercial crop in recent decades in Hawaii, especially on Maui and the Big

Island. The large trees—up to 60 feet tall—bear a hard-shelled nut encased in a leathery husk, which splits open and dries when ripe.

MANGO   From Indonesia and Malaysia comes the delicious mango, a fruit with peachlike flesh. Mango season usually begins in the spring and lasts through the summer, depending on the variety. The trees can grow to more than 100 feet tall. The tiny reddish flowers give way to a green fruit that turns red-yellow when ripe. Some people enjoy unripe mangoes, either thinly sliced or in chutney, a traditional Indian preparation. Note that mango sap can cause a skin rash on some people.

PAPAYA   One of the sweetest of all tropical fruits, the pear-shaped papaya turns yellow or reddish pink when ripe. They are found at the base of the large, scalloped-shaped leaves on a pedestal-like, nonbranched tree whose trunk is hollow. Papayas ripen year-round.

OTHER TREES & PLANTS

BANYAN   Among the world's largest trees, banyans have branches that grow out and away from the trunk, forming descending roots that grow down to the ground to feed and form additional trunks, making the tree very stable during tropical storms. The banyan in the courtyard next to the old Court House in Lahaina is an excellent example of a spreading banyan—it covers two-thirds of an acre.

MONKEYPOD   The monkeypod is one of Hawaii's most majestic trees; it grows more than 80 feet tall and 100 feet across. Seen near older homes and in parks, the leaves of the monkeypod drop in February and March. The wood is a favorite of woodworking artisans.

SILVERSWORD   This very uncommon and unusual plant is seen only on the Big Island and in the Haleakala Crater on Maui. Once a year, this rare relative of the sunflower family blooms between July and September. Resembling a pinecone more than a sunflower, the silversword in bloom is a fountain of red-petaled, daisylike flowers that turn silver soon after blooming.

TARO   Around pools, near streams, and in neatly planted fields, you'll see the green heart-shaped leaves of taro, whose dense roots are a Polynesian staple. The ancient Hawaiians pounded the roots into poi. Originally from Sri Lanka, taro is grown not only as a food crop, but also as an ornamental.

MARIJUANA   This not-so-rare-and-unusual plant—called *pakalolo*, or "crazy weed"—is grown throughout the islands. You probably won't see it as you drive along the roads, but if you go hiking, you might glimpse the feathery green leaves with tight clusters of buds. Despite years of police effort to eradicate the plant, the illegal industry continues. Don't be tempted to pick a few buds, as the purveyors of this nefarious industry don't take kindly to poaching.

THE FAUNA OF MAUI

When the first Polynesians arrived in Hawaii between A.D. 500 and A.D. 800, scientists say they found some 67 varieties of endemic Hawaiian birds, a third of which are now believed to be extinct. What's even more astonishing is what they didn't find—there were no reptiles, amphibians, mosquitoes, lice, fleas, or even a cockroach.

There were only two endemic mammals: the hoary bat and the monk seal. The small **hoary bat** must have accidentally blown to Hawaii at some point, from either North or South America. It can still be seen today on its early evening forays.

The **Hawaiian monk seal,** a relative of warm-water seals found in the Caribbean and Mediterranean, was nearly slaughtered into extinction for its skin and oil during the 19th century. These seals have recently experienced a minor population explosion, forcing relocation of some males from their protected homes in the islets north of the main Hawaiian Islands. Periodically, these endangered animals turn up at various beaches throughout the state. They are protected under federal law by the Marine Mammals Protection Act. If you're fortunate enough to see a monk seal, just look; don't disturb one of Hawaii's living treasures.

The first Polynesians brought a few animals from home: dogs, pigs, and chickens (all were for eating), as well as rats (stowaways). All four animals are still found in the Hawaiian wild today.

BIRDS

More species of native birds have become extinct in Hawaii in the past 200 years than anywhere else on the planet. Of the 67 native species, 23 are extinct and 30 are endangered. Even the Hawaiian crow, **alala,** is threatened.

The **aeo,** or Hawaiian stilt, a 16-inch-long bird with a black head, a black coat, a white underside, and long pink legs, can be found in protected wetlands like the Kanaha Wild Life Sanctuary (where it shares its natural habitat with the Hawaiian coot) and the Kealia Pond.

Endemic to the islands, the **nene** is Hawaii's state bird. It's currently being brought back from the brink of extinction through captive breeding and by strenuous protection laws. A relative of the Canada goose, the nene stands about 2 feet high and has a black head and yellow cheek, a buff neck with deep furrows, a grayish-brown body, and clawed feet. It gets its name from its two-syllable, high nasal call, "nay-nay." The approximately 500 nenes in existence can be seen at Haleakala National Park.

The Hawaiian short-eared owl, **pueo,** which grows to between 12 and 17 inches in size, can be seen at dawn and dusk, when the black-billed, brown-and-white bird goes hunting for rodents. Pueos are highly regarded by Hawaiians; according to legend, spotting a pueo is a good omen.

OTHER LAND FAUNA

GECKOS These harmless, soft-skinned, insect-eating lizards come equipped with suction pads on their feet, enabling them to climb walls and windows to reach tasty insects like mosquitoes and cockroaches. You'll see them on windows outside a lighted room at night or hear their cheerful chirp.

MONGOOSES The mongoose was a mistake in Hawaii. It was brought here in the 19th century to counteract the ever-growing rat problem. But rats are nocturnal creatures, sleeping during the day and wandering out at night; mongooses, however, are day creatures. Instead of getting rid of the rat problem, the mongooses eat bird eggs, contributing to the destruction of the native bird population.

SNAKES Hawaii has but one tiny earthwormlike snake. On the island of Guam, the brown tree snake has obliterated most of the bird population. Officials in Hawaii are well aware of this danger and are committed to preventing snakes from entering the state.

SEALIFE

Approximately 680 species of fish are known to inhabit the waters around the Hawaiian Islands. Of those, approximately 450 species stay close to the reef and inshore areas.

CORAL The reefs surrounding Hawaii are made up of various coral and algae. The living coral grows through sunlight that feeds a specialized algae, which in turn allows the development of the coral's calcareous skeleton. The reefs, which take thousands of years to develop, attract and support fish and crustaceans, which use them for food, habitat, mating, and raising their young. Mother Nature can batter the fragile reefs with a strong storm or large waves, but humans—through seemingly innocuous acts such as touching the coral—have proven far more destructive.

The corals most frequently seen around Maui are hard, rocklike formations named for their familiar shapes: antler, cauliflower, finger, plate, and razor coral. Wire coral looks just like its name—a randomly bent wire growing straight out of the reef. Some corals appear soft, such as tube coral, which can be found in the ceilings of caves. Black coral, which resembles winter-bare trees or shrubs, is found at depths of more than 100 feet.

REEF FISH Of the approximately 450 reef fish, about 27% are native to Hawaii and are found nowhere else in the world. As the islands were born from erupting volcanoes, evolving over millions of years, ocean currents—mainly from Southeast Asia—carried the larvae of thousands of marine animals and plants to Hawaii's reef. Of those, approximately 100 species not only adapted, but thrived.

Some species are much bigger and more plentiful than their Pacific cousins, and many developed unique characteristics. Some, like the lemon or milletseed butterfly fish, are not only particular to Hawaii but also unique within their larger, worldwide family in their specialized schooling and feeding behaviors. Another surprising thing about Hawaii endemics is how common some of the native fish are; you can see the saddleback wrasse, for instance, on virtually any snorkeling excursion or dive in Hawaiian waters. You're likely to spot one or more of the following reef fish while underwater.

Angel fish, often mistaken for butterfly fish, can be distinguished by the spine, located low on the gill plate. Angel fish are very shy; several species live in colonies close to coral for protection.

Blennies are small, elongated fish, ranging from 2 to 10 inches long, with the majority in the 3- to 4-inch range. Blennies are so small that they can live in tide pools; you might have a hard time spotting one.

Butterfly fish, among the most colorful of the reef fish, are usually seen in pairs (scientists believe they mate for life) and appear to spend most of their day feeding. There are 22 species of butterfly fish, of which three (blue-stripe, lemon or milletseed, and multiband or pebbled butterfly fish) are endemic. Most butterfly fish have a dark band through the eye and a spot near the tail resembling an eye, meant to confuse their predators (the moray eel loves to lunch on them).

Moray and conger **eels** are the common eels seen in Hawaii. Morays are usually docile unless provoked, or if there's food or an injured fish around. Unfortunately, some morays have been fed by divers and, being intelligent creatures, associate divers with food; thus, they can become aggressive. But most morays like to keep to themselves, hidden in their hole or crevice. While morays may look menacing, conger eels look downright happy, with big lips and pectoral fins (situated so they look like big ears) that give them the appearance of a perpetually smiling face. Conger eels have crushing teeth so they can feed on crustaceans; in fact, since they're sloppy eaters, they usually live with shrimp and crabs who feed off the crumbs they leave.

One of the largest and most colorful of the reef fish, the **parrot fish** can grow up to 40 inches long. Parrot fish are easy to spot—their front teeth are fused together, protruding like buck teeth and resembling a parrot's beak. These unique teeth allow them to feed by scraping algae from rocks and coral. The rocks and coral pass through the parrot fish's system, resulting in fine sand. In fact, most of the white sand found in Hawaii is parrot-fish waste; one large parrot fish can produce a ton of sand a year. Hawaiian native parrot-fish species include yellowbar, regal, and spectacled.

Scorpion fish are what scientists call "ambush predators." They hide under camouflaged exteriors and ambush their prey when they come along. Several sport a venomous dorsal spine. These fish don't have a gas bladder, so when they stop swimming, they sink—that's why you usually find them "resting" on ledges and on the ocean bottom. Although they're not aggressive, an inattentive snorkeler or diver could feel the effects of those venomous spines—so be very careful where you put your hands and feet in the water.

Surgeonfish, sometimes called *tang,* get their name from the scalpel-like spines located on each side of their bodies near the base of their tails. Some surgeonfish have a rigid spine, while others have the ability to fold their spine against their body until it's needed for defense purposes. Some surgeon fish, like the brightly colored yellow tang, are boldly colored; others are adorned in more conservative shades of gray, brown, or black. The only endemic surgeonfish—and the most abundant in Hawaiian waters—is the convict tang, a pale white fish with vertical black stripes (like a convict's uniform).

Wrasses are a very diverse family of fish, ranging in size from 2 to 15 inches. Several wrasses are brilliantly colored and change their colors through aging and sexual dimorphism (sex changing). Wrasses have the ability to change gender with maturation, from female (when young) to male. Several types are endemic to Hawaii: the Hawaiian cleaner, shortnose, belted, and gray (or old woman).

GAME FISH   Hawaii is known around the globe as *the* place for big-game fish—marlin, swordfish, and tuna—but its waters are also great for catching other offshore fish, such as mahimahi, rainbow runner, and wahoo; coastal fish, such as barracuda and scad; bottom fish, such as snappers, sea bass, and amberjack; and inshore fish, like trevally and bonefish.

Six kinds of **billfish** are found in the offshore waters around the islands: Pacific blue marlin, black marlin, sailfish, broadbill swordfish, striped marlin, and shortbill spearfish. Hawaii billfish range in size from the 20-pound shortbill spearfish and striped marlin to an 1,805-pound Pacific blue marlin, the largest marlin ever caught on rod and reel anywhere in the world.

Tuna ranges in size from small (a pound or less) mackerel tuna used as bait (Hawaiians call them *oioi*) to 250-pound yellowfin ahi tuna. Other species of tuna found in Hawaii are bigeye, albacore, kawakawa, and skipjack.

Some of the best fish for eating are also found in offshore waters: **mahimahi** (also known as dolphin fish or dorado), in the 20- to 70-pound range; **rainbow runner** (*kamanu*), from 15 to 30 pounds; and **wahoo** (*ono*), from 15 to 80 pounds. Shoreline fishers are always on the lookout for **trevally** (the state record for giant trevally is 191 pounds), **bonefish, ladyfish, threadfin, leatherfish,** and **goatfish.** Bottom fishers pursue a range of **snappers**—red, pink, gray, and others—as well as **sea bass** (the state record is a whopping 563 pounds) and **amberjack,** which weigh up to 100 pounds.

WHALES   The most popular visitors to Hawaii come every year around December and stay until spring (April or so), when they return to their summer home in Alaska. Humpback whales—some as big as a city bus and weighing many tons—migrate to the warm, protected Hawaiian waters in the winter to mate and calve.

You can take whale-watching cruises that will let you observe these magnificent leviathans up close, or you can spot their signature spouts of water from shore as they expel water off in the distance. Humpbacks grow to up to 45 feet long, so when they breach (propel their entire body out of the water) or even wave a fluke, you can see it for miles.

Humpbacks are among the biggest whales found in Hawaiian waters, but other whales—like pilot, sperm, false killer, melon-headed, pygmy killer, and beaked—can be seen year-round. These whales usually travel in pods of 20 to 40 animals and are very social, interacting with one another on the surface.

SHARKS   Yes, there *are* sharks in Hawaii, but more than likely you won't see a shark unless you specifically go looking for one. The ancient Hawaiians had great respect for these animals and believed that some sharks were reincarnated relatives who had returned to assist them.

About 40 different species of shark inhabit the waters surrounding Hawaii, ranging from the totally harmless whale shark (at 60 feet, the world's largest fish), which has no teeth and is so docile that it frequently lets divers ride on its back, to the not-so-docile, infamous, and extremely uncommon, great white shark. The most common sharks seen in Hawaii are white-tip reef sharks, gray reef sharks (about 5 feet long), and black-tip reef sharks (about 6 feet long).

MAUI'S ECOSYSTEM PROBLEMS

Maui might be paradise, but even paradise has its problems. The biggest threat facing Maui's natural environment is human intrusion—simply put, too many people want to experience paradise firsthand. From the magnificent underwater world to the breathtaking rain forest, the presence of people isn't always benign, no matter how cautious or environmentally aware they may be.

MARINE LIFE   Hawaii's beautiful and abundant marine life has attracted so many visitors that they threaten to overwhelm it. A great example of this over-enthusiasm is **Molokini,** a small, partially submerged, half-moon–shaped crater off the coast of Maui. In the 1970s, residents made the area a conservation district to protect the unique aquarium-like atmosphere of the waters inside the arms of the crater. Unfortunately, once it was protected, everyone wanted to come here just to see what was worth special protection. Twenty-five years ago, one or two small six-passenger boats made the trip once a day to Molokini; today, it's not uncommon to sight 20 or more boats, each carrying 20 to 49 passengers, moored inside the tiny crater. One tour operator has claimed that on some days, it's so crowded that you can actually see a slick of suntan oil floating on the surface of the water.

People who fall in love with the colorful **reef fish** and want to see them all the time back home are also thought to be impacting the health of Hawaii's reefs. Because of the popularity of home and office aquariums, more and more collectors are taking a growing number of reef fish from Hawaiian waters.

The **reefs** themselves have faced increasing ecological problems over the years. Runoff of soil and chemicals from construction, agriculture, erosion, and even heavy storms can blanket and choke a reef, which needs sunlight to survive. In addition, the intrusion of foreign elements—like breaks in sewage lines—can cause problems for Hawaii's reef. Human contact with the reef can upset the ecosystem as well. Coral, the basis of the reef system, is very fragile; snorkelers and divers grabbing on to it can break off pieces that took decades to form. Feeding the fish can also upset the balance of the ecosystem (not to mention upsetting the digestive systems of the fish). One glass-bottom boat operator reported that divers fed an eel for years, considering it their "pet" eel. One day the eel decided that he wanted more than just the food being offered and bit the diver's fingers. Divers and snorkelers report that in areas where the fish are fed, the fish have become more aggressive; clouds of normally shy reef fish surround divers, demanding food.

FLORA   One of Hawaii's most fragile environments is the rain forest. Any intrusion—from a hiker carrying seeds on his shoes to the rooting of wild boars—can upset the delicate balance in these complete ecosystems. In recent years, development has moved closer and closer to the rain forest.

FAUNA   The biggest impact on the fauna in Hawaii is the decimation of native birds by feral animals, which have destroyed the birds' habitats, and by mongooses that have eaten the birds' eggs and young. Government officials are vigilant about snakes because of the potential damage tree snakes can do to the remaining bird life.

Frommer's Online Directory

by Michael Shapiro & Bruce Gerstman

Michael Shapiro is the author of *Internet Travel 101: How to Plan Trips and Save Money Online* (Globe Pequot). Bruce Gerstman compiled the Maui listings for this directory.

Frommer's Online Directory is a new feature designed to help you take advantage of the Internet to better plan your trip. Part I lists some general Internet resources that can make any trip easier, such as sites for booking airline tickets. It's not meant to be a comprehensive list— it's a discriminating selection of useful sites to get you started. In Part II, you'll find some top online guides specifically for Maui, Lanai, and Molokai, including beaches, outdoor activities, lodging, dining, and entertainment.

1 The Top Travel-Planning Web Sites

Among the most popular sites are online travel agencies. The top agencies, including Expedia, Preview Travel, and Travelocity, offer an array of tools that are valuable even if you don't book online. You can check flight schedules, hotel availability, car-rental prices, or even get paged if your flight is delayed.

While online agencies have come a long way over the past few years, they don't always yield the best prices. Unlike a travel agent, for example, they're unlikely to tell you that you can save money by flying a day earlier or a day later. On the other hand, if you're looking for a bargain fare, you might find something online that an agent wouldn't take the time to dig up. Because airline commissions have been cut, a travel agent may not find it worthwhile to spend half an hour trying to find you the best deal. On the Net, you can be your own agent and take all the time you want.

Online booking sites aren't the only places to book airline tickets— all major airlines have their own Web sites and often offer incentives, such as bonus frequent-flyer miles or Net-only discounts, for buying online. These incentives have helped airlines capture the majority of the online booking market. According to Jupiter Communications, online agencies such as Travelocity booked about 80 percent of tickets purchased online in 1996, but by 1999 airline sites (such as **www. ual.com**) were projected to own about 60 percent of the online market, with online agencies' share of the pie dwindling each year.

Below are the Web sites for some of the major airlines serving Maui's Kahului Airport or Oahu's Honolulu International Airport, where you can pick up an interisland flight to Maui. These sites offer both schedules and flight booking.

Internet Tip

Far more people look online than book online, partly from fear of putting their credit cards through on the Net. Though secure encryption has made this fear less justified, there's no reason you can't find a flight online and then book it by calling a toll-free number or contacting your travel agent. To be sure you're in secure mode when you book online, look for a little icon of a key (in Netscape) or a padlock (Internet Explorer) at the bottom of your Web browser.

Air Canada **www.aircanada.ca**
Air New Zealand **www.airnz.com**
American Airlines **www.aa.com**
Canadian Airlines **www.cdnair.ca**
Continental Airlines **www.flycontinental.com**
Delta Airlines **www.delta-air.com**
Hawaiian Airlines **www.hawaiianair.com**
Northwest Airlines **www.nwa.com**
Qantas **www.qantas.com**
Trans World Airlines (TWA) **www.twa.com**
United Airlines **www.ual.com**
Virgin Atlantic Airways **www.fly.virgin.com**

WHEN SHOULD YOU BOOK ONLINE?

Online booking is not for everyone. If you prefer to let others handle your travel arrangements, one call to an experienced travel agent should suffice. But if you want to know as much as possible about your options, the Net is a good place to start, especially for bargain hunters.

The most compelling reason to use online booking is to take advantage of special offers and Internet-only fares that must be purchased online. Another advantage is that you can cash in on incentives for booking online, such as rebates or bonus frequent-flyer miles.

Online booking works best for trips within North America; for international tickets, it's usually cheaper and easier to use a travel agent or consolidator.

Online booking is certainly not for those with a complex international itinerary. If you require follow-up services, such as itinerary changes, use a travel agent. Though Expedia and some other online agencies employ travel agents available by phone, these sites are geared primarily for self-service.

LEADING BOOKING SITES

Below are listings for the top travel booking sites. The starred selections are the most useful and best designed sites.

Cheap Tickets. **www.cheaptickets.com**
Essentials: Discounted rates on domestic and international airline tickets and hotel rooms.

Sometimes discounters such as Cheap Tickets have exclusive deals that aren't available through more mainstream channels. Registration at Cheap Tickets requires inputting a credit-card number before getting started, so many people elect to call the company's toll-free number rather than book online. Cheap Tickets actually regards this policy as a selling point, arguing that "lookers" who don't intend to buy will be scared off by its "credit card first" approach and won't bog down the site with their

Take a Look at Frommer's Site

We highly recommend Arthur Frommer's Budget Travel Online (**www. frommers.com**) as an excellent travel-planning resource. Of course, we're a little biased, but you will find indispensable travel tips, reviews, monthly vacation giveaways, and online booking.

Subscribe to Arthur Frommer's Daily Newsletter (**www.frommers.com/ newsletters**) to receive the latest travel bargains and insider tips. You'll read daily headlines and articles from the dean of travel himself, highlighting last-minute deals on airfares, accommodations, cruises, and package vacations. You'll also find great travel advice by checking our Tip of the Day or Hot Spot of the Month.

Search our Destinations archive (**www.frommers.com/destinations**) of more than 200 domestic and international destinations for great places to stay, tips for getting there, and what to do while you're there. Once you've researched your trip, you might try our online reservation system (**www.frommers.com/ booktravelnow**) to book your dream vacation at affordable prices.

queries. Despite its misguided credit-card policy, Cheap Tickets is worth the effort, as its fares can be substantially lower than those offered by its competitors.

✪ Expedia. **expedia.com**

Essentials: Domestic and international flight, hotel, and rental-car booking; late-breaking travel news; destination features and commentary from travel experts; deals on cruises and vacation packages. Free (one-time) registration is required for booking.

Expedia makes it easy to handle flight, hotel, and car booking on one itinerary, so it's a good place for one-stop shopping. The hotel search offers crisp, zoomable maps to pinpoint most properties; click on the camera icon to see images of the rooms. But like many online databases, Expedia focuses on the major chains, such as Hilton and Hyatt, so don't expect too many one-of-a-kind resorts or B&Bs here.

Once you're registered, you can start booking with the Roundtrip Fare Finder on the home page, which expedites the process. After selecting a flight, you can hold it until midnight the following day or purchase online. If you think you might do better through a travel agent, you'll have time to try to get a lower price. (You may do better with a travel agent, since Expedia's computer reservation system does not include all airlines.)

Expedia's World Guide, offering destination information, is a glaring weakness—it takes a lot of page views to get very little information. However, Expedia compensates by linking to other Microsoft Network services, such as its Sidewalk city guides, which offer entertainment and dining advice for many of the cities it covers.

Preview Travel. **www.previewtravel.com**

Essentials: Domestic and international flight, hotel, and rental-car booking; Travel Newswire fare sales; deals on cruises and vacation packages. Free (one-time) registration is required for booking. Preview offers express booking for members, but at press time, this feature was buried below the fold on Preview's reservation page.

Preview features the most inviting interface for booking trips, though the wealth of graphics involved can make the site somewhat slow to load. Use Farefinder to quickly find the lowest current fares on flights to dozens of major cities. Carfinder offers a similar service for rental cars, but you can search only airport locations, not city pick-up sites.

Preview has a great feature called the Best Fare Finder; after it searches for the best deal on your itinerary, it will check flights that are a bit later or earlier to see if it might be cheaper to fly at a different time. While these searches have become quite sophisticated, they still occasionally overlook deals that might be uncovered by a top-notch travel agent. If you have the time, explore the options online and then call an agent to see if you can get a better price.

With Preview's Fare Alert feature, you can select up to three routes and receive e-mail notices when the fare drops below your target amount. For example, you can tell Preview to alert you when the round-trip fare from New York to Maui drops below $500. If it does, you'll get an e-mail telling you the current fare.

Minor quibbles: When you search for a fare, hotel, or car (at least at press time), Preview launches an annoying little "Please Wait" window that gets in the way of the main browser window, even when your results begin to appear. The hotel search feature is intuitive, but the images and maps aren't as crisp as those at Expedia. Also, all sorts of extraneous information that's irrelevant to most travelers is listed on maps.

Note to AOL Users: You can book flights, hotels, rental cars, and cruises on AOL at keyword: Travel. The booking software is provided by Preview Travel and is similar to Preview on the Web. Use the AOL "Travelers Advantage" program to earn a 5 percent rebate on flights, hotel rooms, and car rentals.

Priceline.com. www.priceline.com

Priceline lets you "name your price" for domestic and international airline tickets. In other words, you select a route and dates, guarantee with a credit card, and make a bid for what you're willing to pay. If one of the airlines in Priceline's database has a fare that's lower than your bid, your credit card will automatically be charged for a ticket.

But you can't say when you want to fly—you have to accept any flight leaving between 6am and 10pm, and you may have to make a stopover. No frequent-flyer miles are awarded, and tickets are non-refundable and can't be exchanged for another flight. So if your plans change, you're out of luck. Priceline can be good for travelers who have to take off on short notice (and who are thus unable to qualify for advance-purchase discounts). But be sure to shop around first—if you overbid, you'll be required to purchase the ticket and Priceline will pocket the difference.

Travelocity. www.travelocity.com

Essentials: Domestic and international flight, hotel, and rental-car booking; deals on cruises and vacation packages. Travel Headlines spotlights latest bargain airfares. Free (one-time) registration is required for booking.

Travelocity almost got it right. Its Express Booking feature enables travelers to complete the booking process more quickly than they could at Expedia or Preview, but Travelocity gums up the works with a page called "Featured Airlines." Big placards of several featured airlines compete for your attention—if you want to see the fares for all available airlines, click the much smaller box at the bottom of the page labeled "Book a Flight."

Some have worried that Travelocity, which is owned by American Airlines' parent company AMR, directs bookings to American. This doesn't seem to be the case; we've booked there dozens of times and have always been directed to the cheapest listed flight. But this "Featured Airlines" page seems to be Travelocity's way of trying to cash in with ads and incentives for booking certain airlines. (*Note:* It's hard to blame these booking services for trying to generate some revenue; many airlines have slashed commissions to $10 per domestic booking for online transactions, so these virtual agencies are groping for revenue streams.) There are rewards for choosing one of the featured airlines. You'll get 1,500 bonus frequent-flyer miles if you book through United's site, for example, but the site doesn't tell you about other airlines that might be cheaper. If the United flight costs $150 more than the best deal on another airline, it's not worth spending the extra money.

On the plus side, Travelocity has some leading-edge tools. Fare Watcher e-mail is an "intelligent agent" that keeps you informed of the best fares offered for the round-trips of your choice. Whenever the fare changes by $25 or more, Fare Watcher will alert you by e-mail. If you own an alphanumeric pager with national access that can receive e-mail, Travelocity's Flight Paging system can alert you if your flight is delayed. Finally, though Travelocity doesn't include every budget airline, it does include Southwest, the leading U.S. budget carrier.

FINDING LODGINGS ONLINE

While the services above offer hotel booking, it can be best to use a site devoted primarily to lodging in order to find properties that aren't listed on more general online travel agencies. Some specialize in a particular type of accommodation, such as B&Bs, which you won't find on the more mainstream booking services. Other services, such as TravelWeb, offer weekend deals on major chain properties, which cater to business travelers and have more empty rooms on weekends.

All Hotels on the Web. www.all-hotels.com
This site doesn't include *all* the hotels on the Web, but it does have tens of thousands of listings throughout the world. Bear in mind that each hotel listed has paid a small fee (of $25 and up) for placement, so it's not an objective list; it's more like a book of online brochures.

InnSite. www.innsite.com
This site has B&B listings for all 50 U.S. states and dozens of countries around the globe. Find an inn at your destination, have a look at images of the rooms, check prices and availability, and then e-mail the innkeeper if you have further questions. This is an extensive directory of B&Bs, but includes listings only if the proprietor submitted one (*Note:* it's free to get an inn listed). The descriptions are written by the innkeepers, and many listings link to the inn's own Web sites, where you can find more information and images.

Places to Stay. www.placestostay.com
Mostly one-of-a-kind places in the U.S. and abroad that you might not find in other directories, with a focus on resort accommodations. Again, this isn't a comprehensive directory, but it can give you a sense of what's available at different destinations.

✪ TravelWeb. www.travelweb.com
TravelWeb lists more than 16,000 hotels worldwide, focusing on chains such as Hyatt and Hilton, and you can book almost 90 percent of these online. TravelWeb's Click-It Weekends, updated each Monday, offers weekend deals at many leading hotel chains. TravelWeb is the online home for Pegasus Systems, which provides transaction processing systems for the hotel industry.

LAST-MINUTE DEALS & OTHER ONLINE BARGAINS

There's nothing airlines hate more than flying with lots of empty seats. The Net has enabled airlines to offer last-minute bargains to entice travelers to fill those seats. Most of these are announced on Tuesday or Wednesday and are valid for travel the following weekend, but some can be booked weeks or months in advance. You can sign up for weekly e-mail alerts at airlines' sites, or check sites such as WebFlyer (see below) that compile lists of these bargains. To make it easier, visit a site (see below) that will round up all the deals and send them in one convenient weekly e-mail. But last-minute deals

A Handy Tip

While most people learn about last-minute weekend deals from e-mail dispatches, it can be best to find out precisely *when* these deals become available and check airlines' Web sites at that time. To find out when these special offers become available, check the pages devoted to the deals on airlines' Web pages. Because these deals are limited, they can vanish within hours, sometimes even minutes, so it pays to log on as soon as they're available.

aren't the only online bargains—other sites can help you find value even if you can't wait until the eleventh hour.

○ 1travel.com. www.1travel.com
Here you'll find deals on domestic and international flights, cruises, hotels, and all-inclusive resorts such as Club Med. 1travel.com's Saving Alert compiles last-minute air deals so you don't have to scroll through multiple e-mail notices. A feature called "Drive a little using low-fare airlines" helps map out strategies for using alternate airports to find lower fares. And Farebeater searches a database that includes published fares, consolidator bargains, and special deals exclusive to 1travel.com. *Note:* The travel agencies listed by 1travel.com have paid for placement.

BestFares. www.bestfares.com
Bargain-seeker Tom Parsons lists some great bargains on airfares, hotels, rental cars, and cruises, but the site is poorly organized. News Desk is a long list of hundreds of bargains, but they're not broken down into cities or even countries, so it's not easy to find what you're looking for. If you have time to wade through it, you might find a good deal. Some material is available only to paid subscribers.

Go4less.com. www.go4less.com
Specializing in last-minute cruise and package deals, Go4less has some eye-popping offers, such as off-peak Caribbean cruises for under $100 per day. The site has a clean design, but the bargains aren't organized by destination. However, you can avoid sifting through all this material by using the Search box and entering vacation type, destination, month, and price.

Moment's Notice. www.moments-notice.com
As the name suggests, Moment's Notice specializes in last-minute vacation and cruise deals. You can browse for free, but if you want to purchase a trip you have to join Moment's Notice, which costs $25.

Smarter Living. www.smarterliving.com
Best known for its e-mail dispatch of weekend deals on 20 airlines, Smarter Living also keeps you posted about last-minute bargains on everything from Windjammer Cruises to flights to Iceland.

○ WebFlyer. www.webflyer.com
WebFlyer is the ultimate online resource for frequent flyers and also has an excellent listing of last-minute air deals. Click on "Deal Watch" for a roundup of weekend deals on flights, hotels, and rental cars from domestic and international suppliers.

TRAVELER'S TOOLKIT

Seasoned travelers always carry some essential items to make their trips easier. The following is a selection of online tools to smooth your journey.

ATM LOCATORS

Visa (**www.visa.com/pd/atm**)
MasterCard (**www.mastercard.com/atm**)
Find ATMs in hundreds of cities in the U.S. and around the world. Both include maps for some locations and both list airport ATM locations, some with maps.

Intellicast. **www.intellicast.com**
Weather forecasts for all 50 states and cities around the world. Note that temperatures are in Celsius for many international destinations, so don't think you'll need that winter coat for your next trip to Athens.

✪ MapQuest. **www.mapquest.com**
Specializing in U.S. maps but capable of generating maps for dozens of international cities, MapQuest enables you to zoom in on a destination and locate restaurants, hotels, and other attractions on maps.

✪ Net Cafe Guide. **www.netcafeguide.com**
Locate Internet cafes at hundreds of locations around the globe. Catch up on your e-mail, log onto the Web, and stay in touch with the home front, usually for just a few dollars per hour.

2 The Top Web Sites for Maui

ISLAND, SIGHTSEEING & ENTERTAINMENT GUIDES

About.com: Maui. **maui.about.com**
This otherwise generic guide of outside links includes suggestions of wedding planners and an interesting section warning readers about the local shark haunts.

EastMaui.Com. **www.eastmaui.com**
The island photos and dining reviews on this independent guide to Maui's eastern side make it a fine site to preview your stay on the island.

Ecological Guide to Maui Hawaii Vacations. **supak.com/ecomaui/ecomaui.htm**
Visitors seeking environment-friendly hiking and diving tours can find links to tour operators as well as articles on preserving the region's natural ecosystem. The Virtual Tours section includes links to photo galleries and QuickTime video clips that show off the local beauty.

✪ Hawaii Visitors & Convention Bureau: Maui. **www.gohawaii.com/hokeo/ islands/maui.html**
The Maui section of the Visitors and Convention Bureau's online guide is especially strong for its lodging lists. It provides links to individual accommodations, including B&Bs, condos, vacation rentals, hotels, and resorts, with a brief description of each property. A solid Points of Interest section explains many of the island's attractions. Looking to get hitched? Link out to the island's wedding planners.

Maui Arts & Cultural Center. **www.maui.net/~macc/macc/macc12.html**
Learn about Maui culture and read the event schedule to catch an exhibition or show. Performing artists have ranged from world-famous musicians to local cultural troupes.

Maui Cheetah. **www.mauigateway.com/~rw/cheetah.htm**
It's a shame that the Cheetah hasn't updated these pages recently. They're worth browsing for the sections on budget tips, sightseeing, island photos, and restaurant reviews from the *Maui News* "Best of Maui" poll. Check the Maui Movies section for showtimes at the island's six theaters.

Check Your E-mail at Internet Cafes While Traveling

Until a few years ago, most travelers who checked their e-mail while traveling carried a laptop, but this posed some problems. Not only are laptops expensive, but they can also be difficult to configure, incur expensive connection charges, and are attractive to thieves. Thankfully, Web-based free e-mail programs have made it much easier to stay in touch.

Just open an account at a freemail provider, such as Hotmail (hotmail.com) or Excite Mail (mail.excite.com), and all you'll need to check your mail is a Web connection, easily available at Net cafes and copy shops around the world. After logging on, just point the browser to www.hotmail.com, enter your username and password, and you'll have access to your mail.

Internet cafes have become ubiquitous, so for a few dollars an hour you'll be able to check your mail and send messages back to colleagues, friends, and family. If you already have a primary e-mail account, you can set it to forward mail to your freemail account while you're away. Freemail programs have become enormously popular because they enable everyone, even those who don't own a computer, to have an e-mail address they can check wherever they log onto the Web.

Maui Fun in the Sun. **www.maui.net/~mauifun/homepage.htm**
While simultaneously promoting herself, a professional tour guide has organized a personal, practical, and sometimes critical island guide. Consider her suggestions of outdoor excursions, dining, golf, and cultural events.

Maui Historical Society. **www.mauimuseum.org**
Peek into the days of the first foreign settlers on Maui by looking at this site's photos of the Bailey House Museum. Need a ukulele lesson? The Maui Historical Society posts its classes and events.

✪ **Maui Island Currents.** **islandcurrents.com**
Specializing in arts and culture, Island Currents gives the most detailed lowdown on current exhibitions and performance art. Gallery listings are organized by town, while in-depth articles highlight local artists. Consult restaurant reviews from the 1998 *Maui News* "Best of Maui" poll for suggestions and prices.

✪ **Mauimapp: Maui Island Guide.** **www.mauimapp.com**
Though this well-rounded guide serves primarily as a directory of links, you'll find (if you look hard) a link to critical restaurant reviews written by readers and a schedule of events. A map section describes hikes and camping spots around the island. You'll find articles from the Maui Historical Society covering aspects of Hawaiian culture, from pre-state history to the slack key guitar.

✪ **Maui Net.** **www.maui.net**
Extensive directory of links to accommodations, island activities, and shopping. The Activity Desk has links to golf, hiking, airborne activities, and ocean adventures, such as scuba and snorkeling. These links lead to outfitters where you can learn more and set up excursions in advance.

Maui Visitors Bureau. **visitmaui.com**
In addition to providing ad-driven links to lodging, dining, outdoor activities, and shopping, the More for Less section offers a decent list of budget attractions and excursions. Web cams and photos let you virtually experience the ocean and downtown Lahaina.

The Plantsman's Maui Site. pages.prodigy.net/plantsman/contents.htm
This practical resource provides packing tips, advice on taking photos, directions around the island, and a calendar of events. Photos offer a preview to the coast and mountains.

Virtual Field Trip Around Maui. hawaii.ivv.nasa.gov/space/hawaii/vfts/maui/ maui.vft.html
Aerial photos of Maui's amazing topography, including details of Haleakala's summit and crater, as well as ground photos of the Iao Needle.

DINING GUIDES

Dine Hawaii Restaurant Guide: Maui. www.dinehawaii.com/maui
Click around the island map for brief, uncritical listings of island restaurants, which appear to pay for space on this guide.

Maui Guide to Vegan Dining. www.mauidiningguide.com
Organized by region, you can find descriptions, addresses, and phone numbers for places that offer strictly vegetarian and vegan meals. Also see the World Guide to Vegetarianism's listings for Hawaii (**www.veg.org/veg/Guide/USA/Hawaii/index.html**).

✪ Mauimapp: Maui Restaurant Reviews. www.mauimapp.com/restaurant
Straight, honest reviews from patrons who have tried dishes at restaurants on the island. Each review includes the date, and some go into detail about price and service. After you dine, rant and rave for the future visitors.

NEWSPAPERS & MAGAZINES

Lahaina News. www.maui.net/~mauiduck
A calendar of events lists happenings around the isle. Consult the surf report to find the best beach to hang ten.

Maui's Free Press. www.mauisfreepress.com
Giving visitors a local's perspective, this publication's calendar of events lists relevant contact information for forthcoming exhibitions, fairs, and festivals.

BEACHES & OUTDOOR PURSUITS

Fun and Adventure on Maui. www.mauitoday.com
The Activity Owners Association of Hawaii outlines specific tours and suggests tour operators (within the association) for all kinds of outdoor excursions, including biking, jet skiing, scuba diving, and more. Visitors seeking less strenuous fun will find information on whale watching, sunset dinner cruises, and helicopter rides.

Haleakala National Park. www.nps.gov/hale
Rain and dry forests, sub-tropical beaches, and desert make up this spectacular 27,468-acre park. Its most magnificent features include the deep volcanic crater and the summit, which is more than 10,000 feet high. The National Park Service offers directions, accommodations, history, and information about park activities.

Island Golf Review. www.mauigolf.com/maui.html
Offering golf news and resort highlights, the reviews of Maui's courses comprise the best part of this magazine.

Maui A-Z: Beaches. www.maui.net/~tkern/beaches.html
The detailed descriptions and photos of local beaches, organized by region, make this the best section of the Maui A-Z guide. Includes comprehensive tips on scuba diving, snorkeling, and kayaking.

State Parks on the Island of Maui. **www.hawaii.gov/dlnr/dsp/maui.html**
The Hawaii State Department of Land and Natural Resources posts acreage, brief descriptions, and opening hours for the island's state-managed parks.

SIDE TRIPS TO MOLOKAI & LANAI

Aloha Insider: Lanai. **www.theinsider.com/aloha/Lanai/Lanai.htm**
This brief overview of the island includes practical tips on getting around by jeep.

Molokai: The Most Hawaiian Island. **visitmolokai.com**
Enjoy the landscape from a virtual photo tour. Get driving times between various points, and learn about local history while you're at it.

Molokai Visitors Association. **www.molokai-hawaii.com**
Descriptions of accommodations, island attractions and events, and restaurant contact information will give you some ideas for relaxing or taking an adventure.

GETTING AROUND

Aloha Airlines. **www.alohaair.com**
This interisland airline shares flight schedules and information on budget passes. You can reserve online.

Expeditions Lahaina/Lanai Passenger Ferry. **www.maui.net/~paradise/ expeditions/expeditions.html**
Get rates, schedules, and special golf and hotel tour packages for this passenger ferry to Lanai.

Hawaiian Airlines. **www.hawaiianair.com**
Check schedules and reserve online for transpacific or interisland service. Also find rental-car deals and frequent-flyer facts.

Pacific Wings. **pacificwings.com**
Find flight schedules, prices, and contact information for this small interisland airline.

Index

See also separate Accommodations and Dining indexes, below.
Page numbers in *italics* refer to maps.

General Index

DINING

Dining Index

WHEREVER YOU TRAVEL, *H*ELP IS NEVER FAR AWAY.

From planning your trip to providing travel assistance along the way, American Express® Travel Service Offices are always there to help you do more.

Maui

LAHAINA
American Express Travel Service
Westin Maui Hotel, Shop #101
2365 Kaanapali Pkwy.
808/661-7155

WAILEA
American Express Travel Service
Grand Wailea Resort & Spa
3850 Wailea Alanui Dr., Ste. 401
808/875-4526

do more | AMERICAN EXPRESS
Travel

www.americanexpress.com/travel
American Express Travel Service Offices
are located throughout the United States.
For the office nearest you, call 1-800-AXP-3429.